The Selected Works of Edward E. Jones

The Selected Works of Edward E. Jones

Daniel T. Gilbert, Editor
Harvard University

WILEY
www.wiley.com/college/gilbert

Senior Acquisitions Editor   *Tim Vertovec*
Marketing Manager   *Kate Stewart*
Program Assistant   *Kristen Babroski*
Editorial Assistant   *Maureen Powers*
Managing Editor   *Lari Bishop*
Associate Production Manager   *Kelly Tavares*
Production Editor   *Sarah Wolfman-Robichaud*
Illustration Editor   *Benjamin Reece*
Cover design   *Jennifer Fisher*

This book was set in Times by Leyh Publishing LLC and printed and bound by Courier–Westford. The cover was printed by Phoenix Color.

This book is printed on acid free paper. ∞

Copyright © 2004 by John Wiley & Sons, Inc. All rights reserved.

No part of this publication may be reproduced, stored in a retrieval system or transmitted in any form or by any means, electronic, mechanical, photocopying, recording, scanning or otherwise, except as permitted under Sections 107 or 108 of the 1976 United States Copyright Act, without either the prior written permission of the Publisher, or authorization through payment of the appropriate per-copy fee to the Copyright Clearance Center, Inc. 222 Rosewood Drive, Danvers, MA 01923, (978)750-8400, fax (978)750-4470. Requests to the Publisher for permission should be addressed to the Permissions Department, John Wiley & Sons, Inc., 111 River Street, Hoboken, NJ 07030, (201)748-6011, fax (201)748-6008, E-Mail: PERMREQ@WILEY.COM. To order books or for customer service please call 1-800-CALL WILEY (225-5945).

ISBN: 0-471-19226-0

Printed in the United States of America

10 9 8 7 6 5 4 3 2 1

*This volume is dedicated to Mary Ann—
Ned's amanuensis, archivist, and friend.*

Brief Contents

Foreword xix

Notes and Acknowledgements xx

About the Editor xxi

Introduction 1

Part One   The Penetration of Action

Inferential Goals

Chapter 1   Interaction Goals as Bases of Inference in Interpersonal Perception   8

Attribution Theory

Chapter 2   Role Playing Variations and their Informational Value for Person Perception   33

Chapter 3   From Acts to Dispositions: the Attribution Process in Person Perception   47

Chapter 4   Update of "From Acts from Dispositions: the Attribution Process in Person Perception"   85

Chapter 5   Correspondent Inferences and the Attribution Cube: A Comparative Reappraisal   90

Social Cognition

Chapter 6   Afterword: An Avuncular View   118

Chapter 7   The Social in Cognition   126

Part Two   Inferential Anomalies

Correspondence Bias

Chapter 8   The Attribution of Attitudes   140

Chapter 9   The Rocky Road from Acts to Dispositions   162

The Actor-Observer Effect

Chapter 10   The Actor and the Observer: Divergent Perceptions of the Causes of Behavior   179

Chapter 11   How Do People Perceive the Causes of Behavior?   203

Order Effects

Chapter 12   Order Effects in Impression Formation: Attribution Context and the Nature of the Entity   214

Ingroups and Outgroups

Chapter 13   The Perception of Variability within In-Groups and Out-Groups: Implications for the Law of Small Numbers   241

Chapter 14   Polarized Appraisals of Out-Group Members   256

Part Three The Orchestration of Action

Strategic Self-Presentation

Chapter 15 Ingratiation: An Attributional Approach 278

Chapter 16 Toward a General Theory of Strategic Self-Presentation 358

Self-Handicapping

Chapter 17 Drug Choice as a Self-Handicapping Strategy in Response to Noncontingent Success 386

Chapter 18 Control of Attributions about the Self through Self-Handicapping Strategies: The Appeal of Alcohol and the Role of Underachievement 403

Chapter 19 The Framing of Competence 412

Bibliography 427

Contents

Foreword   xix

Notes and Acknowledgements   xx

About the Editor   xxi

Introduction   1

The Penetration of Action   1
Inferential Anomalies   2
The Orchestration of Action   4
Coda   5
References   5

Part One   **The Penetration of Action**

Inferential Goals

Chapter 1   Interaction Goals as Bases of Inference in Interpersonal Perception   8

Some Relevant Properties of the Inference Process   10
Classes of Social Interaction and Their Perceptual Implications   11
   Interactions Classified in Terms of the Reciprocality of Behavior   11
   Interactions Classified in Terms of Mediated Purpose   15
   Relationship Between Formal and Substantive Classes of Interaction   24
The Conditions and Consequences of Set Arousal   26
Summary   30
References   31

Attribution Theory

Chapter 2   Role Playing Variations and Their Informational Value for Person Perception   33

Method   36
   Subjects   36

xi

xii Contents

    Procedure Overview 36
    Stimulus Variations 37
    Impression Rating Scale 38
    Results 39
    Predicted Differences in Perception 39
    Differences in Recall 42
    Perception of Additional Characteristics 43
    Machiavellianism 44
Discussion 44
Summary 45
References 46

Chapter 3   From Acts to Dispositions: The Attribution Process in Person Perception 47

The Naive Explanation of Human Actions: Explanation by Attributing Intentions 48
A Theory of Correspondent Inferences 50
    The Concept of Correspondence 50
    Acts and Their Effects 51
    The Assumed Desirability of Effects 52
    The Determinants of Correspondence 53
    The Calculation of Commonality 55
    Conditions Affecting Desirability Assumptions 57
    Information Gain and the Role of Prior Choice 58
    Correspondence, Choice, and Role Assignment 59
Personal Involvement and Correspondence 61
    The Hedonic Relevance of the Action to the Perceiver 61
    Personalism: The Actor's Intention to Benefit or Harm the Perceiver 68
Summary and Conclusions 82
References 84

Chapter 4   Update of "From Acts from Dispositions: the Attribution Process in Person Perception" 85

References 89

Chapter 5   Correspondent Inferences and the Attribution Cube: A Comparative Reappraisal 90

Correspondent Inference Theory Revisited 91
    Sources of Expected Effect Valence 93
    Some Problems with Correspondent Inference Theory 98
    What Kind of Theory? 103
Kelley's ANOVA Cube: A Brief Summary 105
Correspondence and the Cube: A Comparison 107

Category-Based Expectancies and the Consensus Variable   107
Target-Based Expectancies and Distinctiveness   107
Target-Based Expectancies and Consistency   108
Toward an Integrated Framework for Attributional Processes   110
The Conceptual Variables of an Integrated Attributional Analysis   111
The Action Sequence   111
Summary   115
References   115

Social Cognition

Chapter 6   Afterword: An Avuncular View   118

First and Subsequent Impressions   120
Multiple-Stage Inference Models   120
Reexamining the Person–Situation Trade-Off   121
The Question of Disposition Content   122
Automatic and Controlled Processes   122
Perceiver-Induced Setting   123
References   123

Chapter 7   The Social in Cognition   126

Personal/Cultural Theories, Stereotypes, and Unconscious Ideologies   129
Peripheral Models of Attitude Change   131
Dual Theories of Attribution   131
The Role of Priming in "Unintended Thought"   132
Mental Control and the Return of the Suppressed   132
Cognitive and Behavioral Features of the "Self-Fulfilling Prophecy" in Social Interaction   133
References   136

Part Two   Inferential Anomalies

Correspondence Bias

Chapter 8   The Attribution of Attitudes   140

Experiment I   142
  Method   142
  Results   144
Experiment II   146
  Method   146
  Results   148
Experiment III   152

Method 152
Results 154
Discussion 158
References 161

Chapter 9 The Rocky Road from Acts to Dispositions 162

Underestimated Constraints 169
Information Sequence 171
Explaining the Overattribution Effect 171
Reference Note 177
References 177

The Actor-Observer Effect

Chapter 10 The Actor and the Observer: Divergent Perceptions of the Causes of Behavior 179

Experimental Evidence Consistent with the Proposition 180
The Information Available to Actor and Observer 185
    Effect Data 186
    Cause Data 186
    Historical Data 187
Differences in Information Processing 188
The Naive Psychology of Observers and Actors 192
    The Observer's View: Personality as a Trait Package 193
    What Sustains the Belief in Traits? 194
Personality Traits Are Things Other People Have 198
Motivational Influences on Attribution Processes 199
Summary and Conclusions 200
Bibliography 201

Chapter 11 How Do People Perceive the Causes of Behavior? 203

Laboratory Experiments 204
Field Studies 208
Wider Implications of the Theory 211
References 212

Order Effects

Chapter 12 Order Effects in Impression Formation: Attribution Context and the Nature of the Entity 214

Some Useful Distinctions 216
The Order Effect Paradigm Family: Variations in Judgmental Contexts and
  Their Distinctive Implications 218

Adjective Combinations   218
Reference Scale Anchors and Judgmental Contrast   221
Unfolding Behavior Sequences   226
The Replacement Information Case   232
Underlying Processes: A Speculative Resume   235
Toward Primacy   236
Toward Recency   237
Swing Factors   238
Bibliography   239

Ingroups and Outgroups

Chapter 13   The Perception of Variability within In-Groups and Out-Groups: Implications for the Law of Small Numbers   241

Method   245
Subjects   245
Procedure   245
Results   247
Strength of Prior Impression   247
Predictions and Percentage Estimates   248
Trait Inferences About Target Persons and Target Groups   251
Variability and Liking Measures   252
Discussion   252
Reference Note   255
References   255

Chapter 14   Polarized Appraisals of Out-Group Members   256

Attributional Framework   257
Polarized Evaluations of Out-Group Members   258
Overview of Experimental Studies   260
Experiment 1   261
Method   261
Results   262
Discussion   264
Experiment 2   265
Method   265
Results   267
Additional Evidence   269
Experiment 3   270
Method   270
Results and Discussion   271
Experiment 4   272
Method   272

Results and Discussion   273
General Discussion   273
Reference Note   275
References   275

Part Three   The Orchestration of Action

Strategic Self-Presentation

Chapter 15   Ingratiation: An Attributional Approach   278

A Working Definition   280
Plan of the Essay   280
Tactical Variations with the Subject as Target Person   281
   Complimentary Other-Enhancement   281
   Opinion Conformity   300
   Rendering Favors   304
   Self-Presentation   308
   The Ingratiator's Dilemma Again   313
   Status Differences and Their Implications   316
The Naive Psychology of Ingratiation—or What People Think Will Make Them More Attractive to Others   318
   Making the Horse Drink: Effects of Instructions to Ingratiate   319
   Leading the Horse Near Water: Variations in Dependence   325
Cognitive and Motivational Determinants of Ingratiation   333
   Incentive-Based Determinants   333
   Subjective Probability of Success   335
   Perceived Legitimacy   338
Effects of Ingratiation Overtures   342
   Effects on the Target Person   342
   Effect of Ingratiating Overtures on the Ingratiator   343
   Effect of Ingratiating Overtures on the Quality of Interpersonal Relationships   350
A Few Final Words   353
Bibliography   354

Chapter 16   Toward a General Theory of Strategic Self-Presentation   358

A Definition and Some Exclusions   358
A Taxonomy of Attributions Shaped by Self-Presentational Strategies   362
   Ingratiation   362
   Intimidation   365
   Self-Promotion   367
   Exemplification   371
   Supplication   373
   Summary   374

The Implications of the Phenomenal Self for Strategic Self-Presentation—and Vice Versa   375
    The Phenomenal Self as a Determinant of Strategy Choice   375
    Self-Enhancement, Approval, and Self-Esteem   376
    Performance Authenticity, Self-Handicapping, and Social Feedback   379
    Other Carryover Effects   380
Summary and Conclusions   382
References   384

Self-Handicapping

Chapter 17   Drug Choice as a Self-Handicapping Strategy in Response to Noncontingent Success   386

Experiment 1   390
    Method   390
    Results   393
    Discussion   396
Experiment 2   397
    Method   397
    Results   398
General Discussion   400
References   401

Chapter 18   Control of Attributions about the Self through Self-Handicapping Strategies: The Appeal of Alcohol and the Role of Underachievement   403

Underachievement as a Strategy to Protect Self-Esteem   406
The Choice of the Alcohol Strategy   406
The Competence Image   407
Reactions to Conditional Love Suspicions   408
The Role of Reinforcement Contingency   409
References   410

Chapter 19   The Framing of Competence   412

The Appeal of Attributional Ambiguity   417
    Self-Handicapping   417
    Underachievement   418
    Self-Promotion   420
Concluding Remarks   423
References   425

Bibliography   427

Foreword

Historians are paid to give different accounts of the same events. So it will be in reluctant unison that future historians describe Edward Ellsworth Jones as a giant in the field that he shaped and cherished for nearly forty years. From his early development of attribution theory, the actor-observer effect, and the correspondence bias, to his later work on self-handicapping, social stigma, and strategic self-presentation, Jones built a significant piece of the foundation on which modern social psychology rests. Although his contributions may seem remarkably varied, each was a meditation on some aspect of a single question: How do ordinary people orchestrate and penetrate the mysteries of behavior? That question occupied him for decades, and his deep, delicate, and precise answers have occupied scholars ever since. His death in 1993 brought an untimely end to the steady stream of insights on which social psychology had come to rely, and today we must look backward to partake of his wisdom. This volume allows us to do just that by reprinting Jones's most important and influential shorter works. It does not, of course, reprint all, or even most, of his nearly one hundred chapters and articles, nor does it reprint portions of his books, some of which are among his most significant contributions. But it does provide a selection of the scientific work that has enlightened generations of social psychologists and consigned future historians to poverty.

D. T. G.
July 2, 2003
Cambridge, MA

Notes and Acknowledgements

The preparation of this volume was facilitated by many people, but special thanks are due to Ginnie Jones, Mary Ann Opperman, Joel Cooper, Chris Rogers, Marilynn Oliphant, and Celeste Beck. Those interested in learning more about the work of Ned Jones may wish to read *Attribution Processes, Person Perception, and Social Interaction: The Legacy of E. E. Jones,* edited by J. Cooper and J. M. Darley (1997, APA Press, Washington, D.C.). Ned Jones' papers are preserved in the Archives of the History of American Psychology at The University of Akron, and are available for scholarly study.

About the Editor

Daniel Gilbert is Professor of Psychology at Harvard University. He is the author of numerous research articles, a recipient of the American Psychological Association's Distinguished Scientific Award for an Early Career Contribution to Psychology, a former fellow at the Center for Advanced Research in the Behavioral Sciences, the recipient of research grants and fellowships from the National Institute of Mental Health, the American Philosophical Society, the Guggenheim Foundation, and others. He is co-editor with Susan Fiske and Gardner Lindzey of *The Handbook of Social Psychology*. Professor Gilbert studied with Edward E. Jones at Princeton University from 1981–1985.

Introduction

Edward Ellsworth Jones was born on August 11, 1926, in Buffalo, New York, and was never called anything but Ned. His father was a dean and professor of psychology at the University of Buffalo, his mother was a social activist and passionate voice against injustice, and the two seemed to endow him with their respective scientific and humanitarian orientations. In 1947, after attending Swarthmore College and serving in the army, Ned made two momentous decisions. First, he married Virginia Sweetnam, with whom he raised six children (Sarah, Caroline, Todd, Amelia, Jason, and Janet) and to whom he remained devoted for the remainder of his life. Second, he enrolled at Harvard University where he concentrated his studies in the newly formed Department of Social Relations, earning his A.B. in 1949 and his Ph.D. in 1953, both under the direction of Jerome Bruner. During his graduate training he became involved in a Navy project on psychological warfare against Soviet submarines, which brought him into contact with John Thibaut, who became Ned's good friend and intellectual mentor. In 1953, Ned took a faculty position at Duke University, and in 1977 accepted an appointment as Stuart Professor of Psychology at Princeton University, where he remained until his death in 1993. The work he produced in his four decades of professional life revolved around a trio of topics: The penetration of action (how do people use action to infer the enduring dispositions of others?), inferential anomalies (to what sorts of errors does this inferential process admit?), and the orchestration of action (how do people structure their own action so as to control the inferences that might be drawn about them?). Although some works touched on two or more of these topics at a time, these three topics do provide some lines along which Jones's oeuvre can be roughly carved.

THE PENETRATION OF ACTION

In 1957, Ned attended a conference at Harvard University with such luminaries as Solomon Asch and Fritz Heider. He would often remark that this conference had been an intellectual watershed—a point at which both he and the rest of social psychology abandoned the single-minded focus on the accuracy of interpersonal judgments and became concerned instead with the inferential processes of the judge. Ned thought of those inferential processes as first and foremost grounded in the social interactions they served, and he championed this functionalist theme in the chapter that he and John Thibaut prepared for the conference (Jones & Thibaut, 1958; reprinted here). They suggested that a person's goals during social interaction determine which of a small number of "inferential sets" the person will adopt, and that these inferential sets play a critical role in shaping the person's impressions of his or her interaction partners. In many ways, this early chapter was one of Ned's richest contributions, and students of social inference still find much to appreciate and explore within it.

But even before the chapter appeared in print, Ned recognized that the term "inferential set" was merely a placeholder and he had already turned his attention to developing a more precise understanding of the mental processes by which people learn about each other. His thinking was strongly influenced by Heider (1958), who had suggested that ordinary people think of behavior as a joint product of the actor's enduring predispositions and the situation within which the behavior unfolds, and that the ordinary person uses "attributional rules" to determine which of these caused an actor's behavior. Ned was probably the first to show that people do indeed consider behavior more informative when it occurs in spite of, and not because of, situational demands, and his "astronaut-submariner study" (done in collaboration with his students, Keith Davis and Kenneth Gergen) is widely regarded as the classic demonstration of that axiom (Jones, Davis, & Gergen, 1961; reprinted here). A few years later, Ned folded that axiom into a more general theory, and with Keith Davis offered social psychology its first formal model of this attribution process (Jones & Davis, 1965; reprinted here). In a landmark paper, they introduced their Theory of Correspondent Inferences—a careful articulation of the system of inferential rules by which an observer could determine whether a particular behavior (e.g., a charitable act) provided evidence for the existence of a corresponding disposition (e.g., generosity). The theory suggested that observers use the unique consequences (or "noncommon effects") of an action to determine the actor's intentions, and then use the social desirability of the action to determine whether those intentions were unique enough to provide new information about the actor's enduring qualities. Ned would lightly adjust his theory in the following years (see Jones, 1976, 1978; reprinted here), but by and large he felt that it did a good job of explaining why so much of what people do says so little about them, but why occasionally their character is laid bare by a single word or deed.

The Theory of Correspondent Inferences heralded the beginning of the attributional approach in social psychology, and, with the appearance of Harold Kelley's synthetic chapter in 1967, attribution theory followed dissonance theory as social psychology's premiere theoretical engine. But by the 1980s, psychology had found a new way to talk and think about mental processes, and the old focus on inferential rules was replaced by a new focus on the cognitive operations that instantiated those rules. Ned was an ambivalent convert to this "social cognition" approach. He appreciated its innovative experimental techniques and its emphasis on process, but at the same time he worried that in its quest for experimental and theoretical precision it often ignored much of that which was interesting about social inference in the first place, and he spent many of his later years arguing for a rapprochement between the social cognitive and attributional approaches (Jones, 1993a; 1993b; reprinted here). His own ability to walk the fine line between scientific rigor and conceptual richness was profound and uncommon, and it enabled him to leave an indelible mark on the study of person perception.

INFERENTIAL ANOMALIES

The only thing that Ned liked better than theories were experiments, which he continued to do long past the time when most senior scientists were writing popular books or sketching their memoirs. One of the things he liked best about experiments is that they often proved theories wrong, and he took special delight when the theories they disproved were his own. Although his Theory of Correspondent Inferences suggested that rational observers should not infer dispositions (e.g., a political opinion) from actions that are performed under extreme duress (e.g., a coerced expression of that opinion), Ned and his student, Victor Harris, showed that people do just that (Jones & Harris, 1967; reprinted here). Their studies provided the first empirical evidence for a phenomenon that both Fritz Heider and Gustav Ichheiser had described some years earlier, namely, the tendency for observers to take actors "at face value" even when they are well aware of the social norms that encourage actors to act as they do. Much of Ned's empirical work over the next twenty years was devoted to exploring the causes and consequences of this "correspondence bias" (see Jones, 1979; reprinted here). The fact that attribution theory's rational canon was violated so clearly and often never ceased to intrigue Ned, who turned an experimental anomaly into one of social psychology's magnificent obsessions. His discovery of the correspondence bias led to Lee Ross' (1972) conceptualization of a more general "fundamental attribution error," which in turn set the stage for an explosion of research on biases in social inference.

It was in the spirit of invention that whatever Ned did, he next tried to undo. Having established that observers tend to make a mistake when drawing inferences about others, he sought to turn the phenomenon upside down by showing that observers make precisely the *opposite* mistake when drawing inferences about themselves. In 1969, Ned and six prominent (or soon to be prominent) social psychologists convened for a workshop at UCLA where they presented, debated, discussed, and laid the ground work for a volume that would be titled *Attribution: Perceiving the Causes of Behavior* (Jones, Kanouse, Kelley, Nisbett, Valins, & Weiner, 1972), but that generations of students would refer to more fondly by the color of its cover as "the orange book." The orange book contained many important chapters, but none more important than Jones's chapter with Richard Nisbett on the actor-observer effect (Jones & Nisbett, 1972; reprinted here). Jones and Nisbett argued that people tend to think of their own actions as having been controlled by situational forces, but tend to think of others' actions as expressions of the other's enduring beliefs, desires, and propensities. Their analysis implicated perceptual and cognitive factors rather than emotional or motivational factors as the primary sources of what appeared to be a self-serving pattern of inferences, and in so doing, pioneered a new style of explaining inferential error (see Jones, 1976, reprinted here). Indeed, modern psychology's approach to the topic is still, in many ways, an extension of Jones and Nisbett's.[1]

The correspondence bias and the actor-observer effect were but two of the inferential anomalies that Ned considered and clarified. For example, he made important theoretical advances in the study of order effects in impression formation (see Jones & Goethals, 1972; reprinted here), and performed crucial experiments (with his students, George Quattrone and Patricia Linville) on the ways in which an observer's group membership can influence his or her perception of outsiders (Linville & Jones, 1980; Quattrone & Jones, 1980; both reprinted here). For Ned, theories were standards with

---

[1] One of the maddening things about the orange book was that its chapters were published as separate "learning modules" in 1971 and then together as a book in 1972. Hence, the chapters are often (and properly) cited with two different dates. For the sake of consistency, we have used the 1972 date in all references to the orange book or its constituent chapters.

which human behavior could be contrasted, and he studied deviations from those standards because he felt that social psychology was at its best when it was illuminating and eliminating the gap between *should* and *do*. Ned had seen all too much of cold war brinkmanship and racial intolerance, and he was convinced that these and other social ills often grew out of the innocent mistakes that ordinary people make when they try to comprehend each other's motives, attitudes, and abilities. He spent much of his life dissecting human folly so as to better understand human tragedy, and the considerable improvement in our knowledge of these matters over the last few decades is due in no small part to his efforts.

THE ORCHESTRATION OF ACTION

The only thing Ned loved more than theories were experiments, and the only thing he loved more than experiments were sports—specifically, sports he could win. Ned viewed social interaction itself as a kind of sport in which people work hard to learn the truth about others who work equally hard to prevent them from learning it, and he was a keen observer of the various parries, feints, and triangulations by which people shape others' opinions of them. His early work on this topic found expression in an award-winning book on ingratiation (Jones, 1964) in which he offered a psychological analysis of the mechanics of "getting liked" that put him in the odd but distinguished company of Machiavelli, Dale Carnegie, and Lord Chesterfield. A decade later, Ned found that the attributional approach provided a new way to think about ingratiation, and he and his student, Camille Wortman, recast his 1964 book in attributional terms (Jones & Wortman, 1973; reprinted here). Jones and Wortman argued that if people use attributional logic to "see through" the actions of others, then they should use precisely the same logic to their advantage when they become the objects of observation. In this scheme, the observer and the actor were pitted against each other by nature, like predator and prey, each trying to outflank and outfox his or her opponent. This leitmotif was carried through Jones's analysis of ingratiation and, a decade later, provided the underpinnings for his and Thane Pittman's more general analysis of self-presentational tactics in everyday life (Jones & Pittman, 1982; reprinted here).

One of the self-presentational tactics that interested Ned most was self-promotion—the strategy by which actors attempt to convince observers that they are persons of rare talent and exceptional ability—and in his work with his student, Steven Berglas, Ned showed that when the actor and the observer are the same person, then self-promotion becomes self-deception (Berglas & Jones, 1978; Jones & Berglas, 1978; both reprinted here). Jones and Berglas suggested that people sometimes engineer their own failure so as to preserve the possibility that they have untested skills, and their analysis of these so-called "self-handicapping" maneuvers was both sharp and poignant. Ned was fiercely competitive at the poker table and on the tennis court, but he was in most other settings a gentle, modest man who never quite understood why others seemed to consider his work so interesting or important. That undeserved humility led him to produce a compassionate psychological portrait of the individual who fears discovering his or her own limitations (see Jones, 1989; reprinted here). Although Ned will probably be best remembered for his research on "how observers observe," his writings on "how actors act" are surely among his deepest and most personal works.

CODA

Scientific discoveries seem more inevitable than objects of art. If Watson and Crick had not unraveled the secrets of the DNA molecule then someone else would have done so, but had Van Gogh failed to paint his sunflowers, then those vibrant, haunting pictures would never have been made. Ned Jones was both a scientist and an artist. He discovered enduring truths about us and about our lives together—truths that others might well have found if only they had looked as carefully and as honestly as he did—but his insights were unique. They were not shocking or outrageous. They were not revelations. Rather, they were elegant, simple, astute observations that were so perfectly on the money that those who read one instantly knew that they should have thought of it themselves. When Ned gave someone a birthday present it was never a card-shuffling machine or an electric corkscrew. It was probably a brown tie. Similarly, he did not give us exotic intellectual gifts that will end up in the attic except when they are being trotted out for a history lesson. Instead, he gave us things we really needed. He was the master of telling us what we didn't quite know, and in a too short life, he hit that sweet note again and again and again. The proof is in the pages that follow.

Daniel Gilbert
Cambridge, MA
May 27, 2003

REFERENCES

Berglas, S., & Jones, E. E. (1978). Drug choice as a self-handicapping strategy in response to noncontingent success. *Journal of Personality and Social Psychology,* 36, 405–417.
Heider, F. (1958). *The psychology of interpersonal relations.* New York: Wiley.
Jones, E. E. (1964). *Ingratiation.* New York: Appelton-Century-Crofts.
Jones, E. E. (1978). Update of "From acts to dispositions: The attribution process in person perception." In L. Berkowitz (Ed.), *Cognitive theories in social psychology* (pp. 331–336). New York: Academic Press.
Jones, E. E. (1990). *Interpersonal perception.* New York: W. H. Freeman.
Jones, E. E. & Wortman, C. (1973). *Ingratiation: An attributional approach.* Morristown, NJ: General Learning Press.
Jones, E. E. (1976). How do people perceive the causes of behavior? *American Scientist,* 64, 300–305.
Jones, E. E. (1979). The rocky road from acts to dispositions. *American Psychologist,* 34, 107–117.
Jones, E. E. (1985) Major developments in social psychology during the past five decades. In G. Lindzey and E. Aronson (Eds.), *The handbook of social psychology* (Vol. 1, pp. 47–107). New York: Random House.
Jones, E. E. (1989). The framing of competence. *Personality and Social Psychology Bulletin,* 15, 477–492.
Jones, E. E. (1993a). Afterword: An avuncular view. *Personality and Social Psychology Bulletin,* 19, 657–661.
Jones, E. E. (1993b). The social in cognition. In G. Harman (Ed.), *Conceptions of the human mind: Essays in honor of George A. Miller* (pp. 85–98). Hillsdale, NJ: Erlbaum.
Jones, E. E., & Berglas, S. (1978). Control of attributions about the self through self-handicapping strategies: The role of alcohol and underachievement. *Personality and Social Psychology Bulletin,* 4, 200–206.
Jones, E. E., & Davis, K. E. (1965). From acts to dispositions: The attribution process in person perception. In L. Berkowitz (Ed.), *Advances in Experimental Social Psychology* (Vol. 2, pp. 219–266). New York: Academic Press.

Jones, E. E., Davis, K. E., & Gergen, K. J. (1961). Role playing variations and their informational value for person perception. *Journal of Abnormal and Social Psychology, 63,* 302–310.

Jones. E. E., & Goethals, G. R. (1972). Order effects in impression formation: Attribution context and the nature of the entity. In E. E. Jones, D. E. Kanouse, H. H. Kelley, R. E. Nisbett, S. Valins, & B. Weiner (Eds.), *Attribution: Perceiving the causes of behavior* (pp. 27–46). Morristown, NJ: General Learning Press.

Jones, E. E., & Harris, V. A. (1967). The attribution of attitudes. *Journal of Experimental Social Psychology, 3,* 1–24.

Jones, E. E., Kanouse, D. E., Kelley, H. H., Nisbett, R. E., Valins, S., & Weiner, B. (1972). *Attribution: Perceiving the causes of behavior.* Morristown, NJ: General Learning Press.

Jones, E. E., & McGillis, D. (1976). Correspondent inferences and the attribution cube: A comparative reappraisal. In J. H. Harvey, W. J. Ickes, and R. F. Kidd (Eds.), *New directions in attribution research* (Vol. 1, pp. 389–420). Hillsdale, NJ: Erlbaum.

Jones, E. E., & Nisbett, R. E. (1972). The actor and the observer: Divergent perceptions of the causes of behavior. In E. E. Jones, D. E. Kanouse, H. H. Kelley, R. E. Nisbett, S. Valins, & B. Weiner (Eds.), *Attribution: Perceiving the causes of behavior* (pp. 79–94). Morristown, NJ: General Learning Press.

Jones, E. E., & Pittman, T. S. (1982). Toward a general theory of strategic self-presentation. In J. Suls (Ed.), *Psychological perspectives on the self* (Vol. 1, pp. 231–260). Hillsdale, NJ: Erlbaum.

Jones, E. E., & Thibaut, J. W. (1958). Interaction goals as bases of inference in interpersonal perception. In R. Taguiri & L. Petrullo (Eds.), *Person perception and interpersonal behavior* (pp. 151–178). Stanford, CA: Stanford University Press.

Kelley, H. H. (1967). Attribution theory in social psychology. In D. Levine (Ed.), *Nebraska Symposium on Motivation* (Vol. 15, pp. 192–238). Lincoln: University of Nebraska Press.

Linville, P. W., & Jones, E. E. (1980). Polarized appraisals of out-group members. *Journal of Personality and Social Psychology, 38,* 689–703.

Quattrone, G. A., & Jones, E. E. (1980). The perception of variability within in-groups and out-groups: Implications for the law of small numbers. *Journal of Personality and Social Psychology, 38,* 141–152.

Ross, L. (1977). The intuitive psychologist and his shortcomings. In L. Berkowitz (Ed.), *Advances in Experimental Social Psychology* (Vol. 10, pp. 173–220). New York: Academic Press.

Part One

The Penetration of Action

Inferential Goals
    Chapter 1   Interaction Goals as Bases of Inference in Interpersonal Perception

Attribution Theory
    Chapter 2   Role Playing Variations and Their Informational Value for Person Perception
    Chapter 3   From Acts to Dispositions: The Attribution Process in Person Perception
    Chapter 4   Update of "From Acts from Dispositions: The Attribution Process in Person Perception"
    Chapter 5   Correspondent Inferences and the Attribution Cube: A Comparative Reappraisal

Social Cognition
    Chapter 6   Afterword: An Avuncular View
    Chapter 7   The Social in Cognition

INFERENTIAL GOALS

Chapter 1

Interaction Goals as Bases of Inference in Interpersonal Perception

Edward E. Jones
Duke University
John W. Thibaut
University of North Carolina

It is quite possible to surface after brief immersion in the literature on "social perception" with the impression that people, when they are with other people, are preoccupied with the cognitive task of assessing each other's fundamental nature. This is essential, so the argument is likely to run, because appropriate and adjustive reactions depend on accurate perceptions of the characteristics of the other persons in our social environment. Steiner (1955) has seriously questioned the validity of this latter assumption, which would seem to depend to an important degree on the stimulus attributes chosen as criteria of accuracy. The question thus arises: accurate in what respect? With regard to which set of characteristics?

The development of research and theory dealing with interpersonal perception has thus far been constrained by an overemphasis on perceiving the personality characteristics and behavior tendencies of a particular other. Proceeding on the assumption that the particular

---

Reprinted from *Perception and Interpersonal Behavior*, edited by Renato Tagiuri and Luigi Petrullo, with the permission of the publishers, Stanford University Press.w © 1958 by the Board of Trustees of the Leland Stanford Junior University. References and reference style have been updated by the editor. The original chapter acknowledged the support of the Ford Foundation and the Office of Naval Research.

Chapter 1 Interaction Goals as Bases of Inference in Interpersonal Perception

responses made by another provide the primary clues for drawing inferences about his nature, many research designs in the perception area seem to foster the implication that we view others as though through a reduction screen, to eliminate the disturbing effects of context. In order to be more faithful to the typical situation of social interaction, however, we should recognize that in many interaction situations, considerable information is conveyed by cues about the situation and the roles of the participants. Even if we restrict social perception to the perception of persons per se, we will have to deal with inferences about their behavior in relation to the interaction context.

It also seems unwise to assume that our social effectiveness in an interaction situation grows as a monotonic function of the amount of information available about the other actors. This assumption fails to consider **[151]*** the fact that not all information is equally useful and that a redundancy of cues, when we are only concerned with a few, can operate as distracting noise. A study by Leventhal (1956) provides support for this qualification, and Cronbach (1955) discusses various statistical reasons why an increase in information may sometimes lead to an actual decline in accuracy.

Our present approach rests on the observation that social interactions are rarely communicative free-for-alls which require large amounts of information to be intelligently maintained. For the most part, we interact with others within fairly well-defined situations and in terms of rather constraining roles. Our main requirement, therefore, is for information *relevant* to adequate role performance, and, fortunately for cognitive economy, we need not be indiscriminately attentive to all the cues provided by the other actor(s).

Two assumptions underlying the subsequent development of this argument may now be stated as a conclusion of the foregoing remarks:

1. Interpersonal perception can most fruitfully be treated as both instrumental to social interaction and conditioned by it. Thus the strategic focus in social perception will vary as a function of the type of social interaction it supports. If we can successfully identify the goals for which an actor is striving in the interaction situation, we can begin to say something about the cues to which he will attend, and the meaning he is most likely to assign them.
2. The perceiver in any social situation will act in such a way as to reduce the need for information to sustain the interaction process. This blanket statement, which deserves at least a *ceteris paribus,* implies a general tendency to adopt simplifying strategies in our interactions with others, strategies which are in the service of cognitive and emotional economy. Much stabilization and simplification of the interaction process results from role-playing strategies of various kinds, but other strategies may actually be the expressions of enduring personality characteristics. The unresponsive, passive person has in this sense a lowered need for information when he is interacting with someone else.

In keeping with the focus of the present symposium, our main concern in this paper will be with the inferences one person draws about another person in a social situation, but we shall examine the inference process with consistent reference to the interaction context in which the perceiver finds himself vis-à-vis the person being judged. In particular, we

---

*Bracketed bold numbers refer to original page numbers. Page numbers indicate where the original page ended.

shall discuss some of the conditions and circumstances which affect our assessment of others by giving rise to the premises from which cognitive inferences proceed. We shall attempt to explore, that is, some of the reasons why different inferences are drawn when the same behavior appears in varying social interaction contexts.

SOME RELEVANT PROPERTIES OF THE INFERENCE PROCESS

In some ways it is unfortunate that we have become accustomed to talking about social or interpersonal *perception*. The processes in which **[152]** most of us are interested seem to be primarily those of inference, induction, and deduction, rather than isomorphic reflections of social reality, as the word perception somehow suggests. Recognition that we are mainly interested in the nature of cognitive inferences about interpersonal events points us toward an investigation of the learning processes which lie behind categorization, the attachment of significance to cues, and the cognitive redintegration of wholes through exposure to their parts.

One of the most crucial determinants of the inference process is certainly that of association on the basis of past experience. Thus, the more frequent the occurrence of behavior X and behavior Y in the same stimulus persons, the more likely we are to predict Y when X occurs, or vice versa. Similarly, the more frequently we have associated certain overt behavioral cues with certain internal states or traits, the more will we treat these cues as symptomatic of a trait, a state of mind, or a syndrome. A great deal can be learned about individual differences in association links and patterns through the use of such devices as Osgood's (1952) *Semantic Differential* and Kelly's (1955) *Role Repertory Test*. Both of these devices have actually been applied to the study of problems in interpersonal perception (cf. Bieri, 1955; Leventhal, 1956; Osgood & Luria, 1954). The particular semantic framework in terms of which an individual structures his inferences about interpersonal events is obviously a crucial and suitable focus for detailed empirical study.

In studying the inference process in social perception, however, we should not only be concerned with the most probable if–then sequences of behavior as they are structured by the perceiver. It is also important to examine the conditions which affect the selection of information at the origin of the inference process. Here questions of attention, selective perception, deliberate decisions of relevance, etc., enter the picture. The perceiver does not passively assign equal priority to incoming cues, but actively seeks out information which is relevant to his purposes in the situation of interaction. The perceiver is tuned or set to process certain kinds of information but not others.

Once cue selection has occurred, furthermore, the inference process is not entirely dependent on a stable matrix of associations which are in some mechanical way tripped off by the selected information. Again, depending on the interaction context, the same information may be treated in different ways at different times by the same observer. This is particularly true when we deal with inferences resulting in evaluative conclusions. The same behavior may be viewed with opprobrium in one context and with approval in another. We may dislike a person when he thwarts us but feel quite neutral and objective when he thwarts another.

Thus the context of interaction conditions both the *selection* and the *transformation* of information. In subsequent discussions we shall use the term *inferential set*

(Jones, 1955) to cover these two functions as they are conditioned by the interaction goals of the perceiver. We assume that each participant in an interaction must come to an initial decision (no matter how tentative or erroneous) regarding the nature of the social situation in [153] which he is involved. Out of this decision will evolve a set to attend to, and to utilize in certain ways, the information provided by the other person. This carries us abruptly to the next problem, that of specifying the conditions which arouse various inferential sets and exploring the dimensions along which these conditions appear to vary. This will involve us in an attempt to classify social interaction, but our primary attention will be directed to consequent perceptual variations.

CLASSES OF SOCIAL INTERACTION AND THEIR PERCEPTUAL IMPLICATIONS

Any attempt to classify social interactions will naturally reflect the biases, goals, and theoretical priorities of the classifier. In addition, one can focus on the contents of interaction, the roles of the participants, the formal tempo of the interchange, the fundamental personal needs being served, the contributions of interactive behavior to social equilibrium, and so on. Concerned as we are with the perceptual concomitants of interaction, we have found it useful to work within a two-way classification scheme. On the one hand, there are important variations in the "fullness" or mutuality of interaction—the extent to which the behavior of each actor is contingent on the behavior of each other actor. On the other hand, one can distinguish different interactions in terms of the dominant interpersonal goals of the participants involved. This dual classification scheme is thus both formal and substantive, but we shall attempt to show later that form and substance are empirically interdependent.

Interactions Classified in Terms of the Reciprocality of Behavior

It is customary to speak of social interaction whenever two or more persons are behaving in orientation to each other. The basic defining criterion is simply that the presence of one person affects the behavior of another person. Such a definition covers a broad array of social phenomena, however, and it is necessary to make certain further distinctions based on the degree to which the moment-to-moment behavior of one actor is contingent on the moment-to-moment behavior of the other actor. Although we shall talk hereafter in terms of dyadic situations only, the same considerations should apply in situations of three or more actors. If we reflect on the determinants of behavior in a social situation, we can typically allocate some variance to the general response hierarchy which the actor imports into the situation, to various nonsocial features of the environment, to the social structure of the situation as perceived by the actor, and to the particular behavior of the other actor which becomes a stimulus for the perceiver. The question now becomes, how important a determinant *is* the behavior of the other actor and the personal characteristics he reveals through his behavior? In some social situations, what the other actor says or does plays a minor role in determining what the perceiver says or does. In other situations it may be vitally important. In order to deal with this dimension of variation, we propose three formal types of interaction ranging [154] from the extreme of independent to the extreme of mutually interdependent social behavior: *noncontingent interactions, asymmetrically contingent interactions, and reciprocally contingent interactions.*

A *noncontingent interaction* is actually something of a contradiction in terms, since it implies that/people are interacting in such a way that the behavior of one actor is not a determinant of the behavior of the other actor. However, there is a class of social situations where interaction is simulated in this fashion but where the behavior of each actor is actually quite rigorously determined by detailed role prescriptions. The *appearance* of interaction is accomplished through a simple synchronization of responses, so that both actors do not talk at the same time or in inappropriate orders. In such a situation, we can say that the behavior of each actor is determined by a clearly defined S.O.P. (from the military nomenclature, "standing operating procedure") and thus the content of the other's behavior is irrelevant to the unfolding of his own responses. Many ceremonial interactions, or interactions appearing within highly formalized social organizations, would approximate this extreme. Noncontingent interactions may also arise whenever the participants are characterized by extreme behavioral perseveration or intense personal preoccupation. Thus, noncontingent interactions may be observed between detached schizophrenic patients or mental defectives where the form of social interaction is apparent, but the content of one actor's speech is not contingent on the content of the other's.

When the interaction situation is basically simulated or noncontingent, regardless of its origin, the requirements for social perception in a functional sense are practically nonexistent. Very little sensitivity to the other is required, over and above the minimal amount of monitoring which is essential for temporal synchronization. In this sense, the noncontingent interaction situation is comfortably stable for both participants, and, most important, continuous monitoring of behavioral content is unnecessary. If the perceiver is aware of the S.O.P. which governs himself and the S.O.P. which governs the other, no immediate, instrumental purpose is served by coming to any conclusions about the personality characteristics of the other.

Asymmetrically contingent interactions are considerably more common than noncontingency interactions and also take a greater variety of forms. "Asymmetrical contingency" suggests a type of interaction in which the behavior of one actor is fully contingent on the behavior of another, but the other's behavior is independently determined (as if one person was "shadowing" another). If this were the case, then the situation would be "noncontingent" from one actor's point of view and "fully contingent" as far as the other actor was concerned. This denotation is somewhat misleading, however, and it implies a type of interaction which would be extremely unstable.

It is more meaningful, we believe, to approach asymmetrical contingency [155] interactions by making an initial distinction between standard and variable responders. A standard responder is one whose response potentialities are largely determined by an S.O.P. The S.O.P. does not completely define his behavior, as in the noncontingency situation (except for synchronization cues), but it vastly reduces his range of improvisation. A variable responder, on the other hand, is one whose behavior is unfettered by a constraining S.O.P. and is consequently open to interpersonal influence. With this distinction in mind, then, we can define a situation as asymmetrically contingent when it involves interaction between a standard and a variable responder.

One example of asymmetrical contingency is the typical interaction between an interviewer and a respondent. The interviewer is a standard responder—his behavior is governed by an S.O.P. which may be highly detailed (a schedule of specific questions) or more broadly delimiting (a topic check list). The interviewer's behavior may, at various points, be partly dependent on the respondent's behavior, but he does operate with a set of behavior categories definitely restricted and to some extent sequentially specified by the purpose of his interview. The interviewee, of course, is a variable responder, attuned both to the questions asked and the perceived intent behind them.

Experiments which involve the use of role-playing confederates provide another example, since the naïve subject (variable responder) is confronted with a "stooge" whose behavior is largely determined by an S.O.P. established by the experimenter.

The perceptual consequences of such asymmetrically contingent interactions naturally depend on whether we focus on the cognitive task of the variable responder or the standard responder. Turning first to the latter, the standard responder is of course confronted with a stimulus person whose responses cannot be predicted in terms of any knowledge of a governing S.O.P. If the standard responder's S.O.P. completely specifies his own response sequence, however, there is no need for inference-building information. His behavior is by definition unaffected by the behavior of the variable responder. If the S.O.P. merely restricts the standard responder to a limited set of behavior categories, without specifying the sequence of behaviors, then we have a situation in which a complex stimulus pattern must be "coded" into response-relevant information. In this latter case, the behavior of the variable responder will be perceived in a highly selective fashion. Thus in spite of the complexity of the stimulus, the cognitive burden of the standard responder will be light even if the sequence in which he should make his responses is not specified.

The perceptual implications of being a variable responder depend on the degree to which the responder is aware of the nature of the situation. If he is aware that the standard responder's behavior is covered by an S.O.P., he will presumably concentrate initially on those cues which will help him determine the nature of the S.O.P. The continuity and intensity **[156]** of the variable responder's monitoring will depend on feedback about the complexity of the S.O.P. If the variable responder is unaware of the existence of an S.O.P., he will be in the same position, subjectively, as any actor in a situation of full, mutual contingency.

At least in our democratic, "other-directed" culture, asymmetrical contingency relationships are likely to be quite unstable. Thus some interactions start out being asymmetrically contingent and end up being noncontingent. If we think of the course of an argument between a liberal and a party-line communist, it might well be that the liberal tries to counter the communist's arguments in a flexible and "contingent" way, but the communist responds largely in terms of his own ideological S.O.P. In time, it seems plausible to assume, the liberal will reduce his contingency on the specific content of the communist's argument, and a decline in continuous monitoring will result. In the military, and many other hierarchical organizations, an attempt is characteristically made to push asymmetrical contingency situations in the direction of noncontingent ones by emphasizing the S.O.P.s which govern interactions between status levels.

Other interactions start out asymmetrically contingent and end up being doubly contingent, as in the case where the interviewer is drawn into controversy with the interviewee.

RECIPROCALLY CONTINGENT INTERACTIONS   Here we refer to those "full" interactions in which the behavior of one actor is contingent on the behavior of the other and vice versa. Parsons and Shils (1954) apparently wish to restrict the term interaction to such "double contingency" situations, but we prefer to treat reciprocal contingency as an extreme point on a broad continuum. Nevertheless, reciprocal contingency is neither a rare nor an unimportant phenomenon. In such clearly social situations the full range of human emotions is most likely to be engaged, and the intricate complexities of shared and non-shared perspectives become critically relevant.

As contrasted with noncontingent interactions, the search requirements in reciprocal contingency situations are naturally more demanding as far as interpersonal perception itself is concerned. Because each response of Actor A is partially dependent on the preceding response of Actor B, A will naturally have to monitor continuously the behavior of B. Since the situation is by nature fluid, the perceiver has to be constantly alert to incoming cues from the other in order to respond in an effective manner. There are also two, somewhat contradictory additional implications for interpersonal perception or inference:

1. Actor A and Actor B are by definition in a situation where each, actor is a partial, but only a partial, cause of the other's behavior. If we assume that A and B perceive each other as modifiable from moment to moment, cues of social reinforcement and acceptance by the other actor will take on greater significance because they will be perceived as spontaneous, at least in part. In line with this, inferences about the other's intentions, motives, and "true nature" will take on added significance, i.e., **[157]** will become an increasingly important determinant of interaction behavior. Parsons and Shils (1954) seem to be making the same point when they propose that double contingency interactions imply "the normative orientation of action, since alter's reaction of punishment or reward is superadded to alter's 'intrinsic' or direct behavioral reaction to ego's original selection" (p. 16). Their argument, however, involves a somewhat different derivation.

2. On the other hand, in reciprocal contingency situations the need for information is immediate, and it must be quickly processed since neither actor has much time to think about the preceding act before having to act himself. As a consequence of this "urgency" consideration, we suggest that much of the perceiver's attentive energy will be directed to his own future responses and not to the stable characteristics of the other. Thus the main moment-to-moment problem is not "What is he like?" but "What am I going to do next?"

These two considerations suggest that the perceiver is typically placed in a certain amount of cognitive conflict when in, reciprocal contingency situations. As long as he is in the situation and responding directly to the other person, concentration on his own responses will likely be the dominant factor. Certainly some information about the motives and character of the other actor will "filter through" and in part determine his own reactions, but much of this information will not be processed and evaluated at the time. In retrospect, however, when there is no longer the urgency which comes with response planning and execution, information about the stable characteristics of the other will command greater attention and certain conclusions will likely be drawn about the other actor for future reference. How often do we engage in a pleasant and smooth interchange with some other person only to realize later, upon reflection, that we have been crassly manipulated? It is probably good selling technique to force such a rapid interchange upon the prospect that he cannot devote his full attention to a calm consideration of the merits of the product (or the salesman).

To summarize our position briefly, we feel that certain classificatory distinctions may be made in terms of the degree to which the behaviors of parties to an interaction are mutually contingent. Furthermore, these distinctions appear to have considerable relevance for the continuity and urgency of perceptual search, as well as for the kinds of cues most available as a basis for inference. It is difficult, however, to make any precise predictive statements about the inference process, knowing only the degree of mutual contingency. For this reason, we would like to introduce another, more substantive, basis for classification which will move us closer to empirically verifiable statements.

Interactions Classified in Terms of Mediated Purpose

Certainly the goals or purposes that one person wants and expects to achieve by interaction with another are highly complex in the concrete [158] instance, and difficult to disentangle. It nevertheless seems convenient to classify interactions in terms of three different kinds of goals toward which the interaction is directed: the facilitation of personal goal attainment, the deterministic analysis of personality, and the application of social sanctions.

Assuming that these are important classes of interaction goals, there are characteristic cognitive problems associated with each class of goals. If the goal is facilitation of goal attainment, the associated problem may be summarized by the question, "What is he doing to me or for me that makes me want to approach or avoid him?" The attempt to solve this problem promotes the arousal of what we shall call a *value-maintenance* inferential set, whose selective and transformative properties will be fully discussed below. Given the second goal of analyzing the determinants of personality from the perceiver's point of view arises the functionally related question "How did he get the way he is?" or, "What features in his past experiences cause him to behave as he now does?" The inferential activities to which this kind of concern gives rise may be referred to under the heading *causal–genetic set.* Finally, when the perceiver decides that his goal in the interaction involves the application of social sanctions presumably he becomes concerned with the appropriateness of the stimulus person's behavior in terms of the generalized norms which he considers to be applicable to the present behavior setting. Such a concern conditions the inference process in ways which we shall subsume under the *situation-matching set.*

These distinctions have a variety of implications, many of which will be discussed below, but an important set of implications may be organized around considerations of perceived cause and perceived effect Fritz Heider (1944) has drawn attention to the nature and determinants of personalized "phenomenal causality"—i.e., the location of cause or responsibility in the behaving person—but he has done so, in our opinion, at the expense of underestimating the frequency of situations in which phenomenal causality does not take this form. We know that in some circumstances, particularly those favoring a detached objectivity, causality may be perceived as "distributed" among a variety of determinants including the actor as well as other features of the total situation. The *value-maintenance set,* for example, clearly involves the attribution of substantial cause to the other actor, who is thereby seen as in some personal sense responsible for abetting or thwarting the perceiver. The perceiver in a *causal–genetic set* conceives an act as emanating from a personality which has complex origins in a variety of social, physical, and biological determinants. In the *situation-matching set,* the causal locus of behavior is more or less irrelevant to the inference process, or at least the extent to which causation is phenomenally personalized will depend on other conditions.

In a similar fashion, certain distinctions may be drawn which involve the way in which the actual or most probable *effects* of an act are perceived. Defining the consequences of an act involves the invocation of certain standards or norms of evaluation. The *causal–genetic set,* as we have described [159] it, is alone in its relative avoidance of such evaluation. While the other two sets both involve comparison with a standard, the standard is that of a generalized norm in the *situation-matching set* and one of personal or idiosyncratic criteria in the *value-maintenance set.*

It is now our purpose to show how each of these various sets arises out of particular kinds of interaction situations and how some fairly precise empirical predictions can be derived from a consideration of the interaction context. We now turn, therefore, to a second way of classifying interaction.

FACILITATION OF PERSONAL GOAL ATTAINMENT The search for personal gratification is obviously a ubiquitous feature of social interaction. In general, it is fair to assume that the party to any interaction has a persistent interest in the gratification of his personal needs. H. A. Murray has made a beginning attempt to classify interactions in terms of the various personal needs which are likely to be facilitated or obstructed in behavioral interplay. It may be more fruitful, however, and certainly it is easier, to approach the problem of classification by considering a small number of intermediate interaction goals, each of which may serve a variety of different personality needs. We shall refer in the following four categories, therefore, to the actor's primary purpose in the interaction rather than the specific personal needs which are likely to be fulfilled therein. Each of these four interaction types, all falling under the general rubric of "facilitation of goal attainment," represents an instance of interaction situations in which the *value-maintenance set* is likely to be aroused and maintained.

1. One important goal, which may on occasion dominate the concerns of the actor, is *gaining cognitive clarity about the shared environment.* The main feature of interactions having this as a goal will be the attempt of one actor to elicit information from the other actor about relevant aspects of the environment, and about those characteristics of the other which would qualify him to serve as a reliable information mediator. The actor's primary orientation to the environment is informational, and he is set to use the behavior of others as an extension or surrogate of his own perceptual, reality-testing

apparatus. Festinger's (1954) "A Theory of Social Comparison Processes" deals at length with this pervasive feature of interaction, but his emphasis is on social influence and self-evaluation rather than on the consequences of the social comparison motive for social perception. The findings of a long line of researchers, stemming from Sherif's (1935) and Asch's (1956) work, provide ample evidence that most of us are to some extent influenced by the judgments of others with regard to social reality. A similarly impressive list of findings—many of which are presented in Hovland, Janis, and Kelly (1953) makes it clear that not all sources of social influence are equally effective in causing conformity or attitude change. This suggests the importance of a decision, on the part of the actor, regarding the relevance and reliability of the information provided him.

The implications for social perception, inference, and evaluation are fairly straightforward: the stronger the need for cognitive clarity about the **[160]** shared environment, the more will another be positively evaluated if he is informative and provides reliable evidence about the environment. Thus the perceiver will be particularly sensitive to cues which aid in assessing such personal characteristics as reliability, candor, objectivity, perceptiveness, relevant expertise, etc.

2. A second important goal which may provide a focus for a given interaction is *securing motivational and value support*. Here the main concern of the actor is not with immediately external reality, but rather with the consensual validity of his own values, attitudes, and aspirations. His behavior, therefore, will be directed toward eliciting support and agreement for his views on issues which are important to him. To the extent that the values of others are perceived to be congruent with his own, the actor will feel relaxed, comfortable, and righteous in the interaction. The interaction itself will tend to be leisurely and prolonged, and the actor will give every indication of wanting to maintain his relationship with the other. To the extent that the other's values are perceived to be incongruent, however, the difference in shared perspectives will result in mutual withdrawal and avoidance. No attempt will be made to sustain the interaction. An attempt by Actor *A* to elicit information about the values and attitudes of *B* may be common to several interaction types, but in the present case there is a particular interest in coming to an approach–avoidance decision—"Is he on my side (does he believe the way I do) or not? Is he for me or against me?"

One perceptual implication of this interaction subclass is obvious: the stronger our need to verify and validate our own beliefs and values, the more will others be positively evaluated if they are seen as similar in values to the perceiver. The individual who is secure in his own value orientation, in other words, can afford to be positively attracted to persons with values differing from his own. In general, we do tend to attribute positive characteristics to those perceived to have values congruent with our own. A study by Fensterheim and Tresselt (1953), as well as an unpublished study by Jones, Bruner, and Tagiuri, indicates that this is clearly the case. The further assumption we are making is that the congruence of actors' values will be a much more crucial issue in some interaction settings than in others, and the extent to which the issue is relevant will have important consequences for the inference process.

It should be noted that we are not contending that dissimilarity of values always leads to negative cathexis, or even that similarity of values necessarily leads to positive cathexis. As we shall see below, there are other considerations which affect the relevance for evaluation of value congruence between actors. It is also true that the extent to which congruence is desired by both actors will vary with the particular values involved. Thus a person whose dominant orientation is toward power and exploitation is less likely to be attracted to a person having congruent values than the highly aesthetic person will be attracted to a fellow aesthete. Even the **[161]** power-oriented actor, however, may gain feelings of support and virtue from the knowledge that others are power-oriented too—particularly if some kind of tacit agreement may be reached between actors not to manipulate each other.

3. A third "intermediate" infraction goal is *directly maximizing beneficent social response*. In situations where this goal is dominant, the actor will behave in such a way as to elicit positive affective evaluation from other actors. While it is obvious that Actor *A* will usually be more effective in this activity if he is aware of Actor *B*'s values and criteria for personal evaluation, the basic nature of this goal is the elicitation of cues of liking, acceptance, support, respect, etc. This goal will be pursued regardless of the consequences for obtaining other information or maintaining one's own values and beliefs.

The interaction goal of maximizing beneficent response may be instrumental to a variety of more basic concerns of the actor. The fact that Actor *A* perceives that *B* likes him is comforting to *A* for perhaps two fundamental reasons. On the one hand, when someone else likes you, this more or less automatically increases your potential power or control over his responses to you—i.e., if you know that a person likes you, you also tend to assume that he will "do things for you." On the other hand, to be liked by others is a comforting index of one's own worth and virtue. If *A*'s primary reason for wanting others to like him is that his sense of virtue is thereby enhanced, the *manner* in which he has elicited the "like" response from *B* will take on importance. Thus, if *A* deviously presents a false front to increase the likelihood that *B* will like him, he will not know whether *B* would have liked him otherwise, and therefore *B*'s response will lose its value as an index of *A*'s worth. The cue-eliciting behavior of *A* will presumably be much less relevant if *A* is primarily concerned with the augmentation of his personal power.

A number of perceptual implications stem from these considerations. The stronger a person's need for dependence on others, for control over others, or for establishing his own worth, the more will another person be positively evaluated if he gives signs of liking the perceiver, "choosing" him, or otherwise supporting and accepting him (cf. Tagiuri, 1952). The distinction between liking as a sign of potential nurturance and liking as an index of worth does not suggest any differential implications for perceptual search activities, but the inference process will vary as a function of the perceiver's prior cue-eliciting behavior (the extent to which the perceiver has been deviously ingratiating, etc.). Whatever the source or motive for securing positive affect from others, however, the perceiver will be most sensitive to such traits as friendliness, acceptance, tolerance, and supportiveness.

A recent study by Thibaut and Strickland (1956) indicates quite clearly the value of distinguishing between situations in which the interaction goal is that of gaining cognitive clarity about the shared environment, and situations in which beneficent social response is the dominant issue. In this **[162]** study, subjects whose need for acceptance by others was aroused by pre-experimental procedures showed less resistance to group pressure, in a rigged conformity situation, than subjects who were primarily concerned with their accuracy as individuals. Similar results have been reported by Deutsch and Gerard (1955), and by Jones, Wells, and Torrey (1958).

4. A final interaction goal which we believe needs to be distinguished *is accomplishing some outcome external to the interaction itself.* In a sense, the first of the intermediate interaction goals we have discussed, gaining cognitive clarity about the environment, should fall under the present rubric, but here we are concerned with performance activities which actually effect some change in the environment. The great majority of experiments on group problem solving involve the type of interaction to which we are here referring. There are two variants of this class of interaction, however, that bear separate discussion since their perceptual implications differ.

The first possibility is that Actor *A* is working toward some individually attainable goal which *B* can either prevent or allow *A* to obtain. Thus Actor *A* may be seeking permission to do something which falls within the "gatekeeping" prerogatives of *B*. In such a case, *A*'s interaction strategy might well involve learning the sources of resistance or compliance in *B,* so that activities to produce acquiescence will have more effective direction. The stronger the need to attain the goal in question, the more will the stimulus person (the gatekeeper) be positively evaluated if he gives signs of tractability, permissiveness, and compliance. As Thibaut and Riecken (1955) have shown, this positive evaluation will be especially enhanced if the compliance is perceived to be voluntary or spontaneous rather than forced by the situation or by some power of the perceiver.

A second possibility, however, is that Actor *A* needs supporting activity from *B* in order to obtain a "group goal." In such a case, there will again be some emphasis on tractability, but *A* will also be vitally interested in *B*'s competence and dependability. In order to make precise predictions here about the traits in which *A* will be most interested, a variety of additional considerations would also have to be taken into account: the individual's general desire to lead or to follow, his self-confidence in directing others, etc. In general, however, we might expect *A* to be most sensitive to *B*'s cooperativeness, dependability, and his willingness to work.

A study by Jones and deCharms (1957) provides a demonstration of the arousal of a value-maintenance set in this type of interaction situation. In this study, subjects worked toward the solution of a series of problems in groups.

In half of the groups, all subjects worked toward individual rewards based on their individual performances. In the remaining groups, however, all members had to succeed or no one would obtain a reward. In all cases one member failed by prearrangement, following which the subjects rated each other on a number of personality traits. One finding was that the failing subject was seen as significantly less dependable when his **[163]** failure affected the group (in spite of the fact that his behavior was, of course, identical in both kinds of groups). When the tasks were presented as tests of motivation, this difference was markedly greater than when the tasks were presented as tests of intelligence. The reason for this last finding was apparently that motivation is perceived to be internally caused, i.e., under the control of the actor himself. Competence, on the other hand, represents a more stable, externally imposed cluster of attributes for which the actor cannot be held personally responsible. The assumption that the *value-maintenance set* involves the attribution of cause to the other actor (see above) is thus supported. When *B* behaves in a manner which prevents *A*'s goal attainment, the degree to which the *value-maintenance set* is aroused will depend on the degree to which causation is attributed to the frustrator.

Each of the above interaction subclasses involves the facilitation of personal goal attainment in some instrumental or intermediate way. The range of interactions covered is fairly broad, and we feel that there are few serious omissions as far as most day-to-day interaction situations are concerned. What this implies, in effect, is that most of our interactions, and the social inference activities deriving from them, are apt to proceed largely from value-maintenance sets of varying content. We do not feel, however, that the facilitation of goal attainment is the only activity providing grounds for the substantive classification of interaction types. The remaining two classes add important, and often overlooked, ingredients to the conceptual picture.

DETERMINISTIC ANALYSIS OF PERSONALITY The second broad purpose which may be mediated by social interaction involves a concern with behavior causation. These are the interactions which characteristically give rise to the causal–genetic inferential set, since the main goal of the perceiver is to establish the pertinent historical and situational determinants of a person's behavior, or, more accurately, the personality characteristics giving rise to that behavior.

While the psychotherapist and the psychoanalytically-oriented diagnostician are professionally prone to adopt the causal–genetic set, a concern with behavior and personality determinants is certainly not restricted to these specialized roles. There are many situations in which we are faced with the necessity of making a prediction about another's behavior in order to program our own activities. In some cases, we may predict future behavior on the basis of simple and straightforward generalizations from past behavior. More often, however, prediction is mediated by some kind of personality conception, which provides a matrix from which probability statements may be drawn.

The desire for prediction may stem from a variety of sources other than the need to plan and regulate social interaction with someone else. The interest in understanding the determinants of others' behavior may be [164] simply an expression of aesthetic fulfillment or scientific curiosity. Or, it may stem from a desire for power through social control.

Whatever the particular source of the motive to analyze another's personality determinants, there are several perceptual implications of this type of interaction which merit discussion. All of the situations which we have described as having the goal of "facilitating personal goal attainment" quite clearly involved inferences leading up to an evaluative decision with regard to the stimulus person. Here we turn to a class of situations, however, which do not involve the evaluation of a person in terms of the consequences of his behavior for the perceiver. Since the stimulus person will not be seen as the ultimate causal agent of his own behavior, the often seductive practice of inferring intent from consequence will tend to be inhibited.

It is obvious that not all consequences of a person's behavior are direct reflections of his intentions. Because of his primary interest in personal history and personality factors, the causal–genetic observer has a clear stake in discriminating intended from unintended behavioral consequences. Accidental behavior, or behavior which is completely dictated by the situation, provides little information of relevance to causal–genetic goals.

The observer in the value maintenance set is less concerned with the "true" nature of the stimulus person than he is with the latter's personal meaning or significance for him. Therefore, his overt response to the stimulus person will be dictated by the kind of consequences the stimulus person's behavior has for him. The stronger the consequence, whether positive (e.g., obvious flattery) or negative (e.g., an accidental slur on the perceiver's nationality), the less relevant the underlying intent in conditioning evaluative conclusions.

The situation-matching observer presents the most complicated picture of all, with regard to this issue. In most everyday situations where one is in a position to apply social sanctions to the behavior of others, the intent which underlies "good" or "bad" behavior is a relevant determinant of the application of sanctions (i.e., praise or punishment). The perceiver's cognitive impression of the stimulus person will be quite congruent with the responses made to the stimulus person. There are some situations, however, where the perceiver must fill a clearly prescribed role which constrains him quite automatically to apply positive sanctions to "good acts" and negative sanctions to "bad acts." This might characterize the shop foreman, the ship captain, or the jury member. Such a role often, as one feature of its constraining characteristics, specifically declares the irrelevance of intent for the application of sanctions. So the sanctions presumably will be applied. The sloppy worker will lose his job, the nervous sailor will get shore duty, and the drunk driver who killed a pedestrian will get life imprisonment. But what effect will the behavioral constraints of such a role have on perception and judgment of the stimulus person? [165] This is clearly an empirical question, but our guess is that the observer's *impressions* will be contingent on the intentions of the stimulus person more than on the consequences of his behavior, the reverse being true for his overt sanctioning *responses*. The jury member, for example, may have strong feelings of compassion and personal warmth for the criminal he helps send to the chair. Nevertheless, we would expect some tendency for one's impression to press toward congruence with one's behavior in this case. Intention will only be relevant to a degree which does not conflict too strongly with the prescribed response. Thus, for example, the degree of compassion would be tempered by the seriousness of the crime regardless of the perceived intent behind the criminal behavior.

While the causal–genetic perceiver will thus utilize cues regarding intent as a basis for his inferences, knowledge about intent will be purely instrumental to his analytic purpose. But if intentions are not causes of behavior as far as the determinist is concerned, what are the determinants and how is information about them elicited? It is clear that, even if all the determinants of a particular person's behavior were known, the causal sequence would have to be truncated at some point so as to avoid infinite causal regress. Theories of personality can be characterized, essentially, in terms of the particular schedule of priorities assigned to causal determinants. The layman's phenomenal conceptions of personality or behavior causation are not dissimilar to more systematic theories in this regard. Just as theories of personality differ in structuring and delimiting the causal sequence, so there are differences between individuals in their preference for certain causal determinants rather than others.

Partly because of the great variety of ways in which causation may be attributed in the assessment of personality, it is not possible to make precise predictive statements about the traits to which the causal–genetic perceiver will be most sensitized. It is important to note that, in one sense, the purely causal–genetic perceiver, A, has no intrinsic concern with the stimulus person, B. As we have said before, B is merely the physical locus of converging causal forces. B will not be perceived as deliberately and voluntarily causing his own behavior as is typically the case in the value-maintenance set. Because of this the natural tendency to treat another person as an active, behaving unit may be somewhat inhibited. There will be perceived unity, of course, but it will not be so clearly structured in phenomenal experience nor so completely taken for granted. The unity will tend to be imposed on the stimulus person by the perceiver; the missing links in the inference chain will be supplied by the perceiver's own "theory" of personality. As a consequence, it might be tentatively hypothesized that the causal–genetic observer's inferential conclusions are apt to be more systematic, consistent, and logical than those of the observer in a value-maintenance set. To the value-maintenance observer, contradictory inferences are less apt to be ruthlessly eliminated.

A final consequence of the distinction between emergent and imposed **[166]** unity is that, given an observer in a value-maintenance set, we can make better predictions of the perceiver's inferences by studying the stimulus person than by studying the perceiver. That is, we can assume that perceivers in general will respond to affronts, flattery, or innuendo with similar kinds of reactions. Given a causal–genetic observer, however the inference process can be more fully predicted from a knowledge of the perceiver and his mode of approaching the explanation problem.

THE APPLICATION OF SOCIAL SANCTIONS The third broad purpose which may be mediated by social interactions is that of applying social sanctions to others. In many social situations, an actor may behave as an agent of social control in dispensing social rewards and punishments or in "passing judgment" on the appropriateness of another's behavior. The actor's main goal is to establish whether or not the other person is behaving appropriately whether the person's behavior "matches" the norms which

Chapter 1   Interaction Goals as Bases of Inference in Interpersonal Perception   23

apply in the situation. For this reason, we have spoken of the *situation-matching set* as the cognitive resultant of such interactions. In order to speak of this set having been aroused or adopted, it is not necessary that the perceiver be in a position of authority over the stimulus person or that the perceiver actually be in a position to apply sanctions. The important criterial feature is that Actor *A* evaluates Actor *B* (whether or not it is to his face) positively or negatively in terms of relevant situational norms.

An example will perhaps best clarify some of the differences between situations giving rise to the three different types of inferential set. Let us assume that the stimulus person (*B*) is a suspect in a criminal case. *X*, who is a spectator in the trial courtroom, looks at *B* and says to himself, "I wouldn't want to meet him in a dark alley" or "He looks like a nice, clean-cut chap; the kind of person I'd like to get to know." *Y*, on the other hand, is a court-appointed psychiatrist who is preoccupied with assessing *B*'s sanity and his responsibility for the crime allegedly committed. *Y* might say to himself, "The utter lack of motive for this crime makes me suspect the man's sanity" or "The instability of this man's home environment is clearly a crucial factor behind his impulsiveness and irrationality." *Z*, finally, is a member of the jury. As he looks at *B* he is primarily concerned with *B*'s legal innocence or guilt—deciding *what B* did for one thing, and deciding whether this action violates the law for another. Needless to say, in terms of the foregoing descriptions, we would say that the value-maintenance set is dominant with *X*, the causal–genetic set with *Y*, and the situation-matching set with *Z*. One of the reasons why the courtroom appears to be such a favorite setting for the plot denouement of many plays may be precisely because of the dramatic potential of the dilemma between inferential sets.

While the jurist provides one of the purest examples of roles primarily concerned with social control, there are many other, less specialized roles which also typically involve the application of sanctions. The position of parent, for example, involves an extremely complex set of functions, but **[167]** among these the role of disciplinarian and socializer is clearly very important. Much of the time, the parent's interactions with his child are colored by normative evaluation: is the child obedient and responsible, has he developed the self-control appropriate to his age, etc. Other interaction situations such as those involving fitness evaluations, promotion decisions, school or program failures, etc., are also clearly situation-matching in nature. By the very nature of the role relationship, normative evaluation and the application of sanctions will play a critical in the interactions between superiors and subordinates. If the superior does not, or cannot, apply negative and positive sanctions to the subordinate, it is indeed difficult to see how the hierarchy could maintain itself.

Turning to the perceptual implications of such interactions, we have already discussed some of the conditions affecting the judged importance of intent versus consequence when the two are dissimilar. In general, the situation-matching observer should place less emphasis on whether or not a particular action was intended than should observers in either value-maintenance or causal–genetic sets.

In order to make predictive statements about the inference process of a perceiver in the role of a dispenser of sanctions, it is obviously necessary to know something about how he perceives the norms. Since the perceiver is primarily concerned with the consequences of the other's behavior, perceptions of the person himself involve relatively uncomplicated cognitive requirements. However, this may be more than outweighed by cognitive complexities from another source: the task of evaluating the situation and apprehending the most relevant norms. In any concrete instance, this may be difficult because even though the situation is objectively clear, it may be one to which conflicting norms apply. The dilemma between "universalistic" and "particularistic" standards (Stouffer, 1949; Stouffer & Toby, 1951) is an especially clear example of this. Or the situation may be essentially normless—the perceiver is hard put to trade on any normative precedents or to make generalizations from more clearly structured normative situations. The "brain-washing" phenomenon would seem to be a good example of this, in that the average person does not know whether to refer to turncoats as "traitors" and "cowards" or to conclude that every person has his breaking point. While the government has moved rapidly to shore up the norms for prisoners of war, there was confusion on this score throughout most of the Korean War.

Much of the foregoing may be restated by acknowledging that no norm is categorically imperative. Not only is it unlikely that any situation involves only one norm, or only congruent norms; as implied above, the applicability of a norm is always to some extent dependent on the intentions of the transgressor, the degree to which he was cognizant of the norm in question, and the degree to which extenuating circumstances are involved. Since norms are basically generalizations constructed with reference to recurrent social situations, they are thereby not likely to be totally applicable in any concrete case. It is precisely because norms are not [168] tailor-made that arbitration, personal judgment, and social consensus are typically involved in judicial decisions.

Relationship Between Formal and Substantive Classes of Interaction

Having to this point outlined a dual system for classifying social interactions, it is now pertinent to inquire into the extent to which classification in terms of the formal criteria of contingency is independent of classification in terms of the substantive criteria of mediated goals. As we have presented the classification schemes, they appear to be *logically* independent. That is, it is one thing to classify interaction in terms of the extent to which the behavior of each actor is dependent on that of the other. It is quite another thing to inquire into the content of the actors' expectancies and to assay their goals and purposes in the interaction.

Characteristically, however, there would seem to be an empirical relation between the two modes of classification such that the more specialized roles leading to the causal–genetic and situation-matching sets will be more easily maintained in noncontingent and asymmetrically contingent interactions. Double contingency interactions, on the other hand, are more apt to arouse and perpetuate value-maintenance sets of various types. We have already noted, for example, that inferences about the intentions and motives of others take on added significance in double contingency situations. The evaluation of another person in terms of his motivation is, we have also seen, a critical feature of value-maintenance sets. On the other hand, in situations where the goal of the perceiver is to establish the determinants of another's behavior or to act as an agent of society in the application of sanctions, the mutuality of interpersonal involvement which is assumed to accompany double contingency interactions would seem to add further complication to the cognitive task and make the maintenance of a causal or situation-matching set that much more difficult.

While these relationships are to some extent self-evident, it will probably be helpful to illustrate them in terms of concrete instances. Take, for example, the case of an interviewer concerned with the deterministic analysis of the interviewee's personality. Typically this role would be carried out in the context of asymmetrically contingent interaction. That is, the behavior of the interviewer is determined largely by an S.O.P. which guides him in asking a certain pattern of questions. Even if the "next" question is a function of the last answer, the degree of double contingency is apt to be limited. The stronger the interviewer's S.O.P. the easier it will be to maintain the causal–genetic set. If the interviewer has a weak S.O.P., or if the interviewee forces the interviewer into double contingency by eliciting reactions not covered by the S.O.P. (when the interviewee says, for example, "You seem to know all the answers; why don't you tell me?"), value-maintenance criteria are likely to enter the picture.

A second set of roles—those of the parent, the teacher, the administrator, the foreman, etc.—more definitely suggest the dominance of situation-matching **[170]** in contexts involving role behavior. Persons in each of these roles spend some portion of their time in the application of normative sanctions. Once again, to the extent that the norms are clearly specified by an S.O.P. and do not have to be generated from moment to moment, the situation-matching set can be more easily maintained. An exclusive emphasis on the application of sanctions will tend to break down, however, whenever the child, the student, or the worker succeeds in turning the interaction into a double contingency one. This will tend to happen whenever the target person questions the legitimacy or the rationale of the norms (as when little Johnny says, "Why?" to his mother's request that he clean his room), or when the target person tries to curry favor with the applier of sanctions (the employee buys the foreman a drink). The implication of this increase in the "fullness" of interaction is that value-maintenance criteria will color the application of sanctions. Thus, Johnny may be considered impertinent, and even greater pressure put on him, and the drink-buying employee may be given a high productivity rating by the foreman.

The most natural social context for the arousal of a value-maintenance set is that in which interaction between peers, colleagues, neighbors, "fellow members," etc., is involved. We have already commented on the ubiquitousness of value-maintenance criteria—they obtrude persistently in causal–genetic and situation-matching settings. However, an interesting final consideration concerns what happens to the typical process of interaction over time. It will now be recalled that, in the introduction, we offered the assumption that "the perceiver in any social situation will act in such a way as to reduce the need for information to sustain the interaction process." A derivative of this assumption is the proposition that efforts will be made, during the typical interaction, to reduce the mutuality of contingency. That is, we would expect some kind of drift from double contingency to asymmetrical or noncontingency in the interests of cognitive economy. More specifically, given the desire or need to predict and control aspects of the social environment, the typical person has some investment in maximizing the stability of that environment. The actor in a double contingency situation is by definition faced with the complex cognitive problem of abstracting diverse behavioral determinants. Phenomenally, the behavior of Actor B

is "caused" by Actor *A,* by various features of the situation, and by *B*'s own personal expectancies and intentions in the interaction. As we move away from double contingency, however, into interactions involving stronger and more clearly specified behavioral S.O.P.s, the task of prediction entails more and more exclusively the ability to specify the controlling S.O.P.s. Basically the argument resolves into the proposition that interaction is more predictable between actors who share common conceptions about each other's social role. Beginning with a fresh, fluxional interaction context, then, attempts will be made by each actor to crystallize the S.O.P.s governing each other's behavior and to achieve some consensus about them. [170]

On the other hand, there is counterpressure from another source promoting a value-maintenance set. We have described the value-maintenance set as ubiquitous for the probable and apparent reason that this is the most natural, primitive egocentric orientation. (It may well be fruitful to consider the developmental implications of the different sets herein described. There is, for example, a definite parallel between a value-maintenance orientation and Piaget's stage of egocentrism. Furthermore, it seems true that much of socialization involves the gradual substitution of causal–genetic and situation-matching criteria for more primitive value-maintenance standards.)

While the value-maintenance set is likely to be aroused in a variety of "ego"-involving contexts, orientations in which situation-matching or causal–genetic considerations are dominant seem to require the support of specialized training (legal, psychological, etc.) and/or the force of group pressure for their maintenance. Even with these supports, however, no one would claim that the therapist never expresses anger toward his patient or that the parent never overlooks transgressions which do not prevent the attainment of his own goals.

We have, then, a condition for the development of an equilibrium as far as the temporal trend of interaction, and the accompanying perceptions, are concerned. The expected drift away from mutual contingency is inhibited by the actor's tendency to reinforce those acts of others which have beneficent consequences for him. The expected "regression" to value maintenance is inhibited by the socially important tendency to behave in terms of normative, role-determined requirements.

The implications of this equilibrium between conflicting "drifts" are not at all clear. A logical possibility is that many interactions would "stabilize" at some point between double contingency and noncontingency but that value-maintenance overtones would be quite prominent. This might take the form, for example, of being irritated with a friend solely because he departs from your expectations of him and not because his behavior is intrinsically irritating. Or it might take the form of *A* belittling *B*'s arguments by engaging in a pseudo-psychoanalysis of *B*'s motives or the determinants of his behavior. The underlying desire in this latter case is not to further mutual understanding, but to express value-maintenance conclusions in the guise of a causal–genetic formulation. Whether or not these examples are plausible and representative, it does seem clear that various checking and balancing forces do operate to inhibit or prevent the exclusive, long-term adoption of any inferential set in social interaction.

THE CONDITIONS AND CONSEQUENCES OF SET AROUSAL

Working from the premise that it is the actual process of social interaction which shapes the form and emphases of social perception, it has been necessary to categorize and delimit, to abstract from a complex and ever-changing set of behaviors. In doing so, we have inevitably overemphasized [171] the unitary quality of interaction types and their related inferential sets. A given pattern of interaction is likely to serve several functions for each actor, and we can never expect to find a "pure set" in operation—at least for any psychologically meaningful unit of time. While it is therefore wrong to talk literally about the adoption of a certain inferential set, it is still meaningful to speak of the relatively predominating effects of one set over others in so far as these effects can be reliably indexed.

It was our intention, in the foregoing discussion, to develop a number of themes from which empirically verifiable statements of relationship might be drawn. It is quite clear, however, that the problem of establishing operational indexes for many of the variables introduced will not be easily solved. Indeed, we have deliberately freed ourselves from the responsibility of making detailed empirical statements in favor of a broader conceptual outline. We do believe, however, that many of the relationships implied in the foregoing discussion are testable and some of the evidence for this belief has already been presented. While we have barely scratched the surface in exploring the empirical consequences of the above formulation, there appear at present to be three broad and feasible lines of research.

Our first concern has been with demonstrating that different inferential sets can be aroused experimentally, having at least some of the consequences outlined above. The most straightforward methodology for accomplishing this involves placing different perceivers in different social roles vis-à-vis the person being judged or observed. By holding constant the behavior of the stimulus person, any differences in evaluation or inference may be attributed to the sets themselves. One method of establishing different perceiver roles is, of course, by variations in instruction. In a second experiment by Jones and deCharms, just recently completed, Naval Air Cadets were exposed to a tape-recorded interview between a psychologist and an ex-prisoner of war who had signed several communistic propaganda statements. Subjects in one group were told to imagine that they were members of a judicial board of inquiry empowered to study the case and to decide what the formal charges should be (an attempt to arouse the situation-matching set). Subjects in a second group were told to imagine that they were members of a medical–psychological board of review empowered to determine *why* the prisoner did what he did (causal–genetic set). Other subjects were told to think of him in terms of whether or not they would like the prisoner as a friend (value-maintenance set). A final group of *S*'s were told nothing (control). The adoption of one or another set was further strengthened by requesting the subjects to express a preference among several questions to obtain further information. If the subject under situation-matching instructions chooses a question on the norms and legal precedents involved, we not only have evidence that the instructions were effective (which was true in the experiment [172] described); we also assume that the very act of expressing a preference has given the set further momentum. While the use of instructions for set arousal seems superficial and somewhat naïve, with proper pre-testing and postquestioning it seems to be a moderately effective way of arousing the subject's interest in certain features of the stimulus person rather than in others. There are undoubtedly many other ways of arousing inferential sets, ways which will suggest themselves in the context of a particular experimental problem.

It is obvious that procedures to encourage role simulation will not have the potent perceptual consequences of actual role playing. It is clearly possible to arrange cognitively realistic social situations (with the aid of confederates or other deception devices) in which a certain set is most likely to be promoted. There are two kinds of problems in maintaining experimental control, however. First of all, if any kind of genuine interaction is allowed between naïve subject and confederate, it would be impossible to hold the confederate's (and stimulus person's) behavior constant across replicated subjects. Second, the methodological separation of set and interaction content seems to make conceptual sense as well. If we want to study the effects of set, we confound things by arousing set through variations in the interaction itself. Resulting differences in perception probably will be more a function of shifts in interaction content than of shifts in inferential set—but, in any event, one would never know. For these reasons, we have tended to make the convenient assumption that the *goals* of interaction are present prior to the actual interaction itself. Therefore, in our research we have either held constant or systematically varied the actual content of interaction, while treating set arousal as the independent variable.

As for the dependent or outcome variables, our interest naturally is in measures which reflect the workings and results of the inference process. But the specific outcome variable of interest will depend in an intimate way on the specific design of the experiment: the particular sets that are being compared, the information which has been conveyed in the process of interaction, the relevant personality characteristics of the perceiver, and so on. It is possible to generalize two main types of hypotheses which will determine the outcome variable of interest: sensitivity hypotheses and evaluation hypotheses. It will be noted that these hypotheses are respectively concerned with the selective and transformative function of sets.

Sensitivity hypotheses include specific propositions that people in one set will "pay more attention to" and will be more affected by certain kinds of information presented than people in another set. When set-relevant information is varied, therefore, rating changes will be greater than when the varied information is more relevant to some other set. In the first Jones and deCharms experiment, for example, the confederate is seen as declining more in competence when his low performance prevents the reward attainment of the naïve subjects than when it does not. The interpretation [173] here is that subjects who are interdependent in the solution of problems will be much more "concerned with" each other's problem-solving competence than will subjects who do not share an inevitably common fate.

Evaluation hypotheses propose that the degree to which a person is liked or disliked will be a joint function of the actual information presented by or about him and the set which the perceiver has adopted. There is, of course, a close relationship between sensitivity hypotheses and evaluation hypotheses. Modifying the evaluative potential of set-relevant information will produce a greater shift in evaluative rating than will changes in nonrelevant information.

The attempted arousal of various inferential sets by experimental manipulation is not the only appropriate research tactic. We are quite prepared to assume that some people, or people in different cultures, will find it more difficult to adopt a certain set than others will. This suggests that culture and personality variables are important determinants of set adoption. Not only is this of theoretical importance in its own right, but it provides a means for learning more about the validity of set-arousal procedures. If, for example, highly prejudiced people are hypothetically incapable of adopting a causal–genetic set, we should find them unaffected by arousal procedures designed to promote that set. If subjects at the nonprejudiced extreme of an attitude scale are markedly affected by the procedures, on the other hand, we have a coherent picture in which the predicted effects of one independent variable support the predicted effects of the other independent variable and vice versa. In such a circumstance one's confidence in the validity of the arousal procedures *and* the attitude scale would be enhanced.

Prejudice and authoritarianism are not the only "personality" variables of obvious relevance. In the prisoner-of-war study, a version of the Stouffer–Toby Universalism–Particularism Scale was administered to all subjects to test the hypothesis that universalists would find it easier to adopt the situation-matching set, particularists the value-maintenance set. The results on this point have yet to be analyzed. The dimension of simplicity–complexity of "interpersonal constructs," which has been studied by Bieri (1955) and Leventhal (1956), also suggests itself as a relevant focus for analyzing individual differences in the case of set adoption. The cognitively complex person should prove himself more capable of shifting sets as the occasion demands, and he should adopt the causal–genetic set with less strain than the cognitively simple subject. The experimental choice of the personality or attitude dimension most likely to bring order to the data of individual differences will naturally depend on the particularly experimental design and the content of the social stimulus material. In the first Jones–deCharms experiment, for example, subjects who were low in need for achievement were more negative in their evaluation of a failing confederate than those subjects who were high in need for achievement. While this particular result was unanticipated, it could be plausibly explained **[174]** after the fact. The point is that a variety of personality variables may, at one time or another, seem relevant to the experimenter who wishes to investigate individual differences in interpersonal perception.

While our research to this point has been experimental in nature, a second hopeful avenue of investigation should involve parallel field research. There are a number of hypotheses which can be investigated by studying the perceptual consequences of role adoption in the natural environment. In approaching these "field" problems, of course, it should be useful to employ some of the indexes devised to handle the experimental data in the research discussed above.

One problem of striking interest and importance is the perceptual consequences of the psychotherapeutic role. We need to know a great deal more about the details of the therapeutic interaction process. In terms of our scheme for classifying interaction, the therapeutic relationship is an exceedingly complex one. In a sense, the interaction is doubly contingent and yet the therapist generally operates in terms of a more or less well-defined S.O.P. We are perhaps justified in describing the therapeutic relationship as *simulated* double contingency. While it is generally the therapeutic ideal to keep the interaction simulated, in the sense that the therapist tried to limit his personal involvement, there are several reasons why it is difficult to keep the interaction "asymmetrical."

First of all, in the process of simulating double contingency, the therapist calls for reactions in the patient which are appropriate to double-contingency interactions. It is difficult for the therapist not to be affected by these reactions.

Second, the natural drift away from double contingency is partially inhibited in therapy because of the motive of the therapist to bring about some kind of change in the patient. In order to bring about such change, the therapist has to interact with the patient in a personally relevant and significant way.

Finally, there is a fundamental value of the therapist at stake in such interactions, namely, the importance of being able to bring about a cure or decided improvement in mental condition. The therapist's reputation and self-esteem are anchored to this capacity to change and improve the well-being of another. In the service of this value, the normal drift toward value maintenance is quite likely to produce feelings and reactions which are inconsistent with a purely causal–genetic orientation as well as with keeping the double contingency only simulated. Thus the therapist is apt to feel positive toward a tractable patient and negative toward a resistive one.

Keeping these considerations in mind, it would be most interesting to examine the therapist's perception of his patients *in relation to* the actual content of interaction. The general hypothesis would be that the inferences drawn about the patient by the therapist would depend on the extent to which the patient has threatened, challenged, or vilified the therapist's **[175]** values (used broadly) *and* the extent to which the therapist has been drawn into double contingency throughout the process of therapy.

Another set of problems involves the whole area of role conflict. Using the psychotherapist again as an example, it would be interesting to explore the extent to which the causal–genetic orientation of the therapist's office carries over into interactions with nonpatients, and the extent to which this orientation actually becomes maladaptive. Whether or not fatherhood is an exhausting burden depends, perhaps, on the ease with which the father can shift from the role of disciplinarian (situation matching) to playmate (value maintenance). Situation-matching and value-maintenance conflicts are also clearly involved in many "gatekeeping" roles such as journal editor, critic, personnel selector, etc. Causal–genetic and situation-matching conflicts are presumably prevalent in the observer and student of court cases, and a study of legal precedents themselves, from this point of view, might be most rewarding.

A final area of research would involve a more detailed investigation of the inference process—plotting the actual chain from input through inference to judgment by correlational means. Here the task would be to establish which traits "go with" which other traits in the minds of social perceivers under different conditions of set adoption. Here we would consider the interplay between "search requirements" and "probability considerations," as Bruner (1957) has classified them.

Engaging in research in any of these directions will undoubtedly produce data which call for a restatement of the foregoing conceptual scheme. We would indeed be unhappy if the scheme could encompass any result without needing to be changed. Nevertheless, we do feel that the analysis presented here points up some issues in interpersonal perception which have heretofore been neglected.

SUMMARY

In this paper we have presented a theory of interpersonal perception which is closely geared to the different kinds of social interaction which affect and are affected by one's perception of another. Acknowledging the paramount importance of stimulus content and purely associative inferential linkages in the process of perceiving another, we have concentrated on the role of *inferential sets* as a determinant both of the information selected and the inferential use to which it is put. As a function of the type of interaction in which an individual finds himself, he becomes set to process incoming information about the other person in different ways.

In order to move toward verifiable statements concerning the specific functions that inferential sets might play, we have introduced a two-way classification scheme for handling different kinds of social interaction. One mode of classification is in terms of the rather formal criterion, the degree of contingency between the actors' behavior. Generally speaking, **[176]** the more contingent *A*'s behavior on *B*'s behavior, the greater the need for inferences concerning *B*'s motives and personality.

A second mode of classification is in terms of a more substantive criterion, the personal goal which is mediated by the interaction. Here we proposed three different *kinds* of goals, each giving rise to a different inferential set: (*a*) the facilitation of personal goal attainment, giving rise to the *value-maintenance* set; (*b*) the deterministic analysis of personality, giving rise to the *causal–genetic* set; and (*c*) the application of social sanctions, giving rise to the *situation-matching* set. While formal and substantive classifications are logically independent, it would seem difficult to maintain either a causal–genetic or a situational-matching set under circumstances where there is a high degree of mutual or double contingency.

An attempt was made to describe various hypothetical ways in which the adoption of inferential sets conditions the process of understanding another person. While most of the supporting examples presented were anecdotal, the consequences of the present theoretical position for both laboratory and field research were discussed.

REFERENCES

Asch, S. E. (1956). Studies of independence and conformity: I. A minority of one against a unanimous majority. *Psychological Monographs,* 70, No 9 (Whole No. 416).
Bieri, J. (1955). Cognitive complexity-simplicity and predictive behavior *Journal of Abnormal and Social Psychology,* 51, 263–268.
Bruner, J. S. (1957). On perceptual readiness. *Psychological Review,* 64, 123–152.
Cronbach, L. J. (1955). Processes affecting scores on "understanding of others" and assumed similarity." *Psychological Bulletin,* 52, 177–193.
Deutsch, M., & Gerard, H. B. (1955). A study of normative and informational social influences upon individual judgment. *Journal of Abnormal and Social Psychology,* 51, 629–636.
Fenstcrheim, H., & Tresselt, M. E. (1953). The influence of value systems on the perception of people. *Journal of Abnormal and Social Psychology,* 48, 93–98.
Festinger, L. (1954). A theory of social comparison processes. *Human Relations,* 7, 117–140.
Heider, F. (1944). Social perception and phenomenal causality. *Psychological Review,* 51, 358–374.
Hovland, C. I., Janis, I. L., & Kelly, H. H. (1953). *Communication and persuasion.* New Haven: Yale University Press.
Jones, E. E. (1955). Inferential sets in social perception. *American Psychologist,* 10, 393.
Jones, E. E., & deCharms, R. (1957). Changes in social perception as a function of the personal relevance of behavior. *Sociometry,* 20, 75–85.
Jones, E. E., Wells, H. H., & Torrey, R. (1958). Some effects of feedback from the experimenter on conformity behavior. *Journal of Abnormal and Social Psychology,* 57 207–213
Kelly, G. A. (1955). *The psychology of personal constructs.* New York, Norton. **[177]**
Leventhal, H. (1956). *Effects of setting factors and judges' interpersonal constructs on predictive behavior.* Unpublished doctoral dissertation, University of North Carolina.
Osgood, C. E. (1952). The nature and measurement of meaning. *Psychological Bulletin,* 49, 192–237.
Osgood, C. E., & Luria, Z. A blind analysis of a case of multiple personality using the semantic differential. *Journal of Abnormal and Social Psychology,* 49, 579–591.

32   Part One   The Penetration of Action

Parsons, T., & Shils, E. (1954). *Toward a general theory of action.* Cambridge: Harvard University Press.
Sherif, M. (1935). A study of some social factors in perception. *Archives of Psychology,* No. 187.
Steiner, I. (1955). Interpersonal behavior as influenced by accuracy of social perception. *Psychological Review,* 62, 268–275.
Stouffer, S. A. (1949). An analysis of conflicting social norms. *American Sociological Review,* 14, 707–717.
Stouffer, S. A., & Toby, J. (1951). Role conflict and personality. *American Journal of Sociology,* 41, 395–406.
Tagiuri, R. (1952). Relational analysis: An extension of sociometric method with emphasis upon social perception. *Sociometry,* 15, 91–104.
Thibaut, J. W., & Riecken, H. W. (1955). Some determinants and consequences of the perception of social causality. *Journal of Personality,* 24, 113–133.
Thibaut, J. W., & Strickland, L. H. (1956). Psychological set and social conformity. *Journal of Personality,* 25, 115–129. **[178]**

ATTRIBUTION THEORY

Chapter 2

Role Playing Variations and Their Informational Value for Person Perception

Edward E. Jones, Keith E. Davis and Kenneth J. Gergen
Duke University

Largely under the impetus of Heider's (1944, 1958) persistent concern with phenomenological analysis, much of the recent research in social perception has addressed itself to the naive psychology of the individual perceiver. How do individuals use the behavior of others to infer the probable existence of more enduring personal characteristics? What are the bases for social evaluation that in turn color the impressions one forms of another? What information is ignored and what information is made central in the formation of an impression? A number of investigators have sought a partial answer to these questions by assuming that a basic feature of naive phenomenology is the assignment of observed behavior to psychological causes. It seems logical to propose, for example, that behavior whose locus of causation lies within the person is more relevant to inferences about his particular characteristics than behavior that is induced or constrained by external events. The present investigation was designed to demonstrate this proposition with specific reference to the adoption and performance of social roles.

The concept of role has had a lively and controversial history in the literature of social science. It is often treated as a crucial bridging concept since it concerns the relations

---

From *Journal of Abnormal and Social Psychology,* 63, 302–310. References and reference style updated by the editor.

between social requirements and normative expectations on the one hand, and individual perceptions and behavior on the other. Controversy has surrounded the many attempts to define role, as Levinson (1959) notes, because these attempts have vacillated between viewing role as an aspect of social structure and viewing it as a description of socially relevant individual behavior. In the present paper, the concept of role refers to role demands rather than actual behavior. Role is herein treated as a set of expected behaviors implicit in the instructions to a stimulus person. These instructions define the impression the stimulus person should attempt to create in presenting himself to an interviewer, and variations in behavior given this role definition represent the major independent variable.

The present treatment of role is quite consistent with any other treatment that stresses the shaping of individual responses by social expectations or externally imposed norms. The point has often been made that general adherence to relevant sets of social norms is very important in facilitating social interaction. Particularly in organizational contexts, but by no means exclusively there, many social interactions can be effectively described in terms of the interplay of appropriate role behaviors. Jones and Thibaut (1958) have emphasized the economic significance of such interactions between roles as reducing the need for inferences about idiosyncratic personal characteristics. The complement of this point is that behavior appropriate to role expectations has little informational value in highlighting these individual characteristics.

To follow this line of reasoning a little further, roles facilitate interaction and the social cognitions that support it. The naive person has his own repertoire of role constructs that help to anchor his perceptions of the social environment and to endow it with the necessary stability for planful action. On the other hand, the performance of social roles tends to mask information about individual characteristics because the person reveals only that he is responsive to normative requirements. If these requirements are unclear or conflicting, of course, he may reveal something about himself by the way in which he defines and displays appropriate behavior. The stronger and more unequivocal the role demands, however, the less information is provided by behavior appropriate to the role. Following our introductory comments, this conclusion may be derived from considering probable differences in the attribution of phenomenal causality. When a person's [302]* behavior is very much in line with clear and potent social expectations, we tend to treat it as eternally caused and uninformative with regard to a wide range of personal characteristics. When it departs from normative expectations, on the other hand, we tend to locate the cause for the departure in motivational acts peculiar to the person. We may assume, of course, that he misperceived the expectations, but we would then wish to push on to determine the motivational sources of this perceptual distortion.

From the perceiver's point of view, the behavior of a stimulus person which departs from role expectations takes on special significance for appraising the latter's personal characteristics. In assessing the motives behind such a departure from role, the perceiver must view the sample of behavior available against the background of role specifications. In general, our inferences from behavior to personality must take into account the stimulus conditions eliciting the behavior. This is no less true when the stimulus conditions consist of clearly established role expectations.

---

*Bracketed bold numbers refer to original page numbers. Page numbers indicate where the original page ended.

In attempting to predict the nature and direction of inferences, given a sample of behavior that departs from role expectations, a number of factors must be considered. For one thing, there may be tendencies for the perceiver either to minimize or maximize the nature of the departure. In organizing his impression of the stimulus person, the perceiver may assimilate the latter's behavior sample to the role specifications governing the situation, thus avoiding the problem of inferring unique characteristics. Alternatively, there may be a contrast effect in that the behavior sample becomes cognitively salient and is recalled as departing even more from the role than was actually the case. We are not as yet in a position to choose between these alternative possibilities, or to specify the conditions favoring assimilation versus contrast. The present study does provide a measure of memory distortion, however.

Assuming that assimilation does not occur, or that it occurs incompletely, the perceiver's inferences about unique characteristics rest on his attempt to understand *why* the departure from role expectations took place, Undoubtedly, some departures are intended to achieve a humorous effect (the exchange of "friendly insults" between collaborators on a task); others are intended to play down role characteristics that might be offensive (the "soft-selling" salesman); still others stem from motives of rebellion and nonconformity. In the typical case, however, departure from role suggests a pattern of motivation and skill that is at variance with specific role requirements. The individual does not play the role because, somehow, he cannot or will not. In such cases, personality seems to override role expectations or to color role performance in a unique and significant way. The most probable inference from role departures of this type is that the person reveals something of his "true self" through his failure to perform the expected role.

The present investigation treats this last conjecture as a proposition. An experiment was designed in which stimulus persons were instructed in one of two patterns of role performance. The behavior of the stimulus person was arranged to be consistent with either the first or the second of these patterns, thus creating two experimental treatments where the person's behavior was "in role" and two treatments where it was clearly "out of role." The general hypotheses prompting the study were:

1. Persons performing in line with role expectations reveal little of value for assessing their personal characteristics. When asked to describe such a person, subjects do so with little confidence and tend to avoid extreme statements.
2. Persons whose performance departs from role expectations reveal their personal characteristics through the direction and form of this departure. Their behavior is judged as internally caused and forms the basis for direct inferences about personal characteristics, characteristics that may be judged with confidence.
3. Roles do, however, serve as an organizing function in person perception. Because of its predictive value, in-role behavior is more accurately recalled than behavior that departs from role expectations.

Note that no specific hypothesis was formulated concerning the possibilities of assimilation and contrast, but data bearing on these possibilities are to be presented. [303]

METHOD

Subjects

One hundred and thirty-four male undergraduates participated as subjects in groups ranging in size from 5 to 20. Since the experimental design consisted of four treatment variations, an attempt was made to assign approximately equal numbers of subjects to each condition. The actual cell frequencies varied from 31 to 37. As one attempt to control for individual differences in orientation to others, care was also taken to compose the treatment groups of approximately equal numbers of high, middle, and low scorers on Christie's Mach IV Scale. This scale was originally designed to measure differences in the tendency to endorse Machiavellian sentiments. A high score reflects a tough minded, cynical, and somewhat opportunistic attitude toward others; low scorers are more inclined to value affective involvement with others and to feel that social relations should be governed by strict ethical norms. A description of item content and some sampling comparison data may be found in Christie and Merton (1958). Studies by Jones and Daugherty (1959) and Jones, Gergen, and Davis (1962) provide data on the experimental validity of the scale. Though the present study was not designed to validate the Mach IV Scale, and the scale served mainly as a control variable, the Mach IV score was included as a potential source of variation in the analysis of data. It was felt that the highs and the lows might respond differently to the experimental conditions, though no specific hypotheses involving Machiavellianism were formulated.

Procedure Overview

Each experimental session began with a brief introduction in which the experimenter described the study as a problem-solving task involving judgments of another person. Subjects were instructed to listen carefully to a tape-recorded interview between a psychologist and a student, in which the student would be instructed to play a particular role. The tape recording began with the psychologist giving explicit instructions to the stimulus person (SP) about the interview to follow. Although the recordings were actually based on carefully constructed scripts, an attempt was made to convince the subjects that the SP was given no information about the interview and his role that did not appear on the tape. Thus, the taped instructions emphasized that the SP was to present himself in the interview in such a way as to impress the interviewer that he was ideally suited for a particular job. In interviews played to different groups of subjects one of two jobs requiring radically different personal qualifications was described. In this way the content of the role was manipulated. The SP was told in the recording to "be as honest as you can unless you think another answer would help your chances better of getting the job." In the interview that followed, SP answered some standard questions about his background in a neutral fashion and then responded to a series of choice items some of which were clearly relevant to the job for which he was applying. In responding to these items, the SP either gave answers appropriate to the job description he had been given, or answers which revealed markedly different preferences. Thus, the design involved presentation of four different stimulus patterns, two of which were "in-role" and two of which were "out-of-role."

After listening to the interview, each subject was asked to state his general impression of the SP and to fill out in succession the following dependent variable forms: given the same choice items to which the SP responded in the interview, subjects were asked to reconstruct from memory SP's response to each item; after this choice test form was collected the subject was handed an identical form and instructed to indicate how the SP would have responded if he were being completely honest in describing himself; finally each subject was given a 16-item trait-rating scale and instructed to rate the SP, and indicate his subjective confidence for each rating. The stimulus materials and dependent variable forms are more fully described below.

Stimulus Variations

As implied by the foregoing discussion, the experimental design called for the construction of four separate tapes to be played as the stimulus pattern for independent groups of subjects. These tapes varied along two cross-cutting dimensions: on half of the tapes the job described was that of a submariner, on the remaining half the job was that of an "astronaut" in training for space flights; on half of the tapes the job description was followed by a set of responses appropriate for the submariner job (other-directed pattern), on the remaining half the responses were more appropriate for the astronaut job (inner-directed pattern). The four tapes were actually constructed by separately recording these four segments, always with the same person reading the part of the SP, and splicing them into the following combinations: Submariner–Other, Submariner–Inner, Astronaut–Inner, and Astronaut–Other.

ROLE DESCRIPTIONS   Presentation of the submariner's role was prefaced by a reference to the capacities of atomic submarines and the corresponding qualities necessary for adjusting to the social conditions of submarine life. The following excerpts give both the flavor and some of the content of the role description:

> People at the submarine school are pretty sure they know quite a bit about the kind of person who adapts well to submarine life.... The main thing they look for is stability and good citizenship.... constant cooperation with others is essential ... willingness to tolerate routine ... not supposed to think for himself ... sticks to the rules.... Since submariners are in such constant contact with each other, it's important, of course, that the good submariner enjoys other people around, that he be relaxed and friendly and slow to irritate.

Presentation of the astronaut's role capitalized on the timely issue of sending a single man into space. The role description is suggested again by the following excerpts:

> One of the most difficult requirements of space travel, at least in its early stages, is that it will most likely involve a man's being isolated from virtually all human contact for long periods of time ... looking for men who don't need to have other people around ... inner resources and the ability to maintain concentration without stimulation from others ... alert, imaginative, resourceful....**[304]**

These particular role descriptions were designed, of course, without regard to truth value, solely to emphasize plausibly two sets of qualities that might best be described as other- versus inner-directed.

BEHAVIOR SAMPLES SPs on each of the four tapes responded in an identical fashion until they were asked by the interviewer to take a "choice test which has recently been devised to indicate how well a person will fit into various niches in life…." The test that followed consisted of 22 items, each comprising a pair of statements. The SP was instructed to choose the member of each pair which was more characteristic of himself and to indicate his certainty on an 11-point scale. Half of the items were buffer items not specifically relevant to difference between roles and always answered in the same manner by the SPs. The remaining 11 items were "critical" in reflecting the intended difference between inner- and other-directed response patterns. The following examples indicate some of the pair members endorsed by the SPs in the two behavior samples:

	(C1) Other-Directed	(C2) Inner-Directed
3.	I always like to support the majority.	I like to feel free to do what I want to do.
9.	I would like to be a door-to-door salesman.	I would like to be a forest ranger.
17.	When planning something I always seek suggestions from others.	When planning something I like to work on my own.
21.	I like to know how other people think I should behave.	I avoid situations where I am expected to behave in a conventional way.
22.	I like to settle arguments and disputes with others.	I like to attack points of view that are contrary to my own.

For each of these item pairs, the SP orally endorsed the statement appropriate to the condition and indicated the degree of his certainty. Degree of certainty was predetermined so that the same scale positions were endorsed the same number of times for each behavior sample. This was to equalize any tendency to regress toward or away from less certainty in the memory task.

Impression Rating Scale

The final task of the subjects was to record their impression of the SP in terms of a 16-item rating scale. Each item consisted of two polar adjectives separated by 10 scale points. To the right of each item was a 5-point confidence scale for that item. Thus, subjects were to indicate what they thought the SP was "really like" and how confident they were of each rating. Ten of the items were chosen to reflect five distinct clusters whose contents were relevant to the hypotheses being tested. Each cluster consisted of two items, each suggesting an aspect of cluster meaning but balanced for direction to inhibit tendencies toward response set. Thus the conformity cluster consisted of the pairs "conforming–independent" and "creative–unoriginal." Other clusters were affiliation, intelligence, motivation, and candor. The remaining six items were related to each other only in their strong evaluative tone: warm–cold, popular–unpopular, likable–irritating, etc.

In analyzing the results, cluster scores were derived simply by adding the scale placements for the two component items, naturally reversing the score of one item. Confidence scores were similarly derived by simple addition of scale values.

RESULTS

Predicted Differences in Perception

In line with the general hypotheses of the study, the first specific prediction was that SPs performing out-of-role (Astro–Others and Sub–Inners) would be perceived as revealing their true preferences in the simulated interview more than SPs performing in-role (Astro–Inners and Sub–Others). The most direct test of this hypothesis may be found in the data provided by the subjects in trying to indicate how the SP would have responded in the interview if he was being completely faithful to himself. These data are summarized in Figure 2.1A, and in Table 2.1. It is clear that the prediction is confirmed. The Astro–Other and the Sub–Inner SPs are both seen as revealing their true preferences, though there is a slight and understandable regression toward the mean. Interestingly enough, and quite in line with predictions, the two in-role groups locate the true answers of the SPs almost exactly halfway between the other-directed and the inner-directed pattern. Since behavior appropriate to powerful role requirements generally masks the characteristics of the actor, the perceivers apparently feel that their best guess is a completely neutral one.

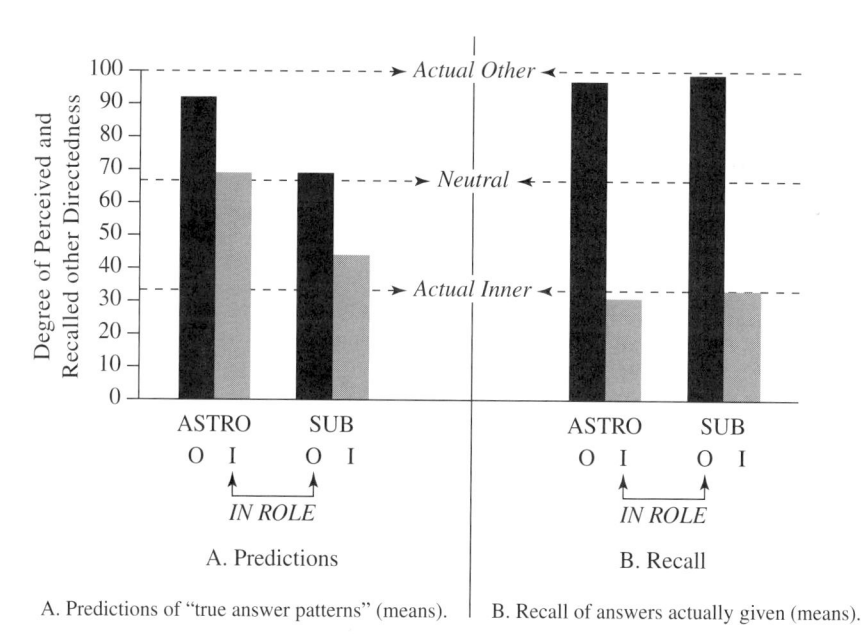

A. Predictions of "true answer patterns" (means). | B. Recall of answers actually given (means).

Figure 2.1 Degree of Perceived and Recalled Other Directedness

Table 2.1 Predictions of SP's True Response
(Summary of Analysis of Variance[a] and t Test Results)

Source	df	MS	F	Group	N	$\bar{X}$	t
A. Astro–Sub	1	1,554.73	63.56**	AO	33	91.12	5.32**
B. Inner–Other	1	1,764.91	64.27**	SO	31	69.26	
C. Mach	2	18.81					
A × B	1	8.63		AI	33	69.15	5.98**
A × C	2	62.67		SI	37	43.92	
B × C	2	31.23					
A × B × C	2	22.84					
Error	122	27.46					
Total	133						

[a]Using the approximation technique for unequal cell frequencies (Snedecor, 1946).
**$p < .001$.

The next issue to be raised is the extent to which these results are restricted to the [305] particular pattern of items covered in the recorded interview. That is, do the highly significant results summarized in Table 2.1 merely reflect rational manipulations of the specific response scale used by the SP, or do they generalize to related measures of perception and inference? Recall that the subjects also filled out a bipolar adjective rating scale, in an attempt to express their appraisal of the SP's true characteristics. The items of this scale were members of small clusters of related traits, varying in their relevance to the dimension of inner–other directedness. Two of the most relevant clusters, by a priori judgment, were attempts to measure perceptions of affiliation and conformity. It was predicted that the two out-of-role SPs would be perceived to differ markedly in both affiliation and conformity and that the two in-role SPs would not. The results, as summarized in Table 2.2, clearly confirm this prediction. The Astro–Other is seen as significantly more affiliative and conforming than the Sub–Inner, and each is seen as differing significantly from its in-role control. Analyses of variance indicate that Machiavellianism contributes to no significant effects and there are no significant interactions between role and behavior sample. This result seems to indicate that genuine perceptual decisions have been made that involve assessing the meaning of the behavior sample provided by the SP against the background of the role-playing instructions imposed on him.

Since the predictions involving the direction and magnitude of perceptual rating differences have been borne out, the next relevant question concerns the confidence with which perceptual judgments were made. The general hypothesis, it will be recalled, predicted that in-role ratings would be less confidently made than ratings of out-of-role behavior. This prediction could be easily tested since the subject rendered a judgment of confidence with respect to each trait rated. The most precise test of the general prediction involves confidence ratings based on the two clusters most relevant to the differences

Chapter Two Role Playing Variations and Their Informational Value for Person Perception 41

between role: affiliation and conformity. When confidence ratings on these clusters are summed for each individual, the **[306]** resulting pattern clearly confirms the hypothesis. As Table 2.3 shows, the interaction between role and behavior sample is highly significant. As for the individual mean comparison, in each case the subjects feel more confident about rating the SP who is behaving out of role than the SP who is behaving the same way *in* role.

Table 2.2 Perceptions of Affiliation and Conformity

	Astro–Other, $n = 33$	Astro–Inner, $n = 33$	Sub–Other, $n = 31$	Sub–Inner, $n = 37$	Comparisons Direction	t
Affiliation						
$\bar{X}$	15.27	11.12	12.00	8.64	AO > SO	4.02**;
SD	2.92	3.81	3.53	4.73	AI > SI	2.12*
Conformity						
$\bar{X}$	15.91	13.09	12.58	9.41	AO > SO	4.02**;
SD	3.22	3.42	3.39	4.95	AI > SI	3.65*

Note: The higher the mean value, the greater the perceived affiliation or conformity. Comparisons between AO and SI are noy tabled, but the differences between these conditions would of course be highly significant.

*$p < .03$.
**$p < .001$.

Table 2.3 Confidence Ratings by Treatments (Analysis of Variance[a] Summary)

		Affiliation and conformity	
Source	df	MS	F
A. Astro–Sub	1	.07	
B. Inner–Other	1	1.62	3.29
C. Mach	2	.26	
A × B	1	8.58[b]	17.42**
A × C	2	.33	
B × C	2	.84	
A × B × C	2	.47	
Within	122	.49	
Total	133		

[a]Using the approximation technique for unequal cell frequencies (Snedecor, 1946).
[b]Results of tests of individual mean comparisons:
AO > SO, $t = 3.30$, $p < .01$; SI > AI, $t = 2.55$, $p = .02$.
**$p < .001$.

Differences in Recall

As one of their tasks, all subjects were asked to reproduce the responses made by the SP in the simulated interview. The fidelity of these attempts at recall was treated in two ways. First, a recall score was computed for each subject involving the degree of discrepancy in scale points for each item, summed without regard to direction. For convenience we may call these absolute error scores. Subjects were expected to make fewer errors in recalling the behavior samples of the in-role treatments than those in the out-of-role treatments. The assumption was that roles, like all categories that summarize relevant information, facilitate cognitive organization and enhance one's ability to predict behavior that is appropriate to the role. In the present case, the behavior sample available in the in-role treatments tended to confirm the expectations established by the role instructions. For subjects in the out-of-role treatments, the role instructions could not be used to organize and predict the behavior which occurred, except insofar as the subjects were led to adopt a clear negative expectation that the behavior was the opposite of that called for.

The results on this measure of absolute recall confirm the hypothesis. The responses of the in-role SPs (Astro–Inner and Sub–Other) are recalled with greater accuracy than the responses of the out-of-role SPs (Astro–Other and Sub–Inner). As Table 2.4 shows, the predicted interaction is significant. ($p < .05$). Most of this interaction effect comes from the two cells in which the SP is other-directed (Sub–Others > Astro–Other, $t = 2.60$, $p < .01$; Astro–Inner > Sub–Inner, $t = .64$, $p < .50$). There is no obvious reason for this difference unless the submariner role was more helpfully predictive in organizing information about the other-directed behavior sample than was the astronaut role in organizing information about the inner-directed sample.

The recall data were also scored to take account of the direction of deviation from accuracy. These data are relevant for answering any questions dealing with the assimilation of recalled responses to categories implied by the roles. In fact, as Figure 2.1B shows, there was no evidence of either assimilation or contrast in directional recall of the SP's interview preferences. Those errors which the subjects did make (see the foregoing data on absolute errors) were quite evenly distributed on either side of the true scale position. As far as the mean-directed error scores are concerned, then, the group recall accuracy was extremely high. **[307]** Of course, we cannot state on the basis of these results that distortions from

Table 2.4 Absolute Recall Errors by Treatments (Analysis of Variance[a] Summary)

Source	df	MS	F
A. Astro–Sub	1	3.89	
B. Inner–Other	1	1.36	
C. Mach	2	.30	
A × B	1	9.59	6.23*
A × C	2	3.61	
B × C	2	.13	
A × B × C	2	1.40	
Within	122	1.54	
Total	133		

[a]Using the approximation technique for unequal cell frequencies (Snedecor, 1946).

[b]The means for the four cells represented by this interaction were:
$\bar{X}$ (Astro–Other) = 12.42;
$\bar{X}$ (Sub–Other) = 9.52;
$\bar{X}$ (Astro–Inner) = 10.00;
$\bar{X}$ (Sub–Inner) = 10.56.

*$p < .05$.

Chapter Two Role Playing Variations and Their Informational Value for Person Perception 43

accurate recall of social behavior are always random distortions, but in the present case there is no evidence for directional errors either toward or away from the role category implied by the instructions to the SP.

Perception of Additional Characteristics

In planning the experiment, it seemed at least conceivable that many subjects would attribute the SP's out-of-role performance in the Astro–Other and Sub–Inner conditions to poor motivation, lack of intelligence, or both. If such were the case, then it would not necessarily follow that the behavior sample provided would be taken as a "true" reflection of the SP's affiliative and conforming tendencies (or the lack thereof). We have seen that most subjects did consider the out-of-role performance to be reflections of these tendencies, but it is still of interest to note their ratings of the SP on trait clusters tapping perceived motivation and intelligence. As Table 2.5 shows, the Sub–Other SP was seen as more highly motivated and intelligent than the Astro–Other SP ($p < .01$), but this expected trend was slightly reversed in the case of the two inner-directed SPs. It would appear, then, that the in-role SP is judged to have greater motivation and intelligence only when the role involves volunteering for the submarine service. There is no obvious reason for this difference in response to the two roles. Perhaps the inner-directed pattern seemed more artificial or obvious in the context of astronaut instructions, or perhaps the meaning of motivation and intelligence became less situation-bound when subjects were asked to appraise a truly inner-directed man.

Also of interest are the ratings of perceived candor. It might be expected that performing out-of-role would be construed as evidence of the SP's frankness and sincerity. The results in Table 2.5 do show a clear difference between in-role and out-of-role SPs with regard to the perception of candor. As expected, the in-role SPs are judged by the average subject to fall at or near the midpoint of the scale (10.00 for the cluster); the out-of-role SPs are seen as significantly more candid in each variation of role instructions.

Table 2.5 Selected Trait and Cluster Means by Treatments with Appropriate Comparisons

Clusters	Astro–Other, $n = 33$	Sub–Other, $n = 33$	Astro–Inner, $n = 31$	Sub–Inner, $n = 37$	Relevant Comparisons
Motivation					
$\bar{X}$	9.97	12.10	9.64	10.92	SO > AO, $p < .01$
SD	3.47	3.66	4.48	4.09	
Intelligence					
$\bar{X}$	8.00	11.13	9.39	9.84	SO > AO, $p < .01$
SD	3.35	4.15	3.72	3.94	
Candor					
$\bar{X}$	12.42	9.68	10.09	12.08	AO > SO, $p < .01$; SI > AI, $p < .05$
SD	4.09	3.61	3.68	3.77	

Results on the remaining traits add little to the picture already presented. For the most part the means fall into a pattern similar to those reflecting perceived affiliation and conformity. That is, the two in-role SPs are perceived to be relatively neutral on most of the evaluative trait dimensions; the Astro–Others are seen as significantly more likable (versus irritating), warm (versus cold), popular (versus unpopular), and helpful (versus disinterested) than the Sub–Inners. This pattern of findings might suggest the operation of a strong "halo" or "generosity" effect favoring those who are perceived as other-directed. However, it must be recalled that the Astro–Other SP is seen as less highly-motivated [308] and less intelligent than the Sub–Other SP, personal attributes that are usually considered to be quite evaluative. Also Astro–Other and Sub–Inner SPs are both seen as more candid than their in-role controls. It seems more likely, then, that evaluative traits like warm, popular, likable, and helpful are linked to other-directedness more by direct association than through an underlying decision that the Astro–Other SP is good and the Sub–Inner SP is bad. This conclusion is supported by two further results: to an extent that is nearly significant, the two out-of-role SPs are seen as more interesting (versus boring) than the two in-role SPs; also the Astro–Inner SP is seen as significantly more conceited (versus self-effacing) than either the Astro–Other or the Sub–Inner SP. While these incidental findings are not all easy to rationalize, they do point up the complexity and subtlety of the cognitive impressions created by the experimental combinations of role and behavior sample.

Machiavellianism

While the study was designed without any consideration of the possible role of Machiavellianism as measured by Christie's Mach IV Scale, it did seem possible that high scorers on the Mach Scale might be generally more sensitive to variations in role instructions and more inclined toward negative evaluation of the SPs who were unable or unwilling to play the prescribed role.

In all of the major analyses, Mach level was included routinely as a potential source of variance. In no case did it contribute to significant main or interactive effects. Either the situational manipulations were simply too powerful for individual differences on this dimension to manifest themselves, or our knowledge of Mach Scale correlates is insufficient to make meaningful predictive statements. In view of the results of a recently completed study by Jones, Gergen, and Davis (1962), the latter alternative seems quite tenable. With respect to one meaningful comparison, however, Machiavellianism does make a significant contribution. The high scorers tend to attribute greater intelligence to the in-role than the out-of-role SPs whereas the low scorers show the reverse pattern in perceiving intelligence. This difference between highs and lows is significant ($t = 2.15$, $p < .05$). A similar trend was noted with regard to perceived motivation, but this fell short of significance ($t = 1.62$, $p < .15$). Though the differences in perceived intelligence are consistent with what little knowledge we do have about high and low Mach scorers, there is little else in the data to suggest that the variable is relevant to the perception of in-role and out-of-role SPs.

DISCUSSION

The results of the present study are unequivocal. Starting from the assumption that individual characteristics are obscured when a person is exposed to strong and demanding stimulus forces, we have reasoned that social stimuli embraced by the role concept may operate in this same way. Thus a person who conforms to salient social expectations reveals little about his basic and distinguishing characteristics. On the other hand, one who rejects or ignores pressures to play a defined role is considered to reflect his true disposition and is perceived with confidence.

It is undoubtedly true that this reasoning is ubiquitous in the psychologist's approach to personality assessment. In many programs of assessment, the patient or subject is exposed to a variety of situational pressures and task demands. Of his responses to these situations, his nonmodal reactions are clearly more informative and carry the most interpretive weight. To take another example, psychological screening for desirable jobs must cope with the problems raised by this study in order to be effective. Since the role constraints for the applicant are often obvious, the interviewer or employer must penetrate to more subtle cues or fall back on projective devices which, though unreliable at best, at least produce the response variety essential for individualized judgment.

It is probably true that short-term social interactions can perfectly well proceed in line with established expectations defining reciprocal roles. If the interaction is self-limiting (as, say, between a hotel guest and his bellhop) there is little need for personalized information to sustain the interaction. When a relationship is more permanent, however, and involves **[309]** the prospect of interactions in varied situations, such information rapidly increases in value. It is to the perceiver's advantage, in such cases, to be especially attuned to out-of-role behaviors and to create situations in which out-of-role behaviors can be most clearly observed. The results of the present study show that such behaviors, rightly or wrongly, are perceived to be peculiarly diagnostic of individual characteristics. Judgments about these personal qualities are presumably most important in governing the perceiver's behavior as he ventures into new situations with the SP.

SUMMARY

An experiment was designed to test the general proposition that behavior which is appropriate to a clearly specified role is relatively uninformative about personal characteristics. Subjects were asked to listen to a recorded interview in which the interviewee was heard being instructed, in two treatment conditions, to respond "as if" he very much desired to be accepted in the submarine service, and in two treatments as if he wished to qualify as a space astronaut. The qualifications of these two positions were described in such a way that dramatically different personal qualifications were required. As the interview proceeded, the interviewee either responded in line with the qualifications described for the astronaut position (inner-directedness) or with those for the submariner position (other-directedness). Thus, in a four-cell design there were two cells of in-role behavior to be judged (Astronaut–Inner and Submariner–Other) and two cells of out-of-role behavior (Astronaut–Other and Submariner–Inner). Reasoning from the importance of distinguishing between self-caused and externally induced behavior in person perception, the following predictions were made:

1. Out-of-role SPs are perceived to be revealing their true characteristics more than in-role SPs.
2. Out-of-role SPs are rated with greater confidence on the dimensions relevant to role performance.
3. The performance of in-role SPs is more accurately recalled than that of out-of-role SPs.

Each of these predictions was strongly confirmed by the results.

REFERENCES

Christie, R., & Merton, R. K. (1958). Procedures for the sociological study of the values climate of medical schools. *Journal of Medical Education,* 33, 125–153.

Heider, F. (1944). Social perception and phenomenal causality. *Psychological Review,* 51, 358–374.

Heider, F. (1958). *The psychology of interpersonal relations.* New York: Wiley.

Jones, E. E., & Daugherty, B. N. (1959). Political orientation and the perceptual effects of an anticipated interaction. *Journal of Abnormal and Social Psychology,* 59, 340–349.

Jones, E. E., Gergen, K. J., & Davis, K. E. (1962). Some determinants of reactions to being approved or disapproved as a person. *Psychological Monographs,* 76 (2, Whole No. 521) 17.

Jones, E. E., & Thibaut, J. W. (1958). Interaction goals as bases of inference in interpersonal perception. In R. Tagiuri & L. Petrullo (Eds.), *Person perception and interpersonal behavior.* Stanford: Stanford University Press, 151–179.

Levinson, D. J. (1959). Role, personality, and social structure in the organizational setting. *Journal of Abnormal and Social Psychology,* 68, 170–180

Snedecor, G. W. (1946). *Statistical methods.* (4th ed.) Ames, Iowa: Collegiate Press. [310]

ATTRIBUTION THEORY

Chapter 3

From Acts to Dispositions: The Attribution Process in Person Perception

Edward E. Jones
Duke University
Keith E. Davis
University of Colorado

Many social psychologists have expressed a central interest in the ties between person perception and interpersonal behavior. The writings of Fritz Heider have exerted a predominant and continuing influence on research designed to illuminate these ties. From his 1944 paper on phenomenal causality to his more recent (1958) book on *The Psychology of Interpersonal Relations,* Heider has persistently concerned himself with the cognitive aspects of social interaction. His writings are especially important for recognizing and identifying the major problems with which [219]* any theory of person perception must contend: causal attribution, cognition–sentiment relations, taking the other's perspective, and so on. Heider's comments are comprehensive, perceptive, and provocative. His exposition does not lend itself readily, however, to the formulation of interrelated prepositional statements. Thus the research which has been done to date is largely demonstrational in significance and dismayingly sparse in quantity. While the

---

Reprinted with permission from L. Berkowitz (Ed.), (1965), *Advances in Experimental Social Psychology,* Vol. 2, New York: Academic Press, 219–266.

*Bracketed bold numbers refer to original page numbers. Page numbers indicate where the original page ended.

studies which we intend to review in this chapter may be seen as islands in the same phenomenological sea, it is not very clear how one navigates between them.

We believe that the kind of systematic, conceptual structure that is needed must involve an analysis of phenomenal causality, or the determinants and consequences of attributing causation for particular actions. In the central portion of this chapter we shall attempt to review, and to some extent reformulate, much of the recent research concerning phenomenal causality and the attribution of intentions. Our first task, however, is to introduce the notion of explaining an action by assigning an intention and to set the stage for the theory of inference which follows.

THE NAIVE EXPLANATION OF HUMAN ACTIONS: EXPLANATION BY ATTRIBUTING INTENTIONS

At the heart of Heider's analysis of naive or "common sense" psychology is the distinction between personal and impersonal causality. We assume that the person-perceiver's fundamental task is to interpret or infer the causal antecedents of action. The perceiver seeks to find *sufficient reason* why the person acted and why the act took on a particular form. Instead of the potentially infinite regress of cause and effect which characterizes an impersonal, scientific analysis, the perceiver's explanation comes to a stop when an intention or motive is assigned that has the quality of being reason enough. "He eats because he is hungry" would not ordinarily bring a request for further explanation. After all, eating is something one would do if one were hungry.

The cognitive task of establishing sufficient reason for an action involves processing available information about, or making assumptions about, the links between stable individual dispositions and observed action. Let us start with the case in which a perceiver observes an action and at least some of its effects. His basic problem as a perceiver is to decide which of these effects, if any, were intended by the actor. Let us first address ourselves to the problem of "if any." In order to conclude that at least some of the effects achieved by an action were intended, the perceiver must first believe that the actor was aware his action would have the observed effects. Thus a first condition in the inference process is the assumption of knowledge on the part of the actor. [220] Consequences of an action which the actor could not have foreseen do not qualify as candidates for what he was trying to achieve. The condition of knowledge is of critical importance within our legal system where it is customary to distinguish among levels of responsibility for a crime: (1) intentional (*P* did *X* to enjoy the immediate effects of *X*), (2) incidental (*P* did *X* as a means of getting to *Y*), and (3) accidental (*X* was a consequence of *P*'s action that he neither intended nor expected).

In addition to assumptions about knowledge of consequences, decisions linking intentional attributes to the effects of action are also affected by the perceiver's judgments of the actor's ability to bring about the effects observed. Simply put, an actor cannot achieve his objectives solely by desiring to achieve them. He must have the capacities or skill to move from his present condition of desire to a subsequent condition of attainment and satisfaction. When a person's actions have certain consequences, it is important for the perceiver to determine whether the person was capable of producing these consequences in response to his intentions. Especially in the case where an actor *fails* to produce certain effects that might have been anticipated by the perceiver,

Chapter 3 From Acts to Dispositions: The Attribution Process in Person Perception 49

there may be ambiguity as to whether the actor did not want to produce the effects, or wanted but was not able to.

Even when effects are achieved, however, the perceiver may have the problem of assessing the relative contribution of luck or chance. When a novice archer hits the bull's-eye, we are more apt to attribute this to luck than to skill. There are other occasions when we do not assign intentions to correspond with effects achieved because we do not consider the actor capable of producing those effects at will. A jury is more likely to believe that a killing is accidental if the average person would have lacked the skill (the marksmanship, the strength, etc.) to bring about the crime deliberately. It was quite possible to believe that Oswald intended to kill President Kennedy and not Mrs. Kennedy or a Secret Service man, because he was known to be an expert marksman. For a further discussion of the problems involved in judging ability relative to difficulty and luck, the reader is referred to Heider (1958).

The perceiver may have certain information about knowledge and ability (he may be informed that Oswald knew the gun was loaded and that Oswald often practiced on a local rifle range), or he may merely assume that knowledge and ability were probably present or probably absent. Whether the perceiver's conclusion about such matters is correct or incorrect, the conclusion obviously will affect his decisions about the actor's intentions in the situation. Knowledge and ability are preconditions for the assignment of intentions. Each plays a similar role in enabling the perceiver to decide whether an effect or consequence of action was **[221]** accidental. The assignment of intention, in turn, is a precondition for inferences concerning those underlying stable characteristics toward which the perceiver presses in attaching significance to action. As Heider (1958) argued, the perceiver ordinarily strives to discover the invariances which underlie manifest actions in order to stabilize the environment and render it more predictable.

We may attempt to summarize the foregoing remarks by the diagram presented as Figure 3.1. It is assumed that the perceiver typically starts with the overt action of another; this is the grist for his cognitive mill. He then makes certain decisions concerning ability and knowledge which will let him cope with the problem of attributing particular intentions to the actor. The attribution of intentions, in turn, is a necessary step in the assignment of more stable characteristics to the actor.

Figure 3.1 attempts to clarify the circumstances under which any intentions will be assigned to explain action. But we now seek to extend the analysis in order to account for the attribution of particular intentions and dispositions on the basis of particular actions. We shall here largely ignore the problems involved in imputing knowledge and ability and concentrate on specific linkages between effects achieved and intentions revealed. We

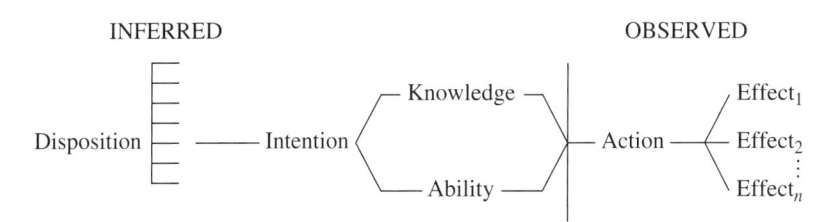

Figure 3.1 The Action–Attribute Paradigm

assume that those consequences of action obviously neither intended by the actor nor within the range of his capabilities will be considered irrelevant by the perceiver.

A THEORY OF CORRESPONDENT INFERENCES

Our purpose is to construct a theory which systematically accounts for a perceiver's inferences about what an actor was trying to achieve by a particular action. In achieving this purpose we view the action as occurring within a particular situational context which defines, in large part, its meaning for the perceiver. In particular, as we shall attempt to show in greater detail below, the meaning of an action—its intentional significance—derives from some consideration of the alternative action [222] possibilities available to but foregone by the actor. As perceivers of action, we can only begin to understand the motives prompting an act if we view the effects of the act in the framework of effects that other actions could have achieved.

Perhaps an example will further clarify our purpose and approach. Let us imagine ourselves as silent observers of an interaction episode in which *A* and *B* are working together on a task. We observe that *A* gives orders to *B*, monitors his performance, and shows his displeasure with the quality and quantity of *B*'s work. The inferences about *A* we would most likely draw from this episode would depend critically on the action alternatives seen to be available to him. If *A* and *B* had come together in a free situation, we would be inclined to see *A* as quite arrogant and domineering. If we were informed that *A* had been given instructions to take a directive leadership role, we would be less likely to regard his dominating behavior as an indication of his personal qualities: that is, our inferences about dominance from his action would be much less *correspondent*.

Such role-playing instructions presumably limit *A*'s freedom to behave in a "revealing" way, that is, in a way which is characteristic of him relative to others. The theory which follows attempts to imbed this consideration of perceived freedom of choice in a systematic framework. We will attempt to extract conceptual commonalities from empirical situations involving different varieties of environmental constraint. Our approach is to cast these "conceptual commonalities" in a form which is amenable to cumulative experimental research.

The Concept of Correspondence

When the perceiver infers personal characteristics as a way of accounting for action, these personal characteristics may vary in the degree to which they correspond with the behavior they are intended to explain. *Correspondence* refers to the extent that the act and the underlying characteristic or attribute are similarly described by the inference. In the example provided in the preceding section, the most correspondent inference is that which assumes with high confidence that domineering behavior is a direct reflection of the person's intention to dominate, which in turn reflects a disposition to be dominant. Thus, to anticipate the broad outlines of the theory to come, correspondence of inference declines as the action to be accounted for appears to be constrained by the setting in which it occurs.

To say that a person is dominant is to say that he is disposed to behave in a dominant fashion in a variety of settings. Of course, the perceiver in the above example would not infer such a dominance [223] disposition if he had not first inferred an intention to dominate. The actor's intention may or may not be conscious and deliberate, but it is marked by some aspect of desire or volition which comes from the person and is not predetermined by environmental forces. Our theory assumes, in using the two concepts of intention and disposition, that correspondence declines as the perceiver moves from inferring intentions to more elaborate inferences about dispositional structures. If the perceiver, having observed a single action, infers intention X with moderate confidence, he cannot be more confident in inferring the underlying disposition X' from the intention X. This would appear to be so because intentions are the data for inferring dispositions, and because an intention may reflect any of several dispositions.

Hopefully, the foregoing discussion has given the reader some general feeling for the meaning of correspondence in the present context. For the sake of theoretical clarity, however, more precise and formal explication is in order. Such an explication may provide a clearer path toward understanding the theory.

All actions have effects on the environment. From the perceiver's point of view, any effect of another person's action is a potential reason why this person had engaged in that action. To infer that the action occurred for X reason is to specify the actor's intention and, indirectly, an underlying disposition. Both intentions and dispositions are attributes of the person. The perception of a link between a particular intention or disposition and a particular action may therefore be called an attribute–effect linkage.

Let us now attempt a more formal definition of correspondence. *Given an attribute–effect linkage which is offered to explain why an act occurred, correspondence increases as the judged value of the attribute departs from the judge's conception of the average person's standing on that attribute.* Turning to the illustration used earlier, the inference that domineering action reflects an underlying trait of dominance is correspondent to the extent that the actor's dominance is seen as greater than that of the average person. This implies, incidentally, that the intention to dominate is out of the ordinary—somehow more intense and noteworthy than we would normally expect.

As a simple example of how the concept of correspondence can be put to use in a research setting, we may provide the perceiver with rating scales designed to measure the strength of the trait attributed to the actor and his confidence in making his rating. The perceiver's certainty that the actor is extreme on a trait which provides sufficient reason for the action's occurrence is, then, the level of correspondence of his inference. **[224]**

Acts and Their Effects

An act is conceived of as a molar response which reflects some degree of personal choice on the part of the actor (if only between action and inaction, though more typically between alternative courses of action) and which has one or more effects on the environment or the actor himself. *Effects* are distinctive (or potentially distinctive) consequences of action. Stated in the broadest terms, they are discriminable changes in the preexisting state of affairs that are brought about by action. Delimiting the unit with which we shall be concerned is more a problem in theory than in practice. If we observe that a man leaves his chair, crosses the room, closes the door, and the room becomes less noisy, a correspondent inference would be that he intended to cut down the noise. One might ask whether the inference that the man intended to reach the door is not also a correspondent inference since "reaching the door" is an effect of crossing the room. But the subordinate parts of a meaningful action sequence do not have to be confused with the effects of an action. In this case, the perceiver is likely to "organize" the action in his mind as beginning with the decision to leave the chair and ending with the closing of the door. It is the effects of the terminal act in a meaningful sequence, then, that provide the grist for our theory.

An act may have only one effect, but usually has multiple effects. When the man closes the door this may reduce the draft, reduce the illumination in his office, and make two students talking in the hall feel a little guilty for interrupting his work. Thus, we are usually dealing with *choice areas* rather than single choices. Important implications for the theory are contained in the fact that "the bitter often comes with the sweet"—an action may be performed to achieve effect x, but effects m, p, t, and z are inextricably produced by the act as well. A choice between two choice areas, then, is a choice between two multiple-effect clusters. The multiple effects in one cluster may or may not overlap extensively with the multiple effects in the second cluster. That is, certain effects may be common to the chosen alternative and to the non-chosen alternative.

If the promising young psychologist Dr. Smedley accepts a position at Harvard rather than Yale, the following effects are obviously common to these two areas of choice: being in the Ivy League, living in New England, joining a university with high prestige and good salaries, living near the sea coast, etc. The theory assumes, then, that these common effects could not have been decisive in the choice, and thus do not provide information which could contribute to correspondent inferences. There are also, of course, distinctive differences between the settings at Yale [225] and Harvard—especially if the perceiver were intimately knowledgeable about the psychology departments of the two institutions—and the perceiver's cognitive accounting of these differences would be the critical determinant of whatever inference was made.

For convenience in representing the structure of the situation in which action occurs, we shall from time to time diagram each perceived choice area as a circle within which the effects of the choice expressed as alphabetical letters may be circumscribed. Common effects may then be represented by the appearance of the same alphabetical letters in different "choice circles." Our hypothetical example of Dr. Smedley's dilemma might be diagrammed as in Figure 3.2.

The Assumed Desirability of Effects

As the perceiver considers the multiple effects of action, he will usually assume that some of the effects were more desirable to the actor, and therefore more diagnostic of his intentions than others. In fact, it is almost always the case that some of the effects of the chosen alternative action are assumed to be undesirable to the actor and some of the effects of non-chosen action are assumed to be desirable. The two major effects of a man's buying a car, for example, are the acquisition of an automobile and the incurring of a substantial debt. The average perceiver, given evidence of such a purchase, will probably assume that the individual desired the car so much that he was willing to go into debt for it, not that he was willing to accept the burden of an automobile for the privilege of being a debtor. [226]

These assumptions by the perceiver tend to operate as hypotheses which bias the inference process. Thus upon observing that an action leads to a normally desirable effect, the perceiver usually will believe that most persons, including the present actor, find that effect desirable. The achievement of this effect will therefore be regarded as

Chapter 3 From Acts to Dispositions: The Attribution Process in Person Perception 53

```
           Dr. Smedley
           /        \
       Harvard       Yale
          |           |
        ( a b c )   ( a b c )
        ( d f   )   ( d e g )
```

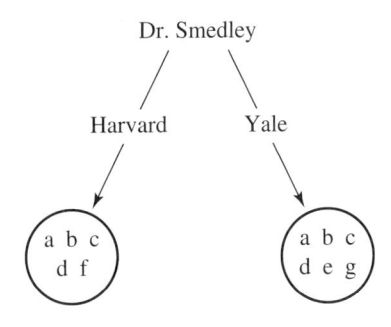

a. Ivy League
b. New England
c. Prestige
d. Good salary
e. Close to New York plays
f. Emphasis on
   interdisciplinary research
g. Emphasis on experimental
   approaches to learning, etc.

Figure 3.2 Smedley's Choice

the actor's most likely intention. The perceiver may, of course, be wrong in his assumptions about people in general. This particular actor may have intended to produce effects in the choice area that most people would be indifferent about or even feel negatively toward. Thus, cultural assumptions or social stereotypes may obscure the true significance of an action.

Let us take a closer look at the consequences for the inference process of assumptions about the desirability of effects. The first step is to distinguish clearly between effects which are assumed to be desirable and those assumed to be undesirable consequences for the average actor. Unless he has evidence to the contrary, the perceiver will assume that the actor has acted in spite of, rather than because of, any negative effects in the choice area. We may go beyond this to assert that any effects in the choice area which are not assumed to be negative will take on greater importance the more negative the remaining effects. Inferences concerning the intention to achieve desirable effects will increase in correspondence to the extent that costs are incurred, pain is endured, or in general, negative outcomes are involved.

Within the range of the supposedly desirable consequences, we still must recognize that effects assumed to be highly desirable are more likely to enter into attribute–effect linkages than effects assumed to be variable or neutral in desirability. However, it is also clear that attribute–effect linkages based on universally desired effects are *not* informative concerning the unique characteristics of the actor. To learn that a man makes the conventional choice is to learn only that he is like most other men. By the definition of correspondence stated above, an inference must characterize the actor's standing as high or low on an attribute relative to the average person, in order to qualify as correspondent. If a choice is explained on the basis of effects in the choice area which anyone would like to produce and enjoy, an attribute inferred to account for that choice will be low in correspondence. In general, we learn more about uniquely identifying intentions and dispositions when the effects of a chosen action are no more universally desired than the effects of a non-chosen action.

The Determinants of Correspondence

It may be helpful to divide the inference process into two aspects (which may in fact be seen as stages in the process). Given an act [**227**] which leads to multiple effects, the perceiver implicitly attaches a probability value to each effect as a candidate for launching the inference process. In other words, the perceiver assumes that certain of the effects achieved are more likely to have been the goal of action than others. In certain cases the probability of all effects but one may be zero, indicating extreme confidence in attributing causation to a particular intention. In other cases, the probability values may be distributed among a range of effects, and since it is possible that the target person acted for more than one reason, the probabilities may add up to more than 1.00. The probability value for any given effect should vary directly as a function of the assumed desirability of the effect and inversely as a function of the number of other effects competing for the perceiver's attention. If the perceiver is asked, then, "What was *A* trying to accomplish?"—his response should reflect this combination of assumed desirability and the number of noncommon effects.

The second aspect or phase is to attach personal significance to the effect or effects singled out as most probable courses of action. In short, what does the action reveal about this particular actor that sets him apart from other actors? By our definition of correspondence, relative extremity of perceiver rating is the crucial measure. Here it seems quite clear that assumed desirability and the number of noncommon effects have conflicting implications. The greater the assumed desirability of the effect in question, the less warrant there is for ratings of relative extremity. The smaller the number of effects in contention, on the other hand, the greater the warrant for extreme ratings. Assumed desirability, then, positively affects the probability of an attribute–effect linkage being chosen to begin the inference process and negatively affects the tendency to assign extreme values to personal characteristics.

The correspondence of an inference, which should directly reflect the amount of information revealed by an action, is thus a function of the two conditions covered by the following explicit formulation: An inference from action to attribute is correspondent *as an inverse function of (a) the number of noncommon effects following the action, and (b) the assumed social desirability of these effects.* This relationship may be stated in simpler terms as a near tautology: the more distinctive reasons a person has for an action, and the more these reasons are widely shared in the culture, the less informative that action is concerning the identifying attributes of the person.

It should be reiterated that correspondence has nothing to do, necessarily, with the accuracy of the inference. The actor may have had no intention of producing an effect which is seen by the perceiver as a prominent consequence of his action. Being able to predict the effects **[228]** of one's own actions is an important precondition for being accurately perceived by others. The theory does not assume, then, that the perceiver and the actor agree on the effects of the latter's action, but focuses on those effects of which the perceiver assumes the actor was aware. The knowledge portion of the attribute-action paradigm (see Figure 3.1) is relevant only in determining which effects the perceiver will include in the choice circle (see Figure 3.2).

There is an interesting relationship between imputations of knowledge and actions leading to socially undesirable effects. We have already noted that when there are both desirable and undesirable effects of an action, more significance is attached to the desirable effects the more numerous and distasteful the undesirable effects "incurred." In a case where the actor produces solely negative effects, however, the situation is quite different. Here the perceiver has two obvious options: he may decide that the actor is truly a deviant type, that he desires those goals which are shunned by others; or he may decide that the actor was unaware of the effects of his action. It seems reasonable to propose, therefore, that in cases where the action–choice circle contains only effects judged to be socially undesirable, the more undesirable these effects the greater the perceiver's tendency to impute ignorance or lack of awareness to the actor. The possibility of imputing ignorance thus sets a limit on the degree of correspondence predicted when actions lead only to socially undesirable effects. (Note that this is quite different from what one would predict in the case where an action leads to effects which are undesirable *for the perceiver* but recognized by him to serve some purpose of the actor. We shall discuss this latter case below under the heading of Hedonic Relevance.)

It may be helpful in summarizing the theory to consider the joint operation of effect desirability and effect commonality as determinants of correspondence, and to do so in the framework of a fourfold table. Such a table is presented in Figure 3.3. As the figure shows, actions which **[229]** lead to effects deemed highly desirable to most persons cannot help but be trivial from an informational point of view. Also, when the number of noncommon effects is high, the perceiver cannot escape from the ambiguity of his data in making inferences either to common or idiosyncratic personal characteristics. In line with the stated theoretical relationship, the high correspondence cell is that in which assumed desirability and the number of noncommon effects are both low.

The Calculation of Commonality

Since the theoretical statement refers to the number of noncommon effects in the chosen alternative, it is important to clarify how effects are identified and their commonality assessed. There are two rather different clusters of problems involved here. One cluster concerns identifying effects and determining whether or not two effects so identified are to be viewed as common. This will simply have to be a matter of cumulative research experience in fractionating and labeling consequences.

The other cluster of problems assumes that we can somehow achieve the necessary identifications and concerns the method of determining how the noncommon effects in the chosen alternative will be sorted out from all others in order to generate reasonably precise predictions. There are essentially three steps involved in sorting out the number of noncommon effects. The first is for the experimenter to lay out (for example, in the graphic manner of Figure 3.2) the different action alternatives that the perceiver is likely to envision in the actor's situation. For each of these alternatives there will be a choice area, a circle containing the distinctive effects of that action. Having identified these circles and the effects they circumscribe, the second step is to pool all the effects associated with the nonchosen alternatives and to compare them with the effects in the choice circle of the chosen alternative. Having done this, one follows through on the assumption

		ASSUMED DESIRABILITY	
		High	Low
NUMBER OF NONCOMMON EFFECTS	High	Trivial ambiguity	Intriguing ambiguity
	Low	Trivial clarity	High correspondence

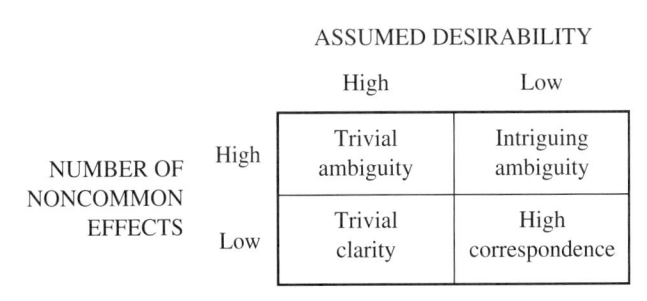

Figure 3.3 Effect Desirability and Effect Commonality as Determinants of Correspondence

that effects which appear in both chosen and nonchosen alternatives cannot serve as a basis for inferences about personal dispositions. One is then left with effects which appear only in the chosen alternative and only in the nonchosen alternative(s). The third and final step is to view the noncommon effects in the nonchosen alternatives as effects which the actor may be trying to avoid. They may thus be transposed, with their sign reversed, and regrouped among the noncommon effects of the chosen alternative. The new total of noncommon effects now serves as the basis for making predictions about the level of correspondence.

In order to illustrate these three stages in the calculation of noncommon effects, let us invent a case involving the choice of a marital partner. We are informed that a Miss Adams, who is ripe for matrimony, [230] has received proposals from three suitors, Bagby, Caldwell, and Dexter. All we know about Bagby is that he is wealthy, he has high status in the community, and he is physically attractive. Caldwell is also quite wealthy, he is physically attractive, and he has often expressed his longing for a houseful of his own children. Dexter is physically attractive like the others, and he is very much the intellectual—widely read and conversationally scintillating. These are the only characteristics of these men that we know anything about, and on the basis of this knowledge we may diagram Miss Adams's choice as in Figure 3.4.

First we lay out those effects presumed to follow from the choice of each man to the exclusion of the other. Then we notice that the three men are physically attractive so we rule out the common effect of sexual enjoyment—we have no information about the importance of [231] this particular characteristic as a determinant of Miss Adams's choice. The remaining effects are regrouped after we receive information about which man has been chosen. The only further distinction is that between effects which are judged to have been wanted by Miss Adams, effects judged to have been unimportant to her, and effects judged to have been *not* wanted or actively avoided. The distinction between lack of importance and undesirability is new; it is based on the commonality of particular effects among the nonchosen alternatives. Thus, if Dexter is chosen, we have no more reason to assume that Miss Adams wanted intellectual stimulation than that she didn't want the responsibilities of wealth. After all, she has avoided two wealthy suitors in favor of one who is not wealthy. Our inference about not wanting wealth, then, would be more correspondent than an inference about not wanting children or not caring about social position. If it were just a matter of not having children, Miss Adams could just as easily have married Bagby. If she was anxious to avoid social position she could have accomplished this by marrying Caldwell. We say these two effects were not *important* to her to suggest that she is willing to forego them in favor of intellectual stimulation, but our evidence that she wanted to avoid these effects is weaker than in the case of wealth.

A further complexity which must be acknowledged is the fact that some or all of the noncommon effects may be correlated or seen by the perceiver to express the same general purpose. At the present stage of developing the theory of correspondence, no formal provision is made for this possibility. To some extent, our flexibility in deciding what we shall call an effect reduces the magnitude of the problem. Thus, certain combinations of discriminable effects may be treated as a more general, unitary effect if each member of the combination has a common significance for the perceiver. The result would be to increase the correspondence and the generality or importance of the

Effects of marriage to be considered:
a. Wealth
b. Social position
c. Sexual enjoyment
d. Children
e. Intellectual stimulation

A. The Choice

                  Miss Adams

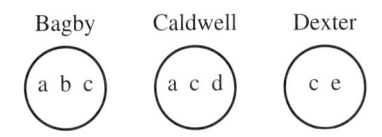

    Bagby   Caldwell   Dexter
    (a b c)   (a c d)   (c e)

B. Elimination of Common Effects (c)

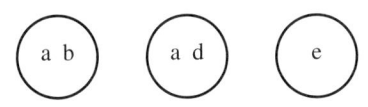

    (a b)   (a d)   (e)

C. Regrouped Noncommon Effects
    If choice is:
        Bagby   b wanted, d and e not important
        Caldwell d wanted, b and e not important
        Dexter   e wanted, a not wanted, b and d not important

D. Inferences:
    If Bagby, Miss Adams is a snob; if Caldwell, Miss Adams is the material type; if Dexter, Miss Adams is an intellectual.

Figure 3.4 Miss Adams Chooses a Husband

ensuing inference. We shall examine this possibility in greater detail when we consider, below, the contribution of hedonic or affective relevance of effects in the inference process and again when we consider sequences of action choices over time.

Conditions Affecting Desirability Assumptions

We have remarked that the perceiver's assumptions or hypotheses about which effects of action were most likely desired by the actor play an important role in the inference process. Those effects perceived to have been high in desirability (i.e., commonly desired by all persons or by all members of a particular cultural group) play a smaller role in the determination of correspondence than those effects which are less [232] universally sought. Without going too deeply into the problem, there are a number of variables which might condition the perceived assumptions that the actor desires the same effects as most persons. Even if we restrict ourselves to the case in which the perceiver confronts the actor for the first time, there may be cues in the circumstances of their encounter and in the appearance of the actor which affect the likelihood of his being seen as desiring the same things most persons would in a given situation. If the situation is so structured that the actor and the perceiver are working for the same objectives, the perceiver may reflect on his own intentions to draw inferences about the most likely aspirations of the actor. Cues about shared perspectives should thus facilitate the formation of definite hypotheses about the actor's motives and desires. Other cues, perhaps reflected in the features of the actor's appearance, might lead the perceiver to assume similarity of intention and disposition before any action has occurred. Or the perceiver's stereotypes about the members of identifiable classes or cultural groups may be triggered by such appearance cues.

Information Gain and the Role of Prior Choice

We now come to one of the most frustrating sources of complexity in calculating non-common effects in the chosen alternative, both for the individual perceiver whose actions the theory concerns and for the theory itself. A person who confronts certain behavior choices has often made previous choices which have brought him to his present decision. There is often a great deal of information contained, then, in knowledge about what alternatives are being considered, above and beyond the information revealed by the actual decision which is made.

Once again, this point can be clarified by an example. Let us consider Miss Adams again, this time caught between the options of going to medical school or to law school. She has been accepted for admission in the two professional schools of comparable universities and the choice is, in that sense, entirely up to her. In comparison, we come upon Mr. Bagby, poised before the choice of going to Duke or to Colorado for graduate study in psychology. Since the Duke and Colorado psychology departments would seem to have much more in common than medical school versus law school, our theory would seem to suggest that any inference we might make about Mr. Bagby after he has chosen would be more correspondent than any comparable inference about Miss Adams. There are many noncommon effects in Adams's chosen alternative, whereas the number of noncommon effects in Bagby's chosen alternative is unquestionably smaller. The hidden factor in this comparison is the fact that considerably more information is contained in the datum that Bagby [233] had already ruled out everything besides psychology, than in the datum that Adams is still struggling with the choice between two basic professions, professions which differ from each other on many different dimensions. The example is thus misleading because Bagby is at a later stage of the choice process than Adams. In order to render them comparable we would have to have more information concerning Bagby's preceding choices, choices which have narrowed the field to psychology.

The example points up the importance of defining correspondence in terms of the information *gained* through the observation of behavior, not in terms of the confidence one has in drawing an inference which may be based on prior information or on knowledge of the culture. If all we know is that Bagby has chosen the Colorado Department of Psychology over the Duke Department of Psychology, we have learned nothing *from the choice itself* concerning the strength of his motivation to become a psychologist.

On the other hand, we might be willing to make some rather confident statements about his love of mountains or the degree of his dislike for hot and humid summers. The facts that there are high mountains and low humidity in Colorado are certainly two of the noncommon effects in the Colorado versus Duke choice.

In dealing with cases of complex behavioral choice in the natural environment, the matter of prior choice is destined to create enormous difficulties in the application of the theory to individual cases. However, in the realm of experimental planning, prior choice presents opportunities for empirical exploration rather than disruptive trouble. The probability of imputing prior choice can either be held constant or systematically varied by suitable experimental arrangements. In the former case for example, subject-perceivers, starting from the same baseline of relative ignorance about a stimulus person, may be exposed to a choice made by that stimulus person under conditions which emphasize the stimulus person's lack of control over the choice presented him.

Correspondence, Choice, and Role Assignment

A recent experiment by Jones et al. (1961) exemplifies the reasoning which underlies the foregoing theory. It is worth reviewing this study before considering some of the more subtle and tentative extensions of the theory into interaction settings marked by personal involvement. The investigation's central purpose was to demonstrate that behavior which conforms to clearly defined role requirements is seen as uninformative about the individual's personal characteristics, whereas a considerable amount of information may be extracted from out-of-role behavior. In other words, inferences based on out-of-role behavior were predicted to be higher in correspondence than inferences from in-role behavior. The [234] reasons for this will become more apparent after the procedures of the experiment are described.

Male undergraduate subjects were exposed to one of four tape-recorded "job interviews" in which the interviewee was instructed (on the tape) to appear very interested in qualifying either as a prospective submariner or as an astronaut. The subjects were aware that the interviewee was being invited to play a role in a fictitious interview situation, but they were not told that the entire interview was carefully written as a prearranged script and was recorded by an experimental accomplice serving as the interviewee.

Those subjects who listened to the recording involving the submariner role, heard the interviewer describe the ideal submariner as obedient, cooperative, friendly, gregarious—in short, as "other directed." The remaining subjects listened to a description of the ideal astronaut as one who does not need other people, who has inner resources—in short, a rather "inner-directed" person. These two interview beginnings were spliced into two different endings, thus creating the four experimental groups. The interviewee either responded with a series of statements indicating extreme other-directedness or he responded with a series of inner-directed statements. On half of the recordings, then, the interviewee–accomplice behaved very much in line with the requirements of the occupational role (astronaut–inner condition, submariner–other condition). On the other half the behavior was distinctly out of line with these requirements (astronaut–other condition, submariner–inner condition).

After listening to these tape recordings, the subjects were asked to rate the interviewee ("What do you think he is *really* like as a person?") and indicate their confidence in the traits they evaluated on their rating scale. The results were striking and unequivocal (see Table 3.1). After the two in-role recordings, the stimulus person was rated as moderately affiliative and moderately independent. In each case the confidence ratings were extremely low. On the other hand, the astronaut–other was seen as very conforming and affiliative, and confidently rated as such. The submariner–inner was seen as very independent and nonaffiliative, again with high confidence. Thus the actual responses of the interviewee were clearly evaluated in the context of the structured setting from which they emerged. If other-directedness is called for, an inner-directed response is highly informative. Inner-directedness in the face of a situation which seems to require it, on the other hand, is difficult to interpret. The same kind of contrast applies to other-directedness in the two settings described, providing a replication of the basic hypothesis within the single experiment.

Now we may ask how the results of the Jones et al. (1961) experiment are to be explained in terms of the foregoing theoretical statement [235] relating cultural desirability and the number of noncommon effects to the degree of correspondence of an inference about personal dispositions. In-role behavior does not lead to confident, correspondent inferences because such behavior has multiple consequences and many of these are high in cultural desirability. Most people want to avoid embarrassing others by not meeting their expectations, most people want to gain the rewards implicit in approval from authority figures, most people wish to manifest their intelligence by showing that they understand what is required of them, and so on. Each of these effects is a "plausible reason" for in-role behavior in the experiment just described. On the other hand, plausible reasons for out-of-role behavior (i.e., those with a reasonable degree of assumed social desirability) are comparatively scarce. One of the few noncommon effects of

Table 3.1 Perceptions of Affiliation and Conformity[a, b]

	Astro–Other (AO), $N = 33$	Astro–Inner (AI), $N = 33$	Sub–Other (SO), $N = 31$	Sub–Inner (SI), $N = 37$	Comparisons Direction	t
Affiliation						
$\bar{X}$	15.27	11.12	12.00	8.64	AO > SO	4.02[d]
SD	2.92	3.81	3.53	4.73	AI > SI	2.12[c]
Conformity						
$\bar{X}$	15.91	13.09	12.58	9.41	AO > SO	4.02[d]
SD	3.22	3.42	3.39	4.95	AI > SI	3.65[d]

[a] Data from Jones et al. (1961).
[b] The higher the mean value, the greater the perceived affiliation or conformity. Comparisons between AO and SI are not tabled, but the differences between these conditions would of course be highly significant.
[c] $p < .05$
[d] $p < .001$.

behavior at variance with role demands is the satisfaction of expressing one's true nature. This effect is also a possible accompaniment of in-role behavior, but in that case it exists in the choice circle along with many other effects. Since there are fewer noncommon effects in the astronaut–other and submariner–inner choices, the effect of "being oneself" forms the basis of a more correspondent inference in these conditions and the interviewee's behavior tends to be taken at face value.

The implications of this study can probably be extended quite generally to cover behavior which is or is not constrained by a well-defined [236] social situation. When certain role requirements are salient, conformity is more rewarding to the actor, more likely to avoid embarrassment and social disapproval, than is nonconformity. The actor may conform for many other reasons as well. Thus, in the case of conformity to role requirements, we do not know the exact reason why the individual behaves the way he does, but there is really no particular mystery in his behavior. This is an example of "trivial ambiguity." On the other hand, behavior which departs from clearly defined role requirements cries for explanation. The fact that the effects of such behavior are presumably low in cultural desirability makes the behavior intriguing to the perceiver. The fact that there are few reasons why a person would behave that way (the action leads to a limited number of noncommon effects) provides the basis for a correspondent inference concerning the intentions and dispositions of the actor.

PERSONAL INVOLVEMENT AND CORRESPONDENCE

In the remaining sections of the chapter, we shall turn to those factors of personal involvement which affect the inference process in person perception. The theory of action implied in the discussion thus far obviously assumes that the actor is concerned with the consequences of his action. It is the very fact that his action choices have motivational significance for *him* that makes these choices informative for the perceiver. But a special and enormously important feature of many person perception settings is that the choice of an actor has significant rewarding or punishing implications for the perceiver. We turn to examine this feature and to consider its implications for our theory of correspondence.

The Hedonic Relevance of the Action to the Perceiver

The actor's behavioral choices may or may not contain effects which have hedonic relevance for the perceiver. The hedonic relevance of an effect is a function of its motivational significance for the perceiver: does the particular action consequence promote or undermine the perceiver's values; does it fulfill or obstruct his purposes? Effects which fulfill a purpose have positive relevance; those which obstruct a purpose have negative relevance. For a *choice* to have relevance means that the algebraic balance of positive and negative effects in the chosen alternative is not equal to the algebraic balance of positive and negative effects in the nonchosen alterative(s). Simply put, the choice proved gratifying or disappointing to the perceiver.

An experiment by Steiner and Field (1960) is conceptually quite similar to the astronaut–submariner study but contains a strong dash of [237] hedonic relevance as an added ingredient. In this study, University of Illinois students met in groups of three to "discuss the desirability of desegregation of public schools and ... attempt to reach agreement among themselves." The major manipulation varied the extent to which the responsibility for presenting certain points of view was assigned by the experimenter. For half of the groups, a confederate of the experimenter was always assigned the role of "a typical Southern segregationist." In the other groups, subjects were encouraged to take into consideration the viewpoint of an N.A.A.C.P. member, a Northern clergyman, and a Southern segregationist, but no role assignments were made. In both cases, however, the confederate gave an identical, pro-segregation performance. From the perceiver's point of view, he apparently chose to express pro-segregation beliefs where no role assignment was made, whereas he had little choice *but* to express the same beliefs in the role assignment condition. Since the subjects themselves were all in favor of integration, the expression of pro-segregationist beliefs would, we assume, be relevant in the negative direction.

The following results would be expected given the theoretical statement that we have developed thus far: (1) perceivers should attribute more intense pro-segregation beliefs to the actor in the choice condition than to the same actor in the assignment condition; (2) perceivers should be more confident of their inferences in the choice condition; and (3) they should evaluate the chooser less favorably than the actor who had the role assigned to him. The investigators do not report the data bearing on the first hypothesis, but the other data make sense only if it were supported. Hypothesis 2 was strongly supported, and both indices bearing on hypothesis 3 were in the predicted direction, though only one treatment difference was significant. In addition, while the fact is not particularly relevant in the present theoretical context, the subjects were apparently more influenced by the remarks of the actor when he chose the role than when he was assigned to it, even though he was better liked in the latter case.

The results confirm very well the expectation derived from the theory of correspondent inferences, and the subjects show the same uncertainty in the role assignment condition as was observed in the in-role treatments of the astronaut–submariner study. Since there are so many objectives served when the actor in the role assignment condition follows his assignment, and since most of these objectives are quite culturally desirable, the perceiver learns very little from the actor's compliance.

Hedonic relevance is involved because the position taken by the actor is contrary to the view held by all perceivers in the experiment. While the experiment does not manipulate the relevance of the action [238] directly, it does alter the subject's evaluative response to the action by altering his interpretation of the act.

It is not as yet clear, however, precisely how relevance enters into the inference process. At the outset, it may be useful to distinguish between the effects of relevance on correspondence, and the joint effects of relevance and correspondence on evaluation by the perceiver. Let us consider each of these in turn. We propose that as relevance increases there is also an increase in the likelihood that inferences will be correspondent. This is because effects which might appear to have little in common in the eyes of most observers might be functionally equivalent to a particular perceiver. Thus, relevance may provide a potent criterion for grouping and packaging the effects of action, thereby reducing the number of unrelated or noncommon effects in the choice circle. The result is an increase in the correspondence of any inference based on that particular choice. This reasoning does not apply in the event that a nonrelevant effect is seen as the probable goal of the action. However, we may assume that the probability of launching the inference from a relevant effect increases directly as a function of the degree of relevance involved.

In addition to the packaging of effects in terms of their positive or negative significance for the perceiver, the number of noncommon effects may be further reduced by *assimilation to the predominant hedonic value*. When the actor makes a choice which is relevant to the perceiver, there will be a tendency for the remaining more or less neutral effects to take on the sign of other effects in the choice circle. This assimilation should operate in such a way as to increase the differentiation between chosen and nonchosen courses of action. The process may be illustrated by changes in the connotative meaning of attributed dispositions. Let us assume that we have identical information concerning the moderately high risk-taking tendencies of Adams and Bagby. If Adams does something which, on balance, goes against our interests, the assimilation hypothesis proposes that risk-taking proclivity might be construed as recklessness and irresponsibility. If Bagby does something that supports our interests and benefits us, riskiness might take on connotations of creativeness and inventive autonomy. This would seem to be an expression of Heider's (1958) general balance principle: Bad actions come from bad people and good is achieved by the good.

Turning now to the joint effects of relevance and correspondence on evaluation by the perceiver, the following proposition suggests itself: If the consequences of an act are predominantly positive, the perceiver will be more favorably disposed toward the actor, the greater the correspondence value of the action. The converse will be true of actions whose effects are negative. In general, ignoring direction for the moment, the **[239]** evaluation of an individual will be more extreme as a joint function of increases in relevance and correspondence.

Since relevance increases correspondence, and since relevance and correspondence affect evaluation, it might seem reasonable to link relevance directly to evaluation. However, relevance may well affect only one condition of correspondence—the commonality of effects—and not the other, the cultural desirability of effects. For this reason it is possible to have high relevance and only moderate correspondence. When, for example, the Russian ambassador to the United Nations makes a speech accusing America of imperialistic ambitions, dollar diplomacy, exploitation of the worker, and so on, it is easy for us to put these remarks into a single package under the label of negative hedonic relevance. And yet, we are sufficiently aware of the norms of cultural desirability among Russian public spokesmen to recognize that none of the ambassador's statements departs very far from these norms.

In terms of the fourfold table presented as Figure 3.3, we are dealing with a case of trivial clarity. Note that relevance is high—the statements chosen by the ambassador have effects almost all of which are an affront to our values as American perceivers. The number of noncommon effects is low—the disparate remarks may be readily packaged as anti-American; and assumed cultural desirability (for a Russian) is high. But we would not predict a particularly intense negative evaluation in this case. Since this particular Russian is just saying what any other Russian would say under the same circumstances, it is rather hard to take special umbrage at his "negatively relevant" remarks. The example helps us to see, then, that a combination of relevance and high correspondence is prerequisite for extreme evaluations to occur.

Relevance controls the direction of evaluation, but is only one of two contributing determinants of its extremity.

RELEVANCE INCREASES CORRESPONDENCE: EMPIRICAL SUPPORT In order to test the hypothesis that relevance increases correspondence in the inference process, it is necessary to present the same action or series of acts in contexts of differing personal relevance for the perceiver. This was done in an experiment by Jones and deCharms (1957) and in another by Kleiner (1960), the results of which we shall briefly summarize.

Two separate experiments, sharing certain basic procedural features were conducted by Jones and deCharms (1957). In the first experiment a trained accomplice was the only member of a group, including four or five naive subjects, who failed the assigned experimental task. In one condition, *individual fate,* the relevance of this failure was minimized. [240] The subjects all received the rewards promised them for succeeding and this was in no way contingent on the accomplice's performance. In another condition, *common fate,* the accomplice's failure prevented anyone from reaping the rewards available. This was, then, a condition of negative hedonic relevance for the naive subjects. The subjects rated the accomplice twice; first, prior to the main experimental inductions and again after his failure was established. We would expect to find, in an index of change in ratings of the accomplice, indications of greater correspondence in the negative relevance than in the minimal relevance condition. In line with this prediction, the accomplice was regarded as being less competent, less dependable, and generally judged in less favorable terms in the common fate (negative relevance) than in the individual fate (minimal relevance) condition. Contrary to expectation, no differences in likability or friendliness occurred as a function of relevance. Perhaps we may cite this pattern of findings to illustrate that relevance may affect certain attributions without necessarily affecting personal evaluation.

A study by Kleiner (1960) varied the positive relevance of constructive member actions by varying the probability of group failure. A previously instructed accomplice then facilitated group goal achievement by solving problems too difficult for the others. We assume that the degree of positive relevance varies directly with the degree of initial threat to the group. Unfortunately for our purposes, Kleiner did not get extensive impression ratings over a variety of traits, but he did get evidence concerning changes in perceived importance of group members. Consistent with the relevance–correspondence hypothesis, the greater the group's need for help, the greater importance attributed to the helpful confederate. Consistent with the second evaluation, the rated likability of the confederate as both a teammate and as someone to socialize with was positively related to the degree of initial need for help.

While there are no other investigations (to our knowledge) that concern themselves directly with the relevance–correspondence hypothesis, there are several closely related studies which increase our confidence in its validity. These are studies in which conditions of *potential* relevance are created by the anticipation of further interaction, but in which impression ratings are taken before the direction of relevance has been established by final action. The general pattern of findings from these studies has been called "facilitative distortion" of perceived attributes—the stimulus person is assigned attributes that are consistent with the positive outcome hoped for in the interaction.

Chapter 3   From Acts to Dispositions: The Attribution Process in Person Perception   65

The classic study was done by Pepitone (1950). Variations in motivation (relevance) were established by having high school students think that their ideas about athletics would be instrumental in obtaining either **[241]** very desirable championship basketball tickets (high relevance) or much less desirable tickets (low relevance). The three judges who evaluated the students' ideas were again accomplices of the experimenter. They varied their apparent approval of the subject in some conditions, and their apparent power to grant him a ticket in others. On the whole, there was a strong tendency for subjects to view the more favorable judges as more powerful than the less favorable judges, though power was ostensibly equated by instructions and the accomplices' careful attention to their prescribed roles. Similarly, when there was a deliberate attempt to vary the judges' power, the more powerful judges were regarded as more approving. We may only assume that such "facilitative distortion" would not have occurred in a non-relevance control group. It *was* true that the high relevance subjects saw the approving judge as more powerful than the low relevance subjects did, which provides direct support for the relevance–correspondence hypothesis, but the remaining differences which might test the hypothesis were not significant.

A similar pattern of facilitative distortions was found in one phase of Davis's (1962) study. Subjects were given pre-information about an individual with whom they were to engage in a series of either cooperative or competitive interactions. For half of the subjects, this information portrayed an essentially submissive person; for the other half, an essentially ascendant person. When the submissive person was to be a *partner,* she was seen as more active, outgoing, forceful, tough, and as less passive, shy, and uncertain of herself than when she was to be an *opponent*. These differential effects did not approach statistical significance in the condition of ascendant information. Perhaps the constraints of clear information were strong enough to inhibit distortion in the latter case.

Other studies also show both facilitative distortion effects and the absence of such effects, but in no study do "pessimistic" distortions occur. There seems little doubt that relevance may increase distortion by causing increases in correspondence which are not based on added information. What we now need is to determine other parameters which influence the relevance–correspondence relationship and thus affect the perceiver's reliance on the available data he obtains from observed action.

RELEVANCE AND CORRESPONDENCE DETERMINE EVALUATION: EMPIRICAL SUPPORT   The second hypothesis concerning relevance was that evaluation is a joint function of the degree of relevance and the level of correspondence. Under a variety of different guises, this hypothesis has received greater empirical attention than the prior hypothesis linking relevance to correspondence. It is not difficult to find ample support for the proposition **[243]** that people like others who benefit them in some way and dislike others who are harmful. But since we have already argued that relevance increases correspondence, this proposition is not a very precise rendition of the second hypothesis. The second hypothesis requires the demonstration that *both* relevance and correspondence are necessary conditions for evaluation, or at least that evaluation will be more extreme when both are present at a high level. Our reasoning implies that evaluation will become more extreme as a function of increases in either relevance or correspondence, as long as the other variable is held constant at some value greater than zero. If an action is expected to be positively or negatively relevant for a perceiver, for example, the perceiver's evaluations should become more extreme when the conditions of judgment give rise to high correspondence.

As one test of this hypothesis, we may return to the second experiment reported in Jones and deCharms (1957). Cross-cutting the common fate–individual fate variation which characterized both experiments, an additional instructional variation was introduced. Half of the subjects were led to believe that the task was such that failure should be primarily attributed to lack of ability. The remaining subjects were told that failure on the particular problems to be solved could only reflect a lack of motivation, a lack of willingness to try hard. In retrospect, we might now see the ability condition as involving less choice for the actor than the motivation condition. After all, if ability and not motivation is involved, then the subject may try heroically, knowing that others are dependent on him and that doing well is important—but still fail. In the ability condition, therefore, his failure would not provide a basis for correspondent inferences about his attitudes toward the group. The individual must have some degree of choice among action alternatives before one may begin to speak of noncommon effects in the chosen alternative.

The results bear out the prediction quite well. An evaluation change index was composed from the combined ratings of the accomplice made by each naive subject before and after the experimental variables were introduced. The traits involved were deliberately chosen to reflect an evaluative "halo effect": competent, intelligent, conscientious, likable, dependable, and so on. When the accomplice supposedly had no choice (in the ability conditions), variations in personal relevance for the perceiver did not lead to differential changes in evaluation. Thus the evaluation change scores in the common fate–ability condition were almost identical to the evaluation change scores in the individual fate–ability condition (see Table 3.2). When the accomplice was presumed to have a choice. On the other hand, relevance was a crucial determinant of evaluation. Subjects in the common fate–motivation condition were significantly more [243] negative in their evaluation change scores than subjects in the individual fate–motivation condition.

It should be emphasized, of course, that the actual behavior of the accomplice was as nearly the same in all conditions as careful pre-training and periodic monitoring could make it. In conclusion, then, the accomplice was negatively evaluated if his

Table 3.2 Change in "Halo Effect," Experiment II[a]

	Groups			
	Common fate		Individual fate	
	Motivation	Ability	Motivation	Ability
$\bar{X}$[b]	23.0	17.3	14.4	18.9
SD	10.68	6.27	2.12	9.53

[a]Data from Jones and deCharms (1957).
[b]The greater the mean change, the more negative the "after" evaluation.

failing performance prevented the others from obtaining rewards *and* he could have avoided failure by trying harder. Not trying hard in this case may have been equivalent to an attitude of indifference to the group, an attitude which (once inferred) would be resented by the group's members.

Perhaps the most celebrated study linking causal attribution and evaluation is that of Thibaut and Riecken (1955). They conducted two separate experiments to explore the proposition that an act of benevolence which is "internally caused" is more appreciated than one which is the inevitable result of environmental circumstances. We would now view internal causation as another way of talking about the perception of choice alternatives available to the actor. A person "internally causes" certain effects in the environment only when he had the option of causing other effects and did not do so.

In each of the Thibaut–Riecken experiments, an undergraduate subject was introduced to two experimental accomplices or confederates, one of whom was apparently much higher in academic or social status than himself and one of whom was lower in status. The subject soon found himself in the position where he needed the help of at least one of the confederates. The experimenter encouraged him to ask for help and required only that he make an identical request of both the high status and the low status confederate. When both of the confederates eventually complied with his request, the subject was asked to explain the compliance [244] and to evaluate each confederate. Since the differences in experimentally manipulated status were perceived as differences in the ability to resist persuasion, the high status confederate was regarded as having more choice in his decision about compliance. The low status confederate, on the other hand, was more likely to be viewed as complying because he felt coerced by the more powerful subject. The norms governing a low status position are such that compliance to those higher in status is often expected. In our terms, then, the behavior of the high status person should lead to more correspondent inferences concerning the intention to help the subject out of a disposition of spontaneous affection or good will

As our hypothesis would predict, holding relevance constant (the subject is benefitted equally by the two confederates), as correspondence of inference (about spontaneous good will) increases, positive evaluation also increases. The benevolence of the high status confederate earns him a greater increase in attractiveness than does the benevolence of the low status confederate. Relevance in the positive direction, coupled with high correspondence in the form of perceived internal causation, results in more positive evaluation.

Incidental findings from two other studies may be mentioned as well. These findings also bring out the relationship between relevance, correspondence, and evaluation. In the study by Davis (1962) briefly referred to above, control groups were run in which subjects anticipated either cooperative or competitive discussions with each other, but no pre-information about the partners was provided beforehand. Each subject rated the other person prior to the interaction on traits which could be combined into an ascendance–submission index, and on likability. In the competitive condition, the more ascendant one's opponent the greater the probability of one's own failure; ascendance has negative hedonic relevance. In the cooperative condition, on the other hand, ascendance has positive relevance since it implies a greater probability of team success. Comparing individual differences in the tendency to assign high first impression ratings on ascendance, we should expect a positive correlation between perceived ascendance and likability in the cooperative condition and a negative correlation between these two sets of ratings in the competitive condition. The correlational values were actually +.60 and –.18 respectively, reflecting a difference between conditions which is significant.

Finally, in an experiment by Jones and Daugherty (1959), some subjects were led to anticipate interacting with one of two persons about whom a fair amount of information was provided via a tape-recorded interview. Others received the same information about the two persons, but it was clear that no subsequent interaction would take place. One [245] of the two interviewees was presented as a rather intellectual, somewhat diffident person, with moderately strong aesthetic interests. The other was presented as a rather opportunistic and conforming, but obviously sociable person. In the no-anticipation condition, in which we may assume that the characteristics of both persons were of minimal relevance, the diffident aesthete was more highly evaluated on a variety of dimensions than was the sociable politician. In contrast, when the subjects were led to anticipate interacting with one of the two, making the relevance of sociability more salient, the subjects' evaluation of the politician markedly and significantly increased. These results, then, suggest that a particular personal attribute (sociability) was assigned approximately the same ratings in the two conditions (varying in the anticipation of interaction) but variations in the relevance of that attribute were associated with shifts in evaluation. If there had been no evidence that the "politician" was sociable, correspondent inferences about him would not have been drawn regarding that disposition and evaluation would not have varied with relevance. It should be emphasized that the obtained differences were not anticipated. However, we view the interpretation as the most plausible one available and are encouraged to think that a replication specifically addressed to the present hypothesis would show the same pattern.

In summary, there seems little question that variations in the relevance of an action to the perceiver have an effect on the process of inferring dispositions which explain the action. Our first hypothesis was that relevance tends to increase correspondence by reducing the number of noncommon effects in the action alternative chosen. We have presented some evidence in favor of this hypothesis, although it is clear that the strength of confirmation depends on other conditions, such as the ambiguity of available information about the actor and the consequent leeway for facilitative distortion. The second hypothesis, which states that personal evaluation varies as a joint function of relevance and correspondence, has received stronger support than the first. Here again, however, much of the evidence is indirect and circumstantial. Hopefully, the present theoretical analysis will point the way toward more precise tests of both hypotheses.

Personalism: The Actor's Intention to Benefit or Harm the Perceiver

An act or a choice may be hedonically relevant to the perceiver even though it is quite clear to the latter that the choice was not conditioned by his unique presence. An actor might express opinions which differ radically from the perceiver's without having any knowledge of the latter's views. Such a choice of opinions may have hedonic relevance for the [246] perceiver, but may not have been offered with any intention to gratify or to spite him. The variable of *personalism* is introduced to distinguish between choices which are conceivably affected by the presence of the perceiver and choices which are not conceivably so affected.

It is usually difficult for a perceiver to judge whether a choice was affected by personalistic considerations. He may, in effect, experimentally arrange conditions of his own presence and absence in an attempt to detect differences in the choice made by the stimulus person. This is often done indirectly, as when the perceiver compares reports of choices made in his absence with his own observations of choices made in his presence. We may try, for example, to find out what others say about us and our beliefs behind our backs. When the actions of another person obstruct our interests, it becomes important for us to determine whether the other sets out specifically to make life unpleasant for us or whether we have been disadvantaged as a by-product of actions primarily directed toward other objectives. Similarly, when others go out of their way to help us, we have an interest in establishing whether they did this because of our uniquely attractive personality or because they would have helped almost anyone under the circumstances.

The distinction between relevance and personalism hinges on the perceiver's imputation of a certain kind of knowledge to the actor: the actor's awareness that the interests of the perceiver are positively or negatively affected by his actions. If such knowledge is *not* imputed by the perceiver to the actor, then we are dealing with a case of "impersonal hedonic relevance."

When a hedonically relevant action is produced in the presence of the perceiver, the latter's problem is to decide whether the act was uniquely conditioned by the fact that he was its target. When there is such evidence of a "unique conditioning," the perceiver is likely to draw strong inferences of malevolence or benevolence, stronger than he would as a bystander. He and only he is the target of the other's highly relevant action; therefore, it is assumed that the other has a special interest in making life easy or difficult for him as a person.

Since the perceiver is going to be so vitally concerned with relevant effects that were deliberately produced for his consumption, such effects should clearly play a special role in shaping his inferences about the actor. We propose that action which is both relevant and personal has a direct and dramatic effect on evaluative conclusions about the actor. One reason for this is that personalism clearly implies choice. If an actor benefits a perceiver, this is a personalistic episode only if it reflects the selection of that particular perceiver as a worthy beneficiary in the face of opportunities to select other targets or other actions. The combination [247] of personalism and positive relevance, then, insures a positive evaluation simply by insuring a correspondent inference of focused benevolence. The special significance of such focused benevolence may lie in the fact that it satisfies the perceiver's needs for information about his worthiness, as well as other needs for security, power over others, and so on. In any event, the receipt of focused benefit or focused harm should generate "halo" effects in the inference process which go beyond the assimilation to hedonic value predicted in the case of impersonal hedonic relevance.

Personalism may, of course, be incorrectly assumed by the perceiver. The most extreme form of distortion along these lines may be seen in paranoia, where innocent actions and actions not conditioned by the perceiver's presence, become the data for inferences concerning ulterior malevolent motivation.

Surprisingly, there are few experiments which precisely assess the role of personalism in the inference process. The above proposition implies that hedonically relevant actions which the perceiver judges to be uniquely affected by his presence will give rise to correspondent inferences to all those attributes captured by a positive or negative "halo" effect. In an experiment specifically concerned with variations in personalism, Gergen (1962) arranged to have coeds receive uniformly positive, reinforcing remarks from another coed under personal versus impersonal conditions. Such remarks probably are hedonically relevant and positive as far as the first coed is concerned.

In the personal treatment, the girls had been previously introduced to each other, had engaged in a pleasant and informative interaction, and the reinforcing person (actually an experimental accomplice) had quite a bit to go on in expressing her positive feelings about the subject. In the impersonal treatment, on the other hand, the subjects were informed that the accomplice had been through some intensive training designed to help her establish rapport in a social interaction. In addition, and in clear contrast with the personal treatment, the accomplice never saw the subject, but interacted with her through a microphone–speaker system while the subject observed her through a one-way mirror. Each subject was ultimately asked to record her impression of the accomplice on a series of evaluative scales. From our proposition concerning the role of personalism in producing high correspondence for evaluative characteristics, we would expect a more positive halo effect in the personal than in the impersonal experimental treatment. There were, however, no significant differences between the subjects' evaluative ratings of the accomplice in the two conditions.

There was some evidence that the subjects felt sorry for the accomplice in the impersonal condition, since she had to operate under the **[248]** rather embarrassing handicap of being seen by the subject without being able to see her. There was also some confusion about whether the subject was to rate the accomplice as she appeared to be or as she "really was." We do not feel, therefore, that the Gergen experiment is a crucial test of the personalism proposition, though some variation of Gergen's procedure would seem to have promise as a fairly direct approach to the problem. It is at least conceivable that the proposition only holds for harmful actions, and that persons are much less sensitive to variations in personalism when positive actions are involved. This may be especially true when these positive actions involve verbal compliments. The reluctance of subjects to assume that a compliment was not intended for them personally is discussed in detail by Jones (1964). In this same source the reader will find a fuller exposition of the Gergen experiment along with results of other dependent variable measures which were more central to his concerns.

FACTORS MITIGATING ONE'S EVALUATION OF AN AGGRESSOR More indirect and yet more promising evidence on the role of personalism comes from experiments concerned with the factors which mitigate one person's reactions to being verbally attacked or insulted by another. The basic paradigm involves comparing perceivers' reactions to the same attacking action when it occurs in different settings. Typically, one setting is designed to bring out reciprocal hostility in the subjects (in the form of highly negative impression ratings) while other settings are arranged to check whether factors which theoretically should mitigate a hostile reaction in fact do. We are especially interested in those studies within this paradigm which exemplify variations in the perceived personalism of the attack.

Chapter 3   From Acts to Dispositions: The Attribution Process in Person Perception   **71**

Provocation by the Perceiver   An obvious mitigating variable which comes to mind is the extent to which the attack is seen as justified by the target person. If the perceiver believes he has done something to earn attack, insult, or rejection, he will presumably be less inclined to appraise his attacker negatively than if the attack was unreasonable or arbitrary. For example, Deutsch and Solomon (1959) found that subjects who were led to believe they had performed poorly on a task were less negative in appraising a stimulus person who rejected them as future work partners than subjects who were led to believe they had performed well.

A similar point is brought out by the results of an experiment by Strickland et al. (1960) on the effects of group support in evaluating an antagonist. Each subject met first with two other subjects who shared his opinions (pro or con) about the role of big-time athletics in university **[249]** life. He then privately chose a series of five arguments to support his position. These were to be transmitted to a person in the next room who was presumably neither for nor against big-time athletics. After this person had a chance to study the arguments, he was interviewed by the experimenter, who probed his feelings about the person who sent the arguments. This interview was broadcast into the subject's room and it contained a strong attack on his intelligence and integrity.

However, prior to his exposure to the broadcast interview (which was actually a standardized tape-recording), the subject learned that his fellow group members either would have chosen the same arguments he did (group support) or would have chosen a very different set (no support). The subject's final ratings of the person in the next room—which tapped into such dispositional characteristics as intelligence, warmth adjustment, conceit, and likability—were affected by this variation in group support. These rating differences were corroborated by free response sketches in which each subject expressed his private feelings about the person. Those whose arguments were supported were more negative in their evaluations of the person in the next room than those whose arguments were not supported.

In neither the Deutsch and Solomon (1959) nor the Strickland et al. (1960) study was the potential for perceiver personalism particularly high. In each, regardless of the experimental condition, a very limited sample of the subjects' behavior was the stimulus occasion for attack or rejection. The subject did not, in other words, expose the full range of his personal characteristics as a preface to the attack received. Nevertheless, the attack was directed toward him ostensibly because of behavior for which he must bear at least some of the responsibility.

We now suggest that an attack in the face of good performance (or group support) is more apt to be viewed as an attempt to harm or to disadvantage the subject than an attack in response to poor performance, because after a poor performance (including the sending of arguments defined as inferior by the group), the attacker will be seen as more constrained to respond negatively. The correspondence value of his hostile action, in other words, will be lowered by the presence in the choice area of effects having more to do with fulfillment of task requirements, candor, and realism than with hostility. Since there are fewer reasons for the antagonist's attack in the good performance setting, and one of these is presumably the antagonist's desire to hurt the subject as a person, correspondence and therefore unfavorability of general impression are high in this latter case.

Evidence of Chronicity Another factor which mitigates a perceiver's evaluation of an antagonist is any evidence concerning the latter's [250] general tendency to be indiscriminately aggressive. If the antagonist is known to be or gives fairly good evidence of being a chronically dyspeptic or uncontrollably negative person, his derogation will have less sting for the target person who bears its brunt.

Two recent experiments by Berkowitz (1960), conducted in quite a different framework from the one we are here proposing, shed some light on the effects of a perceiver's prior knowledge of a particular attack. Since only the first of the Berkowitz studies is particularly relevant to our present concerns, we shall confine ourselves to that.

Pairs of subjects were brought together for a study of first impressions. Through a bogus note exchange, the subject received information first, indicating that the partner was either generally hostile or generally friendly and second, indicating that the partner either liked or disliked the subject personally. The subject recorded his impression of the partner once at the outset of the experiment, once after the general information, and once after the personal evaluation from the partner.

The results showed that if the partner was perceived to be hostile initially, the partner's favorable evaluation of the subject had a decidedly ameliorating effect on the subject's impression, while the unfavorable evaluation changed this impression very little. Similarly, if the subject initially perceived the partner to be friendly, the unfavorable evaluation received from the partner created a striking change of impression in the direction of perceived unfriendliness, while the favorable evaluation resulted in minimal change.

It would appear, then, that the fact of prior knowledge concerning the hostility of the attacker reduces the personal significance of the attack. If we look more closely at the Berkowitz results, however, the point they make is actually rather different from the one we are presently pursuing. If a person who is already seen as generally hostile attacks the perceiver, there will be less of a *decline* (from the second to the third rating) than if a friendly person attacks the perceiver. However, the subject actually ends up liking the hostile attacker less than the friendly attacker, presumably because the evidence concerning the undesirable characteristic, hostility, summates: two hostility indicators are worse than one. The Berkowitz results really do not suggest that the perceiver is less bothered or upset by the attack if he has already decided that the attacker is generally hostile. They merely tell us that the attack is not as unexpected from a hostile person and therefore it contributes less to a change in impression from a point that is more negative to start with. We are dealing here, then, with the attempt on the part of the perceiver–subject to appraise the significance of a particular action choice against background information about different prior choices. [251]

In order to confirm the significance of perceived general hostility as a prior choice factor mitigating the significance of the attack the results would have to show that the generally hostile attacker is better liked by the recipient of the attack than the friendly attacks. However such a finding might be difficult to obtain experimentally. After all, the fact that he is hostile does not make the attacker likable to anybody. It merely means that the attack itself will cause less of a stir.

Evidence from a recent experiment does indicate that someone who starts out being derogatory and continues to act that way is better liked than someone who starts out being favorably disposed to the subject and becomes increasingly derogatory (Aronson and Linder, 1965). In this experiment the subject believed he was overhearing a series of appraisals referring to him with short episodes of social interaction intervening; he was not the target of openly expressed hostility. This may be a critical difference between the Berkowitz design and the Aronson and Linder design. Another difference that may have been crucial is that the former study asked for an intervening rating (which might have "committed" the subject to a particular rating of the attacker) while the latter study did not.

If we return to the conditions of the Berkowitz experiment, it may be too much to expect the hostile attacker to be better liked than the friendly attacker. What is needed is a comparison between the target of the attack and an "innocent" bystander as regards their impressions of the attacker. Because of the general negative significance attached to being hostile, it does not make sense to predict that either the involved subject or the bystander would like the hostile attacker better than the friendly one. However, a more refined and promising hypothesis, still in the spirit of our earlier remarks on the role of personalism, is that the involved subject will dislike the hostile attacker less than the bystander, relative to the discrepancy between their impressions of the friendly attacker.

Emotional Adjustment of the Attacker Such an experimental comparison has yet to be made, unfortunately, but the results of an earlier experiment by Jones et al. (1959) can be interpreted quite nicely in these terms. The procedures of the study by Jones et al. were roughly as follows. At a given experimental session, a pair of female subjects listened to two female stimulus persons allegedly conversing about one of the subjects in an adjacent room. The conversation was actually a carefully written and skillfully acted tape-recording. The stimulus persons were allegedly enrolled in a "senior course in personality assessment" and it was their duty to observe a designated subject through the one-way mirror for a period of time and then to discuss their impressions of that subject. It was clear to them that their remarks would be overheard by [252] the subjects in the adjacent room. One of the stimulus persons was generally neutral or mildly favorable in her comments, but the other stimulus person ("the derogator") was decidedly hostile and clearly had a low opinion of the subject. The subject whose characteristics were not being discussed was instructed to sit aside as a bystander and to pay close attention to the proceedings.

Prior to the attack, both the involved and bystander subject were given some information about the two students who would be observing them from the next room. It was clear upon reading this information that one of these students was quite maladjusted: She had an unstable home life, inadequate emotional resources, and underlying anxiety. The other student was presented as an effective, well-rounded, insightful undergraduate who had reached her present station from a home life that had been happy and rich with support and affection. For one group of subjects (the *derogator–mal* group), the data sheets presented the stimulus person who did not derogate as well adjusted. For a second group of subjects (the *derogator–well* group), the background information sheets were simply reversed.

After the involved and the bystander subjects listened to the tape-recorded discussion, including the derogatory remarks, they were each instructed to rate the two stimulus persons on a number of items. The items with which we are particularly concerned at the present are two reflecting the perceived likability of the stimulus person. The subjects were asked to indicate the extent of their agreement with the two statements: "As a person, she is extremely likable," and "I find it hard to like this person to any extent."

Thus the experimental manipulations created a standard situation in which a subject was derogated by a well-adjusted or a maladjusted person while another subject looked on. The variable of perceived maladjustment was included, in effect, to see whether it would serve as a factor mitigating the subject's response to the derogator. Jones et al. reasoned that the involved subject would be less upset by an attack from a maladjusted person than by an attack from a well-adjusted one. The bystander, on the other hand, was expected to be less concerned in general with the derogation and its implications for inferences about the derogator's personality, and more inclined to prefer the well-adjusted person because she was probably more appealing and talented. The prediction, then, was that there would be a statistical interaction between role (involved versus bystander) and condition of the derogator (maladjusted versus well adjusted).

The data were analyzed in terms of each subject's relative preference for the nonderogator over the derogator, a procedure adopted to reduce [253] that portion of rating variability due to individual differences in scale interpretation or style of responding to the scale items. (Some such device is usually essential in an "after-only" design.) The crucial results are summarized in Table 3.3. It is evident that there is a general dislike for people who are derogatory and a general preference for people who are well adjusted. When these two factors work in the same direction (as in the first column of the table), the discrepancy scores are understandably large. Of greater theoretical interest, when the derogator is well adjusted, the involved subject obviously likes her much less than the bystander subject ($p < .025$). To a slight extent, the average bystander even prefers the well-adjusted derogator to the maladjusted non-derogator (as indicated by the minus sign in that cell). When the derogator is maladjusted, however, the involved

Table 3.3 Joint Effects of Derogator Adjustment and Subject Involvement on "Likability"[a,b]

	Condition	
	Derogator–mal	Derogator–well
Involved subjects		
$\bar{X}$	3.92	2.17
SD	(1.78)	(2.29)
Bystander subjects		
$\bar{X}$	4.33	–.57
SD	(3.17)	(3.96)

[a]Based on discrepancy between ratings of derogator and nonderogator. The larger the mean value, the greater the tendency to dislike the derogator *relative to* the nonderogator.
[b]Data from Jones et al. (1961).

subject actually likes her better than the bystander does (though this difference does not approach statistical significance). The predicted interaction effect is minimally significant ($t = 1.877$; $p < .05$, one-tailed test).

In the context of the present discussion, we would argue that the personalistic significance of the derogation is obviously greater for the involved subject than for the bystander, and that it is greater for the involved subject when the derogator is well adjusted than maladjusted. When the derogator is maladjusted, the involved subject can take comfort in the hypothesis that the attacker's hostility is a symptom of her own problems and she would express similar insults to anyone who came within range. Perceived personalism should be fairly low. When the derogator is well adjusted, the involved subject will be more likely than the bystander [254] to package the insulting remarks into one cluster of highly related hedonic effects, and therefore to assign more correspondent, personalistic meaning to the attack. There is no easy way to escape the inference that the derogator finds the subject personally offensive and is "against her."

The maladjustment treatment in the preceding experiment may be construed in terms of the reduction of freedom to choose which accompanies poor adjustment, and the perception of restraints on choice by the perceiver. Perhaps the prevailing stereotypes of mental health and mental illness contribute to the tendency to perceive the maladjusted person as not responsible for the trouble he may cause others. Under the proper circumstances, however, he may be seen as *more* responsible for causing trouble than the normal, well-adjusted actor. At least such is the implication of some results from the experiment by Gergen and Jones (1963).

Amplification by Ambivalence Gergen and Jones set out to test a set of hypotheses deriving from the assumption that people are ambivalent toward the mentally ill. Many persons expect the mentally ill to have annoying characteristics but inhibit their annoyance because they acknowledge the fact that they are not responsible for their condition and its consequences. Gergen and Jones reasoned that the ambivalence toward a particular mentally ill person would be "split" if a situation were arranged in which his behavior had clear positive or negative consequences for the perceiver. Thus a perceiver should like a benevolent mentally ill person better than a benevolent normal person, and dislike a malevolent mentally ill person more than a malevolent normal person.

In order to test this hypothesis (which was loosely derived from psychoanalytic writings on ambivalence), 64 ambulatory V.A. hospital patients (nonpsychiatric) were given the task of predicting a series of hypothetical consumer choices being made by a patient in the adjoining room. The patient in the next room was alleged to be in the hospital either with a psychiatric illness or with a minor organic ailment. Actually there was no person in the next room, and all the information about him was conveyed by a combination of tape-recorded interviews and feedback through equipment controlled by the experimenter.

The choices of the patient in the adjoining room (hereafter called the stimulus person) were either very hard or very easy to predict. In the *low consequence* (i.e., low relevance) condition, the stimulus person (actually, by a ruse, the experimenter) provided corrective feedback by an informative signal light whenever a prediction error was made. In the *high consequence* condition, prediction errors called forth a raucous buzzer of unpredictable duration. The experimenter also made it clear that he found the buzzer very annoying, implying that it was up to the subject to keep him happy by making the correct predictions. Both before [255] the prediction task and after it was completed, the subject filled out an impression rating scale indicating his current feelings about the stimulus person.

The experimental hypothesis was stated as follows: "Evaluative judgments of a mentally ill stimulus person vary little as a function of predictability unless affective consequences are attached to success and failure of prediction. The role of affective consequences is less important in evaluative judgments of a normal stimulus person. Judgments of the normal should directly reflect variations in predictability, regardless of the consequences of judgment" (Gergen and Jones, 1963, p. 70).

The results presented in Figure 3.5 quite strikingly confirm this complicated hypothesis. There is, as implied by the hypothesis, a significant statistical interaction between the three factors of normality, predictability, and consequence. The most striking thing to note is the extent to which consequence determines perceptions of the mentally ill person. When he is in a position to hurt the subject or to spare him pain—in short, when he is either benevolent or malevolent toward the perceiver—the mentally ill [256] stimulus person is judged very favorably or unfavorably. When there are no such personal consequences for the perceiver, the stimulus person's predictability is not a relevant factor in judging him. (There is also an overall effect of predictability such that, across conditions, the predictable person tends to be evaluated more positively than the unpredictable person.)

Furthermore, it may be shown that the perception of benevolent versus malevolent intentions is involved in the subject's judgments of the high consequence-mentally ill

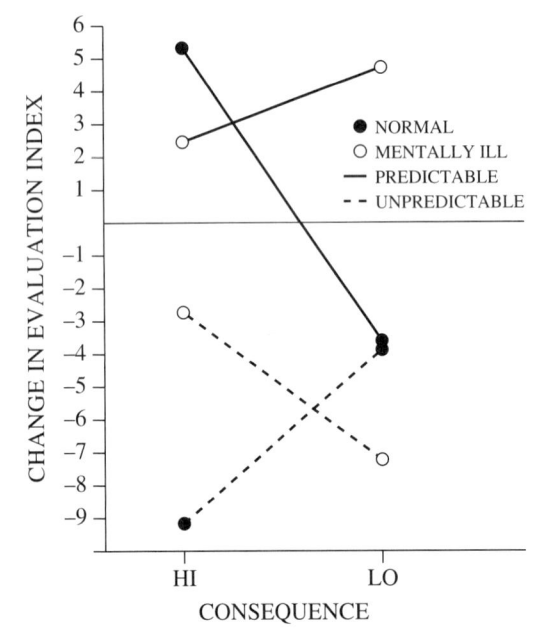

Figure 3.5 Changes in Evaluation as a Function of Mental Status, Predictability, and Consequence (Data from Gergen and Jones, 1963)

person. A variation of the experiment was run in which the stimulus person had supposedly made his consumer choice days before and was not, as alleged in the main experiment, actually in the next room at the time and responding through his own actions to the subject's predictions. In other words, all feedback to the subjects (including the unpleasant buzzer) was openly controlled by the experimenter. The experiment was in all other respects a precise replication of the first version. In this variation, predictability again had a strong effect on average evaluations, but there were no main or interaction differences as a function of consequence or normality. There must, then, be some possibility that the stimulus person is deliberately hurting or sparing the subject for the complex effects noted in the first experiment to occur.

There are many questions raised by the Gergen and Jones experiment. There are also special problems involved in relating these results to the Jones et al. (1959) findings. In interpreting those findings we argued, in effect, that an attack by a maladjusted stimulus person was less devastating than an attack by a well-adjusted stimulus person, because the normal person is perceived to have greater freedom of choice. It is as if evidence concerning maladjustment acts as a damper on the intensity of personal feeling toward the maladjusted person. The Gergen and Jones results, however, seem to show that under certain conditions evidence concerning maladjustment (i.e. mental illness) *amplifies* rather than constricts the intensity of the perceiver's personal feelings. Does this mean that the mentally ill person is assumed to have greater freedom of choice than the normal person in the Gergen and Jones study?

In spite of certain superficial resemblances, the experiments are really quite different in several, crucial respects. In the earlier experiment the very meaning and intensity of the attack is presumably a function of the attacker's adjustment status. To be insulted by a pathetic, perhaps mildly paranoid person is hardly to be insulted at all. In the Gergen and Jones experiment, however, the consequences of the attack are embarrassing, painful, and irritating, regardless of their source. In this case, furthermore, the question of freedom to choose may actually exacerbate rather than mitigate the response to the mentally ill stimulus person. **[257]**

While the data do not force this interpretation on us, there is at least nothing inconsistent in the rating or the postexperimental questionnaire results with the following speculations: When unpredictability hurts, the "why" of the unpredictability becomes a more important issue to the one who suffers. Two possible effects of "buzzing" the subject in the high consequence condition are especially salient, hurting the subject and being honest to one's true preferences for certain consumer objects. In the replication of the experiment, the first of these effects is ruled out by the change in information about the role of the stimulus person. Perhaps it is the case that when the stimulus person is normal, the most likely hypothesis is that he is making "normal choices" and, therefore, that the subject must take at least some of the blame for not being able to figure these out. When the stimulus person is mentally ill, on the other hand, the abnormal choice becomes an instrument of malevolence. Since the choice is a function of abnormality, it is difficult for the subject to maintain the feelings of sympathy which, in the low consequence condition, are sufficient to keep his impression a fairly neutral one. The impression of malevolence may be heightened by the feeling that since the mentally ill person is confused about his choices anyway, the least he can do is to go along with the subject's predictions and not lean on the error buzzer.

Such speculations are obviously no substitute for clear and compelling data on the role of perceived choice in the assignment of benevolent or malevolent intentions. The preceding review of studies involving the effects of personalism, studies mainly focusing on factors which mitigate a target person's response to being attacked, points up the need for additional research into the cognitive consequences of being singled out for benefit or harm. Those of us who have done research on this problem have lacked the kind of integrating framework which is needed to carry out a series of related studies. Perhaps the theory of correspondent inferences will help to provide a focus for the parametric experiments which are needed in clarifying the basic facts about personalism and its implications.

PERSONALISM AND INGRATIATION We have defined as personalistic those actions which are relevant to the perceiver's interests and, as far as the perceiver can tell, are deliberately carried out by the actor because of this relevance. The concept of personalism inevitably implies a certain degree of choice on the part of the actor which is not inherent in the concept of relevance. Since the condition of choice increases the likelihood of correspondent inferences, the coexistence of relevance and personalism should produce rather extreme evaluative judgments. It seems intuitively plausible that someone who helps us will be seen as more generous, helpful, friendly, etc., than someone [258] who helps another in our presence. A comparable line of thought applies to the case of malevolent actions when we have been singled out as their target.

In an attempt to provide a more rational basis for this intuition, we suggest the following distinctions and their consequences. There are three basic decisions which lurk in the wings during an interaction episode: whether to approach the person further and open oneself to him, whether to avoid or ignore him, or whether he must be "coped with," i.e., attacked or fended off. When the effects of an action are relevant in the positive direction, the decision is typically made to approach further. Such a decision is likely to be made whether or not the action is personalistic in addition to being relevant. When the effects of an action are negative, however, the imputation of personalism means that coping may be necessary. In other words, if a person's actions happen to offend you, he can merely be avoided—unless he is intent on offending you and will go out of his way to accomplish this objective. To the extent that coping is required, we would expect greater hostility to be aroused toward the threatening person, and those characteristics associated with malevolence should be inferred with higher correspondence. This might be partly a matter of justifying the hostility and partly a matter of keeping it at a high enough level (through self-reminding instigations) to support coping behavior.

On the basis of this reasoning, it would appear that personalism plays a larger role when an action is harmful than when it is beneficial. The examples we have cited, along with most of the relevant experiments in the literature, describe the response of a perceiver to some form of attack or rejection. However, a number of experiments have recently been completed which deal with first impressions in response to beneficial gestures, compliments, and agreements. These studies raise a new set of considerations which we shall discuss in concluding our treatment of the role of personalism.

We have argued that negative actions lead the target person either to avoid the actor or to mobilize cognitive support for the actions involved in coping with him.

Positive actions, on the other hand, lead to approach behaviors, personal openness, and reciprocation in kind. But a new and complicated problem arises with respect to positive actions. The perceiver must determine their credibility; to what extent does the beneficial act correspond with the intention really to improve the situation of the perceiver as an end in itself? As Jones (1964) has argued in his extended discussion of *ingratiation,* beneficial actions tend to be much more ambiguous than harmful actions when it comes to deciding on the actor's true intention or his ultimate objectives in the situation. The ambiguity of beneficial actions centers around the extent to which ulterior, manipulative purposes may be served by them. [259]

We may now ask, what implications are contained in the theory of correspondent inferences for predicting the cognitive impressions of someone faced with beneficial action? First of all, it is clear that the ambiguity arises because there are at least two classes of effects following from those actions. Actions such as compliments, agreements, and favors may validate the perceiver's self-concept, reduce his uncertainties, offer support against antagonists. Alternatively, or in addition, such actions may have the effect of obligating the perceiver to benefit the actor in return. If the first class of effects is the most salient, the perceiver will attribute to the actor the intention to express his true feelings. From this starting point, correspondent inferences will be drawn to such dispositions as candor, friendliness, likability, and generosity. In short, the perceiver's evaluation of the actor who has complimented him or agreed with him will be positive. If, on the other hand, the second effect, creating obligations to benefit, is salient and noncommon, the actor may be seen as manipulative, self-seeking, conforming, lacking in candor, etc.

Whether the inference process is tipped in the first, positive direction or the second, negative direction depends on the perceiver's reconstruction of the action alternatives available to the actor. This cognitive reconstruction will depend, in turn, on the perceiver's own role as one of the components in the actor's situation. Specifically, if the perceiver does not control any resources which are important to the actor, then the circle containing the effects of the chosen alternative will not contain the effect of "obligating the perceiver to benefit the actor in return." Presumably, then, some such effect as "validating the self-concept" will be salient and the perceiver will be seen as intending an honest compliment or expressing his genuine agreement with the perceiver's opinions.

If the perceiver does control resources important to the actor (i.e., if the actor is dependent on him), it will be hard for him to decide whether he is merely the target of an ingratiation attempt or the target of honest compliments. At the very least, the correspondence of inference to favorable dispositions will be reduced as a function of his own position as a dispenser of valuable resources. Depending on the circumstances, the perceiver may infer flattering or manipulative intentions and assign unfavorable dispositions, or he may infer benevolent intentions reflecting favorable dispositions.

Let us now consider three recent experiments which support the conclusions of the above line of reasoning. Jones et al. (1963) conducted an experiment in which upperclassmen in a campus R.O.T.C. unit exchanged written messages with freshmen in the same unit. This exchange occurred in response to two different sets of instructions, constituting the major treatments of the experiments. In the *ingratiation* condition, both the high and low status subjects were given instructions concerning [260] the importance of compatibility. The experimenter said he was trying to find a number of highly compatible leader–follower pairs to participate in some crucial studies on leadership later in the year. In the *control* condition, the message exchange was presented as part of a first impression study and the importance of "not misleading your partner" was stressed.

The messages that were sent concerned opinions on a variety of issues and eventually contained ratings by each subject of himself and his partner. These messages were actually intercepted and standard information about each subject was conveyed to his partner. Each found the other agreed with him on a variety of opinion issues, presented a rather modest view of himself, and expressed a complimentary view of his partner, the message recipient. On a postexperimental questionnaire (not to be seen by the partner) he was asked to rate the partner with respect to the following trait dimensions: completely sincere–on the phony side, trustworthy–unreliable, and brutally frank–flatterer. Each pair of antonyms was separated by a twelve-point scale. By adding a subject's rating on each of the three traits, he could be given a score ranging from 3 to 36 with a "perceived average" value at 19.5.

The results are presented in Table 3.4. They show that high and low status subjects perceived each other to be equally sincere in the control condition but that the low status subjects attributed significantly greater sincerity to the highs than the highs did to the lows in the ingratiation condition. Restricting our concern to the ingratiation condition, we would say that the inference concerning sincerity is more correspondent for the low status perceivers than for the highs. Relative to the hypothetical average value of 19.5, the empirical mean of 9.62 is more extreme than the mean of 13.05.

This could have been predicted from the theory of correspondent inferences on the grounds that fewer noncommon effects were involved in the high status person's decisions to compliment the low status person than vice versa. Since the low status person [261] was, presumably, in greater need of approval than the high status person, the latter may have been more apt to include "reciprocation of approval" among the effects serving as grist for the inference process. This could, then, have led to reduced correspondence of inference, i.e., ratings of sincerity which were closer to the mean or, in effect, greater perceived flattery.

Such an interpretation is quite post hoc and we offer it to illustrate how the theory might account for such findings rather than as confirmation of the theory. The problem

Table 3.4 Perception of Flattery[a,b]

	High status M	High status SD	High status N	Low status M	Low status SD	Low status N	P_{diff}
Ingratiation	13.05	4.14	19	9.62	3.16	21	.01
Control	11.68	4.46	19	11.85	3.41	20	ns

[a]Mean postexperimental ratings in each condition and differences between them. The higher the mean score, the greater the perceived flattery.
[b]Data from Jones et al. (1963).

is that other assumptions (which we believe are plausible) must be introduced to account for the fact that low status subjects perceive the highs to be more sincere in the ingratiation than in the control condition.

A study by Jones et al. (1963) was more explicitly designed to test the hypothesis that positive, supportive behavior will be taken more at face value as a genuine indication of sincerity and good intentions when the actor is not dependent on the target person. The supportive behavior, in this case, was consistently high agreement with the latter's opinions. Dependence was manipulated in a manner similar to the preceding experiment. Unlike the conditions of that experiment, the subjects were not themselves the targets of agreement, but served in the role of bystanders. Their task was to evaluate a stimulus person who agrees very closely with another person on whom he is obviously very dependent *or* not dependent at all.

In general, when the agreeing person was presented as dependent for approval on the other, he was better liked and was assigned more positive characteristics when he did not agree too closely. When dependence was low, on the other hand, the degree of agreement did not affect the ratings to any significant extent. Once again, the actor's condition of dependence affected the significance attached to highly "ingratiating" behavior. The subjects felt neutral about the high dependent conformist, because they did not know whether he was conforming for strategic advantage or whether his opinion agreement was coincidental. The fact that he was dependent, thus, increased the ambiguity of his behavior by adding the granting of approval to those possible effects of action with which the perceiver had to come to terms in his evaluation.

A study by Hilda Dickoff (discussed in Jones, 1964) also showed quite clearly that an actor who consistently compliments the perceiver is better liked when he is not dependent on the latter. Dependence has no effect when the evaluation received is still positive but contains a few plausible reservations.

The obvious feature of all of these studies is the fact that the same behavior (actions which can be seen as ingratiating in intent) results in quite different inferences depending on the context in which it occurs. **[262]** More specifically, the studies on ingratiation which we have cited share a concern with the variable, dependence, as the contextual conditions whose presence or absence affects causal attribution. Our inference that a complimentary or agreeable person really likes us is apt to be stronger if we are unable to think of anything we have that he might covet. In other words, the compliments or expression of opinions will be taken at face value and correspondence will be high when the actor has no apparent reason to choose the compliment other than his belief that it applies to us.

Now let us return to the notion of personalism and note an apparent qualification of our proposition that personalism increases correspondence. It may appear that when we are dealing with actions that are potentially ingratiating, correspondence *declines* as a function of personalism. Compliments to one's face are harder to evaluate than the same positive statements said behind our back. Opinions which agree with our own are more apt to be taken at face value when expressed prior to our opinion avowals than after such avowals.

We would not argue with the above interpretations in these hypothetical cases. We would claim, however, that personalism is involved in quite different ways in the kind of face-to-face confrontation where ingratiation is an issue and in the case of negative or neutral information. In fact, ingratiation only becomes an issue in the absence of indications that personalism is involved. The person who receives a face-to-face compliment must decide whether that compliment was meant for him because of his unique personal qualities, or was meant for anyone who happened to occupy a position as a potential dispenser of resources. The high status person may have a difficult problem arranging conditions to test the reactions of his subordinates to him as a person; it may be hard for him to get certain kinds of self-validating information. The important point is that actions that may be seen as directed toward him as an occupant of a social position may therefore not be personalistic and the correspondence value of inferences derived from such ambiguous actions is apt to be low.

SUMMARY AND CONCLUSIONS

In the present essay we have attempted to develop a systematic conceptual framework for research on person perception. We have been especially interested in specifying the antecedent conditions for attributing intentions or dispositions, having observed an action. Dispositional attributes are in a general way inferred from the effects of action, but not every effect is equally salient in the inference process. Even if we assume as perceivers that the actor *knew* what the effects of his action would be, we must still engage in the complex analytic process of selectively linking certain effects achieved to certain effects intended. This assignment [263] of intentions can provide sufficient reason for (or explanation of) the action, so that the perceiver may go about his interpersonal business unfettered by a concern with ultimate or infinitely regressive causes.

Our most central assumption in considering the attribution of intentions is that actions are informative to the extent that they have emerged out of a context of choice and reflect a selection of one among plural alternatives. When we pursue the implications of this assumption in some detail it is apparent that the distinctiveness of the effects achieved and the extent to which they do not represent stereotypic cultural values determine the likelihood that information about the actor will be extracted from an action. We have used the term "correspondence of inference" to refer to variations in this kind of informativeness. To say that an inference is correspondent, then, is to say that a disposition is being rather directly reflected in behavior, and that this disposition is unusual in its strength or intensity. Operationally, correspondence means ratings toward the extremes of trait dimensions which are given with confidence.

Having formulated the inference problem in these terms, an obvious research question arises. What are the factors which control the perceiver's judgment that the actor had a choice? Or, more precisely, what conditions influence his judgment concerning the number and distinctiveness (noncommonness) of effects? It is our hope that cumulative, perhaps even parametric research will be stimulated by posing the inference problem in these terms. A study in which the stimulus person either went along with or resisted clearly stated role-demands was presented to exemplify some of the more obvious implications of the theory. The results of the study may be interpreted as showing that a low degree of "psychological" choice is functionally the same thing as having many reasons for making a choice. In-role behavior is supported by too many reasons to be informative about the actor; out-of-role behavior is more informative because the effects of such actions are distinctive (few in number) and not to be dismissed as culturally desirable.

Chapter 3 From Acts to Dispositions: The Attribution Process in Person Perception

In the latter portions of the present essay we have considered the further complexities associated with perceiver involvement which affect theoretical predictions concerning inferred attributes. Our analysis distinguished between two levels of involvement: hedonic relevance and personalism. An actor's choice is hedonically relevant for the perceiver if, on balance, it promotes or thwarts his purposes. An action is personalistic in the perceiver's view, if it was uniquely conditioned by the latter's presence: if conditions are such that the perceiver believes he is the intended consumer of the effects produced by the actor.

In discussing the various effects of relevance, we argued that correspondence generally increases with increasing relevance. Evaluation, in turn, is a joint function of both relevance and correspondence. A small **[264]** number of studies were discussed which seem to shed some light on the impact of relevance. In particular it was noted that if one holds relevance constant (at some value other than zero) and manipulates the variables alleged to increase correspondence, evaluation becomes more extreme. Similarly, by pegging correspondence at a particular level and increasing relevance, the same increase in evaluation extremity may be observed. It should be emphasized, however, that much of the research cited was only indirectly concerned with variations in relevance. More systematic research is needed to establish the conditions under which relevance calls forth positive or negative evaluations. In addition, we need to know much more about the relations between affective and cognitive processes implied by the linkage between relevance and correspondence.

In the final section on personalism, we discussed a study in which this variable was directly and dramatically manipulated, only to acknowledge that the effects were negligible. It will be important to establish the reasons for this curious result by designing other experiments which directly approach different facets of the complex personalism variable. There is, however, indirect or circumstantial evidence which encourages the conviction that personalism and hedonic relevance are not identical in their effects. Specifically, we discussed several experiments which were concerned with the mitigation versus amplification of hostility toward an attacker. Here it is seen that the intensity of hostile reciprocation was affected by factors in the situation which made it more or less likely that personalism was involved. Such factors as sufficiency of provocation and indiscriminateness of the attack, were shown to affect the recipient's evaluation of the attacker. These conditions could be, and were, discussed in terms of the correspondence–noncommon effect theory. Several experiments on ingratiation and the perception of flattery were also discussed in these terms. The main dilemma of the perceiver, when he becomes the target of actions which may be ingratiating in intent, is to determine whether he is being benefited because of his unique personal quality or because of the resources which he may control.

This essay, long as it is, could have been much longer if we had hedged our statements with proper qualifications and dealt fully with the problems which remain in our formulation. We have no illusions that we have finally opened the main door on the mysteries of causal attribution. Our formulation has changed considerably since our work on this essay began, and it will undoubtedly change much more with further thought. We trust it is also obvious that the ability to accommodate old findings from complex experiments is an easy hurdle for any theory to jump. We remain optimistic, however, that the present framework encourages systematic thinking about inferring dispositions from actions and suggests some of the major variables that merit initial consideration. [265]

REFERENCES

Aronson, E. & Under, D. (1965). Gain and loss of esteem as determinants of interpersonal attractiveness. *Journal of Experimental Social Psychology*, 1, 156–172.

Berkowitz, L. (1960). Repeated frustrations and expectations in hostility arousal. *Journal of Abnormal and Social Psychology*, 60, 422–429.

Davis, K. E. (1962). *Impressions of others and interaction context as determinants of social interaction and perception in two-person discussion groups.* Unpublished doctoral dissertation, Duke University.

Deutsch, M., & Solomon, L. (1959). Reactions to evaluations by others as influenced by self-evaluations. *Sociometry*, 22, 93–112.

Gergen, K. J. (1962). *Interaction goals and personalistic feedback as factors affecting the presentation of the self.* Unpublished doctoral dissertation, Duke University.

Gergen, K. J., & Jones, E. E. (1963). Mental illness, predictability, and affective consequences as stimulus factors in person perception. *Journal of Abnormal and Social Psychology*, 67, 95–104.

Heider, F. (1944). Social perception and phenomenal causality. *Psychological Review*, 51, 358–374.

Heider, F. (1958). *The psychology of interpersonal relations.* New York: Wiley.

Jones, E. E. (1964). *Ingratiation.* New York: Appleton.

Jones, E. E., & Daugherty, B. (1959). Political orientation and the perceptual effects of an anticipated interaction. *Journal of Abnormal and Social Psychology*, 59, 340–349.

Jones, E. E., & deCharms, R. (1957). Changes in social perception as a function of the personal relevance of behavior. *Sociometry*, 20, 75–85.

Jones, E. E., Hester, S. L. Farina, A., & Davis, K. E. (1959). Reactions to unfavorable personal evaluations as a function of the evaluator's perceived adjustment. *Journal of Abnormal and Social Psychology*, 59, 363–370.

Jones, E. E.. Davis, K. E.. & Gergen, K. J. (1961). Role playing variations and their informational value for person perception. *Journal of Abnormal and Social Psychology*, 63, 302–310.

Jones, E. E., Gergen, K. J., & Jones, R. G. (1963). Tactics of ingratiation among leaders and subordinates in a status hierarchy. *Psychological Monographs*, 77, No. 3 (Whole No. 566).

Jones. E. E.. Jones. R. G.. & Gergen, K. J. (1964). Some conditions affecting the evaluation of a conformist. *Journal of Personality*, 31, 270–288.

Jones, E. E., Gergen, K. J., Gumpert, P., & Thibaut, J. W. (1965). Some conditions affecting the use of ingratiation to influence performance evaluation. *Journal of Abnormal and Social Psychology*, 1, 613–626.

Kleiner, R. J. (1960). The effects of threat reduction upon interpersonal attractiveness. *Journal of Personality*, 28, 145–156.

Pepitone, A. (1950). Motivational effects in social perception. *Human Relations*, 1, 57–76.

Steiner, I. D., & Field, W. L. (1960). Role assignment and interpersonal influence. *Journal of Abnormal and Social Psychology*, 61, 239–246.

Strickland, L. H., Jones, E. E., & Smith, W. P. (1960). Effects of group support on the evaluation of an antagonist. *Journal of Abnormal and Social Psychology*, 61, 73–81.

Thibaut, J. W., & Riecken, H. W. (1955). Some determinants and consequences of the perception of social causality. *Journal of Personality*, 24, 113–133. [266]

ATTRIBUTION THEORY

Chapter 4

Update of "From Acts from Dispositions: The Attribution Process in Person Perception"

Edward E. Jones
Princeton University

More than 12 years have passed since the original presentation of correspondent inference theory. In the intervening period there have been numerous important developments in our theoretical understanding of person perception, and the attributional approach has been extended to accommodate self-perception, interpersonal conflict, emotional experience, and divergent perceptual perspectives. Kelley's (1967) seminal paper had much to do with these extensions, as did the volume of original essays by Jones, Kanouse, Kelley Nisbett, Valins, and Weiner (1972).

Flexibility rather than hypothetico-deductive rigor has been the strength of the attributional approach, and this adaptive flexibility has made possible the development of numerous attribution-based theories of important psychological phenomena. But in spite of the modest shift toward the attributional analysis of traditional problems in interpersonal relations, the growth of basic attribution theory itself has been somewhat stunted. In 1976, Jones and McGillis (in Harvey, Ickes, & Kidd, 1976) engaged in a tenth anniversary re-examination of correspondent inference theory in an attempt to shore up the weaknesses of that theory and to integrate the Jones and Davis framework

---

Reprinted with permission from *Cognitive Theories in Social Psychology,* (1978) L. Berkowitz, (Ed.), New York: Academic Press, pp. 331–336. References updated by the editor.

with the Kelley model. This brief account will attempt to summarize the major points of that re-analysis and to comment on some of the major empirical consequences of the 1965 paper.

Correspondent inference theory is essentially a theory of information [331]* gain—it concerns changes in one's impressions, brought about by behavioral evidence. An expectation is to some extent violated, and the perceiver must come to terms with the new information reflected in this violation. Correspondent inference theory is an attempt to explain how the expectancy violation might be resolved. The earlier Jones and Davis formulation referred to these expectancies under the heading of cultural desirability, but I now view this as unduly restrictive. The more generic view of an expectancy may be phrased in terms of the prior probability that an actor would desire a certain effect. This prior probability is in turn determined both by assumptions of cultural desirability and by any specific knowledge the perceiver has concerning the actor and his prior behavior. For convenience we may refer to the former as *category-based* expectancies and the latter as *target-based* expectancies, although any given expectancy is very likely to be a combination of the two in the natural world. An exciting challenge for future research is to determine whether these different expectancy origins have different consequences in the event that the expectancy is violated by some act of the target person. In one such attempt, Jones and Berglas (1976) were unable to detect any systematic differences in the combining of action data with category-based versus target-based expectancies.

Whether the prior probability of the target person's desire for an effect or consequence derives from category-based or target-based expectancies, it seems useful to conceive of a valence attached to each of the effects of an observed action. Such a valence has a theoretical value ranging from a –1 to a +1. A maximally undesirable effect will have a –1, indicating the highest probability that the target person would seek to avoid that effect. A +1 valence would signify maximum desirability, either because the effect is universally sought, sought by all members of a category to which the target person belongs, or known to be sought vigorously by him in the past. From the point of view of information gain, pursuit of a low valence effect should lead to greater correspondence of inference, other things equal, than pursuit of a high valence effect.

This reformulation of the cultural desirability variable in terms of a valence measure of a prior probability is intended to extend the generality of correspondent inference theory. The theory can now better handle the problem of what is learned from the actions of a familiar other and is less restricted to the first impression case. The other major theoretical variable—number of noncommon effects—remains as originally stated. Each action is still conceived of as a choice between alternatives. Typically, some of the effects of action [332] are common to the alternatives and should logically be uninformative. Thus, it is the *noncommon* effects that are crucial, and the more there are of these attendant on a given action, the more ambiguous is the meaning of that action. Research has hardly begun on the role of noncommon effect number, though McGillis's study (1974) represents an important step in this direction.

---

*Bracketed bold numbers refer to original page numbers. Page numbers indicate where the original page ended.

Questions concerning the number of noncommon effects are equivalent to those raised by Kelley's (1972) use of the "discounting principle." The greater the number of noncommon effects attendant on a chosen action, the more will any given effect be discounted as a plausible reason for that action. Kelley's augmentation principle also has equivalences in correspondent inference theory, in the notion of costs incurred. To the extent that some of the effects of a chosen act have negative valences, more emphatic or confident inferences will be drawn from the remaining positive effects. These intentional or dispositional inferences will thus be augmented by the presence of negatively valent effects.

The original subtitle of the Jones and Davis paper reads "From Acts to Dispositions," but the theoretical statement is actually more concerned with momentary intentions—inferred reasons for action—than with inferences to durable underlying dispositions. Kelley's (1967) theoretical framework may be more convenient for discussing how dispositions are inferred, because it includes explicit references to consistency over time and modality. When a stable disposition is inferred from a single action combined with an expectancy, this is probably the most tentative kind of hypothesis; one that the perceiver will be motivated to test in the course of further observations of the target person. A comprehensive theory of correspondent inference must eventually incorporate considerations of how behavioral information is combined over multiple observations.

Much of the research spawned by correspondent inference theory has used the theory as a rational baseline model. That is, the theory has been less valuable in pointing to how people actually function in drawing person-perceptual inferences than in providing a logical template for detecting various sources of bias or error. Both functions of the theory—the descriptive and the prescriptive—are illustrated in the research on attitude attribution. Here the basic paradigm has been to present subjects with essays, speeches, or interview comments favoring particular attitudinal positions, and allegedly prepared by target persons under clearly specified conditions of choice or no choice. The subject's task is to infer the target person's "true attitude" by considering the position taken and its context of varying constraint. **[333]** The main results of this line of research are consistent with correspondent inference theory in that attitudes in line with behavior are most strongly inferred when the actor has choice (few noncommon effects) and the behavior is low in prior probability (expected effect valence).

But it is also the case that behavior under no-choice conditions (numerous noncommon effects high in positive valence) leads to significant correspondence as well (Jones & Harris, 1967; Jones, Worchel, Goethals, & Grumet, 1971). Snyder and Jones (1974) have shown that this finding does not derive from artifacts, such as the particular nature of the chosen essay or speech, and that there is even an error of imputing too much correspondence to actual essay writers in a high choice condition.

This tendency for subjects to assess behavior, and subsequently to attribute too much causal significance for the particular behavioral content to internal characteristics of the target person, has been referred to by Ross (1977) as the "fundamental attribution error" [p. 183]. The tendency also played an important role in Jones and Nisbett's (1972) speculations that observers of an action tend to attribute to the actor what the actor himself attributes to the situation.

A recent paper by Snyder and Frankel (1976) has extended the notion of a fundamental attribution error to the attribution of emotions. Specifically, these investigators found that observers of a silent videotape showing a female actor supposedly in an anxiety-arousing situation thought she was more likely to have a durable disposition of anxiety than did observers who watched the same actor in a neutral setting. Thus, information about a situational constraint leads to a stronger dispositional inference rather than the more equivocal one "required" by correspondent inference theory or by Kelley's model. In this case, since the same results are not obtained when subjects are told about the context *after* observing the tape, information about the setting appears to induce perceptions of the (actually neutral) behavior as "anxious," which then gives rise to an inference that seems to belie their origin.

The concepts of hedonic relevance and personalism have received little attention since the Jones and Davis paper. An exception generally confirming our speculations therein is a study by Chaikin and Cooper (1973) that presented in-role and out-of-role behavior vignettes that were positive, neutral, or negative in hedonic relevance for the subjects. The results showed that respect and admiration were affected by the combination of correspondence and hedonic relevance, whereas liking and friendship choice were mediated by considerations [334] of hedonic relevance alone. Subjects disliked a member of the Ku Klux Klan whether he was the son of an Alabama millworker or a northern physics professor. They liked a medical student whether he was the son of a Puerto Rican custodian or the son of a Boston physician. Admiration and respect, however, varied with whether the behavior was in-role or out-of-role.

Jones and McGillis (1976) attempted to integrate correspondent inference theory with Kelley's analysis of variance model, emphasizing distinctiveness, consensus, and consistency. This integration suggests the comparability of distinctiveness and a violated, target-based expectancy. When the expectancy is based on nearly identical past actions, we speak of inconsistency. Circumstance attributions are the equivalent of ignorance—reflected in the knowledge factor in the correspondent inference scheme—since the attributor uses circumstance as a residual category when neither "person" nor "entity" seem appropriate.

More generally, correspondent inference theory and the Kelley analysis of the variance cube make a number of similar, or at least complementary, distinctions. Both theoretical statements approach a lay version of experimental design and analysis. Both the experiment and the attribution episode involve an attempt to isolate distinctive causes for observed behavior. Each proceeds by a combination of comparison and control procedures. The experiment manipulates potential causal variables and compares the effects observed with those effects present in the absence of these variables. The attributor makes use of the experimental logic whenever possible but usually must cope with the natural confounding of potential causes that occurs in the real world.

Although they have much in common, correspondent inference theory and the Kelley cube are divergent in important respects. Correspondent inference theory focuses on the attribution of identifiable personal dispositions and addresses the case in which the attributor is trying to consider a dispositional cause for a perceived act by evaluating the strength of environmental constraints. Kelley, on the other hand, was more explicitly concerned with how personal biases in perception may be corrected or ruled out in the determination of the "true" nature of environmental entities.

I have already noted that Kelley's model incorporates the data from repeated observations in his consistency-over-time-and-modality variable. But Kelley's model has clear weaknesses on the dependent variable side. Combinations of distinctiveness, consensus, and consistency **[335]** result in attributions that "something" about the person, stimulus, or environment caused the behavior. The noncommon effects analysis of correspondent inferent theory provides a mechanism for determining what specifically the "something" is. That is, specific causal factors are focused upon in the noncommon effects analysis, particularly specific causal factors residing in the person.

REFERENCES

Chaikin, A. L., & Cooper, J. (1973). Evaluation as a function of correspondence and hedonic relevance. *Journal of Experimental Social Psychology,* 9, 257–264.

Harvey, J. H., Ickes, W. J., & Kidd. R. F. (1976). *New directions in attribution research.,* Vol. I. Hillsdale, New Jersey: Erlbaum.

Jones, E. E., & Berglas, S. (1976). A recency effect in attitude attribution. *Journal of Personality,* 44, 433–438.

Jones, E. E. & Harris, V. A. (1967). The attribution of attitudes. *Journal of Experimental Social Psychology,* 3, 1–24.

Jones. E. E., Kanouse, D. E., Kelley, H. H., Nisbett. R. E. Valins, S.Weiner. B. (1972). *Attribution: Perceiving the causes of behavior.* Morristown, New Jersey: General Learning.

Jones, E. E., & McGillis, D. (1976). Correspondent inferences and the attribution cube: A comparative reappraisal. In J. H. Harvey, W. J. Ickes, & R. F. Kidd (Ed.), *New directions in attribution research. Vol. 1.* (pp. 389–420). Hillsdale, NJ: Erlbaum.

Jones, E. E., & Nisbett, R. E. (1972). The actor and the observer: Divergent perceptions of the causes of behavior. In E. E. Jones, D. E. Kanouse, H. H. Kelley, R. E. Nisbett, S. Valins, & B. Weiner (Eds.), *Attribution: Perceiving the causes of behavior* (pp. 77–94). Morristown, NJ: General Learning Press.

Jones, E. E., Worchel, S., Goethals, G. R., & Grumet. J. F. (1971). Prior expectancy and behavioral extremity as determinants of attitude attribution. *Journal of Experimental Social Psychology,* 7, 59–80.

Kelley, H. H. (1967). Attribution theory in social psychology. In D. Levine (Ed.), *Nebraska Symposium on Motivation,* 15, 192–238. Lincoln: University of Nebraska Press..

Kelley, H. H. (1972). Attribution in social interaction. In E. E. Jones, D. E. Kanouse, H. H. Kelley, R. E. Nisbett, S. Valins, & B. Weiner (Eds.), *Attribution: Perceiving the causes of behavior* (pp. 1–26). Morristown, NJ: General Leaning Press.

McGillis, D. (1974). *A correspondent inference theory analysis of attitude attribution.* Unpublished doctoral dissertation. Duke University, North Carolina.

Ross. L. (1977). The intuitive psychologist and his shortcomings: Distortions in the attribution process. In L. Berkowitz (Ed.).*Advances in experimental social psychology,* 10, 173–220.

Snyder, M. L. & Frankel. A. (1976). Observer bias: A stringent test of behavior engulfing the field. *Journal of Personality and Social Psychology,* 34, 857–864.

Snyder, M., & Jones. E. E. (1974). Attitude attribution when behavior is constrained. *Journal of Experimental Social Psychology,* 10. 584–600. **[336]**

ATTRIBUTION THEORY

Chapter 5

Correspondent Inferences and the Attribution Cube: A Comparative Reappraisal

Edward E. Jones
Duke University
Daniel McGillis
Harvard University

A little more than 30 years ago, Heider (1944) planted the seed of an attribution theory in his classic paper on phenomenal causality. This contribution was admired as an extension of Gestalt principles to social perception, but with the notable exception of an experiment by Thibaut and Riecken (1955), the idea of using naive causal analysis as a basis for theoretical prediction bore little empirical fruit. Heider's 1958 *Psychology of Interpersonal Relations* transplanted the attribution seed into a richer soil by mixing Gestalt notions with cognitive functionalism, and the result was an accelerated interest in processes and consequences of causal attributions for social behavior.

Influenced both by Heider and the empirical tradition of person perception research, Jones and Davis introduced correspondent inference theory in 1965. Their particular interest was in identifying the variables governing inferences that an act reflects an internal, personal disposition. Shortly thereafter, Kelley (1967) attempted to

---

Reprinted with permission of Lawrence Erlbaum Associates from *New Directions in Attribution Research,* Vol. 1, J. H. Harvey, W. J. Ickes, and R. F. Kidd (Eds.), Hillside, NJ: Erlbaum, pp. 389–420 ©1976. References have been updated by the editor.

Chapter 5 Correspondent Inferences and the Attribution Cube: A Comparative Reappraisal **91**

formulate another variant of attribution theory that would make more immediate contact with such central areas of social psychology as change and social comparison. Not only did Kelley make effective use of Heider's and Festinger's (1954) ideas, but he explicitly extended the concern of attribution theory to self-attribution. In the process, Kelley showed the relevance and compatibility of Bern's "radical behaviorism" (1965, 1972) for the analysis of how one knows his own states and dispositions.

After allowing several years for the digestion of these theoretical proposals, Jones and Kelley joined several other colleagues (Kanouse, Nisbett, Valins, & Weiner) in coauthoring *Attribution: Perceiving the Causes of Behavior.* A highlight **[389]*** of this volume was the ubiquitous acknowledgement of the contributions of Schachter and his colleagues (Davison & Valins, 1969; Nisbett & Schachter 1966; Schachter & Singer, 1962) to an attributional understanding of emotional experience. The book also illustrated the flexibility of attributional notions in their application to domains as diverse as language usage, reactions to success and failure, psychopathology, interpersonal trust, and psychotherapy.

The *Attribution* book was both a reflection and a stimulant of varied research efforts. Nelson and Hendrick's (1974) recent bibliographic survey shows that attribution-oriented studies formed by far the largest category in the social psychology research literature of 1974. The growth of attribution research seems far from peaking and further from decline. A generation of young social psychologists is apparently comfortable with attributional concepts and their use in problem formulation and analysis. But the widespread usage of attributional language and style of approach is one thing, the growth of systematic deductive theory is another. In spite of the growing quantity of attribution research in the last decade, the growth of attribution *theory* has been somewhat stunted. With the thought that it might be an instructive exercise in the direction of theoretical development, we shall conduct a tenth anniversary reappraisal of correspondent inference theory and selective data of relevance. We shall then attempt to relate the theory of correspondent inference to Kelley's attributional formulation in the ultimate interest of solidifying the theoretical structure that will organize existing data and underpin future research.

CORRESPONDENT INFERENCE THEORY REVISITED

The main problem that Jones and Davis wanted to attack was the perception of another's personal attributes. When we see someone acting in a particular setting, how do we decide whether to attribute the cause of the action to the person or the setting? The point of departure was the recognition that people who are not constrained physically or socially will attempt to achieve desirable consequences by their behavior. Therefore, when the actor has behavioral freedom, we should be able to infer his intentions from the consequences or effects of his behavior. This should follow, at least, if the actor is believed to have the knowledge that the particular act will produce the consequences observed. Attributions of probable knowledge are facilitated by any evidence that the actor has the ability to achieve the consequences observed when he desires. After all, if a person cannot reliably achieve a set of effects, an observer is less likely to assume he deliberately intended to achieve them. The accurate attribution of intentions from

---

*Bracketed bold numbers refer to original page numbers. Page numbers indicate where the original page ended.

behavioral effects, then, assumes knowledge, ability, and behavioral freedom. But the problem of attribution is immediately complicated by the fact that a given act invariably has multiple consequences. Not only that, but freedom to choose means there are options chosen and options foregone. Both **[390]** the chosen and the rejected alternatives can, and most often do, have multiple effects. Some of the chosen and foregone effects may be the same; they are *common effects*. Any given action is uninformative with regard to such common effects since they do not provide a discriminating reason for the choice. Thus the only information about intentions is that contained in the *noncommon effects* of action. Something in the combination of noncommon effects chosen and foregone has guided the actor's behavior in the observed direction. As a first approximation, we might say that a dispositional inference is correspondent to the extent that an act and the disposition are similarly described by the inference (for example, "his domineering behavior reflects an underlying trait of dominance").

But correspondent inference theory is not just concerned with the attribution of intentions or other dispositions; it is concerned with information *gain* as a function of behavioral observation. In Bayesian terms (cf. Ajzen, 1971; Ajzen & Fishbein, 1975), correspondence reflects changes in the subjective probability of inferring a disposition given observed behavior. The perceiver may begin either with an expectancy based on normative considerations or one based on prior behavior of the same actor. Thus he may ask, what makes this actor differ from other actors? Or he may ask, what do I know about the actor now that I did not know about him before? A correspondent inference may be formally defined in the following terms: *Given an attribute–effect linkage which is offered to explain why an act occurred, correspondence refers to the degree of information gained regarding the probability or strength of the attribute.* Jones and Davis (1965, p. 234) originally stated that "correspondence increases as the judged value of the attribute departs from the judge's conception of the average person's standing on that attribute" (for example, "he is more dominant than most people"). To this earlier formulation we would now like to add, "or the judge's prior conception of where the actor stood on that attribute" (for example, "he is more dominant than I thought he was").

When correspondence is defined as information gain, it is obvious that we need to consider more than just whether behavioral effects are noncommon. We also have to consider whether, and to what extent, they fit the judge's prior expectations concerning people in general, or this particular actor. This determinant was originally described by Jones and Davis in terms of effects assumed to be desired in the culture. But the more generic case concerns the prior probability that the particular actor would desire a particular effect. This might be based on assumptions about cultural desirability, or it might be based on prior knowledge about the actor. Whichever may be the case, it seems useful to conceive of a valence attached to each effect having a possible range from -1 to $+1$. A maximally undesirable effect would have a valence of -1, indicating the highest probability that the individual concerned would seek to avoid that effect. A $+1$ valence, on the other hand, would signify the highest probability of effect desirability. From the point of view of information gain, pursuit of a low valence effect should lead **[391]** to greater correspondence of inference, other things equal, than pursuit of a high valence effect.

Considering together the uniqueness and valence of the effects pursued, it now should be clear that correspondence of inference is greatest when the number of noncommon effects is low, and their valence is low or negative. The basic predictions of correspondent inference theory can be summarized, if oversimplified, in terms of the 2 × 2 design presented in Table 5.1. Correspondence is seen here as the joint inverse function of effect commonality and effect valence, as long as we keep in mind that the latter refers to the expected or assumed valence for the actor prior to his act. This relationship can be more simply described as a near tautology: the more distinctive reasons a person has for an action and the less surprising or unexpected these reasons are, the less informative the action is concerning the identifying attributes of the person. The table emphasizes that highly expected actions are trivial from an informational point of view. Also, inference ambiguity obviously increases when the number of potential determining effects increases.

With the few exceptions noted, this presentation is but a cryptic summary of the exposition presented at greater length in Jones and Davis (1965). The reader who is being exposed to these ideas for the first time may wish to retreat to that source. Jones and Davis (1965) also considered the operation of motivational sources as affecting correspondence of inference. There may be consequences for the perceiver as well as for the actor. Effects of action may be *hedonically relevant* in that the perceiver benefits from the action he has just observed or is disadvantaged by it. This could happen in the absence of any intention of the actor to help or hurt the perceiver. But the actor could also be *personalistic* in his provision of relevant effects, clearly intending benefit or harm for the perceiver. In spite of the potential importance of motivational effects on attribution, the present chapter will focus on the purely cognitive aspects of information processing. Readers interested in the effects of hedonic relevance [392] and personalism are referred to Jones and deCharms (1957) and Chaikin and Cooper (1973).

Sources of Expected Effect Valence

We would like to extend the theory from a conceptualization of initial contact with a stranger's behavior to a more general statement concerning information gain in person perception. One criticism of the earlier Jones and Davis formulation is that the analysis was concerned with the single behavioral episode, and there was no provision for inferences following more extended experience with a given target person. Indeed, their paper might better have been subtitled "From Acts to Intentions" than "From Acts to Dispositions." A disposition is inferred when an intention or related intentions persist or keep reappearing in different contexts.

Table 5.1 Expected Valence and Effect Commonality as Determinants of Correspondence

Number of noncommon effects	Expected valence	
	High	Low
High	Trivial ambiguity	Intriguing ambiguity
Low	Trivial clarity	High correspondence

The shift from assumed cultural desirability to assumed or expected valence makes it possible to treat correspondence of inference, or information gained, at any stage in a relationship. But is this extension legitimate, and can we treat prior probability inferences about the actor himself in the same way as inferences based on normative considerations? In order to explore the applicability of the theory to these two different cases, we introduce the distinction between category-based expectancies and target-based expectancies.

A category-based expectancy derives from the perceiver's knowledge that the target person is a member of a particular class, category, or reference group. In the case of extreme prior information poverty, the perceiver at least knows that the actor is a human being of a particular sex and approximate age. From this knowledge the perceiver doubtless can generate at least crude expectancies about probable attribute–effect linkages. Usually, of course, the perceiver has much more information to guide his expectancies, information that locates the actor in a sociocultural network. This might be information about occupation, group affiliation, country or state of origin, or social class and educational level. Whatever the particular pattern, the actor may be typically located as a member of overlapping categories, each contributing to a refinement of expectancies against which the actual behavior of the person will be judged. Feldman (1972) and Feldman and Hilterman (1975) have shown that such category combinations as race and occupation interact to produce different stereotypic impressions.

These category-based expectancies tend to be probabilistic: "since he is a Russian, the chances are he favors state ownership," "women are apt to be more submissive than men," "he has narrow lapels, chances are 60–40 that he is a Republican." As these examples show, category expectancies are obviously held with varying degrees of probability. At one extreme, we are dealing with stereotypes where the probabilistic nature of the expectancy is simply ignored, and the individual actor is endowed with a characteristic believed to be modal in whatever "category" he represents. With extreme stereotyping, behavioral data **[393]** may be entirely ignored or severely distorted to fit the expectancy (cf. Secord, Bevan, & Katz, 1956). At the other extreme, the perceiver may have the vaguest kind of expectancy which is quickly discarded in the face of behavioral data and assigned no weight whatsoever in the inference process. Brigham (1971) and Mann (1967) have shown that ethnic group stereotypes may or may not predict attributions toward individual ethnic group members on specific stereotyped traits, a reflection of this variation in the probabilistic nature of category-based expectancies.

Target-based expectancies are derived from prior information about the specific individual actor. The perceiver's task is to extrapolate from one set of judged dispositional attributes (traits, motives, attitudes) to a set of attributes relevant to the behavior observed. This extrapolation most likely follows the paths of the perceiver's "implicit personality theory." Target-based expectancies are formed with particular readiness in the attitude realm. From a single statement of support for George Wallace, we may readily infer a whole set of expected attitudes. Someone who opposes abortion is probably also in favor of restrictive laws governing massage parlors. Pro-busing advocates are more likely than those who oppose busing to favor the legalization of marijuana. The network that generates target-based expectancies is undoubtedly, in part, a product of the perceiver's experiences with dispositional contingencies in others, and partly a product of logical implication.

Target-based expectancies are conceived of as probabilistic in the same way that category-based expectancies are. They undoubtedly range in strength from those which call for a direct generalization from prior behavior to those which must filter through an elaborate perceived dispositional structure.

Do these different kinds of expectancies operate differently in their influence on the attribution process? It first must be noted that category-based expectancies shade into target-based expectancies when the category is a voluntary membership or reference group. To know that the actor belongs to the ACLU is to have prior knowledge of his behavior. This should, then, really be classed as target-based information. But disregarding this kind of overlap, what evidence is there that this is a distinction of consequence?

The most well-developed line of research on correspondent inference theory is a series of studies dealing with attitude attribution. The typical paradigm presents a statement, an essay, or a speech authored by a target person under conditions of high or low environmental constraint. Crosscutting the constraint or choice variable is a variation in whether the statement reflects an expected or unexpected position. The subject's task is to estimate the true attitude of the target person. In terms of the theory, it is important to note that the constraint variation is a manipulation of noncommon effects; there are more reasons for making the statement in the no-choice than in the choice condition, since the no-choice case includes all the reasons of the choice case plus those associated **[394]** with obedience to authority, avoidance of embarrassment, not appearing to misunderstand the instructions, and so on.

The crosscutting variation of statement direction is a manipulation of expected valence. In the three experiments by Jones and Harris (1967) expectancies were category based. For example, in one experiment a college student target person gave a pro-integration or pro-segregation speech. In some cases, the target person was from the rural South, and in other cases, from the industrial North. Jones and Harris reasoned that a pro-segregation speech would be generally unexpected from a contemporary undergraduate, and even more unexpected from a northerner than from a southerner.

In a study by Jones, Worchel, Goethals, and Grumet (1971), on the other hand, expectancy was more directly manipulated by varying the related attitudes of the target person; the expectancy was thus target-based. A pro- or anti-marijuana essay was attributed to a target person who had already endorsed a cluster of opinions concerning potential interference with an individual's rights to live his own life and control his own destiny. It was assumed, and the results support the assumption, that someone favoring personal freedom and autonomy would most likely favor the legalization of marijuana.

Regardless of whether the manipulated expectancy was category or target-based, the results were basically the same in each of the various attitude attribution experiments. Correspondence was higher in the choice/unexpected than in the no-choice/unexpected conditions. That is, the attributed attitude was more in line with the behavior when noncommon effects were low and the expected valence of the position taken was low. In addition, in each of the attribution of attitude studies cited (and in several others described in Snyder & Jones, 1974), there was a main effect of speech direction even in the no-choice condition. Even the highly constrained target person was attributed an attitude in line with his statement, though much less strongly than his choice counterpart.

In a recent experiment, Jones and Berglas (1976) sought to compare directly subjects' responses to category-based versus target-based expectancies under different orders of receiving information. In all cases, the target person made a statement directly supporting a particular attitudinal position. The target person was also identified by either a category-based or a target-based expectancy. This expectancy was either strong or weak, as determined by pre-testing with a similar subject population. The expectancy was either confirmed or disconfirmed by the statement. Examples of the stimulus materials are as follows:

1. Category-based expectancies (strong)
   a. Confirming: Actor is a female judge
   b. Disconfirming: Actor is a North Carolina deputy sheriff [395]
2. Target-based expectancies (strong)
   a. Confirming: Actor argues that homosexuals should not be discriminated against by employers
   b. Disconfirming: Actor argues that anything including violence must be used to prevent busing

Finally, there was an order variation. Half of the subjects were exposed to the expectancy first, followed by the statement, and then asked to attribute the target person's true attitude. The remaining half were given the statement first, followed by the expectancy information.

The results showed that a strong order effect appeared. When the expectancy preceded the statement, it was essentially ignored, and played no role in attitude attribution. When the expectancy followed the statement, however, the attribution was much less correspondent with the statement. What is of interest in the present context is the fact that this recency effect was almost identically strong with either category-based or target-based expectancies, and the strength of the expectancies did not play a significant role either.

THE SEARCH FOR A CONTRAST EFFECT The Jones and Berglas experiment was one of a number of studies searching for a contrast effect in attitude attribution. A contrast effect is defined by comparing an expectancy confirmation case to an expectancy discontinuation case. There is contrast when the discontinuing behavior leads to a more extreme inference than the confirming behavior. Let us suppose that we hear two people make similar statements favoring the unionization of municipal employees. The first person is a self-made financier, the second a postal clerk. We would speak of contrast if the financier were judged to be more liberal, more pro-union than the postal clerk. His behavior is contrasted with the prior expectancy, and the resulting inference moves further toward the liberal end of the scale than an inference based on the same behavior in the confirmation case.

It should be noted that correspondent inference theory would not necessarily make this strong a prediction. Although the theory does predict greater correspondence in the disconfirming case, this refers to information gain rather than the final extremity of the scale rating. Thus, relative to an initial rating of the financier on liberalism, the rating after his pro-union statement should show greater movement toward the liberal extreme

Chapter 5 Correspondent Inferences and the Attribution Cube: A Comparative Reappraisal   97

than the postal clerk's rating after the same statement. The possibilities, including assimilation, the opposite of contrast, are spelled out in Figure 5.1. Correspondence is measured by the changes calculable from the differences between items 3 and 4 and between items 2 and 5. In the contrast case, correspondence is obviously greater (+7) than the assimilation case (+3). But even the assimilation case is more correspondent than the confirmation case (+2).

As a sociopsychological phenomenon, a plausible case can be made for contrast. First, there is the simple possibility akin to psychophysical judgmental [396] contrast: the disconfirming behavior is so perceptually salient because of its surprise value that its distance from the expectancy is exaggerated (cf. Sherif & Hovland, 1961). In addition, depending on the nature of the expectancy, various costs may be involved in taking a stand that is unexpected or unusual. The financier who favors unionization may suffer ridicule or disfavor within the paneled walls of his club. The white busing advocate from a small town in Alabama most likely has had to pay often and heavily for his maverick views. From the costs presumably incurred, one might infer greater intensity of belief for the southerner than for the young northerner who favors busing on general liberal ideological grounds. When expectancies are derived from reference group norms—and especially when these norms are supported by group sanctions—contrast effects might be more likely.

Following this reasoning, our initial hunch was that contrast is more likely after discontinuation of category-based expectancies than of target-based expectancies. One is

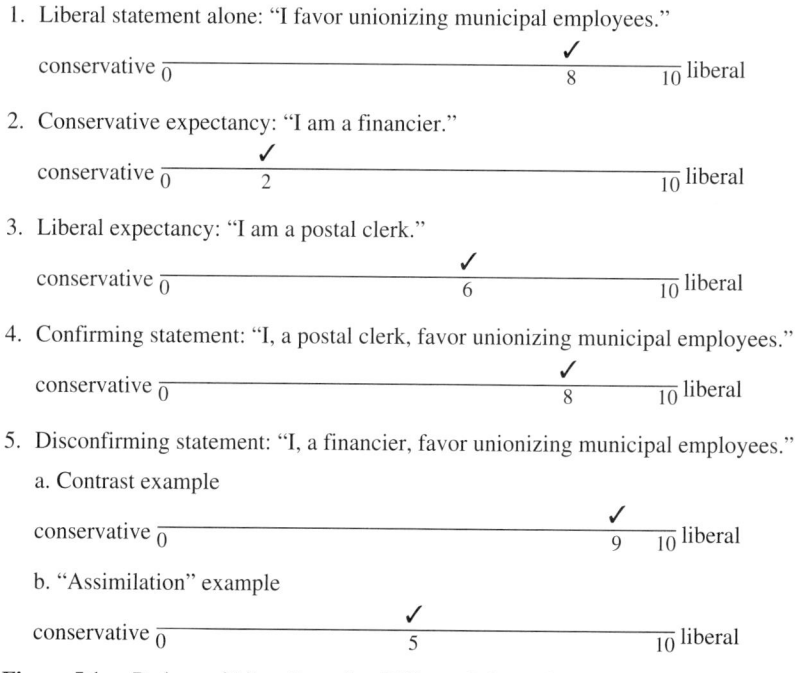

1. Liberal statement alone: "I favor unionizing municipal employees."
   conservative $_0$ ———————————— ✓ ———— liberal
                                    8    $_{10}$

2. Conservative expectancy: "I am a financier."
   conservative $_0$ —— ✓ ——————————————— liberal
                    2                      $_{10}$

3. Liberal expectancy: "I am a postal clerk."
   conservative $_0$ ——————— ✓ —————— liberal
                              6         $_{10}$

4. Confirming statement: "I, a postal clerk, favor unionizing municipal employees."
   conservative $_0$ ———————————— ✓ ———— liberal
                                    8    $_{10}$

5. Disconfirming statement: "I, a financier, favor unionizing municipal employees."
   a. Contrast example
   conservative $_0$ —————————————— ✓ —— liberal
                                      9    $_{10}$

   b. "Assimilation" example
   conservative $_0$ ———————— ✓ ———————— liberal
                              5            $_{10}$

Figure 5.1 Ratings of Liberalism after Different Information about a Category-Based Expectancy and Expressed Opinions toward the Unionization of Municipal Employees

more likely to find a maverick in a group than to find a person with highly inconsistent attitudes or traits. However, there is at present absolutely no evidence to support this hunch. In fact, the only attitude attribution study that obtained anything like contrast involved *target*-based expectancies. Jones *et al.* (1971) found some marginal evidence that target persons writing essays on marijuana were judged to have attitudes more in line with their essays [397] when the essays discontinued target-based expectancies than in the confirmation case. This only happened in those conditions where the target person had a choice to write an essay on either side. Thus an anti-autonomy target person choosing to write an essay favoring marijuana legalization was seen as more pro-marijuana than a pro-autonomy target person writing the same essay.

This isolated finding of contrast was not robust, and we have not been able to replicate it in several classroom demonstration follow-ups. On three other occasions, we were unable to produce contrast effects with category-based expectancies. Jones and Harris (1967) had speeches on desegregation delivered by northerners versus southerners. The northerner was judged uniformly more liberal on the race issue. McGillis (1974) had black and white target persons voting for candidates supporting more minority employment. There was no evidence that the white voter was seen as more in favor of minority employment than the black voter. In fact the opposite was the case. Jones and Berglas (1976) also found no evidence for contrast.

Thus far, then, the contrast phantom has proved very elusive. At least in the attitude attribution realm, subjects seem readier to integrate information through a form of compromise (à la Anderson, 1974) than to contrast behavior with expectancy. But the principle of incurred costs does seem to predict contrast in other realms. In a persuasion study by Mills and Jellison (1967), the communicator who violated expectancy by delivering a speech against the interests of his audience was seen as more honest and sincere. He was also significantly more persuasive. Feldman (1972) found that black professionals were judged to be more "professional" than white professionals. This is consistent with the assumption that blacks have to incur more costs to achieve professional status. We are not yet in a position to identify the precise conditions favoring contrast, but it looks as though obvious perceived cost is an important ingredient.

It should be emphasized again that neither contrast nor category–target expectancy differences are basic correspondent inference theory predictions. In fact, it is comforting, in a way, that there appear to be no systematic differences between the effects of discontinuing category-based versus target-based expectancies. For the moment we can assume that correspondent inference theory holds regardless of the expectancy source. It is, however, premature to abandon the search for expectancy source differences. We hope others will join us in the search for such effects since the consequences of expectancy discontinuation represent such a crucial problem in the study of person perception and stereotyping.

Some Problems with Correspondent Inference Theory

BOUNDARY CONDITIONS FOR EXPECTANCY EFFECTS The theory tells us that behavior which disconfirms prior expectancy is more likely to lead to a correspondent inference than is confirming behavior. It must be remembered, however, that [398] inferences from effects back to intentions assume both knowledge and ability. There are undoubtedly cases where the expectancy is so strong and the disconfirmations so drastic that it is easier for the perceiver to question the knowledge assumption than for him to engage in cognitive gymnastics to achieve a correspondent inference. We therefore propose that as the discrepancy between expectancy and behavior grows, the perceiver will be increasingly skeptical concerning the knowledge assumption. And we would expect this skepticism to be positively accelerating, growing very slowly under low discrepancies and very rapidly as the discrepancy increases further. This skepticism factor is reminiscent of Osgood and Tannenbaum's (1955) credibility correction. They reasoned that a statement departing too far from expectation about the source will appear incredible and be discounted. A clear example of the skepticism factor was found by McGillis (1974) in his study of voter choice and attitude attribution. The procedure was to present a voter choosing between two candidates for the governorship of an unspecified state. The candidates, in turn, were alleged to favor passage of certain specified bills. The design varied both the number of noncommon effects and their prior probability. The two candidates either supported three identical bills and a different fourth (low noncommon effects) or one identical bill and three that were different (high noncommon effects). The voter was presented as black or white, and it was always the case that Candidate *A* favored a preventive detention bill whereas Candidate *B* favored a bill requiring preferential hiring of minorities by state agencies. This was the manipulation of expectancy or prior probability. It was assumed that subjects would expect the white voter to prefer *A* and the black voter *B*. This assumption was reinforced for the subject by some bogus poll data provided to him. A final variable was the inclusion or omission of further information concerning the degree of the voter's commitment to the chosen candidate. In the high commitment treatment, it was alleged that the voter organized publicity drives and spoke at public rallies on behalf of his candidate. In the low-commitment treatment this information was omitted.

The major predictions were derived directly from correspondent inference theory. Attitude ratings on the issue relevant to voter choice were expected to be most extreme (most correspondent) in the conditions of low noncommon effects and low prior probability. For example, the white voter who chose the candidate favoring preferential minority hiring, with three other bills supported in common by the two candidates, was predicted to be, and was, seen as very pro-minorities. Also in line with prediction, commitment intensified this tendency.

In spite of the general support for the theory, certain reverse tendencies were discovered in the black voter conditions. Specifically, in the low noncommon effects condition, neutral attributions were made when the black voter supported the candidate favoring preventive detention and rejected the candidate favoring preferential hiring for minorities. But this only happened in the low-commitment condition. [399] We suggest that this is probably an excellent example of the skepticism factor in operation. One way to handle the extreme discontinuation of a black voting against his own interests is to assume that he was unaware of some of the positions endorsed by his chosen candidate. This would be especially likely in the low noncommon effects condition where there are no other differences between the issues supported by the candidates. However, this skepticism about voter awareness can hardly be maintained in the commitment condition, where it seems inconceivable that a voter would get deeply involved in campaigning for a candidate without knowing his position on issues of critical importance.

Another boundary condition concerns *differential* knowledge of the target person and his environment. If a perceiver has firm prior knowledge about the target person and the latter behaves in a highly unexpected way, the perceiver may attribute his behavior to the situation rather than change his conception of the person. If expectations about the situation are firmer than those about the actor, there should be a change in person attribution. Bell, Wicklund, Manko, and Larkin (1976) confirmed this hypothesis in a pair of experiments. In one, for example, they found that negative behavior from a positively regarded actor (an expectancy created by the experimenter) was attributed more to the situation than to the person. Bell *et al.* proposed that, in general, attributions will flow toward that aspect of the total person–environment complex about which the least is known. This may be true because it is harder to change a firm expectancy than one which is very vague and tentative.

PRIOR CHOICE AND EFFECT MAGNITUDE   Jones and Davis were aware of an apparent absurdity that followed from a literal application of correspondent inference theory. There are occasions when it seems intuitively that much more information is gained when noncommon effects are numerous than when they are scarce. The example they invented pictured Miss Adams confronting the choice between medical school and law school at comparable universities and Miss Bagby trying to decide whether to enroll as a psychology graduate student at Duke or Colorado. Most people have the subjective experience of learning more from Adams's choice than from Bagby's. And yet, there are many more noncommon effects separating the law–medicine choice. As Jones and Davis (1965) point out, however, "the hidden factor in this comparison is… that considerably more information is contained in the datum that Bagby has already ruled out everything but psychology, than in the datum that Adams is still struggling with the choice between two basic professions, professions which differ from each other on many different dimensions [pp. 233–234]." In a sense, then, the effects common to the two psychology departments were noncommon effects when one backtracks to the decision to pursue a career in psychology.

This kind of consideration creates substantial problems at times when we try to apply correspondent inference theory to the analysis of attribution in the **[400]** complex real world. Here choice is piled upon choice and presumably effects can shift from common to noncommon with a simple shift in temporal perspective.

Another way of approaching the Adams–Bagby comparison is to argue that some effects are more significant or important than others. A career choice is more important than a choice between two psychology departments where the choice is based, say, on a slight preference for mountain air. We view this as a defeatist alternative, however, because the problems of measuring effect importance are staggering. Hopefully, a retreat to this position can be avoided by equating importance to the number of positively valenced effects. In most cases effect magnitude can be seen to imply a quantity of discrete effects. Life versus death, for example, is a momentous decision for the potential suicide candidate because of the almost infinite number of effects of being alive.

Tying these considerations together, we might conclude that early choices in a behavior sequence are more likely than later choices to involve the exclusion of large numbers of noncommon effects. This may or may not be actuarially true. We can certainly think of cases where trivial or preliminary choices (sharpening the pencil) precede more important

Chapter 5 Correspondent Inferences and the Attribution Cube: A Comparative Reappraisal 101

subsequent choices (choosing a topic to write about). Whether the choice is early or late in a behavior sequence, however, a more "important" choice implies that one learns less about more whereas with the "less important" choice he learns more about less. Thus, there seems to be a trade-off between the number of intentions about which one might make tentative inferences and the precision or confidence with which one can make them. This is inherent in the basic theoretical argument about noncommon effects. But we suspect that this is a point where the logic of the theory may be at odds with the cognitive-processing tendencies of the perceiver. At least it is an interesting question whether social perceivers overuse and are overaffected by ambiguous information. Thus, perceivers may feel better informed about the total personality of a target person whose behavioral choice involves many effects and yet not be able to rate him as confidently on any particular dimension. If a target person does something that has five effects, in order to achieve one of them, the perceiver may conclude that he was disposed to achieve all five. Perceivers, in other words, may think they have learned more about a person from his choices than is warranted by the number of possible permutations and combinations that are involved in the chosen and rejected alternatives. They may have a low threshold for making solid inferences from behavioral data that are worthy only of the most tentative hypotheses.

This consideration is related to Jones and Nisbett's (1972) proposition that observers tend to attribute dispositions in circumstances where actors attribute their behavior to the situation. Jones and Nisbett argued that this was true both because actors typically know much more about their past behavior in similar situations and because actors and observers take a different perspective toward the information that is available. Now we are suggesting a further, more subtle reason for actor–observer differences. The actor is in a much better position **[401]** than the observer to choose among effects achieved in explaining his intentions. In particular, if there are high-valence effects, the actor will be content to consider these as a sufficient explanation for his behavior. High-valence effects are usually effects which anyone would seek, that is, effects called for by the situation. The observer, on the other hand, may be more equally drawn to all effects and be motivated to include for consideration those that have low valence in the general population. Why might this be so? Because, whereas the actor is typically interested in seeing himself as rationally responsive to his changing environment, the observer has a special interest in discovering those dispositions that uniquely identify the actor. The actor's interest is in normalization; the observer's interest is in individualization.

We can summarize these speculations by suggesting that observers attach too much significance to each possible effect and become prematurely locked into inferential conclusions. If we add to this a further tendency for the observer to be drawn toward low-valence effects, we have one set of conditions that supports the actor–observer difference proposition. Whether or not one wishes to connect the present speculations with the earlier stated propositions, this is an intriguing area for further study because it suggests that observers are over-individuating in their inferences and overconfident about inferential validity. The subjective feeling that one has gained more information about a person in a high-effect than a low-effect situation may, in other words, be an illusion and support biased inferences. The high-effects case is analogous to an experiment in which the experimental and control groups differ from each other on many grounds. The trained experimenter is careful not to draw premature conclusions about the reason for any observed differences.

EFFECTS CHOSEN AND EFFECTS FOREGONE   Jones and Davis do not go into detail concerning the cognitive operations involved in identifying the common and noncommon effects of action. There is no question that the identification of effects is an arbitrary enterprise dependent on momentary perspective (see above). But at another stage in the operations specified by the theory, the perceiver must combine information on noncommon effects chosen and noncommon effects foregone. Figure 5.2 presents an example of a target person choosing Act X over Act Y. The effects of each act and their attached valences are listed in the "choice circles." The target person's choice of X mildly disconfirms the perceiver's expectancy (indicated by the total valence). In general, then, this episode has the potential for a correspondent inference. But now the trouble begins. Effect b is common and can be ignored. This leaves not only the effects e and f of the choice alternatives; the foregone effects a, c, and d must also be considered as reasons for the choice. Considering only effects f and c, the perceiver does not know whether the target person was trying to attain f, avoid c, or both. This, in concrete form, is the question of this section. Other [402] things being equal, do perceivers attach as much weight to foregone as to chosen alternatives?

Newtson (1974) has addressed a very similar question in an elegant experiment on the number of noncommon effects remaining and eliminated by a choice. Based on careful pre-testing, Newtson selected three behavior alternatives, each having either one or two specified effects. Two target persons (Alex and Bob) were said to have chosen Alternative 3, "babysit for a professor." One effect of choosing this alternative was always listed as "in order to ingratiate himself with the professor." In the design, some subjects were given this as the only effect "remaining" after the choice. Other subjects were given this effect (ingratiation) plus "in order to get some extra studying done for all his courses." In the cases where Alex was said to have chosen to babysit for two reasons and Bob for one, Bob was seen as more ingratiating, in line with correspondent inference theory and the role of noncommon effect number.

In addition to varying the number of effects remaining, Newtson varied the number of effects eliminated by the choice to babysit. The alternatives were to go to the beach

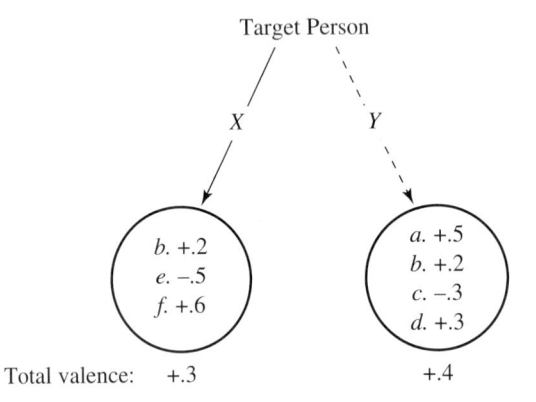

Target Person

X   Y

b. +.2   a. +.5
e. −.5   b. +.2
f. +.6   c. −.3
                d. +.3

Total valence: +.3   +.4

Figure 5.2   A Hypothetical Choice of Act X over Y

or to work in the library filling in for a friend. Each of these alternatives had one or two specified effects. In the case where Alex's choice to babysit eliminated four effects (two for each alternative) and Bob's choice eliminated only two, Alex was judged more ingratiating. Thus, the fewer the effects remaining and the more the effects foregone, the more correspondent the inference will be. The role of eliminating the effects follows directly from an information-theory analysis. It also follows from an "incurred cost" analysis that the more things Alex is willing to give up in order to babysit, the more ingratiating he must be. **[403]**

The crucial part in Newtson's experiment was a clear-cut comparison of correspondence resulting from varying the number of effects eliminated versus varying the number of effects remaining. In the case where Alex's choice to babysit eliminates two effects with one remaining (*E*2, *R*1), he is judged to be more ingratiating than Bob, whose choice eliminates four effects but leaves two remaining (*E*4, *R*2). Newtson (1974) was led to the conclusion that "while persons can respond to both effects chosen and effects foregone, they apparently prefer to respond to effects chosen [p. 495]." Newtson related this to the well-established tendency in concept formation research for subjects to prefer positive instances of the concept to negative ones and to make better use of the former even when technically the information conveyed is identical.

It should be noted that this effect of varying the number of alternatives foregone should work only when the alternatives are attractive (better than nothing with valences greater than zero). While it appears to be true that the more positive the alternatives foregone, the more significant is the meaning of the choice; it is also true that the more negative the alternatives foregone, the more ambiguous is the meaning of the choice. In Steiner's (1970) term, perceived decision freedom is low to the extent that foregone alternatives are negatively valenced. When this negative valence clearly outweighs the positive valence of the chosen alternative, the behavior becomes "obvious," and there is no information gained.

What Kind of Theory?

Correspondent inference theory is essentially a rational baseline model. It does not summarize phenomenal experience; it presents a logical calculus in terms of which accurate inferences could be drawn by an alert perceiver weighing knowledge, ability, noncommon effects, and prior probability. But the role of the theory has been as much to identify attributional bias as to predict precisely the course of the social inference process. In a similar vein, Edwards (1968) has stated regarding decision theories that "they specify what an ideal decision-maker would do and thus invite comparison between performances of ideal and real decision-makers [p. 34]." The theory cannot be invalidated by experimental results any more than game theory can be invalidated by the choices of players in a prisoner's dilemma game. Of course, it may turn out that the theory is not very useful in stimulating research, and it might, of course, prove vulnerable to logical criticism as well.

Use of the theory as a rational baseline model can best be seen, perhaps, in the attitude attribution research outlined above. The main results of this line of research are consistent with correspondent inference theory in that attitudes in line with behavior are most strongly inferred when the actor has choice (low noncommon effects) and the behavior is low in prior probability (expected effect valence). But we have also noted that behavior under no-choice conditions [404] leads to significant correspondence as well. A repeated finding has been that actors writing, for example, "pro" essays under no-choice instructions are seen as more pro than actors writing no-choice "anti" essays, regardless of the topic involved and, within wide limits, regardless of the strength or persuasiveness of the essay.

Such a finding becomes interesting only after obvious sources of artifact are systematically ruled out. One might argue, for example, that the actors really have some choice in the no-choice condition. They are not, after all, acting at gunpoint. They are going along with their instructor's examination question, the debating coach's assignment, the experimenter's request, and so on. Snyder and Jones (1974) showed, however, that no one, in fact, refuses these simple requests to compose a persuasive speech or essay even when the composition runs directly counter to his own attitude; and, when the statements are exchanged so that actors become perceivers, they still assign attitudes in line with the constrained behavior. What this means, of course, is that perceivers are very inaccurate in making dispositional inferences about actors who are highly constrained. Instead of predicting an average or modal attitude, they are influenced by the direction of the opinion expressed. Correspondent inference theory provides a rational baseline in terms of which this inaccuracy can be assessed.

Similarly, the Newtson (1974) study presented above showed that perceivers make greater use of effects chosen than effects foregone. Jones and Davis were noncommittal about the role of foregone effects in the inference process, but there seems to be no purely logical reason why chosen and foregone effects should not be equally weighted. The fact that empirically they are not becomes psychologically interesting.

As a final example, Snyder (1974) studied the attribution of anxious disposition (what clinicians sometimes refer to as trait anxiety) by having subjects observe a target person who allegedly was or was not going to be shocked in a few moments. Both correspondent inference theory and Kelley's (1971a) discounting principle would argue that more state anxiety would be perceived in the shock situation, but because the anxiety can be "explained" by the anticipated shock, trait anxiety would not be inferred. In fact, given a standard facial expression captured on videotape (as was the case in Snyder's study), the attribution of trait anxiety should be greater when no shock is involved. Snyder reasoned, on the other hand, that subjects would use cues about the shock setting to infer momentary anxiety in the target person and, when asked about anxious disposition, they would erroneously use the anxiety state inference to assign an anxiety trait. He found this to be true with his female subjects and, in a more recent replication (personal communication), the hypothesis was confirmed for males as well. Here is an instance, then, where correspondent inference theory was used as a kind of logical straw man to show how people make inappropriate use of situational data in the attribution of emotional dispositions. [405]

In short, a theory can serve a variety of purposes. Correspondent inference theory has been useful both as a source of deductions that have been confirmed and as a model against which to identify and study attributional biases.

KELLEY'S ANOVA CUBE: A BRIEF SUMMARY

Kelley's (1967) theory has a different goal than that of correspondent inference theory. Kelley has stated the nature of this difference as follows:

> The observer's focus in the two [theories] is essentially at opposite ends of the person–environment polarity. In my earlier analyses... the person is concerned about the validity of an attribution regarding the environment. He applies the several criteria in an attempt to rule out person-based sources of "error" variance. In the problems specified by Jones and Davis the observer has exactly the opposite orientation. He is seeking for person-caused variance (that caused by the particular actor under scrutiny) and is doing so he must rule out environmental or situation-determined causes of variations in effects. [p. 209].

This divergence between the theoretical efforts is illustrated by the differences in dependent measures used in experiments to test them. In the attitude attribution experiments testing correspondent inference theory, specific attitude or trait attribution scales are used as dependent measures, and subjects are requested to indicate the degree to which the target person possesses the given attitude or trait. In research to test Kelley's theory, on the other hand, dependent measures reflect the theory s orientation towards allocating causal attributions to either the person or the environment. For example, in McArthur's (1972) experiment, dependent measures included "something about the person (for example, John) probably caused him to make response X (for example, laugh) to stimulus Y (for example, the comedian)" and "something about the stimulus probably caused the person to make response X to it." These measures provide global attributions regarding the perceived locus of causality for the observed behavior. Jones and Davis in their noncommon effect analysis provide a potential means for determining what the "something" is.

The four attributional criteria for decisions about causal allocation discussed by Kelley (1967) are (a) distinctiveness, (b) consensus, (c) consistency over time, and (d) consistency over modality. Kelley has discussed the use of these criteria both with respect to self- and other-attribution. In either case, the perceiver wishes to determine whether his (or the other's) response to a stimulus is caused by properties inherent in the stimulus, by properties of the actor, or by circumstantial factors.

By distinctiveness, Kelley refers to whether the individual (self or target person) responds differentially to different entities (or stimuli). Thus, in cases of high distinctiveness, the individual would tend to respond uniquely to the given [406] stimulus. The consensus variable involves whether or not the same response is produced by other people in the presence of the given stimulus. A high consensus would imply, in Kelley's terms, that the majority of individuals respond similarly in the presence of the stimulus. A low consensus could exist either if there were random responding or if there were a consensus differing from the target person's reaction. The consistency over time variable refers to whether the target person responds similarly to the stimulus whenever it is presented in similar circumstances, while the consistency over modality variable concerns whether the target person responds similarly to the stimulus regardless of the type of situation in which the stimulus is presented.

Kelley embeds these variables in a factorial cube for presentational purposes and treats their influence on attributions by analogy to the analysis of variance. In this analogy, the distinctiveness variable is the numerator of the F ratio, standing for the between-conditions term in the analysis. The greater the difference in response to different entities, the more the response to one entity is determined by that entity. Consistency and consensus, on the other hand, are within-conditions "error" variance, and belong in the denominator of the F ratio. These are the variables that inform about the stability and replicability of the effects being considered. The greater the inconsistency and lack of consensus, the larger the distinctiveness variation has to be to influence attribution significantly.

McArthur (1972) has manipulated the distinctiveness, consensus, and consistency variables factorially in an experiment presenting vignettes of accomplishment, emotion, opinion, and action. Her predictions were in line with those presented in Kelley (1967). Person attribution was predicted to be most frequent when a response was characterized by low distinctiveness, low consensus, and high consistency. Stimulus attribution was predicted to be maximized when a response was characterized by high distinctiveness, high consensus, and high consistency. Attribution to the specific circumstances in which the response occurred was predicted in cases of low consistency. McArthur's results supported the predictions based upon Kelley's theory for person attribution, stimulus attribution, and circumstance attribution.

In subsequent essays, Kelley (1972a, 1972b) has elaborated on the determinants of attribution, especially emphasizing the dichotomous possibilities of self versus other and person versus situation as causal loci. In his discussion of "Attribution in Social Interaction," Kelley (1972a) emphasized the covariation principle that underlies the effects of distinctiveness. Thus, an effect that occurs in the presence of one entity and not others is presumed to be caused by that entity.

In his consideration of various attributional "rules," Kelley (1972a) discussed the discounting effect and its obverse, the augmentation principle. The discounting effect holds that "the role of a given cause in producing a given effect is discounted if other plausible causes are also present [p. 8]." This can be mapped **[407]** completely into the operation of noncommon effects as a variable in correspondent inference theory. In discussing the augmentation principle, Kelley (1972a) stated that: "if for a given effect, both a plausible inhibitory and a plausible facultative cause are present, the role of the facilitative cause will be judged greater than if it alone were presented as a plausible cause of the effect [p. 12]." This principle can be restated in terms of expected negative valence or cost. Jones and Davis (1965) make the point that "any effects in the choice area which are not assumed to be negative will take on greater importance the more negative the remaining effects. Inferences concerning the intention to achieve desirable effects will increase in correspondence to the extent that costs are incurred, pain is endured and, in general, negative outcomes are involved [p. 227]."

While these are obvious points at which Kelley's analysis converges on that of correspondent inference theory, it is not as immediately evident how the analogical analysis of variance (ANOVA) cube relates to the noncommon effects, prior probability analysis of attribution. In the concluding section, we shall try to integrate the two theoretical statements with the eventual goal of stressing points of overlap and complementarity, as well as points of divergence where interesting empirical problems may lie.

CORRESPONDENCE AND THE CUBE: A COMPARISON

Category-Based Expectancies and the Consensus Variable

McArthur manipulated consensus in her vignettes simply by stating whether the target person's action was in agreement or disagreement with the majority. We have already discussed the attitude attribution research in which prior probabilities were manipulated by variations in category-based expectancies. It seems clear that these variables are operationally similar and that they play similar roles in the two theoretical analyses. Consensus, according to Kelley, has to do with veridicality, with the likelihood that behavior is caused by the situation or entity rather than the person. If everyone likes the movie, then the movie and not its viewers must be the prepotent causal factor. Prior probability variables in correspondent inference theory are treated in much the same way: behavior in line with expectation is not informative concerning the person. One only knows that he is like everyone else—by implication, that he places the same value and interpretation on the situation in which he finds himself.

There is no question that category-based expectancies play a significant role in attitude attribution research. We have already alluded to repeated experiments in which correspondence was greatest where consensus (prior probability deriving from category-based expectancy) was lowest. McArthur's results suggest, however, that consensus is a relatively weak determinant of internal versus external [408] attribution in the fictitious settings with which she was concerned. Nisbett and Borgida (1975) have recently shown that there are remarkable insensitivities in the use of consensus data. Subjects appear unwilling to use data about the distribution of others' behavior to infer the responses of individual persons. McArthur suggested that consensus data may be more informative than distinctiveness when a person is evaluating his own behavior, but less informative when he is evaluating others'. The uninformativeness of consensus information in the perception of others may stem from the fact that the perceiver himself forms a limited consensus for evaluating the target person. In any event, the Nisbett and Borgida data certainly do not fit well with the attitude attribution data, and the reasons for this are not obvious. It may be that Nisbett and Borgida's subjects interpreted their task as one of not being fooled or misled by group data in dealing with individuals. This interpretation would be less likely in an attitude attribution study where the consensus manipulation is more implicit and poses a sociological problem for the subjects to solve.

Target-Based Expectancies and Distinctiveness

An obvious difference between correspondent inference theory and Kelley's cube is that Jones and Davis considered a given act in relation to other *potential* acts available to the target person whereas Kelley considered several already occurring acts and the information that could be abstracted concerning the comparability of responses across entities. There is obviously no point in trying to argue that these are equivalent cognitive operations. But if we shift again from the common effects part of the analysis to prior probability, there is some comparability between target-based expectancies and distinctiveness. McArthur's (1972) low-distinctiveness case involved information such as "John also laughs at almost every other comedian," whereas the obverse high-distinctiveness case stated "John does not laugh at almost any other comedian." This information was to be used in combination with the fact that John laughed at the specific comedian. As in the case of target-based expectancy manipulations (Jones et al., 1971), subjects were required to extrapolate from the target person's previous actions regarding similar stimuli to develop an expectancy regarding his response to the present stimulus. The low-distinctiveness case can be compared to the high prior probability case of Jones et al., and the high-distinctiveness case is comparable to the low prior probability manipulation. In all cases, the subject's expectancy is based on his information regarding the target person's prior behavior toward similar stimuli. But here we confront a serious problem. In the Jones et al. study, the most correspondent inference is made when the person chooses to write an essay supporting marijuana legalization when she was expected to be against it, and vice versa. Distinctiveness thus leads to personal attribution in that case. The opposite is the case in McArthur's experiment. Here, the person who laughs nondistinctively at all clowns is seen as most personally **[409]** responsible for laughing at a particular clown. Why does the analogy between target-based expectancy and distinctiveness break down in this case?

The answer may lie in a consideration of the degree of similarity among the entities involved. In the Jones et al. (1971) study, subjects were confronted with a target person who made different responses to very similar attitude issues. In the McArthur study, the high-distinctiveness target person endorses one among all clowns, and clowns are known to differ greatly. Perhaps if the distinctive reaction were to one of several highly similar clowns, the cause would be located in the person. If, on the other hand, a very diverse group of opinions were endorsed by the same target person, we would make a personal attribution in line with McArthur's finding. We would say that the target person is a "yea sayer," or that he is response-acquiescent. This seems to be the analogy most consistent with the McArthur results.

Another way of reconciling the apparent conflict in predictions is to consider more carefully the situation in which a target person makes a statement toward Issue *A* which disconfirms the expectancy established by his previous statements toward related Issues *B*, *C*, and *D*. Perhaps an entity attribution to *A* (as Kelley and McArthur would predict) is the first step toward a correspondent inference that the target person really feels strongly about *A*. That is, the attributor must first see *A* as a distinctive issue before he can assign a special strength to the target person's attitude toward *A* in a direction opposite to his perceived attitudes toward *B*, *C*, and *D*. Otherwise, the target person must be seen as simply inconsistent.

Target-Based Expectancies and Consistency

This brings us rather naturally to our next comparison between target-based expectancy and the consistency variable. If it were stated that a specific behavior was performed consistently in the same or similar settings, this could be treated either as an example of target-based prior probability manipulation or as equivalent to Kelley's consistency over time and modality variable. McArthur (1972) manipulated the consistency variable in her experiment by stating (for a typical high-consistency manipulation) "in the past, John has almost always laughed at the same comedian" or (for a low-consistency manipulation) "in the past, John has almost never laughed at the same comedian." The comparable manipulation in Jones *et al.* was to inform subjects that, for example, the target person was against censorship, in favor of liquor by the drink, for student control of universities, for permissiveness in childrearing, *and* chose to write an anti-marijuana speech.

A conflict of predictions again arises if we try to equate these two manipulations. As noted above, Jones *et al.* predicted and found high correspondence (equivalent to high person attribution) in the unexpected behavior case. McArthur predicted (from Kelley) that person attribution would be facilitated by high consistency. We could avoid the conflict between these two predictions [410] by emphasizing the differences between the respective manipulations of expectancy violation and inconsistency. They are not, of course, the same operations. But if we were to bring the opinion topics closer and closer to the marijuana issue (presenting, say, attitudes toward LSD, alcohol, and amphetamines), the manipulations begin to converge. Correspondent inference theory can handle the shift from strong person inferences after violated expectancies to weak person inferences after inconsistency by introducing the boundary condition of knowledge or the skepticism factor. When the expectancy violation reaches a particular threshold of extremity, the perceiver may be forced to decide that the target person was unaware of what he endorsed or at least of the consequences and implications of his endorsement.

But we know from the McArthur study that the typical inference from inconsistency is "something about the particular circumstances," and there is no specific provision for this inference in correspondent inference theory. Since the theory is explicitly concerned with attributions of personal dispositions, it does not distinguish between stimulus and circumstance. Both would be treated together as category-based valence effects. In effect, subjects' use of the "circumstance"-dependent variable is nothing more than a confession of ignorance. Inconsistency cannot be caused either by the entity or the person, since both remain constant as the actor's response changes. Therefore, the perceiver has failed to identify the relevant entities, and he can only retreat to a residual category in assigning causation.

Presumably, a more complete analysis of the setting in terms of the full range of action effects would eliminate the difference between stimulus and circumstance. Since the person has behaved differently in commerce with the same entity, we can say that his behavior has had different effects at two different times. Then the problem is to identify what is different about the total context of action at Time 1 and Time 2. This amounts to analysis of potential but foregone action alternatives. We suggest, then, that a careful noncommon effects analysis may rule out the need for circumstance attributions. A circumstance refers to features of a situation that suggests various response options. If these, often very subtle, features can be made prominent by the perceiver in his analysis, then he may not need to resort to a circumstance attribution.

TOWARD AN INTEGRATED FRAMEWORK FOR ATTRIBUTIONAL PROCESSES

It is clear from the preceding discussion that correspondent inference theory and the Kelley ANOVA cube make a number of similar, or at least complementary, distinctions. Both theoretical statements approach a lay version of experimental design and analysis. The experiment and the attribution episode each involves an attempt to isolate distinctive causes for observed behavior. Each proceeds by a combination of comparison and control procedures. The experiment manipulates **[411]** potential causal variables and compares the effects observed with those effects present in the absence of these variables. More complicated experimental designs are often generated by the need to eliminate the confounding of potential causes. The attributor makes use of experimental logic whenever possible, but he usually must cope with the natural confounding of potential causes that occurs in the real world. The kinds of attributional analyses we have described in this chapter are similar to the kinds of "quasi-experimental" designs that Campbell and Stanley (1963) talk about.

Although they have much in common, correspondent inference theory and the ANOVA cube are divergent in important respects. We have noted that correspondent inference theory focuses on the attribution of identifiable personal dispositions and addresses the case in which the attributor is trying to establish the cause for a single behavior episode. While some prior probability manipulations have provided information regarding the earlier behavior of the target person, the theory does not explicitly incorporate the impact of information regarding the target person's past behavior. This factor is systematically dealt with by Kelley, whose theory is concerned with judgments based upon behavioral data gathered over multiple behavior episodes. We have already noted the importance of consistency information in the attribution process. Kelley (1967) has stated, "it has been postulated... that physical reality takes precedence over social reality information... the implication is that the consistency criteria may be more important to the individual than the consensus criterion [p. 207]." In her analysis of the proportion of the variance accounted for by the various independent variables in her experiment, McArthur (1972) observed that consistency information accounted for more of the total variance than consensus information. This finding argues for the importance of including the consistency variable in an integrated theory of attributional processes.

Kelley's theory is also limited. This point is illustrated by the dependent measures used to test the theory. Kelley's theory was designed to provide global attributions either to the person, the stimulus, or the circumstances in which the behavior occurred. Thus, dependent measures result in attributions that "something" about the person, stimulus, or environment caused the behavior. The noncommon effects analysis of correspondent inference theory provides a mechanism for determining what specifically the "something" is. That is, specific causal factors are focused upon, in the noncommon effects analysis, particularly specific causal factors residing in the person. Perhaps, each theory would gain analytic power by incorporating variables of the other. The following integrated framework is offered as an attempt in this direction.

The Conceptual Variables of an Integrated Attributional Analysis

The following terms are proposed as concepts in an integrated framework of attribution theory. Each is described in terms of an observer trying to understand [412] the behavior of another, but the same terms can also be used by an actor in a self-attribution process.

I. Prior probability variables (expected effect valences)

    A. Category-based expectancies (*consensus*). Based on inferences derived from the target person's membership in a social category such as sex, age, occupation, or ethnic origin. May be further differentiated into:

    Type 1: Stereotypic. Category membership suggests a modal behavior expectancy or the presence of one categorizing feature (obesity) suggests other correlated features (jolliness).

    Type 2: Normative. There is a modal behavior expectancy created and maintained by social sanctions against deviance. Thus, behavior departing from a normative expectancy incurs personal cost.

    B. Target-based expectancies. Based on inferences drawn from knowledge about the behavior of the specific target person at other times. May be further differentiated into:

    Type 1: Replicative. Expectancy derived from previous observation of behavior in identical situation. Helps to validate ability and knowledge assumptions (*consistency over time*).

    Type 2: Conceptual replicative. Expectancy derived from previous observation of consistent behavior toward the same entity in conceptually similar but descriptively different settings (*consistency over modality*).

    Type 3: Structural. Expectancy derived from observing correlated responses to other entities seen as related through attitude structures or implicit personality theory (*distinctiveness*).

II. Noncommon effect variables. Derived from an analysis of the observed consequences of actions undertaken and plausible action alternatives foregone. Each effect carries a valence denoting its desirability or prior probability as a purpose of action (see I above).

III. Knowledge and ability variables. Evaluation of the target person's awareness that his action was going to produce the resulting effects. As the overall prior probability of the observed action (relative to alternative actions) declines, skepticism concerning knowledge increases in a positively accelerating fashion. Ability may be separately inferred from expressive behavior or other indicators of the skill apparently required, but both ability and knowledge are validated by consistency over time.

The Action Sequence

In this final attempt at theoretical integration, we can imagine an attributional "flowchart" in which the above variables are embedded. It is important to emphasize that perceivers do not make attributions from every act they observe. [413] And when attributions are drawn, many of the steps in the sequence depicted in Figure 5.3 may be bypassed or occur at different points in the order of events. The sequence is not expected to bear much of a relationship to the phenomenology of a naïve perceiver. Many attributional routines and subroutines run themselves off as overlearned inference paths. Also, it is usually the case that the attributor must work with very incomplete data, and Kelley (1972b) has made some ingenious suggestions about the "schemata" people use in such cases. The depicted sequence is a somewhat idealized version of how dispositions are inferred from acts. It includes the variables that might be consciously reviewed and analyzed in a setting where the perceiver has unlimited time and where it is important that inferences be made as precisely and validly as possible.

With these caveats in mind, then, let us review the various steps in the sequence and note how they fit into the previous discussions of correspondent inference theory and the Kelley ANOVA cube. First of all, of course, there is the observation of a target person acting in commerce with his environment. We can imagine the environment as consisting of multiple entities at any point in time. The perceiver's first cognitive problem is to resolve the situation into a figural entity and a background context. This context includes a sense of the setting as well as a residual or interactive category known as circumstances. The target person is assumed to direct his action toward the figural entity, though contextual factors may be recognized as influential in determining the nature (direction, intensity, etc.) of the inference.

This first step in the process is, no doubt, a crucial one, and the choice of figural entity is quite probably determined by the purposes of the perceiver as well as by objective, Gestalt properties of the situation. Jones and Thibaut's (1958) analysis of inferential sets is quite relevant here, as are papers by Zadny and Gerard (1974) and by Jeffery and Mischel (unpublished).

The next step in the depicted sequence is a noncommon effects analysis. At this point, our idealized perceiver considers the act in its context of other responses to the situation that might reasonably have occurred. In particular, the analysis concerns consequences brought about by the act and consequences foregone. It is out of this pattern of actual and potential effects that the perceiver weaves a preliminary picture of what the target person was trying to accomplish in the situation.

Although valences are shown as attached to each effect, their value is determined in the next stage of prior probability analysis. The perceiver relates his observations and effect analyses to expectations derived both from social placement (recall and estimates of how others would have acted) and his recall of prior acts by this target person in the same or similar situations. Expectations derived from social placement may or may not involve normative sanctions. Such sanctions would appear as negative valences in cases where the individual's behavior violates reference group norms. The generation of category-based and target-based expectations not only determines the valences to be attached [414] to effects, but the information shaping the expectancies is also used to validate the assumption of knowledge and ability. In order to know what to make of his effect analysis, the perceiver must consider the evidence regarding intentionality. Did the target person know that his actions would have the effects obtaining? And the closely related questions, does he have the power, ability, and control to produce the

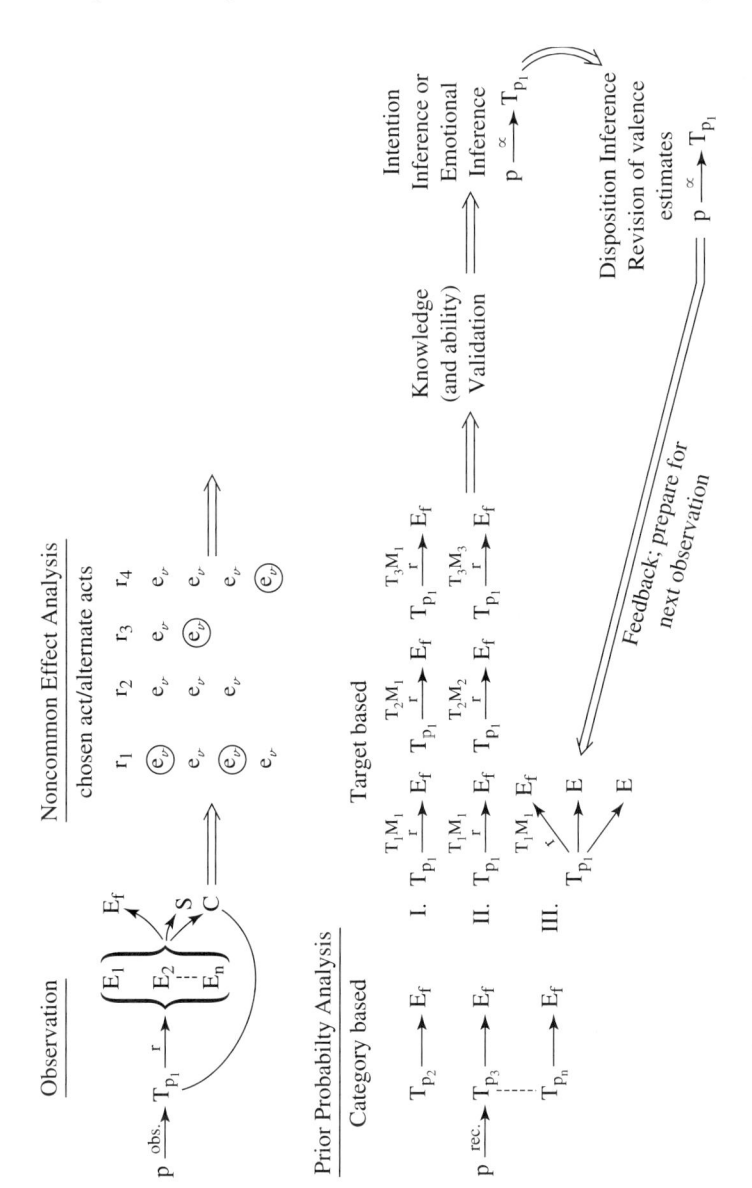

Chapter 5 Correspondent Inferences and the Attribution Cube: A Comparative Reappraisal **113**

Figure 5.3 Action Sequencer in an Integrated Attributional Framework

Key: p, perceiver; T_p, target person; e, effect; ⓔ, noncommon effect; v, valence; obs., observe; rec., recall; $\propto$, attribution; T, time; M, modality; E, entity; E_f, figural entity; S, setting; C, circumstance.

act at will? Consistency information is valuable here, since effects persistently striven for are not likely to be accidental or unanticipated consequences. Also, effects persistently achieved betoken ability rather than luck. As we have noted, skepticism concerning knowledge grows at an accelerating rate as the observed action departs from the action expected. Consistency information becomes increasingly important as a test of knowledge when expectancies are disconfirmed.

The perceiver then infers an intention or emotion. Correspondent inference theory has dealt exclusively with intentional, instrumental behavior. It has been assumed that the individual is acting to achieve certain desired effects. But many actions are expressive *re*actions to the mere presence of a figural entity. Although McArthur (1972) has shown that there are some differences in the use of consistency, consensus, and distinctiveness information for emotions versus actions (emotions yielded significantly more stimulus attributions), the process of emotional attribution may be tentatively encompassed by the depicted framework This may be done by including expressive emotional reactions among the effects of commerce with the figural entity and its situational context.

The next step is to proceed from the transient intention or emotion to a dispositional inference. It is at this step that causal allocation decisions become critically important. In ANOVA jargon, the variance is allocated between entity, setting, circumstance, and person. The greater the variance assigned to the person, the greater the correspondence between inferred intention and inferred disposition. This suggests that correspondence may be a two-step inference. The first step concerns the relationship between perceived effects and inferred intent: he dominated the group and really intended to. The second step concerns the relationship between intention and disposition: he was intentionally dominant in this situation and is really a dominant character in general.

One way to conceive of the dispositional inference is to imagine the resetting of valences. In the above example, all those effects involving influence over others should be assigned more positive valences for this particular target person. Valence pattern is another way of talking about personality structure, and when a perceiver makes a correspondent inference, he is inferring a pattern of valences that is somewhat different from the pattern inferred as a "prior probability." This newly inferred pattern is fed back into the perceiver's expectancies to govern the prior probability analysis of the next behavior episode with the same target person.

Once again, it should be stressed that there is considerable arbitrariness in any specification of a sequence from observation to dispositional inference. **[416]** Hopefully, however, by concretizing the steps in this way, we can show more explicitly the relationships between correspondence inference theory and Kelley's cube. In spite of the apparent complexity of the flowchart, it is, of course, merely a series of signposts that point to further complexities. The problem of effect identification and analysis remains as nettlesome as ever, and perhaps the inclusion of emotion creates new difficulties that, at the moment, are unforeseen. The relationship between act and expected act, and whether the resultant inference is a product of contrast, assimilation, or information integration, is an intriguing problem about which much more needs to be known. The links between intention or emotion and disposition have not been systematically explored, and Snyder's (1974) data (discussed earlier) suggest that a distinction between emotion and intention may be very crucial in considering this link. Finally, there is the intriguing problem of the impact of the inference drawn about the target person on category-based expectancies. When our stereotypes are discontinued by behavior, under what circumstances do they shatter or disappear, and when do they become even more rigid ("the exception proves the rule")? Hopefully, the integrated framework will suggest where these and other meaningful research questions may be lurking.

SUMMARY

In the present chapter, we have been primarily concerned with modifying correspondent inference theory to bring it more in line with Kelley's theoretical statements on attribution and with experimental data generated in the past decade. A major change has been the substitution of the concept of expected valences for the more restricted notion of assumed desirability. The valence concept permits reference to target-based expectancies and thus opens up the possibility of dealing with more extended behavior sequences. A correspondent inference constitutes a shift in expected valences so that the target person is seen as desiring certain consequences more or less than before the behavioral observation. Certain problems with the theory remain: locating the threshold of skepticism concerning the actor's knowledge of his behavioral effects, dealing with the question of prior choice and effect magnitude, and determining the relative importance of effects chosen and effects foregone. By means of an idealized attributional flowchart, we have attempted to encompass the various subprocesses of person perception. The would-be attributor appraises the effects of the observed act and of plausible alternative acts, considers the effects in terms of his prior expectancies of people in general and the actor in particular, validates the knowledge-of-effects assumption, and makes inferences about intentions and ultimately more stable dispositions. These dispositional attributions become expectancies influencing subsequent attributional inferences when more behavior by the same actor is observed. The integrated framework proposed seems to [417] accommodate existing data and helps to identify the points at which intriguing research problems remain.

REFERENCES

Ajzen, I. (1971). Attribution of dispositions to an actor: Effects of perceived decision freedom and behavioral utilities. *Journal of Personality and Social Psychology* 18, 144–156.

Ajzen, I., & Fishbein, M. (1975). A Bayesian analysis of attribution processed. *Psychological Bulletin* 82, 261–277.

Anderson, N. H. (1974). Cognitive algebra: Integration theory applied to social attribution. In L. Berkowitz (Ed.), *Advances in experimental social psychology* (Vol. 7). New York: Academic Press.

Bell, L., Wicklund, R.A., Manko, G., & Larkin, C. (1976). When unexpected behavior is attributed to the environment. *Journal of Research in Personality* 110(3), 316–327.

Bern, D. J. (1965). An experimental analysis of self-persuasion. *Journal of Experimental Social Psychology* 1, 199–218.

Bern, D. J. (1972). Self-perception theory. In L. Berkowitz (Ed.), *Advances in experimental social psychology* (Vol. 6). New York: Academic Press.

Brigham, J. C. (1971). Racial stereotypes, attitudes, and evaluations of and behavioral intentions toward Negroes and Whites. *Sociometry* 34, 360–380.

Campbell, D. T., & Stanley, J. C. (1963). *Experimental and quasi-experimental designs for research.* Chicago: Rand–McNally.

Chaikin, A. L., & Cooper, J. (1973). Evaluation as a function of correspondence and hedonic relevance. *Journal of Experimental Social Psychology* 9, 257–264.

Davison, G. C., &. Valins, S. (1969). Maintenance of self-attributed behavior change. *Journal of Personality and Social Psychology* 11, 25–33.

Edwards, W. (1968). Psychological aspects of decision making. In D. Sills (Ed.), *International encyclopedia of the social sciences.* New York: MacMillan.

Feldman, J. M. (1972). Stimulus characteristics and subject prejudice as determinants of stereotype attribution. *Journal of Personality and Social Psychology* 21, 333–340.

Feldman, J. M., & Hilterman, R. J. (1975). Stereotype attribution revisited: The role of stimulus characteristics, racial attitude, and cognitive differentiation. *Journal of Personality and Social Psychology* 31, 1177–1188.

Festinger, L. (1954). A theory of social comparison processes. *Human Relations* 7, 117–140.

Heider, F. (1944). Social perception and phenomenal causality. *Psychological Review* 51, 358–374.

Heider, F. (1958). *The psychology of interpersonal relations.* New York: Wiley.

Jeffrey, K., & Mischel, W. *Effects of purpose on the organization and recall of information in person perception.* Unpublished manuscript, Stanford University, California.

Jones, E. E., & Berglas, S. (1976). A recency effect in attitude attribution. *Journal of Personality* 44(3), 433–448. **[418]**

Jones, E. E. & Davis, K. E. (1965). From acts to dispositions: The attribution process in person perception. In L. Berkowitz (Ed.), *Advances in experimental social psychology* (Vol.2), New York: Academic Press.

Jones, E. E., & deCharms, R. (1957). Changes in social perception as a function of the personal relevance of behavior. *Sociometry* 20, 75–85.

Jones, E. E., & Harris, V. A. (1967). The attribution of attitudes. *Journal of Experimental Social Psychology* 3, 1–24.

Jones, E. E., Kanouse, D. E., Kelley, H. H., Nisbett, R. E., Valins, S. & Weiner B. (1972). *Attribution: Perceiving the causes of behavior.* Morristown, New Jersey: General Learning.

Jones, E. E., & Nisbett, R. E. (1972). The actor and the observer: Divergent perceptions of the causes of behavior. In E. E. Jones, D. E. Kanouse, H. H. Kelley, R. E. Nisbett, S. Valins, & B. Weiner (Ed.), *Attribution: Perceiving the causes of behavior* (pp. 79–94). Morristown, NJ: General Learning Press.

Jones, E. E. & Thibaut, J. W. (1958). Interaction goals as bases of inference in interpersonal perception. In R. Tagiuri & L. Petrullo (Eds.), *Person perception and interpersonal behavior.* Stanford, California: Stanford University Press.

Jones, E. E., Worchel, S., Goethals, G. R., & Grumet, J. F. (1971). Prior expectancy and behavioral extremity as determinants of attitude attribution. *Journal of Experimental Social Psychology* 7, 59–80.

Kelley, H. H. (1967). Attribution theory in social psychology. In D. Levine (Ed.), *Nebraska Symposium on Motivation.* Lincoln: University of Nebraska Press.

Kelley, H. H. (1972a). Attribution in social interaction. In E. E. Jones, D. E. Kanouse, H. H. Kelley, R. E. Nisbett, S. Valins, & B. Weiner (Ed.), *Attribution: Perceiving the causes of behavior* (pp. 1–26). Morristown, NJ: General Leaning Press.

Kelley, H. H. (1972b). Causal schemata and the attribution process. In E. E. Jones, D. E. Kanouse, H. H. Kelley, R. E. Nisbett, S. Valins, & B. Weiner (Ed.), *Attribution: Perceiving the causes of behavior* (pp. 151–174). Morristown, NJ: General Learning Press.

Mann, J. W. (1967). Inconsistent thinking about group and individual. *Journal of Social Psychology* 71, 235–245.

McArthur, L. (1972). The how and what of why: Some determinants and consequences of causal attribution. *Journal of Personality and Social Psychology* 22, 171–193.

McGillis, D. (1974). A correspondent inference theory analysis of attitude attribution. Unpublished doctoral dissertation. Duke University, North Carolina.

Mills, J., & Jellison, J. M. (1967). Effect on opinion change of how desirable the communication is to the audience the communicator addressed. *Journal of Personality and Social Psychology* 6, 98–101.

Nelson, C. A., & Hendrick, C. (1974). Bibliography of journal articles in social psychology. Mimeo Kent State University.

Newtson. D. (1974). Dispositional inference from effects of actions: Effects chosen and effects foregone. *Journal of Experimental Social Psychology* 10, 489–496.

Nisbett, R. E., & Borgida, E. (1975). Consensus information and the psychology of prediction. *Journal of Personality and Social Psychology* 32, 932–943.

Nisbett, R. E., & Schachter, S. (1966). Cognitive manipulation of pain. *Journal of Experimental Social Psychology* 2, 227–236.

Osgood, C. E., & Tannenbaum, P. H. (1955). The principle of congruity in the prediction of attitude change. *Psychological Review* 62, 42–55.

Schachter, S., & Singer, J. E. (1962). Cognitive, social and psychological determinants of emotional states. *Psychological Review* 69, 379–399.

Secord, P. F., Bevan, W., & Katz, B. (1956). The Negro stereotype and perceptual accentuation. *Journal of Abnormal and Social Psychology* 53, 78–83.

Sherif, M., & Hovland, C. I. (1961). *Social judgment: Assimilation and contrast effects in communication and attitude change.* New Haven: Yale University Press.

Snyder, M. (1974). The field engulfing behavior: An investigation of attributing emotional states and dispositions. Unpublished doctoral dissertation. Duke University, North Carolina. **[419]**

Snyder, M., & Jones, E. E. (1974). Attitude attribution when behavior is constrained. *Journal of Experimental Social Psychology* 10, 585–600.

Steiner, I. (1970). Perceived freedom. In L. Berkowitz (Ed.), *Advances in experimental social psychology* (Vol. 5). New York: Academic Press.

Thibaut, J. W., & Riecken, H. R. (1955). Some determinants and consequences of the perception of social causality. *Journal of Personality* 24, 113–133.

Zadny, J., & Gerard, H. B. (1974). Attribution intentions and informational selectivity. *Journal of Experimental Social Psychology* 10, 34–52. **[420]**

SOCIAL COGNITION

Chapter 6

Afterword: An Avuncular View

Edward E. Jones
Princeton University

I have been invited to generate a few paragraphs of historical perspective, perhaps in acknowledgment of my persistent interest in the issues confronted by the contributions to this special issue. The editors of this remarkable collection of articles have rightly assumed that this is a propitious moment to take stock of recent developments in the focal area of social cognition that is concerned with dispositional inferences. The collection takes on particular interest because the articles deal with a more venturesome social cognition than that depicted by its critics, one attuned to the interplay among beliefs, goals, expectancies, and evolving information needs over time.

To place this depiction of a newly liberated social cognition in an appropriate context, let me step back a bit and try to characterize the changes in person perception research and theorizing over the past 20 years. For many of us, the attributional approach was initially appealing because the idea of exploiting naïve psychology seemed to promise a fruitful break with psychometric approaches to diagnosis and judgmental accuracy, and to open the door to concerns with cognitive events embedded in everyday social interactions. Thus, the naïve psychology that Heider (1958) attempted to introduce pointed to concerns with interpersonal affairs such as envy, attraction, trust, and competence. This initial excitement of teasing out the psycholinguistics of interpersonal relations soon gave way, first to formal theories of attributional inference (Jones & Davis, 1965; Kelley 1967), and then to a new excitement when these theories failed to capture the reasoning processes of the naïve psychologists whose wisdom we were

---

Reprinted with permission of Sage Publications Inc. from *Personality and Social Psychology Bulletin,* 19, 657–661, copyright © 1993. References have been updated by the editor.

relying on to buttress the attributional paradigm (Jones, 1979; Ross, 1977). The discovery and repeated confirmation of dispositional overemphasis ("correspondence bias") identified the first and most prominent of several systematic biases noted as violations of the more rational attributional models. Soon there were not only additional attributional biases (self-serving, false consensus, etc.), there were also the important heuristic short cuts identified by Tversky and Kahneman (1974) as additional dislocations of the reasoning process. As many reviewers have noted, this concern with cognitive fallibility came to dominate the adolescent stage of attributional interest during the 1970s. Attribution theorists like me seemed intrigued by the mysteries being exposed by attributional research. Perhaps with a little more self-satisfaction than was justified, we were more or less content to show that our independent variables had consequences on the dependent variable side, and that these could not easily be dismissed as instances of experimenter demand or other artifacts.

As social psychology moved deeper into the 1970s, the broader cognitive revolution outside the field began to have an impact on research and theorizing about interpersonal inferences. A new breed of social cognition proponents (typified by Norman Anderson and Robert Wyer) wanted to talk about and explain what kinds of things happen between independent and dependent variables. They wanted to focus on how information was processed and what mental models and knowledge structures gave rise to the most fruitful predictions. In their "postattributional" zeal, the new proponents of information processing borrowed extensively from the methods and materials of cognitive science. Their well-meaning efforts toward greater control and the use of within-subjects designs, however, pushed these researchers increasingly toward the use of adjective strings and contrived vignettes that were, at best, remotely related to the complexities of interpersonal relations.

Increasing complaints about the absence of the social in social cognition resulted in a variety of therapeutic efforts. Several of these efforts challenged the preeminence of cognitive factors (Zajonc, 1980), whereas others complained about the substitution of an interest in person memory (e.g., Ostrom, 1989) for the earlier interest in attributional inference. The major attempts [**657**]* to recapture the social in social cognition included an infusion of symbolic interactionist themes in research on self-presentation, self-conception, and self-fulfilling prophecies (Jones & Pittman, 1982; Snyder, 1984; Swann, 1987); a resuscitation of interest in affect, motives, life tasks, and social decisions (Cantor & Kihlstrom, 1987); and the attempt to break away from experimental methods by redirecting the concern of social psychologists toward close and enduring relationships (Kelley *et al.*, 1983).

Articles in the present collection make occasional references to these developments but can more appropriately be seen as reflecting a rapprochement between attributional and information-processing approaches. (Such a rapprochement is also apparent in the differences between the first and second editions of *Social Cognition,* Fiske & Taylor, 1984, 1991.) To oversimplify, champions of the information-processing approach have influenced attributionists to care more about just how and when attributional decisions are made: Is behavior categorization always attributional? Is there a typical sequence of

---

*Bracketed bold numbers refer to original page numbers. Page numbers indicate where the original page ended.

cognitive events in person perception? Which stage in the sequence is most vulnerable to interference? Where and how do motives and emotions enter and affect the process? Attributionists, in contrast, have helped to sustain awareness of the social embeddedness of dispositional inference processes: the social purposes served by attributions, the role of perceivers as actors, and the issues involved in self-definition, maintenance, and protection. Many of the present articles reflect this rapprochement between attributional and information processing approaches and verify its importance in furthering our understanding of dispositional inference processes and their consequences.

To be more specific, now, I shall try to identify the major themes that seem to characterize recent concerns in the domain of interpersonal perception—many of which are captured by articles in the present collection.

FIRST AND SUBSEQUENT IMPRESSIONS

Those who focus exclusively on first impressions can be, and have been, accused of taking the easy way out. Perhaps we can take comfort in the fact that even first impressions inevitably involve prior expectancies. Therefore, we might defensively argue, first impressions contain in essence the ingredients of more fully developed impressions. Nevertheless, the researchers' task of getting from initial impressions to longer-term understanding is as crucial as it is daunting. The increasing focus on expectancy effects is a step in the right direction, and the numerous recent stereotype studies, and those concerned with behavior confirmation, have shaped our understanding in constructive ways. Still, the gap between information integration at the initial stages of impression formation and the kinds of understanding developed in close relationships remains substantial. Perhaps the gap can never be completely filled because of the difficulty of applying experimental methods in attempts to understand evolving or long-term relationships, each with its own idiosyncratic history, but surely any attempt to understand the immediate and reverberating effects of prior expectancies will provide useful, if only partial, insights into the vicissitudes of long-term relationships.

MULTIPLE-STAGE INFERENCE MODELS

Clearly one of the most significant developments in the last decade has been the emergence of multiple-stage models leading to the ultimate attribution of stable personal dispositions. The degree of consensus favoring such models is remarkable, and to judge by many of the present articles, the idea that there are at least two separate stages has become almost part of our established cultural wisdom. Although the two stages are differently described by different modelers, there remains substantial agreement that a process of descriptive behavior categorization precedes the more elaborate process of cognitive inference when decisions about personality dispositions are at issue. The initial stage may or may not be viewed as a kind of ecological imperative (as implied by Baron & Misovich, 1993), but there seems little question that some kind of initial behavior identification process occurs before the more elaborate "reasoning" processes featured in models of dispositional attribution. Furthermore, the distinction is important because different variables control the cognitive outcomes at the different stages that have been identified. In addition, it has been established that the behavior identification stage is a feature of automatic, relatively effortless perception, whereas dispositional inferences can be easily disrupted by competing demands on the perceiver's cognitive resources. The models of Trope (1986) and Gilbert (1991) have been especially influential in sharpening the distinction between information-processing stages.

And yet, the distinctiveness of these stages should not be exaggerated. Bassili (1989) makes the interesting suggestion that behavior identifications may "auto-prime" dispositional inferences. Newman and Uleman (1993) contend that behavior identifications are essentially incomplete trait inferences. Gilbert himself notes the tendency for perceivers to inflate their categorizations of behavior, a state of inferential readiness that leads easily to premature dispositional inference. The relationships between behavior categorization and dispositional inference are fascinating and extremely important, and they remain ripe for further study. [658]

REEXAMINING THE PERSON–SITUATION TRADE-OFF

Though extensively featured in Trope's theory of dispositional inference, the person–situation trade-off has invited comment from many of the other contributors to this collection. Trope has elegantly pointed out the conflicting influence of perceived situational constraint at the identification and dispositional inference stages of interpersonal perception (see Trope & Liberman, 1993; Higgins and Winter, 1993; as well as Dix, 1993) alert us to the role of prolonged situational influences on attributed dispositions. Whereas situational constraint is in a discounting relationship with dispositions in the short run, prolonged situational constraint can be converted into personal traits or values, evading the discounting process.

Shoda and Mischel (1993) attack the discounting principle even more forcefully, citing perceivers' tendencies to deal with if–then contingencies. They contend that perceivers are cognitive social theorists, trading in goals and contingencies rather than in traits. Their critique of the discounting principle (and implicitly the basic assumptions of correspondent inference theory) rests on a view of situations as enabling or "affording" (cf. Baron & Misovich, 1993) rather than constraining. Clearly, situations can be both. If a situation presses all or most actors to react in a certain way, the reaction is uninformative about individual differences in the disposition to act. If the person chooses the situation that then constrains him or her, or if the situation affords an opportunity to display a disposition, obviously we must go beyond the simplified version of discounting contained in the noncommon effect principle of Jones and Davis (1965) or in Kelley's (1967) discounting principle. Trope and Liberman's (1993) distinction between inherent and extraneous situational inducements is relevant in this context, though it does not completely capture the diverse roles that situational factors can play in a perceiver's naïve psychology.

There are many other complexities attendant on considering the relationship between situational and personal factors. As I have argued elsewhere (Jones, 1990), we need more sophisticated theories of situational influence to inform our understanding of the varied role of context in dispositional inference.

THE QUESTION OF DISPOSITION CONTENT

For many years I have been uneasy with our tendency as social psychologists to speak grandly of dispositions as the end product of the attribution process, without stopping to distinguish among traits, goals, values, and beliefs. Even among the fuzzy category that we designate as traits, there are important differences in the evidence required and the opportunities afforded for the behaviors constituting such evidence. This is driven home nicely by Reeder (1993) and by Gidron, Koehler, and Tversky (1993). Students of the self-fulfilling prophecy in social interaction have been forced (somewhat reluctantly, perhaps) to appreciate the fact that trait expectancies differ greatly in their availability for behavior confirmation—the crucial step in the fulfillment of the expectancy's promise. Thus traits closely related to approach/avoidance (e.g., *sociable, hostile*—"frequency traits" in Reeder's taxonomy?) may lend themselves to behavior confirmation more readily than morality traits that are high in scope (to use Gidron, Koehler, and Tversky's term). If a setting does not provide an opportunity for expectancy-confirming behavior, or if negative characteristics are easy to conceal, the sequence of prophecy fulfillment will not occur (Jones, 1986, 1990). The lesson implied by these considerations of content is that our "implicit personality" theories need work. We need to be better informed of the naïve psychology of personal dispositions and to be more sensitized to the different consequences of different kinds of attributed dispositions.

AUTOMATIC AND CONTROLLED PROCESSES

An inherent feature of all multi-stage theories of person perception and dispositional attribution is the realization that some processes are more automatic than others. Bargh (1989) has cautioned us not to use the notions of awareness and its absence too loosely, but there is a broad consensus that perceivers cannot control or account for much of what happens in social information processing. The emphasis may be on the evolutionary reality of affordances, as we automatically respond to the informative social environment (Baron & Misovich, 1993). Less mysteriously, the emphasis may be on well-developed, "overlearned" knowledge structures (Abelson, 1981; Hilton & Slugoski, 1986; Wyer & Srull, 1986; Read & Miller, 1993). Or, more specifically, we may adopt a straightforward functional approach and refer to the automatic identification of social behavior as a preparation for adaptive inferences: We encode behavior in attribution-relevant terms (Trope, 1986).

There is nothing really new about the realization that actors cannot always identify the causes of their own actions. Lewin was careful not to assume phenomenal awareness of all features in the causal life space, and Heider also left room for causal inferences outside of awareness. What *is* new is the rapidly accumulating evidence that the effect of influence-out-of-awareness may be more profound than previously suspected. In the present context of interpersonal perception, the extent of this "profound influence" can only reduce the importance of classic attributional models featuring rational **[659]** analysis. Or, at least, such models must be allocated to a more restricted domain in the manner of Trope (1986), Gilbert (1991), Hamilton (1988), and others. After all, if the initial categorization of behavior-in-situation is seriously affected by the priming of irrelevant recent experiences, or by the misapplication of prior expectancies, or by the misreading of situational constraints, then the attribution process that follows may be burdened with too much to correct. (And, alas, among other consequences of the new focus on behavior identification and perception, studies of how we integrate trait adjectives become even less relevant to our understanding of interpersonal perception.)

Experimental research to reveal further evidence of automatic processes at work hardly needs more of a push from me. I suspect that such research [along with its obverse: investigations such as Wegner's (1992) explorations of thought suppression and control] will capture increasing attention in the years to come. As part of this increased attention to the early, more automatic stages of person perception, I think we will also learn much more about the role of physical attraction, age, gender, ethnicity cues, and nonverbal stimulus inputs.

PERCEIVER-INDUCED SETTING

I have identified, and fondly endorsed, the growing rapprochement between attributionists and social cognitivists, but both kinds of researchers need to move more boldly into the domain featuring consequences of overt perceiver actions. Much has been gained by our receptivity to the methods and theories of mainstream cognitive science. However, we social psychologists have not paid enough research attention to the distinctive role that perceivers play in creating the situations in which their social perceptions take place. To some significant, if unknown, extent, we create our own social reality, and any account of person perception that ignores this cannot be taken seriously as a full and complete analysis. Research on the self-fulfilling prophecy sequence is a relevant example of taking the perceiver's behavioral role seriously. In addition, Gilbert and I (1986) have introduced the term *perceiver-induced constraint* and have shown, in a number of contexts, how active perceivers do a poor job of calibrating their own contributions to situational constraint. Gilbert (e.g., 1989) has gone on to verify an implication from our earlier studies that social interaction depletes perceiver resources, enhancing the relative influence of less effortful automatic processes and resulting in increased correspondence bias.

Further steps are needed, perhaps along the lines suggested by Baron and Misovich (1993). They note that we perform "event-activity tests," that we learn to act so as to reveal affordances. Such suggestions strike me as cogent and researchable. Active perceivers not only constrain target persons, they afford opportunities for diagnostic revelations. Over time, perceivers can indeed implement what amount to experimental designs, in coping with the response variations of others—particularly those responses that have personalistic significance for the perceiver. Do perceivers do this? And if they do, how well do they do it? A few of the present articles have much to say about the active perceiver and the consequences of his or her actions. But to draw attention truly to the social in social cognition, the mutual interaction between behavior and cognition needs to be more systematically addressed.

REFERENCES

Abelson, R. P. (1981). The psychological status of the script concept. *American Psychologist,* 36, 715–729.
Bargh, J. A. (1989). Conditional automaticity: Varieties of automatic influence in social perception and cognition. In J. S. Uleman & J. A. Bargh (Eds.), *Unintended thought* (pp. 3–51). New York: Guilford.

Baron, R. M., & Misovich, S. J. (1993). Dispositional knowing from an ecological perspective. *Personality and Social Psychology Bulletin,* 19, 541–552.

Bassili, J. N. (1989). Trait encoding in behavior identification and dispositional inference. In J. N. Bassili (Ed.), *On-line cognition in person perception* (pp. 61–89). Hillsdale, NJ: Lawrence Erlbaum.

Cantor, N., & Kihlstrom, J. F. (1987). *Personality and social intelligence.* Englewood Cliffs, NJ: Prentice-Hall.

Dix, T. (1993). Attributing dispositions to children: An interactional analysis of attribution in socialization. *Personality & Social Psychology Bulletin,* 19, 633–643.

Fiske, S. T., & Taylor, S. E. (1984). *Social cognition.* Reading MA: Addison-Wesley.

Fiske, S. T., & Taylor, S. E. (1991). *Social cognition* (2nd ed.). New York McGraw-Hill.

Gidron, D., Koehler, D. J., & Tversky, A. (1993). Implicit quantification of personality traits. *Personality & Social Psychology Bulletin,* 19, 594–604.

Gilbert, D. T. (1989). Thinking lightly about others: Automatic components of the social inference process. In J. S. Uleman & J. A. Bargh (Eds.), *Unintended thought* (pp. 189–211). New York: Guilford.

Gilbert, D. T. (1991). How mental systems believe. *American Psychologist,* 46, 107–119.

Gilbert, D. T., & Jones, E. E. (1986). Perceiver-induced constraint: Interpretations of self-generated reality. *Journal of Personality and Social Psychology,* 50, 269–280.

Hamilton, D. L. (1988). Causal attribution viewed from an information-processing perspective. In D. Bar-Tal & A. W. Kruglanski (Eds.), *The social psychology of knowledge* (pp. 359–585). Cambridge: Cambridge University Press.

Heider. F. (1958). *The psychology of interpersonal relations.* New York: Wiley.

Higgins, E. T., & L. Winter. (1993). The "acquisition principle": How beliefs about a behavior's prolonged circumstances influence correspondent inference. *Personality and Social Psychology Bulletin,* 19, 605–619.

Hilton, D. J., & Slugoski, B. R. (1986). Knowledge-based causal attribution: The abnormal conditions focus model. *Psychological Review,* 93, 75–88.

Jones, E. E. (1979). The rocky road from acts to dispositions. *American Psychologist,* 34, 107–117.

Jones, E. E. (1986). Interpreting interpersonal behavior: The effects of expectancies. *Science,* 234, 41–46.

Jones, E. E. (1990). *Interpersonal perception.* New York: W. H. Freeman.

Jones, E. E., & Davis. K. E. (1965). From acts to dispositions: The attribution process in person perception. In L. Berkowitz (Ed.), *Advances in experimental social psychology* (Vol. 2, pp. 21–266). New York: Academic Press.

Jones, E. E., & Pittman, T. S. (1982). Toward a general theory of strategic self-presentation. In J. Suls (Ed.), *Psychological perspectives on the self* (pp. 231–262). Hillsdale, NJ: Lawrence Erlbaum.

Kelly, H.H (1967) Attribution theory and social Psychology. In D. Levine (Ed.), *Nebraska Symposium on Motivation* (Vol. 15 pp. 192–241). Lincoln: University of Nebraska Press.

Kelly H.H., Berscheid, E., Christensen, A., Harvey, J. H., Huston T. L., Levinger, G. Mclintock, E., Peplau L. A., & Peterson, D. R. (Eds.). (1983). *Close Relationships.* San Francisco: W. H. Freeman. **[660]**

Newman, L. S., & Uleman, J. S. (1993). When are you what you did? Behavior identification and dispositional inference in person memory, attribution, and social judgment. *Personality and Social Psychology Bulletin,* 19, 513–525.

Ostrom, T. M. (1989). Three catechisms for social memory. In P. R. Solomon, G. R. Goethals, C. M. Kelley, & B. R. Stephens (Eds.), *Memory: Interdisciplinary approaches* (pp. 201–220). New York: Springer-Verlag.

Read, S. J., & Miller, L. C. (1993). Rapist or "regular guy": Explanatory coherence in the construction of mental models of others. *Personality & Social Psychology Bulletin,* 19, 526–540.

Reeder, G. D. (1993). Trait-behavior relations and dispositional inference. *Personality & Social Psychology Bulletin,* 19, 586–593.

Ross, L. (1977). The intuitive psychologist and his shortcomings: Distortions in the attribution process. In L. Berkowitz (Ed.), *Advances in experimental social psychology* (Vol. 10, pp. 174–221). New York: Academic Press.

Shoda, Y., & Mischel, W. (1993). Cognitive social approaches to dispositional inferences: What if the perceiver is a cognitive social theorist? *Personality and Social Psychology Bulletin,* 19, 574–585.

Snyder. M. (1984). When belief creates reality. In L. Berkowitz (Ed.), *Advances in experimental social psychology* (Vol. 18, pp. 248–306). New York: Academic Press.

Swann, W. B., Jr. (1987). Identity negotiation: Where two roads meet. *Journal of Personality and Social Psychology,* 53, 1038–1051.

Trope, Y. (1986). Identification and inference processes in dispositional attribution. *Psychological Review,* 93, 239–57.

Trope, Y., & Liberman, A. (1993). The use of trait conceptions to identify other people's behavior and to draw inferences about their personalities. *Personality & Social Psychology Bulletin,* 19, 553–562.

Tversky, A., & Kahneman, D. (1974). Judgment under uncertainty. Heuristics and biases. *Science,* 185, 1124–1131.

Wegner, D. M. (1992). You can't always think what you want: Problems in the suppression of unwanted thoughts. In M. P. Zanna (Ed.), *Advances in experimental social psychology* (Vol. 25, pp. 193–225). San Diego, CA: Academic Press.

Wyer, R. S., Jr., & Srull, T. K. (1986). Human cognition in its social context. *Psychological Review,* 93, 322–359.

Zajonc, R. B. (1980). Feeling and thinking: Preferences need no inferences. *American Psychologist,* 35, 151–175. **[661]**

SOCIAL COGNITION

Chapter 7

The Social in Cognition

Edward E. Jones
Princeton University

A number of historians who have tried to characterize the past 25 years in American psychology have referred to the cognitive revolution. Indeed, George Miller deserves a major amount of credit for helping to wean mainstream psychology away from rat mazes, pigeon boxes, and hours of deprivation. Yet to the social psychologist, the idea of a "cognitive revolution" can inspire an ironic chuckle. As my good friend Bob Zajonc (1980b) claimed a decade ago, social psychology has always been cognitive. Indeed, how could it be otherwise? If we define social psychology in terms of responses to a social environment—that is, an environment of people in action and of the symbolic products of their action—it is impossible to avoid the basic assumption of "subjectivism." We deal in social situations, and the only meaningful way to describe a social situation is to try to get a handle on how that situation is perceived and interpreted by the actors in it.

The origins of this recognition, of the recognition that a social psychology must be grounded in social perception and social cognition, are numerous and diverse. Some 65 years ago, Thomas and Thomas (1928) introduced the term *definition of the situation*, arguing that "if men define situations as real, they are real in their consequences" (p. 572). For psychologists in general, and for social psychologists in particular, Bartlett provides a more recent starting point. His 1932 book *Remembering* is certainly a major precursor of contemporary cognitive psychology. It specifically set the stage for studies

---

Reprinted with permission of Lawrence Erlbaum Associates, from G. Harman (Ed.), *Conceptions of the human mind: Essays in honor of George A. Miller* (pp. 85-98). Hillsdale, NJ: Erlbaum., ©1993. References have been updated by the editor.

of the role of motivation and expectancy in perception, celebrated in the so-called "new look" of the Bruner and Postman experimental program immediately after World War II. Although Bartlett's claim that people interpret complex verbal material in terms of experienced-based schemata would hardly have [85]* surprised the even earlier students of the psychology of testimony or rumor, Bartlett nevertheless brought such considerations into the mainstream of psychological research and provided a number of useful descriptive labels for summarizing common tendencies for assimilation to a pre-established cognitive framework.

Bruner and his colleagues (e.g., Bruner, 1951) added explicit motivational and psychodynamic factors to the mix, at the same time emphasizing the idea that we can be affected by situations without being aware of how they are affecting us. Then we come to those giants who had such an enormous impact on the evolution of social psychology: Lewin and Heider. It is important to note that although both recognized the great value of phenomenal reports by others, each was careful to permit a vague and unspecified arena of situational influence lying outside phenomenal awareness. For Lewin (e.g., 1951), the life space or the psychological field was completely deterministic, but not all elements of the life space were contained in the phenomenal awareness of the individual. Similarly, Heider's (1958) analysis of naïve psychology was viewed as an important tool of method, but he also wanted to leave room for influences outside the phenomenal awareness of the person. Heider's approach really involved a kind of semantic psycholinguistics: He sought wisdom in the accepted meanings of, and the relations between, a limited number of everyday concepts such as desire, ability, effort, envy, dislike, own, benefit, or owe.

Lewin, as all good psychologists are supposed to know, contrasted the Aristotelian and Galilean approaches to scientific understanding. The Aristotelian approach led in the direction of trait psychology and those formulations in the field of personality emphasizing past experience and correlation approaches to interpretive factors or clusters. Lewin didn't look kindly on efforts in that direction. The Galilean approach that Lewin favored has clearly won out in the social psychological mainstream. His focus on the "life space"—essentially a psychological environment full of valences and pressures and opportunities and boundaries—and his meta-theory depicting a field of psychological forces, set the stage for an experimental approach, and thus the controlling aspects of situational contexts became focal mediating research constructs.

The experimental game to be played—the game that was made implicit by Lewin and made more explicit by his student Festinger—involves the imaginative construction of situations that have roughly the same significance—the same meaning with reference to their goals or concerns or motives—for a chosen sample of subjects (who usually happen to be, for matters of convenience, college students). It is not easy to characterize exactly how this game is played in some simple string of sentences, but as experimental social psychology has evolved, one central research theme has been the discovery of subtle and important situational influences that occur [86] outside the awareness of our subjects. Indeed, if people were more routinely aware of the situational influences that affect their behavior, social psychology would be a less important,

---

*Bracketed bold numbers refer to original page numbers. Page numbers indicate where the original page ended.

or at least a very different, discipline. The "induced-compliance" paradigm in cognitive dissonance research (e.g., Festinger & Carlsmith, 1959), Milgram's (1974) obedience research, studies of the nonintervening bystander (Latané & Darley, 1970), just to cite a few famous and familiar examples, seem to require that subjects share a certain profound innocence concerning the constraining structure of the situation.

Psychology's cognitive revolution has its counterpart in a more modest minirevolution within social psychology, celebrated under such labels as social cognition or information-processing. Some very bright and industrious people are attempting to push beyond the earlier notions of attribution theory to characterize the ways in which socially relevant information is selected, encoded, stored, structured, and retrieved. I admire many of these sophisticated efforts, efforts that can involve very elaborate flow charts and that generate research contributing to our understanding of how things are remembered and retrieved. Nevertheless, these approaches have yet to convince me that they indeed can handle what is truly social about social cognition. So, in spite of the recent upsurge in information-processing approaches within social cognition, much of social psychological research and theorizing remains strongly flavored by the phenomenal causality approach of naïve psychology.

In other words, there is still plenty of mileage to be gained by trying to capture the naïve psychology of causal attribution based on the assumption that if we can characterize the ways in which people perceive causes and effects in their everyday environment, we can understand why they behave the way they do. This is not at all incompatible with an information-processing approach, but it does tend to focus more on situational input and interpretive response outputs than on the delineation of intervening cognitive transformations. Gilbert (1989, p. 191) put it rather dramatically: "None [of the attribution theories] ... specifies what actually happens when an attribution is made—which chutes open, which bells go 'ding,' which lights wink on and off."

But, there is a paradox lurking. If we join Lewin, Heider, and many others in realizing that naïve psychology is not to be equated with phenomenal awareness, then how much does it help to know how people think the environment is organized in cause-and-effect terms? Well, of course, the naïve psychology of causal attribution does carry us a long way. There is considerable overlap between how we perceive the environment and how it is, in fact, "structured for our use." However, where can we fit the realization that our dearly beloved field of experimental social psychology thrives on just those patterns of situational influence of which the individual remains unaware? [87]

A further dose of some recent history may be useful at this point. The attributional approaches promoted by Heider (1958), Kelley (1967), and myself (Jones & Davis, 1965) were originally attempts to characterize the ways in which people actually think about and respond to the ongoing social situation. In a very broad and rather crude sense the theories were quite successful in enabling the prediction of large classes of behavior. They appeared to capture a sizable chunk of common sense. However, as the attributional approach held sway during much of the 1970s and the 1980s, it was the failures of prediction that became more intriguing. What started out to be deductive theories often became normative baselines against which the "irrationality" of individual actors could be identified. The most prominent example of a predictive failure involves the robust tendency toward dispositionalism—a tendency that seems to push away from the appropriate recognition of situational determinants of another's behavior toward a clearly biased emphasis on individual differences. If perceivers see a person acting completely in line with situational constraints, in a way that even they realize could be entirely determined by those constraints, they nevertheless are inclined to make a dispositional attribution and to assume that some individual propensity contributed to the individual's actions. This has been variously called the "fundamental attribution error" (Ross, 1977) and "correspondence bias" (Jones, 1990b), the latter term referring to the fact that we tend to see behavior as corresponding to a disposition while tending to underplay the role of situational influences.

So it can be said that attribution theories were partly true, and when they weren't true, they should have been true. When our theories failed to predict, we could say, "Ah ha! This is a normative baseline and isn't it intriguing that people don't respond the way they logically should?" So we attributionists, in a sense, had our cake and could eat it too. As the attribution literature began to expand in the 1970s, the identification of various attributional biases began to merge with substantial evidence of decision-making heuristics that often resulted in logical or arithmetic errors of judgment. Nisbett and Ross (1980), much influenced by the work of heuristics of Tversky and Kahneman (1974), captured many of these vagaries of human inference in an important book about 10 years ago.

More recently, the interests of social psychologists in those areas of behavioral influence that lie outside of awareness have begun to focus on phenomena that are strongly reminiscent of the distinction between automatic and controlled processing. They also seem to remind us that "subliminal perception" is alive and healthier than ever. The following are a few examples of how this distinction seems to be affecting contemporary social psychology. [88]

PERSONAL/CULTURAL THEORIES, STEREOTYPES, AND UNCONSCIOUS IDEOLOGIES

Some 15 years ago, the work of Nisbett and Wilson (1977) attempted to make clear the role of implicit personal and cultural theories in the interpretation of behavior. They provided a number of intriguing demonstrations of the different contexts in which people are influenced by subtle environmental arrangements while remaining unaware that these demonstrable influences were, in fact, present. Just to pick one simple example, women faced with four identical sets of panty hose arranged on a table in front of them had a strong tendency to evaluate the right-hand set as the most attractive. When asked whether their ratings were affected by the positions of the panty hose, virtually all subjects denied such influence and were often annoyed with the researcher for even suggesting such a factor.

More recently, there has been considerable interest and concern with the role of unconscious ideologies and of the influence of stereotypes, again operating below or outside the level of awareness. It is fairly easy to generate anecdotal evidence regarding the operation of unconscious ideologies—for example, assumptions about gender differences or race differences. The following is a now familiar puzzle:

> A father and his son were driving to a ball game when their car stalled on the railroad tracks. In the distance, a train whistle blew a warning. Frantically, the father tried to start the engine, but in his panic, he couldn't turn the key, and the car was hit by the onrushing train. An ambulance sped to the scene and picked them up. On the way to the hospital, the father died. The son was still alive, but his condition was very serious and he needed immediate surgery. The moment they arrived at the hospital, he was wheeled into an emergency operating room, and the surgeon came in, expecting a routine case. However, on seeing the boy, the surgeon blanched and muttered, "I can't operate on this boy—he's my son."

Of course, in this enlightened age most of us catch on quickly that the surgeon is the boy's mother, but a decade or so ago, this case proved to be a puzzling riddle even for presumably liberated academics. The general point thus remains an important one, even though underlying stereotypes and ideologies can clearly change in content and accessibility.

Some recent research by Devine (1989) even suggests that nonprejudiced people are quite aware of the stereotypes underlying racism and in fact are influenced by racist ideology in important, if subtle, ways—even though they would vigorously deny the validity of the ideology and would score low on any prejudice scale. **[89]**

After establishing that both high- and low-prejudiced subjects (as identified by a scale measuring "implicit racism") were equally aware of a stereotype concerning Black Americans, Devine exposed both highs and lows to a subliminal version of the stereotype. Specifically, subjects were asked to identify the quadrant of a tachistoscope on which a stimulus appeared over a series of trials. Each "stimulus" was, in fact, a word. In one condition, 80% of the words were taken from the Black American stereotype. Examples were: Blacks, Negroes, poor, lazy, athletic, musical, busing, and oppressed. In another condition, only 20% of the words were derived from this stereotype. Subsequent memory probes made it clear that those words were, in fact, presented below the level of reportable awareness.

This procedure was followed by a "second experiment" in which the same subjects were asked to form an impression of Donald, a well-traveled target person in other experiments on priming, who was briefly described in "ambiguously hostile" terms. For example, one sentence described him as demanding money back from the clerk immediately after his purchase. Another noted that he refused to pay rent until his apartment was painted.

In conveying their impression of Donald, subjects in the 80% condition tended to rate him as more "hostile," "dislikable," and "unfriendly," than subjects in the 20% condition. Whether the raters were high or low in prejudice made no difference. Thus, when subjects were primed below the level of awareness with many features of the Black American stereotype, even nonprejudiced subjects were inclined to see the innocent Donald in very negative terms.

In a further study, when asked to list their conscious associations to the category *Black Americans,* high- and low-prejudiced subjects behaved very differently.

High-prejudiced subjects were quite willing to generate a number of negative traits; low-prejudiced subjects were much more inclined toward positive labels and corrective beliefs.

Thus, Devine seemed to show that people are affected by their knowledge of stereotyped content, even when they disagree with the validity of the stereotype. This is a little scary (and it deserves to be replicated). It points to the discrepant functioning of automatic and controlled processing in a crucial area of social judgment.

PERIPHERAL MODELS OF ATTITUDE CHANGE

In the area of attitude-change theory and research, the elaboration likelihood model of Petty and Cacioppo (1986) is an explicit recognition that attitude change can occur in two contexts, or perhaps on two levels. One context involves explicit awareness and the rational consideration of relevant information; the other context involves symbols such as the good looks or the irrelevant fame of the communicator that primes and triggers [90] reactions outside of the level of awareness. An example in one textbook (Worchel, Cooper. & Goethals, 1989) is that of the commercial in which Robert Young, who played Marcus Welby on television, advises people to drink decaffeinated coffee, saying explicitly, "I'm not a doctor, but I play one on TV." If anyone was influenced to switch to the advertised brand of coffee, they would be hard-put to provide a rational explanation for this behavior.

DUAL THEORIES OF ATTRIBUTION

A number of intriguing dual theories of attribution have recently emerged that essentially distinguish between the identification of perceived behavior in attribution-relevant terms and the subsequent cranking up of the attribution process itself. For example, McArthur and Baron (1983) borrowed heavily from Gibson's (1979) emphasis on the analysis of stimulus structures to argue that much of the information contained in the social environment is also prestructured to convey immediately the stable meaning of events. There is a strong evolutionary flavor to their reasoning, as they suggest that certain kinds of information are critically important in a given ecological niche. Because it is so adaptive to differentiate male from female and friend from foe in the social environment (just as animals need to distinguish prey from predator), such information comes to us in prestructured forms as a consequence of its adaptive importance over a long sequence of generations.

Trope (1986) made a more explicit distinction between the identification and cognitive labeling of an observed action event—and the causal attribution of why it is occurring and what underlying motive or disposition it may represent. People label an overture as "friendly" through an immediate, automatic act of identification. Then, perhaps, they tackle the problem of deciding whether this is a real friendly guy or just a dedicated used-car salesman. Neither the individual nor the psychologist looking at the individual can clearly explain exactly why this automatic identification process occurs.

Along these same lines, one can hardly help but be intrigued by the research of Johansson (1973) and his colleagues who showed how perceivers can identify males and females, dancers and walkers, and other patterns of mundane motor activity, from extremely limited information conveyed by pin points of light attached to target persons who are otherwise in complete darkness. This is no calculated inference; it is an immediate apprehension.

THE ROLE OF PRIMING IN "UNINTENDED THOUGHT"

Social cognition has been much affected by the legacy of procedures from cognitive science. Therefore, it is not surprising that the varied and diverse [91] operations of cognitive priming have reached into and had effects on social psychology. A recent volume by Uleman and Bargh (1989) entitled *Unintended Thought* summarized many of these priming studies—studies showing the automatic or unwitting influence of exposure to information in the recent past that helps to frame interpretation of events in the present. Earlier work of Higgins (Higgins, Rholes, & Jones, 1977) and more recent work of Bargh (1982, 1989) warned that impressions of a new acquaintance at one moment in time may be heavily influenced by supposedly unrelated recent experiences—experiences that make certain interpretations about the acquaintance more accessible than others. There are many other intriguing chapters in this volume that provide a helpful summary of the amount of work that's going on in the area of automatic thought processes. These include, for example, chapters on the role of affect, the consequences of attempting not to think of something, implications of reduced or strained cognitive resources for social inferences, and the evidence for spontaneous trait inferences.

Bargh (1989) raised the interesting question of whether people must simply give in and be passive victims of these automatic processes and comes up with an interesting metaphor: "that of the ambitious royal advisor upon whom a relatively weak king relies heavily for wisdom and guidance. The actual power of decision always rests with the king, who by no means has to follow the preferred advice; yet the counselor who 'has the king's ear' wields the real power over decisions and the policy of the kingdom" (p. 40). I'm not sure whether this is better than Freud's metaphor of the Id and the Ego, but I present it as a possible contemporary alternative.

MENTAL CONTROL AND THE RETURN OF THE SUPPRESSED

In a recent paper on the social foundations of mental control, Wegner and Erber (1992) discussed some of the many instances in which private thoughts diverge from their public expression. The linkage between behavioral control and thought control is fascinating and problematic. Usually, there are felt pressures on the individual to bring his or her thoughts in line with behavior—to make the behavior more "authentic"—so people try to concentrate on thoughts that support socially appropriate actions and suppress thoughts and emotions that undermine such actions. Unfortunately, Wegner's research on thought suppression indicates how difficult it is not to think about something—as in "don't think about a white bear," or "try not to think about sex." One of Wegner and Erber's main conclusions is that in trying to suppress thoughts in the interests of social accommodation or the avoidance of depressed mood, people tend to become obsessed with the very thoughts they are trying to suppress.

Without disputing this tendency of voluntarily suppressed thoughts [92] to rebound or resurface, our own research (Jones, 1990a) does point to some subtle conditions under which uncharacteristic actions—such as responding in a very self-deprecating manner in an interview—can carry over, at least temporarily, to a depressed private view of the self. This occurs when the interviewee is cajoled (subtly induced rather than required) to present himself or herself unfavorably, suggesting the operation of cognitive dissonance reduction processes at work once again.

COGNITIVE AND BEHAVIORAL FEATURES OF THE "SELF-FULFILLING PROPHECY" IN SOCIAL INTERACTION

Finally, to return to the more purely social, there is the so-called "self-fulfilling prophecy" in social interaction. This effect occurs when a perceiver's expectancy or a hypothesis about another person leads to actions by the perceiver that elicit confirmatory actions in the target person. If I wanted to mention one single feature that helps to distinguish the social psychological approach from "mainstream" cognitive science, I would mention the extent to which people participate in producing or creating their own social reality—not just by imagining or perceptually distorting it in some congenial way, but by adding their own behavior to everything else that is going on. A moment's thought makes clear that, in the real world, people provide part of the stimulus environment to which others are responding. They can, thus, produce very different environments in a family gathering or a faculty meeting by responding pessimistically or optimistically, by acting aggressively or passively, by being gauche or tactful, or by smiling or frowning.

Much of our own recent research indicated that people are terrible at dealing with the implications of their own contributions to the social environment (e.g., Gilbert & Jones, 1986). Each should, as lay students of human behavior, show some signs of discounting the diagnostic significance of reactions to their own constraining remarks or actions. Our data emphasize that people are dispositionalists even here—that they tend to take at face value, and make dispositional attributions to account for, actions of others that they have clearly brought about by their own influence.

The following is a striking experimental example of the perceiver's failure to discount his or her own constraining influence, as described by Jones (1986, p. 234):

> In a simulated interview situation, 26 Princeton undergraduate subjects believed that their roles as interviewers were to signal interviewees to read answers to questions concerning social or political issues. On each of several trials, the subject, in an isolation booth, asked a question and then pressed a button to signal for either a liberal or a conservative response. It was made clear to the interviewer that the statements on each issue had been previously **[93]** prepared for the experiment and that the interviewee was merely complying with instructions in reading them verbatim. The results showed a strong tendency toward correspondence bias: even though the perceivers were obviously aware that they had induced the responses they heard, they tended to attribute to the interviewee attitudes consistent with the opinions expressed. On a 15-point scale anchored at the end points by the phrases "extremely liberal" and "extremely conservative," 10 out of 13 subjects faced with a predominantly conservative

responder rated him on the conservative side, whereas the predominantly liberal responder was rated on the liberal side by 10 out of 13 subjects in that condition. Thus the subjects, who could and logically should have distributed their responses around the midpoint, gave ratings systematically biased in the direction of the responses they had induced and heard.

Gilbert, a collaborator in the experiment, has gone on to document the importance of attentional allocation in such failures to discount situational requirements. In a series of studies (Gilbert, 1989), he showed that people are particularly prone to attribute constrained behavior to a personal disposition of the actor when operating under "cognitive load." Subjects who must keep strings of digits in mind, or who must anticipate their own impending action, or who must exert mental control over their negative feelings—such "cognitive loaded" subjects do an especially poor job of discounting the influences of strong situational pressures when evaluating a highly constrained role-player performing on video or audiotape. Gilbert (1991) cited this as an instance of a broad and fundamental cognitive tendency to believe-as-we-encode, prior to a subsequent stage of certification (acceptance), rejection, or skeptical adjustment—which can be, and often is insufficient, in any event. When this subsequent, more inferential stage is disrupted by cognitive load, perceived action is taken at face value and attributed to a correspondent disposition. Thus, Gilbert has become a shameless Spinozan while rejecting the Cartesian view that perception and evaluation are totally separate processes.

The failure to recognize one's own constraining influence is essential to the role of "behavior confirmation" in the self-fulfilling prophecy. If I very tentatively expect a male acquaintance to be especially friendly, for example, I will probably approach that person with a smile and nonverbal warmth cues that follow from my expectancy. Even if the other fellow does not really have a characteristically friendly disposition, he may—indeed he probably will—respond with the friendliness initially expected. The problem arises when I take his response as independent verification of my tentative expectancy, so that behavioral confirmation now locks in the erroneous impression. If I were wise enough to say to myself, "well, he seems like a friendly person, but he's probably just responding to my friendly overture," the expectancy of friendliness would at least not receive [94] the strong added impetus conferred by behavior that unequivocally confirms the expectancy.

Where does all this seem to be leading? Probably more than in any other domain of psychology, social psychologists have been intrigued more by the mysteries of mental functioning than by attempts to characterize what happens in a systematic or rigorous way. To understand why this is so, one has to understand the socialization of social psychologists. We all have to cope with the fact that everyone is a social psychologist, or thinks he is (a fact noted by Krech and Crutchfield as long ago as 1948). Each of us has his or her own theory of social events and of individual behavior and personality. When a social psychologist reports a research conclusion, two common reactions are: "Of course, that's so obvious! Why would anybody want to waste his good time studying something we already know?" or alternatively, "That's ridiculous, you couldn't possibly be right. *Cherchez le fluke or le artifact.*" Most of us would rather hear the latter than the former. We are deathly afraid of being accused of "bubba psychology"—the psychology of what one's grandmother knew—and most are therefore pushed perhaps unduly toward a seeming preoccupation with errors, biases, failures to predict, and so on—the little and not-so-little pathologies of everyday life.

A more benign way of putting it is that we social psychologists are pushed in the direction of intriguing mysteries. It is almost as if we are more interested in deepening the mystery than reducing it. The information-processing approach, mentioned briefly in the beginning of this chapter, may lead us out of the wilderness, perhaps with the aid of computer stimulation models, but thus far, this approach is saddled (and tethered) with the charge that the procedures pay too heavy a price of foregoing social relevance in order to obtain methodological rigor.

I should not, of course, imply that social psychology can be equated with social cognition. Yet certainly, the more that we can learn about social cognition, the better off we shall be in trying to understand such things as close relationships or interdependence, mixed motive negotiations, attitude change and social conformity, and so on. I share with the social cognition students a basic interest in the perception of persons, an interest I have pursued in various ways for 40 years. It does seem to me that if we can understand how persons are perceived, then many of the other problems of social psychology would fall into place. This, at least, is the justifying premise of my recent book, *Interpersonal Perception* (1990b). I would like to think that our own work featuring the perceiver as an actor, as part of the ongoing social situation, is an attempt to move beyond those sterile social cognition approaches—approaches that feature word lists and scenarios—in order to capture the early stages of relationship development. Once again, I am particularly intrigued by the distinctive feature of social **[95]** psychology, namely, that people create their own social reality. The behavior of others cannot be conveniently separated from whatever is done to elicit it.

After rambling over this rocky terrain, I now focus more specifically on the topic that I accepted as my particular assignment—namely, how the mind is treated in social psychology. I have, of course, implicitly been talking about this, but perhaps a few summarizing statements are in order:

1. *Level of Abstraction: Staying Close to Phenomenal Experience.* Most social psychologists resist the kinds of fine-grain analyses that lend themselves readily to physiologizing or to computer simulation. Most of us have lived with a felt necessity for such molar concepts as categories, expectancies, goals, inferences, reasons—in short, terms borrowed from the naïve vocabulary of persons who are asked to explain themselves, to explain their actions, their beliefs, or their preferences. Most of us take for granted that psychologists, like real people, can account for sizable proportions of human behavior by such an appeal to naïve psychology and the phenomenal experience of others.

2. *Capitalizing on Information-Processing Errors.* The mind doesn't always work the way grandma thought. Just as perception psychologists have learned much through the analysis of illusions and perceptual breakdowns, social psychologists have studied and been intrigued by instances in which mental processes get derailed and generate socially consequential errors and gaffes. Once more, though the derailments are systematic and predictable, they are not always well understood. In many cases, one is stuck with a kind of functionalism. Thus, heuristic biases such as availability and representativeness are explained as the misapplications of normally useful and efficient (energy-saving) information-processing, tactics.

3. *Automaticity and Primitive Constructs.* Beyond the reaches of phenomenal causality analysis are the many routine instances of social perception or "identification" that almost seem hardwired. Functional explanations, in this case, are often joined with notions of experiential repetition as well as evolutionary presumptions. There are those who want to build more and more functional wiring into the human propensity to navigate successfully in the social environment. How does the perceiver know that Johansson's revolving lights represent a woman and not a man walking? How do perceivers process anger and friendliness before trying to interpret the behavior in some explanatory context? Or how, in Zajonc's (1980a) terms, are people wired to evaluate and emote before they fully cognize?

4. *Serving as the Conscience of the Field.* Social psychologists have continually forced perception psychologists and cognitive psychologists to take account of context. To many laborers in the cognitive science vineyard, this is just an annoying and burdensome source of inexplicable complexity. [96] To us, it is the essential ingredient of a true understanding of mental processing, and we are sustained by the challenge of social, temporal, and personal expectancy contexts as they affect cognitive interpretations of the social reality in which all of us live.

REFERENCES

Bargh, J. A. (1982). Attention and automaticity in the processing of self-relevant information. *Journal of Personality and Social Psychology,* 43, 425–436.

Bargh, J. A. (1989). Conditional automaticity: Varieties of automatic influence in social perception and cognition. In J. S. Uleman & J. A. Bargh (Eds.), *Unintended thought* (pp.3–51). New York: Guilford.

Bartlett, F. C. (1932). *Remembering.* Cambridge: Cambridge University Press.

Bruner, J. S. (1951). Personality dynamics and the process of perceiving. In R. R. Blake & G. B. Ramsey (Eds.), *Perception: An approach to personality* (pp. 121–147). New York: Ronald Press.

Devine, P. G. (1989). Stereotypes and prejudice: Their automatic and controlled components. *Journal of Personality and Social Psychology,* 56, 5–18.

Festinger, L., & Carlsmith, J. M. (1959). Cognitive consequences of forced compliance. *Journal of Abnormal and Social Psychology,* 58, 203–211.

Gibson, J. J. (1979). *The ecological approach to visual perception.* Boston: Houghton Mifflin.

Gilbert, D. T. (1989). Thinking lightly about others: Automatic components of the social inference process. In J. S. Uleman & J. A. Bargh (Eds.), *Unintended thought* (pp. 189–211). New York: Guilford.

Gilbert, D. T. (1991). How mental systems believe. *American Psychologist,* 46, 107–119.

Gilbert, D. T., & Jones, E. E. (1986). Perceiver-induced constraint: Interpretations of self-generated reality. *Journal of Personality and Social Psychology,* 50, 269–280.

Higgins, E. T., Rholes, W. S., & Jones, C. R. (1977). Category accessibility and impression formation. *Journal of Experimental Social Psychology,* 13, 141–154.

Heider, F. (1958). *The psychology of interpersonal relations.* New York: Wiley.

Johansson, G. (1973). Visual perception of biological motion and a model for its analysis. *Perception and Psychophysics,* 14, 201–211.

Jones, E. E. (1986). Interpreting interpersonal behavior: The effects of expectancies. *Science,* 234, 41–46.

Jones, E. E. (1990a). Constrained behavior and self-concept change. In J. Olson & M. Zanna (Eds.), *Self-inference process: The Ontario Symposium,* (Vol. 6, pp. 69–86). Hillsdale, NJ: Erlbaum.

Jones, E. E. (1990b). *Interpersonal perception.* New York: Freeman.

Jones, E. E., & Davis, K. E. (1965). From acts to dispositions: The attribution process in person perception. In L. Berkowitz (Ed.), *Advances in experimental social psychology* (Vol. 2, pp. 219–266). New York: Academic Press.

Kelley, H. H. (1967). Attribution theory in social psychology. *Nebraska Symposium on Motivation,* 14, 192–241.

Krech, D., & Crutchfield, R. S. (1948). *Theory and problems of social psychology.* New York: McGraw-Hill.

Latané B., & Darley, J. M. (1970). *The unresponsive bystander: Why doesn't he help?* New York: Appleton-Century-Crofts.

Lewin, K. (1951). *Field theory in social science* (D. Cartwright, Ed.). New York: Harper & Bros.

McArthur, L. Z., & Baron, R. M. (1983). Toward an ecological theory of social perception. *Psychological Review,* 90, 215–238. **[97]**

Milgram, S. (1974). *Obedience to authority.* New York: Harper & Row.

Nisbett, R. E., & Ross, L. (1980). *Human inference strategies and shortcomings of social judgment.* Englewood Cliffs, NJ: Prentice-Hall.

Nisbett, R. E. & Wilson, T. D. (1977). Telling more than we can know: Verbal reports on mental processes. *Psychological Review,* 84, 231–259.

Petty, R. E., & Cacioppo, J. T. (1986). The elaboration likelihood model of persuasion. In L. Berkowitz (Ed.), *Advances in experimental social psychology* (Vol. 19 pp. 123–205). New York: Academic Press.

Ross, L. (1977). The intuitive psychologist and his shortcomings: Distortions in the attribution process. In L. Berkowitz (Ed.), *Advances in experimental social psychology* (Vol. 10, pp. 174–221). New York: Academic Press.

Thomas, W. I., & Thomas, D. S. (1928). *The child in America: Behavior problems and programs.* New York: Knopf.

Trope, Y. (1986). Identification and inference processes in dispositional attribution. *Psychological Review,* 93, 239–257.

Tversky A., & Kahneman, D. (1974). Judgment under uncertainty: Heuristics and biases. *Science,* 185, 1124–1131.

Uleman, J. S. & J. A. Bargh (Eds.). (1989). *Unintended thought.* New York: Guilford.

Wegner, D. M., & Erber, R. (1992). The hyperaccessibility of suppressed thoughts. *Journal of Personality and Social Psychology,* 63, 903–912.

Worchel, S., Cooper, J. & Goethals, G. R. (1989). *Understanding social psychology* (4th ed.). Pacific Grove, CA: Brooks/Cole.

Zajonc, R. B. (1980a). Cognition and social cognition: A historical perspective. In L. Festinger (Ed.), *Restrospections on social psychology* (pp. 180–204). New York: Oxford.

Zajonc, R. B. (1980b). Feeling and thinking: Preferences need no inferences. *American Psychologist,* 35, 151–175. **[98]**

Part Two
Inferential Anomalies

Correspondence Bias
    Chapter 8   The Attribution of Attitudes
    Chapter 9   The Rocky Road from Acts to Dispositions

The Actor-Observer Effect
    Chapter 10   The Actor and the Observer: Divergent Perceptions of the Causes of Behavior
    Chapter 11   How Do People Perceive the Causes of Behavior?

Order Effects
    Chapter 12   Order Effects in Impression Formation: Attribution Context and the Nature of the Entity

Ingroups and Outgroups
    Chapter 13   The Perception of Variability within In-Groups and Out-Groups: Implications for the Law of Small Numbers
    Chapter 14   Polarized Appraisals of Out-Group Members

CORRESPONDENCE BIAS

Chapter 8

The Attribution of Attitudes

Edward E. Jones and **Victor A. Harris**
Duke University

> ABSTRACT: Three experiments were conducted within the framework of correspondent inference theory. In each of the experiments the subjects were instructed to estimate the "true" attitude of a target person after having either read or listened to a speech by him expressing opinions on a controversial topic. Independent variables included position of speech (pro, anti, or equivocal), choice of position vs. assignment of position, and reference group of target person. The major hypothesis (which was confirmed with varying strength in all three experiments) was that choice would make a greater difference when there was a low prior probability of someone taking the position expressed in the speech. Other findings of interest were: (1) a tendency to attribute attitude in line with behavior, even in no-choice conditions; (2) increased inter-individual variability in conditions where low probability opinions were expressed in a constraining context; (3) that this variability was partly a function of the subjects' own attitudes on the issue; (4) that equivocation in no-choice conditions leads to the attribution that the equivocator opposes the assigned position. The main conclusion suggested is that perceivers do take account of prior probabilities and situational constraints when attributing private attitude, but perhaps do not weight these factors as heavily as would be expected by a rational analysis.

From *Journal of Experimental Social Psychology,* 3, 1–24.

When a person verbalizes an opinion, he may or may not hold an underlying attitude that "corresponds" to that opinion. The degree to which opinions and attitudes—or more generally, acts and dispositions—are seen as correspondent is a function of the relative weight assigned to internal versus external causal factors (cf. Thibaut and Riecken, 1955). Loosely stated, a person will be perceived to hold attitudes that correspond with his opinion statements when the statements seem to have been freely offered and not coerced by situational pressures.

Jones and Davis (1965) have attempted to develop a systematic statement of the attribution process in person perception which extends this [1]* common-sense reasoning. Building on Heider's earlier work (1944, 1958), they have proposed a theory of *correspondent inferences* to clarify the major variables involved in extracting information about dispositions from observed acts. An inference about an attribute is correspondent to the extent that the attribute and a sample of observed behavior are similarly described by the inference and the attribute serves as a "sufficient explanation" for the behavior. A "sufficient explanation" is one that accounts for the occurrence of an act to the reasonable satisfaction of the perceiver. Correspondent inferences imply a circularity in such explanations: "he dominated the meeting because he is dominant," "he cries because he is in pain," "he voted for prohibition because he is against the sale and consumption of alcohol."

But more than circular reasoning is involved in decisions about correspondence as defined in the theory. Since Jones and Davis were interested in the information *gained* about a person through the opportunity to observe him act, not every inference that takes behavior "at face value" is highly correspondent. If everyone were in favor of prohibition, and the perceiver was aware of this beforehand, he would gain no information about person A from observing him vote for prohibition. The concept of correspondence should reflect person A's distinctiveness on the dimension in question. It is not that he (like everyone else) favors prohibition; our inference becomes correspondent when we attribute to A more intense feelings about alcohol than we attribute to the average person. Correspondence is high when the act tells us something in a direct way about the person that we did not know beforehand. To paraphrase the formal definition of correspondence offered by Jones and Davis (1965): Given an inference that assigns an attribute to account for an act, the correspondence of that inference increases as the judged value of the attribute departs from the judge's conception of the average person's standing.

In the original presentation of correspondent inference theory, Jones and Davis (1965) couched their analysis in terms of the effects of action, the uniqueness of a given act–effect linkage, and the assumed social desirability of the effects achieved. For our present purposes a simpler terminology will suffice, one which is easily mapped into the more general original statement. Given the fact that a person expresses himself on some opinion issue, the inference that he believes what he says, and that not everyone would say it, is correspondent. Correspondence should be high when perceived choice is high and the prior probability of the act occurring is low. This should be the condition where maximum information is gained from behavior (cf. Berlyne, 1965)—what a person says is unexpected or at variance with the norm

---

*Bracketed bold numbers refer to original page numbers. Page numbers indicate where the original page ended.

and he seems to have said it [2] "on his own hook." Information gain is lowest when the person expresses highly conventional opinions under conditions where it would be extremely difficult for him to express any other opinions.

An alternative way of stating the relationship between perceived choice, prior probability, and correspondence conceives of the first two as orthogonal independent variables and the latter as the dependent variable. The crucial hypothesis to be tested by the experiments to be presented below is: When a person expresses a modal (high probability) opinion, attribution of underlying attitude will not vary as a function of perceived choice; when an unexpected or unpopular opinion is expressed, correspondent attribution will vary directly with the amount of choice perceived. We are predicting, then, a particular kind of statistical interaction between the amount of perceived choice and the prior probability of an opinion's being expressed, in determining the correspondence of resulting inferences about opinion-related attitudes.

This hypothesis is hardly paradoxical, though it does propose that persons perform a kind of implicit information theory calculus in making sense out of the behavior of others. The information contained in a statement (act) goes up as the prior probability of the statement goes down, assuming that the speaker was not forced, bribed, or otherwise constrained to make the statement. But does the average perceiver, in fact, follow this prescription? Relevant experimental evidence is sparse. Steiner and Field (1960) conducted an experiment in which an accomplice expressed pro-segregation opinions in a group discussion. In some cases, he chose his role with apparent freedom; in other cases he was assigned the role by the experimenter. Other group members were more confident in their assignment of pro-segregation beliefs to the accomplice in the choice condition. They also liked the accomplice less, probably because the subjects were Northern college students who themselves were against segregation. In effect, the Steiner and Field (1960) study tests half of the proposed hypothesis, whereas the present experiments attempt to show that choice is not an important variable when the prior probability of the behavior being observed is high. A number of other studies (e.g., Jones and Davis, 1961; Bem, 1965; Thibaut and Riecken, 1955; Jones, Davis, and Gergen, 1961) are indirectly relevant in assessing the role of perceived choice in correspondent attribution. They do not, however, provide a direct test of the theory.

Such a test requires a design in which a stimulus person states either an expected or an unexpected opinion under conditions of high versus low perceived choice. Three closely related experiments were conducted within this general design; the subjects' primary task in each was to estimate the true attitude of the person making the statement. [3]

EXPERIMENT I

Method

In the first experiment subjects were asked to read a short essay in "Castro's Cuba" and to record their estimates of the essayist's true attitude toward Castro. The essay itself was either pro-Castro or anti-Castro; it had either been written under conditions of free choice or by assignment from a course instructor. The two variables of *choice* and *behavior direction* thus comprised a two-by-two factorial design. This basic design was repeated in each of the three experiments, though there were variations from experiment to experiment in the manner in which the cross-cutting variables were manipulated.

SUBJECTS Thirty-six males and 15 female students served in the experiment in one group session. They were volunteers from the introductory psychology course at Duke University who received course credit for their participation.

PROCEDURE Each subject was handed a mimeographed pamphlet that contained an essay on Castro's Cuba, a prior statement manipulating the choice variable, and a final questionnaire. The experimenter then explained the purpose of the experiment as "an attempt to determine if people can make valid judgements of another's personality and attitudes on the basis of very limited information." The subjects were led to believe that a variety of personal materials written by the same undergraduate student were distributed among them. They were told, "Some of you have an excerpt from the person's autobiography, which was originally written to accompany his college application. Others have in your pamphlet, a short essay prepared for a creative writing course. The essay deals with conflicting values in contemporary society.… The remainder of you have an answer from a political science hour exam." The subjects were then told to glance at the material to identify their condition. They were led to believe that the conditions would be compared to see which kind of written material produced the most valid impression, as measured by "a lot of additional information that you do not know about." The experimenter went on to state that other target persons would be evaluated by other subjects.

Actually, each subject was in the "political science exam" condition. His task was to read the examination answer and attempt to judge the true attitude of the "target person" toward the topic. The experimenter concluded his orienting overview with some brief remarks identifying the author of the materials as a student at the University of North Carolina, a resident of the state, and the son of an automobile salesman. The mimeographed material began with a reproduction of the exam question. This instructed the target person in one of three ways: (a) "Based on the past week's discussion and lectures, write a short cogent *criticism* of Castro's Cuba as if you were giving an opening statement in a debate"; (b) "… short cogent *defense* of Castro's Cuba as if …"; (c) "… short cogent essay either defending *or* criticizing Castro's Cuba as if …" This constituted the *choice* manipulation, with subjects in conditions where the target person received either (a) or (b) instructions considered as "no choice" subjects.

The essay that followed was approximately 200 words. It was either pro-or anti-Castro, and in the no choice condition, the direction of the essay was always that called for by the examination question. Although the essay was typed, there **[4]** were occasional spelling errors, false starts, and cross-outs. The experimenter explained that this would provide information about the "style and approach" of the target person. The essay itself was neither polished nor crude: it had a C+ quality. Embodying a few reasonable and familiar arguments. For example:

> *Pro-Castro essay*
> "… the people of Cuba now have a share in the government and are demonstrating their ~~feeling by their actions~~ approval by their tremendous response to the trials of building a new society from the wreckage left by the exploiters of foreign industry."
>
> *Anti-Castro essay*
> "Castro can and does attempt to take over our neighbors and convert them to communist sattelites by using methods of infiltration sabotage and subversion. "

RESPONSE MEASURES The essay was followed in the booklet by (a) a 12-item semantic differential scale for rating various personal qualities of the target person; (b) a 10-item Likert-type scale for the subject to use in estimating the target person's true attitude toward Castro: and (c) a second copy of the same scale for the subject to record his own attitude.

Results

The subjects' own attitudes toward Castro were roughly comparable (not significantly different) from condition to condition. Not surprisingly the scores clustered at the anti-Castro end of the scale, with very few scores beyond the midpoint in the pro-Castro direction.

The main response measure of interest is the prediction by the subject of the target person's true attitude. This measure was taken in the form of scale ratings on ten items concerning Castro and Cuba. Five were stated in a pro-Castro direction (e.g., "Cuba has as much right as any other country to choose her own form of government free from outside interference by the United States"), five in an anti-Castro direction (e.g. "The communist government of Cuba is one which cannot be tolerated by the U. S. and must at all costs be destroyed"). Subjects indicated degree of predicted agreement or disagreement with each statement on a seven-point scale. The maximum score (pro-Castro) was thus 70; the minimum score (anti-Castro) was 10. Since the pro-Castro items were **[5]** more indirect and permissive toward differing viewpoints than the anti-Castro items, the scale has no true neutral point.

Table 8.1 presents the means and standard deviations of the subjects' prediction ratings. A number of things are clear by inspection. The direction of the speech was of great importance in guiding the prediction ratings. This was especially true in the choice conditions, as one would expect, but it was also true in the no choice conditions to a highly significant extent ($t = 5.32$, $df = 10.76$, $p < .001$). It is also clear that within each speech condition, correspondence between speech direction and attributed attitude was greater when the speaker had choice than when the essay direction was assigned ($p < .01$ in both cases). An equally obvious fact is that the variances are heterogeneous, that of the No Choice-Pro condition being almost 10 times as large as the next largest variance. Because of this heterogeneity, all the statistical comparisons mentioned above were evaluated

Table 2.1 Means[a] and Variances for Attributed Attitude Scores

		Speech direction		p_{diff}
		Pro-Castro	Anti-Castro	
Choice	N	13	13	
	$\overline{X}$	59.62	17.38	< .001
	s^2	13.59	8.92	
No choice	N	10	15	
	$\overline{X}$	44.10	22.87	< .001[b]
	s^2	147.65	17.55	
p_{diff}		< .01[b]	< .01	

[a]Possible range from 10 (extreme anti) to 70 (extreme pro). The average subject's "own score" was 32.23, $s^2 = 35.54$.
[b]Degrees of freedom, and therefore probability values, adjusted for unequal population variances.

with the reduced degrees of freedom called for when t tests are performed under an assumption of unequal population variances (cf. Walker and Lev, 1953, pp. 157–158).

The inflated variance in the No Choice-Pro condition is of interest in its own right, for it is precisely in this cell that the largest variance might be expected. From the subjects' perspective, this should be the condition of greatest ambiguity: the behavior direction is at variance with population expectations, but the target person was told to behave that way. What does he really believe? Apparently some subjects put more weight on the behavior direction than the context, others discounted the behavior almost entirely because of the context.

The main hypothesis was that the difference between Choice and No [6] Choice means would be greater for subjects hearing the pro-Castro speech than for those hearing the anti-Castro speech. While the mean differences in the pro-Castro condition were larger, both Choice-No Choice comparisons were significant (as noted above), and the predicted difference between differences did not approach significance. The hypothesis was not confirmed.

Returning to the inflated variance in the No Choice-Pro condition, one might wonder whether the subjects' own attitudes toward Castro affected their predictions of the target person's true attitudes. There is some slight evidence that this was so. The correlation between own and imputed attitude was +.50 in the No Choice-Pro condition; in the other conditions the comparable correlations ranged from –.12 to +.05. Because of the small N's involved, none of these correlations differ significantly from zero.

The semantic differential ratings revealed little information of interest. There were twelve 7-point scales involving such antonyms as bad-good, worthless-valuable, weak-strong. Scores were totaled for each subject to provide a measure of favorability of trait attribution. There was a significant tendency ($p < .05$) for subjects in the No Choice conditions to feel more positively toward the target person than those in the Choice conditions. This may be understood as a sympathy reaction to a student forced to take a particular side on a touchy issue in writing an examination essay.

Perhaps the most striking result of the first experiment was the tendency to attribute correspondence between behavior and private attitude even when the direction of the essay was assigned. If the subjects fully understood the conditions under which the essay was written, their tendency to be affected by the essay content in attributing an attitude to the target person would seem to reflect incomplete or distorted reasoning in the No Choice conditions. Perhaps some of the subjects were inattentive and did not clearly understand the context of choice or no choice in which the exam essay was written. Perhaps some felt that the assignment to write an exam essay on Cuba was unlikely and were skeptical of the cover story. In order to check on these possibilities, a second experiment was conducted.

The main hypothesis of the first experiment was not confirmed at least in part because the choice variation affected attitude attribution more than was expected in the anti-Castro essay conditions. In spite of the fact that subjects in the four conditions had comparable "own" attitudes, as measured by a simple one-way analysis of variance, those in the Choice-Anti condition did have the most pro-Castro attitudes. The mean "own score" in that condition was greater by t test than the means in each of [7] the other three conditions. The effects of this fortuitous event cannot be estimated, but its occurrence provides another reason for replicating the first experiment before rejecting the main experimental hypothesis.

EXPERIMENT II

Method

The second experiment included a modified replication of the four basic conditions of the first experiment plus eight additional conditions. Before describing the new conditions, the procedural modifications of the basic replication will be described.

CHANGES IN BASIC PROCEDURE In order not to depart too radically from the conditions of the first experiment the issue of Castro's Cuba was retained along with the notion of free choice versus assignment by an authority. The differences were:

1. *Context of behavior.* The essay was presented as the first draft of an opening statement in a college debate, with appropriate specifications to make this cover story plausible. We assumed that the subjects would realize that debaters often try to defend positions in which they do not believe. The topic of the debate was written on the blackboard in all cases as, "Resolved that Castro's Cuba is a legitimate member of the family of nations and that the United States should not interfere with the sovereign rights of another country." The choice-no choice manipulation was delivered orally: the debater had either been directed by the team advisor to argue a specified side of the topic or was given his choice of sides.

2. *Behavior itself.* The "essays" were changed very little in content, though they were distributed as Xerox copies of the handwritten original rather than in mimeograph form.
3. *Judgment task.* Subjects were again told that the experimenter was interested in their ability to judge beliefs and personality on the basis of limited information. However, no mention was made of other subjects working from different materials on the same target person.
4. *Respond measures.* The scale for measuring imputed and own attitudes toward Castro was identical. The semantic differential items were modified to increase their relevance. Such items as poor–rich, sane–insane, and dirty-clean were eliminated in favor of such items as foolish–wise, trite–original, and disorganized–organized. A final questionnaire was also included to check on the experimental manipulations.

ADDED CONDITIONS The results of the first experiment raised a number of questions concerning the choice manipulation and how it was perceived by the subjects. In the added conditions, an attempt was made to increase the salience of the choice manipulation by requiring the subject himself to write a pro- or anti-Castro essay before reading the target person's. In condition 5 (the first four replicated the basic design, as noted above), subjects were instructed to write a pro-Castro debate opening speech and then were exposed to a No Choice-Anti target person; in condition 6, subjects were instructed to write an anti-Castro speech and were then exposed to a No Choice-Anti target person; and in condition 7 subjects were instructed to write a pro-Castro speech and were then exposed to a No Choice-Pro target person. These additions [8] represented a compromise in design, since the major purpose was to make the subjects in the No Choice conditions aware of how it feels to be assigned a particular side of the debate, and the remaining combinations of subject and target person instructions were not expected to be equally informative.

Five additional conditions were added in which, regardless of what the target person was instructed to do, the resulting speech was ambivalent. It combined both pro- and anti-Castro arguments in a balanced presentation. Pre-instructions to the subject and to the target person were varied to generate these five conditions. The full design of Experiment II is presented in Table 8.2, along with the means and *N*'s for each of the twelve conditions. The ambivalent speech conditions were included to explore the attribution of attitude when behavior is out of line with role prescriptions. Presumably someone who is instructed to write a pro-Castro debate opener, but in fact writes an ambivalent statement, should be seen as strongly anti-Castro. The obverse should also be true: an ambivalent statement following anti-Castro instructions should lead to predictions of pro-Castro attitude.

ADMINISTRATION OF EXPERIMENT A total of 97 subjects (male and female volunteers from the introductory psychology course) were run in 11 experimental sessions during a 1-week period. The number of subjects signing up for a particular session could not be entirely predetermined, and two sessions were sometimes required to fill one condition. Otherwise two conditions, which differed only in the direction of the debate statement being evaluated, were run in the same session.

Results

The subjects' own attitudes were again predominantly anti-Castro, and this time the mean "own scores" in each condition were almost identical. There is no question that the subjects were attentive to the choice manipulation. When asked how much choice the target person perceived he had (on a 9-point scale) there was very little overlap between the Choice and the No Choice distributions ($t = 8.09, p < .001$). Whether or not the subject himself was instructed to write an essay (in the choice-salience conditions) did not affect the attribution of choice perceived by target person.

Turning to the major dependent variable, attribution of attitude toward Castro, the mean attribution scores for all 12 conditions are presented in Table 8.2. Comparing conditions 5 and 6 with condition 1, and condition 7 with condition 2, it is clear that there were no systematic effects on the choice-salience manipulation. Since this was the case, all No Choice-Anti conditions were combined, and all No Choice-Pro conditions were combined, to produce the data presented in Table 8.3. These data may be compared

Table 8.2 Design of Experiment II

	Instructions to Subject	Instructions to Target Person	Target Person's Performance	$\bar{X}$	N
A. Basic conditions					
1. NCA	—	NCA	Anti	21.78	9
2. NCP	—	NCP	Pro	38.57	7
3. CA	—	C	Anti	22.89	9
4. CP	—	C	Pro	57.67	9
B. Salience-of-choice conditions					
5. Pro-NCA	Pro	NCA	Anti	25.89	9
6. Anti-NCA	Anti	NCA	Anti	23.56	9
7. Pro-NCP	Pro	NCP	Pro	43.75	8
C. Salience-ambivalent conditions					
8. Pro-NCA-a	Pro	NCA	Amb	42.00	7
9. Anti-NCA-a	Anti	NCA	Amb	39.33	9
10. Pro-NCP-a	Pro	NCP	Amb	33.00	7
11. Pro-C-a	Pro	C	Amb	40.00	7
12. C-C-a	C	C	Amb	42.86	7
				Total N	97

Note: C stands for free choice, NC for assignment by the debate captain, A for anti-Castro speech, P for pro-Castro speech, and a for ambivalent speech.

directly with those presented in Table 8.1. (The attribution data for the ambiguous speech conditions will be deferred for later consideration.)

Once again there were striking effects for direction of speech. These effects were significantly greater when the target person was given a [9] choice, but the pro–anti difference was highly significant even when the debate side was assigned. Once again the variances were heterogeneous, and since the greatest variability recurred in the No Choice-Pro condition this replicated the pattern of variances in Experiment I. The mean values seem to provide strong support for the main hypothesis that degree of [10] choice makes a greater difference when the behavior has a low prior probability. An interaction t test, adjusting the degrees of freedom to compensate for heterogeneity of variance, is significant ($t = 3.37$, $df = 36.1$, $p < .01$). This test compares the means in the following way: (57.67–41.33) > (23.74–22.89), cf. Table 8.3, and thus appropriately ignores the direction of the differences in each column. Otherwise the interaction test would merely show that the means are further apart in the first row than in the second row, or that the differences between speeches is greater when choice is allowed. As we have already noted above, this form of the interaction is also significant, linking degree of correspondence of inference directly to degree of choice.

EFFECTS OF MAKING AN AMBIVALENT SPEECH When a target person is directed to make an anti-Castro presentation and equivocates in his argumentation, he should be seen as relatively pro-Castro. The same ambivalent speech under pro-Castro directions should result in the attribution of an anti-Castro attitude. The results of conditions 8, 9, and 10 bear out this hypothesis (see Table 8.2). When conditions 8 and 9 are combined (since both require the target person to give an anti-Castro

Table 8.3 Experiment II: Means[a] and Variables for Attributed Attitude Scores

		Speech direction		
		Pro-Castro	Anti-Castro	p_{diff}
Choice	N	9	9	
	$\overline{X}$	57.67	22.89	< .001
	s^2	21.00	34.86	
No choice	N	15	27	
	$\overline{X}$	41.33	23.74	< .001[b]
	s^2	134.81	50.12	
p_{diff}		< .001[b]	n.s.	

[a]Possible range from 10 (extreme anti) to 70 (extreme pro). The average subject's "own score" was 31.67, $s^2 = 82.25$.
[b]Degrees of freedom, and therefore probability values, adjusted for unequal population variances.

speech) and contrasted with condition 10, the difference is significant ($t = 2.07$, $df = 21$, $p < .05$). The target person who gave an ambivalent speech under free choice conditions was seen to be rather in favor of Castro, as one would expect. In spite of the differences noted, the effects on attitude attribution of having the target person violate instructions are far from overwhelming. The target person who gave an ambivalent speech under anti-Castro instructions was seen as no more in favor of Castro than the one who gave a pro-Castro speech under pro-Castro instructions. The target person who responded ambivalently under pro-Castro instructions was seen as much more in favor of Castro than the target person who slavishly followed anti-Castro directions. This seems to be further evidence that the average subject in these experiments attaches insufficient weight to the constraining force of authoritative directions to behave in a certain way.

OWN AND ATTRIBUTED ATTITUDE Table 8.4 presents the pattern of correlations between the subjects' own attitudes toward Castro and the attitudes imputed to the target person. There are several points of interest in the table, though conclusions drawn from correlations with such small N's are obviously risky. First of all, there is a dramatic replication of the correlation between own attitude and imputed attitude in the No Choice-Pro condition. Apparently we may venture the conclusion that when a subject attempts to predict attitude in a situation with conflicting cues (where the behavior tells him one thing and the context tells him another), he tends to fall back on his own attitudes as a guide for his estimate. Note, however, that this was only true in the no-salience [11] condition. When the prediction task was preceded by the task of writing a pro-Castro speech under directions, the correlation vanishes. Having to write a speech against one's own position seems to reduce the significance of that position when it

Table 8.4 Experiment II: Relationship between Own Attitude toward Castro and Imputed Attitude (Product Moment Correlations)

		Pro-Castro	Anti-Castro	Ambivalent	
Choice	N	9	9	14	
	r	−.03	.09	−.61*	
				Instructions	
No choice– No Salience	N	7	9		
	r	.93**	.37	Pro	Anti
No choice– Salience	N	8	18	7	16
	r	−.51	.33	.64	−.43*

*$p < .05$.
**$p < .01$.

comes to imputing the attitude of a target person operating under the same prescription. Perhaps the subjects in the No Choice-Salience condition were alerted to concentrate more on the speech itself, being sensitive to any nuances or signs of sincerity in the arguments presented.

The other intriguing feature of the correlational data is the tendency for own position to be *negatively* related to imputed position when an ambiguous speech was given, unless the instructions were to give a pro-Castro speech. In order to account for this, we present the following *post hoc* speculation. The target person in the Pro-Ambivalent condition does not follow instructions slavishly, and is therefore seen as quite anti-Castro on the average. Perhaps this is what the anti-Castro subject thinks he might do in the same circumstances, thus causing him to assimilate the target person's attitude to his own. The target person who writes an ambivalent speech when told to write an anti-Castro speech, or told to choose one side or the other, reveals himself as moderately pro-Castro. Here there seems to be a contrast effect: the more anti-Castro the subject, the more he judges the speech (and therefore the debater) to be pro-Castro. These speculations are based on rather complex assumptions, but the reasoning is compatible with the judgmental theory of Sherif and Hovland (1961) further elaborated by Berkowitz (1960). This theory proposes that opinion positions close to one's own will be judged as closer than they are; the extremity of more distant positions will be exaggerated. The semantic differential results were essentially negative. The tendency to respond more favorably to the No Choice target person noted in the first experiment did not replicate. [12]

The second experiment established the main hypothesis much more firmly than the first, and did so under better controlled, and probably more involving, conditions. The choice variable does seem to make a greater difference in attributing correspondence when a noncustomary act is being assessed than when the act is customary or highly normative. Once again, the direction of the act had a striking effect even when the actor had no choice. What are the determinants of this tendency to overemphasize the content of behavior when attributing attitude? Two major possibilities suggest themselves. First, the subjects may perceive that the target person has an important degree of choice even in the No Choice condition. Perhaps the examination question (described in the first experiment) was one of several alternative possibilities. In the second experiment, the debater could have refused the assignment, quit the debating team, or maneuvered for another issue, if he really found it distasteful to argue on behalf of Castro. On the other hand, students are familiar with settings, like the debate context, where a person has good and compelling reasons to argue against his own private attitude. Also, the average subject in the No Choice-Pro condition affirmed on the postexperimental questionnaire that the target person had very little choice (average of 2.08 on a scale where 7.00 represents complete freedom).

A more likely possibility is that the speech content conveys information about the talent of the speaker, his familiarity with the issues involved, and his experience at concocting, say, pro-Castro arguments. Where does the material come from that goes into the speech? In the first experiment, presumably, developments in Cuba had been discussed in class along with arguments attacking and defending the regime. In the second experiment, the debater presumably had access to various resource materials in preparing his speech. Nevertheless, in neither case was it crystal clear that the preparation of arguments was merely a matter of putting together information assembled by others.

Perhaps the pro-Castro statement was so constructed that it was hard for the subjects to believe that the arguments were not spontaneous, and at least partly believed by the target person.

The third experiment was designed with a number of purposes in mind. First, it was necessary to show that the results were not a peculiar function of the particular speeches used or of the Cuban issue. In order to test the generality of the findings, an entirely different attitudinal area was tapped. Second, it was important to make more explicit the fact that stock arguments prepared by others were available for composing the speech. Finally, an attempt was made to vary the reference group of the target person so as to manipulate directly the probability that he would express [13] opinions in a certain direction. To accomplish these objectives, subjects were exposed to tape-recorded speeches for or against segregation, delivered by a Northerner or a Southerner, who did or did not have prior choice. The design was thus a $2 \times 2 \times 2$ factorial with eight experimental conditions.

EXPERIMENT III

Method

ADMINISTRATION OF EXPERIMENT The subjects were 125 male volunteers drawn from the same introductory psychology course and recruited by the same incentive conditions (fulfilling a course requirement for experimental participation) as in the previous two experiments. Four subjects were dropped from the analysis, three for suspecting the cover story and one for elementary failure to follow instructions. Once again, the number of subjects signing up for a particular session could not be entirely predetermined. Each condition included data from at least two, but no more than three, experimental sessions. There were no significant between-session effects within conditions.

RATIONALE The purpose of the experiment, the subjects were told, was to "determine the predictability of a target person's attitudes on various issues given information about his attitudes on other issues." In order to explain the origin of the tape recordings to be played, the experimenter's introduction included a rather complex cover story describing the recruitment of ten target persons: An advertisement had been placed in the student newspaper at the University of North Carolina asking for volunteer upperclassmen to participate as research subjects. Accepted volunteers were promised $2.50 for "about a half-hour's work." The advertisement invited interested participants to leave their name and phone number at a particular box number. Of those that responded, the cover story continued, ten were selected as target persons because data were available (from a large-scale survey of undergraduate opinion conducted by the sociology department) on their attitudes toward segregation and other issues. Appointments were arranged to meet with each of these persons in their dormitory rooms. After the experimenter arrived there, the target person was asked to study a list of arguments for and against segregation, to construct a speech based on these arguments, and to deliver the speech in a convincing manner into a portable tape recorder. As in the previous two experiments, the target person was either given his choice of constructing a pro- or anti-segregation speech or he was instructed to take a particular side. Each target, person was reassured that he would receive $2.50 for approximately a half-hour's work.

The latter portions of this cover story were conveyed on the tape recording itself, in the form of instructions to the particular target person. The arguments he was asked to study were allegedly taken from the Letter-to-the-Editor section of a daily newspaper. In all cases, the target person asked whether he was supposed to use the arguments provided for him and was told "you can use any arguments you wish from the list but you don't have to use the list at all if you don't want to." The experimenter emphasized that he did not necessarily endorse any of the arguments on the list. **[14]**

The entire tape recording, including the speech itself, was a carefully scripted playlet in which the target person presented himself as a junior political science major from either Sandersville, Georgia, or from New Brunswick, New Jersey. The target person's accent was accordingly very southern or very northeastern.[1] At the end of the speech, which either favored or opposed segregation, the experimenter (on the tape) asked the target person to sign a voucher for the $2.50, explained that the tapes would be used as stimulus materials in an attitude perception project at Duke, and secured his permission to use the recording for this purpose without ever, of course, revealing his identity.

The Speeches The scripted speeches were as comparable as possible except for their direction and conclusion. They were constructed so that the same "facts" were discussed from different perspectives. For example:

Pro-segregation
It is a standard argument of the "do-gooders" and others that the reason for the Negro's weaknesses is due not to innate factors but rather to environmental conditions.... This argument is completely fallacious.

Negroes while contributing far less than their share to the development of America, have contributed far more than their share to crime statistics and welfare lists.
Etc.

Anti-segregation
It is a standard argument of the "die-hard" segregationists that Negroes are innately inferior to whites and that environmental factors are of little account. Such an argument is completely fallacious....

The fact that a high percentage of Negroes are involved in major crimes and on welfare case lists is but further evidence of the awful effects of segregation and deprivation.
Etc.

Each speech was approximately 375 words in length.

Attitude Prediction Measure A 15-item Likert scale was constructed to measure the subject's own attitude toward segregation and his attribution of attitude to the target person. This scale contained three 5-item subsets in scattered order. Subset A consisted of statements taken directly from the speeches (e.g., "The Negro is innately inferior to the white"). Subset B consisted of statements directly referring to the segregation issue, but not specifically mentioned in the speeches (e.g., "Integration threatens one of the basic principles of democracy, the right of each citizen to choose his own associates").

---

[1]We are indebted to Thomas Hammock and Lloyd Stires for their effective portrayals of the target persons.

Subset C consisted of statements making no explicit reference to the segregation issue but reflecting a more pervasive conservatism—a liberalism likely to be highly correlated with attitude toward segregation (e.g., "A union should be free to organize workers whether or not the management wants it to," and "The federal government has long overstepped its legal authority as defined by the Constitution and has consistently infringed on constitutionally guaranteed states' rights").

The attitude scale was constructed in this manner to determine whether the independent variables of choice and speech direction would affect attribution in areas related to, but not specifically mentioned in, the speech. Do the subjects conceive of an underlying attitude structure when predicting the target person's behavior, or do their attributions merely reflect the explicit content of the speech? While the choice of items was *a priori*, we were successful in selecting items for [15] subsets B and C that the average subject, used in the same manner as the A items. For all subjects combined, the attribution of segregationist attitude on A correlated with attribution in the same direction on B, $r = .90$, $df = 120$; A correlated with C, $r = .85$; B with C, $r = .81$ (all p values $<.001$).

An additional reason for constructing the scale in three parts was the possibility of testing a rather subtle hypothesis concerning behavioral departures from reference group norms. How do subjects perceive a Southerner who chooses to construct an integrationist speech, or a Northerner who chooses to act like a segregationist. Perhaps a more coherent attitude structure is assigned to such a "maverick" because his position differs from the expectations of his community of origin and does not simply reflect reference group norms. The Northerner who espouses the cause of integration may be judged to be a "knee-jerk liberal" who passively reflects reference group norms without fighting through to a coherent attitudinal integration. The same kind of conclusion ("knee-jerk racist"?) may also be applied to the Southern segregationist. These considerations suggest the following hypothesis: (1) The "maverick" who chooses to differ with the assumed position of his community reference group will be perceived to have a more correspondent attitude than one who chooses to stand with his reference group; thus the Southern integrationist will be seen as more pro-integration than the Northern integrationist and the Northern segregationist will be seen as more in favor of segregation than his Southern counterpart. (2) There will be a higher correlation among the subsets of the attitude scale for "mavericks" than for "knee-jerk liberals" or "knee-jerk racists." In other words, if the "maverick" is seen as anti-segregation, he will also be seen as basically liberal; if he is seen as pro-segregation, he will also be seen as basically conservative.

Postexperimental Questionnaire   After the subject recorded his attitude predictions ("please try to predict how the target person would honestly respond to the following statements"), he was asked to indicate his own attitude on the same 15-item scale. Finally, each subject answered seven questions in the form of 9-point scales, each designed to check on some aspect of the subjects perceptions of the experiment.

Results

Once again, the subjects were very attentive to the choice manipulation. When asked how much choice the target person perceived he had (on a 9-point scale), there was very little overlap between the Choice and the No Choice distributions ($t = 10.63$, $p < .001$).

ATTRIBUTION OF ATTITUDE TOWARD SEGREGATION As noted above, the attitude scale for measuring attribution was constructed of three subsets of items varying in degree of remoteness from the arguments specifically mentioned in the speech. As might have been expected from the high overall correlations among these subsets (see above), attribution to each subset was highly comparable within experimental conditions. This can be verified both by close inspection of Table 8.5 and by the fact that significance levels for all statistical tests are roughly the same whether they refer to subset A, B, C, or the combined total. [16] For convenience, we shall concentrate on the total attribution scores, except where interesting differences among the subsets emerge.

For the third time, there were striking effects for direction of speech. Whether the speech was made by a Southerner or a Northerner, and whether or not he had choice, all differences between the pro-segregation speech and the anti-segregation speech were highly significant. The interactive effects of choice and speech direction were again significant, but the interaction took the same form for Southern and Northern target persons. That is, the target person with a choice was seen as more pro when he made a pro speech and more anti when he made an anti speech than the target person without a choice.

For those subjects exposed to the Northern target person, the main hypothesis was that choice would affect attribution when a pro-segregation speech was made but not when an anti-segregation speech was made. The obverse was predicted for those exposed to the Southerner: choice would affect attribution when an anti-segregation speech was made but not under pro speech conditions. The Northern target person data in Table 8.5A fall into the predicted pattern on each item subset and the total. In each case, the predicted interaction, obtained by comparing the pro (no choice minus choice) difference with the anti (choice minus no choice) difference, was significant. For subset A, $(t = 2.30, p < .05)$; for B, $(t = 3.64, p < .01)$; for C, $(t = 3.90, p < .001)$; and for all items combined, $(t = 3.80, p < .001)$. Degrees of freedom were adjusted in each case to accommodate heterogeneity of variance. Clearly, at least for the Northern target person, attributions to related attitudinal issues are affected by the experimental variables to an extent that is at least as great as when issues mentioned in the speech are involved.

A glance at the data summarized in Table 8.5B indicates that the main hypothesis was definitely not confirmed in the case of the Southern target person. In each condition, the Southerner was seen as more in favor of segregation than his Northern counterpart, as one would expect. The overall Southern–Northern difference was highly significant, $(t = 4.86, p < .001)$. However, the Southern pattern of means was an attenuated version of the Northern pattern rather than its obverse. When the Southerner made a speech under No Choice conditions, the attributed attitude was less extreme whether the speech was in a pro- or anti-segregation direction. The subjects did not readily assume the Southerner was a pro-segregationist when he had no choice but to make a pro speech.

A plausible explanation of this failure of prediction is available. Perhaps the prior probability that a college student from Georgia is pro-segregation is not strikingly high, especially one who has gone "north" to enroll at the University of North Carolina. Some support for this salvaging [17] speculation may be found in the actual attitude scale scores of subjects from the South. The home states of 100 subjects could be readily ascertained

Table 8.5 Experiment III Means[a] and Variances for Attributed Attitude Scores

A. Northern target person

		Pro-segregation				Anti-segregation			
		A[b]	B	C	Total	A	B	C	Total
Choice	$\bar{X}$	10.05	13.80	13.80	37.65	31.52	29.76	28.76	90.06
	s^2	38.95	29.46	16.36	212.66	9.07	10.53	6.41	50.43
					$N = 20$				$N = 17$
No choice	$\bar{X}$	16.36	21.00	22.36	59.73	31.14	30.86	27.50	89.50
	s^2	47.14	34.54	17.32	162.82	5.28	3.41	12.68	31.65
					$N = 11$				$N = 14$

B. Southern target person

		Pro-segregation				Anti-segregation			
		A	B	C	Total	A	B	C	Total
Choice	$\bar{X}$	8.25	9.31	11.31	28.88	28.33	27.46	25.00	80.80
	s^2	11.81	12.72	18.34	75.72	34.75	26.38	23.33	191.89
					$N = 16$				$N = 15$
No choice	$\bar{X}$	13.93	17.13	16.80	47.87	25.38	25.62	22.15	73.15
	s^2	46.19	31.72	22.69	231.40	65.16	45.16	27.21	402.30
					$N = 15$				$N = 13$

[a]Possible range (subsets A, B, C) from pro-segregation 5 to anti-segregation 35. Possible range for total scores: 15 to 105.
[b]Refers to item subsets ranging from A (explicitly in speech), through B (mentions segregation), to C (segregation not explicitly mentioned).

from the Duke student directory. Fifty-seven of these were from Southern states, while 43 were from the North. The average scale score of Northern subjects ($\bar{X} = 80.42$) was significantly higher than that of the average Southerner ($\bar{X} = 70.07$; $t_{\text{diff}} = 3.49$, $p < .001$). The Southern subject was, not surprisingly, more in favor of segregation. Of greater interest for our present argument, however, is the greater variability among Southerners ($s^2 = 260.42$) than Northerners ($s^2 = 166.01$), significant at the .06 level. Thus, being a college student from a Southern town is not a very informative objective indicator of attitude toward segregation. The attribution results suggest that the subjects were aware [18] of attitudinal variability among Southern college students (from a neighboring university) and were especially responsive to the evidence that the target person had chosen his speech. The No

Choice Southerner is an ambiguous stimulus object, a conclusion that is supported by the fact that subjects were more variable in attributing attitudes to this target person than to others. It may be noted in Table 8.5 that the two largest variances (total score columns) appear in the two No Choice Southerner conditions.

OWN AND ATTRIBUTED ATTITUDE Although subjects were assigned to conditions through their own initiative in signing up for particular times, there were some rather peculiar variations among subjects exposed to Southern target person. Those in the Choice-Pro and No Choice-Anti conditions were significantly more against segregation than those in the No Choice-Pro and Choice-Anti conditions. No such pattern emerged in subjects exposed to Northern target person. However, among the latter subjects, those hearing the anti-segregation speech ended up significantly more opposed to segregation than those hearing the pro-segregation speech. Since the subjects filled out the own attitude questionnaire after hearing the speech and after making their attribution ratings (as was the case in the two preceding experiments as well), it is impossible to estimate the extent to which they may have been influenced by the speech. The pattern of "own attitude" scores is reproduced in Table 8.6, but we demur from any attempt to interpret the differences between conditions.

Table 8.6 Experiment III: Subjects' Own Attitudes toward Segregation ($\bar{X}$), and Correlations between Own and Attributed Attitude (r), by Conditions

A. Northern target person

Speech direction

	Pro-segregation			Anti-segregation		
	$\bar{X}$	r	N	$\bar{X}$	r	N
Choice	69.70	.09	20	76.70	.49*	17
No choice	64.91	.60*	11	78.36	.60*	14

B. Southern target person

Speech direction

	Pro-segregation			Anti-segregation		
	$\bar{X}$	r	N	$\bar{X}$	r	N
Choice	86.50	.06	16	71.53	.24	15
No choice	69.60	.38	15	84.15	.07	13

Note: Significant comparisons across conditions. Northern target person: Anti versus Pro, $F = 6.67$, $p < .05$; Southern target person: interaction $F = 13.78$, $p < .001$; Northern versus Southern: $F = 3.87$, $p < .10$.
*$p < .05$.

Also presented in Table 8.6 are the correlations between own and attributed attitude for each experimental condition. Each correlation is positive, suggesting a general tendency to assimilate the target person's attitude to one's own. This tendency reaches significance in only three conditions, all involving the Northern target person. In the two previous experiments, the highest correlation between own and attributed attitude occurred in the condition where No Choice was combined with Pro-Castro speech (low prior probability behavior). The present correlational results neither replicate nor disconfirm the proposition that the correlation is highest when ambiguous or conflicting information is presented. The correlation *is* high for subjects in the Northern-No Choice-Pro condition, but it is also high in two other Northern conditions. The correlations among subjects exposed to the Southern speaker are low and nonsignificant.

Perceptions of the "Maverick's" Attitude Structure   We proposed in introducing this experiment that correspondence of attribution would be especially high in the case of the "maverick" who chooses to differ with the assumed position of his community reference group. A second hypothesis, developed from the same reasoning, was that the intercorrelations among item subsets would be higher for "mavericks" than for those who choose the expected speech direction, the "knee-jerk liberals" and 'knee-jerk racists." We have already noted that there is no support for the first of these hypotheses. The Southerner who chooses to give a pro-integration speech is not seen as more in favor of integration than the Northerner who chooses pro-integration; the Northerner who chooses pro-segregation is not seen as more of a segregationist than his Southern counterpart. Perhaps the reasoning behind this hypothesis confused extremity with certitude. The pro-integration Southerner may be more confident that he is right, without being more extreme in his dedication to integration. There is no evidence in the present study that would support this alternative, however.

The second hypothesis does receive some support. Table 8.7 presents the intercorrelations between item subsets for each experimental condition. These correlations are generally positive and, as we have already noted the three overall correlations are very high. Those correlations especially involved in the second hypothesis are italicized in the table and the probabilities of the observed differences are indicated. The correlation between subsets for the "mavericks" (Southern-Choice-Anti, [20] and Northern-Choice-Pro subjects) did tend to be higher than the correlations for the remaining choice subjects in five of six comparisons. Two of these were statistically significant. While these results suggest that further research on the attribution of a coherent attitude structure to the "maverick" might be fruitful, the evidence in support of the hypothesis is only suggestive.

DISCUSSION

We have presented three experiments involving the same general design. In each case, subjects were asked to rate the true attitude of a target person from a set of his opinion statements. The content of these statements was either in the direction expected from such a target person or in the opposite direction. The target person either chose to

Table 8.7 Experiment III: Correlations between Item Subsets, Attributed Attitude Scores, by Conditions

Condition	N		A–B	B–C	A–C
NNCA	14		.00	.11	.43
SNCA	13		.74**	.76**	.93***
NNCP	11		.62*	−.41	.34
SNCP	15		.72**	.61*	.43
SCA[a]	15		.83***	.53	.43
NCA	17		.48	.21	.56*
		p_{diff}	n.s.	n.s.	n.s.
SCP	16		.23	.07	.69**
NCP[a]	20		.74***	.68***	.74***
		p_{diff}	< .05	< .05	n.s.
Total	121		.90***	.81***	.85***

[a]"Mavericks."
*$p < .05$.
**$p < .01$.
***$p < .001$.

express opinions in the direction he did, or was instructed by an authority figure to do so. Our main interest was to test the hypothesis from correspondent inference theory (Jones and Davis, 1965) that degree of choice would affect attribution more when the opinions expressed were in an unexpected direction than when their prior probability was high. Figure 8.1 summarizes the findings that bear on this hypothesis in a form that facilitates comparing the similarities and differences from experiment to experiment. Confirmation was clear in the second experiment and for the Northern target person in the third experiment. The difference between differences was in the predicted direction in Experiment I, but was not significant. In Experiment [21] III, we presented evidence to suggest that a Southern college student's attitudes toward segregation are difficult to predict if all the predictor knows is that the student was born in the South. Objectively, there is high variability among Southerners on the segregation issue and the subjects seem to be aware of this. In general, given fairly determinate expectations about the target person's most probable private attitude, the hypothesis may be considered confirmed.

A striking feature of the results in each experiment was the powerful effect on attribution of the content of opinions expressed. While the subjects do take account of choice and prior probability, as correspondent inference theory proposes, they also give substantial weight to the intrinsic, or "face value," meaning of the act itself in their attributions of attitude. This is true even when the act occurs in a No Choice context. The question is whether this tendency reflects an irrational bias that is inherent in person perception, or whether it is a function of specific, removable cues in the

160 Part Two Inferential Anomalies

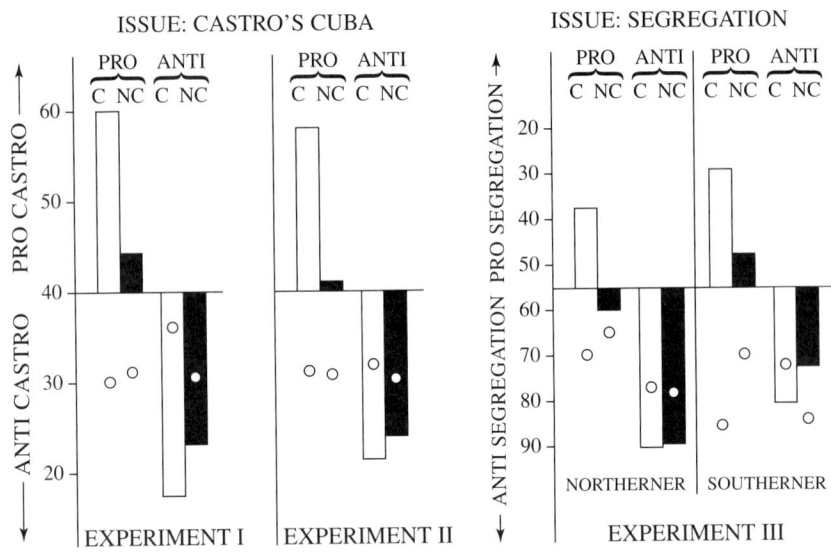

Figure 8.1 Attribution of attitude in each of three experiments. The dividing midline in each case represents the arithmetic midpoint of the possible scoring range; it bears no necessary relation to the psychological neutral point. The symbol O superimposed on each column refers to the mean "own rating" for subjects in that condition.

three procedures. Heider (1958) comments on the common tendency to assign too little significance to the determining context of action in social perception.

> It seems that behavior, in particular, has such salient properties, it tends to engulf the total field rather than be confined to its proper position as a local stimulus whose interpretation requires the additional data of a surrounding field (p. 54).

Perhaps behavior did "engulf the field" in the present experiments, but **[22]** this describes the results without really explaining them. We have already wondered (in the introduction to Experiment III) whether the amount of choice perceived in the No Choice conditions is enough to have significant effects. Obviously, the target persons did have the ultimate option to refuse their instructor in Experiment I, their debate captain in Experiment II, or the dormitory visitor in Experiment III. Nevertheless, it seems fair to assume that each subject himself would agree to express false opinions under comparable circumstances of authoritative assignment, and the subjects' postexperimental ratings of choice indicated their awareness of strong external constraints on the target person's behavior.

An important area of choice does remain, however, even in the No Choice condition. This is the choice between various ways of expressing the directed opinion. The arguments advanced in each essay or speech were not specified in detail by the constraining authority; an unknown degree of freedom to select and organize arguments remained even in the third experiment. In planning the present experiments, we assumed that this minimal ambiguity was necessary to bring out the specific interaction that was the test of our major hypothesis. If the target person had been merely handed a speech to read under very strong external constraints, his compliance would have conveyed little or no information to the subjects. Under these circumstances we would have expected no difference between No Choice-Pro and No Choice-Anti conditions. Were the constraints to extend to every detail and facet of an observed performance, the prediction that attribution is uninfluenced by performance would be a trivial one. The present experiments show that when the major decisions about the direction and form of behavior are made for the target person, his performance is still a powerful source of variation in the attribution results. Short of some extreme degree of specification, behavior does engulf the field, and it is difficult for the perceiver to assign appropriate weights to the situational context.

We are led to conclude that correspondence in attributing underlying attitudes to account for expressed opinions is high when the opinions are unexpected and expressed in a context of free choice. However, the content and direction of the opinions exert a clear inference on attribution, even when choice is drastically reduced. In a context that permits the target person some very minimal degree of spontaneity, the perceiver seems to view his performance as more informative than a rational analysis of act and context would suggest. This bias may have important implications for interpersonal relations, and we might propose a hypothesis for further research that distortion, in the form of assigning too much significance to performance, increases as the objective constraints on a target person's actions increase. [23]

REFERENCES

Bem, D. J. (1965). An experimental analysis of self-persuasion. *Journal of Experimental Social Psychology,* 1, 199–218.
Berkowitz, L. (1960). The judgmental process in personality functioning. *Psychological Review,* 67, 130–142.
Berlyne, D. E. (1965). *Structure and direction in thinking.* New York: Wiley.
Heider. F. (1944). Social perception and phenomenal causality. *Psychological Review,* 51, 358–374.
Heider, F. (1958). *The psychology of interpersonal relations.* New York: Wiley.
Jones, E. E., and Davis, K. E. (1965). From acts to dispositions. In L. Berkowitz (Ed.), *Advances in experimental social psychology* (pp. 219–266). New York: Academic Press.
Jones. E. E., Davis, K. E., and Gergen. K. J. (1961). Role playing variations and their informational value for person perception. *Journal of Abnormal and Social Psychology* 63, 302–310.
Sherif, M., and Hovland. C. I. (1961). *Social judgment: Assimilation and contrast effects in communication and attitude change.* New Haven: Yale University Press.
Steiner. I. D., and Field, W. L. (1960). Role assignment and interpersonal influence. *Journal of Abnormal and Social Psychology,* 61, 239–246.
Thibaut. J. W., and Riecken, H. W. (1955). Some determinants and consequence of the perception of social causality. *Journal of Personality,* 24, 113–133.
Walker, H. M., and Lev, J. (1953). *Statistical inference.* New York: Henry Holt. [24]

CORRESPONDENCE BIAS

Chapter 9

The Rocky Road from Acts to Dispositions

Edward E. Jones
Princeton University

> ABSTRACT: This article examines the attributional error of overestimating dispositions as a cause of behavior, with reference to the attitude attribution paradigm. Earlier experiments were open to criticism on artifactual grounds, but the overattribution-to-persons tendency has proved to be a remarkably robust and easily replicated phenomenon. It can be undermined or overcome when the perceived constraints on behavior are extreme or when instructions specifically set the subject to consider the importance of situational factors. The functional significance of the attributional error is not clear, though it probably stems from a perceptually generated hypothesis that is insufficiently adjusted for contextual constraint.

When I was first asked to submit a title for this address, I too readily slipped into a play on the title of my earlier essay with Keith Davis (Jones & Davis, 1965) and came up with the ambiguous "rocky road" metaphor. The road to our understanding of attributional vicissitudes is indeed rocky, but when we think in terms of the attributor, the cognitive road from acts to dispositions is perhaps not as rocky as it should be. That is the main thrust of the story I have to tell.

Reprinted with permission of the American Psychological Association ©1979 from *American Psychologist*, 34, 107–117. References have been updated by the editor.

Chapter 9   The Rocky Road from Acts to Dispositions   163

Getting from acts to dispositions, or more generally, making inferences from behavior about personality, is a ubiquitous activity of paramount significance for all of us. Understanding how people make inferences about others' stable characteristics from observations of their behavior in various contexts is also one of the most fundamental problems in social and clinical psychology. Social psychologists are perhaps especially interested in the role of context in sharpening or muting the dispositional significance of behavior. One of Heider's (1944) most celebrated insights was that although "changes in the environment are almost always caused by acts of persons in combination with other factors, the tendency exists to ascribe the changes entirely to persons" (p. 361). This was later summarized by the caption "behavior engulfs the field" (Heider, 1958), by which I presume he meant to emphasize the salience of observed action and the actor as well. Exploring the fundamental tendency to underestimate the role of context in person perception has shaped much of the research in attribution in the past 15 years. By 1977, enough consistent evidence had accumulated for Lee Ross to refer to the overestimation of personal or dispositional factors as "the fundamental attribution error" (p. 184).

I would like to concentrate here on the fruits of a particular experimental paradigm, that of attitude attribution, to examine the light it sheds on the determinants of the fundamental attribution error. As applied to the attribution of attitudes, the notion that behavior engulfs the field means, of course, that expressed opinions are taken at face value much more than they should be. There are multiple reasons for endorsing a particular stand, and only some of these are correlated with possession of an attitude that truly corresponds to the stand endorsed. We sometimes say things for strategic effect, in the interest of some objective that is temporarily more important than faithful self-expression. We may endorse popular positions to avoid public disagreement. We may take stands in the interests of consistency with role constraints. To the extent that people, as observers, underestimate the role of contextual factors, there is error not only in interpersonal understanding, but potentially in the appraisal of those features of reality mediated by social comparison. We supposedly make dispositional attributions to facilitate our control over the social environment and to enhance predictability. But the existence of a fundamental attribution error suggests that this subjective feeling of control is purchased at the high cost of premature closure both about the [107]* actors we observe and about the reality that they mediate.

When we broadly consider the range of conceivable acts and conceivable dispositions, the fundamental attribution error may create havoc in the courts, the schoolroom, and the family, to say nothing of the special arenas of counseling and diagnosis. Greater concessions to situational pressure and greater ambiguity tolerance may be the ultimate beneficiaries of the sustained analysis of the fundamental attribution error and its determinants. Here, however, I concentrate on the determinants themselves and restrict myself largely to the attitude realm.

The initial attitude attribution study (Jones & Harris, 1967) was an attempt to verify correspondent inference theory (Jones & Davis, 1965). This theory states that behavior

---

*Bracketed bold numbers refer to original page numbers. Page numbers indicate where the original page ended.

will be taken at face value when it does not generate multiple highly expected effects. Correspondent inferences are those that assume underlying dispositions are directly conveyed in behavior—the heart is on the sleeve. A clear implication of the theory is that behavior under free-choice conditions is more diagnostic than behavior under constraint. Another implication is that choices should play a greater role when action is unexpected—when it departs from the norm. Jones and Harris described three studies in which subjects, hereafter called observers, were presented with written or spoken opinion statements allegedly made by an unknown target person under free-choice versus no-choice conditions.

In the studies that exemplify the attitude attribution paradigm, choice has been restricted in a variety of ways. In the so-called no-choice condition, observers have been told variously that the target person was asked by his political science professor to defend a particular position in an exam answer, that the person was told by the debating team advisor to prepare a position statement, or that the person was instructed to prepare a persuasive argument on a designated side of a controversy by an experimenter employing him for high fees to construct useful experimental materials. In all cases, an attempt has been made to construct plausible and legitimate no-choice contexts in which 100% compliance would normally be expected. The task of the observers is to infer the true, private, underlying attitude of the target person who constructed the essay or speech. It is typically pointed out that the target person had the opportunity to examine relevant arguments on both sides of the controversial issue before preparing his statement. In the initial Jones and Harris studies, the degree of choice and the prior probability of the stand taken were both shown to be influential in the attribution of attitude, and thus the major predictions were confirmed. This may be seen in Figure 9.1, which presents results from the second experiment conducted by Jones and Harris (1967).

Although the early attitude attribution research tended to confirm correspondent inference theory, Figure 9.1 also shows an interesting result not predicted by the theory, but anticipated by Heider: Behavior in the no-choice conditions still has highly reliable effects. This finding has been replicated across several different issues and choice contexts (Jones & Harris, 1967; Jones, Worchel, Goethals, & Grumet, 1971; Miller, 1974, 1976; Snyder & Jones, 1974). Figures 9.2 and 9.3 show the replicabiliІу of this effect.

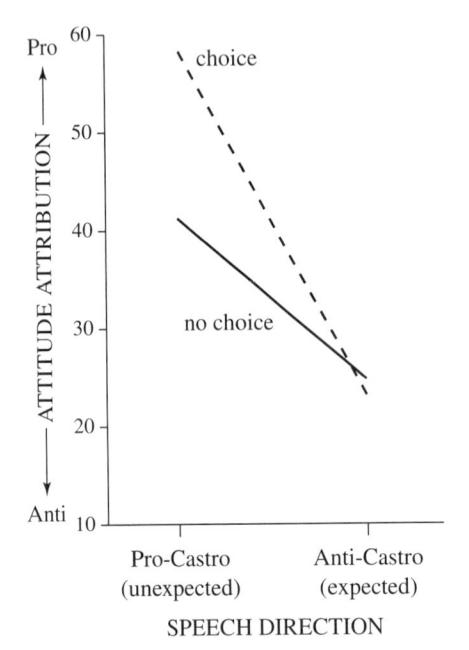

Figure 9.1 Attitude attributed to a target person who prepared a debate draft favoring or attacking Fidel Castro under choice or no-choice instructions from the debating team advisor. (Data from Jones & Harris, 1967.)

Figure 9.2 shows the same data pattern as Figure 9.1 does, but with a different issue—attitudes toward [108] segregation. The target person was a Northern male college student, and in 1966 we assumed observers would expect him to be against segregation. The results show the effects predicted from correspondent inference theory—the choice line is steeper, and there is greater spread when the speech is in the unexpected direction. When we look at the no-choice line alone, the fundamental attribution error is clear.

Figure 9.3 shows the same pattern within yet another attitude context, the legalization of marijuana, only here the observers' expectancy was specifically manipulated by prior information about the target person's related attitudes. The right panel of the figure is the obverse of the left. Both show the expected effects of choice, expectancy, and the fundamental attribution error.

Because these findings fit our intuitions as well as the notion of behavior engulfing the field they were taken seriously as a springboard for Jones and Nisbett's (1972) proposition that, relative to actors explaining their own behavior, observers of that behavior underestimate the importance of contextual or situational factors.

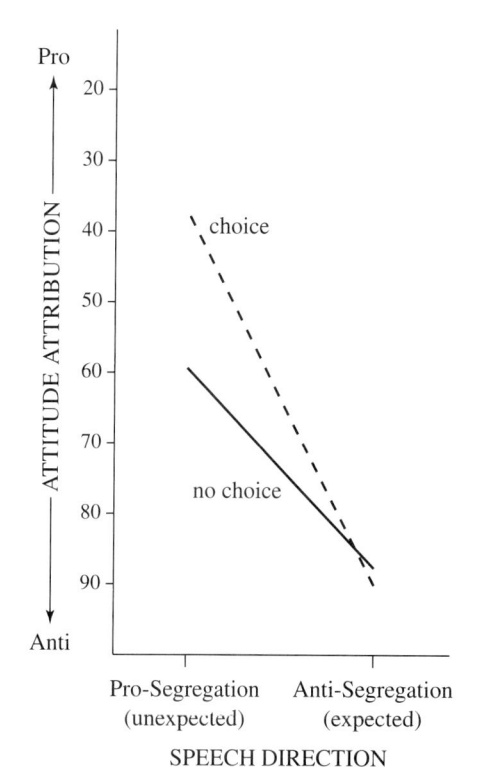

Figure 9.2 Attitude attributed to a target person, described as a Northern college student, making a speech favoring or opposing segregation under choice or no-choice instructions. (Data from Jones & Harris, 1967.)

But a number of alternative explanations soon asserted themselves, and many of these raised the possibility of artifacts inherent in the peculiar conditions of this kind of experiment. A vulnerable point in these initial experiments was the fact that the behavior sample was constructed by the investigators for use in the experiments. Though we tried to avoid esoteric information and overly compelling rhetoric in the stimulus materials used and though observers were told that the target person was provided with sample arguments, it was possible that we had inadvertently impressed observers with the target person's expertise—an expertise that provided a clue concerning the target person's true attitude. In addition, Kelley (1972) speculated that in this series of studies, "context factors have not been manipulated as strongly or clearly as has the behavior itself" (p. 18). Kelley went on to suggest that there may have been a fair amount of choice perceived in the no-choice condition.

Snyder and I (1974) sought to answer the implied criticisms of perceived expertise and perceived freedom by a series of experiments in which essays, composed by actual naïve subjects, were substituted for those heretofore scripted by the [109] investigators.

166 Part Two Inferential Anomalies

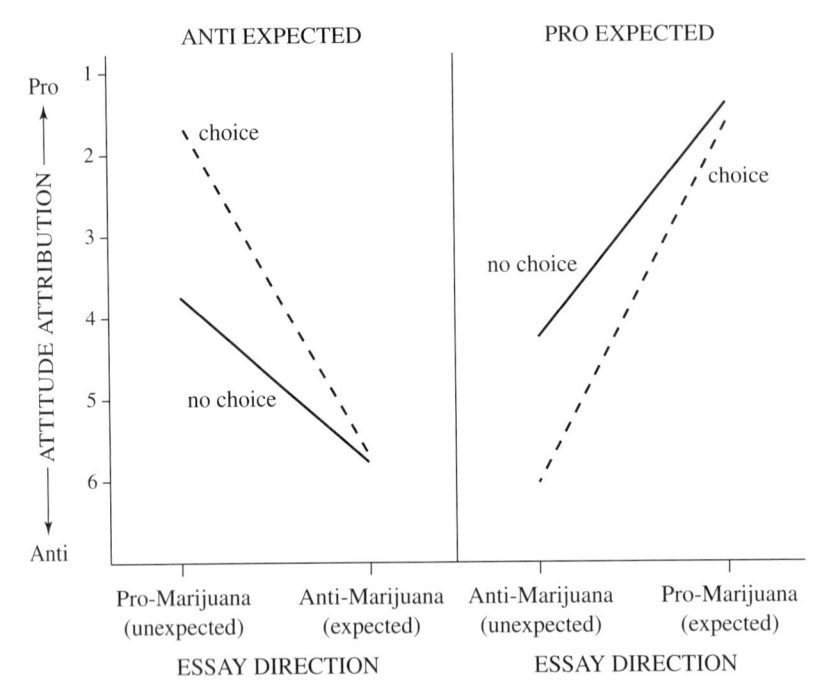

Figure 9.3 Attitude attributed to a target person writing an essay favoring or opposing legalization of marijuana under choice or no-choice instructions. The essay direction was either in line with or opposed to expectations. (Data from Jones, Worchel, Goethals, & Grumet, 1971.)

Subjects were asked to write an essay taking a designated position. In some cases, the assigned position favored, and in other cases, it opposed their private view. It is important to note that *no* subject refused the assignment. Thus, in terms of consensus, our no-choice-condition instructions in the previous experiments were, in fact, sufficiently constraining to have induced 100% compliance. When subjects received essays written under the same no-choice conditions that governed their own essay preparation, and this was made clear to them, they still made the fundamental attribution error of assigning a true attitude in line with behavior. From the evidence of 100% compliance, I would argue that observers seriously err if they draw a correspondent inference based on the assumption that only an actor not opposed to a position would agree to endorse it when so instructed. This assumption is, in fact, incorrect.

A number of other features of the Snyder and Jones (1974) study and related experiments are worth reviewing: (a) Observers' attributions are not influenced systematically by their own prior attitudes. (b) Changes in the observers' own attitudes following their exposure to the target person's statement are not essential to the overattribution effect. (c) The strength of essays prepared by naïve target persons is actually unrelated to their true attitudes. (d) Within wide limits, the quality, strength, or persuasiveness of the essay has little effect on observer attributions. In one study (Schneider & Miller, 1975), the manipulated enthusiasm of a speaker on videotape had no effect, even in no-choice conditions. (e) Finally, variations in the *degree* of constraint also have remarkably small effects.

Chapter 9   The Rocky Road from Acts to Dispositions   **167**

Snyder and Jones (1974) showed that if observers are told the specific arguments provided to the target person and these arguments appear in the essay, overattribution is reduced to a marginal effect. Furthermore, if it is clear to the observer that the target person has merely copied, in his own handwriting, an essay written by someone else, the error is finally wiped out. However, if the target person delivers an essay on either video or audiotape that is explicitly described as having been written by someone else (Miller, 1976), the fundamental attribution error persists. This is shown in Figures 9.4 and 9.5.

Figure 9.4 shows the declining strength of the effects of speech direction with increasing constraint. Here the attitude issue was the federal provision of free medical care. The leftmost bar shows the effects of opposing or defending medical care under low constraint; that is, when the observers are led to understand that the target person [110] is perfectly free to write an essay on either side of the issue. As usual, this is the greatest difference. The striped portion of the choice bar is the amount of the difference between oppose and defend conditions that represents the true difference in attitudes between naïve target persons who chose to defend federal aid and those who chose to oppose it. It may thus be seen that the remaining error is at least as great as the now familiar error in the no-choice bar to its right.

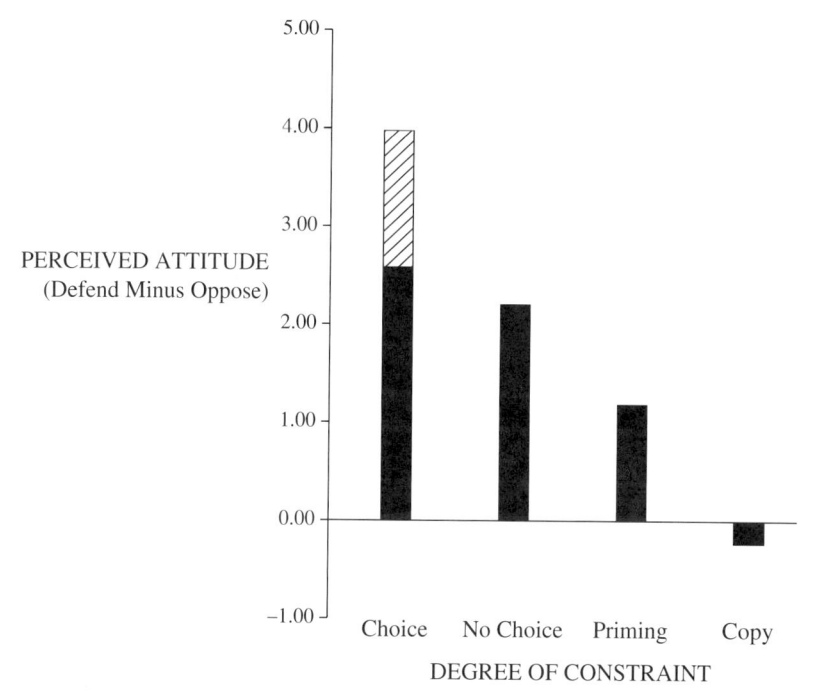

Figure 9.4   Difference in perceived attitude in defense of versus opposition to free medical care by the federal government, as a function of the degree of constraint. The striped portion of the choice bar reflects that portion of the difference in perceived attitude attributable to the difference in actual attitude. (From "Attitude Attribution When Behavior Is Constrained," by Melvin Snyder and Edward E. Jones, *Journal of Experimental Social Psychology,* 1974, 10, 585–600. Copyright 1974 by Academic Press, Inc. Reprinted by permission.)

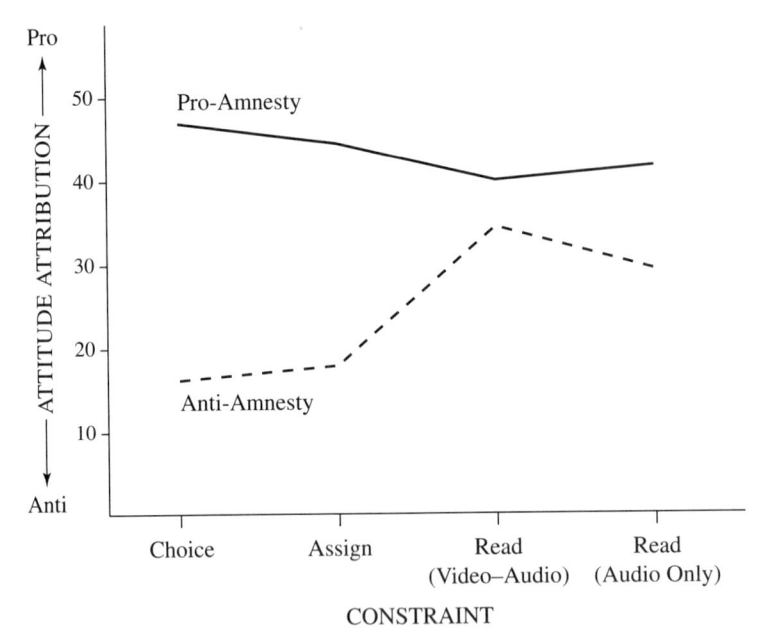

Figure 9.5 Attitude attributed as a function of essay direction (for or against for draft evaders), constraint level, and target person. (Adapted from Miller, 1976.)

When priming information was provided to the no-choice target persons, the increase in constraint was registered in a decline of error below the probability value of .15. The point of current interest is the complete absence of any bias when the target person merely copied an essay composed by someone else.

Figure 9.5, adapted from one presented by Miller (1976), concerns the attribution of attitudes toward amnesty for draft evaders as a function of both the direction of a speech delivered on videotape and the degree of constraint. Here, surprisingly, there is almost as large a gap between pro- and anti-conditions in the assign as in the choice condition. In the two read conditions, the target person was presented as reading an essay prepared by someone else, either with or without the visual picture of the reader during the delivery. A significant difference remains even under these conditions of extreme constraint.

From the Miller studies, it appears that even when the explicit content of a speech is prepared by someone other than the target person, attitudes are attributed to him or her in line with the thrust of the arguments. There appears, then, to be a difference in the extent to which written versus oral behavior engulfs the field. It seems reasonable to assume that an oral or videotaped delivery makes the person more salient than does a handwritten copy of the attitudinal statement.

There is another way to approach the potential criticism that the context manipulations in these experiments were much weaker than the behavioral manipulations. This criticism may be countered by an experimental procedure that reduces the behavior manipulation to zero. Melvin Snyder and I had a hunch that people sometimes infer a generalized emotional disposition from an emotional state that is itself inferred only because of contextual or situational cues. In concrete terms, a target person might be judged to be angry because we have observed that he or she was provoked in the extreme by someone else, even though he or she shows no signs of anger. Such an inference is reasonable, but then to infer that our abused target person is dispositionally hostile would be a strange attributional error—one that would clearly be inconsistent with correspondent inference theory and Kelley's discounting principle, both of which emphasize that situational attributions are the complement of personal attributions. Thus, anger that is clearly understandable in terms of situational provocation should not be attributed to a generalized hostile disposition. Nevertheless, we predicted that emotional dispositions are sometimes inferred from emotional states that, in turn, are inferred solely because of situational cues. In other words, we predicted that observers may dissociate an emotional state from its situational source and misattribute it to a disposition of the actor.

In his dissertation, Snyder (1974) presented a videotape of a male target person taking a word association test. Half of the observers believed that the target person anticipated receiving electric shock in the next portion of the experiment; the other half did not. Female observers who thought that the target person anticipated being shocked not only perceived him as being more apprehensive at the end of the word association test but also attributed to him more of a disposition to be anxious—as measured in a variety of different formats. The behavior was of course identical across variations in information about whether the target person was or was not anticipating shock.

In a conceptual replication of this effect, Snyder and Frankel (1976) exposed male observers to videotapes without sound tracks, showing a female target person being interviewed. Some of the observers thought they were watching a student being interviewed about sex, and some thought the interview was about politics. It was assumed that the sex topic would be judged to be more anxiety-provoking than politics. After viewing the tape, observers were asked to rate how upset and uncomfortable the interviewee was. They were then asked to evaluate her dispositional anxiety by a number of different measuring formats. As predicted, not only was the target person judged to be more anxious when the topic was assumed to be sex, she was also judged to have a generally anxious disposition in that condition relative to the politics conditions. Interestingly enough, and in line with correspondent inference theory and the discounting principle, when the interview topic [111] was announced *after* the observers had viewed the tape, precisely the opposite occurred. Greater dispositional anxiety was attributed after the politics-interview cue than after the sex-interview cue. This suggests strongly that perceptions of behavior are influenced by prior information about the context, but behavior is not seriously distorted in retrospect. These results are portrayed in Figure 9.6. They clearly provide a very stringent test of the engulfing process in that a disposition is inferred from an act that is itself inferred from contextual manipulations alone.

UNDERESTIMATED CONSTRAINTS

Snyder and Jones (1974) argued that the fundamental attribution error grows out of the perceptual salience of action against the contextual ground:

> Since the behavior is figural against the situational ground, it may be natural for the observer to emphasize its production by the actor, and therefore to exaggerate the latter's responsibility for it.... The behavior and the behavior products of others are relatively unfamiliar, novel, and thus draw attention to themselves. (p. 598).

170 Part Two Inferential Anomalies

[Figure: Graph showing EMOTIONAL DISPOSITION (apprehensive, nervous, anxious) on y-axis from -1.0 to 1.5, and ALLEGED INTERVIEW CONTEXT (Sex or Politics) on x-axis. Two lines: "Information before" slopes downward from Sex to Politics; "Information after" slopes upward from Sex to Politics.]

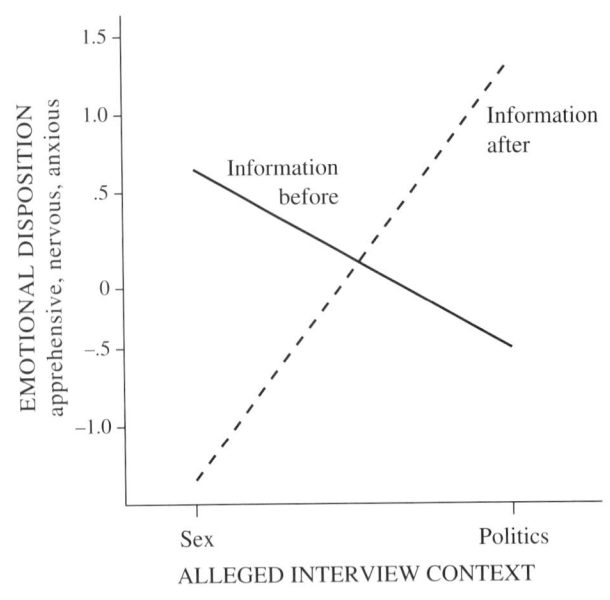

Figure 9.6 Attribution of the disposition to be anxious as a function of interview context (sex or politics) and order of information presentation. (Data from Snyder & Frankel, 1976.)

As a correlate of this behavioral salience, we might expect observers to overestimate the degree of choice that is actually present in the no-choice conditions of the attitude attribution experiments. It is difficult to check this expectation because it is hard to know how to interpret a mark on a scale from complete choice or freedom to no choice or complete constraint in anything but relative terms. In an absolute sense, the no-choice target person retains considerable choice—he or she may refuse to write the essay, presumably incurring only the perceived cost of losing face or money. Some observers may assume that anyone who really felt strongly opposed to the position he or she was asked to defend would decide not to incur these costs. Therefore, the observer may view the target person as belonging to a self-selected group of actors with views at least moderately in line with their statements. As defined by consensus, however, the degree of remaining choice for the no choice target person in reality is quite limited—apparently, everyone complies with a request to write or deliver a viewpoint as long as the auspices are reasonable (providing materials for an experiment, taking an assigned side in a debate, answering essay questions on an exam, and so on). Though it is hard to know, then, what significance to attach to absolute positions on the freedom–constraint scale, most studies do show that the target person with high choice is rated closer to the complete-freedom end of the scale than the target person with no choice is to the complete-constraint end of the scale.

In an informative study by Miller, Mayerson, Pogue, and Whitehouse (1977), subjects in the high-constraint conditions were asked what factors led them to make their particular judgment of attitude. Only 28% acknowledged the constraining instructions, and those who did avoided the overattribution error. Unfortunately, it is not clear whether the remaining no-choice subjects were aware of the instructions and discounted them, or whether they simply did not attend to them in the first place. For the majority of subjects, however, constraint instructions appear to be of low salience.

INFORMATION SEQUENCE

The differential salience of behavior and instructions might conceivably be a function of the order in which information is presented to the subject. In all of the experiments cited thus far, the constraint instructions preceded the behavior, which was followed by the crucial ratings of attributed attitude. Perhaps the temporal proximity of the behavior and the attribution rating is an important condition for minimizing the effects of earlier information about constraint. Jones, Riggs, and Quattrone (1979) recently investigated the role [112] of sequence by comparing attitude attributions to the author of an essay when the essay follows information about the choice context, with the situation when the essay is followed by the context. The issue was the use of affirmative action quota systems as part of college admissions procedures, and observers were exposed to the essays in mimeographed booklets. Whether it was presented after or before the essay, the choice context was introduced by the phrase, "You might be interested in knowing that the essay was written under the following instructions: ...." Choice or no-choice instructions to the target person followed. As usual, it was pointed out that the target persons had materials from which to form their essays. Somewhat to our surprise, overattribution to the target person under no-choice conditions was *greater* when the essay was presented first than under the more typical conditions where the essay followed the choice context instructions. Also, in the essay-first condition, the no-choice essays were judged more extreme, and the no-choice target person was seen as having written under less constraint. These results are apparent in Figure 9.7. They are reminiscent of the perseverance effect explored by Ross, Lepper, and Hubbard (1975). It appears that when no-choice instructions are introduced as a corrective constraint after an initial impression has been formed on the basis of an essay, the instructions have relatively less impact than when the subjects are aware of the no-choice context while being exposed to the essay. Regardless of the particular interpretation of this finding, there is no question that the overattribution effect in attitude attribution studies is not simply a function of the recency of the information about behavior.

EXPLAINING THE OVERATTRIBUTION EFFECT

Most of the explanations of why observers do not go far enough in recognizing the "sufficient" causal significance of the no-choice instructions are either artifactual alternatives or explanations that are one step removed from data descriptions. The artifactual alternatives, such as essay extremity, reflected expertise, order effects, weak constraint manipulation, and attitude change in the observer that is projected, are not without interest in their own right. To paraphrase William McGuire, today's artifact is tomorrow's grant proposal. Nevertheless, such artifactual explanations have largely been ruled out or have been found to be nonessential for the effect to occur. Thus, we are mostly left with descriptive explanations such as "behavior engulfs the field" or with those emphasizing the salience of action.

172 Part Two Inferential Anomalies

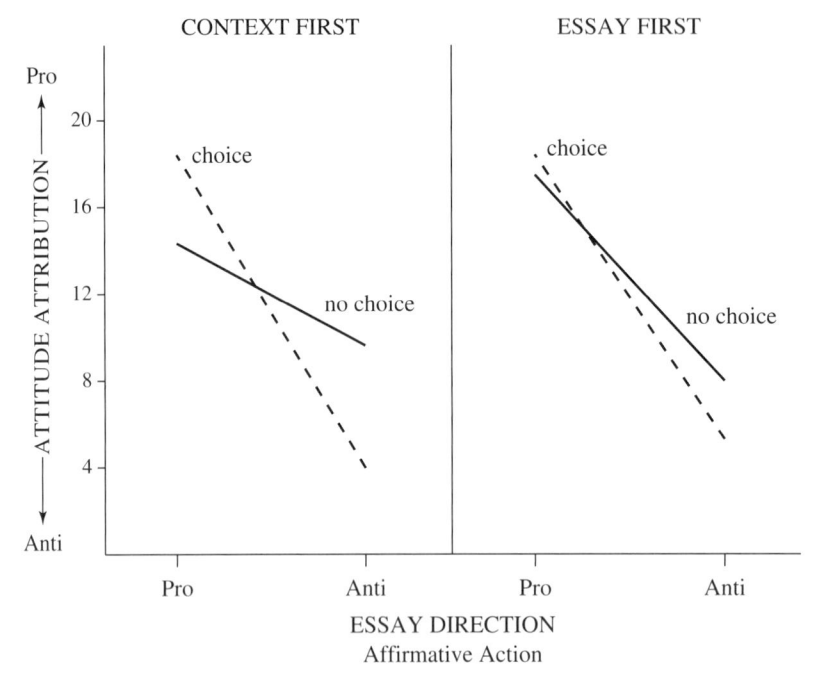

Figure 9.7 Attribution of attitude toward affirmative action minority quotas as a function of information order and degree of choice. (Data from Jones, Riggs, & Quattrone, in press.)

Though there is mounting evidence that people are more likely to make causal attributions to salient features of their environment than they are to nonsalient features (Taylor & Fiske, 1978), it is not entirely evident that the salience of behavior should lead to person attribution rather than to situation attribution. One would surmise that other contextual factors might affect whether the admittedly salient behavior is seen as part of a connected causal unit embracing the person or one involving the commanding provocation of the situation. What might these other factors be?

We have seen that the fundamental attribution error is a replicated, robust empirical tendency. Often, however, we learn more about the causes of a phenomenon by seeking out those exceptions that clarify genotypic determinants and point to more fundamental functional relations. This is the tack recently taken by Quattrone (Note 1). In an ingenious experiment, he set out to demonstrate that there is at least one set of conditions under which people make unnecessary overattributions to the situation. The colorful subtitle of his paper is "When Behavior Engulfs the Person." The origins of attribution theory lie in Holder's extension of the perceptual-unit concept to encompass unit formation based on perceived cause and effect. Specifically, the actor and his act, in Heider's view, are perceived as a causal unit, and this perception [113] is a very natural, fundamental gestalt. What is more reasonable, after all, than the brute, palpable fact that there can be no action without an actor? The notion that situations can cause action is abstract and derivative, almost metaphoric in its implications. At best, situations capture and direct the energies provided by the organism. Situations are contextual shapers; they vary as more or less potent background conditions but they nevertheless remain part of the background. If we add to these primitive perceptual priorities the likely fact that socialization pressures capitalize on the importance of taking one at his word or listening politely to others and attending to the content of their remarks, the basis for an omnipresent attributional bias is perhaps apparent.

Quattrone reasoned, however, that a causal unit linking behavior to the situation could be made salient through arrangements designed to influence the set of the subject. He varied the standard attitude attribution paradigm by presenting unambiguous evidence concerning the attitude of the target person toward marijuana *before* presenting an essay on marijuana legalization supposedly written by the target person and perfectly congruent with his prior attitude, whether it was for or against. In a context purportedly probing experimenter effects, the subject-observers were asked to estimate the extent to which the target person might have been influenced in presenting his views by subtly conveyed cues from the experimenter, by the nature of the materials provided to the target persons, or by the experimenter's own attitude toward the issue. Quattrone's basic finding was that in spite of the fact that essay direction and content were totally explainable in terms of the stated prior attitude of the target person, the subjects saw the situation created by the experimenter as also facilitating the target person's behavior in writing the essay. We not only have an example of overexplanation, in other words, we have an apparent instance of overattribution to the situation. As Figure 9.8 shows, when the subject is given a sufficient attitudinal reason why a target person with complete freedom of choice would write an essay strongly favoring a particular position, he or she nevertheless attributes the essay direction, in part, to subtle influences from the experimenter. This situational attribution is only slightly greater when no prior attitude is mentioned. In this latter case, of course, some attribution of the statement to situational influences is perfectly reasonable.

We may note, however, the lengths to which Quattrone went in designing this experiment to sensitize the subjects to the possibility of an environment–behavior causal unit:

1. The experimental cover story stressed the possibility of subtle experimenter influences in psychological experiments, though it made clear that such influences were probably present in some and absent in others and that subjects might also react against any experimenter influence. The subjects were thus alerted to the task of discerning such influences if they were present. Note the contrast between this and the typical attitude-attribution-study cover story, which emphasizes impression formation and presumably sets the subject to consider whether the expressed opinion is correspondent to an attitude in the same direction. We must face the possibility that the overattribution effect or the fundamental attribution error may be in part a function of the set to perceive a personality, to be sensitized to individuating information. Of course, we may still argue that such sensitizing conditions predominate in our everyday interactions and that the fundamental attribution error is not, therefore, just a laboratory [114] phenomenon created by special setting instructions.

174 Part Two Inferential Anomalies

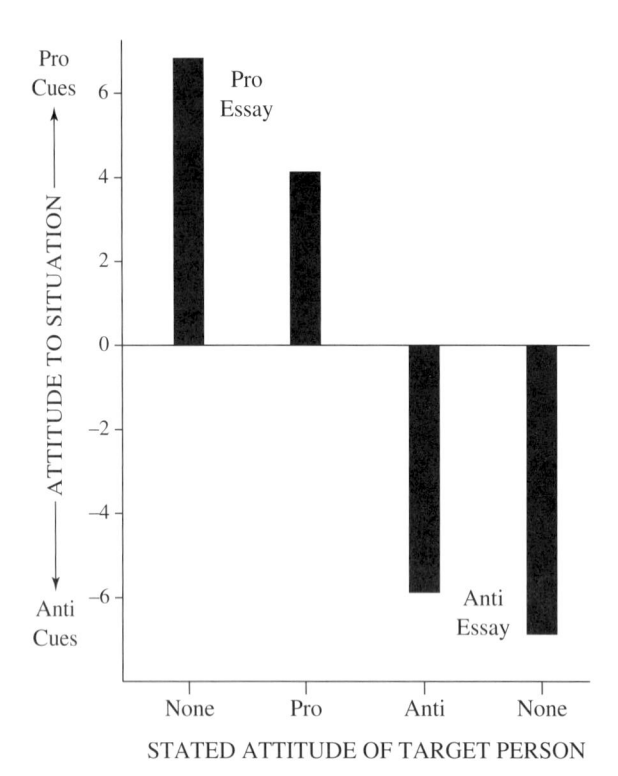

[Figure: Bar chart showing ATTITUDE TO SITUATION (Pro Cues to Anti Cues, scale -6 to 6) on y-axis and STATED ATTITUDE OF TARGET PERSON (None, Pro, Anti, None) on x-axis. Bars show approximately: None/Pro Essay ≈ 6.5; Pro/Pro Essay ≈ 4; Anti/Anti Essay ≈ -6; None/Anti Essay ≈ -6.5.]

Figure 9.8 Attribution of essay favoring or opposing saccharin ban to the situation established by the experimenter, as a function of information about the target person's prior attitude. (Data from Quattrone, Note 1.)

2. The major dependent measures were scaled along dimensions that could be readily mapped into the pro–con dimension on the essay itself. Subjects were asked, for example, to infer the extremity and direction of the experimenter's subtly conveyed cues to have the target person write an essay on a particular side of the legalization of marijuana controversy. The scale ran from –6 (pressure opposing legalization) to +6 (pressure favoring legalization). Thus the bridge between the behavior and the situation was made as navigable as the bridge between behavior and true attitude in the typical attitude attribution study.

3. Finally, and perhaps most important, it should not escape notice that the measure of situational influence was actually a measure of the experimenter's behavior as well as his inner state. The experiment may be interpreted as substituting, by a novel structuring of set inferences about the experimenter's behavior for inferences about the target person's behavior. Thus the cover story and the questions helped to redefine who the actor was in the experimental situation.

The Quattrone experiment helps us to place the overattribution bias in a broader perspective. It is quite clear that such bias is not always the effect of some unique cause.

There is not a single fundamental antecedent to go with the fundamental error. It is much more reasonable to expect that such biases can result from different combinations of shifting determinants and that some will be stronger in some settings than in others. In summary, however, the following factors merit singling out:

1. I accept the role of behavioral salience and am willing to argue that, in most settings, behavior is seen as naturally connected with the actor as origin. The actor and his act form a natural cognitive, if not perceptual, unit, especially when the actor is seen or heard in the process of emitting his or her own behavior.

2. The slightly less natural but still normal presumption is that the actor–act unit reflects a correspondent disposition. This is neither a necessary nor an inevitable inference but perhaps becomes the most readily available hypothesis the observer has to account for the behavior he or she observes. I propose that this hypothesis becomes the point of departure for further corrective inferential work. The correspondent inference becomes the anchor for an adjustment process in dealing with other personal and situational explanations for the behavior. This adjustment occurs, less extreme correspondent dispositions are attributed in the high-constraint conditions, but it is insufficient. As noted by Tversky and Kahneman (1974), such *insufficient adjustment* is a common error in the processing of sequentially presented information. I am suggesting that salience as well as temporal priority create "anchorhood." When the two coincide, as in our experiment where the constraint information followed the essay, the adjustment is understandably even less sufficient. In this appeal to insufficient adjustment, I realize I have called on one error as an explanation for another, but the anchor–adjustment heuristic appears to be a more basic cognitive phenomenon than the fundamental attribution error itself, and it ties the latter into a broad literature of conservatism in judgment and decision-making.

3. The natural salience of an act–actor unit may itself be undermined by contextual factors that set the observer to consider as his or her task the possible role of situational determinants. Among other things, such set manipulations may weaken the hypothesis of correspondence and create competing anchors in the attribution process.

To conclude, I have presented data generated primarily by the single paradigm of attitude attribution research. The advantages of staying within a restricted paradigm are those associated with cumulative and overlapping findings. Alternative explanations can be carefully scrutinized, and the search for underlying cognitive processes can move forward. I hope, of course, that the theoretical reasoning derived from these related studies can usefully be applied to a broader range of phenomena designated as the fundamental attribution error. The compellingness of actors–action unit formation may be illustrated in a variety of mundane contexts, as well as in more exotic illusionary realms. Ross (1977) argued convincingly that the classic forced-compliance effect in dissonance research must be based on the tendency of experimental subjects to fall victim to the fundamental attribution error when appraising their own actions. Otherwise, subjects would be aware that the contextual arrangements set in motion by the experimenter provided a perfectly sufficient explanation for their compliant behavior. Similarly, Asch's conformity studies, Milgram's obedience research, and the studies by Darley and Latané of bystander intervention excite our interest because [115] the responses of most subjects are nonobvious—that is, they are nonobvious unless we take the fundamental attribution error into account.

Ross, Amabile, and Steinmetz (1977) showed how even the most blatant role assignments may be ignored in rushing to a conclusion linking acts to a disposition. In their fascinating study, subjects were openly assigned by random procedures to be either the questioner or the contestant in a quiz game. In front of the contestant, the questioner was explicitly urged to compose a number of "challenging but not impossible questions," tapping the contestant's general knowledge. After having difficulties with such questions, typical contestants see the questioner as extremely knowledgeable, much more knowledgeable than they see themselves or than the self-rating of the questioner. Neutral observers are equally convinced of the superior knowledgeability of the questioner. Thus, the inherent bias or constraint in a sample of questions deliberately chosen to reflect the questioner's knowledge *and* the contestant's ignorance is strikingly ignored.

Beyond the arena of social psychological research, there are ubiquitous anecdotal instances of the fundamental attribution error. We may note the compelling illusion of Mortimer Snerd as behavior origin, even when we are perfectly aware that the dummy's remarks originate with the ventriloquist. Dancers and actors achieve considerably greater public acclaim and attention than choreographers, directors, and playwrights, yet the origin of this action is much more diffused or shared than this differential fame would suggest. As a bizarre variant of this, one wonders how a jury could give proper weight to the situational forces that carried Patty Hearst into bank robbery after the members had seen the videotape shots of her entrance brandishing a gun.

The journey from acts to dispositions is apparently often taken in unthinking haste and leads commonly to unwitting error. But what are the social consequences of this omnipresent tendency and how is it embedded in the broader story of cognitive evolution? Is some adaptive purpose served by overattribution to the person? It is tempting to say that such overattribution facilitates effective action, that it increases opportunities for control. But how does it do these things? How can this ubiquitous proneness to attributional error really facilitate control? This leaves us saying, perhaps, that at least it promotes the illusion of control and is therefore comforting. But again, how does it do this? Why should we feel more in control when we think we understand a personal disposition than when we think we understand the situational context of behavior?

A slightly more subtle way of potentially explaining the error is to speculate that the mistake of overindividuating the social environment is less costly than assuming that people are typical until they clearly demonstrate otherwise. But what would be the basis for this differential error cost? In what ways would we be handicapped by a focus on norms and situational constraints?

Perhaps the error is the product of cognitive inertia. Perhaps it reflects the misapplication of a heuristic that is normally useful. Most of the time, people presumably mean what they say, or at least, it is socially adaptive for the listener to assume that they do. The attribution error appears, then, in the form of inappropriate generalization. A strategy that is normally in the service of what Goffman (1955) called "face-work" is extended into an experimental situation where the focus is ostensibly on accuracy but where the costs for inaccuracy are negligible. The strategy originally grows out of the realization that to challenge the integrity or veracity of a proponent is a social rupture fraught with anxiety and embarrassment.

Finally, we know all too little about the relations between attribution and action. Do errors of attribution produce errors of action? It is conceivable that overt behavior is better tuned to the full range of causal influences than is a response to an attributional questionnaire. We must explore these and other related questions about the social consequences of attributional errors, and perhaps the convenience of the attitude attribution paradigm and the reproducibility of the results it yields will continue to prove useful in moving toward more general theoretical explanation.

REFERENCE NOTE

1. Quattrone G. (1970). *Overattribution and unit formation: When behavior engulfs the person.* Manuscript submitted for publication. [Editor's note: This manuscript was eventually published as Quattrone, G. A. (1982). Overattribution and unit formation: When behavior engulfs the person. *Journal of Personality and Social Psychology,* 42, 593–607.]

REFERENCES

Goffman, E. (1955). On face-work: An analysis of ritual elements in social interaction. *Psychiatry,* 18, 213–231.
Heider, F. (1944). Social perception and phenomenal causality. *Psychological Review,* 51, 358–374.
Heider, F. (1958). *The psychology of interpersonal relations.* New York; Wiley. **[116]**
Jones, E. E., & Davis, K. E. (1965). From acts to dispositions: The attribution process in person perception. In L. Berkowitz (Ed.), *Advances in experimental social psychology* (Vol. 2, pp. 219–266). New York: Academic Press.
Jones, E. E., & Harris, V. A. (1967). The attribution of attitudes. *Journal of Experimental Social Psychology,* 3, 1–24.
Jones, E. E., & Nisbett, R. E. (1972). The actor and the observer: Divergent perceptions of the causes of behavior. In E. E. Jones, D. E. Kanouse, H. H. Kelley, R. E. Nisbett, S. Valins, & B. Weiner (Ed.), *Attribution: Perceiving the causes of behavior* (pp. 79–94). Morristown, NJ: General Learning Press.
Jones, E. E., Riggs, J. M., & Quattrone, G. (1979). Observer bias in the attitude attribution paradigm: Effect of time and information order. *Journal of Personality and Social Psychology,* 37(7), 1230–1238.
Jones, E. E., Worchel, S., Goethals, G. R., & Grumet, J. (1971). Prior expectancy and behavioral extremity as determinants of attitude attribution. *Journal of Experimental Social Psychology,* 7, 59–80.
Kelley, H. H. (1972). Attribution in social interaction. In E. E. Jones, D. E. Kanouse, H. H. Kelley, R. E. Nisbett, S. Valins, & B. Weiner (Ed.), *Attribution: Perceiving the causes of behavior* (pp. 1–26). Morristown, NJ: General Leaning Press.
Miller, A. G. (1974). Perceived freedom and the attribution of attitudes. *Representative Research in Social Psychology,* 5, 61–80.
Miller, A. G. (1976). Constraint and target effects in the attribution of attitude. *Journal of Experimental Social Psychology,* 12, 325–339.
Miller, A. G., Mayerson, N., Pogue, M., & Whitehouse, D. (1977). Perceivers' explanations of their attributions of attitude. *Personality and Social Psychology Bulletin,* 3, 111–114.
Ross, L. (1977). The intuitive psychologist and his shortcomings: Distortions in the attribution process. In L. Berkowitz (Ed.), *Advances in experimental social psychology* (Vol. 10, pp. 173–220). New York: Academic Press.
Ross, L., Amabile. T. M., & Steinmetz, J. L. (1977). Social roles, social control, and biases in social-perception processes. *Journal of Personality and Social Psychology,* 35, 485–494.
Ross, L., Lepper, M. R., & Hubbard, M. (1975). Perseverance in self-perception and social perception: Biased attributional processes in the debriefing paradigm. *Journal of Personality and Social Psychology,* 32, 1004–1013.

Schneider. D. J., & Miller, R. S. (1975). The effects of enthusiasm and quality of arguments on attitude attribution. *Journal of Personality,* 43, 693–708.

Snyder, M. L. (1974). The field engulfing behavior: An investigation of attributing emotional states and dispositions (Doctoral dissertation. Duke University. 1074). *Dissertation Abstracts International,* 34, 6259B–6260B, (University Microfilms No. 74-13,496).

Snyder, M. L., & Frankel, A. (1976). Observer bias: A stringent test of behavior engulfing the field. *Journal of Personality and Social Psychology,* 34, 857–864.

Snyder, M., & Jones, E. E. (1974). Attitude attribution when behavior is constrained. *Journal of Experimental Social Psychology,* 10, 585–600.

Taylor, S. E., & Fiske, S. T. (1978). Salience, attention, and attribution: Top of the head phenomena. In L. Berkowitz (Ed.), *Advances in experimental social psychology* (Vol. 11, pp. 249–288). New York: Academic Press.

Tversky, A., & Kahneman, D. (1974). Judgment under uncertainty: Heuristics and biases. *Science,* 185, 1124–1131. [117]

… THE ACTOR-OBSERVER EFFECT

Chapter 10

The Actor and the Observer: Divergent Perceptions of the Causes of Behavior

Edward E. Jones
Duke University
Richard E. Nisbett
University of Michigan

When a student who is doing poorly in school discusses his problem with a faculty adviser, there is often a fundamental difference of opinion between the two. The student, in attempting to understand and explain his inadequate performance, is usually able to point to environmental obstacles such as a particularly onerous course load, to temporary emotional stress such as worry about his draft status, or to a transitory confusion about life goals that is now resolved. The faculty adviser may nod and may wish to believe, but in his heart of hearts he usually disagrees. The adviser is convinced that the poor performance is due neither to the student's environment nor to transient emotional states. He believes instead that the failure is due to enduring qualities of the student—to lack of ability, to irremediable laziness, to neurotic ineptitude.

When Kitty Genovese was murdered in view of thirty-nine witnesses in Queens (New York), social scientists, the press, and the public marveled at the apathy of the residents of New York and, by extension, of urban America. Yet it seems unlikely that the

---

Reprinted with permission of Simon & Schuster Elementary Group © 1972 from *Attribution: Perceiving the causes of behavior,* Jones, E. E., Kanouse, D. E., Kelley, H. H., Nisbett, R. E., Valins, S., & Weiner, B. (Eds.). Morristown, NJ: General Learning Press. References have been updated by the editor.

witnesses themselves felt that their failure to intercede on the woman's behalf was due to apathy. At any rate, interviewers were unable to elicit comments from the witnesses on the order of "I really didn't care if she lived or died." Instead, the eyewitnesses reported that they had been upset, but felt that there was nothing they could or needed to do about a situation that in any case was ambiguous to them.

In their autobiographies, former political leaders often report a different perspective on their past acts from that commonly held by the public. Acts perceived by the public to have been wise, planful, courageous, and imaginative on the one hand, or unwise, haphazard, cowardly, or pedestrian on the other, are often seen in quite a different light by the autobiographer. He is likely to emphasize **[79]*** the situational constraints at the time of the action—the role limitations, the conflicting pressures brought to bear, the alternative paths of action that were never open or that were momentarily closed—and to perceive his actions as having been inevitable. "Wise moves" and "blunders" alike are often viewed by the leader as largely inescapable under the circumstances. The public is more inclined to personalize causation for success and failure. There are good leaders who can cope with what the situation brings and bad leaders who cannot.

In each of these instances, the actor's perceptions of the causes of his behavior are at variance with those held by outside observers. The actor's view of his behavior emphasizes the role of environmental conditions at the moment of action. The observer's view emphasizes the causal role of stable dispositional properties of the actor. We wish to argue that *there is a pervasive tendency for actors to attribute their actions to situational requirements, whereas observers tend to attribute the same actions to stable personal dispositions.* This tendency often stems in part from the actor's need to justify blameworthy action, but may also reflect a variety of other factors having nothing to do with the maintenance of self-esteem. We shall emphasize these other, more cognitive factors, but include also a consideration of the role of self-justification.

The proposition that actors attribute their behavior to situational constraints while observers attribute the behavior to dispositions of the actor is best characterized, perhaps, as an actuarial proposition. We acknowledge at the outset that there are undoubtedly many exceptions. In our opinion, though, there are good theoretical reasons for believing that the proposition is generally correct. We wish to explore what we believe to be powerful cognitive forces impelling actors to attribute their behavior to the environment and observers to attribute that same behavior to characteristics of the actor. The proposition has not been fully tested, but there are a few experiments that provide data consistent with it. We will now describe these experiments in order to supplement our selected anecdotes.

EXPERIMENTAL EVIDENCE CONSISTENT WITH THE PROPOSITION

Jones, Rock, Shaver, Goethals, and Ward (1968) compared the attributions made by actor-subjects with those made by observer-subjects in a rigged IQ testing situation. To collect their observer data, Jones et al. asked each subject and an accomplice to take an

---

*Bracketed bold numbers refer to original page numbers. Page numbers indicate where the original page ended.

IQ test "designed to discriminate at the very highest levels of intelligence." The items were quite difficult and some were insoluble. Success and failure feedback for both the accomplice and the subject was reported after each item. The items were ambiguous enough to permit feedback that bore no necessary relation to the performance of the subject. The pattern of "successes" was such that, at the end of the series, the subject believed he had solved ten of the thirty items, with success scattered randomly throughout the test. In one of the experimental conditions, it was made to appear that the accomplice had solved fifteen randomly scattered problems. In another condition, it was also made to appear that the accomplice solved fifteen problems, but many more of the initial problems were solved than final problems. In a third condition, the accomplice again solved fifteen problems, but he had many more successes at the end than at the beginning. Special pains were taken to assure the subjects that the items were of equal difficulty, and the evidence suggests these assurances were accepted.

Whether the accomplice solved more problems at the beginning of the series (descending condition) or at the end (ascending condition) had a pronounced influence on (a) the subject's recall of the accomplice's performance, (b) the subject's prediction about the number of problems the accomplice would solve on a later, similar series, and (c) the subject's estimate of the accomplice's intelligence. If the accomplice solved a great many problems at the beginning of the series, the subject perceived him as more intelligent, distorted his overall performance on the test in a more favorable direction, and predicted that he would do better on the later series than if the accomplice solved few problems at the beginning. For most of the measures, in most of the variations of the experiment reported by Jones et al., the randomly successful accomplice was judged to be intermediate between the descending and ascending accomplices.

Jones et al. interpreted their data as evidence of a strong primacy effect in the attribution of ability: early information was weighted heavily and later evidence was essentially ignored (see Jones & Goethal, 1972). For our purposes, the important point is that ability attributions were made at all. This fact serves as the background against which to evaluate the results of a variation in which the tables were turned and the accomplice randomly solved the ten problems while the subject solved fifteen problems, either in random order, in descending order, or in ascending order.

When the feedback patterns were thus reassigned, the results were markedly different. In the descending [80] and ascending conditions it was apparently impossible for the subjects to resist the conclusion, despite the experimenter's initial disclaimer, that the item difficulty had changed over the series. Descending subjects believed that the items got more difficult and ascending subjects believed they got less difficult. These beliefs apparently affected subjects' expectations about their performance on a future series. Ascending subjects predicted they would do better on the later series than did descending subjects, completely reversing the direction of observers' predictions. As would be expected, subjects' judgments about their own intellectual ability were unaffected by the experimental manipulations.

The pattern of attributions is therefore quite different for actor and observer. In identical situations, the actor attributes performance to variations in task difficulty, the observer to variations in ability.

The experiments by Jones et al. present data for actors and observers in identical situations. Another set of experiments, while lacking data on actors themselves, indicates that observers are remarkably inclined to see behavior in dispositional terms. Three experiments were conducted by Jones and Harris (1967). In the first of these, they asked their college student subjects to read essays or listen to speeches presumably written by fellow students. Subjects were asked to give their estimates of the communicator's real opinions. They were told either that the communicator had been assigned one side of the issue or that he had been completely free to choose a side. It is the "no choice" conditions that are of most interest to us here. In one case, the impression of no choice was created by telling subjects they were reading essays written for a political science course in which the instructor had required the students to write, for example, a "short cogent defense of Castro's Cuba." In another experiment subjects believed they were reading the opening statement by a college debater whose adviser had directed him to argue a specified side of the Castro topic. In a third experiment, subjects believed they were hearing a tape recording of a subject in a psychology experiment who had been instructed to give a speech favoring or opposing segregation. Questionnaire responses showed that subjects easily distinguished between choice and no choice conditions in the degree of choice available to the communicator.

Despite the fact that the subjects seem to have clearly perceived the heavy constraints on the communicator in the no choice conditions, their estimates of the true opinions of the communicator were markedly affected by the particular position espoused. When subjects read an essay or speech supporting Castro's Cuba, they inferred that the communicator was pro-Castro. If the communication opposed Castro's Cuba, they inferred that the communicator was anti-Castro. Across the three experiments, the effect of taking a pro versus anti stand was a highly significant determinant of attributed attitude in no choice conditions, though the effect of position taken was roughly twice as great when the communicator had complete choice.

These results are extremely interesting if they may be taken as evidence that observers attach insufficient weight to the situational determinants of behavior and attribute it, on slim evidence, to a disposition of the actor. It may be, however, that something about the content of the speeches caused the subjects to infer that the communicator actually held the opinion he was advocating. If the communications were quite eloquent and drew on esoteric sources of knowledge, it would not be surprising to learn that observers inferred that the communicator held the opinion he was delivering. This does not seem to be the proper explanation of the results, however, in view of the following facts: (a) the communications were designed to be "neither polished nor crude;" "of a C+ quality" in the case of the political science essay; (b) in each experiment, it was made clear that subjects had access to study materials to help them formulate their arguments; (c) in a later series of experiments, Snyder (unpublished data) found that when the communications used were the actual products of students under no choice conditions, the same effects found by Jones and Harris were obtained. A crucial feature of Snyder's experiments was that each subject wrote a no choice essay himself, to be delivered to another subject. Thus, the subjects should have been clearly aware of the constraints involved and of the ease or difficulty of generating arguments for a position opposite to that privately held.

The Jones and Harris experiment provides evidence, then, that observers are willing to take behavior more or less at "face value," as reflecting a stable disposition, even when it is made clear that the actor's behavior is under severe external constraints.

Chapter 10 The Actor and the Observer: Divergent Perceptions of the Causes of Behavior **183**

These results have been replicated both by Snyder and more recently by Jones, Worchel, Goethals, and Grumet (1971) with "legalization of marijuana" as the issue.

A second study providing data for observers only has been performed by McArthur (1970). Her study is quite relevant to our proposition, if one is willing to lean heavily on intuitions about the causal attributions that would be expected of actors. Subjects were given a simple, one-sentence description of an action, such as "George translates the sentence incorrectly," **[81]** "While dancing, Ralph trips over Jane's feet," "Steve puts a bumper sticker advocating improved automobile safety on his car." They were then asked why this action probably occurred: Whether it was something about the person that caused him to act this way ("Something about *George* probably caused him to translate the sentence incorrectly"), or something about the *stimulus* ("Something about the *sentence* probably caused George to translate it incorrectly"), or something about the *situation* ("Something about the *particular circumstances* probably caused George to translate it incorrectly"). If subjects found none of these simple explanations to be the likely one, they were allowed to give whatever explanation they thought necessary to account for the behavior. These were then coded into complex explanations involving both person and stimulus, both person and circumstances, both stimulus and circumstances, or all three. (As it happened, only the person–stimulus combination was resorted to with very great frequency.)

It seems likely that if one were to ask a random sample of people who had mistranslated sentences, tripped over feet, or placed bumper stickers on their cars why they had performed their various actions, a rather high fraction of explanations would be pure stimulus attributions or mixed stimulus–circumstance attributions. We would expect answers such as "That sentence was difficult to translate," "It was dark and Jane doesn't cha-cha the way I do," "The AAA sent me this catchy bumper sticker in the mail." For McArthur's vicarious observers, however, such reasons were extremely infrequent, amounting to only 4 per cent of the total attributions. By far, the greatest proportion of reasons given—44 per cent for each of these particular actions—were pure *person* attributions: George translates the sentence incorrectly because he is rather poor at translating sentences and Steve is the sort who puts bumper stickers on his car.

McArthur also presented her subjects with statements about emotional experiences, such as "John laughs at the comedian," "Sue is afraid of the dog," "Tom is enthralled by the painting." One would expect that in a random sample of people found laughing at comedians, being frightened by dogs, or being enthralled by paintings, most of the actors would explain their experiences in pure stimulus terms: The comedian is funny; the dog is scary; the painting is beautiful. For McArthur's observers, however, only 19 per cent of the attributions were pure stimulus attributions and the most frequent attributions (45 per cent of the total) were *person–stimulus interactions:* "Sue tends to be afraid of dogs and this is a very large one." Interestingly, one of the emotion items did produce a very high proportion (52 per cent) of pure stimulus attributions: "Mary is angered by the psychology experiment." Since subjects were at that moment participating in a psychology experiment, it is tempting to conclude that they were responding as actors rather than as observers.

It is possible that some unintended feature of McArthur's highly artificial situation forced attributions away from the stimulus and toward the person. Perhaps a different sample of statements or a more extended account of the behavior would yield different results.

Nevertheless, the willingness of her subjects to invoke explanations involving dispositions of the person seems striking. One's strong intuition is that the actors themselves, in real-life situations of the type described to McArthur's subjects, would rarely interpret their behavior in dispositional terms.

McArthur (1970) completed a second experiment that is less open to criticism on methodological grounds. Subjects were induced to perform a particular act, and a written account of the actor and the surrounding circumstances was presented to observers. It was then possible to compare the attributions made by the actor subjects with the later attributions made by observer subjects. McArthur obtained the consent of subjects to participate in a survey concerning interpersonal relationships and then asked the subjects why they had agreed to participate. As we would expect, subjects were inclined to attribute their participation to the importance of the survey and were not likely to attribute their participation to a general disposition to take part in such surveys. Observers exactly reversed this pattern, attributing subjects' participation primarily to a personal inclination to take part in surveys and only secondarily to the value of the survey.

McArthur's study comes very close to being a direct test of the proposition that actors attribute cause to situations while observers attribute cause to dispositions. It suffers, however, from the interpretive difficulty that information about the actor's behavior was given to observers only in printed, verbal form. Two studies by Nisbett and his colleagues avoided this problem by examining situations where more nearly equivalent forms of information were available to actors and observers.

In the first of these studies, Nisbett and Caputo (1971) asked college students to write a brief paragraph stating why they had chosen their major field of concentration and why they liked the girl they dated most frequently. Subjects were asked to write similar brief paragraphs explaining why their best friends had chosen their majors and girl friends. It proved possible to code all of the answers, à la McArthur, into either stimulus attributions ("Chemistry is a high-paying field," "She's a very warm person") or person attributions ("I want to make a lot of money," "I like warm girls"). When answering for himself, the average subject listed roughly the same number of stimulus and person reasons for choosing his major and twice as many stimulus as person reasons for choosing his girl friend. When answering for his best friend, subjects listed approximately three times as many person as stimulus reasons for choosing the major and roughly the same number of stimulus as person reasons for choosing the girl friend. Thus, when describing either choice of a major or choice of a girl friend, subjects were more likely to use dispositional language for their best friends than for themselves.

In a final study, Nisbett, Legant, and Marecek (1971) allowed observer subjects to watch actor subjects in a controlled laboratory setting. Subjects were Yale co-eds. Those designated as actors believed they were to participate in a study on decision-making. Subjects designated as observers believed their task would be to watch the subject make decisions and then make judgments about the subject's reasons for making her decisions. Prior to the fictitious decision-making study, the experimenter met with the actor and two confederates, who presumably also were going to be subjects in the decision-making study. The observer sat in the background, with instructions simply to observe the (real) target subject. The experimenter, after some introductions and throat-clearing, said, "Before we begin the study, I happen to have sort of a real decision for you to make." The experimenter explained that the "Human Development Institute" at Yale would be sponsoring a weekend for the corporate board and some of their prospective financial backers. The wives of these men would need entertainment and campus tours for the weekend. As a consequence, the Institute had asked the psychology department to recruit students to help with this chore. After elaborating on details of time, place, and specific activities, the experimenter solicited the help of the two confederates and the actor. The confederates were always asked first, and, in order to boost compliance rates on the part of actors, always willingly volunteered.

The amount of money offered to volunteers was manipulated—either $0.50 per hour or $1.50 per hour—with very large effects on compliance rates. Only about a fifth of the low-payment actors volunteered, while two-thirds of the high-payment actors volunteered. Volunteers' rates were thus determined in a major way by a purely extrinsic factor: the amount of money offered for compliance.

Actor and observer were then led to separate rooms where they were asked detailed questions concerning the actor's reasons for volunteering or not volunteering. The questions included an item designed to tap the extent to which the actor's behavior was considered an expression of a general disposition to volunteer or not volunteer for worthy activities: "How likely do you think it is that you (or the subject) would also volunteer to canvas for the United Fund?" Observers of volunteering actors thought that the actors would be more likely to volunteer for the United Fund than observers of nonvolunteering actors. Actors themselves did not think they were any more likely to help the United Fund if they were volunteers than if they were nonvolunteers. Thus, in this experimental situation, observers infer dispositions from observation of the actor's behavior, while actors themselves do not.

This last experiment is useful in pointing out the relationship between our proposition and the proposal by Bem (1965, 1967) emphasizing the *convergent* perceptions of actors and observers. In all important respects, according to Bem, people use the same kinds of evidence and follow the same logic whether they are making self-attributions or deciding about the characteristics of others. Actors are self-observers, viewing their own behavior in terms of the surrounding context and inferring what their attitudes and feelings must have been. We agree that actors often reflect on their own actions to check on the direction and intensity of their attitudes and feelings, but contend that actors are much more likely than observers to see those actions as constrained by the situations. We feel it is frequently the case that, as in the experiment just described, observers make dispositional inferences from behavior that is interpreted quite differently by actors. To support this contention, we shall now examine what we believe to be differences in the information available to actor and observer and differences between the two in the processing of the available information.

THE INFORMATION AVAILABLE TO ACTOR AND OBSERVER

It is a truism that the meaning of an action can be judged only in relation to its context. It is central to our argument that the context data are often quite different for actor and observer, and that these differing data prompt differing attributions. The kinds of data available for the attribution process may be conveniently broken down into effect data and cause data. Effect data are of three broad types: data about the nature of the act itself (what was done), data about the environmental outcomes of the act (success or failure, reaction of the recipient of action, and so on), and data about the actor's experiences (pleasure, anger, embarrassment). Cause data are of two broad types: environmental causes (incentives, **[83]** task difficulty) and intention data (what the actor meant to do, how hard he was working to do it). This categorization is useful for pinpointing the areas where discrepancies are likely to occur in the information available to actor and observer.

Effect Data

Under the category of effect data, it seems clear that actor and observer can have equivalent information about the nature of the act and about environmental outcomes. The observer may know that the actor has delivered an insult and that the recipient is angered. The observer can, however, have no direct knowledge of the experiential accompaniments of the act for the actor. The observer's knowledge about the actor's feelings is limited to inferences of two types: attempts to read inner experience from physiognomic and gestural cues, and judgments based on the observer's knowledge of what others and he himself have felt in similar situations. The observer may infer from the actor's flushed face that he spoke in anger, or he may guess that an insult of the type delivered would probably only be spoken by someone in a great rage. Of course, expressive behavior may not be witnessed by the observer at all. If it is not, then he simply has no information on this score. If it is, his knowledge of the experience of the actor may range from superior in rare cases—a parent may know better than his child that the child is disappointed over a failure or frightened of moving to a strange city—to quite inferior or utterly wrong. In many circumstances actors are motivated to conceal their inner feelings. In others, misperceptions derive from unrecognized individual differences in expressive style. Knowledge of the actor's feeling states is therefore never direct, usually sketchy, and sometimes wrong.

Cause Data

Under the category of perceived causes, it seems clear that there can be equal or nearly equal knowledge of the proximal environmental stimuli operating on the actor. The observer, for example, may know that the recipient of the actor's insult had previously taunted the actor. In principle such knowledge can be as complete for the observer as for the actor. In practice such completeness is probably rarely approximated, if only because of the likelihood that the actor is responding to events more extended in time than those available to the observer. The particular taunt that triggered the actor's outburst may have been the straw that broke the camel's back—the latest in a series of frustrations. The observer is more likely to work instead with the data from one slice of time. Even so, the discrepancy in information about the causal role of the environment is probably rarely as great as the discrepancy in knowledge about the experiential accompaniments of the action. Nor is the discrepancy as great as it is with the second type of data concerning causality—the intentions of the actor.

Like the actor's feeling states, his intentions can never be directly known to the observer. In attempting to determine whether the insult was a spontaneous outburst produced by rage or a calculated move to embarrass and motivate the recipient, the observer may infer intentions from the actor's expressive behavior or from the "logic" of the situation. But, as with feeling states, knowledge of intentions is indirect, usually quite inferior, and highly subject to error.

Historical Data

As the previous section indicates, it is never really possible to divorce a given act from a broader temporal context. Much of the discrepancy between the perspectives of observer and actor arises from the difference between the observer's inferred history of everyman and the concrete individualized history of the actor himself. The actor has been exposed to a sequence of experiences that are to a degree unique, but the observer is constrained to work with the blunt conceptual tools of modal or normative experience.

Kelley (1967) has proposed that naïve causal inference resembles the scientist's analysis of variance. The attributor possesses three different kinds of information that correspond to different causal possibilities: consensus information (do other actors behave in the same way to a given stimulus?); distinctiveness information (does the actor, and do other actors, behave in the same way to other stimuli?); and consistency information (does the actor, and do other actors, behave in the same way to the given stimulus across time and situational contexts?). The attributor then makes use of whatever information he has available in the "analysis of variance cube" formed by these three dimensions and makes the best causal inference he can. In Kelley's terms, the observer always lacks some of the distinctiveness and consistency information the actor possesses by virtue of knowing his own history. The observer may approach the actor's knowledge of these dimensions if he knows the actor well, but he cannot reach it. If the actor is unfamiliar to him, he knows nothing at all of this data set.

Because the actor knows his past, he is often diverted from making a dispositional attribution. If the actor insults someone, an observer, who may **[84]** assume that this is a typical sample of behavior, may infer that the actor is hostile. The actor, on the other hand, may believe that the sample is anything but typical. He may recall very few other instances when he insulted anyone, and may believe that in most of these instances he was sharply provoked. The actor's knowledge about the variability of his previous conduct—associated, in his mind, with different situational requirements—often preempts the possibility of a dispositional attribution. We suspect that because of the differences in the availability of personal history data, actors and observers evaluate each act along a different scale of comparison. The observer is characteristically normative and nomothetic: He compares the actor with other actors and judges his attributes accordingly. The actor, on the other hand, is more inclined to use an ipsative or idiographic reference scale: This action is judged with reference to his other previous actions, rather than the acts of other actors.

There is, in summary, good reason to believe that actors and observers often bring different information to bear on their inferences about the actor and his environment. Typically, the actor has more, and more precise, information than the observer about his own emotional state and his intentions. (We say "typically" rather than "obviously" because there are occasions when the actor might be defensively unaware of his own motives, motives that are readily discernible to the observer.) Moreover, in the absence of precise knowledge of the actor's history, the observer is compelled to deal with him as a modal case and to ignore his unique history and orientation.

The difference in information available to actor and observer probably plays an important role in producing differential attributions, but this is not the whole story. There are good reasons for believing that the same information is differentially processed by actors and observers.

DIFFERENCES IN INFORMATION PROCESSING

While it hardly seems debatable that actors and observers operate much of the time with different background data, the contention that actors and observers differ fundamentally in the *processing* of available data is bound to be more controversial. We believe that important information-processing differences do exist for the basic reason that *different aspects of the available information are salient for actors and observers and this differential* salience *affects the course and outcome of the attribution process.*

The actor and the observer are both reaching for interpretations of behavior that are sufficient for their own decision-making purposes. With unlimited time, and using the kinds of probes that emphasize a full deterministic picture of an action sequence, observers can probably reach attributional conclusions very similar to those of the actor. In the heat of the interaction moment, however, the purposes of actor and observer are apt to be different enough to start the inference process along distinctive tracks. Conceptualization of this problem depends to some extent on the kind of action–observation situation we are considering. Two extreme cases are the mutual contingency interaction (Jones & Gerard, 1967), where each actor observes, and is affected by, the other, and the asymmetrical case of passive observation, where running behavioral decisions are thrust exclusively upon the actor while the observer's only task is to record and interpret—as if from behind a one-way screen.

We shall later examine the differences between these two situations, but a very important feature is common to both: the action itself—its topography, rhythm, style, and content—is more salient to the observer than to the actor. In establishing the reasons for this, we may begin with the observation that action involves perceptible movement and change (by definition), and it is always, to some extent, unpredictable. While the environment is stable and contextual from the observer's point of view, action is figural and dynamic. The actor, however, is less likely to focus his attention on his behavior than on the environmental cues that evoke and shape it. In part, this is because the actor's receptors are poorly located for recording the nuances of his own behavior. Many response sequences are preprogrammed and prepackaged, as it were, and do not require careful monitoring. The actor need not concern himself with his response repertory until there is conflict among the demands of the environment. Even then he will resolve the conflict in terms of perceived stimulus requirements. In short, the actor need not, and in some ways cannot, observe his behavior very closely. Instead, his attention is directed outward, toward the environment with its constantly shifting demands and opportunities.

These attentional differences should result in differences in causal perception. The actor should perceive his behavior to be a response to environmental cues that trigger, guide, and terminate it. But for the observer, the focal, commanding stimulus is the actor's behavior, and situational cues are, to a degree, ignored. This leaves the actor as the likely causal candidate, and the observer will account for the actor's responses in terms of attributed dispositions.

The effect of these differential attribution tendencies [85] is amplified by bias from another source, the tendency to regard one's reactions to entities as based on accurate perceptions of them. Rather than humbly regarding our impressions of the world as interpretations of it, we see them as understandings or correct apprehensions of it. The nature of this bias is perhaps easiest to see with young children, where it is much more extensive and profound than for adults. Philosophers and other adults make a distinction between the properties of entities that a three-year-old child does not make. The distinction is between those properties that have an existence apart from the transaction of a human being with the object and those properties that are the result of such a transaction. Properties of the former type include the bulk, shape, mass, and motion of an object. Most philosophers and almost all scientists and laymen would agree that such properties have an existence apart from the perception of them. Philosophers since the seventeenth century have designated these as primary qualities and have distinguished them from what are called secondary qualities, including taste, odor, sound, and color, which have no existence apart from the interaction of a sense organ with the object. The layman, it is important to note, does not ordinarily distinguish between primary and secondary qualities unless corrected by a philosopher. He does, however, distinguish in principle between the primary and secondary qualities on the one hand, and what may be called evaluations on the other. Evaluations include judgments such as those concerning the goodness, beauty, or propriety of an object or action. Adults realize, at least intellectually, that evaluations do not have the status of perceptions, but are only interpretations or reactions.

How is it that a three-year-old correctly learns the distinction between evaluations and primary qualities, and incorrectly learns to group the secondary qualities with primary qualities instead of with evaluations? The answer seems to be that the child learns that certain of his reactions to objects meet invariably with consensual validation, while others do not. Once he learns the designation "blue," his judgment that an object is blue is almost never contradicted. He eventually learns, however, that not everyone agrees with his evaluations of objects as pretty, funny, or good. In terms of Kelley's (1967) analysis of variance analogy, the child comes to learn that certain of his reactions to entities are shared by all others, and that he himself has those same reactions at all times and under all circumstances. Simultaneously, he learns that there are certain other types of reactions that may or may not be shared by others and that he himself does not invariably have. Before the analysis of variance cubes begin to fill in, however, the child believes that clowns are funny in the same way that balls are round. Funniness is experienced as a property of the clown.

It seems clear that the distinction between evaluations and primary qualities is never fully made. We never quite get over our initial belief that funniness is a property of the clown and beauty is in the object. The probable reason for this is the fact that there remains a considerable degree of consensus even for our most subjective evaluations. Almost always, at least some people agree with our evaluations, and sometimes almost everyone agrees with our evaluations. Phenomenologically, the distinction between evaluations and primary qualities is merely a quantitative one, just as the initial basis for learning the distinction—the degree of consensus—is quantitative. Just as we erroneously feel that secondary qualities are primary, we continue to feel that our subjective evaluations are in some sense perceptions.

This confusion between what is inherent in the object and what is a reaction elicited by it comes close to what Heider labels "egocentric attribution":

> Attribution to the object ... means more than the dependence of p's pleasure on the object. It also means that there is something enjoyable about the object. The attractiveness is a quality of the object, just as is the sweetness of a fruit or the roughness of a terrain. Consequently, p's expectations, and therefore beliefs, refer not only to his own reactions to x on future occasions, but also the reactions of other people. The basic scheme is as follows: "Since my pleasure was aroused by x, x is positive, and therefore everyone will like it." An expectation of similarity between the reactions of others and the self is thus egocentrically determined (1958, p. 158).

Our responses to immediately impinging stimuli are therefore biased in two ways: they are too salient and they are too "real." These biases should have a pronounced effect on the interpretations given by an actor and an observer to the actor's behavior. The actor will experience his behavior as proceeding naturally from the attractions, compulsions, and restraints in his environment. For the observer, it is not the stimuli impinging on the actor that are salient, but the behavior of the actor. The observer will therefore tend to see the actor's behavior as a manifestation of the actor, as an instance of a quality possessed by him. For the actor to interpret his behavior as the result of a disposition, he would have to weight the impact of the immediate environment less heavily, regard his knowledge about the environment as mere evaluations that may or may not be shared, and recognize that others might not respond as he does to this particular environment. For the observer to interpret the actor's behavior as a response to his environment, he would have to weight the vivid, sense-impression [86] data of the behavior itself less heavily and strain his empathic abilities to allow himself to imagine the vividness for the actor of the environmental cues he confronts. To the extent that actor and observer fail to accomplish these tasks, the actor will overattribute his behavior to the environment and the observer will overattribute the behavior to qualities of the actor.

The quotation from Heider is but one reflection of our debt to him, but we wish to demur from the tone of Heider's analysis. The term "egocentric attribution" and Heider's discussion of the concept make the process sound willful and motivated, or at best the result of self-satisfied laziness. We hold that the individual comes by "egocentric attribution" honestly for the most part. All of our evaluations would be "egocentric attributions" were it not for the fact that we occasionally learn that our evaluations are not shared. The illusion that our reactions are perceptions is sustained, in part, by the apparent consensus accompanying most of our reactions, a consensus that may rest as much on transmitted cultural norms as on the compelling features of objective "reality."

Another of Heider's observations is closely related to our present discussion:

> It seems that behavior ... has such salient properties that it tends to engulf the field rather than be confined to its proper position as a local stimulus whose interpretation requires the additional data of a surrounding field—the situation in social perception (1958, p. 54).

What we have said about the observer's perspective on the actor's behavior clearly echoes Heider's idea. Again, however, we differ with Heider about the explanation for

Chapter 10 The Actor and the Observer: Divergent Perceptions of the Causes of Behavior

this phenomenon. Heider appears to believe that behavior engulfs the field because the observer often cannot see all the environmental stimuli operating on the actor and because the observer often has not seen that the actor displays different behavior in other circumstances. We have already seconded this opinion in the section dealing with differences in available information, but we also believe that behavior engulfs the field in part because the salient, vivid stimulus for the observer is the actor's behavior. Even when the stimuli influencing the actor's behavior are visible to the observer, he ignores them to an extent.

Our differences with Heider are clearly minor and involve primarily subtleties of emphasis. It should be noted, however, that our analyses have different starting points. We prefer to derive the notion that behavior engulfs the field from the assumption that, for the observer, behavior is figural against the ground of the situation. And we prefer to derive the concept of egocentric attribution from the assumption that the primitive belief in evaluations as perceptions is never outgrown.

It is now time to return to the distinction between passive and active observers, and to consider the implications of this distinction for our discussion. By definition, the passive observer is not in a position to respond to the actor, and the actor is unaware of his specific presence. The observer may be affected by the actor, but the actor cannot be affected by the observer—there is asymmetrical contingency. This is the situation of the moviegoer, the TV watcher, and the concealed observer behind a one-way screen. The passive observer may have any of a number of purposes that make him more attentive to certain kinds of information than others. As Lazarus (1966) and Aderman and Berkowitz (1970) have shown, it is possible to affect the amount of empathy shown by the observer for the actor by simple variations in observational instructions. Presumably, the more the observer is set to empathize with the actor, the more similar their attributional perspectives will be. Unless the observer has a strong empathy set, however, we would expect him to show the general observer tendency to underestimate the role of the environment, if only because of the differential salience of behavioral and situational information.

For the observer who is at the same time an actor, the tendency toward heightened salience of action should become more pronounced for several reasons. The fact that the observer is also caught up in action suggests that he will not be in a position to make leisurely appraisals of the setting and its contributions to unfolding behavior. Rather than being in a set to understand and evaluate the relative contributions of person and environment, the actor–observer will be tuned to process those cues that are particularly pertinent for his own next responses. Short-run behavior prediction is of paramount importance to the observer who is preparing his next act, and we suggest that the actor's behavior is more likely to seem pertinent for such predictions than the situational context evoking it. The acting organism probably does not operate at the peak of potential cognitive complexity, but it is likely to be attracted to convenient simplifying assumptions about the environment. One such simplifying assumption is that action implies a disposition to continue acting in the same manner, and to act in such a manner in other situations as well.

A second consideration arises from the fact that the observer's presence and behavior may affect the actor's responses in ways not discerned by the observer. It is difficult for the active observer to evaluate the significance of his own presence because he is not often afforded clear comparative tests—tests that pit the stimulus contributions he generally makes [87] against the stimulus contributions of others. In the situation we are now considering, where the observer is also an actor, the observer is likely to exaggerate the uniqueness and emphasize the dispositional origin of the other's responses to his own actions, actions the observer assumes to be perfectly standard, unexceptional, and unprovocative.

A final feature of the mutual contingency interaction is that the surrounding environment is roughly the same for each actor—observer. Therefore, the extent to which each actor behaves differently in the same situation should cause *each* to attribute the other's actions to internal, dispositional factors. If actor *A* is attuned to the reality of the situation, and sees himself as behaving accordingly, any variations in *B*'s behavior will be attributed to *B*'s idiosyncratic interpretations of that reality.

In summary, the observer and the actor are likely to take different perspectives toward the same information. For the observer, the actor's behavior is the figural stimulus against the ground of the situation. The actor's attention is focused outward toward situational cues rather than inward on his own behavior, and moreover, those situational cues are endowed with intrinsic properties that are seen to cause the actor's behavior toward them. Thus, for the observer, the proximal cause of action is the actor; for the actor, the proximal cause lies in the compelling qualities of the environment. Finally, the tendency for the observer to attribute action to the actor is probably increased to the extent that the observer is also an actor, and to the extent that both the observing and the observed actor are tied together in a mutually contingent interaction.

THE NAIVE PSYCHOLOGY OF OBSERVERS AND ACTORS

The preceding discussion is likely to raise, in the reader's mind, a question as to who is correct, the actor or the observer. In the typical case, is behavior really caused by the actor or elicited by the environment? Put in these simplified terms, the question is of course unanswerable. All behavior is, in one sense, caused or produced by the actor. Except perhaps in acts such as the patellar reflex, all action involves some form of explicit or implicit decision process suggesting volition or personal causation.

The more pertinent and answerable question concerns the extent to which a particular setting is likely to evoke the same response across many persons. According to either the logic of Kelley's (1967) analysis of variance cube, or of Jones and Davis' (1965) correspondent inference theory, a situation that evokes a response common to many persons is likely to be seen as causing the behavior. Situations that evoke varied or unique responses are much less likely to be seen as causal. Obviously, when a person acts in a similar fashion on many different occasions, the act is seen to reflect a personal disposition.

It is obviously safer to talk about *phenomenal* causality than to raise any questions concerning accuracy or objective causality. Nevertheless, it is interesting to consider the many occasions on which the observer appears to violate the rules, set up for him by Kelley and by Jones and Davis—to make a dispositional inference when the data do not allow it. Without insisting that the actor is usually right, we can point to many instances where the observer's interpretation of behavior is simply wrong. The observer is wrong when he infers that an attitude is consistent with an essay written in response to a legitimate request. He is wrong when he thinks the nonintervening bystander is apathetic, or infers that the subject who agrees to help out for a handsome fee is a chronic volunteer. In each of these cases, the observer seems to underestimate the power of the situation and to overestimate the uniqueness of the (in fact modal) response.

The Observer's View: Personality as a Trait Package

It is interesting to speculate on the possible implications of the observer's bias for the conception of personality structure held by most people in our society, and indeed by most personality psychologists. At bottom, this conception is an Aristotelian view of personality as a collection of traits, that is, the most general kind of dispositions. Does this conception err by overemphasizing individual differences at the trait level and slighting the impact of situational variance?

Mischel (1968) argues persuasively that such overemphasis is common. He reviews the evidence on the existence of several dimensions of behavior usually presumed to be manifestations of a trait—honesty, dependency, attitudes toward authority, rigidity or intolerance for ambiguity, persuasability, and so on. Using the restricted empirical criterion of predictability from one behavior that is presumed to reflect the trait to another such behavior, Mischel finds little evidence that traits exist anywhere but in the cognitive structure of observers. For example, in the early, but very sophisticated and ambitious honesty study of Hartshorne and May (1928), children were exposed to a variety of temptations in a variety of settings, including the opportunity to cheat on a test, steal money, and lie to save face. Despite the fact that there was some reliability of behavior (for example, the correlation between cheating by copying the answer key on one test in school and copying **[88]** the answer key on another test was .70), there was very little generality of honesty across settings. It was rare for correlations across different behaviors, and especially for different behaviors across different settings, to exceed .30. This means, of course, that the improvement in predicting dishonesty in one situation by virtue of knowing about behavior in another situation is negligible. Mischel reviewed many other studies attempting to find behavioral generality across settings usually presumed to reflect a given trait. With the rather clear exception of abilities and ability related traits, no disposition was found to be immune from the indictment of low generality.

The trait concept fares no better when it is examined in terms of attempts to predict behavior from paper and pencil trait measurements. When trait scores are obtained from questionnaire self-reports, they rarely predict, with any accuracy, behavior that is presumed to tap the trait dimension. Mischel facetiously proposes that the term "personality coefficient" might be used to describe "the correlation between .20 and .30 that is found persistently when virtually any personality dimension inferred from a questionnaire is related to almost any conceivable external criterion involving responses sampled in a *different* medium—that is, not by another questionnaire" (p.78). Thus, when we ask a person what his position is on a trait, or when we infer it from his response to questionnaire items, we learn almost nothing about his actual behavior.

What Sustains the Belief in Traits?

Mischel therefore contends that there is little evidence for the existence of the broad trait concepts that have been such a standard part of our psychological vocabulary for centuries. From our position of lesser expertise, we agree that a conception of personality emphasizing behavior generality is inadequate and misleading. How does it happen, then, that students of personality have persistently embraced a trait construction of behavior? Why has it taken forty years of negative findings on the question for anyone to propose seriously, in a textbook on personality, that these trait dimensions may not exist? One answer is that the conclusion is based on inadequate data; another, that the traits have not been measured properly; or still a third, that the wrong traits have been examined. Another answer, and this is a conclusion that Mischel and the present writers prefer, is that traits exist more in the eye of the beholder than in the psyche of the actor.

If we are to uphold the position that personality traits are overattributed, then it is incumbent upon us to account for the widespread belief in their existence. Beliefs in a trait psychology are especially perplexing when held by personality psychologists who have worked in the area and watched the negative evidence accumulate. If the belief in traits is mistaken, there would have to be very strong forces operating to sustain it. We believe there are such forces and have already dealt with two of them: (1) the information-processing biases that conspire to make behavior appear as a manifestation or quality of the actor and (2) the informational deficit of the observer, which prevents disconfirmation of the trait inference. We believe there are still other important reasons for the illusion. In discussing these reasons, it will be helpful to categorize them into sources of informational bias, sources of information-processing bias, and sources of linguistic bias. The discussion draws heavily on similar arguments made by Mischel (1968, 1969), and to a lesser extent, on ideas expressed by Heider (1958) and Icheiser (1949).

INFORMATIONAL BIAS Apart from the general ignorance one has about the range of behaviors that another person can exhibit, and apart from one's general ignorance of the environmental forces operating on him, there are some quite specific and systematic information deficits that help to turn ignorance into error. As Mischel (1968) notes, most of the people we observe are seen only in a very few roles. Within those already narrow confines, we are likely to see them in a biased sample of situations: when they are at their best or at their worst, when they are at their most harassed or their most relaxed, in their work moods or their play moods, in the morning or in the evening, in the company of people they like or with people they dislike. Those of us who are embedded in a bureaucracy may be especially prone to confuse responses to role requirements with personality dispositions. Bank presidents are usually surprised when the drab, black-suited teller absconds with the funds and is found living it up in Tahiti. To the extent that role and situational factors produce behavior that can be labeled as conforming, hostile, thrifty, brave, clean, or reverent, observers are likely to see the individual as being a conforming, hostile, thrifty, brave, clean, or reverent person.

Beyond the sampling bias produced by roles and situations, one carries with him, into a relationship with others, a bias in the form of oneself. To the extent that one's own behavior is a restricted sample of possible behaviors, it will evoke a restricted sample from the other person in turn. This point has been anticipated in our previous discussion of the "active observer" and is similar to one made by Kelley and Stahelski (1970). They point out that one's own behavior may evoke complementary responses in another [89] that one then mistakenly perceives as a manifestation of the other's personality. One may unwittingly shape the other's behavior in a variety of ways: by one's own role- and situation-determined behaviors toward the other, by implicitly communicated expectations and hopes about his behavior, and by a host of personal characteristics such as one's abilities, physical appearance, mannerisms, or social status.

INFORMATION-PROCESSING BIAS Much has been written about the human tendency toward cognitive balance or consistency. Surely the tendency toward consistency must play some role in the observer's assignment of traits. A person who is aggressive in one setting should, to be "consistent," be aggressive in other settings. To see dependence and independence in the same actor may lead to greater subtleties of categorization, or it may lead to misperception of the evidence so that it becomes more consistent. In short, all the cognitive mechanisms of inconsistency reduction can be put to work in the service of dispositional accounts of action. It is not surprising that personal consistency is exaggerated in the eye of the beholder.

The tendencies toward primacy and assimilation discussed by Jones and Goethals (1972) also operate to create illusions of consistency. Out of his needs to impose structure on the environment, the observer often makes premature commitments to the nature of those entities he is observing. Within certain limits of discrepancy, therefore, inconsistent information will be seen as more consistent than it deserves to be. Even beyond these limits, contradictory data can be treated as anomalous, even as the exception that proves the rule.

Mischel (1968) points to still another factor that may encourage us to see people as being more of a piece than they are. The simple fact that another person is physically continuous, always looks more or less the same, and has the same mannerisms, may encourage the impression that there is continuity in his behavior as well. The fact of physical constancy may produce the illusion of behavioral, and therefore dispositional, consistency.

LINGUISTIC DISTORTIONS Language probably facilitates the inference of traits in several ways. Once we have labeled an action as hostile, it is very easy to move to the inference that the perpetrator is a hostile person. Our language allows the same term to be applied to behavior and to the underlying disposition it reflects. It is possible to imagine that we all have little syllogistic subroutines through which we constantly generate trait inferences from act labels: "o has behaved x-ly; people who have the x trait behave x-ly; o has the x trait." The application of the syllogism will lead to an erroneous trait inference whenever we overlook the fact that there are other reasons for behaving x-ly besides having the trait of x. Which is to say, often.

It may also be noted that our vocabulary is rich in dispositional or trait terms (the Allport–Ogbert list includes over 18,000 terms) and quite impoverished when it comes to describing the situation. Among personality theorists H. A. Murray (1938) has shown as much sensitivity to this problem as anyone, but his list of environmental "presses" is merely adapted from a complementary list of needs. In social psychology, Roger Barker (1968) has stood almost alone in attempting to develop a descriptive taxonomy for behavior settings. His important effort is undoubtedly much impeded by the inadequate resources placed at his disposal by the English language.

The momentum of our linguistic machinery undoubtedly does not stop with the inference of a single trait. Passini and Norman (1966) have shown that the same factor structure is obtained for trait ascriptions to total strangers as for trait ascriptions to well known acquaintances. This would seem to indicate that we carry trait-intercorrelation matrices around in our heads, or to put it in a more traditional way, that we have implicit personality theories (Jones, 1954; Cronbach, 1955). We tend to assume that trait x is, in general, associated with trait y. This means that we may pass from observation of an act that we label as x-like to the inference of an x trait to the inference of a y trait because of our assumption that traits x and y are correlated.

THE RARITY OF DISCONFIRMATION Informational bias, processing bias, and linguistic bias all operate, therefore, in such a way as to generate trait inferences where there may be no traits. Are there no mechanisms that can curtail and reverse the errors? There probably are. Certainly the better we know someone, the more restraints there are against facile trait ascription. There are probably sharp limits, however, to the power of additional information to disconfirm a trait ascription. Once we have decided that a person is hostile or dependent, a wide variety of behaviors can be construed as support for this supposition, including even behaviors commonly taken as implying the opposite of the trait ascription. A kind behavior on the part of a "hostile" person may be perceived as insincere, manipulative, or condescending. We are probably all rather adept at the maintenance of a trait inference in the face of disconfirmatory evidence. When practiced by some psychoanalytic writers, the maneuvering can be truly breathtaking.

It might be argued that discussion with others provides ample opportunity for disconfirmation of a trait [90] inference. The individual may find in such discussion that his trait inferences are not shared. This is undoubtedly true. We can all think of instances where our beliefs about another person have been altered by hearing about someone else's experiences with that person. There are good reasons to expect that our erroneous trait inferences will more often receive consensual validation, however. To the extent that another person resembles oneself in role, status, personal and physical characteristics, he is likely to have the same sorts of experiences with a given person that one has had oneself, and therefore to have made the same trait inferences. It seems likely, moreover, that the more similar two people are the more probable it is that they will discuss the personality of someone they know mutually. The chairman of a department does not often exchange opinions with graduate students on the intelligence or warmth of assistant professors. Finally, when one's trait inferences are flatly contradicted by another person, everything we have said implies that one is likely to explain the contradiction in terms of the dispositions of the person who is contradicting him: "I wonder why John is unable to see the essential kindness of Mary."

In summary, the observer, even when he is a professional psychologist, is apt to conceive of the personalities of others as a collection of broad dispositions or traits, despite the scant empirical evidence for their existence. This conception appears to result from deficits and biases in the information available to the observer, and to a variety of biases in the processing of information at the perceptual, cognitive, and linguistic levels. It should be noted, however, that the low empirical validity of the trait concept may be of importance only to the psychologist. The observer, in his daily life, may achieve fairly high predictability using trait inferences that the psychologist can show to be erroneous. If the observer is habitually insulted by a given actor, it may make little difference to the observer whether the reason for this consistent behavior is the hostility of the actor, the actor's dislike of the observer, or the fact that the observer sees the actor only in the early morning when the actor is always grouchy.

The Actor's View: Personality as a Value Matrix There has been relatively little research on the actor's view of his own personality structure. The individual's implicit theory of his own personality has not usually been singled out for study by personality theorists, probably because it is generally assumed that actors regard themselves only as "instances" of personalities generally. Much that we have said about the actor's perspective on his own behavior prompts the suggestion that this assumption may not be correct.

Mischel has noted that "Dispositional theories try to categorize behaviors in terms of the hypothesized historical psychic forces that diverse behaviors supposedly serve; but it is also possible to categorize the behaviors in terms of the unifying, evoking, and maintaining conditions that they jointly share" (1969, p. 1016). Mischel, of course, prefers the latter conception of individual differences as the more nearly accurate account.

We would suggest that the actor's view of his own personality is close to the conception preferred by Mischel. Consistent with the actor's strong preference for assigning causal significance to the situation, he tends to focus on Mischel's "evoking and maintaining conditions" as the stimuli guiding his own behavior. Whereas observers operate as trait psychologists, actors may operate as contingent reinforcement theorists, mapping their behavioral plans in terms of perceived reinforcement potentials. The observer, we have argued, processes actions in a nomothetic, taxonomic way, and is thus likely to construe behavior on what Allport (1937) would call a common trait basis. The actor, if he thinks of himself as having traits at all, is likely to see an "individual trait" (the term again is Allport's), expressing the congruity of interrelated purposes. When the actor steps back to view himself, he is probably inclined to emphasize not the superficial topography of behavior but the underlying purposes mediated by the behavior. The actor is consequently more likely to conceive of his personality as a configuration of value sand strategies than as a collection of response dispositions. When the actor compares himself to others, we might expect him to believe that he differs chiefly in the priorities that he assigns to his goals,and in the particular, means he has devised to achieve them.

We have criticized the observer harshly for his errors, and to be fair we should note that the actor is also likely to make some mistakes. We have already observed that people fail to distinguish between primary and secondary qualities, and tend to blur the distinction between perceptions and evaluations. The actor probably consistently errs by ignoring the role of his own biases in responding to situations. In Lewinian terms, the actor locates the valence in the object rather than the need in himself. If the observer assumes that people are more different than they are, the actor probably assumes that he is too much like everyone else—that the qualities he sees in the environment [91] are really there, and not a product of his own motives and expectancies.

In quite another sense, however, the actor is likely to conceive of himself as more unique than he is. Each actor lacks knowledge of the population base rates for various experiences, beliefs, and motives. There may exist, in effect, a sort of pluralistic ignorance of the human condition. If so, it might account for what Meehl (1956) has called the "P. T. Barnum effect," the readiness of the client to accept as uniquely applicable a clinician's assessment of himself that could in fact apply to almost everyone. Stagner (1958) and Ulrich, Stachnick, and Stainton (1963) have capitalized on this kind of egocentric attribution in clever demonstrations of the susceptibility of businessmen and college students, respectively, to allegedly tailor-made diagnoses of their personality. Each subject was given an identical personality description ("Some of your aspirations tend to be pretty unrealistic"; "Sexual adjustment has presented some difficulties for you") and asked to comment on its accuracy. The great majority of the subjects were impressed by what they perceived as a penetrating analysis, with some expressing the view that they had been helped by these insights into their characters.

PERSONALITY TRAITS ARE THINGS OTHER PEOPLE HAVE

If it is true that actors and observers have different conceptions of personality structure along the lines we have discussed, then it should be the case that each individual perceives every other individual to have more stable personality traits than he himself possesses. He should view others as having generalized response dispositions, but himself as acting in accord with the demands and opportunities inherent in each new situation. In order to test this proposition, Nisbett and Caputo (1971) constructed a variant of the standard trait description questionnaire. A list of twenty polar adjectives ("reserved–emotionally expressive;" "lenient–firm") was presented to subjects, along with the option, for each dimension, "depends on the situation." Each of the male college student subjects was asked to check one of the three alternatives for each trait dimension for each of five people: himself, his best friend, an age peer whom the subject liked but did not know well, his father, and (to fill in the remaining cell of the young–old, familiar–unfamiliar matrix) the television commentator Walter Cronkite. In line with anticipations, subjects were likely to use the "depends on the situation" category for themselves, but quite willing to assign traits to the other stimulus persons. Neither degree of acquaintance nor similarity in age was a very potent determinant of the willingness to ascribe traits to others: subjects assigned traits in about equal numbers to each of the other stimulus persons.

We have already discussed a large number of cognitive factors that would be expected to produce Nisbett and Caputo's findings. Perhaps we should add to the list the individual's desire for control over his environment. Brehm (1966) has written, at some length, on the strength of man's desire to see himself as free, in varied ways, and the "reactance" created by threats to behavioral freedom. The perception of freedom is probably best maintained by simultaneously ascribing traits to others and denying them in oneself. When the observer infers the existence of a trait, this gives him the happy, if sometimes illusory, feeling of predictability of behavior and therefore of control over the environment. On the other hand, the individual would lose the sense of freedom to the extent that he acknowledged powerful dispositions in himself, traits that imperiously cause him to behave consistently across situations.

The reader may have noticed that this last paragraph represents virtually our only consideration of traditional motivational concepts. In the final section, we will discuss, in some detail, the role of motives that are perhaps even more powerful than reactance.

MOTIVATIONAL INFLUENCES ON ATTRIBUTION PROCESSES

Perhaps we have gone as far as we can go by acting as though man's motives are exclusively cognitive—that all he wants is to test and structure reality so that he can respond appropriately to it. There are many other motives that affect information processing, the most obtrusive of which is probably the motive to maintain or enhance one's self-esteem. Our examples of actor–observer differences in processing information have more frequently involved blameworthy than praiseworthy acts. Is it possible that most of the facts may be explained by merely invoking the notion that actors try to excuse their reprehensible actions by blaming them on circumstances, whereas observers are coldly, perhaps gleefully, ready to put the shoe of blame on the actor's foot? Have we perhaps erected a fanciful cognitive edifice to surround and obscure this simple principle of human pettiness?

Our answer is a qualified no. We have emphasized—perhaps overemphasized—the role of cognitive and perceptual factors in developing our major theme. We have argued that both actors and observers are concerned with processing useful information and suggested that action cues and situation cues are utilized differentially by them. We would now like to acknowledge that motivational factors may often [92] serve to exaggerate the broad tendencies that we have tried to describe. At the same time, however, we would also like to express the opinion that motivational factors may often mute those tendencies.

Perhaps the simplest way of describing what we believe to be the relationship between the divergent biases of actor and observer, and motivational factors, such as the desire to maintain self-esteem, is to suggest that the biases are generally found even when the act in question is neutral affectively and morally, and when the observer holds a neutral opinion toward the actor. If the action is reprehensible, the tendency of actors to attribute it to the situation is undoubtedly enhanced ("You would have done the same in my shoes."). If the action is praiseworthy, on the other hand, this tendency is probably muted, and perhaps often reversed ("Class will tell."). We also readily grant that, when the observer has a favorable opinion of the actor who performs a praiseworthy act, a dispositional inference is more likely. (Alan Jay Lerner's father is supposed to have responded to an opening night patron's comment that his son was a lucky man, "Yes, and I've noticed that the harder he works, the luckier he gets.") The tendency to infer dispositional causes is undoubtedly also enhanced when the observer dislikes the actor who performs a blameworthy act. ("What can you expect from people like that?") Again, however, the observer's bias can just as easily be reversed, as when the observer likes the perpetrator of bad acts ("The other boys made him do it") or dislikes the performer of good acts ("You must have caught him in a good mood").

Whether it is ecologically more frequent that our proposition is set back, or given a boost by motivational factors, depends on parameters we are not likely ever to know, such as the relative frequency of blameworthy and praiseworthy acts, and the probability of liking actors versus disliking them. The more answerable question is whether or not the attributional biases exist when there is no reason to assume that motivational purposes are served by them. As should be clear, we strongly believe this to be so. As Leventhal has pointed out, a set of stimuli may give rise to both motivational and cognitive processes. It is unwarranted to assume in such an instance that one set of processes determines, or even affects, the other. In fact, we suspect that the attributional biases often hold even when motivational purposes are thwarted by them. The accidental hero seems often to be quite convinced that others would have been heroic in the same spot. The selfless missionary and the Nobel scientist are probably well aware of external incentives and ulterior motives that cloud the picture of virtue conveyed by their actions.

However powerful motivational factors may be, it should be noted that here, as in other psychological contexts, there is an inherent conflict between the "pleasure principle" and the "reality principle." Jones and Gerard (1967) have discussed the general conflict between these two orientations under the heading of the "basic antimony," and suggest that the pleasure principle is dominant in the postdecisional phase, whereas the reality principle is dominant when action and choice are still possible. We may want to believe that we are responsible for our good acts, always and exclusively, but such a belief is not very adaptive in the long run.

It should be emphasized, finally, that we have dealt with only a few of the motives that interact with attribution processes. The individual, whether he is an actor or an observer, is a self-esteem enhancer, a balance maintainer, a dissonance reducer, a reactance reliever, a seeker after truth, and more. The relative strength of these motives, in competition with one another and with more purely cognitive processes, is a problem best pursued empirically.

SUMMARY AND CONCLUSIONS

Actors tend to attribute the causes of their behavior to stimuli inherent in the situation, while observers tend to attribute behavior to stable dispositions of the actor. This is due in part to the actor's more detailed knowledge of his circumstances, history, motives, and experiences. Perhaps more importantly, the tendency is a result of the differential salience of the information available to both actor and observer. For the observer behavior is figural against the ground of the situation. For the actor it is the situational cues that are figural and that are seen to elicit behavior. Moreover, the actor is inclined to think of his judgments about the situational cues as being perceptions or accurate readings of them. These cues are therefore more "real" as well as more salient than they are for the observer. Behavior is thus seen by the observer to be a manifestation of the actor and seen by the actor to be a response to the situation.

The observer often errs by overattributing dispositions, including the broadest kind of dispositions—personality traits. The evidence for personality traits as commonly conceived is sparse. The widespread belief in their existence appears to be due to the observer's failure to realize that the samples of behavior that he sees are not random, as well as to the observer's tendency to see behavior as a manifestation of the actor rather than a response to situational cues. A variety of additional perceptual, cognitive, and linguistic processes help to sustain the belief in traits.

It is suggested that the individual's view of his own personality [93] differs from his view of the personalities of others. The individual may be inclined to view his own personality as consisting of "individual traits," values, goal priorities, and means of attaining goals. The actor may simultaneously view his own personality as being more unique than it is, and his own behavior as being more appropriate to given situations than is the behavior of others.

BIBLIOGRAPHY

Aderman, D. & Berkowitz, L. (1970). Observational set, empathy, and helping. *Journal of Personality and Social Psychology,* 14, 141–148.
Allport, G. W. (1937). *Personality: A Psychological Interpretation.* New York: Holt.
Barker, R. G. (1965). Explorations in ecological psychology. *American Psychologist,* 20, 1–14.
Bem, D.J. (1965). An experimental analysis of self-persuasion. *Journal of Experimental Social Psychology,* 1, 199–218.
Bem, D.J. Self-perception: An alternative interpretation of cognitive dissonance phenomena. *Psychological Review,* 74, 183–200.
Brehm, J. (1966). *A theory of psychological reactance.* Academic Press.
Cronbach, L. J. (1955). Processes affecting scores on understanding of others and assumed similarity. *Psychological Bulletin,* 52, 177–193.
Hartshorne, H. & May, M.A. (1928). *Studies in the nature of character, Vol. I. Studies in Deceit.* New York: Macmillan.
Heider, F. (1958). *The psychology of interpersonal relations.* New York: Wiley.
Icheiser, G. Misunderstanding in human relations: A study in false social perception. *American Journal of Sociology,* 55, part 2, 1–70.
Jones, E.E. (1954). Authoritarianism as a determinant of first impression formation. *Journal of Personality,* 23, 107–127.
Jones, E. E., & Davis, K. E. (1965). From acts to dispositions: The attribution process in person perception. In L. Berkowitz (Ed.), *Advances in experimental social psychology.* Vol. 2. (pp. 219–266). New York: Academic Press.
Jones, E.E. & Gerard, H.B. (1967). *Foundations of social psychology.* New York: Wiley.
Jones, E. E., & Goethals, G. R. (1972). Order effects in impression formation: Attribution context and the nature of the entity. In E. E. Jones, D. E. Kanouse, H. H. Kelley, R. E. Nisbett, S. Valins, & B. Weiner (Ed.), *Attribution: Perceiving the causes of behavior* (pp. 27–46). Morristown, NJ: General Learning Press.
Jones, E.E. & Harris, V.A. (1967). The attribution of attitudes. *Journal of Experimental Social Psychology,* 3, 1–24.
Jones, E.E., Rock, L., Shaver, K.C., Goethals, G.R., & Ward, L.M. (1968). Pattern of performance and ability attribution: An unexpected primacy effect. *Journal of Personality and Social Psychology,* 10, 317–340.
Jones, E.E., Worchel, S., Goethals, G.R., Grumet, J. (1971). Prior expectancy and behavioral extremity as determinants of attitude attribution. *Journal of Experimental Social Psychology,* 7, 59–80.
Kelley, H. H. (1967). Attribution theory in social psychology. In D. Levine (Ed.), *Nebraska Symposium on Motivation.* Vol. 15. (pp. 192–238). Lincoln: University of Nebraska Press.
Kelley, H. H. (1972). Attribution in social interaction. In E. E. Jones, D. E. Kanouse, H. H. Kelley, R. E. Nisbett, S. Valins, & B. Weiner (Ed.), *Attribution: Perceiving the causes of behavior* (pp. 1–26). Morristown, NJ: General Leaning Press.
Kelley, H.H., & Stahelski, A.J. (1970). The social interaction basis of cooperators' and competitors' beliefs about others. *Journal of Personality and Social Psychology,* 16, 66–91.
Lazarus, R.S. (1966). *Psychological stress and the coping process.* New York: McGraw-Hill.
Leventhal, H. (1970). Findings and theory in the study of fear communications. In L. Berkowitz (Ed.)., *Advances in Experimental Social Psychology* (Vol. 5, pp. 119–186). New York: Academic Press.
McArthur, L.Z. (1970). *The how and what of why: Some determinants and consequences of causal attribution.* Unpublished Ph.D. dissertation, Yale University. [Editor's note: This manuscript was later published as McArthur, L. Z. (1972). The how and what of why: Some determinants and consequences of causal attribution. *Journal of Personality and Social Psychology,* 22, 171–193.]

Meehl, P.E. (1956). Wanted—a good cookbook. *American Psychologist,* 1, 263–272.

Mischel, W. (1968). *Personality and assessment.* New York: Wiley.

Mischel, W. (1969). Continuity and change in personality. *American Psychologist,* 11, 1012–1018.

Murray,H.A. (1938). *Explorations in personality.* Oxford: Oxford University Press.

Nisbett, R.E., & Caputo, G.C. (1971). Personality traits: *Why other people do the things they do.* Unpublished manuscript. Yale University. [Editor's note: This manuscript was later published as part of Nisbett, R. E., Caputo, C., Legant, P., & Maracek, J. (1973). Behavior as seen by the actor and as seen by the observer. *Journal of Personality and Social Psychology,* 27, 154–164.]

Nisbett, R.E., Legant, P., & Marecek, J. (1971). *The causes of behavior as seen by actor and observer.* Unpublished manuscript, Yale University. [Editor's note: This manuscript was later published as part of Nisbett, R. E., Caputo, C., Legant, P., & Maracek, J. (1973). Behavior as seen by the actor and as seen by the observer. *Journal of Personality and Social Psychology,* 27, 154–164.]

Passini, F.T., & Norman, W.T. (1966). A universal conception of personality structure? *Journal of Personality and Social Psychology,* 4, 44–49.

Stagner, R. (1958). The gullibility of personnel managers. *Personnel Psychology,* 11, 347–352.

Ulrich, R.E., Stachnick, T.J., & Stainton, N.R. (1963). Student acceptance of generalized personality interpretations. *Psychological Reports,* 13, 831–834. **[94]**

THE ACTOR-OBSERVER EFFECT

Chapter 11

How Do People Perceive the Causes of Behavior?

Edward E. Jones
Duke University

Finding the causes for behavior is a fundamental enterprise of the psychologist. But it is an enterprise he shares with the man on the street. Our responses to others are affected by the reasons, or *attributes,* we assign for their behavior. At least this is the basic assumption of the attributional approach in social psychology, an approach that concerns itself with phenomenal causality—the conditions affecting how each of us attributes causes for his own and others' behavior. The hope is that if we can better understand how people perceive the causal structure of their social world, we can better predict their responses to that world. If A attributes B's anger to the fact that B has lost his job, A is less likely to reciprocate. If a teacher attributes a student's poor performance to lack of motivation, he is more likely to express open disappointment than if his attribution were to lack of ability. A supervisor's appreciation of a subordinate's compliments is more or less alloyed by his attribution of ulterior motives.

The attributional approach (Jones et al. 1972) is essentially a perspective, or a framework, rather than a theory. The perspective owes much of its current prominence to the seminal writings of Fritz Heider. However, prepositional statements have been spawned within the framework, and there are some identifiable theoretical positions. Davis and I outlined a theory of *correspondent inferences* in 1965, which is especially concerned with inferences about the dispositions and intentions of a person drawn from

---

Reprinted with permission of from *American Scientist,* 64, 300–305. Copyright © 1976. References updated by the editor.

observing his behavior in particular contexts. Simply put, the theory states that causal attribution will be made to an actor to the extent that he is not bound by circumstances and is therefore free to choose from a number of behavioral options. If a person has choice, and if his actions depart in any way from expectations, the perceiver–attributor should gain information about his motives and personality. Under these conditions, we might say that the person reveals himself in his actions. We can make a correspondent inference that ties an act to a causal disposition: "He dominated the meeting because he is dominant"; "He cries because he is in pain"; "He voted for ERA because he believes in full civil liberties for women."

Two years later, Kelley proposed a comprehensive theory of *entity attribution,* which was the complement of correspondent-inference theory. Whereas Davis and I wanted to explain how attributions to the person can be made by ruling out environmental explanations, Kelley wanted to show how we decide whether an actor's response is caused by the entity to which it is directed rather than by some idiosyncratic bias on his part. Both approaches accepted the division of person and situation as reflecting the terms in which the naïve attributor is supposed to make his causal allocations.

In 1972, Nisbett and I rather recklessly proposed that actors and observers make divergent attributions about behavioral causes. Whereas the actor sees his behavior primarily as a response to the situation in which he finds himself, the observer attributes the same behavior to the actor's dispositional characteristics. This proposition had grown out of a number of informal observations as well as a sequence of experiments on attitude attribution. Let me digress for a moment to summarize briefly this line of research.

LABORATORY EXPERIMENTS

Nine separate experiments were run within the same general paradigm with college undergraduates from widely separated universities. Each followed a procedure in which subjects were given a short essay or speech favoring a particular position, and were asked to infer the underlying attitude of the target person who produced it. In one experiment, the statement was presented as an answer to an examination question; in another, it was identified as the preliminary statement of a debater; in still others, the statement was attributed to paid volunteers recruited for personality research (cf. Jones and Harris 1967). The statements used in each experiment involved a particular social issue, such as the viability of Castro's Cuba, marijuana legalization, desegregation and busing, liberalized abortion, or socialized medicine.

The experimental conditions were created by varying whether the target person could choose which side of the [317]* issue to write or speak on, and whether or not the side was the expected or popular position. Some subjects were informed that the target person was assigned to defend a particular side of the issue (by his instructor, the debating coach, or the experimenter). Others were told he had been free to choose either side. The statement itself took one or the other side of the issue. In the typical experiment, then, there were four experimental groups: pro-position with choice, anti-position with choice, pro-position with no choice, and anti-position with no choice. For any given sample of subjects, one of the sides (pro or anti) was more popular or expected than the other.

---

*Bracketed bold numbers refer to original page numbers. Page numbers indicate where the original page ended.

All of the experiments showed remarkable stability in supporting the predictions one would make from correspondent inference theory. Attitudes in line with behavior were more decisively attributed to the target person in the choice than in the no-choice condition, but degree of choice made a greater difference if the essay or speech ran counter to the expected or normative position. This is illustrated in Figure 11.1, which presents the results from an early study (1967) dealing with attitudes toward Fidel Castro. Subjects read an essay presumably written as an opening statement by a college debater, but actually it was scripted beforehand as an unremarkable pro or anti summary, the kind of thing an undergraduate debater might write after minimal study of the issue. The subject was also told either that the target person had been directed by the team advisor to argue a specific side of the debate, or that he was given his choice of sides.

After digesting the essay and noting the context in which it was produced, each subject was instructed to rate the target person's true attitude toward the Castro regime. From Figure 11.1 it is apparent that choice has an effect, but only in the pro-Castro condition, where the debater's position was not in line with the expected attitude of a college student in the late sixties.

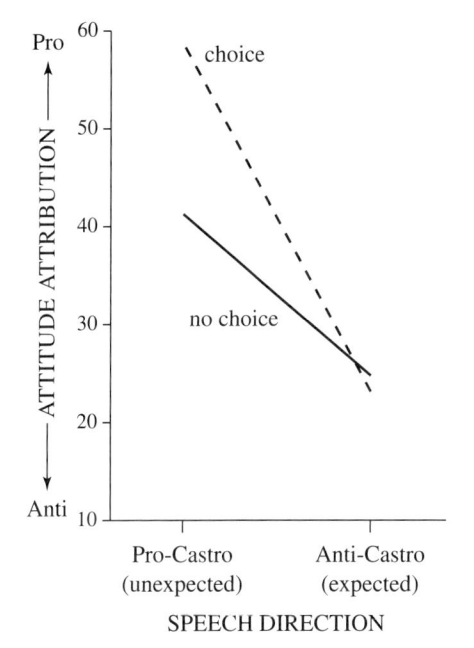

Figure 11.1 In this attitude-attribution experiment, target persons presented short speeches either for or against the Castro regime in Cuba. Some were said to have chosen which side to support (choice condition); others were said to have been required to take the position endorsed (no-choice condition). Observers then rated what they felt was each target person's true attitude toward Castro; the possible range was from 10 (extreme anti) to 70 (extreme pro). Observers rating pro-Castro target persons in the "choice" condition saw their true attitude as more decisively in favor of Castro than observers rating Castro supporters in the "no choice" condition. Choice was a negligible factor when the speech opposed the Castro regime. At the time the experiment was conducted, most subjects—both target persons and observers—held anti-Castro views. Data from Jones and Harris (1967).

For our present purposes, what is most interesting is a finding that could not have been predicted by correspondent inference theory: even in the no-choice conditions, subjects tended to attribute attitudes in line with the speech. They seemed to attach too little weight to the situation (the no-choice instructions) and too much to the person. Although several alternative explanations quickly suggested themselves, these were effectively ruled out by additional experiments (Jones et al. 1972; Snyder and Jones 1974). I became, and remain, convinced that we are dealing with a robust phenomenon of attributional bias, and that persons as observers are all too ready to infer underlying dispositions, like attitudes, from behaviors, like opinion statements, even when it is obvious that the statements are produced under constraint.

Although these results were compatible with the hypothesis that actors and observers have divergent perspectives, they said nothing, of course, about the actor. But there is abundant evidence from other social psychological experiments that actors do not adjust their attitudes to make them consistent with their behavior if they are required (given little or no choice but) to defend the opposite of their initial position on an issue (cf. Aronson 1969; Bem 1972). Their behavior can be adequately explained by an attribution to the situation.

Nisbett and his associates (1973) set out to test the actors–observer proposition more directly. They found, in a questionnaire study, that people assign more traits to others than to themselves, a finding quite consistent with the notion that observers see personal dispositions in others but believe their own behavior depends primarily on the situation. Nisbett and his group also conducted an experiment in which some subjects were turned into actors and some into observers. The actors were asked to volunteer to take distinguished visitors around the Yale campus, while observers monitored the actors' responses to the volunteering request. Actors who volunteered were judged by the observers to be more likely to agree to canvas for the United Fund (an instance of response generalization implying a "volunteering trait") than those who did not volunteer. There was a slight reversal in this trend when the actors themselves were asked whether they would volunteer to canvas. By inference, then, the observers assumed that someone who volunteers in one setting will volunteer in others—they attributed a volunteering disposition to the actor.

Nisbett and I (1972) incorporated these data and tried to elucidate some of the reasons why the actor–observer divergence might occur. As a starting point, it may be helpful to consider the observer's orientation. In the attitude-attribution paradigm, and in the volunteering experiments, we confront the observer with a brief sample of behavior produced in a particular setting. The actor is aware of a history of his prior actions in similar settings and is likely to compare the present behavior to previous behavior. Differences in his behavior over time can readily be attributed to the situation. The observer, on the other hand, is typically ignorant about details of the actor's history and is likely to take a cross-sectional, or normative, view, asking himself, "How do this person's reactions differ from those I would expect from others, from the average, from the norm?" Thus the observer's orientation [318] is individuating; he seeks out (and exaggerates?) differences among people, perhaps because this gives him a feeling of control against the unexpected. His error seems to lie in failing to see the situation as a completely sufficient cause of the behavior observed. Heider (1958) must have had something similar in mind when he talked about the tendency for behavior to "engulf the field." Behavior belongs to the person; the "field" acts on everyone.

In addition to the observer's relative poverty of information, it is also true that the same information will be processed differently by actors and observers. For the observer, in general, action is dynamic, changing, unpredictable, and therefore *salient*. In the attitude-attribution paradigm, the essay appears to stand out as the unique product of the writer. It must, since it is the only concrete information the perceiver has about the writer, reflect the writer's characteristics in a number of ways. That is what "the experiment" is about: the subject is in the position of wondering how good he is at estimating a person's true attitudes. The actor who writes a counterattitudinal essay has faced situational pressure and succumbed to it. The observer knows in some intellectual sense that the pressure was there, but he is so drawn to the essay as the focus of his judgment task that he infers too much about the individual and his uniqueness.

There is good evidence, finally, that *perceptual focusing* leads to attribution (Duncker 1938; Wallach 1959). Of special relevance here is a study by Storms (1973). He set out to investigate whether observers and actors could be induced to exchange perspectives with the aid of videotape replay. As is the case with most important experiments, the design was elegantly simple. Two experimental subjects (actors) held a brief get-acquainted conversation while two other subjects were each assigned to observe a different actor. Television cameras were pointed at each actor, but after the conversation the experimenter appeared to notice that only one had been working properly.

During the next phase of the experiment, all subjects observed the intact videotape replay of the conversation (focusing on one of the actors) and then made a series of attributional judgments. Thus, one actor had the same orientation toward the other actor that he had in the conversation—he was looking at the other on the video replay. The other actor was looking at himself on the replay. He had become a self-observer. When asked to account for the target person's behavior in terms of the contributions of personal characteristics and characteristics of the situation, the actors observing themselves were much more inclined to attribute their behavior to dispositional influences. Attributions by the two observers varied depending on their new orientation. The original observer of the non-taped actor was asked to account for his target person's behavior after looking at the other actor. In this changed orientation, he attributed his target person's behavior to situational factors. The other observer, who watched the taped subject originally as well as in phase two, assigned much greater dispositional influence to his target person.

To summarize these findings, then, attribution seems to follow along with perceptual focus, or perspective. It appears that we attribute causality to whatever or whomever we look at, at least when we are asked. The implications of this fact for persistent interpersonal misunderstandings are obvious. In a persuasive communication setting, for example, the communicator thinks he is describing reality, whereas the target person thinks he is expressing his personal biases.

The results of Storms's experiment also suggest that seating arrangements might be extremely important in a discussion group. In fact, this has been demonstrated by Taylor and Fiske (1975). In their experiment, subjects observing a two-person "get-acquainted" discussion between two confederates of the experimenter were seated in such a way that some faced one discussant, some faced the other, and some observed both from a 90° angle. These differences in literal perspective strongly affected the observer–subjects' attributions of causality for various aspects of the conversation. Specifically, the discussant directly in the observer's line of sight was assigned greater personal causality. When the discussants were both observed from the side, equal personal causality was assigned.

In an even more subtle manipulation of perspective, Hansen et al. (1975) presented videotaped shots of a person solving a jigsaw puzzle or playing chess. The shots either viewed the puzzle or chessboard from the point of view of the actor, or from an angle perpendicular to that of the actor. Once again, the observer focusing on the actor attributed greater behavioral causality to him. The observer with the same angle of vision as the actor attributed the game outcome to the situation.

These experiments essentially converted observers into actors by letting them literally see what the actor saw. Could the same result be achieved by a shift in *psychological* perspective? Regan and Totten (1975) showed college women a videotaped "getting-acquainted" discussion, telling half of them to empathize with discussant *A* (the target person) and to try to imagine how *A* felt as she engaged in the conversation. The remaining subjects were given no such instructions. Using the same measures that Storms had used, Regan and Totten confirmed their hypothesis that empathy-inducing instructions produce a shift toward attributing behavior causation to the situation. This was especially true in a condition where the subject could see only the target person on the tape, though she could hear the other discussant as well. Thus, the authors argue, the divergence of perspective between actors and observers is founded in more than differences in available information. It derives, at least in part, from differences in the ways in which the same information is processed.

Arkin and Duval (1975) have also found that the subjects' attention can be manipulated to affect their causal attributions. Actors in a picture-judging experiment attributed their preferences more to various features of the situation than to themselves (whereas observers were more inclined to attribute the preferences to the actor as a person). However, these differences were reversed when actors felt that they were being videotaped. The self-consciousness induced by the presence of a TV camera apparently shifted the causal assignment from the situation to the self. This is quite in line with the Duval and Wicklund (1972) theory of *objective self-awareness,* which suggests that [319] an actor's causal attributions are a function of whether or not his attention is focused on himself.

FIELD STUDIES

It is quite apparent that something interesting is happening here, and the evidence that perceptual perspective influences causal attribution seems reliable and replicable. But, the reader might demur, is this one of those hothouse laboratory phenomena that is overwhelmed by other variables in the more chaotic and complex natural environment? Obviously, we should not expect to find a quick answer to this question, but a recent study by West et al. (1975) shows the predicted basic pattern of actor–observer differences in a dramatic field experiment simulating the Watergate burglary attempt.

Undergraduate criminology majors at a state university were contacted by a man whom they knew as a local private investigator. He arranged a meeting with each subject at which detailed plans of a business burglary were presented. The subject was asked to participate in breaking into the offices of a local firm to microfilm a set of records. In one condition of the experiment, the subjects were told that a competing local firm had offered $8,000 for a copy of designs prepared by the first firm. The subjects were told that they would be paid $2,000 for their participation in the crime. In other conditions, the experimenter presented himself as working for the Internal Revenue Service and said that the records would allegedly show that the firm was trying to defraud the U.S. government. Of the subjects exposed to the IRS cover story, half were told that they would receive immunity from prosecution if caught; the other half were told that there would be no immunity. After an elaborate and convincing presentation of the plan, subjects were asked to come to a final planning meeting. Their assent or refusal was the major dependent measure of the experiment. Once the subjects either agreed or did not agree to participate in the burglary, the experiment was then over and they were given extensive debriefing concerning the deceptions involved and the purpose of the experiment. (Readers interested in the ethical problems of this experiment will find a considered view presented by West and his colleagues, 1975, and comments by Cook, 1975, who tries to place the experiment in the more general framework of ethical problems in psychological research.)

Not surprisingly, whether the subject thought he or she would be granted immunity if caught was a crucial determinant of the frequency of compliance. Nearly half (45 percent) of the subjects in the immunity condition agreed to attend the final planning session. It is somewhat surprising that only 1 out of 20 subjects in the IRS no-immunity condition complied, whereas 4 out of 20 subjects in the reward condition agreed, although this difference was not statistically significant.

In addition to the involved subjects, a large sample of role-playing "observers" were asked to imagine themselves in the situation of the subject. They were given a very detailed description of experimental events in the condition to which they were assigned and asked whether they would or would not comply. About 18 percent of these observer subjects said that they would have agreed, and there was no difference as a function of the various conditions. Of special interest in the present context, all subjects (actors and role-players) were asked to explain *why* they did or did not agree to move closer toward the burglary. Whether the actors were compliers or noncompliers, they attributed their decision to environmental factors more than to personal dispositions. The role-playing observers, on the other hand, were much more likely to attribute the decision to dispositions in the actor. This was true whether they were asked to explain the decision of a complying or a noncomplying actor. Thus the actor–observer divergence in this case is not simply a matter of the actor's being inclined to rationalize his "criminal" behavior by blaming the situation.

In another, less dramatic, field study, McGee and Snyder (1975) followed their hunch that there are interesting attributional differences between those who salt before and those who salt after tasting their food. Restaurant patrons were approached after placing themselves in one of these two categories by their salting behavior, and were asked to rate themselves on a series of polar adjectives like realistic–idealistic, cautious–bold and energetic–relaxed. Each adjective pair was followed by another option, "it depends on the situation." As predicted, the before-tasting salters tended to check more traits as characteristic of themselves than the after-tasting salters, who were much more inclined to check "it depends on the situation." (It should be emphasized that none of the traits made any reference to eating behavior, taste, and so on.) When asked why they salted their food, the two types also diverged: the before-salters explained their behavior in terms of personal characteristics, whereas the after-salters tended to refer to the food.

Snyder and Monson (1975) have also shown that subjects classified as high "self-monitors" expect themselves to behave variably across different hypothetical situations. Low "self-monitors," on the other hand, expect to show greater cross-situational consistency. The authors classified their subjects by means of the score attained on a self-descriptive questionnaire, describing different hypothetical situations: low self-monitors endorsed items such as "My behavior is usually an expression of my true inner feelings, attitudes, and beliefs" and "I would not change my opinions (or the way I do things) in order to please someone else or win their favor," whereas high self-monitors endorsed items such as "I'm not always the person I appear to be" and "I may deceive people by being friendly when I really dislike them." On another questionnaire, describing different hypothetical situations, low self-monitors expected their behavior and environment in these different situations to be much more stable than did the high self-monitors. There is some evidence, then, that Nisbett's and my proposition must be qualified: *some* actors tend to attribute their actions to themselves, whereas others—more faithful to the proposition—typically make situational attributions.[1]

There are other experimental results which seem more drastically at odds with our proposition. Most of these studies (e.g. Wolosin et al. 1975) involve the perception of behavioral freedom as the main dependent variable. Under some conditions, at least, actors will rate themselves as freer of situational influence than observers would rate them. Thus, if the attributional question is phrased in terms of whether the situation has *required* the actor to behave in a certain way, or if it strongly implies the giving up of his freedom and control, actors will claim greater freedom and responsibility whereas observers will see themselves as relatively constrained. If the question is more neutral with regard to relinquishing control, however, actors will see their behavioral decisions as responses appropriate to the opportunities and constraints of the environment (cf. Bell 1973).

There is an important philosophical distinction between "reasons" and "causes" (discussed at length by Beck, 1975) that is relevant here. Apparently, under most conditions, actors do not like to think that their behavior is *caused* by either the environment or the personality. At the less deterministic level of *reasons,* however, they are more likely to attribute their behavior to situational rather than to personal factors, though to some extent, we all realize that both factors are involved.

Monson and Snyder (1975) raise a caveat that deserves to be mentioned. They point out that most actor–observer studies have been laboratory experiments in which the actor's behavior is, in fact, "controlled" by a situational manipulation. Thus, Nisbett and his colleagues (1973) induced actors to volunteer to lead sightseeing tours by offering to pay them. In such a case, it is not surprising that the actor—who, most would agree,

---

[1]Editor's note: There was a typographical error in the original article that rendered this paragraph unintelligible. I have deleted three words and inserted one sentence to restore the author's original meaning. I thank Mary Snyder for help with this task.

is more sensitive to situational variations—tends to attribute his behavior to the setting. He is right. The monetary incentive was "responsible" for his behavior. On the other hand, Monson and Snyder point out that in the natural environment, people are not placed in situations so much as they choose them. Or, as Wachtel (1973) has argued, the situational forces to which actors respond are often of their own making. To the extent that this is true, actors may see their behavior, even though it varies from situation to situation, as dispositionally caused, whereas observers who see only the variation with situations may, if anything, underestimate the dispositional role.

This is an intriguing point, and it has some support in empirical data. For example, experimental evidence supports the fact that actors attribute their choice *among* situations to personal, dispositional factors. Once in the situation, however, they see their behavior as controlled by its salient cues (cf. Gurwitz and Panciera 1975). It remains true, however, that even in the natural environment we often find ourselves in situations which we may have long ago selected, but which we do not control in any detail. We should be wary of an easy translation from the laboratory to real life, but we should be equally careful not to assume that the laboratory is some irrelevant microcosm.

WIDER IMPLICATIONS OF THE THEORY

I think the balance of the evidence provides rather remarkable support for our "reckless" proposition. To say that actors attribute to situations what observers assign to dispositions is obviously not a law of behavioral science. But it is a useful guiding hypothesis that holds under a surprising range of conditions. The proposition can be subverted by special motivational factors (such as wanting to claim personal responsibility for a success) or by special knowledge on the part of the actor that he selected among many situations the one to which he now exposes himself. In the absence of these special conditions, however, our proposition seems to be robust and quite general. The proposition derives its validity in part from differences in perceptual perspective, and in part from differences in the information available to actors and observers.

The major implication of the observer bias in attitude-attribution studies is that such a bias sows the seeds for interpersonal misunderstandings. It seems reasonable to assume that the more two people get to know each other, the more capable they become of taking each other's perspective; there should be a gradual merging of actor–observer orientations. In more transient interactions, however, we may all be victims of a tendency to misread role for personality. If our research has any generalization value at all, it is very likely that we assign to another's personality what we should be viewing as a complex interaction between person and situation. Particular roles within society or within an organization may call for certain patterns of behavior that are then used as a clue to what the role player is really like. What the reviewed research shows is that people make some allowance for the determining significance of roles and other situational pressures, but the allowance undershoots the mark. As a consequence, people who may be arbitrarily assigned to a group role, or assigned to a role on the basis of some initial response to strong environmental pressures, may have attributed to them a set of unwarranted personality characteristics to explain the role-induced behavior. Furthermore, once the group members make these attributions, their behavior toward the target person may constrain him to meet their expectations by "taking on" the personality they have assigned him. This is in the nature of a self-fulfilling prophecy: I expect John to behave in a certain way, and I give off subtle cues to ensure that he does.

In recent years, a number of social scientists have pointed to, and commented on, the tendency in the field of psychology toward overattribution to the person. Mischel (1968, 1969) has essentially argued that there is not enough personal consistency across situations to warrant the personality psychologist's confident attribution of traits and attitudes to individual subjects or clients. Anthropologists D'Andrade (1974) and Shweder (1975) have also criticized individual difference psychology, claiming (with supportive evidence) that personality impressions follow the conceptual logic of the perceiver but do not fit the behavior of the persons being judged. The present research results point in the same direction by at least hinting at the pervasiveness of personal overattribution.

One final question might be raised: If such a pervasive attributional bias does exist, how come we get along as well as we do in the world? And how come the tendency doesn't get corrected by feedback and eventually drop out? One answer to the first question is, Maybe we don't get along so well. The Peter Principle (Peter and Hull, 1969) is a striking example of attributional bias. A man gets promoted to his level of incompetence because the manager doesn't realize that a good performer in one setting may be incompetent in another. There may be other human costs incurred by the person who is misread by others, costs associated with the strain of meeting false expectations.

Perhaps one reason the bias persists uncorrected is that predictions from [321] personality often overlap with, or converge on, predictions from situations. Much of our social life is more highly structured than we realize. Because we often see particular others in a restricted range of settings, cross-situational consistency is not an issue. Furthermore, we as observers are always a constant in the situation, which gives a farther impetus to behavioral consistency. In situations restricted to a standard setting, it makes no difference whether the prediction of behavioral continuity is based on attributions about personality or perceptions of situational requirements. There is no opportunity for corrective feedback. It is also the case that social behavior is notoriously ambiguous as feedback, and many an observer can tailor his perceptions of behavior to previously made personality attributions. We are probably all rather adept at maintaining trait inferences in the face of disconfirming behavioral evidence. When practiced by some psychoanalytic writers, the maneuvering can be truly breathtaking.

REFERENCES

Arkin, R. M., & Duval, S. (1975). Focus of attention and causal attributions of actors and observers. *Journal of Experimental Social Psychology,* 11, 427–438.

Aronson, E. (1969). The theory of cognitive dissonance: A current perspective. In L. Berkowitz, (Ed.), *Advances in Experimental Social Psychology:* (Vol. 4, pp. 1–34). New York: Academic Press.

Beck, L. W. (1975). *The actor and the spectator.* New Haven: Yale University Press.

Bell, L. G. (1973). *Influence of need to control on differences in attribution of causality by actors and observers.* Unpublished dissertation, Duke University.

Bem, D. J. (1972). Self-perception theory. In L. Berkowitz, (Ed.), *Advances in Experimental Social Psychology,* (Vol. 6, pp. 2–62). New York: Academic Press.

Cook, S. W. (1975). A comment on the ethical issues involved in West, Gunn, and Chernicky's "Ubiquitous Watergate: An attributional analysis." *Journal of Personality and Social Psychology,* 32, 66–68.

D'Andrade, R. (1974). Memory and the assessment of behavior. In H. M. Blalock (Ed.), *Measurement in the social sciences.* Chicago: Aldine.

Duncker, K. (1938). Induced motion. In W. D. Ellis (Ed.), *A sourcebook of Gestalt psychology* (pp. 161–172). New York: Harcourt, Brace.

Duval, S., & R. A. Wicklund. (1972). *A theory of objective self-awareness.* New York: Academic Press.

Gurwitz, S. B., & Panciera, L. (1975). Attributions of freedom by actors and observers. *Journal of Personality and Social Psychology, 32,* 531–539.

Hansen, R. D., Ruhland, D.J., & Ellis, C.L. (1975). *Actor versus observer: The effect of perceptual orientation on causal attributions for success and failure.* Unpublished manuscript.

Heider, F. (1958). *The psychology of interpersonal relations.* New York: Wiley.

Jones, E. E., & Davis, K.E. (1965). A theory of correspondent inferences: From acts to dispositions. In L. Berkowitz, (Ed.), *Advances in Experimental Social Psychology,* (Vol.2, pp. 219–266). New York: Academic Press.

Jones, E. E., & Harris, V.A. (1967). The attribution of attitudes. *Journal of Experimental Social Psychology, 3,* 1–24.

Jones, E. E., Kanouse, D. E., Kelley, H. H., Nisbett, R. E., Valins, S., & Weiner, B. (Eds.). (1972). *Attribution: Perceiving the causes of behavior.* Morristown, NJ: General Learning Press.

Jones, E. E., & Nisbett, R. E. (1972). The actor and the observer: Divergent perceptions of the causes of behavior. In E. E. Jones, D. E. Kanouse, H. H. Kelley, R. E. Nisbett, S. Valins, & B. Weiner (Ed.), *Attribution: Perceiving the causes of behavior* (pp. 79–94). Morristown, NJ: General Learning Press.

Jones, E. E., Worchel, S., Goethals, G.R., & Grumet, J. (1971). Prior expectancy and behavioral extremity as determinants of attitude attribution. *Journal of Experimental Social Psychology, 7,* 59–80.

Kelley, H. H. (1967). Attribution theory in social psychology. In D. Levine (Ed.), *Nebraska Symposia on Motivation* (pp.192–240). Lincoln: University of Nebraska Press.

McGee, M. G., & Snyder, M. (1975). Attribution and behavior: Two field studies. *Journal of Personality and Social Psychology, 32,* 185–90.

Mischel, W. (1968). *Personality and assessment.* New York: Wiley.

Mischel, W. (1969). Continuity and change in personality. *American Psychologist, 24,* 1012–1018.

Monson, T. C., & Snyder, M. (1975) *Actors, observers, and the attribution process: Toward a reconceptualization.* Unpublished manuscript. [Editor's note: This manuscript was later published as Monson, T. C., & Snyder, M. (1977). Actors, observers, and the attribution process: Toward a reconceptualization. *Journal of Experimental Social Psychology, 13,* 89–111.]

Nisbett, R. E., Caputo, C., Legant, P., & Maracek, J. (1973). Behavior as seen by the actor and as seen by the observer. *Journal of Personality and Social Psychology, 27,* 154–165.

Peter, L. J., & Hull, R. (1969). *The Peter principle.* New York: Morrow.

Regan, D. T., & Totten, J. (1975). Empathy and attribution: Turning observers into actors. *Journal of Personality and Social Psychology, 32,* 850–856.

Shweder, R. A. (1975). How relevant is an individual difference theory of personality? *Journal of Personality, 43,* 455–484.

Snyder, M., & Jones, E.E. (1974). Attitude attribution when behavior is constrained. *Journal of Experimental Social Psychology, 10,* 585–600.

Snyder, M., & Monson, T.C. (1975). Persons, situations, and the control of social behavior. *Journal of Personality and Social Psychology, 32*(4), 637–644.

Storms, M. D. (1973). Videotape and the attribution process: Reversing actors' and observers' points of view. *Journal of Personality and Social Psychology, 27,* 165–175.

Taylor, S. E., & Fiske, S.T. (1975). Point of view and perceptions of causality. *Journal of Personality and Social Psychology, 32,* 439–445.

Wachtel, P. (1973). Psychodynamics, behavior therapy, and the implacable experimenter: An inquiry into the consistency of personality. *Journal of Abnormal Psychology, 82,* 324–334.

Wallach, H. (1959). The perception of motion. *Scientific American, 201,* 56–60.

West, S. G., Gunn, S.P., & Chernicky, P. (1975). Ubiquitous Watergate: An attributional analysis. *Journal of Personality and Social Psychology, 32,* 55–65.

Wolosin, R. J., Esser, J., & Fine, G.A. (1975). Effects of justification and vocalization on actors' and observers' attributions of freedom. *Journal of Personality, 43,* 612–33. **[322]**

Chapter 12

Order Effects in Impression Formation: Attribution Context and the Nature of the Entity

Edward E. Jones
Duke University
George R. Goethals
Williams College

The attribution process substitutes inferred structure for observed flux. Acts, appearances, and all manner of manifestations are potentially grist for the process. Such observable events are organized by the attributor into a conception of the underlying entities to which they appear to refer. In the interpersonal realm, a basic task of the attributor is to allocate the determinants of observed action to the person or to the environment. Does an act reflect some distinctive characteristic of the actor, and thus help us to identify the nature of his particular dispositions, or does it primarily reflect the evocative power of the environment?

A programmatic essay by Jones and Davis (1965) considers a rational strategy for making personal versus environmental attributions. When attributions are made to the person, we may speak of "correspondent inferences," since the inferred disposition corresponds to the act observed, and the former is seen to have caused the latter. The Jones

---

Reprinted with permission from Jones, E. E., Kanouse, D. E., Kelley, H. H., Nisbett, R. E., Valins, S., & Weiner, B. (Eds.), *Attribution: Perceiving the causes of behavior.* Morristown, NJ: General Learning Press. © 1972 by General Learning Press, a subsidiary of Simon & Schuster Elementary Group.

and Davis paper restricts itself, however, to the frozen moment in time when one unit of information, one act, is the input of the attribution process. The question of how behavioral data are combined is obviously a next step in the inquiry. There are many ways to approach the analysis of how inputs are combined in the inference process; this study considers what might be learned from a fresh look at an old and convenient comparative design, the order effect paradigm.

The order effect paradigm can be simply described as comparing responses to one sequence of information with responses to the same information presented in reverse order. It is clear that information within an interpersonal episode is neither produced nor perceived all at once. Since this is the case, it is reasonable to ask whether the attribution process is in systematic ways affected by the [27]* order in which information is received.

Reasonable to ask, that is, if one does not expect a simple answer. When information occurs in a particular temporal sequence, an attributor may organize it in such a way as to yield primacy, recency, or something in between. These crude outcome categories are like large earthenware vessels into which hard-to-identify and ill-assorted determinants may be poured. To change the metaphor, the order effect paradigm is an overcrowded crossroads where a variety of theoretical principles converge from a variety of angles. Since both primacy and recency are multiply determined, it is possible to get either effect for several reinforcing reasons, or it is possible that the competition between primacy determinants and recency determinants results in a neutralizing standoff.

The study of order effects has moved from the question of primacy versus recency to a more sophisticated inquiry into the conditions under which one or the other effect may be expected. But the search for determining conditions has favored the easily controlled and varied over the more naturalistic and context-relevant determinants. Especially in the able hands of Norman Anderson, the order effect inquiry has become increasingly precise and increasingly detached from the problems actually confronting an attributor in a natural interpersonal setting. Anderson's contributions have been important, as we shall see, but it is time to look carefully at the boundary conditions within which they were produced.

Primacy versus recency is not a gripping theoretical issue in its own right. Information order, like time, age, and number of siblings, is not a conceptually unitary psychological variable. The appropriate justification for studying order effects is that sequence transformation experiments can provide occasions for observing the attribution process at work. In the impression formation realm, the order effect paradigm typically presents information about a target person in such a sequence that the implications of the early information are very different from the implications of the later information. There is built-in information conflict, and the interest is in how it is resolved by attributional processes. If time or order do not enter into the resolving process, there will be neither primacy nor recency. When primacy or recency obtains, any one of a number of factors may be operating; ranging from cognitive tendencies "wired into" the human organism to hypotheses developed by the perceiver from his particular experiences with different sequential event orders. In an effort to redress the

---

*Bracketed bold numbers refer to original page numbers. Page numbers indicate where the original page ended.

bias of the literature, we shall emphasize the latter portion of this range, focusing on some of the principles that may give rise to sequence-related hypotheses in forming an impression of an actor. The discussion will enter a realm of greater confusion and complexity than the traditional primacy–recency literature, but hopefully with the compensating gain of viewing the order effect paradigm in terms more appropriate to naturalistic predictions.

The major proposition we shall attempt to document is that *the information, conveyed by the order of events itself, is contingent on the context in which these events unfold, and on the nature of the entity being considered as an attributional target.* The role of primacy versus recency has been investigated under different guises in many different content domains. There are, at present, several nonintersecting subliteratures dealing with order effects, and it is our hope that by examining the implications of the above proposition for these various problem areas, certain general conclusions about order and attribution can be reached. Before embarking on such a review, however, some attention should be given to the general problems of comparability when evaluating different experiments dealing with the effects of order. In the following section, therefore, we consider several potentially important distinctions of method that should be kept in mind during the subsequent comparative review.

SOME USEFUL DISTINCTIONS

We have stated that the order effect paradigm can be simply described as comparing one sequence of information with the same information presented in reverse order. In the analysis of specific empirical studies, however, this simplicity breaks down both with respect to the information items being compared and the response measures used in making the comparison. We assume at the outset that different kinds of information will produce different kinds of order effects. Even restricting ourselves to the impression formation domain, one would intuitively hesitate to predict the same effects of order from trait-adjective sequences (Anderson, 1965), paragraphs describing inconsistent behavior (Luchins, 1957), and the direct observation of the behavior itself (Jones, Rock, Shaver, Goethals, & Ward, 1968). These different kinds of materials certainly present the observer with different inference problems (see Anderson & Norman, 1964). At the very least, the observer of unfolding behavior is faced with an additional problem of moving from observed acts to inferred dispositions, and therefore of assessing the role of the environment at each point in the ordered sequence of acts. [28]

Attending to these distinctions between different types of information suggests a more fundamental difference between the sequence in which information is generated by a target person and the sequence in which it is received by a perceiver. While it sometimes happens, of course, that we learn about someone's recent exploits before we learn about his past, the natural sequence of behavior observation coincides with the sequence of behavior production: in the typical acquaintance process, where one person observes another's actions over time, the order of generating and receiving information is confounded. What happened first in time is perceived first in time. To our knowledge, there are no published studies that have explored the consequences of this confounding, but it should make some difference in those temporally extended settings where orderly changes in performance are expected from the effects of practice, warm-up, fatigue, or indeed in any setting where changes in the stimulus environment may be inferred. We shall subsequently describe an experiment comparing behavior sequences that explicitly preserve or scramble the order in which the behaviors occurred. For the moment, it will suffice to bear in mind the distinction between confounding and separating orders of producing and receiving information.

In addition to these important potential differences in the nature and context of entity manifestations, the effects of information order may be measured in several different ways. We are primarily interested in measures of attributed personal characteristics, but this does not move us very far toward a clear understanding of the most appropriate measure on any experimental occasion. The most straightforward measure of attribution would presumably involve ratings of the entity on dimensions relevant to the axis of change in the stimulus sequence. Depending on the dimension, of course, we may be asking "how warm?" or "how intelligent?" or "how liberal?" is the person. Subtle differences in how these questions are asked may have implications for the fate of primacy versus recency. An important issue is whether order effect differences in attribution ratings represent shifts in the meaning of the judgmental language used or true differences in the perception of the entity being judged. As Campbell, Lewis, and Hunt (1958) have shown, it makes a difference whether the judgments obtained are in relativistic terms (heavy versus light, sweet versus salty) or in absolute terms that are extensive and have some anchorage outside the particular experimental situation (ounces, inches, degrees temperature in Fahrenheit).

The fact that there are no all-purpose, interchangeable, attribution measures makes it difficult to make all but the crudest comparisons across attributional domains. A partial solution to this problem is available as long as the investigator sticks to dimensions that have clear evaluative implications, and compares good-to-bad with bad-to-good sequential orders. Under such conditions, *general evaluative ratings* can serve as useful measures of the effect of order. Much of the work with positive and negative trait-adjectives has used evaluative ratings as a dependent variable, and with notable success as judged by the criterion of cumulative and comparable results. Such judgments, however, hardly meet the test of being couched in a language that is absolute and extra-experimentally anchored.

Presumably, various *behavior prediction measures* should be correlated with both the direct attributive and the evaluative measure of order effects. If the investigator has doubts about the reliability and validity of simple ratings of, say, intelligence, he can ask the subject to predict the target person's performance on a relevant subsequent task. The more intelligence is attributed to the target person, in all probability, the higher will be the predicted performance. A variant of this kind of measure is concurrent subjective probability estimation. As subjects are exposed to a series of events, they can be asked to estimate the probability after each event that the next will be an X or a non-X (a good trait or a bad trait, a success or a failure). Insensitivity to objectively shifting probabilities can then become a measure of primacy (see Peterson & DuCharme, 1967).

Finally, it would seem almost mandatory to insert, somewhere in the design, a *measure of recall*. The chances are that a person who recalls more of the positive adjectives than the negative ones will have a more favorable view of the person being described than the person remembering more of the negative traits. One recalled as solving many problems will be seen as more intelligent than one recalled as solving just a few. Distortions in memory in a primacy or recency direction can obviously affect attribution when, as is usually the case in the order effect paradigm, items are systematically arranged to convey different information at the beginning than at the end. Though one should not accept a simple measure of recall as a direct measure of attribution, recall distortions may be sufficient explanation for any primacy–recency effects observed. (It is also quite possible, of course, that recall distortions can be an *effect* of prior attributional decisions.)

Unfortunately, we are presently in no position to distinguish clearly among these various measures or [29] to predict their differential sensitivity to order. It may be, however, that order affects evaluation differently than it does descriptive attribution, and that behavior predictions perform differently than either. One would expect these various measures to be highly intercorrelated, but the fact that they might not be is reason enough to raise the dependent–variable issue before embarking on the following review. The reader should be warned also that no attempt will be made to provide a comprehensive survey of the voluminous order effect literature in the different content areas in which it has been generated. Those examples that raise issues and provoke speculation will be featured.

THE ORDER EFFECT PARADIGM FAMILY: VARIATIONS IN JUDGMENTAL CONTEXTS AND THEIR DISTINCTIVE IMPLICATIONS

Adjective Combinations

In 1946, S. E. Asch described a series of studies in which subjects were asked to make summary impression ratings of a person allegedly described by a series of traits. In one group of these studies, some subjects were exposed to a list of traits and others to the same list in reverse order. An example: intelligent–industrious–impulsive–critical–stubborn–envious. Comparison of impressions suggested by the two sequences revealed a primacy effect. Asch explained his primacy findings in terms of the directional implications of item content: "It is not the sheer temporal position of the items which is important as much as the functional relation of its content to the contents of the items following it" (p. 272). With these studies, the order effect paradigm was born, and the effects of order were given a structural interpretation in terms of meaningful interactions among trait meanings, with the earlier traits exerting a directional force on the later ones.

The interpretation suggested by Asch seemed so reasonable, apparently, that no one readily perceived the seeds of controversy in any relevant alternative explanations of the primacy effects obtained. Asch was essentially arguing that no particular trait adjective has a fixed meaning, and the overlapping connotations of adjectives appearing late in a series are selectively processed in terms of the connotative implications of earlier adjectives. Bruner, Shapiro, and Tagiuri (1958) presented some data to show that impressions inferred from lists of traits could be very reliably predicted from an arithmetic averaging of their independent meanings, but their report was an isolated addendum to Asch, rather than a systematic reexamination of his suggested interpretation.

Some fifteen years after Asch's classic study, Anderson and his colleagues published the first in a series of studies exploring the effects of the order of evaluative adjectives on the favorability of resulting impressions. Working with traits selected for their valence on the basis of judges' ratings, Anderson and Barrios (1961) presented over sixty sets of six adjectives to each subject and asked him to rate his impression of the person being described by each set on a scale ranging from +4 (highly favorable) to –4 (highly unfavorable). The sets were composed of adjectives that either abruptly or gradually changed from positive to negative or vice versa. Strong primacy effects were observed across all sets, and though these effects declined with repeated judgment trials, they did not disappear. Furthermore, it did not seem to make any difference whether the transition of valence within the set was abrupt or gradual.

Anderson's subsequent studies have used the order effect paradigm in an effort to discriminate between different models of information processing. The main conclusion of the most relevant studies (Anderson, 1962, 1968) is that adjectives presented in this manner do not interact to form a new gestalt structure. The connotation of one adjective does not depend on the other adjectives in the set, as Asch had argued. If one assigns a given favorability value to each adjective (based either on the consensus of judges or on the subject's own preratings), the resulting impression of the set can be closely approximated by calculating the arithmetic mean of the values. When the set is so arranged that there is a systematic shift in valence, primacy effects arise because subjects assign differential weights to early and late adjectives: "the net influence of an adjective decreases linearly with its ordinal position in the set" (Anderson, 1965).

The implications of Anderson's weighted average model are similar to the implications of Asch's "change in meaning" interpretation, and it is not immediately obvious how one could crucially test their relative power of prediction. Anderson's weighted average model might be preferred on the grounds of parsimony alone—it requires fewer individualized, content-specific assumptions. In addition, however, the weighted average, linear decrease model implies that subjects "tune out," or even if they remain attentive late in the series, they discount inconsistent information in other ways. Support for an attention decrement explanation of primacy is seen in studies by [30] Anderson and Hubert (1963), Stewart (1965), and Hendrick and Costantini (1970), where instructions designed to equalize attention over the entire list appear to wipe out primacy. One could not have predicted these differences from a change-in-meaning position.

In general, Anderson should be commended for introducing elegant refinements into the design and analysis of order effects, and for his sensitivity to qualifications and alternative explanations. Nevertheless, several cautionary words are in order before we rush to apply the weighted average, linear decrease model to the general case of impressional attribution. It is quite clear that the test of any information-processing model requires data, and these data have to be generated in a particular judgmental context with particular kinds of informational content. Anderson has chosen to work with the impression formation context as a convenience, but in the interests of precision and elegance he may have worked himself away from a number of significant variables that affect the natural attribution process in the domain of interpersonal judgment.

First of all, the strategy of using elaborate counter-balance designs in which each subject responds to numerous trait-adjective lists creates important difficulties that limit the generality of Anderson's conclusions about averaging and interaction among the traits used. Since the kind of interaction effects suggested by Asch may or may not result in primacy, the averaging across adjective lists may obscure the kinds of strong interactions that might be expected with certain trait combinations only. One might describe the typical primacy effects of an Anderson experiment as the residual of various operations designed to rule out the vagaries of *particular* trait interactions.

Anderson and Jacobson (1965) did compare impressions formed from trait combinations involving antonyms (honest–deceitful) with those formed from traits that are merely of different affective value (honest–reckless). Because the traits were read by the subject in both regular and reversed orders, however, the implications of this variation for order effects was explicitly ruled out. Different conditions were established in which instructions either encouraged or suppressed discounting. When discounting was encouraged by suggesting that all traits might not be equally valid, the antonym-inconsistency lists departed more from the weighted average model than the affective-inconsistency lists. In attempting to track down the particular patterns of differential weighting that resulted from the discounting tendency, Anderson and Jacobson were led to modify their earlier attacks on the interactive argument: "even though the averaging formulation shows promise in accounting for the impression response data per se, it cannot completely account for (the form of differential weighting observed). In this respect, it would appear that the adjectives do interact in forming the impression, a conclusion in harmony with the views of Asch (1946)" (p. 539). The best conclusion would seem to be that the effects of trait interactions have not been properly tested in relation to order of presentation, and any final choice among inferential models seems premature at this point.

POSSIBLE EFFECTS OF INSTRUCTIONS Problems may arise not only by commitments to particular items of information in the trait lists, but also by commitments to particular instructions that provide the judgmental context. Anderson has not been entirely consistent in how he presents the adjectives to be combined, but in no instance has he made an effort to convince the subjects that the traits refer to real persons. In the typical case, the subject is to think of the adjectives as having been given by different persons who knew the target person well. The lists are either explicitly or implicitly hypothetical. Except in the Anderson and Jacobson (1965) study, furthermore, the instructions typically have indicated that all adjectives of a set should be considered as having equal importance. Perhaps it is not surprising that the combination of a hypothetical judgment setting and instructions about equal weighting should lead to confirmation of a weighted average model. One might contend that the subjects are simply following the direct implications of experimental instructions, or being responsive to "experimenter demand." It is true, however, as Anderson and Jacobson argue, that this is not completely preordained by the circumstances, since the meaning of the traits is not fixed, and assimilation and contrast effects could occur. Such effects, of course, imply interactions among trait meanings.

A related observation is that only in the Anderson (1968) study is any mention made to the subjects about the meaning of order. Here "the serial presentation procedure was explained by analogy to real life in which one customarily gets to know a person step by step" (p. 365). This seems a halfhearted effort in the direction of the earlier described natural confounding of information generated and received. It is perhaps not incidental that this most recent Anderson study is the only one in which the results show more recency than primacy in the various order effect comparisons. In none of the other studies in this [31] program is anything said about order, but this does not mean that subjects are oblivious to various shared and idiosyncratic connotations of presentational order. A subject might conceivably assume that the experimenter put the most important adjective first, or the most useful, or the most generic. Otherwise, why not simply put the terms in alphabetical order? This may appear to be dangerously close to nit-picking, but such a hypothesis, even if entertained by only a minority of the subjects, could contribute to the typical primacy effects observed when adjectives are presented in a sequence presumably determined by the experimenter.

Have Anderson and his colleagues ever discovered how to produce recency effects in the impression formation domain? In a study especially designed to distinguish between the applicability of averaging and additivity models, Anderson (1968) employed adjective lists involving less affective contrast than in all the previous studies of presentational order. The affective transitions ran from extremely favorable traits to moderately favorable traits, or from extremely unfavorable to moderately so. In this study, as we have noted above, explicit mention was made of the natural meaning of order in the acquaintance process. The results came out in favor of the averaging versus the additive formula. In brief, the moderate traits pushed the impression toward neutrality rather than toward the even more extreme judgments that would be predicted if the favorability values of the traits were simply added. The results also showed a general tendency toward recency.

Anderson attributes the prevalence of recency to the lack of affective inconsistency in the trait lists. The discounting mechanism, which he favors as an explanation of primacy, is not brought into play because there is insufficient affective inconsistency among the traits. He does not consider the possibility that the explicitly serial presentation might have contributed to recency. In our view, this remains a possibility even though the lack-of-inconsistency explanation may have more inherent plausibility.

To say that Anderson favors the discounting hypothesis does not necessarily imply that he rejects the hypothesis of attention decrement. His weighted average model is compatible with either process, and both are preferred to a "new gestalt," change-of-meaning explanation. In his 1965 paper with Jacobson, Anderson attempted to relate the discounting and attention decrement explanations by suggesting that decreased weights for the later adjectives might be caused at least in part by decreased attention (p. 539). Hendrick and Costantini (1970) have proposed that discounting should vary with the degree of inconsistency between traits, whereas attention decrement should be independent of inconsistency and perhaps dependent only on the length of the series. If this assumption is granted, their results support an attention decrement hypothesis in that instruction to pronounce each trait (an attention-equalizing manipulation) converts primacy into recency. There is no support for discounting in their data, however, since the effects of order were unrelated to the degree of discrepancy among the traits.

Reference Scale Anchors and Judgmental Contrast

While we have emphasized the Anderson research program because of its quality and coherence, there are a host of other studies employing trait-adjective combinations in an impression formation context. If one were to have a run-off of primacy versus recency conclusions, primacy effects would win hands down. But another important research literature suggests that recency should be the predicted outcome under a wide range of conditions and is not just an anomalous exception to the primacy law. This derives from the tradition of research on psychophysical scale construction and the judgment of weight, brightness, pitch, numerosity, opinion extremity, and so on. It is appropriate to ask how this line of research relates to that, featuring the combination of adjectives.

Anderson makes an interesting stab at bringing the two sets of data together. In an attempt to account for the findings of recency obtained in his 1968 experiment discussed above, he concluded that recency is the generally expected outcome when information is presented in a sequence, and a

> necessary though not sufficient condition for primacy would be inconsistency among the stimulus items. Whether this view has any generality is difficult to say since the primacy-recency area is especially marked by conflicting results.... However, since most work in this area has, in fact, used stimuli of mixed polarity, conflicting results might be expected on the present view. With such stimuli, tendencies toward primacy and toward recency could be operating together and the net resultant would depend heavily on experimental details (p. 361).

The conclusion that recency is the generally expected outcome derives partly from the serial position learning literature, and partly from the literature on contrast effects in the judgment of stimuli in a series. From the former, we can extract the common sense principle that recent events are more easily remembered than more remote ones, though the [32] serial learning data show primacy effects as well as recency effects, with the items in the middle being most subject to retention difficulty because of retroactive and proactive inhibition. Miller and Campbell (1959) contend that recency will tend to win out over primacy when the measure of memory or impression occurs immediately after the end of the sequence, but their argument refers to longer time spans than those with which we shall be concerned.

The literature on assimilation and contrast in the psychophysical tradition seems more directly relevant to our problem than the nonsense syllable learning and retention literature. In the typical psychophysical judgment task, a subject is confronted with a series of objects that can be arrayed along the same attributive dimension. By any of a variety of methods (paired comparison, single stimuli, and the like) he is asked to locate specific objects along this dimension. There is some objective way to measure the true intensity value of each stimulus being judged—either by physical measurement in the classical psychophysical case or consensual judgment in the case of "goodness" or attitudinal extremity. Since this is so, it is possible to plot relations between the objective stimulus values presented and the subjective judgments given.

One of the conditions known to affect these relations is the item context preceding the particular item being judged. The preceding items serve as an "anchor" in terms of which a given item is judged. If the preceding items do produce anchoring effects, these may be either in the direction of contrast or assimilation—the judged item can either appear less like the items preceding it (contrast) or more like these items (assimilation) as judged against some objective criterion. The next step is to realize that assimilation is a sufficient condition for a primacy effect when the task is to summarize the characteristics or nature of the entire series, and contrast is a sufficient condition for recency. Thus, in a series of trait adjectives that are ordered from positive to negative, the later, negative adjectives might be judged more negative because of the anchoring effect of the earlier positive items. This would be a contrast effect and it would lead to recency when the subject attempted to rate his impression of the person described by the adjectives.

Restricting our consideration to sequences of changing information about a person, there are several theoretical positions that would expect contrast, and therefore recency, to characterize summarizing judgments in such a case (Johnson, 1944; Helson, 1947; Volkmann, 1951). The basic contention of each of these theorists is that earlier stimuli are in one way or another integrated into an expectancy or adaptation level in terms of which later stimuli are judged. No particular provision is made for assimilation in these theoretical statements. A more complicated position is taken by Sherif and Hovland (1961) and Sherif, Sherif, and Nebergall (1965), who propose that either contrast or assimilation can occur, depending on the discrepancy between the value of the stimulus being judged and the anchor. When the stimulus is close in value to the anchor, it will be assimilated to the anchor. Beyond some critical discrepancy value, however, the stimulus will be contrasted with the anchor and the discrepancy between the two will be magnified. Where this critical point is that separates assimilation from contrast depends on a number of factors discussed in detail by Sherif and Hovland. In general, the width of the assimilation range depends on the breadth and ambiguity of the cognitive categories involved. If a new stimulus falls near, but within the defining boundary of the category defined by the anchoring stimuli preceding it, it will be assimilated to the typical instance of that category (Bruner, 1957). If it falls outside the defining category boundary, contrast formation should occur (Berkowitz, 1960; Jones and Gerard, 1967).

What are the implications of the Sherif and Hovland argument for the analysis of order effects in impression formation? We have said that assimilation and contrast provide sufficient conditions for primacy and recency. Obviously, however, primacy and recency can occur without any implied distortion of the value of early- or late-appearing stimuli. In fact, Anderson's weighted average formula does not take assimilation or contrast into account; such factors would imply shifts in the meaning or scale value of at least some of the traits being assessed and would thus fall outside Anderson's model. If we accept the possibility of assimilation and contrast effects, however, then we can draw some interesting inferences about the relation of such effects to primacy–recency as a function of the entity being judged and the context of judgment.

In order to understand what might be involved, assume once again that we confront subjects with items of information in a sequence. If we insist to the subject that these items definitely refer to, describe, are manifestations of, the entity, such an insistence would presumably set up pressures toward assimilation—that is, toward judging each item as more similar to early (or modal) items than if the items were in isolation. If there is some reason to believe that different entities are being described together, or **[33]** that the manifestations are not equally valid or reliable, the effects of assimilation, in this sense, should be much weaker and contrast, in fact, could result. As an example of contrast effects where different entities are being judged in sequence, consider an experiment by Bieri, Orcutt, and Leaman (1963). These investigators presented sequences of contrived clinical cases in such a way that a case of moderate pathology was preceded by two cases of high or low pathology. As predicted, moderate cases preceded by high cases were judged less pathological than moderate cases preceded by low cases—the third case in the sequence was contrasted with the preceding two anchoring cases.

Actually, most cases of psychophysical judgment emphasize the relative or absolute evaluation of individual stimulus items and the subject is not asked to view the items as manifestations of some underlying entity. If items x, y, z are being independently judged as entities X, Y, Z, we should expect contrast. If items x, y, z are presented as manifestations of the same entity, however, there should be more pressures toward assimilation. It is the latter circumstance that characterizes the typical impression formation situation, and studies by Anderson and Lampel (1963) and Anderson (1966) clearly indicate the effects of viewing discrepant information samples as manifestations of the same entity. Subjects were told to rate each of three adjectives in terms of "how much you like the traits implied by the adjective." In some cases, they made these ratings after initially being told that the adjectives described a certain person and having rated their liking for that person. Subjects who made these initial ratings showed a "positive context effect" in their subsequent individual trait ratings. In other words, a favorable trait in combination with two unfavorable traits was judged as less favorable only when the traits were allegedly descriptive of the same person. We would venture to substitute the word "assimilation" for "positive context effect," though it is true that the results do not prove that the traits actually changed their meaning. The assimilation may be, then, more like a composite rating of the person and the traits—even though the instructions point only to the trait.

As we have already noted, assimilation (or a "positive context effect") is not automatically guaranteed in single entity situations because the manifestations to be judged may be differentially valid or referable to causal factors besides the entity itself. This is quite possible when the task is to form an impression from samples of behavior over time, because behavior may be attributed either to the person or the evoking situation. In the Anderson paradigm, the traits being evaluated may be seen as a joint function of the person being described and the person who (hypothetically) gave the description. Any suggestion that the traits are not equally valid should break up the tendency toward assimilation. Primacy effects may still occur for other reasons, however, since the chances are good that the later traits will be discounted entirely (rather than distorted through assimilation) if they are in conflict with the earlier traits.

A recent experiment by Thibaut and Ross (1969) is of special interest because it bears on these issues and introduces still another consideration, namely the extent to which the subject is *committed* to his initial impression—in this case, an impression of an artist's ability. An experimental manipulation committing the subject to an initially good or bad impression of the artist should promote assimilation of subsequent disconfirming information. In order to study the effects of commitment in comparison to appropriate control conditions, identical sequences of information were presented with different cover stories. The investigators presented twenty 16 × 16 matrixes containing varying proportions of 0's and 1's. Subjects were exposed either to an ascending series with a generally increasing proposition of 1's in the successive matrixes, or to a descending series in which the proportion of 1's is decreased. There were three conditions of judgment to which different subjects were assigned. In the *preference* condition, each matrix was said to represent the ratings of a particular painting by sixteen nontrained judges assessing sixteen esthetic attributes as good ("1") or bad ("0"). Each matrix in the series of twenty was alleged to refer to a different painting by the same artist. The subject's task was to announce how good he thought each picture was after seeing the judges' ratings using a preference scale ranging from 0/16 to 16/16. After observing the entire series of slides, each subject also evaluated the artist himself on a number of bipolar adjective scales. It may be noted that the trial-by-trial rating task is similar to the typical psychophysical judgment of individual stimuli, whereas the second rating task is more like the typical impression judgment.

In the *commitment* condition subjects initially ranked a series of seventeen reproductions of "representative" paintings by different artists. They then proceeded exactly as in the preference conditions except that the ascending series of matrix ratings was said to be of paintings by the artist whom the subject had ranked second from the worst and the descending series by the artist ranked third from the best.

In the *attribute* condition, subjects were merely [34] asked to estimate for each slide the proportion of 1's in the matrix from 0/16 to 16/16. Since the subjects in the other two conditions were asked to express their own judgments of the goodness of the painting in these same proportional terms, the dependent variable was comparable in all conditions. In all conditions, subjects were then exposed to a second series of slides that were actually the same twenty, in reverse order. Thus, subjects went from an ascending to a descending series or vice versa. A separate control group of subjects was exposed to a random series of matrixes (neither ascending nor descending) in the attribute condition.

The main results were presented in terms of the average value assigned to each judgment over the twenty matrixes in a series. On the first series of twenty slides, contrast effects were obtained in the preference and attribute conditions, as predicted, and a slight but nonsignificant assimilation effect occurred in the commitment condition. In the second series (presumably judgments of another group of twenty paintings by a different artist), there was a strong assimilation effect in the commitment conditions, but the contrast effect was no longer observed in the preference and attribute conditions. This is quite in line with previous findings (Bieri, Orcutt, & Leaman, 1963; Campbell, Lewis, & Hunt, 1958) that practice with alternating anchors reduces contrast. In the Thibaut and Ross study apparently the joint effects of practice and commitment were necessary to produce a full assimilation effect.

Results on the final ratings of the artist paralleled in almost every way the results summarizing the subjects' ratings of individual painting matrixes. Thus, in the present case at least, judgments of the individual paintings seem to be remembered when it comes to making an overall appraisal of the artist. Or to put it in another way, the summary judgment of the artist seems to have been affected by assimilation and contrast effects in the preceding judgment of his work.

The Thibaut and Ross study makes several points that are congenial to our main proposition. First of all, the context of judgment is obviously important. The more strongly the subject is committed to his initial judgment, the more he will tend to assimilate subsequent discrepant information. Secondly, without special manipulations of commitment, contrast appears to be facilitated by successive judgment instructions. Although the subjects in the preference condition are encouraged to think they are judging appraisals of productions by the same artist, they are also making successive stimulus judgments comparable to those of psychophysical rating tasks where contrast is a typical finding. Finally, it is of interest to note that overall judgments of the artist summarize the preceding individual matrix judgments, thus converting contrast into recency.

It is not at all clear that the results would have been the same if the procedures had asked *only* for a final summarizing judgment. Given such a procedure, Anderson and others (such as Hendrick & Costantini, 1970) might argue that the early matrices would be more salient and the later ones affected by attention decrement. Perhaps the successive matrix judgments, in other words, prevent attention decrement and therefore primacy—except when the power of commitment to an initial impression is sufficiently strong.

Unfolding Behavior Sequences

In the introduction to this paper, we drew attention to the confounding that typically exists in the natural environment between the order in which information is generated by a target person and the order in which the information is received for processing by an attributor. As an example of what might be involved in such confounded sequences, let us consider a study in which we put together a video tape consisting of twenty-one brief conversational vignettes involving two undergraduate students. Each vignette featured the same student expressing his views about other people in general and certain acquaintances, in particular. These vignettes showed the student as either very accepting and benevolent or as rejecting and pessimistic about human nature. In one condition (the accept–reject sequence), the early statements by and large extolled the charity of human nature whereas the later statements were more generally cynical and malevolent. A few transitional statements were placed in the middle to enhance credibility. In another condition, the sequence was reversed (reject–accept). Crosscutting these sequence variations were instructions designed to vary whether the student's actions were seen in the natural order in which they occurred. Half the subjects were told that the original sequence of these comments had been preserved on the tapes—they occurred at various points during the semester when these two students met once a week as part of a "get acquainted experiment." Thus, the subjects given these instructions could imagine that the target person changed in his outlook over the semester, or perhaps that his initial uneasiness in the relationship wore off, revealing his true personality, or that he changed the expression of his outlook when he found out about the beliefs of [35] his conversational partner. The remaining subjects were told that the vignettes were scrambled and arranged in random order. All subjects were subsequently asked to fill out the same impression rating scale designed to measure attributed benevolence–malevolence, and to write a paragraph describing their overall impression of the target person.

Did the instructions about order have any effect? First of all, there were some marginal differences between the summed benevolence–malevolence ratings. The random arrangements yielded a significant primacy effect: the target person was seen as more benevolent after the accept–reject sequence than after the reject–accept sequence. In the "sequence–preserved" conditions, neither primacy nor recency was observed. What is of particular interest is that few of the subjects in the random condition were able to develop reasonable hypotheses to explain the variation in expressed views. The free-impression paragraphs were analyzed to determine whether subjects had entertained any hypotheses to account for the behavior shift and, if so, what these hypotheses were. In the random conditions, nearly 80 percent of the subjects did not develop any resolving hypotheses about the dispositional characteristics of the target person. They either wrote matter-of-fact descriptions of the behavior they had observed (70 percent), or presented polarized impressions that ignored half of the information received (10 percent). The remaining random condition subjects recorded what might be called *diagnostic* impressions, most of which had a pejorative twist ("he's very confused in his values," "he strikes me as very insecure," "… muddle-headed").

In the sequence-preserved condition, on the other hand, almost 60 percent of the subjects developed hypotheses to account for the inconsistency of the student's opinions and 40 percent of the total number (as opposed to zero percent in the random conditions) made references to external events or the setting of the taped interaction. Fourteen out of the seventeen subjects who developed these hypotheses gave greater weight to the later information, manifesting a recency effect. They either supposed that the target person's outlook was changed by something that had happened during the semester in which the conversations took place—that there was a real change in the target person— or they felt that he was cautious or defensive at first, and as he became more relaxed, his true self was more clearly expressed. Three of the sequence-preserved subjects saw the target person as a chameleon, a hypothesis suggesting a weak primacy effect, since the target person would presumably start out being himself and later change to whatever position was being advocated by his partner. These conflicting hypotheses, plus the number of subjects who gave purely descriptive (25 percent) or polarized (18 percent) impressions, produced a wide range of responses to the benevolence–malevolence rating task in the sequence-preserved conditions. Thus, there was no overall tendency toward primacy or recency, as we noted above.

A final point of interest in the data is that it made some difference in the choice of hypotheses whether the sequence was accepting–rejecting or rejecting–accepting. Somewhat surprisingly perhaps, subjects observing the rejecting–accepting sequence were more prone to conclude that the target person was initially nervous and defensive than subjects in the accepting–rejecting sequence. There were not enough subjects in any such refined hypothesis subcategory to confirm a definite "interaction effect," but it seems highly plausible that the effects of confounding the sequence generated with the sequence received should vary as a function of the particular content and particular sequential direction involved.

The results of this study provide support for our basic proposition by showing that subjects do relate the changing manifestations of an entity to imagined external events when this possibility is made salient by instructions. It is important to realize that not all subjects do this, and some, in fact, seem curiously insensitive to the role of order in the sequence-preserved condition. But it seems self-evident that more clear-cut differences between random and sequence-preserved conditions could be obtained by more clearly structuring the interaction context (suggesting, for example, that the target person was undergoing intensive psychotherapy during the time span of the observed interviews). Thus, more pains could have been taken to specify the influence potential of the particular program of conversations.

In addition, sharper differences might have emerged if the dimension of behavioral variation had been more salient conceptually, and perhaps more clearly exemplified by the observed episodes. The malevolence–benevolence continuum may be organized into very different cognitive structures by different subjects. Also, the kinds of comments presented in the videotaped conversations were necessarily noisy, imperfect indicators of one's position on the continuum. In order to maintain credibility, the comments had to be varied, concrete, and not blatantly self-contradictory. For example, in one of the "benevolent" segments the target person made an appreciative remark about someone who had stopped [36] and helped him with a flat tire. Such a reminiscence night reflect benevolence, by the logic of salience and selective recall, but it is also a response determined by the characteristics of an external entity, the helper himself.

Finally, and of broader theoretical interest, the malevolence–benevolence disposition is a rather unstable one in most persons. We all have good moods and bad moods, and charity can rapidly give way to cynicism. It may be that the more unstable the attribute that supposedly underlies an unfolding behavior sequence, the less pressure there will be toward assimilation and primacy.

For this reason, it is appropriate to review the results of a series of experiments on the attribution of ability (Jones, Rock, Shaver, Goethals, & Ward, 1968). Ability as a dispositional construct obviously differs from benevolence–malevolence in many respects. One of the most crucial differences is that ability is a more stable attribute and its manifestations may be somewhat more reliable, and diagnostic ability does not come and go like our moods of optimism and pessimism; only the conditions favorable to its manifestations come and go. One implication of this fact is that a reliable glimpse of talent may assure us that the person "has it in him," even though we may never see him perform as capably again. Once high ability is attributed, therefore, subsequent declines in performance may be explained away in terms of motivational variations, outside distractions, neurotic problems, and so on. The person who performs well after we have decided he is low in ability may cause us to revise our estimate of his talents. It is also common, however, to find excuses for his belated excellent performance and attribute it to luck, the help of others, or dogged perseverance. There is some reason to believe that the "late bloomer" never gets the fair shake he may deserve, while the one who starts off on the right performance foot may gain a lasting impressional edge.

Let us consider the experimental situation designed by Jones et al. (1968). Subjects observed a stimulus person attempting to solve a series of thirty multiple-choice progressions and analogies. All items were described as of equal difficulty level (in terms of college norms) and they were varied and discrete like most intellectual aptitude test items, so that practice and learning effects would not be expected. The stimulus person always solved fifteen correctly, but in some cases he solved more of the later items (ascending series). In all cases, the subjects then predicted his success on a second series of unfolding items much like the first series. After this, subjects were asked to rate the intelligence of the stimulus person and to recall the number of correct answers given in the first series of thirty problems. A final questionnaire included ratings of attributed motivation, perception of item difficulty level, and other relevant probes.

In four separate experiments along these general procedural lines, primacy effects were obtained though some experiments showed stronger effects on one measure of order effects than on another. In general, subjects confronting a descending performer predicted that he would solve more on the second series, and judged him to be more intelligent. These indications of primacy were maintained whether or not the subject himself solved the problems along with the stimulus person (and thus might be motivated to belittle the latter's performance) and whether or not the subjects made successive item-by-item estimates of the subjective probability of success on the next item.

How might this primacy effect in ability attribution be explained? We may begin by ruling out a few likely alternatives. One possibility is that subjects judging the descending stimulus person assumed that he lost interest in the task after an early display of mastery. If such were the case, the subjects might conclude-that the stimulus person did poorly toward the end of the series almost *because* he was so bright, and therefore bored. The items were very difficult however, and it is hard to imagine highly selected college students not being motivated to do their best in such a situation of public intellectual evaluation—and, in fact, the subjects rated the descending performer and the ascending performer as equally (and highly) motivated.

Another possibility is that the subjects got bored and ceased to pay attention to the performer's changing fortunes. This would be the *attention decrement* explanation of primacy, an explanation receiving some support in the adjective combination literature. If such "tuning out" actually occurred, however one would surely expect the primacy effect to be reduced in a condition where subjects are asked to make subjective probability estimates of success before each trial. In fact, the addition of such a condition led to an increase rather than a decrease in primacy. Furthermore, as judged by the accuracy with which they were able to track changes in the objective probability of success, subjects in the probability estimation condition clearly maintained their attention, throughout. A simple inattention explanation is hard to defend in the face of these data.

It is possible that subjects related the different patterns [37] of performance to changes in the difficulty level of the items—in spite of instructions to the contrary. In fact, however, subjects in each of the experiments judged the items to be of equal difficulty level throughout the series.

The explanation of *discounting* proposed by Anderson and Jacobson (1965) is distinct from that of attention decrement and would suggest that, in some ways, subjects view later performance successes as unreliable or invalid indicators of ability. Such an explanation is perhaps plausible when subjects are trying to integrate discrepant traits ascribed by different acquaintances of the target person—it is easy to assume that some acquaintances knew the person better or were more discerning judges. It is more difficult to see how the discounting hypothesis might apply in performance evaluation when there is no evidence for motivation decrement or variations in problem difficulty.

The explanation for primacy that seems most convincing to us is one that stresses the phenomenal status of ability as a stable disposition and the information assuring that the items were of equal difficulty. The equal difficulty instructions should imply to the subjects that initial performance would be a valid indicator of performance to come—unless there was some change in the performer's motivation or ability. No change in motivation was perceived, and ability is assumed to be a stable personal attribute. We posit, for these reasons, an initial expectancy that successes will be equally distributed over the thirty trials. Such an expectancy should bias the recall of performance in the direction of a more equal spread of successes. A final assumption of assimilation to the initially observed proportion of successes would be sufficient to account for the observed primacy effect. In short, the subjects expect the early trials to tell them what the later ones will be like and, in spite of their attention to the evidence of these later trials, there is some assimilation in memory to bring this evidence more in line with the projected forecast.

The best evidence for this interpretation is in the recall data. After predicting trial-by-trial success over the second series of thirty items (viewed as a behavioral measure of attributed ability), subjects were asked to recall how many of the *first* thirty items the stimulus person had correctly solved. This measure showed consistent distortion of recall in favor of a greater number of successes for the descending stimulus person. In one experiment—which, incidentally, asked for successive probability judgments during the first series—the average subject recalled that the descending performer was correct on 20.6 of the 30 initial trials, whereas the ascending performer was recalled as solving 12.5. In both cases, of course, the true number was 15. The magnitude of distortion is rather remarkable, and such distortion provides a sufficient explanation for the primacy effect in ability attribution. It is possible that an attributional decision about ability leads to subsequent distortion of recall, but it seems much more likely that recall distortion leads to differential attribution. It might be noted, along these lines, that the recall data make even less plausible the interpretation of perceived motivational decline in the descending case. If the descending stimulus person were seen to fail on the later items because he was not trying, there would be no reason to see him as solving many more items than he in fact did.

Our favored explanation, then, is that of short-term memory assimilation to the expected proportion of successes and failures. This expectancy is jointly a function of the phenomenal stability of intelligence, an equal distribution assumption, and forecast data from the early trials. The evidence rules out a number of alternative interpretations and is consistent with the one we are offering; nevertheless, the evidence hardly makes an airtight case.

The memory assimilation interpretation does not rest on any quality peculiar to the attribute of intelligence aside from its relative stability. We hope we can make experimental predictions on the basis of variations in such general attributes as entity stability and do not have to construct new functional relations for each new entity being studied. The present interpretation should, then, apply in any judgmental setting where the subject is led to expect an equal distribution of the manifestations of a stable entity. Our next step was to conduct a follow-up experiment that imported these features into a setting of impersonal judgment.

Jones, Goethals, Kennington, and Severance (unpublished) tried to design the experiment as a close analogue of the ability study. It was introduced to the subjects as a study in information processing, "to see how well people can predict subsequent events on the basis of earlier information." The subjects' specific task was to turn over thirty cards, one at a time, after predicting, in each case, whether the card would be an ace or a non-ace. To set the stage for this task, subjects were shown an array of thirty-card decks and told that the decks had been doctored so as to contain anywhere from three to twenty-seven aces. The subject was asked to choose one of these decks at random and to shuffle the deck several times, being careful not to look at the card values while doing so. After the deck [38] was shuffled, a previously prepared deck was surreptitiously substituted just before the prediction task was to begin. This contained fifteen aces in the same ascending or descending order as successes in the ability studies.

After the subject went through this prearranged deck attempting to predict ace versus non-ace before each turnover, he was given an interpolated task consistent with the experimental rationale of forecasting events in a series. The specific task was to predict whether the next checker, taken from a large canister, would be red or black. After this interpolated task, the subject was asked to recall how many aces there had been in the deck of cards he had exposed and to indicate the distribution of these aces across thirty trials.

The result was a primacy effect: more aces were recalled in the descending than in the ascending condition. Furthermore, it was clear from the distributional memory data that subjects tended to exaggerate the number of late-appearing aces in the descending condition and to underestimate the number of late aces in the ascending condition. The estimates over the first ten trials were quite accurate. In short, there was fairly clear evidence of assimilation of late-appearing to early information.

Is this really an apt analogy to the ability situation? In arguing the affirmative, we would point out two crucial features of the setting and procedure. First of all, the attribute of "aceyness" is indeed stable in the sense that we intend to use that term. The number of aces in the chosen deck is fixed—like the ability of the performer in the earlier studies—and there is no apparent way that the number could change in the course of the experiment. Second, the shuffling procedure is similar to the equal-difficulty instructions of the ability studies in assuring the subjects that, except for random fluctuations, the distribution of aces should be equal. The actual distribution, of course, departed considerably from randomness, but as long as the subject retained the equal distribution expectancy he should have recalled the series as less lopsided than it actually was, adjusting primarily the later trial data to the earlier established expectancy about the probable proportion of aces in the deck.

A next step would be to manipulate directly the stability of the entity, to see if increasing instability leads to decreasing primacy. Alternatively, one might manipulate the expectancy of an equal-distribution of positive manifestations of the entity. The benevolence–malevolence experiment was one effort in this direction, but for several acknowledged reasons that study does not make clearly the point we seek to establish. Another alternative would be to stay within the framework of ace prediction while attempting to manipulate expectations concerning the stability of aceyness and the distribution of aces. Specifically, a deck could be created so that it would be difficult to predict "aceyness" from an initial sample of turned-up cards. This was attempted in an experiment also reported in Jones, Goethals, Kennington, and Severance. The procedure in the crucial condition involved having the subject choose a red-backed deck and a blue-backed deck from large arrays of both. Each deck contained twenty cards and (allegedly) anywhere from zero to twenty aces. After the subject shuffled each deck carefully several times, the decks were rather casually combined into one by the experimenter and handed back to the subject with instructions to predict whether the next card would be an ace or a non-ace. Again, the experimenter substituted a prepared deck containing either an ascending or descending series of aces. The backs of the cards showed, furthermore, that the two subdecks were unevenly distributed throughout the pack and the subject could see that more red (or blue) cards appeared early in the series. The cards were arranged in such a way, then, that there was a correlation between color of back and "aceyness."

This changing, or unstable entity, condition was compared to two control conditions, each featuring stacked decks with the same patterns of ascending and descending aces. In the first, the subjects chose one from among several large (forty-card) single-color decks, each allegedly containing anywhere from zero to forty aces. In the second, decks of two colors were again combined, but there was no correlation between card color and probability of being an ace. Unlike the changing entity deck, therefore, the red and blue backs were evenly distributed over the entire series. In all conditions, subjects engaged in the same task of turning over each card in turn and predicting the probability that the next one would be an ace.

The results of this final card-monitoring study showed that significant primacy in recalling the total number of aces occurred in both control conditions. As predicted, there was no primacy in the crucial condition in which card color provided a clue to the changing frequency of aces. Such clues make salient the fact that there is no reason to expect the later cards exposed to replicate the early cards in terms of the predominance of aces. If the entity is unstable or changing, in other words, strong expectancies should not form on the basis of early instances, and [39] without such expectancies primacy by the assimilation route would not be expected.

A major difference between our assimilation to expectancy proposal and the hypotheses of discounting or attention decrement is that the focus is on memory rather than initial information input. Evidence from both the ability and the card studies shows that subjects' memories are distorted in the direction of primacy even after they have made successive probability judgments that show sensitivity to the cumulative impact of preceding trials. What happens, we propose, is that the data across trials are equally attended to, but in the five- to ten-minute delay between exposure to the final item and questions about "how many aces?," the subject has made subtle adjustments to bring data in line with expectancy. (Perhaps it is appropriate to recall here that Miller and Campbell (1959) would predict the increase of primacy with an increasing delay between the event and its measurement—at least up to some point.) The extent to which assimilation and thus primacy will occur depends jointly on the stability of the entity and on cues suggesting how entity manifestations will be distributed. Finally, once these assimilative memory distortions have occurred, a variety of other attributional consequences can follow. The fact that the drift of memory toward expectancy is the culprit does not make the phenomena of primacy trivial or uninteresting since the attributional consequences that follow may be significant indeed. It often makes a great difference whether we judge someone to be intelligent or even, especially when the stakes are high, whether we feel we are dealing with a truly acey deck.

There are a few additional studies of the effects of order on the interpretation of unfolding behavior, but most of these are studies in which one person comments on his increasing or decreasing attraction for another. These studies will be briefly discussed because they bring up an important consideration that we have thus far ignored, the extent to which the information contained in later behavior replaces or subsumes the information contained in earlier behavior.

The Replacement Information Case

Aronson and Linder (1965) designed an experiment in which subjects were exposed to different patterns of sequential feedback reflecting the attitudes of a target person toward them. The procedures involved an elaborate, but plausible scenario wherein one female subject overheard another female subject, actually an experimental accomplice, making remarks about her to the experimenter. The subject heard these remarks from an adjacent room while she was busy at the task of recording the number of plural nouns in the accomplice's remarks. This activity fit the cover story presenting the experiment as one involving an attempt to increase the use of plural nouns through reinforcement from the experimenter. Between each of seven sets of remarks, the subject entered the accomplice's room and engaged her in conversation for three minutes. The subject believed she was doing this to see whether the increased use of plural nouns would generalize to someone other than the reinforcer. Actually, this periodic contact was a crucial feature of the experiment because it gave the accomplice a pretext for changing her mind and presumably endowed the evaluative remarks with greater personal significance for the subject.

There were four experimental conditions in the main study. As subjects listened to the accomplice's remarks about them, they learned that she (*a*) thought highly of them throughout the experiment (steady positive treatment), (*b*) started out negatively disposed but became increasingly favorable (gain treatment), (*c*) thought highly of them initially but became increasingly cool (loss treatment), or (*d*) remained unfavorable throughout (steady negative treatment). At the end of the seven conversational and monitoring episodes, the subject was led to the office of a final interviewer, who asked several questions to assess the subject's evaluation and final impression of the accomplice.

The results of the major assessment question showed that the subject liked best the accomplice in the gain treatment, next most, the accomplice who gave steady positive feedback, next, the steady negative accomplice, and least, the accomplice in the loss treatment. The accomplice in the gain treatment was liked significantly better than the accomplice in the steady positive treatment. The steady negative and the loss conditions were not significantly different. Aronson (1969) interprets these results in the framework of "gain–loss theory," and suggests that the subject's attraction for the accomplice is a function of the latter's responsibility for *changes* in the subject's self-esteem. He proposes that the accomplice in the gain treatment may be better liked because she first upsets the subject, raising her uncertainty level, and then reduces uncertainty. Some alternatives to this anxiety reduction hypothesis are (*a*) that the gain accomplice establishes greater credibility through her discrimination, (*b*) that the subject feels rewarded for her strivings to secure a more favorable **[40]** impression after a bad start (an efficacy reward explanation), and (*c*) that the final feedback values are seen in contrast to the expectancies established by the initial values (a contrast effect explanation).

A study by Landy and Aronson (1968) at least reduces the likelihood that a discrimination hypothesis is sufficient to account for the Aronson and Linder results. They found that a discriminator was liked better than a nondiscriminator and a positive evaluator was liked better than a negative evaluator. There was no interaction effect, as the discrimination hypothesis would require. A recent study by Mettee (1971b), however, suggests that Landy and Aronson may have manipulated judgmental variability under the guise of "discrimination" without affecting perceived credibility, supposedly a main component of the term's meaning. Cognitive contrast may contribute in a small way to the effects observed, but it seems insufficient in view of the explicit nature of the evaluative remarks and the fact that such remarks should be fairly clearly anchored within the range of feedback received and observed in everyday life. The efficacy interpretation could be evaluated by a replication in which the subject's own remarks were prerecorded and played episodically to the stimulus person. Thus, the subject could not vary his behavior in response to early negative feedback. Regardless of the specific hypothesis preferred, and several processes may be operating in various combinations in the situation, the fact remains that the Aronson and Linder results give a recency effect in both change conditions. This is especially clear when we note that the gain and loss conditions were maximally discrepant on the dependent variable liking measure.

Mettee (1971a) conducted a follow-up experiment to investigate the effects of varying the *importance* of the internally changing evaluations received by a subject. In the general setting of an experiment on the effects of knowledge of results upon group decision–making processes, subjects were exposed to two successive evaluations of their responses to the legendary Johnny Rocco case. Half of the subjects were asked first to comment on a very specific aspect of the case and then received highly favorable or unfavorable written comments from the leader. The remaining subjects were asked to comment more generally on the decision that should be made and to base their decision on a general philosophy regarding love and punishment as disciplinary methods. These subjects also received either favorable or unfavorable evaluations of their responses. Following this initial feedback stage, each half of the sample was then given the instructions the others had received initially and these always received feedback opposite to that initially given. Mettee's intent was to expose each subject to a combination of positive and negative feedback, and to endow one feedback message with more significance than the other because it was based on a more important sample of behavior and concerned with more general and more personal issues. After exposure to one of four information combinations (defined by the fourfold table of major–minor, gain–loss feedback), all subjects were asked to rate the leader in terms of their liking for him as a person.

Unlike the Aronson and Linder study, Mettee asked his subjects to rate the target person after each feedback message received. It is not clear, therefore, whether the final ratings on the two experiments can be meaningfully compared because of the commitment possibilities inherent in making the intervening rating. However, as Table 12.1 shows, the results are very different indeed from those obtained by the Aronson and Linder procedure. Some aspects of these results are trivial and do little more than validate the manipulations of feedback importance and order. What is interesting is the evidence for a primacy effect. The appropriate comparisons are those conditions in which exactly the same information is conveyed, but in opposite sequences. Thus the experimenter in the "small loss" condition is better liked than the "large gain" experimenter.

Table 12.1 Final Liking Ratings of the Evaluator

Group	Mean	SD
Small loss + + / −	3.29	1.16
Large gain − / + +	2.20	1.45
Large loss + / − −	1.10	1.55
Small gain − − / +	.62	1.38

Source: D. R. Mettee, 1971a.

Why should these results be essentially the opposite of the Aronson and Linder results? Rather than focus on the differential importance of the information units per se, Mettee suggests that his feedback units were essentially independent of each other and contributed to an additive resolution of the evaluational conflict. The positive evaluation had to be looked *at in conjunction with* the negative evaluation, and vice versa, in order for the subject to determine the experimenter's overall opinion of him. In contrast, the gain and loss sequence of the Aronson and Linder experiment involved successive information units that *replaced* the preceding units. To an important extent, the accomplice's expression of liking for the subject after seven conversational episodes [41] subsumed his report of liking after six, five, four, and so on episodes. Rather than seeing these as an added bit of information that needed to be integrated by the subject, he was dealing with the latest word in a pattern of cumulative readings of the accomplice's attitude toward him.

In a more recent experiment, Mettee and Taylor (unpublished) attempted to compare reactions to replacement information with reactions to independent information. The procedure involved two-part interviews with female subjects; the interviews were punctuated by prerecorded evaluative remarks allegedly delivered by a male experienced in evaluating female "datability." In the replacement conditions, the second half of the interview dealt with expansions of topics covered during the first half. In the independent conditions, the second half of the interview covered entirely new topics. Gain, loss, steady positive, and steady negative feedback patterns were presented in both replacement and independent contexts. The main measure of the subject's final liking for her evaluator showed primacy in the independent information conditions and recency (replicating Aronson and Linder's results) in the replacement conditions.

Unfortunately, the Mettee and Taylor experiment is not conclusive because, in the interests of plausibility. the second-half feedback remarks were noticeably different in content (and possibly in affective intensity) in the two contexts. Nevertheless, the results certainly encourage belief in the hypothesis, and the hypothesis is itself very plausible. It is not difficult to see, for example, that the adjective lists used by Anderson and others are typically combinations of independent information units. This is implied, at least, by the instructions stating that the adjectives each come from a different person who is well acquainted with the person being judged. If the ability attribution studies had dealt with a skill that was susceptible to rapid improvement with practice, this would have certainly implied a replacement unit judgmental set—the one who was doing well at the end should be judged as the most capable, or at least should be expected to continue to do well on the next series of trials. Certain equivocal results in the order effect literature may reflect the fact that a mixture of independent and replacement unit cues have been combined in the same experiment. Perhaps this was one of the difficulties with the benevolence–malevolence experiment. Some subjects treated the sequential information as independent and additive, whereas others saw the later information as growing out of, and replacing, the earlier impression. The replacement unit concept is important to bear in mind in any ongoing interpersonal situation to the extent that any comment or reaction builds on, or subsumes, previous behavior.

UNDERLYING PROCESSES: A SPECULATIVE RESUME

It is not an easy task to summarize the foregoing remarks, much less embed them in a coherent account of the principles involved in order effects. At least the reader has been forewarned that primacy, recency, and the absence of either can come about as the resultant product of a variety of processes. Hopefully, we have teased out some of these processes by commenting on the antecedent conditions that appear to produce order effects, and by attempting to juxtapose experimental traditions that have heretofore only touched each other gently in passing. About all we can do now is identify the major processes that seem to be involved in determining primacy or recency and make a few common sense remarks about each. Perhaps this hurried Cook's tour will serve as an interim substitute for the more extensive journey that awaits additional comparative research.

Toward Primacy

The three major processes involved in primacy effects are *attention decrement, discounting,* and *assimilation*. Attention decrement may result from distraction or from the increase of fatigue in processing sequential information, or it may be a more active process protecting against the disturbing implications of incongruity. The subject, in other words, may actively block out or ignore incompatible information.

More commonly, one would imagine, selective attention favoring early events probably occurs to the extent that there is cognitive overload—too much to remember. If the subject has to make a decision about holding on to one impression at the expense of another, it is not surprising that the initial impression has an advantage in the competition. This may be especially true when the subject is bored and has no particular incentive to do the best job he can with the complex information presented to him.

Presumably, the impetus for discounting depends unequivocally on the extent to which the information really is incompatible. At least this is Anderson's suggestion, and it has been exploited experimentally by Hendrick and Costantini (1970). Our assumption [42] has been that while incongruity may provide the impetus for discounting, its likelihood of occurrence should be enhanced by any factors in the context that permit judgments of differential reliability or validity.

Anderson's instructions—that not all traits are equally valid—facilitated discounting. One could imagine other cues that operate in a first-impression setting, causing the receiver to attribute early actions to the person and later, incompatible ones to the situation. This presumably is a common attributional tendency and it clearly may operate to preserve an initial impression of ability, attitude, or personality.

Primacy effects that result from attention decrement are not of theoretical interest, if all they show is that subjects become inattentive during an experimental series. Discounting maneuvers may also be theoretically trivial if the judging context is such that subjects can easily explain away recent information as unreliable. Assimilation is a more mysterious and pervasive phenomenon. We have tried to relate assimilation in the order effects domain to the general notion of cognitive assimilation. This general notion, going back to Bartlett and beyond, assumes that information creates or finds its way into preexisting categories. These categories are like hypotheses about the nature of reality being confronted. Once a categorical decision is made, subsequent evidence is distorted to fit the category or to confirm the hypothesis—as long as it is not too discrepant from the category's typical instance. Unlike discounting or attention decrement interpretations, assimilation implies that the value, intensity, or frequency of later units is shaped by the categories (expectancies) established by early information. Primacy is more than a function of assigning lower weights to more recent events.

Any factor that contributes to the speed with which a category can be formed and to the degree of confidence with which it is held should increase the tendency toward assimilation. As we have seen, this includes a variety of procedures designed to increase the subject's commitment to his initial judgment. Commitment puts the subject in a postdecisional phase in which consistency is of greater importance than accuracy (Festinger, 1964; Jones & Gerard, 1967).

Cognitive categories are more readily formed when the entity being judged is stable and its manifestations are assumed to be equally distributed over time. Unstable entities with capricious, cyclical, or a periodic manifestations should contribute to the suspension of conclusive attributional judgments, and the avoidance of the kind of premature closure on which assimilation apparently depends. Such considerations have intriguing implications for the question of which kinds of personal attributes are most likely to be prematurely judged in a developing relationship and what are the consequences of such selective distortion for interpersonal harmony and disharmony.

As indicated above, assimilation probably depends in a critical way on the discrepancy between items of unfolding information. All who make some attempt to deal with the concept of assimilation recognize that there is some point of information discrepancy beyond which assimilation cannot take place. Considerably more research is needed to determine the effects of discrepancy size and even to develop measures of discrepancy when dealing with semantic interactions among traits. One might propose, for example, a curvilinear hypothesis relating discrepancy magnitude to primacy. If later manifestations are only slightly different from earlier manifestations in their entity implications, they should be readily assimilated in value. The later manifestations should, in effect, be seen as more like the earlier manifestations than, in fact, is the case, giving rise to a primacy effect. With slightly greater discrepancies, however, we might expect contrast to occur. Later items should exert a disproportionate influence on the category (entity, expectancy) being formed and should bring about recency. But beyond some point of moderate discrepancy, the processes of incredulity, denial, and discounting should give rise to primacy again.

Toward Recency

Three major kinds of processes seem to favor recency. First there are those processes that appear to be a simple and direct reflection of *recall readiness.* There is abundant evidence that immediate past events are better remembered than more remote events. The extent to which this is true depends on how remote the early events are that we want to use for comparison, and how close the recent events are to the point at which the impression is being measured. One would expect natural sequences of events occurring over long periods of time to lend themselves more to recency than to primacy.

When short, circumscribed time spans are involved, the more relevant process may be that of judgmental *contrast.* Early information creates anchoring expectancies in terms of which later experiences are judged. The extent of contrast can vary with the pattern and range of information presented, the nature of the judgmental language being used, the amount of practice with other sequences in the same domain, and [43] so on. The typical setting for attaining contrast effects is one in which the subject is required to make independent judgments of items in terms of an attribute scale. Contrast arises under circumstances where those items are presented in a systematically biased, rather than a random, or counter balanced, order. To the extent that the later-appearing items are contrasted with the earlier, anchoring, items, one might expect a resultant impression of the series to show recency. This requires that the judgment of the earlier anchors does not change in retrospect before the summarizing, impressional judgment is made—that the contrast is irreversible.

A number of *content-* and *context-related hypotheses* are also potential preconditions for recency. If the entity is known to be capable of progressive changes or development, its later manifestations are obviously more significant than earlier manifestations for interactions with the entity. Maturation, growth, learning and practice effects, profiting from experience, in general—each of these factors can contribute to a tendency to attribute greater significance to more recent entity manifestations. Alternatively, the content and context of judgment may trigger off hypotheses that discredit early information for different reasons. If there are warm-up effects, if the individual is shy and unrevealing at first, early manifestations should be relatively ignored. Finally, the ordered content may be presented in a form that suggests that early information is being superseded by later information. We have noted this when information about liking is involved, but there may be other instances in which later behavioral data explain or subsume earlier evidence.

Swing Factors

When one considers the role of content and context, as this essay is recommending, the problem of order effects becomes more relevant to interpersonal behavior and much more complicated to analyze. Within the confines of an experimental design, information value can be manipulated with a fair amount of precision. For example, some attempt can be made to equalize the importance and level of information while systematically varying favorability. In the natural information environment, however, the person is exposed to considerably more chaotic data patterns that vary simultaneously on a number of different dimensions. If we listen to one person inform us about another, he is likely to range from behavior description through evaluation to inferences about motives and back again to description. Mixtures of positive and negative information can also take infinite forms and assume a great variety of intensity values.

There is certainly no question that some items of information assume priority over others or, to use Asch's term, some traits have a dominant centrality in the formation of an impression. Primacy or recency can obviously be affected by the position at which such central determinants fall. There are many reasons—plus some data (Ritchie, McClelland, & Shimkunas, 1967)—supporting the likelihood that unfavorable information is given greater weight than favorable information when units of different value are being combined. The centrality of an item, furthermore, may interact with its position in a sequence.

The possibilities for running into trouble when attempting to predict the effects of order in a complex natural setting are thus real ones. Our present effort has been less concerned with developing prescriptions for prediction than with using the order effect paradigm to suggest some of the processes underlying impression formation. There is much more to be understood, but our review points up enough consistencies across different traditions of research to suggest that some progress has been made and more is in the offing. At the very least, it is a kind of progress to realize that things are not as simple as they seem and to identify some of the reasons why. [44]

BIBLIOGRAPHY

Anderson, N. H. (1962). Application of an additive model to impression formation. *Science,* 138, 817–818.
Anderson, N. H. (1965). Primacy effects in personality impression formation using a generalized order effect paradigm. *Journal of Personality and Social Psychology,* 2, 1–9.
Anderson, N. H. (1966). Component ratings in impression formation. *Psychonomic Science,* 6, 279–280.
Anderson, N. H. (1968). Application of a linear-serial model to a personality-impression task using serial presentation. *Journal of Personality and Social Psychology,* 10, 354–362.
Anderson, N. H., & Barrios, A. A. (1961). Primacy effects in personality impression formation. *Journal of Abnormal and Social Psychology,* 63, 346–350.
Anderson, N. H., & Hubert, S. (1963). Effects of concomitant verbal recall on order effects in personality impression formation. *Journal of Verbal Learning and Verbal Behavior,* 2, 379–391.
Anderson, N. H., & Jacobson, A. (1965). Effect of stimulus inconsistency and discounting instructions in personality impression formation. *Journal of Personality and Social Psychology,* 2, 531–539.
Anderson, N. H., & Lampel, A. K. (1965). Effect of context on ratings of personality traits. *Psychonomic Science,* 3, 433–434.
Anderson, N. H., & Norman, A. (1964). Order effects in impression formation in four classes of stimuli. *Journal of Abnormal and Social Psychology,* 69, 467–471.
Aronson, E. (1969). Some antecedents of interpersonal attraction. In W. J. Arnold and D. Levine, (Eds.), *Nebraska Symposium on Motivation.* Lincoln, NE: University of Nebraska Press.
Aronson, E., & Linder, D. (1965). Gain and loss of esteem as determinants of interpersonal attractiveness. *Journal of Experimental Social Psychology,* 1, 156–172.
Asch, S. E. (1946). Forming impressions of personality. *Journal of Abnormal and Social Psychology,* 41, 258–290.
Berkowitz, L. (1960). The judgmental process in personality functioning. *Psychological Review,* 67, 130–142.
Bieri, J., Orcutt, B. A., & Leaman, R. (1963). Anchoring effects in sequential clinical judgments. *Journal of Abnormal and Social Psychology,* 67, 616–623.
Bruner, J. S. (1957). On perceptual readiness. *Psychological Review,* 64, 123–152.
Bruner, J. S., Shapiro, D., & Tagiuri, R. (1958). The meaning of traits in isolation and in combination. In R. Tagiuri and L. Petrullo, (Eds.), *Person Perception and Interpersonal Behavior.* Palo Alto, CA: Stanford University Press.
Campbell, D. T., Lewis, N. A., & Hunt, W. A. (1958). Context effects with judgmental language that is absolute, extensive, and extra-experimentally anchored. *Journal of Experimental Psychology,* 55, 220–228.
Festinger, L. (1967). *A Theory of Cognitive Dissonance.* New York: Row Peterson.
Helson, H. Adaptation level as a frame of reference for prediction of psychophysical data." *American Journal of Psychology,* 60, 1–29.
Hendrick, C., & Costantini, A. F. (1970). Effects of varying trait inconsistency and response requirements on the primacy effect in impression formation. *Journal of Personality and Social Psychology,* 15, 158–164.
Johnson, D. M. (1944). Generalization of a scale of values by the averaging of practice effects. *Journal of Experimental Psychology,* 34, 425–436.
Jones, E. E., & Davis, K. E. (1965). From acts to dispositions: The attribution process in person perception. In L. Berkowitz, (Ed.), *Advances in Experimental Social Psychology: Vol. 2.* New York: Academic Press.
Jones, E. E., & Gerard, H. B. (1967). *Foundations of Social Psychology.* New York: Wiley.
Jones, E. E., Goethals, G. R., Kennington, G. E., and Severance, L. J. *Primacy and assimilation in the attribution process: The stable entity proposition.* Unpublished manuscript, Duke University. [Editor's note: This paper was subsequently published as Jones, E. E., Goethals, G. R., Kennington, G. E., & Severance, L. J. (1972). Primacy and assimilation in the attribution of process: The stable entity proposition. *Journal of Personality,* 40, 250–274.]
Jones, E. E., Rock, L., Shaver, K. G., Goethals, G. R., & Ward, L. M. (1968). Pattern of performance and ability attribution: An unexpected primacy effect. *Journal of Personality and Social Psychology,* 10, 317–340.
Landy, D., & Aronson, E. (1968). Liking for an evaluator as a function of his discernment. *Journal of Personality and Social Psychology,* 9, 133–141.

Luchins, A. S. (1957). Primacy–recency in impression formation. In C. I. Hovland, (Ed.), *The Order of Presentation and Persuasion.* Yale University Press.

Mettee, D. R. (1971a). Changes in liking as a function of the magnitude and affect of sequential evaluations. *Journal of Experimental Social Psychology,* 7, 157–172.

Mettee, D. R. (1971b). The true discerner as a potent source of positive affect. *Journal of Experimental Social Psychology,* 7, 292–303.

Mettee, D. R., & Taylor, S. E. *Affect conversion versus affect change as determinants of the gain–loss liking effect.* Unpublished manuscript, Yale University. [Editor's note: This paper was subsequently published as Mettee, D. R., Taylor, S. E., & Friedman, H. (1973). Affect conversion and the gain-loss liking effect. *Sociometry,* 36, 494–513].

Miller, N., & Campbell, D. T. (1959). Recency and primacy in persuasion as a function of the timing of speeches and measurements. *Journal of Abnormal and Social Psychology,* 59, 1–9.

Peterson, C. R., & DuCharme, W. M. (1967). A primacy effect in subjective probability revision. *Journal of Experimental Psychology,* 73, 61–65.

Richey, M. H., McClelland, L., & Shimkunas, A. M. (1967). Relative influence of positive and negative information in impression formation and persistence. *Journal of Personality and Social Psychology,* 6, 322–327. **[45]**

Sherif, C.W., Sherif, M., &. Nebergall, M. S. (1965). *Attitude and attitude change.* Philadelphia: Saunders.

Sherif, M., & Hovland, C. I. (1961). *Social judgment assimilation and contrast effects in communion and attitude change.* New Haven: Yale University Press.

Stewart, R. H. (1965). Effect of continuous responding on the order effect in personality impression formation. *Journal of Personality and Social Psychology,* 1, 161–165.

Thibaut, J., & Ross, M. (1969). Commitment and experience as determinants of assimilation and contrast. *Journal of Personality and Social Psychology,* 13, 322–329.

Volkmann, J. (1951). Scales of judgment and their implications for social psychology. In J. H. Rohrer and M. Sherif, (Eds.), *Social psychology at the crossroads.* New York: Harper. **[46]**

INGROUPS AND OUTGROUPS

Chapter 13

The Perception of Variability within In-Groups and Out-Groups: Implications for the Law of Small Numbers

George A. Quattrone and **Edward E. Jones**
Princeton University

> ABSTRACT: Hypothesis: An observer's tendency to generalize from the behavior of a specific group member to the group as a whole is proportional to the observer's perception of the group's homogeneity, at least when the observer lacks a clear preconception on the behavioral dimension witnessed. Subjects from two rivalrous universities viewed target persons alleged to be students either at their own university or its rival. Each of three such target persons made a simple decision within a different decision scenario. After observing the decision made, each subject made estimates of the percentage of people likely to make the same decision in the parent group. The results confirmed the main predictions: (a) Percentage estimates tended to be consistent with the target person's decisions; (b) the degree of consistency was greater for out-group than for in-group target persons; and (c) both of these effects were clearest for the decision scenario where subjects' preconceptions about the most likely decision were weakest.

Reprinted with permission of the American Psychological Association © 1980 from *Journal of Personality and Social Psychology,* 38, 141–152.

> Given a thimbleful of facts, we rush to make a generalization as large as a tub. (Gordon Allport, 1954, p. 8)
>
> Women are more like each other than men [are]. (Lord, not Lady, Chesterfield)

An individual's beliefs about the attributes and characteristic behaviors of group members are often implicitly probabilistic. One may believe, for example, that roughly 60% of all undergraduate males would prefer to read *Playboy* rather than *Time,* or that a good 85% of all Scots are cheap. How might these percentage estimates be affected by the individual's witnessing the behavior of a group member? According to the "law of small numbers" (Tversky & Kahneman, 1971), observers would tend to generalize unduly from the actor's behavior and his inferred dispositions to those deemed typical of the actor's group as a whole. Thus, an individual's estimate concerning the percentage of undergraduate males preferring *Playboy* over *Time* would be somewhat greater had the individual just observed an undergraduate male choose the former and reject the latter, than had the individual just observed the opposite selection. Let us refer to the difference in percentage estimates due to the particular behavior observed as the "law of small numbers" (LOSN) effect. Nisbett and Borgida (1975) report data consistent with this effect.

We propose that the magnitude of the LOSN effect depends on the firmness of the individual's preconception about the target group on the behavioral dimension witnessed, and on the individual's perception of the target group's general variability, the extent to which its members are believed to differ from one another when viewed over all dimensions. Let us develop our argument by considering the information an observer may employ when making percentage estimates [141]* after having witnessed a member of the group engage in some behavior, such as making a decision between two alternatives. In trying to estimate the percentage of members of the actor's group who would make the same or the alternate decision, the observer may consider what caused the actor's behavior. If the choice seems to have been preordained by the nature of the setting—in short, it is in reality no choice at all—then the LOSN will automatically apply, and the variability of the group will, in this instance, be irrelevant. To the extent that the situation clearly permits variability of choice, the actor's decision presumably reveals something about his own values, traits, or motives. When this happens, the LOSN effect will be magnified in proportion to the observer's perception of the group's homogeneity. If the observer perceives the members of the actor's group as "pretty much all alike," then he may infer that the preferences, traits, values, or motives mediating the actor's decision prevail within the actor's group. A perception of variability, however, would undermine such facile generalizations from the actor's behavior and related attributes to those considered typical of the group.

The LOSN effect and its possibly greater magnitude for target groups perceived as relatively homogeneous may also depend on the observer's impression of the actor's group prior to viewing the decision. With a firm preconception about the percentage of members who would choose each of the two options, the observer may place relatively little weight on the information derived from one particular actor's decision. The observer's

---

*Bracketed bold numbers refer to original page numbers. Page numbers indicate where the original page ended.

tendency to rely more on a prior impression than on the actor's behavior, then, should minimize the LOSN effect as well as any tendency for this effect to be larger for groups perceived as generally homogeneous across its members. With merely a vague, tentative, or nonexistent preconception, however observers may place relatively more weight on the information extracted from the actor's decision, enlarging both the LOSN effect overall, and the tendency for this effect to vary with the group's perceived homogeneity.

An additional question remains. What determines the preconception of a group's variability? There is clearly no single determinant of whether one group is perceived to be more or less variable than another. A contributing condition is the sheer act of categorization. Tajfel (1969) and Taylor, Fiske, Etcoff, & Ruderman (1978) have demonstrated that categorization leads to increased between-category variability and decreased within-category variability. Other plausible determinants of perceiving more variability within one group than another include the size and inclusiveness of the groups (e.g., Christians vs. Chassidic Jews), the personality relevance of group-defining criteria (religion vs. hair color), and whether the group members have salient identifying symbols (Shriners vs. historians at a convention).

Our present hypothesis is that beyond these (and no doubt other) determinants of perceived variability, an important additional determinant is whether the perceiver is or is not himself a member to the group being perceived. We propose that, in general, people perceive more variability within in-groups, social categories of which they are members, than within out-groups, social categories of which they are not members. Thus the common observation that "they all look alike but we don't" may extend from the realm of physical appearance to the realm of personality attributes. What are some of the major reasons why this might be so?

First, we may note that the information a person acquires about different social groups varies in quantity and nature. Because the members of a group generally interact more frequently with in-group than with out-group members, the in-group member is more likely to have been exposed to the full range of attributes and personal lifestyles characterizing the group members. Moreover, the in-group member, because of his relatively impoverished store of data about others, may wish to abstract as much stable information as he can from his rare encounters with the out-group. An ingenious experiment by Campbell (1956) suggests that, at incomplete stages of learning, people may try to maximize their acquisition of information by [142] focusing on the similarities, and by overlooking the differences among a set of variable entities. Thus an individual may not only be ignorant about how the members of an out-group differ from one another; he may also be disproportionately aware of how they are all alike.

But frequent exposure to the members of a particular group is not alone sufficient to induce a perception of variability. By virtue of his particular relationship to the target group, an out-group member may have quite a few encounters with a mere subsample of the target group's members. This subgroup (e.g., psychologists who appear in Sunday supplements or on the Merv Griffin Show) may have much in common, while not particularly representing the group as a whole. In addition, intergroup encounters are more likely than intragroup encounters to occur in a restricted range of situations where the participants may be bound to constraining roles. Because the perceiver may not fully realize the impact of such situational constraints on the behavior of others (Jones, 1979), he may mistakenly attribute the observed behavioral uniformity among an out-group's members to their actual dispositional invariance. And since people may attend preferentially to the very behavioral dimensions relevant to adequate role performance (Jones & Thibaut, 1958; Zadny & Gerard, 1974), they may fail to notice the heterogeneous attributes displayed along dimensions on which behavior is free to vary.

An individual's fellow in-group members, sharing similar episodes with the out-group, may, through their consensual agreement, subjectively validate the individual's experiences and his inferences about the out-group's homogeneity. Of course, the in-group may do more than merely validate the individual's own impression. They may also supply him with "information" about out-groups and exert influence to enforce agreement. Such culturally transmitted, category-based expectancies (Jones & McGillis, 1976) are often framed in stereotypic terms. Moreover, an individual may find it desirable to discover homogeneity within an out-group, so as to provide himself with an unequivocal hypothesis about how to behave toward each of its members. At the same time, the individual may find it desirable to discover heterogeneity within in-groups, so as to be free of constraining expectations, and so as to avoid a sense of being indistinguishable from others. Finally, by acting toward all out-group members in a manner shaped by expectations about them, the individual may launch a chain of events culminating in the confirmation of his beliefs (Allport, 1954; Rosenthal & Jacobson, 1968; Snyder, Tanke, & Berscheid, 1977). There are several additional reasons why disconfirmatory evidence may be ignored and why an impression of homogeneity may persevere in the face of contradictory data. These are discussed in Quattrone's more detailed essay (Note 1).

An experiment was conducted to test some of the hypotheses raised in the present report. In this study, sophomore males from Princeton University and from Rutgers College viewed a videotape consisting of three scenarios. In each scenario, a distinct target person was shown making a decision between two behavioral alternatives that differed depending on the scenario. The three target persons were described as sophomore males, all sampled from either Princeton University or Rutgers College. Depending on condition, subjects observed the target persons select one set of options or the complementary set of options. Thus, three between-subjects factors, each with two levels, were crossed factorially: subject's group (Princeton/Rutgers), target persons' group (Princeton/Rutgers), and decision made (Set A/Set B). Scenario expectancy strength served as a within-subjects variable with three levels. Labels for the levels of the scenario variable (weak, moderate, firm) corresponded to the strength of subjects' preconceptions about the target groups on the three decisional dimensions. After subjects viewed the entire videotape, they were asked to estimate the percentage of members of the target persons' group who chose each of the two options for each of the three decisions. We made the following predictions:

1. There will be a main effect for decision. That is, collapsing over the scenario variable, [143] we expect the percentage estimates to be consistent with the target persons' decision, corresponding to what we have referred to as the LOSN effect.
2. Again collapsing over the scenario variable, there will be a three-way interaction among subject's group, target persons' group, and decision. The form of the interaction will indicate that percentage estimates reflect the target persons' decisions to a greater extent when the target persons are described as

out-group members than when they are described as in-group members. This prediction follows from our propositions that (a) the LOSN effect is proportional to the individual's perception of the target group's homogeneity and (b) out-groups are perceived as less variable than are in-groups.

3. The magnitudes of the main effect for decision and the three-way interaction will depend on the particular decisional dimension on which the percentage estimates are being made. The main effect and the interaction should be largest for the dimension about which subjects have weak preconceptions and smallest for the dimensions about which subjects have firm preconceptions. These considerations predict an interaction between decision and scenario's linear component and a four-way interaction among subject's group, target persons' group, decision, and scenario's linear component.

METHOD

Subjects

Fifty-four sophomore males from Princeton University and 41 sophomore males from Rutgers College participated in a study entitled "decision making." For their participation, Princeton students received cash and Rutgers students received experimental credit. Subjects were run at their own institution in small groups ranging in size from 1 to 5 participants. All subjects within a session served in the same experimental condition. Except, of course, for the subject's group variable, subjects were assigned randomly to condition, each composed of from 9 to 14 subjects. The data from one Princeton student, who recognized an actor on the videotape, were not analyzed, leaving a total of 94 subjects.

Procedure

After all the subjects for a session had arrived, the experimenter discussed various psychological consequences of making decisions and expressed his current interests in (a) how accurately ordinary people can predict the decision to be made by others and (b) how accurately people can, having observed or not observed a decision, infer a target person's self-description. Subjects then viewed a videotape, intermittently stopped for them to make various ratings. The tape was introduced to some subjects as having been made at Princeton and to other subjects as made at Rutgers. The tapes were allegedly filmed during sessions of three previous experiments on decision making, each involving 100 male sophomores. The target persons acting on the tape, all actually Princeton upperclassmen recruited for the purposes of the present study, were said to have been randomly selected from subjects participating in their respective experiments and to have been unaware of their being videotaped until the completion of their session. The three alleged experiments corresponded to the three levels of the scenario variable, and they were presented to subjects in three counterbalanced orders, following a Latin square. (The order in which the scenarios were shown produced no theoretically interesting main effects or interactions and will not be further discussed.) For the "weak expectancy" scenario, subjects viewed a target person having to decide whether to wait alone or to wait with other subjects while his experimenter fixed a broken dial on a biofeedback machine. In the "moderate expectancy" scenario, a target person chose to work on a set of either mathematical or verbal problems for his alleged experiment investigating the effects of noise on intellectual performance. The "firm expectancy" scenario faced a target person with the options of listening to rock music or to classical music during his experiment on auditory perceptual sensitivity. Various internal measures were used to validate our manipulation of predecisional expectancy strength.

Each scenario followed the same basic format. A target person was shown listening attentively as the experimenter (who also served as experimenter in the present investigation) explained the procedures to be followed in the fictitious experiment. After the experimenter had asked the target person to make his decision, the tape was turned off long enough for subjects to try to predict the target person's decision. Predictions were made on 21-point scales that had endpoints labeled with the two relevant options. (Except for the percentage estimates, all other dependent measures were also taken from 21-point scales with labeled endpoints.) The tape was then turned on again and subjects witnessed the decision the target person was said to have actually made. The decision manipulation was here introduced. Subjects in the Set A condition witnessed the target person choose to (a) wait alone in the weak scenario, (b) work on verbal **[144]** problems in the moderate scenario, and (c) listen to rock music in the firm scenario. Subjects in the Set B condition witnessed the complementary set of alternatives chosen (i.e., wait with the other subjects, work on the mathematical problems, and listen to classical music, respectively). Subjects were then asked to infer how the target person rated himself along several personality scales chosen for their apparent relevance to the decision. The scales used for each scenario follow: (a) weak expectancy scenario—sociable/unsociable, talkative/quiet, and tense/relaxed;[1] (b) moderate expectancy scenario—methodical/unmethodical, creative/uncreative, sensitive/insensitive, emotional/unemotional, mathematical/verbal; and (c) firm expectancy scenario—hip/straight, snobbish/down-to-earth, conventional/unconventional, concerned with image/unconcerned with image, self-righteous/non-self-righteous.

After subjects had inferred the target person's self-description, the tape was turned on again. A second target person, allegedly drawn from the same experiment as the first, was shown waiting for the experimenter to arrive. After having observed this target person for about a minute, subjects were asked to predict his decision and self-description on the basis of "whatever cues seem relevant." The second target person was included to assess whether the decision and inferred self-description of the first target person would be generalized to another member of his group irrespective of whether generalizations to the group as a whole were made (cf. Nisbett & Borgida, 1975). After this basic procedure was repeated for all three scenarios, the videotape monitor was turned off, and subjects were instructed to complete the pages remaining in their booklets. On rating scales with endpoints labeled with the decisional alternatives for each of the three scenarios, subjects responded to the following questions: (a) What decision do you think the average Princeton (or Rutgers, depending on the target persons' group affiliation) undergraduate male made in this situation? (b) What decision do you think you

---

[1] Two other scales were inadvertently omitted from the dependent measure questionnaire by secretarial error.

would have made in this situation? and (c) Whom do you like as people more? Those who prefer.... In addition, subjects were asked to estimate how many of the 100 participants chose each of the two options (i.e., a percentage estimate).

Subjects also rated the average Princeton (Rutgers) undergraduate male on a set of 25 personality scales. These included the 13 scales subjects used to infer the target persons' self-description, as well as the 2 scales relevant to the weak expectancy scenario that were previously omitted: shy/bold and independent/conforming. These scales were used to test whether traits attributed to specific target persons would be generalized to the group as a whole. The remaining 10 scales, dispersed randomly among the set of 25, were chosen to discriminate between the expected stereotypes for Princeton versus Rutgers undergraduate males. The endpoints of these scales follow, showing first here, but not necessarily in the booklet, the trait we expected to be seen as more typical of Princeton students: conservative/liberal, upper class/lower class, wealthy/poor, intelligent/stupid, school-oriented/party-oriented, ambitious/unambitious, articulate/inarticulate, cosmopolitan/provincial, well dressed/poorly dressed, and conceited/modest. These measures were taken to see whether a target group would be rated in line with its stereotype to a greater extent by out-group than by in-group members, a result that would certainly be consistent with the in-group/out-group hypothesis.

Subjects then responded to two final questions. The first required subjects to rate the variability of the target persons' group on a scale anchored with endpoints "They're pretty much all alike," and "They're all completely different from one another." On the second scale, subjects indicated how much they liked the average Princeton (Rutgers) undergraduate male. After all subjects in a session completed their booklets, the group was debriefed.

RESULTS

Strength of Prior Impression

We viewed several measures as informative with respect to the strength or firmness of our subjects' prior impression. First, we reasoned that for scenarios eliciting only a tentative prior impression, subjects would do more random guessing when asked to predict the first target person's decision. Alternatively, subjects might develop vague hunches concerning the presumed personality attributes of the target person. Since the information about the target person was so minimal, subjects would be likely to disagree in their personality assessments. Whether based on random guessing or ill-informed hunches, subjects' predictions should not gravitate toward any common decisional alternative. Consequently, the variance in their predictions should be relatively large, and the grand mean should deviate little from the scale's midpoint. We reasoned further that the stronger their preconception, the less subjects' predictions about the first target person in a scenario would differ from their predictions about the second. The first three rows of Table 13.1 present results for each scenario on measures suggested by the above [145] reasoning. (The F values for the linear trends displayed in the final column of Table 13.1 as well as the F values given for all other analyses presented in this report, are based on the assumptions and methods of the multivariate general linear model as presented in Morrison, 1967.) Our predictions were generally confirmed. It is important

Table 13.1 Measures of Predecisional Expectancy Strength and Magnitude of Law of Small Numbers Effect as a Function of Scenario

	Scenario			
Measure	Weak	Moderate	Firm	lin F (1, 70)[a]
1	.26	3.82	5.19	47.70**
2	32.04	16.06	14.13	
3	5.92	3.98	3.82	9.65**
4	26.60	12.92	11.24	10.72**
5	16.77	5.55	−2.16	4.06*

Note: 1 = Absolute extent to which the grand mean of predictions about the first target person's decision deviated from the scale's midpoint.
2 = Variance in predictions about the first target person's decision.
3 = Mean absolute difference in decision predictions for both target persons within a scenario.
4 = Magnitude of the law of small numbers effect (i.e., main effect for decision).
5 = In-group/out-group difference in Measure 4 calculated so that positive numbers indicate greater generalization for out-group target persons.

[a]The 16 df corresponding to the order variable's effects were included in each of these analyses. Hence, the within-cell error estimates are based on 70 (92-24) instead of 86 (94-8) df.

*$p < .05$.
**$p < .01$.

to note that these analyses were done separately for each combination of subject group by target group. These separate analyses produced results almost identical to those displayed in Table 13.1 with one consistent exception. By all three criteria, undergraduates from Rutgers considered themselves, and were considered by others, to prefer rock music to classical music to a greater extent than were undergraduates from Princeton.

Predictions and Percentage Estimates

For each scenario, five dependent measures directly concerned predictions and estimates about decisions (as opposed to trait inferences): (a) predictions about the first target person observed, (b) predictions about the second target person observed, (c) predictions about the average member of the target persons' group, (d) percentage estimates, and (e) conjectures about subjects' own likely decision. (Measures c and d gave virtually identical results, $r = .84$, and thus only the percentage estimates will be discussed.) As a control against the inflation of Type I error rates, these multiple responses were subjected to three multivariate analyses of variance (MANOVA), one for each scenario. The fruits of these analyses are presented in Table 13.2. Here it is evident that the main effect for decision was highly significant across all three scenarios. Univariate

Table 13.2 Ratios Obtained from MANOVA Contrasts

Source of Variance	Scenario		
	Weak	Moderate	Firm
Subjects' group (A)	1.19	< 1	4.36*
Target persons' group (B)	1.17 12.65**	1.22 7.92**	5.09** 5.50**
Decision (C)	< 1	< 1	< 1
A × B	1.21	1.42	< 1
A × C	1.15	< 1	1.83
B × C	2.43*	< 1	1.72

Note: All p values are based on distribution of $F(5, 66)$.
*$p < .05$.
**$p < .001$.

analyses revealed that these effects were due almost entirely to subjects' percentage estimates, estimates that reflected what we have referred to as the LOSN effect. These percentage [146] estimates are displayed in Table 13.3. The univariate main effects for decision are significant at beyond the $p = .001$ level.

Although not apparent from an already crowded Table 13.3, it is particularly interesting that the decision variable had absolutely no effect on subjects' predictions about the decision to be made by the second target person shown within a scenario. Thus, whereas the first target person's decisions clearly generalized to estimates about the behavior of his group as a whole, these decisions did not affect predictions about the behavior of specific members of his group, a finding reminiscent of Nisbett and Borgida's (1975) data. These authors found that subjects were prone to generate base rates that reflected the behavior of a few sample cases, but were not at all prone to base their predictions of individual cases on experimentally provided base rates.

The multivariate analyses also uncovered a three-way interaction among subject's group, target persons' group, and decision for the weak expectancy scenario. The pertinent columns in Tables 13.3 show that this significant result reflects the predicted in-group/out-group difference in subjects' fidelity to the law of small numbers: For the weak scenario, the decision of an out-group member had a greater effect on categorical percentage estimates than did the decision of an in-group member, $F(1, 70) = 5.30, p < .03$. The interaction was also significant for subjects' conjectures about the decision they themselves might have made in the depicted situation: Their conjectures reflected the out-group target person's decision more than the in-group target person's decision, $F(1, 70) = 6.54, p < .02$. At first glance, this greater consistency with the out-group appears ironic. If we consider the fact, however, that there was a stronger tendency to perceive consensus among out-group members, the finding makes more sense. Perhaps the subjects were more strongly influenced by the greater imputed consensus, even though it involved a consensus among out-group members.

Let us examine the specific predictions we made concerning subjects' percentage estimates. [147] Collapsing over the scenario variable (see Table 13.3), we find a highly significant main effect for decision that strongly confirms Prediction 1 of a general LOSN effect, $F(1, 70) = 96.88$, $p < .001$. Again collapsing over scenarios, we find a three-way interaction among subject's group, target persons' group, and decision that falls just short of significance, $F(1, 70) = 3.82$, $p = .055$, providing at least tentative support for Prediction 2 that subjects would show the LOSN effect more strongly for out-group than for in-group targets. More important, the main effect for decision and the three-way interaction are both qualified by their interactions with scenario's linear component. As we proceed from the weak expectancy scenario through the moderate expectancy scenario to the firm expectancy scenario, we find that the LOSN effect and the predicted in-group/out-group difference in subjects' adherence to this effect become smaller: for Decision × Scenario, linear $F(1, 70) = 10.72$, $p < .005$; for Subject's Group × Target Persons' Group × Decision × Scenario, linear $F(1, 70) = 4.06$, $p < .05$. The magnitudes

Table 13.3 Percent of Target Person's Group Estimated to Choose Set A Options

Set of Decisions Observed	In-group P/P	In-group R/R	Out-group P/R	Out-group R/P
Weak scenario				
A. Wait alone	55.00	56.44	59.42	71.60
B. Wait with others	44.31	30.69	28.37	32.68
Difference	10.69	25.75	31.05	38.92
Moderate scenario				
A. Verbal problems	49.42	53.50	47.42	53.07
B. Math problems	41.93	40.69	37.62	31.49
Difference	7.49	12.81	9.80	21.58
Firm scenario				
A. Rock music	70.05	86.39	75.80	73.77
B. Classical music	55.42	76.39	73.67	55.58
Difference	14.63	10.00	2.13	18.19
Combined scenario				
Set A	58.16	65.44	60.88	66.14
Set B	47.22	49.26	46.55	39.92
Difference	10.94	16.18	14.33	26.22

Note: P = Princeton. R = Rutgers. P/R = Princeton subjects viewing Rutgers targets, and so on. Combined = Set A decisions averaged over scenarios.

of the main effect for decision and of the three-way interaction are given in the last two rows of Table 13.1. It is evident that their relative sizes parallel the ordering of the measures presented in the first three rows of Table 13.1 that were previously discussed.

Table 13.2 also shows multivariate main effects for subject's group and target persons' group that were significant for the firm expectancy scenario. These reiterate the point made earlier that Rutgers students were especially thought to prefer rock to classical music, whereas the perceived rock preference of Princeton students was less marked. Quite consistent with the proposed effect of expectancy strength on the LOSN effect, Table 3.3 shows that, for the firm scenario, the main effect for decision was greater for Princeton target persons than for Rutgers target persons.

Trait Inferences About Target Persons and Target Groups

Acts led to inferred dispositions—at least if we make the reasonable assumption that inferences made about the target person's self-descriptions tap indirectly subjects' own perceptions of him. Analyses performed on indices derived from summing the traits attributed to the decision-making target persons revealed main effects for the decision variable that were quite reliable for the weak expectancy scenario, $F(1, 86) = 97.31$; for the moderate expectancy scenario, $F(1, 84) = 152.03$; and for the firm expectancy scenario, $F(1, 84) = 25.42$, all $ps < .001$. Taken individually, 11 of the 13 trait attributions showed a main effect for decision, confirming our hunches that the traits selected were indeed perceived as relevant to the target persons' decisions. At the same time, these results indicate that the subjects did not see sufficient constraint in the decision situations to negate the drawing of dispositional inferences from the decision made. The decision variable had no effect on attributions made to the second target person observed within a scenario, the one not shown making a decision. Subjects, once more, did not generalize from the inferred dispositions of one person to those of another member of his group.

Did these trait inferences generalize to the target persons' group as a whole? Recall that subjects were asked to rate the target persons' group on a set of 15 personality scales chosen for their relevance to the target persons' decisions. A summary index of these ratings shows a main effect for decisions, with subjects rating the average member of their target group more in line with the observed (Set A or Set B) choice, $F(1, 70) = 5.46, p < .03$. Taking indices for each scenario individually, we find that the main effect for decision was significant only for the weak expectancy scenario, $F(1, 70) = 5.29, p < .03$, although the interaction between scenario and decision did not approach significance, $F(2, 140) < 1$. Also for the weak expectancy scenario, we found a three-way interaction among subject's group, target persons' group, and decision, $F(1, 70) = 4.46, p < .04$: Attributions made to the group as a whole reflected the target person's decision only when the target group was an out-group (see Table 13.4). The appearance of this interaction

Table 13.4 Attributions Made to Average Member of Target Person's Group on Index of Traits Relevant to the Weak Expectancy Scenario

	Decision	
Status	Wait alone	Wait with others
In-group	9.88	9.96
Out-group	10.89	9.58

Note: High numbers refer to traits consistent with the decision to wait alone.

only within the weak scenario did result in a significant four-way interaction among [148] subject's group, target persons' group decision, and scenario $F(2,140) = 3.19, p < .05$.

Variability and Liking Measures

Subjects rated the variability of the target persons' group. By this measure, subjects showed absolutely no tendency to rate the in-group as more variable than the out-group. In addition, affective factors apparently played no role in subjects' percentage estimates. That is, their percentage estimates could not be predicted from their liking for the target persons' group and their liking for the sorts of people who would choose one alternative over the other. For example, subjects who liked Princeton students and who preferred mathematical to verbal people did not surmise that Princeton consisted of more mathematical types than did subjects who also liked Princeton students but whose personal preferences were reversed. The often-found affective bias in favor of the in-group (see Brigham, 1971, for a review) was replicated in the present study, however. Subjects did indeed indicate greater liking for the in-group ($M = 12.92$) than for the out-group ($M = 11.02$); $F(1, 70) = 7.83, p < .01$, for the interaction between subject's group and target persons' group.

DISCUSSION

The major findings of the present investigation can be summarized as follows:

1. Subjects' estimates about the number of members of a target group who would make a particular behavioral decision were consistent with the decision made by one of the group's members, especially if the target person was a member of an out-group rather than of an in-group.
2. This tendency to generalize from a decision made by a group member to the probability of a similar decision being made by other members (the LOSN effect) was especially strong when the group under consideration was an out-group, but only when a weak expectancy scenario was involved. In other words, when subjects did not have a clear prior expectancy concerning the target person's most likely response (in the wait-alone vs. wait-together scenario), they were more influenced by a member's decision in making inferences about decision tendencies in the out-group than in the in-group. The LOSN appears to be a joint function of a weak category-based expectancy and the perceived homogeneity of the target group.
3. Subjects made inferences about the target person's self-description by selecting traits consistent with his decision. Moreover, a summary index of traits attributed to the target persons' group as a whole also reflected the particular decision witnessed. Taken on a scenario-by-scenario basis, however, the effect of decision on these group attributions was significant only for the weak expectancy scenario. In this scenario, it was also found that traits were generalized from the target person to his group only if it was an out-group. Again, the particular combination of a weak category based expectancy and out-group membership of the target person appears to facilitate an *attributional* LOSN effect as well as a behavior–prediction effect.

Although these main findings were clearly predicted, there were also some anomalous findings that are difficult to interpret. Although the particular decision of the first target person in a scenario clearly affected subjects' percentage estimates, this decision just as clearly had no effect on predictions within the same scenario about the decision to be made by a second "randomly chosen" member of the target group. Instead, predictions about the second person were correlated with predictions about the first person ($r = .36$, $p < .001$), which of course were [149] made before the first person's decision. Predictions about the second target person in a scenario were also correlated with percentage estimates for his group ($r = 46$, $p < .001$), as were predictions about the first target person ($r = .48$, $p < .001$). We thus have a peculiar collection of facts to interpret: (a) Predictions for both first and second target persons in a scenario correlate with percentage estimates for the group, rendering it unlikely that subjects are ignoring base rates when making their predictions; (b) percentage estimates are clearly affected by the first target person's decision; and yet (c) predictions of the second target person's decision are not affected by the first one's decision.

If the decision affected percentage estimates, why did the subjects not use these newly calibrated estimates to form their inferences about the second target person in each scenario? One possibility is that subjects may not have reformulated their percentage estimates until they were asked. Since their predictions about the second target persons preceded these estimates, their predictions may have been based exclusively on their initial category-based expectancies.

Alternatively, the failure of the first target person's decision to affect predictions concerning the second target person's decision may reflect a mixture of generalization to the group with something akin to the "gambler's fallacy." Some subjects, in other words, may have felt it important to characterize the group's distribution as a whole by emphasizing the independence of the two group members. This might reflect a broader belief that two subjects (two heads, two good poker hands) are not likely to repeat each other, given less than 100% consensus.

Subjects also failed to rate the members of the in-group as any more variable than the members of the out-group. Moreover, regardless of in-group/out-group status, there were no consistently significant correlations between subjects' rating of the target group's variability and the extent to which their percentage estimates reflected the target persons' decisions. Taken by themselves, these data might raise questions about the validity of the hypotheses that motivated the present investigation. But other studies, notably an impressive series of experiments initiated by Nisbett and Wilson (1977), have pointed to the inability of subjects to provide accurate reports of the actual determinants of their choice behavior. People are not very good at describing their higher order cognitive processes. More importantly, we have been collecting additional data over the past few years that lend convergent support to the proposition concerning in-group/out-group differences in the perception of variability. In one study, conducted at Duke University, it was found that premedical or nursing students considered their own groups as consisting of more distinct types of people than did the corresponding out-groups ($p < .01$). In another study run at Duke, we found that differences in subjects' endorsements of the statements, "To a large degree, all leftists (rightists) are alike," were affected by the subjects' own political orientation as measured by an attitudinal questionnaire ($p < .025$). The results of this study, unlike the results obtained on the similar measure in the present investigation, were consistent with our proposition. Finally, it may be recalled that subjects in the present study rated the average member of the target person's group on a set of 10 traits chosen for their relevance to differences between the Princeton and Rutgers undergraduate male stereotype. The main effect for target person's group was significant for all 10 traits, and the means fell in the expected direction. These ratings were then summed into an index. It was found that the average member of each institution was rated more in line with its stereotype by out-group than by in-group members, $F(1, 70) = 6.85$, $p < .02$.

These additional findings attest to our belief that the term "the perception of a group's variability" is hardly univocal in its definition and perceptual implications. To assess an individual's perception of a group's variability we may look at (a) the number of subgroups or types believed to compose the group, (b) the extent to which traits consistent with the group's stereotype are attributed [150] to the average member of the group, (c) the readiness with which the individual displays the LOSN effect along dimensions previously considered irrelevant to the group, and (d) direct ratings of the group's variability. Unfortunately, we are at present far from knowing much about the conditions under which each of these measures will shed light on in-group/out-group differences in social perception.

Although many questions remain unanswered by the data herein reported, the present experiment does move us further toward understanding the purely cognitive bases of stereotype formation. Without for a moment denying that stereotypes are often fueled by affective rationalization, the present results cannot easily be cast in these terms. Although there were significant in-group preferences by both subject groups, these preferences played no discernible role in the stereotype formation observed in the weak expectancy condition. Here we saw that when an out-group member makes an unprovocative decision either to wait alone or with others, subjects end up with a perception of his group as rather solitary or rather sociable, respectively. We have, in a way, given birth to a benign stereotype. Furthermore, our data suggest that such stereotypes are likely to arise in precisely those areas where an in-group member observing an out-group member has the *least* prior knowledge and there is no broader consensual norm governing prior expectancies. It is less clear, however, how people put these generalizations about groups to use. At least in the present instance, it does not seem to be a simple matter of leaping from one group member to another through a general group stereotype. Somewhat surprisingly, the stereotype is generated, but it does not immediately affect expectancies concerning specific, other out-group members. Such disjunctions between group and individual expectancies have been previously noted (cf. Brigham, 1971), and the finding raises some hope that even people with group stereotypic expectations can suspend judgment about individual members. Wilder's (1978) data further suggest that individuating information about out-group members tends to inhibit invidious discrimination toward the out-group.

Nevertheless, group stereotypes can obviously lead to negative actions that affect each member of a group adversely, even if the stereotypes were to ignore or discount his stereotype each time he made a judgment of a specific group member. Explicit or implicit quota systems in hiring, education, or housing may place minority group members at an obvious disadvantage even though our experience with individual minority members leads us to see each person as an exception to the stereotype.

REFERENCE NOTE

1. Quattrone, G. (1976). *They look alike, they think alike, they dress alike. We don't: Ingroup/outgroup differences in the perception of variability.* Unpublished manuscript, Duke University.

REFERENCES

Allport, G.W. (1954). *The nature of prejudice.* Cambridge, Massachusetts: Addison-Wesley.
Brigham, J. C. (1971). Ethnic stereotypes. *Psychological Bulletin,* 76, 15–58.
Campbell, D.T. (1956). Enhancement of contrast as a composite habit. *Journal of Abnormal and Social Psychology,* 55, 350–355.
Jones, E. E. (1979). The rocky road from acts to dispositions. *American Psychologist,* 34, 107–117.
Jones, E. E., & McGillis, D. (1976). Correspondent inferences and the attribution cube: A comparative reappraisal. In J. H. Harvey, W. J. Ickes, & R. F. Kidd (Eds.), *New directions in attribution research* (Vol. 1, pp. 389–420). Hillsdale, NJ: Erlbaum.
Jones, E. E., & Thibaut, J. W. (1958). Interaction goals as bases of inference in interpersonal perception. In R. Tagiuri, & L. Petrillo (Eds.), *Person perception and interpersonal behavior* (pp. 151–178). Stanford, CA: Stanford University Press.
Morrison, D.F. (1967). *Multivariate statistical methods.* New York: McGraw-Hill.
Nisbett, R. E., & Borgida, E. (1975). Attribution and the psychology of prediction. *Journal of Personality and Social Psychology,* 32, 932–943.
Nisbett, R. E., & Wilson, T. D. (1977). Telling more than we can know: Verbal reports on mental processes. *Psychological Review,* 84, 231–259.
Rosenthal, R., & Jacobson, L. (1968). *Pygmalion in the classroom: Teacher expectation and pupils' intellectual development.* New York: Holt, Rinehart & Winston. **[151]**
Snyder, M., Tanke, E.D., & Berscheid, E. (1977). Social perception and interpersonal behavior: On the self-fulfilling nature of social stereotypes. *Journal of Personality and Social Psychology,* 35, 656–666.
Tajfel, H. (1969). Cognitive aspects of prejudice. *Journal of Social Issues,* 25, 79–98.
Taylor, S. E., Fiske, S.T., Etcoff, N. L., & Ruderman, A. J. (1978). Categorical and contextual bases of person memory and stereotyping. *Journal of Personality and Social Psychology,* 36, 778–793.
Tversky, A., & Kahneman, D. (1971). Belief in the law of sınall numbers. *Psychological Bulletin,* 76, 105–110.
Wilder, D.A. (1978). Reduction of intergroup discrimination through individuation of the out-group. *Journal of Personality and Social Psychology,* 36, 1361–1374.
Zadny, J., & Gerard, H. B. (1974). Attributed intentions and informational selectivity. *Journal of Experimental Social Psychology,* 10, 34–52. **[152]**

INGROUPS AND OUTGROUPS

Chapter 14

Polarized Appraisals of Out-Group Members

Patricia W. Linville
Carnegie-Mellon University
Edward E. Jones
Princeton University

> ABSTRACT: The present research developed and tested a model that predicts differential appraisal of in-group and out-group members. This model assumes that people have a more complex schema regarding in-groups than out-groups, and consequently, that appraisals of out-group members will be more extreme or polarized than appraisals of in-group members. A series of experiments tested this model, as well as predictions derived from attribution principles. In Experiment 1, white male and female subjects read and evaluated a law school application containing incidental information about the applicant's race and gender. A black applicant with strong credentials was judged more favorably than an otherwise identical white applicant, supporting a prediction derived from the augmentation principle. In Experiment 2, an applicant with weak credentials was included in the design. Results supported the prediction that out-group members would be evaluated more extremely: When the application credentials were positive, the out-group

---

Reprinted with permission from *Journal of Personality and Social Psychology,* 38, 689–703. Copyright © 1980 by the American Psychological Association.

member (a black or opposite-sex applicant) was evaluated more favorably than the in-group member (a white or same-sex applicant). When the application credentials were weak, the out-group member was evaluated more negatively. Experiments 3 and 4 provided support for the two assumptions underlying the complexity–extremity hypothesis: First, white subjects demonstrated greater complexity regarding whites than blacks. Second, greater complexity resulted in evaluative moderation.

Social scientists have long recognized the role of normal cognitive processes in the formation and use of stereotypes (cf. Allport, 1954; Lippmann, 1922). The present research coincides with a recent renewal of interest in the cognitive bases of stereotypes (e.g., Hamilton, 1979; Taylor, in press; Wilder, in press). The experiments reported here were designed to explore the cognitive bases of social evaluations in which race and gender play a role. In particular, we asked college students to evaluate the application materials of persons who had recently gained admission to a prestigious law school.

Two separate approaches to social cognition are investigated here. The first is the attribution perspective regarding facilitating and inhibiting factors affecting performances. Specifically, the augmentation and discounting principles (Kelley, 1972) yield predictions regarding evaluations of applicants depending on the perceived advantages or obstacles faced in the application process. The second approach is a new framework that grew out of the empirical findings in the initial studies reported here. We propose that the extremity of the evaluation of an applicant depends on the richness and complexity of the evaluator's conception of the applicant's social group.

ATTRIBUTIONAL FRAMEWORK

The initial studies were designed to examine the possible contribution of an attributional perspective to understanding the evaluations of individual out-group members who have been the potential beneficiaries of affirmative action programs. Kelley's (1972) discounting principle, as well as the principle of noncommon effects [689]* (Jones & Davis, 1965), states that the role of a given cause in producing an effect is discounted to the degree that other causes are present. The acceptance of a black or female applicant may be attributed either to the applicant's high ability and motivation, or to the perceived lower acceptance thresholds generated by affirmative action pressures. Insofar as awareness of these affirmative action pressures activates the discounting principle, the competence of recent black, and perhaps female, applicants accepted to law school will be viewed with greater reservations than the competence of white male applicants with otherwise identical credentials.

Such a prediction assumes a clear public perception that acceptance thresholds are indeed currently lower for black than for white applicants and for females than for males. The discounting prediction also assumes that affirmative action policies are perceived as more facilitating for black admissions than earlier cultural deprivations are inhibiting. If subjects are more aware of, and concerned with, the probable cultural deprivations of blacks, the salience of these experiential handicaps may outweigh the salience of affirmative action boosts to minority admissions.

---

*Bracketed bold numbers refer to original page numbers. Page numbers indicate where the original page ended.

Minority applicants thus could be the beneficiaries of what Kelley (1972) has called the augmentation principle. This principle states that the extremity of an attribution based on one effect of an action will increase to the extent that causal factors are also present that would normally inhibit the action. To the extent that persons perceive blacks or women as the victims of early environmental constraints, they will conclude that such an applicant's ability and motivation must have been unusually strong to overcome the normally inhibiting obstacles to success in the application process. Thus, the competence credentials of recent black and female applicants will be viewed with greater strength and certainty than those of white male applicants.

Unfortunately, then, one attribution principle (augmentation) leads to the prediction that greater capability will be attributed to a black law school matriculant, whereas another attribution principle (discounting) leads to the prediction of less capability for a black than a white law school matriculant with identical credentials. A preliminary study focused on these alternative predictions. White college students were presented with three law school applications of accepted applicants. The first two applications were identical for all subjects, but on the third application, incidental information about the race (black/white) and sex of the applicant was varied. In their evaluations of this third, crucial application, subjects rated the black applicant as being significantly more motivated and more active than the white applicant. Although there were no significant differences in perceived ability or liking, a multivariate analysis across the various evaluative scales showed a significant main effect for race. Thus, in general the black applicant was rated more favorably than the white applicant. This was in spite of the fact that subjects clearly perceived, in response to a postexperimental questionnaire, that advantages were conferred on blacks in the admissions process.

From an attributional point of view, one may infer that the augmentation principle won out over the discounting principle: blacks were given credit for overcoming earlier cultural obstacles in spite of the apparent help they may have received in the admissions process itself.

POLARIZED EVALUATIONS OF OUT-GROUP MEMBERS

A second way of looking at this preliminary finding is not in terms of the perceived advantages or obstacles faced by the applicant, but rather in terms of certain assumptions about how we think about and perceive out-group members. Viewed from this perspective, subjects evaluated an out-group member (a black applicant) more favorably than an in-group member (a white applicant). This is interesting in light of the relatively consistent findings showing that in-groups receive more favorable ratings than outgroups, even when the classification is made on an arbitrary and essentially meaningless basis (for a review, see Brewer, 1979). On the other hand, Feldman (1972) and McGillis and Jones (Note 1) both found favoritism toward the out-group, showing that white subjects rate a black professional higher on occupationally relevant traits than a comparable white professional. **[690]**

The particular stimuli used in these studies suggest an integrative explanation. The crucial application in the preliminary study, as well as materials in the Feldman (1972) and McGillis and Jones (Note 1) studies, contained nothing but laudatory information about the target person. Thus, positive information leads to more favorable ratings of an out-group than an in-group member. Negative information, however, may lead to less favorable ratings of an out-group member. Thus instead of a uniform favorability bias toward either in-groups or out-groups, the direction of the bias may depend on the information about the group member.

A rationale for this prediction may lie in the nature of prior knowledge structures concerning in-groups and out-groups. Such structures may be referred to as cognitive schemas to emphasize their structural and organizing features (see Hastie, 1981; Taylor & Crocker, 1981, for reviews on social schemas). In particular, we propose first, that people have a more complex schema regarding their own groups than other groups. Second, we propose that, as a result of this greater complexity, people tend to make more moderate judgments regarding in-group members than out-group members. (Tesser's 1978 proposal that evaluations are likely to polarize over time when a schema is complex is not inconsistent with the present prediction, which refers to the comparison of in-group and out-group evaluations at a particular point in time.)

Presumably, in-group schemas are more complex and differentiated, because perceivers must come to terms with a larger collection of diverse instances involving persons in their own group. This rich background of experience with the in-group generates a larger number of dimensions along which individual members may be characterized. Our knowledge of out-groups, on the other hand, being based on fewer and less varied experiences, generates fewer dimensions.

Why might complex schemas result in evaluative moderation? With a complex schema, a relatively large number of attributes or dimensions will be used in encoding a stimulus. The more attributes of a stimulus one considers, the more likely that some attributes will be perceived as good and others will be perceived as bad. For example, a favorable applicant is likely to be viewed as good in most respects but poor in a few others. Likewise, a weak applicant is likely to be viewed as poor in most respects but good in a few others. Thus, judgments based on a greater number of evaluative considerations are more likely to be mixed, resulting in evaluative moderation. Judgments based on fewer dimensions, however, are less likely to be mixed, resulting in evaluative extremity. That is, a favorable applicant is more likely to be viewed as simply good in all respects, and a weak applicant to be viewed as poor in all respects. (For further elaboration of this argument, see Linville, 1979.)

Schema complexity may also influence the relative impact carried by specific new information. Because schemas concerning the in-group are rich and highly differentiated, evaluative information about a particular in-group meets the inertia of a complex expectancy and has relatively little impact on one's impression of that member. Cognitive schemas for out-groups, on the other hand, are relatively simple and impoverished. One's impression of an out-group member may be heavily influenced by the evaluative significance of specific information concerning that member. Thus, specific favorable or unfavorable information has more impact on appraisals of out-group members.

With a complex schema, given information may also be perceived as incomplete and unsatisfactory. When a white male is told a little bit about a white male law school applicant, he may feel that the information is trivial compared to the many things that he would like to know, and is prepared to know, about someone like himself. Perceived lack of information on so many aspects may lead to reserved or suspended judgments. Because out-group schemas are relatively simple and characterized by fewer dimensions, new information may carry more impact and lead to confident and extreme judgments.

To be more descriptive and less analytical, we argue that people perceive and evaluate out-group members in relatively global, approach–avoidance terms. To suggest the extreme case, out-group members are perceived [691] as either good or bad. In-group members, on the other hand, cannot be so readily categorized, because they are perceived as good in some respects and bad in others.

This reasoning puts the twin problems of prejudice and stereotyping in a new and interesting light. People do not merely embrace beliefs that all blacks, Episcopalians, Turks, or Canadians are bad (or good). We suggest that relative lack of familiarity breeds a tendency to be highly influenced by data relevant to evaluation. Affectively relevant information may lead to greater polarization with a less differentiated schema. We do not deny the existence of "knee-jerk prejudice" in some persons toward some categories of persons. But for most persons, the evaluative side of intergroup relations may be closely tied to the cognitive side—and particularly to the lack of differentiated categories for storing evaluative data and placing them in perspective.

Other theoretical positions predict, and accompanying data document, polarized reactions to out-group members. Gergen and Jones (1963) reasoned that ambivalence toward certain stigmatized groups such as the mentally ill would amplify a person's feelings toward a mentally ill person when the behavior of the person has clear consequences for the perceiver. That is, if the behavior is nonconsequential, evaluative reactions will be suspended or moderate. If there are consequences for the perceiver, however, evaluation consonant with the consequences (positive or negative) will be more extreme when the target person is stigmatized than when he or she is not. The results of their experiment supported this prediction of ambivalence leading to evaluative polarization. This polarization effect, however, was presumably a function of the affect aroused by conflict resolution; it was not mediated by the more purely cognitive factors featured in the present treatment.

Dienstbier (1970) found that when socially desirable values were ascribed to a black target person, he was liked more than a white target person (i.e., positive prejudice). When socially undesirable values were ascribed to a black target person, however, he was liked less than a white target person (i.e., negative prejudice). Positive prejudice correlated with flexibility and liberal attitudes. These correlations cannot, however, explain negative prejudice in response to negative descriptions.

Recently, Katz and Glass (1979) have summarized a series of investigations that generally provide tentative support for a response amplification theory similar to the ambivalence formulation of Gergen and Jones (1963). They provide no evidence concerning the mechanisms involved, however, and their theoretical assumptions are not directly tested. Thus, the present research was designed to shed some light on both the polarization effect and its underlying mechanism.

OVERVIEW OF EXPERIMENTAL STUDIES

Experiment 1 was designed to test the attributional implications for evaluations of accepted law school applicants. The experiment was planned to extend the preliminary results with a more discerning and informative set of dependent variables. White college students read and evaluated a routinely favorable law school application containing incidental information about the applicant's race and gender. Since the results of Experiment 1 suggested that subjects' responses depended on an in-group–out-group distinction for both race and gender variables, we became intrigued by the possibility of affective polarization as a function of the information provided about the specific target person.

The remaining studies were therefore designed to explore this new theoretical possibility. Experiment 2 was designed to test directly the out-group polarization hypothesis, pitting this against the generalizability of the apparent augmentation effect. Experiments 3 and 4 were planned to test directly the two assumptions underlying the out-group polarization hypothesis: first, that white subjects have a more complex schema regarding whites than blacks; and second, that greater schematic complexity leads to less extreme evaluation.

EXPERIMENT 1

Method

SUBJECTS   Introductory psychology students at Duke University (40 white males and 40 white females) volunteered to evaluate law school applicants as part of their research participation requirement. **[692]** Subjects were run in small groups of two to eight per session and were randomly assigned to experimental conditions.

STIMULUS MATERIALS   Each subject was given a booklet containing portions of three law school applications that provided incidental information about the applicant's sex and race (white or black). The actual letterhead of a prestigious law school appeared at the top of each page to enhance the appearance of a realistic application. To add further to this realistic appearance, authentic law school application questions were incorporated into the booklets, and the answers of different applicants were typed on different typewriters. Rating scales followed each of the three applications. The first two applications (by a white male and a white female) were fillers to disguise the purpose of the study and were identical for all subjects. The third application contained the crucial information regarding the applicant's sex and race. This third application, presumably submitted by a student accepted to law school in 1974, included the applicant's college honors and activities, draft status, and ethnic identification (supposedly requested by the Department of Health, Education, and Welfare). There was also an essay written by the applicant describing why he or she wanted to study law. The quality of the applicant's essay, honors, and activities was good but not outstanding for a law school applicant to a prestigious school. This final application was identical across conditions except for incidental information about the applicant's sex and race. Sex of the applicant was varied on the draft question, and race of the applicant was varied on the DHEW ethnic identification question. Ratings of the third applicant only were analyzed.

PROCEDURE   On arrival at the experimental room, subjects were informed that the study was sponsored by the (fictitious) National Law School Association's Committee on Admission Procedures. The experimenter explained that the committee's primary interest was in evaluating policies and methods regarding the selection of law students. She added that the goal of this particular study was to discover which portions of a law school application are the most diagnostic of a student's future performance in law school.

Subjects were informed that they would read portions of three successful applications. They were told that different groups of subjects would read different portions of an application and then would evaluate that applicant. The experimenter added that names and personal information had been deleted to maintain confidentiality. Subjects were instructed not to put their names on the rating scales. They were assured that their ratings were completely anonymous and that their evaluations would have no conceivable consequences for the applicants. The experimenter emphasized that their honest impressions were desired. Subjects were asked not to try to second-guess the evaluations of other subjects or the law student's professors but instead to make judgments that reflected their own feelings about the applicant.

DEPENDENT MEASURES After reading each application, the subject rated the applicant on 16 bipolar adjective scales reflecting traits relevant to law school performance. Each scale consisted of a 5 in. (12.7 cm) line whose endpoints were marked with a bipolar trait. Subjects were instructed to place an X at the point on the line that best described the applicant's standing in comparison with other law students. After each subject had completed his or her evaluations of the final applicant, the booklet was collected and the experimenter gave the subjects a final questionnaire to explore perceptions of affirmative action facilitation and early inhibiting obstacles. This questionnaire included items pertaining to perceived difficulty in gaining acceptance and perceived early deprivation.

Results

VALIDATING THE MANIPULATIONS The race of the crucial applicant was correctly remembered by 91% of the subjects, with percentages ranging from 70%–100% across conditions. The applicant's sex was correctly recalled by 93% of the subjects. The condition percentages ranged from 80%–100%

PERCEIVED OBSTACLES TO ACCEPTANCE In an attempt to distinguish clearly between early deprivation obstacles and specific law school acceptance obstacles, subjects were asked: (a) "Do you think that it was easier or harder for the applicant to gain acceptance to law school than it would be for the average student applying that year?" and (b) "To what extent did the applicant probably face obstacles in developing his or her potential in early environment and prior schooling?" Analysis of variance indicated that the black applicant was believed to have faced greater early obstacles, $F(1, 72) = 13.77$, $p < .001$, but had an easier time gaining acceptance to law school than the white applicant, $F(1, 72) = 6.57$, $p < .01$. Whereas affirmative action programs were judged to be effective for blacks, females were seen as discriminated against relative to males. Both male and female subjects tended to think that the male applicant had an easier time gaining acceptance to law school than the female applicant, $F(1, 72) = 3.48$, $p < .07$. Subjects perceived no difference in early obstacles faced by females compared to males. **[693]**

An examination of cell means in conjunction with the relevant F ratios (see Table 14.1) reveals that the black–white "early obstacles" difference was greater in the black direction than the "application obstacles" difference was in the white direction. This

Table 14.1 Mean Rating of Early Obstacles and Application Obstacles as a Function of Applicant Race: Experiment 1

	Condition		
Measure	White applicant	Black applicant	F[a]
Early obstacles	4.78	6.18	13.77
Application obstacles	6.13	5.03	6.57

Note: Higher scores indicate greater early obstacles and greater application obstacles.

[a] Degrees of freedom are 1, 72.

provides some support for our surmise in accounting for the apparent augmentation of motivation and activeness in the preliminary study. A black applicant was given extra credit for overcoming early obstacles, and this credit was not neutralized by the greater perceived likelihood of acceptance of blacks in the application process.

EVALUATION OF THE APPLICANT In the analysis that follows, 15 trait measures were involved. A competence item was omitted because its factor loading was inconsistent across studies. These measures were factor analyzed using varimax rotations. Three factors emerged that had eigenvalues greater than 1.0. The items that loaded heavily on Factor 1 appeared to reflect an ability dimension and included the traits *creative in thought, good writer, intelligent, articulate speaker, logical or analytical,* and *astute judgment.* The items that loaded heavily on Factor 2 appeared to reflect a motivation dimension and included the traits *hard-working, persistent, motivated,* and *dedicated.* The items that loaded heavily on Factor 3 appeared to reflect an activity dimension and included the traits *aggressive, resourceful,* and *a leader.* Only a likability trait loaded heavily on a fourth factor. A multivariate analysis of these three factors and the separate likability trait revealed a main effect for race, $F(4, 69) = 3.43$, $p < .01$, and a Race × Sex of Applicant × Sex of Subject interaction, $F(4, 69) = 3.86$, $p < .01$.

Looking more closely at the effects of race on the separate factors, the black applicant was rated as being more able, motivated, [695] active, and likable than the white applicant with identical credentials and background data. Univariate analyses were significant for the motivation factor and the likability trait (see Table 14.2).

The role of subject and applicant sex was much more complicated than the role of race. There were significant Race × Sex of Applicant × Sex of Subject interactions on the motivation index, $F(1, 72) = 8.26$, $p < .01$, and on the likability trait, $F(1, 72) = 10.90$, $p < .001$. These triple interactions did not modify the main effect for race. An inspection of the means shows a consistent cross-sex effect for the white, but not for the black applicant on the three factors and the likability trait (see Table 14.3). Subjects of both sexes (all of whom were white) were more positive toward the opposite-sex white applicant. A multivariate test within white applicants only revealed a significant interaction between sex of subject and sex of applicant, $F(4, 69) = 3.11$, $p < .02$. The interaction within black applicants only was not significant. The univariate interaction

Table 14.2 Mean Ratings of Ability, Motivation, Activeness, and Liking as a Function of Race of Applicant: Experiment 1

	Condition		
Measure[a]	White applicant	Black applicant	F[b]
Ability factor	23.45	25.58	2.97
Motivation factor	26.14	29.64	9.50*
Activeness factor	21.95	24.32	3.05
Liking	23.55	27.80	10.90**

Note: Higher scores indicate greater positive ratings.
[a]Each measure reflects an index averaged across the number of variables in that index.
[b]Degrees of freedom are 1, 72.
*$p < .01$.
**$p < .001$.

Table 14.3 Mean Ratings of White Applicant as a Function of Subject and Applicant Sex: Experiment 1

	Condition			
	Male subjects		Female subjects	
Measure[a]	In-group (male applicant)	Out-group (female applicant)	In-group (female applicant)	Out-group (male applicant)
Ability factor	22.73	25.37	22.18	23.53
Motivation factor	23.10	28.45	24.23	28.78
Activeness factor	21.28	23.45	20.70	22.38
Liking	21.60	27.40	21.10	24.10

Note: Higher scores indicate more of the factor or quality listed.
[a]Each measure reflects an index averaged across the number of variables in that index.

test within white applicants was significant for the separate motivation factor, $F(1, 72) = 9.33$, $p < .01$, and the likability trait, $F(1, 72) = 5.84$, $p < .05$. Thus, when rating applicants of their own race, both males and females were more favorable toward the opposite-sex candidate than toward the candidate of their own sex.

Discussion

The results of the race variable are quite straightforward and generally replicate the results of the preliminary study. In both experiments, subjects of both sexes (all of whom were white) viewed the black candidate of either sex more favorably than the comparable white candidate: more able, more motivated, more active, and more likable. These results may be accounted for by the augmentation principle, if one assumes that a black applicant is given extra credit for overcoming early obstacles. These results throw doubt on several explanations that predict biases against a black applicant, including the discounting principle, in-group favoritism, and a generalized negative stereotype concerning the native endowment of blacks.

A plausible alternative to the augmentation explanation, however, is that subjects simply wish to appear unprejudiced toward commonly identified ethnic groups such as blacks. Subjects may either wish to conceal their prejudice from the experimenter or adopt a private denial mechanism that leads to compensatory favorability in rating blacks. Either possibility would operate in the same direction as the augmentation principle in the present case. However, mere concealment from the experimenter seems unlikely because of the stress on rating anonymity and the use of dummy applications to reduce the salience of race. Both alternatives are further weakened if we examine the data from subjects evaluating the white applicant. Prejudice concealment appears to be an unlikely explanation for the more favorable view of cross-sex applicants. Furthermore, female favorability toward males can hardly be explained by the augmentation principle, since there is no clear reason for females to see male applicants as having overcome more early obstacles than females.

Both the race and sex data are consistent, however, with the hypothesis that out-group members will be evaluated more extremely. That is, when the information is positive, as in the preliminary study and Experiment 1, the out-group member will be evaluated more favorably; when the information is negative, the out-group member should be evaluated less favorably than the in-group member.

A straightforward comparative test of the augmentation and the out-group polarization hypotheses is possible with the addition of a negative application condition. The augmentation account predicts more favorable ratings for a black applicant regardless of the favorability of the application. The polarization account predicts an entirely different interactive pattern given application material that is, for an accepted law school applicant, unexpectedly negative. The white subjects should be more negative toward the black candidate with weak credentials than an identically weak white candidate. Similarly, subjects should be more negative toward the opposite sex candidate with weak credentials than toward the same-sex candidate. Thus, the second experiment varied the strength of the application material to test directly for an [695] out-group polarization effect. To the extent that negative polarization occurs for the black candidate with weak credentials, the present results (and presumably the earlier results for comparable subjects) cannot be attributed to a simple desire to conceal one's prejudice or convince oneself of its absence.

EXPERIMENT 2

Method

Subjects were 96 white male and 96 white female Duke University undergraduates who volunteered for an experiment entitled "evaluation of law school applications." The cover story and instructions of the experiment were identical to those in Experiment 1. In addition to varying the applicant's sex and race, however, favorability of the application information was also varied. The format of the application remained identical, but the third applicant's credentials were now either more positive or more negative than in the previous experiment.

As in the first experiment, subjects read an application of a student presumably accepted by a prestigious law school in 1974. Page 1 contained information regarding college honors and activities, draft status (denoting sex of applicant), and ethnic identification (denoting race of applicant). Page 2 again contained the applicant's essay. A third page consisting of a faculty evaluation was added in Experiment 2.

Favorability of the applicant's credentials was manipulated by varying scholastic honors and activities, the articulateness of the essay, and the strength of the faculty evaluation. Scholastic honors of the strong applicant included graduating Magna cum Laude and receiving the Outstanding Senior Thesis Award in Political Science, whereas the honors of the weak applicant included only being placed on the Dean's List. The strong applicant was Vice-President of the Student Political Union, editor of the campus newspaper, and a member of the debating team. In contrast, the weak applicant was a member of the Student Political Union, the yearbook staff, and a fraternity or sorority.

The recommendation for the strong applicant read in part as follows:

> I am delighted to write a letter of reference for Ms. [name blacked out], who is applying to your law school, and I recommend her without the slightest reluctance. I have had her as a student in two courses. In one of these (Econometric Analysis) she received an A, in the other (Mathematical Economics) an A–, in spite of a weak background in Calculus.... There is no question ... concerning her intrinsic interest in the intellectual problems of juxtaposing regulation and freedom within a legal framework. Obtaining a law degree seems rather incidental to a further exploration of these matters at an advanced level.... I like her as a person and feel she is well suited for the many personal challenges that a typical law career generates. My guess is that she will ... prove to be a solid addition to your roster of successful graduates.

In contrast, the recommendation for the weak applicant read in part as follows:

> I have agreed to write a letter of reference for Ms. [name blacked out], who is applying to your law school, but I do so not without some reluctance. I have had her as a student in two courses. In one of these (Economics of the Business Firm) she received a B+, In the other (Economic Doctrines and Public Policy) a B–, after a very shaky start. In neither course was I able to discern whether she truly had the ability to do better with greater effort or whether she was in fact working close to her capacity. I hope you receive other letters from those who have worked more closely with her on a tutorial basis.... It is not entirely clear to me ... whether she has an intrinsic interest in the intellectual problems of the legal profession or whether she is more concerned with the extrinsic gains of obtaining a law degree.... In spite of my ambivalence, I would like to say that this is an attractive and agreeable young woman. She speaks with self-assurance and is a patient and responsive listener. I like her as a person and only wish I could be more confident about the

intensity of her dedication and the depth of her intellectual commitment. My guess is that she will surprise some people here ... and prove to be a solid addition to your roster of successful graduates.

For male applicants, the appropriate pronouns were used.

DEPENDENT MEASURES After reading the application, subjects evaluated the applicant on the same trait scales given in Experiment I. After the application booklet had been collected, a final questionnaire was given that included the same items given in Experiment 1 in addition to several new items designed to aid in the interpretation of the main results.

Results

VALIDATING THE MANIPULATIONS In response to the question "How positive was the information about this applicant?" the strong application was evaluated more positively than the weak application, $F(1, 176) = 364.61, p < .001$. The race of the applicant was correctly identified by 91% of the subjects, with percentages ranging from 75% to 100% correct across conditions, and 99.5% of the subjects correctly identified the sex of the applicant. **[696]**

EVALUATION OF THE APPLICANT In the analysis that follows, the same trait measures used in Experiment 1 were involved. These measures were again factor analyzed using varimax rotations. The same three factors emerged having eight values greater than 1.0. These again included an ability factor, a motivation factor, and an activeness factor. Again, the likable trait alone loaded heavily on a fourth factor.

A multivariate analysis was conducted on the three trait factors (ability, motivation, activeness) and the likability trait. This analysis revealed a significant main effect for strength of application, $F(4, 173) = 66.35, p < .001$. The Race × Strength interaction approached significance, $F(4, 173) = 1.87, p < .12$, and the Sex of Applicant × Sex of Subject × Strength interaction was significant, $F(4, 173) = 2.90, p < .05$. These were the three predicted effects. Also as predicted, no main effects for race or for sex of the applicant were observed.

Univariate results showed significant effects of application strength on the ability, motivation, and activeness factors ($ps < .001$). Subjects did not differ significantly in their liking for the strong and weak applicant.

Recall that we predicted a polarization effect whereby out-group members would be rated more extremely (in a direction determined by the favorability of information) than in-group members. Thus, white subjects who read a strong application would rate a black applicant higher than a white applicant; those reading a weak application of a black applicant should be more negative in their appraisal than those reading the same application for a white applicant. Similarly, males viewing a female's application and females viewing a male's application should show the polarization effect. **[697]**

The univariate Race × Strength interaction approached significance for the ability factor, $F(1, 176) = 3.24, p < .07$, but was not significant for the motivation factor, $F(1, 176) = 2.14, p < .15$. The activeness factor showed no such interaction. The predicted interaction was significant for the likable trait, $F(1, 176) = 4.85, p < .05$. Consistent with the polarization hypothesis, the strong black applicant was liked more and the weak black applicant was liked less than the comparable white applicants.

Results of the Race × Strength interaction for individual trait items can be seen from the means in Table 14.4. Although the number of significant findings (and the multivariate results) is disappointing, the consistency of the interactive pattern is striking. When the credentials of the applicant were strong, the black applicant was rated more positively than the white applicant on 14 of the 15 traits. When the credentials of the

Table 14.4 Mean Ratings of Trait Factors as a Function of Strength of Application and Race of Applicant: Experiment 2

	Strong credentials		Weak credentials	
Measure	White applicant	Black applicant	White applicant	Black applicant
Factors[a]				
Ability factor	28.10	30.22	18.70	18.18
Motivation factor	31.77	33.18	23.86	23.00
Activeness factor	28.07	28.92	20.71	20.73
Liking	28.58	31.96	30.15	29.71
Individual traits				
Creative in thought	24.73	29.75	19.71	19.08
Good writer	28.67	30.17	12.83	14.08
Intelligent	28.19	29.71	16.98	14.96
Articulate speaker	28.63	30.92	18.60	17.75
Logical and analytical	28.79	29.67	20.04	19.48
Astute judgment	29.60	31.10	24.04	23.71
Hard-working	33.40	33.92	24.35	23.90
Persistent	30.33	31.71	24.04	21.29
Motivated	31.60	33.83	24.23	24.52
Dedicated	31.73	33.27	22.83	22.29
Aggressive	27.90	26.69	20.23	19.56
Takes initiative	27.19	28.19	21.77	20.69
Resourceful	28.94	30.54	21.81	22.06
Leader	28.27	30.27	19.02	20.60

Note: Higher scores indicate more of the trait or factor designated.

[a]Each measure reflects an index averaged across the number of variables in that index.

applicant were weak, the black applicant was rated more negatively than the white applicant on 11 out of 15 items.

Turning to the evidence on polarization for cross-sex pairings, the significant multivariate effect of the Sex of Subject × Sex of Applicant × Strength interaction noted previously provided strong support for the polarization hypothesis as far as general rating favorability was concerned. In univariate analyses, however, the same interaction was significant only for the activeness factor, F (1, 176) = 4.70, $p < .05$. Reference to Table 14.5 shows that both male and female subjects rated the opposite-sex applicant more extremely in both a positive (active) and negative (passive) direction than the same-sex applicant. The pattern of sex interaction findings does not precisely replicate the pattern obtained in Experiment 1. Looking at the white applicant data alone, there is no tendency (as was found in the prior experiment) for cross-sex polarization on the ability, motivation, and liking items. Rather, the effect now occurs only on the activeness items. We have no obvious explanation for why this is so, but one reasonable possibility suggests itself. In the second experiment, the positive applicant was more positive than the standard applicant of the first experiment. This may have affected the results by creating a ceiling effect on ability and motivation items. There was less specific information relevant to the activeness items, and perhaps these items were therefore more sensitive to the polarization tendency.

We thus have some evidence that polarization occurs when white subjects look at black applicants and when white males and females look at applicants of the opposite sex. The evidence is equivocal in that the specific factors that are most sensitive to polarization are difficult to anticipate or interpret. Nevertheless, there is a general evaluative extremity effect that is detectable in both the race and the sex data, thus offering suggestive support for the polarization tendency in cognizing and evaluating out-group members.

ADDITIONAL EVIDENCE

Because of the novelty of the polarization hypothesis and the fact that it received only modest support in the second experiment, additional analyses and experiments were

Table 14.5 Mean Ratings of Activeness Factor as a Function of Strength of Application, Sex of Subject, and Sex of Applicant: Experiment 2

	Male subjects		Female subjects	
Credentials	In-group (male applicant)	Out-group (female applicant)	In-group (female applicant)	Out-group (male applicant)
Strong	27.92	29.21	26.99	29.88
Weak	20.91	19.80	21.82	20.35

Note: Higher scores indicate higher ratings on the activeness factor.

conducted to provide more direct evidence concerning the validity of the theoretical assumptions involved. We hypothesized that people manifest greater complexity in their thinking about in-groups than out-groups. Additional analyses of data from Experiment 2 are consistent with this theoretical suggestion.

In factor analytic terms, greater complexity should be reflected in more numerous independent [698] dimensions. For this reason, the individual trait measures were factor analyzed separately for the white and the black applicant conditions to examine whether white subjects used more dimensions in analyzing the white (in-group) than the black (out-group) applicants.

For the white applicant condition, three factors emerged with eigenvalues greater than 1.0; for the black applicant condition, there were only two. Considering the 120 correlations between the individual trait measures, 95 correlations were higher in the black applicant condition than in the white applicant condition. Turning to the separate factor analyses for the same-sex and opposite-sex applicants, a similar pattern was found. For the same-sex condition, three factors emerged with eigenvalues greater than 1.0; for the opposite-sex condition, there were only two. Again considering the 120 correlations between individual trait measures, 94 were higher in the opposite-sex condition than the same-sex condition. These results, though suggestive at best, are consistent with the hypothesis that people employ fewer independent evaluative dimensions in construing and analyzing out-group compared to in-group members. Two additional studies were conducted to test more directly the major assumptions of the polarization hypothesis.

EXPERIMENT 3

To conduct an independent check on the differential schematic complexity regarding one's own group compared with another group, Experiment 3 was designed to measure complexity directly and to test the hypothesis that white subjects have a more complex schema regarding whites than blacks. Complexity is operationalized here in terms of the number of independent dimensions a person uses to represent stimuli in a domain (see Scott, 1962, 1969). Subjects completed a trait-sorting task that measures dimensional complexity regarding a specific domain. White male subjects sorted personality traits into groups representing traits that belong together. Half the subjects were instructed to think about white undergraduates while performing the task; half were instructed to think about black undergraduates. According to the hypothesis, white undergraduates will use a larger number of independent conceptual dimensions when describing white than black undergraduates.

Method

SUBJECTS   One hundred and three white male undergraduates volunteered to participate as part of their research participation requirement. All subjects were tested in small groups of two to six subjects.

COMPLEXITY INSTRUMENT   A measure of dimensional complexity patterned after Scott's index (1962, 1969) was developed to examine the number of independent conceptual dimensions employed with respect to a specific domain (e.g., black or white social groups). The task involved a trait-sorting method used in multidimensional scaling tasks (see Rosenberg & Sedlak, 1972) in which subjects sort traits that go together into groups. Each subject's trait sort was used to calculate Scott's H, an information-theory-based measure of conceptual complexity.[1] This measure may be interpreted as the minimum number of independent binary dimensions needed to produce a trait sort equal in complexity to that of the subject's. A pretest sample of black and white undergraduate males was used to generate the personality traits. Some were asked to describe white male undergraduates, some were asked to describe black male undergraduates, and others were asked to describe male undergraduates. From the complete set of traits generated, 40 were selected that had the property of being frequently used to describe both black and white undergraduates. This procedure was designed to optimize equal latitude in forming trait groups for each race.

PROCEDURE Each subject received a packet of 40 randomly ordered cards, each containing the name of a personality trait. The experimenter instructed the subject to sort the traits into groups representing traits that belong together. No limit was set on the number of groups formed or the number of traits sorted into a group. The experimenter instructed subjects to "continue forming groups until you think that you have formed the important ones. Form as many groups as you find meaningful." The same trait could be placed in as many groups as desired, but subjects did not have to use every trait. The experimenter emphasized that there was no right or **[699]** wrong answer. To ensure anonymity, subjects did not put their names on the recording sheet. After, these general instructions, some subjects were told to think about white male undergraduates while performing the sorting task; others were told to think about black male undergraduates.

Table 14.6 Number of Categories and Scott's H as a Function of Race of Target Group: Experiment 3

	Target group	
Measure	White	Black
Number of categories	7.50	6.46
Scott's H[a]	3.30	3.03

[a]Scott's H, which reflects dimensional complexity, may range between 1 and $\log_2 n$ (here, $\log_2 40 = 5.32$).

Results and Discussion

White subjects formed more groups when thinking about white than black males, $t\,(101) = 1.95$, $p < .05$ (see Table 14.6). Considering the main measure of dimensional complexity, white subjects scored higher on Scott's H when thinking about white males than black males, $t\,(101) = 2.19$, $p < .03$. Thus, as predicted, white male undergraduate subjects demonstrated greater complexity regarding white compared to black male undergraduates in their sorting behavior.

---

[1]Scott's H was calculated for each subject as follows:

$$H = \log_2 n - \frac{1}{n} \Sigma n_4 \log_2 n_4$$

where n = total number of traits (here 40); n_4 = the number of traits that appear in a particular combination of groups.

EXPERIMENT 4

The previous study provided support for the first assumption that people have greater schematic complexity regarding members of their own group than another group. Schematic complexity was measured in terms of the number of conceptual dimensions used in thinking about a specific domain (e.g., a social group). Experiment 4 directly tested the second assumption that greater complexity results in more moderate evaluations. Schematic complexity was manipulated through task instructions directing subjects' attention to either two or six dimensions relevant to law school application essays. If the assumption is correct, subjects in the simple two-dimension condition should make more extreme overall evaluations of the essays than subjects in the complex six-dimension condition.

Method

SUBJECTS   Forty undergraduate subjects, approximately equal numbers of males and females, volunteered as part of their research requirement. All subjects were tested in small groups of two to six persons.

MATERIALS   A pretest sample of subjects read four law school application essays, then listed important dimensions relevant to the essays. From these responses, a group of 14 dimensions were chosen. A second group of pretest subjects first read the essays and then rated the importance of these dimensions. Six dimensions were chosen for their importance and independence: sincerity, writing style, experience, motivation, specificity of presentation, and organization.

PROCEDURE   Subjects received a booklet containing three law school application essays supposedly written by separate applicants describing why they wanted to study law. The first two were fillers and identical for all subjects. The third, crucial essay was either strong or weak in terms of the ideas expressed and the general quality of the writing. The essays were quite similar to those used in Experiment 3. No personal information regarding the applicant's race or gender was provided. After reading each essay, subjects read an instruction sheet asking them to think about the essay during the next 4 minutes in terms of "the following characteristics." Half the subjects were instructed to think about the essay in terms of six characteristics (all six dimensions were listed); the other half were instructed to think about two characteristics (all possible pairs of the six dimensions were randomly distributed among subjects in this condition).

Subjects were informed that they would read an identical instruction sheet after reading each essay. During the carefully timed 4-minute period, subjects were not allowed to reread the essay. Immediately following this 4-minute period, subjects turned to a separate sheet instructing them to give only their *overall* evaluation of the essay on a scale with endpoints marked favorable and unfavorable. Subjects followed this procedure for all three essays, but only the ratings for the final essay (which varied in favorability) were analyzed.

Note that subjects never rated or expected to rate the essays on the separate characteristics. Care was taken to show subjects the rating sheet prior to making any ratings and to emphasize that they were only to mark their overall evaluation. This procedure should minimize any experimental demand for consistency between subjects' ratings along several dimensions and their overall rating of that essay. At the end of the session, the experimenter fully debriefed all subjects. **[700]**

Results and Discussion

The strong essay was rated more favorably than the weak essay, $F(1, 37) = 54.17$, $p < .001$. As predicted, complexity interacted with essay favorability, $F(1, 37) = 6.22$, $p < .02$ (see Table 14.7). Subjects provided with two dimensions were more extreme in their evaluations than those provided with six dimensions. When the essay was strong, subjects with a simple two-dimensional schema rated it more favorably than subjects with a more complex six-dimensional schema. When the essay was weak, subjects with a simple schema rated the essay less favorably than subjects with a complex schema. If these assumptions concerning schemas are correct, the six-dimensional condition is analogous to the in-group condition in Experiment 2, whereas the two-dimensional condition is analogous to the out-group condition. Thus, the same pattern of results has been found for evaluations of law school application materials when directly manipulating dimensional complexity as when manipulating social group status: Greater complexity results in less extreme evaluations.

GENERAL DISCUSSION

We have presented evidence to support a hypothesis of relative polarization in the evaluation of an out-group member as a function of the evaluative implications of specific information about him or her. Thus, an out-group member with strong credentials will be evaluated more positively than an in-group member with the same credentials, and an out-group member with weak credentials will be evaluated more negatively than an in-group member with weak credentials. The evidence for such an effect is not entirely compelling because of the marginal significance values of the hypothesized interactions and the difficulty of predicting on which evaluative index the polarized affect will reveal itself most strongly. Nevertheless, the striking thing is the relative comparability of the polarization evidence both for race and gender out-groups and the directional consistency of the mean differences regardless of the index involved.

Table 14.7 Evaluation of Essay as a Function of Essay Favorability and Number of Suggested Dimensions: Experiment 4

Measure	Six dimensions (complex schema)	Two dimensions (simple schema)
Strong essay	27.91	37.50
Weak essay	14.50	10.50

Note: Higher scores indicate more positive ratings.

The polarization hypothesis is based on the assumptions that (a) people have more complex cognitive schemas regarding their own group than regarding other groups, and (b) the evaluative significance of new information has less impact the greater the complexity of the applicable schema. We have presented experimental evidence supporting the validity of both assumptions.

The earlier polarization hypotheses of Gergen and Jones (1963) and Katz and Glass (1979) derive from quite different assumptions. Gergen and Jones proposed an energy summation basis with clear psychoanalytic overtones. There is affective or motivational conflict in responding to stigmatized persons, and information that tips the balance in either a positive or negative direction will draw on the total energy involved in both sides of the conflict. Katz and Glass favor different assumptions of self-concept threat. In their view, the initial ambivalence toward stigmatized persons is anchored in conflicting aspects of the self-image. People want to see themselves as humane and yet discerning in their evaluation and treatment of others. Having friendly feelings for a discredited, unworthy other threatens the self-image of discernment. Having hostile feelings toward one who is less fortunate threatens the self-image of humaneness. Favorable information about a stigmatized person poses a threat to discernment. This threat may be handled by denial of the self-image aspect that conflicts with the incoming information (in this case discernment), along with response amplification in the positive direction. In the case of negative information, **[701]** there is similar threat to the humane self-image and comparable denial in the interests of threat reduction.

There is no a priori reason to assume that polarization, insofar as it occurs, must have a single origin. In the present experiments, however, the motivation-rich notions of ambivalence and self-image threat would seem to be largely neutralized by respondent anonymity and the fact that our subjects neither interacted, nor expected to interact with, the target person. One of Gergen and Jones's (1963) major findings was that stigmatized and normal target persons are evaluated similarly if their behavior does not have hedonic consequences for the evaluator. Because of the assumed low hedonic relevance of the present experiments for most subjects, we prefer a more cognitive explanation for the amount of polarization that did occur. In future research on response amplification, or ambivalence, we suggest that investigators consider differences in the complexity of cognitive schemas before embracing more heavily freighted dynamic or motivational explanations.

Although the present evidence for polarization in the negative direction is not overpowering, there is clear and replicated evidence for more favorable ratings of an out-group member with strong credentials than of an in-group member with the same strong credentials. How can this be reconciled with the considerable body of research (reviewed by Brewer, 1979) suggesting that even the most arbitrary categorizations of subjects into groups can produce more *favorable* in-group than out-group ratings? We suggest that a crucial mediating factor for explaining the discrepancy that is found in the literature between negative and positive reactions to out-groups is the amount and kind of information provided about the individual being evaluated. Most of the studies showing favoritism toward the in-group either involve ratings of the group as a whole or ratings of individuals based on extremely scanty information. Even strongly held stereotypes may be set aside, or may interact in complex ways, with individuating information about specific group members. The present data as well as those of Feldman (1972), and McGillis and Jones (Note 1), are consonant with Brigham's (1971) caveat that "there is not a simple relationship between the expression of ethnic stereotypes and their use in behavior toward specific ethnic group members" (p. 29). The present experiments suggest that out-group stereotypes, because they represent relatively simple cognitive structures, may be highly vulnerable to individuating information with evaluative implications. Thus out-group members, even more than the members of one's own group, may be the beneficiaries of favorable information just as they may be the victims of information shaded in a negative direction.

REFERENCE NOTE

1. McGillis, D. B., & Jones, E. E. (1976). *Ethnicity, occupation, and region as determinants of stereotypic attribution.* Unpublished manuscript, Duke University.

REFERENCES

Allport, G. W. (1954). *The nature of prejudice.* Cambridge, Mass.: Addison-Wesley.
Brewer, M. B. (1979). In-group bias in the minimal intergroup situation: A cognitive-motivational analysis. *Psychological Bulletin,* 86, 307–323.
Brigham, J. C. (1971). Ethnic stereotypes. *Psychological Bulletin,* 76, 15–38.
Dienstbier, R. A. (1970). Positive and negative prejudice: Interactions of prejudice with race and social desirability. *Journal of Personality,* 38, 198–215.
Feldman, J. M. (1972). Stimulus characteristics and subject prejudice as determinants of stereotype attributions. *Journal of Personality and Social Psychology,* 21, 333–340.
Gergen, K. J., & Jones, E. E. (1963). Mental illness, predictability, and affective consequences as stimulus factors in person perception. *Journal of Abnormal and Social Psychology,* 67, 95–105.
Hamilton, D. L. (1979). A cognitive–attributional analysis of stereotyping. In L. Berkowitz (Ed.), *Advances in experimental social psychology* (Vol. 12). New York: Academic Press.
Hastie, R. (1981). Schematic principles in human memory. In E. T. Higgins, C. P. Herman, & M. P. Zanna (Eds.), *Social cognition: The Ontario symposium on personality and social behavior.* Hillsdale, N.J.: Erlbaum.
Jones, E. E., & Davis, K. E. (1965). From acts to dispositions: The attribution process in person perception. In L. Berkowitz (Ed.), *Advances in experimental social psychology* (Vol. 2). New York: Academic Press.
Katz, I. A., & Glass, D. C. (1979). An ambivalence–amplification theory of behavior toward the stigmatized. [702] In W. Austin & S. Worchel (Eds.). *The social psychology of intergroup relations.* Monterey, Calif.: Brooks/Cole.
Kelley, H. H. (1972). Attribution in social interaction. In E. E. Jones, D. E. Kanouse, H. H. Kelley, R. E. Nisbett, S. Valins, & B. Weiner (Ed.), *Attribution: Perceiving the causes of behavior* (pp. 1–26). Morristown, NJ: General Learning Press.
Linville, P. W. *Dimensional complexity and evaluative extremity: A cognitive model predicting polarized evaluations of outgroup members.* Unpublished doctoral dissertation, Duke University.
Lippmann, W. (1922). *Public opinion.* New York: Harcourt Brace.
Rosenberg, S., & Sedlak, A. (1972). Structural representation of perceived personality trait relationships. In A. K. Romney, R. N. Shepard, & S. Nerlove (Eds.), *Multidimensional scaling: Theory and applications in the behavioral sciences: Vol. 2. Applications.* New York: Seminar Press.
Scott, W.A. (1962). Cognitive complexity and cognitive flexibility. *Sociometry,* 25, 405–414.
Scott, W.A. (1969). Structure of natural cognitions. *Journal of Personality and Social Psychology,* 12, 261–278.
Taylor, S. E. (1981). A categorization approach to stereotyping. In D. L. Hamilton (Ed.), *Cognitive processes in stereotyping and intergroup behavior.* Hillsdale, N.J.: Erlbaum.
Taylor, S. E., & Crocker, J. (1981). Schematic bases of social information processing. In E. T. Higgins, C. P. Herman, & M. P. Zanna (Eds.), *Social cognition: The Ontario symposium on personality and social behavior.* Hillsdale, N.J.: Erlbaum.

Tesser, A. (1978). Self-generated attitude change. In L. Berkowitz (Ed.), *Advances in experimental social psychology* (Vol. 11). New York: Academic Press.

Wilder, D.A. (1981). Perceiving persons as a group: Categorization and intergroup relations. In D. L. Hamilton (Ed.), *Cognitive processes in stereotyping and intergroup behavior.* Hillsdale, N.J.: Erlbaum. **[703]**

Part Three

The Orchestration of Action

Strategic Self-Presentation
    Chapter 15   Ingratiation: An Attributional Approach
    Chapter 16   Toward a General Theory of Strategic Self-Presentation

Self-Handicapping
    Chapter 17   Drug Choice as a Self-Handicapping Strategy in Response to Noncontingent Success
    Chapter 18   Control of Attributions about the Self through Self-Handicapping Strategies: The Appeal of Alcohol and the Role of Underachievement
    Chapter 19   The Framing of Competence

STRATEGIC SELF-PRESENTATION

Chapter 15

Ingratiation: An Attributional Approach

Edward E. Jones
Duke University
Camille Wortman
Northwestern University

> Let another man praise thee, and not thine own mouth. [Old Testament: Proverbs. XXVII, 2]
>
> Do not offer a compliment and ask a favor at the same time. A compliment that is charged for is not valuable. [Mark Twain]
>
> Obsequiousness begets friends; truth hatred. [Terence, from Andria (*The Lady of Andros*), 1. 68]
>
> Modesty is becoming to the great. What is difficult is to be modest when one is nobody. [Jules Renard]
>
> Praise yourself daringly; something always sticks. [Francis Bacon, (*Apothegms*)]

Both classic and contemporary literatures are full of epigrams and maxims offering advice on how to conduct our interpersonal relations. Much of this advice suggests ways of making ourselves more attractive to others or, as we would say, spells out the

---

Reprinted by permission. © 1973 by General Learning Press, a subsidiary of Simon & Schuster Elementary Group.

various tactics of ingratiation. There is considerable agreement about [1]* the kinds of actions that others find endearing. People like to be praised, agreed with, served, and so on. But the supreme irony is that tactics obviously designed to enhance attraction are going to be less effective precisely in those settings where attraction is most important. We shall refer to this later as the "ingratiator's dilemma," but merely note at the moment that attraction-seeking can be a very complex business indeed.

The purpose of this essay is to provide a systematic examination of ingratiation and to locate its facets in the conceptual framework of contemporary social psychology. Toward this end, we describe the tactics that are likely to be employed for the purpose of ingratiation, present a theoretical analysis of the conditions that favor or inhibit its practice, and discuss both the short-term and long-term effects of ingratiating overtures on the target person who receives them and on the ingratiator himself.

If anyone tells us that we are behaving in an ingratiating manner, we will probably be less than pleased. The word evokes connotations of dissimulation and deceit in social communication and self-presentation. We think of an ingratiating person as one who is overconcerned with the effects of his behavior on others. The pejorative connotations of the term doubtless stem from the common belief that ingratiation involves manipulative intent and deceitful execution. It is the illegitimate and the seamy side of interpersonal communication.

But how does one know what types of behavior are "legitimate" in an interpersonal relationship? What is needed in this attempt to frame a working definition of ingratiation is some notion of the normative base line from which ingratiation departs. The baseline of legitimacy may be viewed as an implicit contract between the two (or three, or n) persons involved. There are many ways to describe this contract. For example, Goffman (1955) has suggested that interactions are governed by the implicit agreement that each will help the other maintain face. Each actor enters into communication hoping and expecting to act out a "line" with the tacit support of the other. This involves the actor in "face-work"—actions that smooth over potentially embarrassing threats to the projected faces. The ingratiator may be viewed as an individual who exploits this face-work contract while seeming to validate it. The contract states that each will honor the other's claim to face, and this is presumably to be accomplished by developing a common definition of the situation that will support both faces. The ingratiator never violates the contract openly by insults, cutting candor, or direct challenges to the other's face. Instead, he publicly sends out reassuring signals that he accepts the contract, while privately working toward another goal: making himself attractive to the other.

Another characteristic of the ingratiator is that while leading the target person to believe that the current setting is his primary focus, he is looking ahead to possible interactions with the target person in the future. Goffman suggests that "much of the activity during an encounter can be understood as an effort on everyone's part to get through the occasion and all the unanticipated and unintentional events that can cast participants in an undesirable light, ... and...to bring the encounter to a satisfactory close" (1955, p. 229). But the ingratiator has a broader temporal perspective. He is intent on building up a relationship that will be beneficial to him, and he therefore desires to leave the present interchange with a better face than when he entered it.

---

*Bracketed bold numbers refer to original page numbers. Page numbers indicate where the original page ended.

This process of improving face has clear implications for shifts in the relative power of the ingratiator and his target person. Interpersonal relationships are characterized by mutual dependence. Each can help and each can hurt the other. In many relationships, however, one party has less power, is more dependent, than the other. It is under such conditions of power asymmetry that the more dependent person is motivated to augment his power.

When we consider what strategies are available to him, we can see that some merely confirm the asymmetry, whereas others may be effective in modifying the asymmetry in the direction of more equal power. Compliance is an example of a dependence-confirming tactic. The worker who dutifully does everything he is told and never questions the supervisor seems to be saying, in effect, that he accepts the power asymmetry and considers the supervisor's directions to be perfectly reasonable. Ingratiation, on the other hand, is power-enhancing or dependence-reducing. If the dependent person can increase his attractiveness in the eyes of the more powerful person, the latter will be inhibited from providing negative outcomes that were originally part of his behavior repertory. "In other words, as the dependent person becomes more attractive, the powerful person cannot punish him without greater cost to himself. This, in effect, means that his power has been reduced" (Jones, 1965).

A Working Definition

On the basis of the preceding discussion, then, we can define ingratiation as *a class of strategic behaviors illicitly designed to influence a particular other person concerning the attractiveness of one's personal qualities.* Ingratiating actions are illicit because they are [2] directed toward an objective that is typically not contained in the implicit contract that underlies social interaction.

The ingratiator's task is essentially that of manipulating the attributions made by the target person. His ultimate goal is to make himself attractive, but his personal resources and the setting in which he finds himself may dictate the particular attributions sought after. He may seek attraction by attempting to elicit attributions of friendliness, or perceptiveness, or integrity, while avoiding attributions of ulterior motivation. The ingratiator, to be successful, must operate with all the wisdom of an applied social psychologist in trying to manipulate the outcomes of another's attribution process.

Plan of the Essay

Now that we have defined what we intend to mean by ingratiation, we will proceed to a more detailed analysis of its shaping conditions and vicissitudes. First, we shall take a careful look at potentially ingratiating behaviors from the target person's perspective. We will describe experiments in which subjects are exposed to a confederate engaged in various attraction-seeking tactics and are asked to indicate how much they like him. This should give us some feel for the kinds of tactics that are likely to be effective in eliciting interpersonal attraction.

In the next section, we shall ask how individuals behave when they are trying to make themselves attractive to another. We will review a series of experiments that have used one or more of the ingratiation tactics as the dependent, or response, variables.

Subjects in these experiments are typically placed in a situation that requires them to interact with a confederate of the experimenter. In some of the studies, half of the subjects are explicitly instructed to try to create a positive impression, while the remaining subjects are told to be "honest" and "accurate." The subjects are then given a chance to describe themselves, flatter the target person, or agree with his opinions, and the responses of the two groups are compared. Other studies are more implicit in attempting to elicit ingratiating overtures: a subject's dependence on another individual is experimentally varied. Subjects in one condition are placed in the situation of needing the other's approval or attraction, and their responses are compared with those of subjects who have nothing to gain by impressing the target person.

Then we shall examine the cognitive and motivational determinants of ingratiation. The discussion emphasizes the incentives for engaging in ingratiation, the subjective probability of successfully increasing one's outcomes through attraction-seeking strategies, and the perceived legitimacy of attempting to curry favor. The subject's estimation of these three factors is expected to determine whether or not he engages in ingratiating behaviors. In a final section, we shall consider both the short-term and long-term effects of ingratiation. We will first discuss how ingratiating overtures are likely to affect the target person who receives them. A target person may often be motivated to believe that the positive feedback he is receiving from another is genuine. Even if he wants to know the "truth" about himself, he is likely to have a difficult time distinguishing between valid self-information and false praise. Next, we will focus on the effects of ingratiation on the ingratiator himself. We will consider the effects of his ingratiating overtures on both his attitudes toward himself and his feelings about the target person. We will conclude by pointing out some of the ways that ingratiation is likely to affect the quality of our interpersonal relationships.

TACTICAL VARIATIONS WITH THE SUBJECT AS TARGET PERSON

Ingratiation can, according to the present definition, at least, take all or any of the forms by which interpersonal attraction may be solicited. In considering the kinds of communication that might make a person more attractive to another, we suggest that there are four major classes of ingratiation tactics: other-enhancement, opinion conformity, rendering favors, and self-presentation. In our discussion of the probable effectiveness of these tactics in various situations, we will cite experiments that have used them as independent variables and measured the subject's attraction to the stimulus person employing them. When research findings are not available (and this will often be the case), we will rely on our own intuitions concerning the target person's likely response. In so doing, we will consider carefully what attributions of causality the target person is apt to make when the ingratiator employs a given tactic in a certain situation. In order to sharpen the discussion, we shall often write as though we are giving advice to the ingratiator on how to succeed. This should not be taken as an endorsement of ingratiation, but recognized as an expository convenience.

Complimentary Other-Enhancement

The first class of tactical variations involves communication of enhancing evaluative responses to the target person. This class of tactics probably comes closest [3] to the meaning of flattery in its everyday usage. The ingratiator finds ways to express a positive evaluation of the target person and emphasizes the latter's various strengths and virtues. He may distort and exaggerate the target person's admirable qualities, but such direct duplicity is not an essential ingredient of behaviors in this class. The ingratiator may call attention to positive attributes that do, in fact, characterize the target person, but through errors of omission, he may fail to develop the negative side of the ledger. While it is fruitless to specify the particular responses that are likely to bring attraction out of other-enhancement, we may single out this class of tactics as one designed to convey the impression that the ingratiator thinks highly of the target person.

The effectiveness of other-enhancement as a tactic in the service of attraction-seeking seems to derive from the premise that people find it hard not to like those who think highly of them. Such a premise has been put forth by Heider who maintains that a dyad is unbalanced if one party likes the other, but is disliked by him (1958, p. 202). Heider's system implies that if one person perceives that the other likes or respects him, that one person will have a tendency to move toward liking the other. If no such movement occurs, the target person will feel the subjective discomfort or strain that imbalance can bring. In fact, a large number of studies have confirmed the fact that subjects change in the direction of greater attraction toward a stimulus person who expresses his approval of them (see, e.g., Jones, Gergen, & Davis, 1962; Lowe & Goldstein, 1970).

Can we expect a target person to react favorably to us if we tell him how wonderful he is and how much we like him? The answer undoubtedly depends on the surrounding circumstances. The target person's evaluation of an individual who compliments him will depend on the motives he attributes to the individual. When another compliments us, there are many possible explanations for his behavior—only one of which is that he likes us and really believes we have the virtues he has mentioned.

Suppose, for example, that a young woman is told by her date, during the course of the evening, that she is a "beautiful, sensitive person." How is she likely to react to such a compliment? There are a number of attributions she might make about her date's comment. First, she may decide that the comment was made not because her date really feels that way, but because he wants something from her—in other words, because he has manipulative intentions. If the young woman makes an attribution of this type, her opinion of the young man will not only fail to increase, but may very well decrease.

A second possible attribution that "the young woman may make is that her date is "the kind of person who always makes positive comments to others." There is obviously a great deal of individual variation in the way individuals respond to each other. At one extreme is the individual who is perpetually grouchy and usually responds to others in a negative or nasty way. At the other end of the continuum is the individual who appears to be good-natured and responds to everybody in a positive and pleasant manner. Just as we are unlikely to take an insult from the former type of person as evidence that we are inadequate, we will probably not accept a compliment from the latter type of person as evidence of our basic worth. If the young woman attributes her date's compliment to the fact that he is positive to everyone, he will probably gain little in interpersonal attractiveness.

A third attribution that a young woman may make when she is complimented by her date is that his response was triggered by the situation, and really has little to do with her attractiveness. There are many situations in which it is "normative" to compliment someone. For example, when a young man picks up his date for the senior prom, it is probably normative for him to mention how nice she looks. Indeed, if he said nothing about her appearance, she would very likely be disappointed and hurt. Likewise, it is normative to congratulate someone after he has received a raise or a promotion. It is normative to tell mothers that their babies are cute. It is normative to tell a woman who has just come from the hairdresser that her hair looks nice. And so on. While not complimenting someone when such behavior is called for by the social situation may lead to a decrease in interpersonal attraction, a compliment of this type probably does not lead to much of an increase. It is accepted as one of the normal routines of face-work.

A fourth possible attribution the young woman may make when she is complimented by her date is that he is "just trying to be nice" or "trying not to hurt my feelings." Thus, she may not believe that her date is being entirely honest when he tells her how beautiful she is, but may nevertheless attribute benign motivations to him. We are generally appreciative when someone is thoughtful and considerate of our feelings, since this implies that he feels positively toward us. Therefore, the attribution that the ingratiator is "just trying to be nice" is likely to result in feelings of increased attraction to him.

Last but not least, the young woman may conclude that her date really means what he said—that he really does think she is a beautiful and sensitive person. Of course, an ingratiator who succeeds in leading the target person to believe that his compliment is sincere, [4] and in this way conveys his genuine high regard for the target person, will probably be quite successful in eliciting the target person's attraction. In a study by Jones, Bell, and Aronson (1972), subjects were led to believe that they were seeing true physiological indicators of another person's attraction for them. Under these conditions, where there is no question of the genuineness of the other's attraction, the results overwhelmingly show that liking and disliking are reciprocated.

In summary, if we want a target person to respond to us with increased attractiveness, there are a number of things that we should keep in mind. We should take great care to avoid compliments under circumstances that will lead him to conclude that we merely "want something" from him. We should also avoid complimenting others in front of the target person in such a way that he concludes that we are the kind of person who is positive to everyone. Finally, we should seek out situations where compliments are not routine so that the target person will not conclude that anyone would compliment him in that situation. We should compliment the target person so that he will conclude that we feel high positive regard for him—either because we are trying to "be nice" and not "hurt his feelings" or, preferably, because we genuinely believe the positive things we are saying about him and are not uniformly as positive to others.

FACING THE CREDIBILITY PROBLEM How should an ingratiator structure his compliment in order to increase his chances that the target person will make the desired attribution? First, he might play down his dependence on the target person in order to reduce the suspicion that he needs, or expects, to be benefited by him. This may be a matter of timing his remarks so that the benefit desired is not a salient issue at that moment. For example, a student who is interested in ingratiating himself with the professor is unlikely to be very successful if he says, "I'm really enjoying your course this semester. It's one of the best courses I've ever had. By the way, would you mind completing this recommendation form for me?" One way to avoid the attribution of manipulative intentions on our part is to arrange to have the compliment mediated by a third party. The advantages of such a strategy were noted early by Lord Chesterfield, who recommended to his son an "... innocent piece of art; that of flattering people behind their backs, in the presence of who, to make their own court, much more than for your sake, will not fail to repeat and even amplify the praise to the party concerned. This is, of all flattery, the most pleasing and consequently the most effectual" (1901, I, p. 179). We suggest that it is the "most pleasing" because credibility is established through the mediation process—there is, in such cases, no evidence that the originator of the compliment wanted, or expected, to have the compliment repeated.

It also seems obvious that a compliment is likely to be more effective if it is inherently plausible. Such ploys as telling our obese uncle that he "certainly is looking trim," or telling a hostess that her meal was delicious when the meat was burned to a crisp and the Jello never jelled, are unlikely to be very effective. Such implausible compliments are likely to lead the target person to conclude either that we are complimenting him for "ulterior purposes" or that we have extremely poor judgment.

Keeping in mind that we want our compliment to be plausible, a number of questions arise. First, what traits shall we select when we compliment the target person? Should we choose traits about which the target person is quite certain and secure, or traits about which he has serious doubts? Although compliments about the former may appear to be more "plausible" to the target person, compliments about the latter may be more appreciated by him. Lord Chesterfield puts the matter this way:

> Men are most and best flattered upon those points where they wish to excel, and yet are doubtful whether they do or not.... The late Sir Robert Walpole, who was certainly an able man, was little open to flattery upon that head, for he was in no doubt himself about it; but his prevailing weakness was, to be thought to have a polite and happy turn to gallantry; of which he has undoubtedly less than any man living; it was his favorite and frequent subject of conversation; which proved, to those who had any penetration, that it was his prevailing weakness. And they applied to it with success (1901, 1. p. 27).

Although no research has yet been focused on this question, we would agree with Chesterfield that a person is likely to be especially susceptible to compliments on those dimensions on which he is hungry for praise, as long as the compliments are not implausible.

SELF-ESTEEM AND THE RESPONSE TO COMPLIMENTS A related problem, and one that has received a considerable amount of attention, is whether a person's reactions to praise or censure depend on his overall level of self-esteem. Some investigators (e.g., Backman & Secord, 1959; Deutsch & Solomon, 1959) have argued that individuals with high self-esteem will respond more favorably to praise than those with low self-esteem. In other words, individuals will like those who like them only if they like themselves (cf. Heider, 1955), and individuals with low self-esteem will prefer a negative evaluator to a positive one. Others (e.g., Dittes, 1959; Harvey & Clapp, 1965; Walster, 1965) have suggested that individuals with low self-esteem will be especially susceptible to or grateful for compliments [5] since they are generally uncertain and dissatisfied with themselves. Although a number of experiments have been conducted on this problem, the results are inconclusive. Deutsch and Solomon (1959) manipulated subjects' self-esteem by leading them to believe that they had performed either extremely well or very poorly on two intellectual tasks. They then received evaluative comments concerning their performance from another subject. Half of the subjects received a note from another that was quite positive ("You are the person I most prefer to have on my team"). The remaining subjects received a negative note. Subjects were then asked to evaluate the person who had sent them the note. Subjects in the high self-esteem condition liked others who rated them positively better than those who had low opinions of their performance. In contrast, subjects in the low self-esteem condition did not prefer others who gave them positive feedback. However, they did not clearly prefer the negative feedback either. Deutsch and Solomon attributed their findings to the joint operation of two motives: a "consistency" motive (persons like others who evaluate them in a similar manner to the way they evaluate themselves) and a "positivity" motive (people like those who approve of them and dislike those who disapprove of them). They maintained that, for persons with positive self-evaluations, both consistency and positivity led the individual to like the positive evaluator better than the negative one. They suggested that, in the case of the person with low self-regard, the consistency and positivity motives operated in opposing directions and, as a result, the subjects had no strong preference for either the positive or the negative evaluator.

Skolnick (1971) recently attempted to replicate Deutsch and Solomon's experiment. Although his procedure was very similar to that employed by Deutsch and Solomon, his results were quite different. Skolnick found a main effect for evaluation, indicating that the positive evaluators were liked better than negative note writers, regardless of the recipient's self-esteem. In addition, and quite in contrast with Deutsch' and Solomon's results, persons in the failure group who received a positive note evaluated the note writer more favorably than persons in the success group who received the same note. The author suggested two reasons why his results may have differed from those of Deutsch and Solomon. He argued that the procedure used by Deutsch and Solomon may have generated suspicion and incredulity concerning the evaluations. He also suggested that the subjects used by Deutsch and Solomon (telephone operators) may have been less upset by a negative evaluation on a task that purportedly measured their intelligence than the subjects in his own experiment (college students).

Jacobs, Berscheid, and Walster (1971) were also interested in the question of whether high and low self-esteem individuals respond differentially to evaluations from others. They maintained that low self-esteem individuals are usually receptive to affection when they realize it is being offered, but that it is difficult for them to recognize positive comments from others. In a clever experiment, they manipulated male subjects' self-esteem and then exposed them to a positive, negative, or ambiguous evaluation by a female peer. After hearing the girl's evaluation of him, each subject was asked to indicate how much he liked the girl.

The results indicated that when the subjects were rejected by the girl, low self-esteem individuals showed a tendency to dislike her more than did high self-esteem subjects; when the message was ambiguous, high self-esteem subjects liked the girl more than low self-esteem subjects. When the subjects were accepted, the evaluation of the girl was not significantly different for low and high self-esteem subjects. The authors suggest that the reason low self-esteem subjects liked the ambiguous evaluator less than high self-esteem subjects is because they interpreted her comments to be negative, more or less assimilating the ambiguous remarks to their negative self-concept. Unfortunately, the investigators did not include a dependent measure on which subjects were asked how negative the evaluator's comments were, so there is no direct evidence on the mediating process.

However, if Jacobs, Berscheid, and Walster's conclusion is valid, their results are of potential importance to the ingratiator. The ambiguous comments employed in this study were relatively positive (e.g., "I think we might hit it off if we ever were to meet"). Therefore, their results imply that, unless an ingratiator's comments are extremely favorable, a low self-esteem individual will interpret them as negative and react negatively to the ingratiator. Of course, extremely favorable comments may alert the target person to the fact that the ingratiator is trying to win his approval. This suggests that successful ingratiation attempts toward target persons with low self-esteem are likely to be a real problem. A highly positive comment may tip him off that an attempt is being made to curry favor, and anything less positive might be interpreted as negative.

The results of this experiment revealed that low self-esteem subjects reacted more negatively to rejection than high self-esteem subjects. Similar results have been obtained by the majority of investigators who have focused on the question (see, e.g., Jones, Hester, Farina, & Davis, 1959; Rosenbaum & deCharms, 1960). However, both the experiment by Jacobs, Berscheid, [6] and Walster and an earlier study by Dickoff (1961) found no difference in the perception of positive feedback by high and low self-esteem individuals. Skolnick (1971), on the contrary, found that low self-esteem individuals responded more favorably to positive feedback than high self-esteem individuals. The same may be inferred from Walster's study (1965). To complicate matters further, Deutsch and Solomon (1959) found the reverse: The low self-esteem subjects in their experiment were less favorable to a positive evaluator than the high self-esteem subjects were.

How can we account for this contradictory pattern of results? In a recent attempt to integrate the findings in this area, Steven Jones (1973) favors what he calls "esteem theory": Low self-esteem people are generally more favorable toward others who approve of them than high self-esteem people. He suggests that the tendency for highs to like approving others and lows to like disapproving others (consistency theory) obscures this basic esteem tendency when (1) the feedback is not entirely clear (à la Jacobs, Berscheid, & Walster, 1971) or (2) when the recipient anticipates a future performance where his level of competence will be exposed.

It is unlikely that this attempted resolution will settle the matter, since there remain contradictory findings that are difficult to explain away. One problem is that when a subject responds a certain way in a given experiment, it is difficult to know why he is doing so. For example, if a low self-esteem individual fails to increase his liking for a person who compliments him, is this because (1) he is indeed more favorably disposed toward those who see him as he sees himself; (2) he feels that the compliment is not credible and therefore questions the ingratiator's motives, his judgment in making such a statement, or both; or (3) he interprets the compliment as a negative remark and assumes that the ingratiator is negatively disposed toward him? Unfortunately, none of the experiments discussed previously has included dependent measures aimed at assessing the target person's view of the compliment, its plausibility, or the motives of the individual delivering it.

It is probably safe to say that if a person is quite convinced that he is poor in some ability or unworthy in some area, compliments that tell him that he is good in this area will appear incredible to him and raise suspicions of ulterior motivation. To the extent that a person is uncertain about an attribute he would like to possess, however, or to the extent that he needs reassurance about such an attribute, he presumably will respond to compliments concerning the attribute with increased attraction for the communicator.

Some evidence for this reasoning is provided in study by S. C. Jones and Schneider (1968). Subjects were told that the experiment concerned social sensitivity and were asked to take a test to measure this ability. The certainty of their self-appraisal was manipulated by giving the subjects false feedback concerning their performance. The test had four sections. Subjects in the certain condition were informed that they had done poorly on all four sections. Subjects in the uncertain condition received a low score on the first section, but were not given any information concerning their performance on the remaining sections. Subjects were then told that they would answer some items from the test orally, and that their answers would be evaluated by the other subjects who were present. Subjects received evaluations from one peer that were primarily positive and evaluations from another peer that were primarily negative. In addition to receiving evaluations, the subjects sent evaluations to the peers. The main dependent measure was whether the evaluations sent to the peers were positive or negative. As Table 15.1 shows, subjects in the certain condition sent slightly more positive evaluations to the negative evaluator, while subjects in the uncertain condition sent more positive evaluations to the positive evaluator.

Although there remain many loose ends in the attempt to relate self-esteem variations to the reciprocation of attraction, there is one straightforward prediction tested by Dickoff (1961) that concerns how subjects respond to compliments exceeding their self-esteem when the complimentor does or does not have something to gain from the subject. Dickoff exposed her female subjects to an evaluation from a female graduate student who had observed them through a one-way mirror. She manipulated whether the person giving the evaluation had anything to gain by impressing the subject. Subjects in the "accuracy" condition were led to believe that the person evaluating them would try to be as accurate as possible. Subjects in the "ulterior motive" condition were told that the person evaluating them wanted them to participate in a study of her own and that she was going to ask them [7] to do so after the experiment. The intent of these instructions was

Table 15.1 Percentage of Positive Evaluations Sent to Others as a Function of Certainty and Evaluations Received from Others[a]

	Received	
	Positive evaluation	Negative evaluation
Certain	67.1	71.1
Uncertain	67.0	61.7

[a]Adapted from Jones and Schneider (1968).

to make the evaluator dependent on the subject's good will and so suggest that an ulterior motive might govern her relations with the subject.

Each subject entered the lab individually and was first asked some questions about her personal history and her values, while the graduate student observer watched from behind a one-way mirror. Subjects were told that the graduate student would evaluate them on a scale containing several triads of items. Each triad consisted of a positive, a neutral, and a negative personal trait. Subjects were told that the graduate student evaluator would choose the item in each set that she felt was most characteristic of the subject.

In reality, the graduate student evaluator was a confederate of the experimenter, and her evaluation was planned beforehand to create the various experimental conditions. For one-third of the subjects (positive condition), the graduate student responded with a uniformly favorable evaluation by always choosing the most positive attribute to apply to the student. For one-third of the subjects (self-concept condition), the graduate student's responses were identical to those made by the subject herself in an earlier group testing session. For remaining subjects (neutral condition), the graduate student systematically avoided all positive attributes in favor of uniformly choosing the neutral one on each item. Thus, the situation was one in which some subjects received an evaluation that was extremely positive and uniformly so, some subjects learned that the other person had very much the same impression of them that they had of themselves, and some learned that the other person had a rather evasive and, by implication, negative impression of them. The major dependent-variable measure was a 20-item rating scale on which each subject recorded her impression of the graduate student observer after learning the student's evaluation of her. The subject was also asked to jot down her impression of the observer in her own words.

The results of this experiment are summarized in figure 15.1, where the mean attraction scores are plotted for each of the experimental conditions. Here it may be seen that there is a general relationship between the favorability of the evaluation received by the subject on the one hand, and the evaluation given to the observer by the subject on the other hand. It is especially clear that people respond in kind when they receive a relatively negative evaluation. In support of our reasoning, the instructions varying the observer's dependence on the subject had an effect on attraction when a uniform dose of positive evaluation was administered by the evaluator. It may be inferred by comparing the two positive condition means that

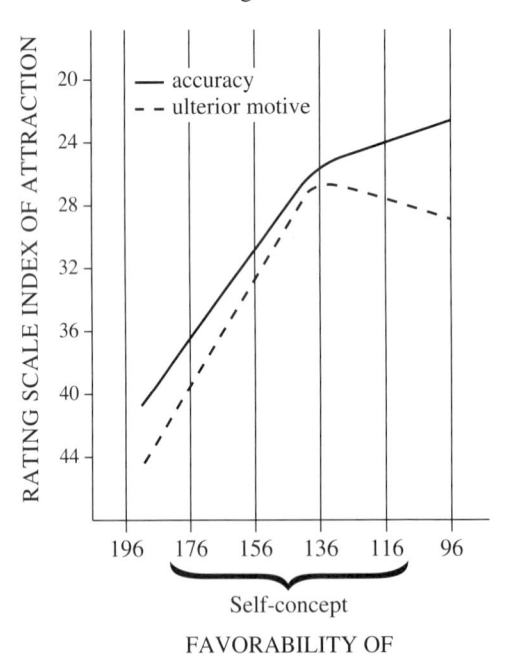

Figure 15.1 Mean Rating Scale Attraction Scores

other-enhancement begets attraction as long as there is no reason to believe that the observer is motivated to benefit himself.

A closer examination of the subjects' ratings on other dimensions and of their free descriptions of the evaluator also sheds some light on this problem. It is clear that the positive evaluation conveyed somewhat different meanings to subjects in the two instructional conditions. For subjects in the accuracy-positive condition, the favorable evaluation tended to be attributed to the observer's naiveté, her congenital optimism, and her kindheartedness, but no manipulative intentions were cited. The accuracy-positive observer was better liked, even though the accuracy–self-concept observer was judged to be brighter and more perceptive, than the accuracy-positive observer. In contrast, the free descriptions of subjects in the ulterior-motive–positive condition conveyed the implication that the observer was behaving out of weakness, insecurity, and fear of being rejected by the subjects. Impressions of the observer in the neutral conditions were uniformly **[8]** negative in tone, though the observer was usually given credit for her honesty and candor.

Taken as a whole, Dickoff's results suggest that when it is clear to the target person that an individual has something to gain by impressing him, the tactic of being very flattering or complimentary will not be particularly successful.

Comparable results have been obtained by Lowe and Goldstein (1970), who found that a positive evaluator was well liked only if subjects thought he was trying to be accurate. Positive evaluations from subjects known to be approval-seeking were not nearly so successful in eliciting interpersonal attraction.

THE DISCERNING INGRATIATOR The preceding discussion has mentioned some factors that are likely to determine whether the target person responds to compliments with increased attraction or concludes that the compliments are designed for the sole purpose of obtaining some benefit within his power to bestow. If an ingratiator avoids complimenting the target person when the benefit desired from him is salient, picks an attribute to admire about which the target person is insecure, but makes sure that his compliment is plausible, he should reduce the probability that the target person will attribute ulterior motivations to him. But, in addition to avoiding the conclusion that he is manipulative and self-seeking, the ingratiator should also try to avoid the attribution that he is complimenting the target person because he is the kind of person who always says complimentary things to everyone. How can the ingratiator structure his compliment so as to reduce the probability that the target person will draw this inference?

If an ingratiator wants to avoid the attribution that he is always positive, or positive to everyone, he should try to convey by his compliments that he is discerning—in other words, that he is selective in giving praise and gives it only when he sincerely believes it is truly merited. One way of doing this is to concoct a judicious blend of the bitter and the sweet. For example, the ingratiator may acknowledge negative attributes in the target person of which the latter is fully aware and then go on to emphasize positive attributes of which the target person is uncertain. Or he may criticize the target person on unimportant or trivial points and compliment him on dimensions that are important to him. Some risk is involved in employing this tactic, since it requires that the ingratiator correctly intuit the target person's certainty about his own weaknesses and his willingness to acknowledge them.

A second way that an ingratiator may avoid the attribution that he is being positive because he is "a positive person" is to start off with a neutral or negative stance toward the target person and to become more positive over time. This tactic is likely to be especially important if the ingratiator is interacting with the target person for the first time. Imagine that you are talking with someone at a cocktail party. If he is friendly and positive toward you from the moment he opens his mouth, you will not necessarily conclude that he is being friendly because he is specifically attracted to you. Instead, you probably will conclude that he is just a friendly person. On the other hand, if he is not particularly friendly or positive toward you at the beginning of the conversation but becomes so after some time has elapsed, you will probably attribute his positive behavior to the fact that he has come to like you, and you will respond to him with increased attractiveness.

Some support for this reasoning comes from an experiment by Aronson and Linder (1965). During the experimental session, female subjects were induced to participate in a series of seven brief interactions with a female confederate of the experimenter. After each of these interactions, the subject was given a chance to overhear the confederate tell the experimenter her impression of the subject, presumably unaware that the subject was listening. The confederate was best liked in a condition in which her early appraisals of the subject were uncomplimentary but became quite positive over time. The subject's liking was significantly greater in this "negative–positive" condition than in a "positive–positive" condition characterized by uniformly complimentary appraisals. The results are summarized in Table 15.2.

Aronson and Linder discussed a number of possible explanations for their results. One of them has already been mentioned in this paper—we may like a negative–positive evaluator better than a consistently positive one because we regard him as more discerning. If an evaluator is uniformly positive to us, we can dismiss this behavior as being a function of his particular style of response. But if he begins by being negative and [9] then becomes more positive, he has demonstrated his ability to make discriminations, and we may therefore be more apt to take his evaluations personally.

In order to examine the validity of the discernment hypothesis as an explanatory mechanism for Aronson and Linder's results, Landy and Aronson (1968) conducted the following experiment. Subjects were led to expect that they would observe and evaluate a male peer, who was actually a confederate of the experimenter. After engaging in a brief interaction with the confederate, subjects were permitted to overhear him either praise or criticize them to the experimenter. Subjects were then asked to watch the confederate perform an art judgment task in which he revealed that he was either a discerning individual (his judgments were quite variable) or a nondiscerning person (his judgments were all pretty much the same). The authors suggested that if the discernment notion accounts for Aronson and Linder's results, the discerning individual should be liked best when he evaluated the subject positively and liked least when he evaluated the

Table 15.2 Mean Values on a Scale of Liking for Confederate[a]

Experimental condition	Mean[b]
1. Negative–Positive	+7.67
2. Positive–Positive	+6.42
3. Negative–Negative	+2.52
4. Positive–Negative	+0.87

[a]Adapted from Aronson and Linder (1965).

[b]Scale ran from extreme dislike (−10.0) to extreme like (+10.0).

subject negatively. However, no significant interaction was obtained. The findings revealed two main effects: Positive evaluators were liked better than negative ones, and discerning individuals were liked better than nondiscerning ones.

Mettee has suggested that Landy and Aronson did not adequately test the discernment notion, since "discriminating among art objects may simply have no bearing whatsoever upon a source's credibility, and hence his discernment status, as an interpersonal evaluator" (Mettee, 1971a, p. 293). Mettee has argued that we will like a discriminator (one who makes negative as well as positive evaluations) better than a nondiscriminator (one who always makes positive judgments) only if a discriminator's interpersonal judgments are perceived as more valid and credible than the nondiscriminator's, and he reports an experiment that provides some support for his reasoning (1971a).

A second reason why we may prefer a negative–positive evaluator to a consistently positive one is because of the feelings of effectance or competence (cf. White 1959) that arise as a result of changing someone's opinion toward us. If we are trying to get someone to like us, evidence that they have changed their opinion of us from negative to positive implies that we have been very successful. A third possible reason cited by Aronson and Linder to account for their results is an anxiety-reduction hypothesis. This explanation suggests that when a person expresses a negative opinion toward us, we feel hurt. If his behavior then becomes more positive, his new behavior is rewarding not only because it is positive, but also because it has reduced the anxiety that was aroused previously. Consistent with this hypothesis, Aronson and Under (1965) found that subjects within the negative–positive condition who were upset by the initial negative evaluations liked the confederate more than the subjects who were not upset. However, an internal analysis of this type is never conclusive, since there may be many reasons why anxious people like others, reasons having nothing to do with the experimental setting.

The only other evidence pertaining to the anxiety-reduction hypothesis is from two recent studies by Hewett (1972). In the first of these studies, subjects received either a positive or a negative evaluation from person A. They then received a positive evaluation from person B. The anxiety-reduction hypothesis predicts that person B will be more liked for his positive comment if the subject has just received a negative evaluation, since in this case the positive comment reduces anxiety. However, Hewett found person B to be no more appreciated for his positive comment if the subject has just received a negative comment than if he has just received a positive one.

Before we worry too much about the particular mechanism that may account for Aronson and Linder's results, we should point out that a number of investigators have been unable to replicate their findings. The two experiments by Hewett (1972) and an experiment by Taylor, Altman, and Sorrentino (1969) exposed subjects to evaluations of themselves from another individual. None of these experiments found a person whose evaluations had changed from negative to positive to be better liked than one whose evaluations were consistently positive. However, one aspect of the procedure in these three studies was quite different from that employed by Aronson and Linder. In Aronson and Linder's experiment, the subjects overheard the evaluations. The evaluator communicated her feelings about the subject to a third party and was presumably unaware that the subject could hear her comments. In both of the experiments by Hewett and the study by Taylor, Altman, and Sorrentino, the evaluations were communicated directly to the subject. As Hewett has pointed out, it may be considered rude and tactless to express negative feelings directly to an individual. The person who does so is not only giving information about his appraisal of the subject, but is also conveying some information about himself. An evaluator who conveys negative information directly to the subject gives the subject two possible reasons to dislike him—he holds a negative opinion of the subject and is also rude and tactless. If the evaluator subsequently changes his mind and comes to view the subject more favorably, this may remove one source of the subject's dislike for the evaluator, but not the [10] other. Even if this alternative is embraced, however, a recent report by Tognoli and Keisner (1972) indicates a failure to replicate Aronson and Linder's findings when their original conditions are followed to the letter.

Obviously, more research is necessary before we can draw conclusions regarding the validity of the results obtained by Aronson and Linder, or the explanatory mechanism behind them. Furthermore, it is important to realize that the method employed by Aronson and Linder, Hewett, and Taylor and his associates has been one in which the confederate began with a negative opinion of the target person and gradually shifted to a more positive view. No research has compared the reaction of a subject who received positive information about some of his traits and negative information about others with a subject who received only positive information. A study approaching such a condition was done by Mettee (1971b). He asked subjects to answer some questions about a real-life decision problem. One group of subjects first received a positive evaluation about a major aspect of their work and received a negative evaluation about a minor aspect. Unlike the Aronson and Linder study, the two aspects discussed were independent of each other. Attractiveness ratings were obtained from the evaluator after each of the evaluations. As would be expected, subjects indicated a high degree of attraction for the evaluator after receiving the "major" positive evaluation. Interestingly, they did not change their evaluation of him after he later delivered a "minor" negative evaluation. Since Mettee's design did not include a condition in which subjects received a major positive evaluation followed by a minor positive one, it is not clear whether subjects receiving a mixture of positive and negative information regarded the source more highly than they would have if they had received only positive information. Interestingly, however, subjects who received a major positive evaluation followed by a minor negative one, rated their evaluator much more highly than subjects who first received a minor negative evaluation followed by a major positive one. This suggests that the order in which our statements are made, as well as how positive and negative they are, is likely to affect the target person's response. In comparison with Aronson and Linder's experiment, it also suggests that the effects of order are contingent on the independence of the bits of information presented in sequence. In Mettee's experiment, the early information carried more weight, whereas later information (presumably supplanting the earlier information) was more important in Aronson and Linder's study.

Taken as a whole, these studies suggest that making both positive and negative statements about a target person in order to enhance one's credibility is likely to be an extremely risky strategy. If enticed into this strategy, we should probably attempt to restrict our negative comments to rather minor faults that the target person is quite willing to acknowledge. Mettee's experiment (1971b) suggests that whatever negative comments we do make should be made after we have praised an individual in some important area. Furthermore, we should make sure that these negative comments are made in such a way that they in no way imply that we are rude, tactless, or inconsiderate. Otherwise, any gain in credibility that we get for giving negative feedback is bound to be offset by the attribution of negative traits to us.

Are there any less risky ways of complimenting another, so as to avoid the attribution that you are the kind of person who is "always positive"? One possibility is to locate a person in reference to others and point out that you think he is better than they are. This should convey to him that you don't evaluate everyone favorably. Another way of creating the impression that you do not flatter everyone is to avoid complimenting others in the presence of the target person. Imagine for a moment that you are a young woman and have just arrived at a party. You are greeted enthusiastically by a male acquaintance who tells you how lovely you look and how glad he is to see you. Such a compliment is likely to be quite effective in eliciting interpersonal attraction. But if you happen to overhear this young man telling another woman that she looks beautiful tonight and that he is glad to see her, much of the effect of his compliment to you is likely to be diminished. Although no research has been conducted on this topic, we assert that if an individual sees another compliment others as well as himself, he will draw the inference that the person is the kind of individual who is positive to everyone and his compliments will contribute little toward increasing his interpersonal attractiveness.

ON BEYOND THE NORM The preceding discussion has focused on how an ingratiator can avoid the attributions that he is manipulative and self-seeking, and that he is the kind of person who is always complimentary. In addition, the ingratiator should try to avoid the attribution that he is complimenting the target person because it's the normative thing to do—because anyone in his situation would be complimentary. As we have mentioned previously, some situations exert strong pressures on an individual to be complimentary. Suppose you see a woman with a new baby. Even if her offspring is the ugliest baby you've ever seen, the situation is one that calls for complimentary behavior on your part. Or suppose you meet an old friend who has had a new hairdo or a nose job. Most people would [11] probably find themselves telling her how marvelous she looks, even though they may not really think so. A hostess who has obviously spent hours preparing dinner will probably be told by her guests that the food is wonderful, even if it compares unfavorably with a TV dinner.

We do not mean to imply that complimenting an individual when such behavior is called for by the situation will never be effective in enhancing one's attractiveness, but the most reasonable conclusion is that such circumstances make it much easier to lose ground than to gain it. While a target person who receives a compliment of this type may not be sure whether we really feel positively toward him, a target person who doesn't receive a compliment when it is called for by the situation is likely to conclude that we feel negatively toward him, if only because we don't seem to care about how *he* feels toward *us*. Suppose, for example, that after wearing your hair long for many years, you decide on a different style. So one day you go walking into the office or the classroom with a new haircut. If someone says to you, "I like your hair," it will be hard for you to tell whether he really does like your hair or whether he is just responding to the normative requirements of the situation. However, suppose he doesn't even comment on your new haircut. Or, worse yet, suppose the individual says, "You got your hair cut," but provides no value judgment. You will probably conclude that he does not like your haircut.

The ingratiator should always compliment the target person when such a response is called for by the situation, since not complimenting him may imply negative feelings. In delivering his compliment, he should try especially hard to convey his sincerity, perhaps by the aptness or tailor-made quality of his compliment. By adopting this strategy, he would probably dispel the target person's doubts that he is just being polite.

One situation that exerts strong pressures on us to be complimentary to others is when they ask us what we think of them. Suppose, for example, that your roommate says, "I just blew all of my money on this new dress. How do you like it?" Or suppose an individual asks us about an even more important attribute, such as whether we think he is attractive to members of the opposite sex. By and large, when people ask us what we think of them, they do not necessarily crave the truth. We often sense that they would prefer our compliments to our candor and act accordingly. It is commonly understood that such information-seeking is often motivated by the need for support rather than by the need for genuine appraisal. Therefore, the target person himself is likely to be aware that the more avidly he seeks information from others, the more invalid it is likely to be. It would seem that the ingratiator, bent on convincing a target person of his genuine admiration for him, would arrange to deliver spontaneous compliments as well as to respond with praise whenever the bait is offered. In fact, the ingratiator may learn from the fishing-for-compliments episodes just what the target person's areas of uncertainties are and exploit this knowledge in subsequent spontaneous praise.

So far, our discussion of other-enhancement has centered around compliments. But there are many other ways of conveying to a person that we like him. Most of these strategies are more subtle than verbal compliments, and therefore they may be more effective—especially in situations in which the ingratiator is dependent on the target person and the target person is on guard for ingratiating behaviors.

GESTURES THAT MAY ENHANCE THE OTHER First, there are a number of nonverbal behaviors that an individual can employ. He can smile when he meets the target person. As Dale Carnegie has pointed out, "Actions speak louder than words, and a smile says, 'I like you. You make me happy. I am glad to see you'" (1940, p. 72). Carnegie considered smiling so important that he advised his readers to "... force yourself to smile. Act as if you were already happy, and that will tend to make you happy" (p. 74). He mentions a technique employed by Franklin Bettger, former third baseman for the St. Louis Cardinals and at one time one of the most successful insurance men in America: Before entering a man's office he always pauses for an instant and thinks of the many things he has to be thankful for, and works up a great big honest-to-goodness smile, and then enters the room.... This simple technique, he believes, has had much to do with his extraordinary success in selling insurance (p. 75).

Another nonverbal behavior that is likely to convey to a person that we like him is continued eye contact especially while he is talking to us. Most of us have had the jarring experience of talking to someone at a cocktail party while the other person was looking all around the room. Lack of eye contact conveys to a person that you don't really care very much about what he is saying and would like to find someone more interesting to talk to or something more interesting to talk about. In addition to maintaining eye contact, we probably convey to a person that we like him by such behaviors as leaning toward him while he is speaking and nodding our heads when he makes a point.

INDIRECT VERBAL COMPLIMENTS   In addition to these nonverbal behaviors, there are a number of verbal [12] behaviors that may convey to a target person that we like him. For example, we can respond to his statements with such reinforcers as "Really," "That's very interesting," or "That's a good point." Of course, any of these strategies may backfire if they are carried to extremes. If you never stop smiling, nod your head continually, and say "Right on" every time the target person opens his mouth, you will probably not be very successful in eliciting interpersonal attraction.

An additional strategy for subtly conveying to an individual that you like him has also been mentioned by Carnegie: calling the person by name. Calling a person by name can imply that we would like the relationship to move to a more intimate level. Recently, Kleinke, Staneski, and Weaver (1972) have conducted a series of experiments to determine how individuals react to a person who uses this strategy. They argue that an individual will elicit a positive reaction by using the target person's name only if he is not dependent on the target person. They maintain that if the ingratiator obviously has something to gain by impressing the target person, the target person will attribute the ingratiator's behavior to ulterior motivation and will react negatively when called by name. In order to test their reasoning, these investigators conducted two experiments in which a naive subject was asked to react to an individual who called him by name. In the first study, a highly attractive woman interviewed two men simultaneously. She called one by name several times during the interview, but called the other by name only once. The authors reasoned that since the interviewer was not dependent on the subjects in this experiment, using one's name should elicit attraction. The results supported their reasoning. The subjects who had been assigned to the condition in which they were called by name stated that they liked the interviewer significantly more than subjects who had not been called by name. In a second experiment, a man and a woman subject were placed alone in a room for 15 minutes to "get to know each other." Half of the men were instructed to call the woman by name as frequently as possible during the conversation. The remaining subjects were told not to use the woman's name. In this study, using the target person's name produced a negative reaction. Men who used the woman's name were rated less positively by the women than men who did not. They were viewed as significantly more motivated to make a good impression and significantly less genuine than subjects who did not. Furthermore, the women rated them as significantly less desirable as future discussion partners than subjects who did not use their names. The authors suggest that the subjects in the second experiment were more dependent on the target person for approval than were subjects in the first experiment. They argue that since the female interviewer in the first experiment had nothing to gain by making a positive impression on the undergraduate male subjects, the men who were called by name took this as a reflection of the interviewer's positive feeling for them. Another possibility not mentioned by the authors, is that subjects in the first experiment responded more favorably when they were called by name because they heard the interviewer interact with another person and *not* call him by name. Subjects in the second experiment who were called by name may have thought that the male undergraduate was the kind of person who uses immediacy with everyone, and may have failed to react positively for that reason.

Another subtle way of conveying to a person that you like him and find him interesting is to encourage him to talk about himself. As Carnegie has pointed out,

"Remember that the man you are talking to is a hundred times more interested in himself and his wants and his problems than he is in you and your problems" (1940, p. 93). If the person is involved in a discussion of a topic other than himself, an ingratiator can convey positive feelings for him by listening attentively, by asking questions, and by sticking to the speaker's subject. We should try to convey by both our verbal responses and our nonverbal behaviors that we are deeply interested in what the speaker is saying. Few things are as uncomplimentary as looking bored, yawning, or interrupting to ask what time it is while the target person is telling us about something he finds interesting and important.

Still another subtle means of conveying to a person that we think highly of him is to ask him for advice. Such a request is likely to imply that we respect the target person's judgment and is especially effective if they act as though the advice will be taken. A related strategy is asking the target person to do a small and reasonable favor for us. This tactic is likely to convey that we feel good about our relationship with the target person, since it is not customary to ask people to do favors for us unless our relationship is a relatively good one.

In addition to asking individuals to do favors for us there are other strategies that convey to a person that our relationship with him is a good one. One way of conveying a sense of closeness with another is through the use of the "friendly insult." Small talk among close friends (especially men) is often peppered with barbs, derogation, and sarcasm. The use of friendly insults implies that the target can take it as well as dish it out and, probably more important, that he does not [13] really have the deficit or liability suggested by the insult. The insult, at worst, is intended as a gross and humorous exaggeration. A second way to suggest to a target person that we consider him a friend is to reveal an intimate personal experience or feeling to him. Self-disclosure on our part implies respect for the other's understanding, tolerance, or discretion. It also implies that we trust the target person, that we do not fear exploitation by him, and that we would like the relationship to continue and deepen.

In recent years, a number of experiments have been conducted to test the relationship between self-disclosure and interpersonal attractiveness. Unfortunately, the results of these studies have not been particularly consistent. In a study by Worthy, Gary, and Kahn (1969), female subjects entered the lab in groups of four and were asked to fill out attractiveness measures on one another. They then were given a set of seven questions that had been scaled for intimacy. They were asked to send a note to each other subject containing a question and an answer. The subject could thus choose how self-disclosing she would be to each of the other subjects. This procedure was repeated with a different set of questions for ten trials. Then subjects were again asked to fill out an attractiveness measure on one another. The results revealed that those who had made more intimate disclosures were better liked.

Since this study was correlational in nature, the results should be interpreted with some caution. Disclosing subjects may be liked for reasons quite remote from the act of intimate disclosure. Furthermore, the results of later studies have not provided support for the hypothesis that high-disclosing others are liked more than low-disclosing others. Schneider and Eustis (1972) conducted an experiment in which subjects were told that they would receive information about their partner. Half of the subjects were told that their partner had scored high on a test measuring his general willingness to be intimate with other people. The remaining subjects received information that their partner had scored low on this test. Subjects were asked how much they liked their partner. Interestingly, this question produced no significant differences between conditions. These results suggest that the fact that someone is a kind of person who is revealing is not enough to enhance his interpersonal attractiveness. Perhaps a person must emphasize by the nature of his disclosure that he likes and trusts the recipient in order for the disclosure to increase his interpersonal attractiveness.

Ehrlich and Graeven (1971) also examined the relationship between disclosure and liking. Male subjects were paired with a confederate who posed as another subject. Their interaction was structured by having each person speak alternately for two-minute periods. The confederate spoke first and used scripts to control his intimacy level. No systematic relationship was found between the subjects' degree of liking for the confederate and the confederate's disclosing behavior. Ehrlich and Graeven suggest that, in future studies on this topic, more attention should be paid to the contents of the disclosure. Self-disclosure may lead to interpersonal attraction only when the disclosure reveals similarity between the individuals or such characteristics as good-naturedness, poise in adversity, and basic humility.

We agree with Ehrlich and Graeven that the content of the disclosure is likely to be an important factor in determining whether the disclosure results in increased or decreased attractiveness. If the content reveals to an individual that the ingratiator is dissimilar to him or possesses negative traits, the target person may be unlikely to enhance his view of the ingratiator. Suppose, for example, a woman discloses to you that she has had an abortion. You may feel pleased that she likes and trusts you enough-to confide in you. But if you feel that abortions are immoral, you may dislike the discloser for this reason. The net effect of her disclosure, then, may be to decrease her interpersonal attractiveness if the disclosure suggests to you that she possesses traits or characteristics that are undesirable.

All in all, we would expect self-disclosure to be effective in increasing interpersonal attraction when it conveys to the recipient that the discloser likes and trusts him. Unfortunately, most of the studies on self-disclosure have not assessed the subject's attributions concerning the target person's behavior. As is true with most forms of other-enhancement, there are many other attributions that the target person may make when an individual is disclosing to him. One factor that may influence an individual's attributions to a disclosing person is the length of the relationship with him. Once one of us went to a car dealer to purchase a new car. Before we had been talking to the salesman for five minutes, he revealed to us that his relationships with his fellow salesmen were bad, that his son was a midget with a bone disease, and that his wife thought he was sexually perverse. We were not sure whether this was a new sales technique, or whether the salesman was simply very odd. Because his comments had occurred so early in the relationship, it was difficult for us to think that he was intimate because he liked and trusted us. Beyond this, of course, the content of the revelation was unsettling to say the least.

Most experiments have examined the reactions of relative strangers to one another. Perhaps subjects [14] have trouble viewing the willingness to disclose personal information under these circumstances as a compliment. Particularly when the disclosure is extreme in nature, we may conclude that it reflects negative characteristics of the discloser rather than anything about his feeling for us. Some support for this reasoning comes from a recent experiment by Cozby (1972). This experiment attempted to test the relationship between disclosure and liking over a wider range of intimacy values than has generally been employed. Unfortunately, he used a role-playing methodology in which subjects were asked to imagine that a girl had been asked to choose ten things about herself from a list containing 70 such topics. Items on the list had been scaled for intimacy. Each subject was given a list of the items presumably chosen by another girl. For one treatment, these items were generally low in intimacy (e.g., "her favorite TV program"). A second treatment used medium intimacy items (e.g., the things she enjoys most in life), and a third used high intimacy items (e.g., "her greatest romantic disappointment"). Each subject was exposed to each of the three treatments. Following each treatment, they were asked to indicate how much they liked the girl and to rate her on a number of scales. The results revealed a curvilinear relationship between disclosure and liking, with subjects expressing the most liking for the girl who selected items of medium intimacy. Interestingly, the high-disclosing other was rated as more maladjusted than the medium other, but there was no significant difference between maladjustment ratings for the medium and low conditions. The high-disclosing other, in comparison with the medium discloser, was also rated as less intelligent, more anxious, and less discreet. These results suggest that making self-disclosing statements to another is unlikely to be effective ingratiation strategy if the statements are too self-revealing. Instead of conveying to the target person that the ingratiator likes, respects, or trusts him, the ingratiatior may convey that he is maladjusted, indiscreet, and anxious. It is possible that such negative trait attributions would not be made to a high-disclosing other at later stages of a relationship.

Of course, even these more subtle types of other enhancement may convey to a target person that we have manipulative intentions, that we are the kind of person who is always positive, or that we are only being positive because of the situation. The suggestions we made earlier for avoiding these attributions when complimenting another should apply to these more subtle strategies as well.

THE NEGATIVE EFFECTS OF PRAISE In our discussion of other enhancement as an ingratiation strategy, we have mentioned some ways of avoiding the attribution that one is manipulative and self-seeking, that he is complimentary to everyone, or that he is just being complimentary because of the situation. Are there any other conclusions that the target person might draw when he receives a compliment—conclusions that lead him to react negatively rather than positively to praise? Farson (1963) has argued that praise often functions to establish a distance between two people rather than draw them together. He has pointed out several possible negative effects of praise. First, he maintains that praise may make a person feel awkward by placing him in a difficult social situation. When someone tells us how great we are, how should we respond? Should we agree with the praiser? If we do, we are likely to seem immodest. Should we say, "No, I'm really not very good?" Then we may seem too self-deprecating and we may seem to doubt the praiser's judgment. Or should we merely thank the praiser for his compliment? In responding to praise, we want to convey that we appreciate the compliment, that we are not conceited enough to believe it is completely true, but that we are not self-deprecating enough to think it is totally false either. Conveying all of these things simultaneously is not likely to be easy. Second, Farson has mentioned that praise may imply a low level of expected performance. Thus, praising one's performance on a very simple task may carry almost insulting implications. Third, he argues that praise may lead to apprehension over future evaluation. Praise may create an unrealistic set of expectations about future performances and prove ultimately frustrating to the target person (S. C. Jones & Ratner, 1967).

The ingratiator would probably do well to keep these negative effects of praise in mind and to structure his compliments so as to avoid them. For example, he may avoid making the recipient feel awkward by complimenting the recipient individually rather than in a group, and by making his compliment as specific and discerning as possible. He can try to phrase his compliment so that it does not imply a low level of expected performance. For example, he can say. "I knew this was going to be a good dinner, but I didn't expect anything this fantastic." Furthermore, he can try to compliment the target person on performances that are nonrecurring and therefore unlikely to lead to anxiety about future evaluation on the part of the target person.

Before concluding our discussion of other enhancement and the effects of praise, we would like to mention an interesting study by Kipnis and Vanderveer (1971). In this experiment, male subjects were recruited to act as "the boss" in an industrial simulation experiment. Subjects were informed that they would **[15]** supervise four technical high school students who were in another room. Actually, these student "workers" did not exist, and their output was preprogrammed by the experimenter. Subjects could communicate with their workers by microphone and were told that their workers could communicate with them by sending notes along with their work output.

To evaluate the influence of ingratiation, the behavior of three of the workers was varied as follows. One of the workers was a superior worker. His output greatly exceeded that produced by the other workers. A second worker was an average worker. A third worker performed the same as the average worker, but sent ingratiating messages to the leader. He sent a note indicating that he thought the boss was a "nice guy" and one indicating that the leader could count on him for help.

In addition to these three workers, the investigators included a problem worker in their design. For one-third of the subjects, this worker's output was low, and it was made clear that his poor performance was due to ineptitude. A third of the subjects were led to believe that the worker's output was poor and that his performance was due to a poor attitude toward the job and the supervisor. The remaining subjects participated in a control group in which this worker's performance was satisfactory, and his output was as good as the average worker's. The subjects were permitted to use any of several forms of power in dealing with the workers, including promising or actually awarding pay increases. In addition, subjects were asked to evaluate the performance of each of the workers. The authors predicted that the leader would allocate more rewards to an ingratiating subordinate when also faced with a hostile, rather than merely an inept, subordinate.

As Table 15.3 shows, the subjects awarded almost twice as many pay raises to the compliant workers in the poor-attitude condition than in the inept or control conditions. However, the prediction that the ingratiator would receive more pay raises than noningratiators in the poor-attitude condition, but not in the control condition, was not supported. The superior worker received significantly more pay raises than either the average worker or the ingratiator. The ingratiator received marginally more pay raises than the average worker ($p < .10$). Interestingly, while the ingratiator was

Table 15.3 Mean Number of Pay Raises Awarded to Compliant Workers[a]

Condition	Superior worker	Average worker	Ingratiator	Total
Control	1.1	0.4	0.6	2.1
Inept	1.0	0.6	0.8	2.4
Poor attitude	1.5	1.1	1.4	4.0

[a]Adapted from Kipnis and Vanderveer (1971).

Table 15.4 Mean Number of Promises of Pay Raises to Compliant Workers[a]

Condition	Superior worker	Average worker	Ingratiator	Total
Control	1.1	0.4	0.9	2.4
Inept	1.6	0.8	1.7	4.1
Poor attitude	1.1	1.4	0.9	3.4

[a]Adapted from Kipnis and Vanderveer (1971).

only marginally effective in receiving more pay raises, he was very effective in eliciting promises of pay raises (Table 15.4). The ingratiator received as many promises of pay raises as the superior worker in all conditions and significantly more promises of raises than the average worker in the control and inept conditions. It is as if the false coin of ingratiation is repaid by unfilled promises.

Analysis of the performance evaluation data reveals that both the ingratiator and the superior worker were given significantly higher performance evaluations than the average worker. The ingratiator's performance evaluation scores were not significantly lower than those of the superior worker, suggesting that the ingratiator's flattery was successful. The authors point out that, in situations where task performance is less readily measured in absolute terms, one would expect the ingratiator to be even more successful in earning extra rewards.

Opinion Conformity

A second class of tactics available to the ingratiator involves expressing agreement with the target person. Whereas the tactic of other-enhancement attempts to capitalize on the proposition that persons like those who appear to like them, the conformity tactic follows another proposition: Persons like those whose values and beliefs appear to be similar to their own. In general, research has supported the assertion that we prefer others with similar attitudes (see, e.g. Byrne, 1961; Byrne & Rhamey, 1965; Byrne & Griffit, 1966; Clore & Baldridge, 1970; Griffit & Veitch, 1971).

SIMILARITY AND ATTRACTION There are a number of reasons why individuals may like those whose views are similar to their own. Byrne (1969) has maintained that attitudinal similarity leads to interpersonal attraction because it provides evidence that one's view of the world is correct. Johnson and Johnson (in press) **[16]** have found that subjects who perceive another as having similar attitudes expect the other to cooperate more in a goal-interdependent situation than do subjects who perceive the other as having dissimilar attitudes. Thus, their study suggests that we may like those with similar attitudes because we expect them to facilitate our goal attainment.

The tactic of opinion conformity ranges from simple agreement with expressed opinions, through more elaborate attempts to articulate the position presumed to be held by the other, to the most complex forms of behavior imitation. In considering the kinds of conformity that are likely to be effective as ingratiation strategies, we will once again keep in mind the attributions of causality that the target person is likely to make when the ingratiator agrees with him. Of course, many of the points that we made in the section on other enhancement should be valid here. The ingratiator should try to avoid the impression that he is conforming because he wants something from the target person. This can be accomplished by agreeing with the target person at times when the benefit desired from him is not salient. A second way that an ingratiator can structure his conformity so as to avoid the attribution that he is agreeing for ulterior purposes is to attempt to anticipate opinions of the target person that are as yet unexpressed. If the target person says he thinks there should be more "law and order," and you indicate your agreement with his position, he may infer that you are agreeing in order to impress him. But if you cleverly intuit from his short hair, his manner of dress, and his other attitudes that he feels this way, and then spontaneously mention how concerned you are about the problem of law and order, such an attribution on his part is probably less likely.

When it is clear to the target person that the ingratiator would have something to gain by impressing him, the ingratiator should try especially hard to avoid the appearance of slavish agreement. A study by Jones, Jones, and Gergen (1963) clearly supports this bit of folk wisdom.

A problem may arise for the ingratiator, however, if the target person expresses opinions that happen to be identical to the ingratiator's views. If he indicates that he agrees with the target person, the target person may view this agreement as an ingratiation attempt. What should an individual do under these circumstances? Should he be true to his opinions and agree with the target person at the risk of having his intentions misunderstood? Or should he vary his opinions in order to avoid the attribution that he is agreeing for ulterior purposes? As we shall see in the next section, R. G. Jones and E. E. Jones (1964) conducted an experiment in which they tried to face subjects with this dilemma.

FINDING THE RIGHT MIXTURE The ingratiator should also try to avoid the attribution that he is conforming because he is "the kind of person who always agrees with everyone." He can accomplish this by agreeing with the target person on some issues, while disagreeing on others, or by disagreeing with other people in the presence of the target person.

Gerard and Greenbaum (1962) conducted an experiment that provides interesting evidence in this connection. In their study, each subject was confronted by repeated disagreement from two of three peers on judgments concerning unambiguous stimuli.

The judgments of these two peers always preceded the subject's judgment, while the third peer's judgment always followed the subject's. The third peer either agreed with the subject on each judgment, agreed with the first two peers and disagreed with the subject, or, depending on the treatment condition, he began to agree with the subject after initially disagreeing with him for varying periods of time. Once he began to agree with the subject, he continued to agree with him from that point on. The major dependent variable was the subject's impression of this third peer.

The results indicated that the subject was most unfavorable in his evaluation of the peer when the latter always disagreed with him. It was also found that the subject was most favorable when the peer always agreed with him. Data from the "switch" treatments showed that the peer was liked relatively more when the switch was quite early or quite late than when it was moderately late. Gerard and Greenbaum argue that positive evaluation of the early switcher has the same basis as affection for the peer who always agreed: It occurs because we generally like those who support our views. Positive evaluation of the late-switching peer contrasted sharply with the negative evaluation of a peer who never switched. Gerard and Greenbaum suggest that the relatively positive reaction to the late-switching peer is a function of the degree of uncertainty reduction that he provides. Presumably, the longer the subject goes without an ally, the more uncertain he becomes and the more gratified he is when someone finally agrees with him.

The effect of anxiety or uncertainty reduction on interpersonal attraction has also been investigated by Stapert and Clore (1969). In their study, subjects were shown attitude surveys of five other individuals and were asked to indicate how much they liked each individual. One group of subjects was exposed to surveys that were in agreement with their attitudes; the other groups of subjects were exposed to one, two, three, or four disagreements before being exposed to an agreeing survey. Attraction toward an agreeing stranger was found to be greater when he was preceded [17] by disagreement than when he was not. Unlike Gerard and Greenbaum's results, however, an individual appreciated an agreer no more when he had been exposed to several disagreements than when he had been exposed to one or two.

Another possible mixture involves changing one's stance from one of disagreement to one of agreement. Jones and Wein (1972) have shown in the opinion agreement realm what Aronson and Linder (1965) showed in the reciprocation-of-attraction realm. Subjects were exposed to beliefs expressed by a confederate who either started out similar and became dissimilar, or vice versa. The dissimilar–similar confederate was better liked than the similar–dissimilar confederate, in spite of the fact that the total amount of agreement was identical. The mechanism for this effect may be a form of uncertainty reduction, but it is not likely that much anxiety is aroused when one discovers that a single other person disagrees with his opinions on a series of controversial topics. Jones and Wein offer an explanation in terms of positive and negative expectancy violation. When a dissimilar person agrees with us, this may add special credibility to the agreed-with beliefs. When a similar person disagrees with us, on the other hand, the disagreed-with beliefs are clearly threatened. It is not surprising, then, that we express more attraction to the one who bolsters than to the one who undermines our beliefs.

Taken together, these studies suggest that agreeing with someone in a way that reduces his anxiety or uncertainty, may increase interpersonal attraction. Jones and

Wein (1971) and Gerard and Greenbaum (1962) did not find, however, that a person who agrees after disagreeing is better liked than one who is agreeable all the time. Therefore, the ingratiator would probably do well to reduce anxiety by agreeing after someone else has disagreed with the target person, rather than agreeing after he himself has disagreed.

Another experiment that bears on this topic is one conducted by Sigall (1970). The purpose of his study was to determine whether you will like someone more if you are effective in changing his opinion than if he has always agreed with you. Subjects in his experiment were asked to deliver a persuasive message to a person who was either very close to their own opinion or very far from their opinion. They were selected because their opinions ranged from 26 to 29 on a 30-point scale. The listener, who was actually a confederate of the experimenter, either changed from 23 to 24, changed from 8 to 13, or changed from 13 to 18. In the first condition, there is agreement without effectance. (i.e., evidence of the subject's effect on the listener). In the second, there is effectance, but the subject remains in general disagreement. In the third condition there is both effectance and final agreement.

In addition to the confederate's opinion, Sigall manipulated how ego-involved the subject was in delivering the message to the confederate. Half the subjects were asked to read a prepared speech; the remaining subjects were instructed to organize their own speech. The results revealed that in the latter (high-involvement) case, the subjects liked the confederate better in the effectance–no agreement condition, but low-involvement subjects liked the confederate better in the agreement–no effectance condition. Not surprisingly, subjects liked the confederate best when both agreement and effectance occurred. Sigall's results show that similarity is not always a paramount determinant of attraction and suggests that the would-be ingratiator be alert to those occasions when he can reward the target person's persuasive efforts by publicly moving toward agreement with him.

In many settings the ingratiator has the opportunity to agree on some issues while disagreeing on others. Are there any clues from the literature concerning what kinds of issues are likely to be most effective in eliciting interpersonal attraction? Byrne, Nelson, and Reeves (1966) manipulated the extent to which opinions could be verified by objective evidence and found that the relationship between opinion similarity and interpersonal attraction was higher when opinions were unverifiable than when they were verifiable. It has already been mentioned that one reason why conformity is likely to be effective is that it provides evidence to the target person that his view of the world is correct. When objective means of validation are not available, one's agreement is likely to be an especially potent source of information concerning reality. Therefore, conforming on opinions that are unverifiable is likely to be especially effective as an ingratiation strategy.

A second possibility is that an individual may appreciate agreement more if his stand on the issue is unusual or counternormative than if it is a stand that most people would take. For example, an individual who believes that the world is about to end may be especially gratified when he meets another who shares this unusual view. Varying the a priori likelihood of attitudinal similarity, as well as the similarity itself, should provide some interesting possibilities for future research. There is one study that does bear on the point. Jellison and Zeisset (1969) found that subjects were especially attracted to those who were similar to them in possessing special taste sensitivity when that sensitivity was presented as a rare characteristic. [18]

In summary, a potential ingratiator should carefully appraise the situation before deciding what kind of opinion conformity to manifest. If it is clear to the target person that the ingratiator is dependent on him for some favor or other benefit, the ingratiator should try to anticipate the target person's opinions before they are expressed. This should be more effective than agreeing with the target person after he has mentioned his opinion or changing one's mind to agree with the target person, since these tactics may signify that one has manipulative intentions. If the benefit desired from the target person is not salient, and especially if the target person is very involved in arguing for his position, opinion change might be a better strategy. By agreeing on important issues while disagreeing on trivial ones, or by disagreeing with other people in the presence of the target person, the ingratiator can avoid the attribution that he is the kind of person who agrees with everyone. And in choosing issues to conform on, the ingratiator would probably be wise to concentrate on those that are unverifiable by objective evidence, and especially on those where the target person's stand is the unusual, the minority position. Conformity on these issues is likely to be a potent source of information about reality, likely to reduce anxiety or uncertainty, and, therefore, likely to be quite effective in enhancing one's attractiveness.

COMBINATIONS OF SIMILARITY AND BEING LIKED We have suggested that opinion conformity is likely to be a successful ingratiation strategy because people like those who agree with them, and we have cited several experiments showing a relationship between attitudinal similarity and interpersonal attraction. Before concluding this section, however, we should point out that a recent study by Jones, Bell, and Aronson (1972) suggests that the relationship may be very complicated when similarity occurs in the context of being liked or disliked. They present some evidence that a dissimilar other who likes you may be more attractive to you than a similar liker, whereas a similar other who dislikes you will be seen as especially unattractive. To complicate matters further, this preference for the dissimilar other holds only when the target person is herself attractive and the subject therefore is highly involved in the impression she creates.

Most of the studies relating similarity to attraction have provided the subject with little information about the confederate except for his attitudes. Jones, Bell, and Aronson's study suggests that similarity of attitudes may become a less important determinant of attraction as the target person obtains more information about the ingratiator. Even if future research demonstrates this to be the case, however, the ingratiator will still be able to use opinion conformity in those situations where the target person has little information about him, such as during the early stages of their relationship.

Rendering Favors

A logical candidate for the status of an ingratiation tactic is the giving of favors, since persons are likely to be attracted to those who do nice things for them. The idea of linking favors to attraction seeking is so embedded in our culture that the term "apple polisher" is in very wide use. Like compliments, favors may convey to a target person that we like and respect him and suggest that his welfare is important to us. They also may convey that the favor-doer is a kind and thoughtful person. Thus, the ingratiation strategy of rendering favors overlaps slightly with the complimentary other-enhancement tactics discussed previously, and the self-presentation strategies to be discussed in the next section.

We have been arguing that the effectiveness of any ingratiation strategy is likely to depend on the attributions that the target person makes concerning the ingratiator's motives. Concerning favors, there is actually some evidence to support this assertion. Studies by both Greenberg & Frisch (1972) and Nemeth (1970) have indicated that receiving help has no effect on attraction or reciprocity unless it is clear to the recipient that the donor intended to benefit the recipient. In the experiment by Greenberg and Frisch, subjects received either deliberate or accidental help from an experimental confederate. In the deliberate help condition, the confederate gave the subject information that he needed to solve a problem, along with a note indicating that he thought the subject might find the information helpful. In the accidental-help condition, the confederate sent a note to the subject asking a question. This note happened to contain some information that the subject needed to solve a problem. More help was reciprocated in the deliberate-help condition than the accidental-help condition. Interpersonal attraction also increased more in the deliberate help condition than in the accidental-help condition. Evidence that these results were mediated by attributions of the donor's intent comes from the fact that subjects in the deliberate-help condition rated the other student as being more concerned about them and more motivated to help them than subjects in the accidental-help condition. Comparable results were obtained in an experiment by Nemeth (1970).

It is hardly surprising that we will appreciate another's help more if he has made an effort to help **[19]** us than if his help has been accidental. At the very least, these results suggest that the ingratiator should make it clear to the recipient that he intended to be helpful. However, we would maintain that attribution of intent to be helpful is not sufficient to insure attraction. The ingratiator should try to convey, by his favor, that he thinks highly of the target person, and that he himself is a thoughtful and considerate person. He must avoid the attribution that he is performing the favor because he desires some benefit in return. The trouble with favors, from the ingratiator's point of view, is that they make so salient the questions of obligation, reciprocation, and exchange. Less subtle than conformity or judicious compliments, favors can make the ulterior motives of the favor-giver all too transparent.

One condition under which a favor is likely to signify manipulative intentions is if it is very obvious that the ingratiator is dependent on the target person, or if the benefit desired is salient to the target person when the favor is performed. A favor also may signify manipulative intentions on the part of the donor if it is performed under "inappropriate" circumstances. Studies by both Schopler and Thompson (1968) and Kiesler (1966) have indicated that a person's reaction to a favor is strongly influenced by the appropriateness of the favor for the situation.

In Schopler and Thompson's experiment, female subjects were recruited for a marketing study. They were interviewed purportedly to get their reaction to a new product—a blouse designed especially for college students. One independent variable was whether subjects received a favor from the interviewer. On the interviewer's desk there was a jar containing a single rose. Half of the subjects were given this rose as a favor with the comment, 'This is from my garden. I would like you to have it." The remaining subjects received no rose. The second independent variable was the appropriateness of the favor. Half of the subjects were told that the interview would be formal; the remaining subjects were told that it would be informal. It was reasoned that a favor would be viewed as appropriate behavior in the informal, but not in the formal, interviewing situation. At the end of the interview, the interviewer explained that his company wished to have some volunteers participate in a home test of the blouse and launder it by hand. Subjects were asked to indicate how many times they would be willing to wash the blouse on a scale ranging from one to 50. After the interview was completed, they were given a questionnaire designed to assess the interpersonal attractiveness of the interviewer.

For the measure of washing the blouse at home, the results showed that the effects of the favor depended on the formality of the setting. In the formal condition, subjects who received a favor consented to fewer washings than those not receiving a favor. In the informal condition, subjects receiving a favor agreed to do more washings than those who had not received a favor. These results do not appear to be mediated by liking. Subjects in the informal interview conditions were found to like the interviewer significantly more than subjects in the formal interview conditions, but there was no differential effect of favor giving. However, subjects in the appropriate (informal) favor condition did see the interviewer as more generous than subjects in any other conditions.

Kiesler (1966) found that when performing a favor is in accord with role requirements, attraction will be greater when the favor is performed than when it is not and when withholding a favor is in accord with role requirements, attraction will be greater when the favor is withheld than when it is not. Unfortunately, neither Kiesler nor Schopler & Thompson included dependent measures to determine the recipient's attributions of the donor's motives. In the Schopler and Thompson study, however, the attribution of generosity is certainly consistent with what one would expect from more direct questions about motivation. Perhaps this gives us a clue that when a favor is performed under inappropriate circumstances, it alerts the recipient to the possibility of manipulative intentions. Of course, it is also possible that a person who does a favor under inappropriate circumstances is viewed as something of a fool, and reciprocation does not occur for that reason.

Schopler and Thompson suggest that a favor is inappropriate in a formal or highly structured situation. Of course, there are many other situations in which a favor may be viewed as inappropriate by the recipient; appropriateness may vary with the recipient; appropriateness may vary with the magnitude of the favor and the nature of the relationship between the donor and the recipient. If someone offers to perform an extremely costly favor for us, we are likely to be embarrassed and suspicious about his intentions. For example, suppose a young woman is told by her date that he is going to Florida for the weekend and would like her to come along at his expense. Except among the best of friends, costly favors are highly unusual. Such a favor may seem inappropriate to the recipient and then alert her to the possibility of exploitative intentions.

We have suggested, in previous sections of the paper, that an ingratiator should try to avoid the attribution that he is the kind of person who compliments everyone or who agrees with everyone. Should an [20] ingratiator also try to avoid the attribution that he is the kind of person who does favors for everyone? Of course, if an ingratiator wishes to convey by his favor that he thinks highly of the target person, then he should avoid doing favors for others in the target person's presence. But if he wishes to have the target person view him as a thoughtful and considerate person, then the ingratiator can, and probably should, do favors for others in the target person's presence. Which of these two courses of "attribution management" a potential ingratiator should follow probably depends on the target person's traits and values. If the target person especially admires thoughtfulness and sensitivity in others, the latter technique would probably be the best.

A condition under which a favor is *not* likely to be an effective ingratiation strategy is suggested in a study by Brehm and Cole (1966). The purpose of their experiment was to show that when an individual receives a favor that reduces his freedom, he will experience "psychological reactance" and therefore not manifest the normal tendency to return the favor. Each subject arrived at the lab to find a confederate posing as another subject. The experimenter announced a delay, and the confederate asked if he could leave for a few minutes.

During his absence, the subject was told that in addition to the regular experiment, he would be asked to fill out a first impression rating of the other subject. The importance of making an accurate impression of the other was experimentally varied. Half of the subjects were told that it was extremely important that their ratings be accurate. The remaining subjects were led to believe that it was not at all important. In addition to the importance of the freedom to make an accurate judgment, the authors manipulated whether the subject received a favor from the confederate. For half of the subjects, the confederate returned to the lab with a single soft drink, which he gave to the subject. The remaining subjects received no such favor. After the confederate returned to the lab, he and the subject went inside and were asked to make the first impression ratings of one another. These ratings consisted of 11 scales of antonym pairs, and a number of questions designed to assess the degree to which the subject liked the confederate. The experimenter then gave the confederate 50 sheets of paper and asked him to stack them in piles of five. A dependent measure of helping was how soon, if at all, the subject helped the confederate.

The results revealed that when it was important to the subject to maintain his freedom to make an accurate judgment, he was far less likely to return a favor than if it was not important. As table 15.5 shows, of those subjects receiving favors, 14 out of 15 returned the favor and helped the confederate stack the papers in the low importance condition. In the high importance condition, only 2 out of 15 reciprocated the favor. In the no-favor conditions, about half of the subjects helped the confederate and half did not. The percentages were the same in the low and the high importance condition. Examination of the adjective scales and attraction data suggest that the helping results are not mediated by interpersonal attraction.

These results suggest that if what the ingratiator wants from the target person is a favor done for him, he should avoid

Table 15.5 Number of Subjects Who Helped the Confederate Stack Papers[a]

	Low importance	High importance
No favor		
Helped	9	7
Did not	6	8
Favor		
Helped	14	2
Did not	1	13

[a]Adapted from Brehm & Cole (1966).

performing a favor himself that restricts the target person's freedom. For example, suppose the target person is an employer, and the ingratiator wants a job. In this situation, it is likely to be very important to the target person that he be able to make an accurate judgment of the ingratiator's traits. If the ingratiator performs a favor of some sort for the target person, this favor may arouse psychological reactance in the target person, since it would restrict his freedom to make an unbiased judgment. The present results suggest that by performing a favor for the target person under these circumstances, the ingratiator would actually reduce his chances of getting the job. It is interesting that while performing a favor that restricts another's freedom leads the other to avoid performing a favor in return, it apparently does not affect the other's feelings of attractiveness for the individual.

In conclusion, performing a favor is likely to be an effective ingratiation strategy as long as it does not signify manipulative intentions. The clever ingratiator can avoid this problem by doing favors only when the benefit desired is not salient and by taking care not to perform a favor under circumstances that may seem "inappropriate" to the recipient. If the ingratiator is trying to convey by his favor that he thinks highly of the target person, he should avoid performing favors for others in the target person's presence. However, [21] performing favors for others in full view of the target person may be an effective way of establishing to the target person that the ingratiator is kind, considerate, thoughtful, and therefore deserving of any largesse the target person can bestow. If the ingratiator wants something from the target person, he should consider whether a favor is likely to threaten the target person's freedom to make an unbiased judgment about him. He should carefully avoid performing favors under these circumstances, since a favor that reduces freedom seems to make the target person less likely to benefit the ingratiator than no favor at all.

Self-Presentation

A fourth tactic of ingratiation involves the explicit presentation or description of one's attributes to increase the likelihood of being judged attractive. In the present context, self-presentation refers both to making explicit statements about one's traits, characteristics, or behaviors (e.g., I am the kind of person who …) and to behaving in such a way as to imply that one possesses certain characteristics. For example, a person can present himself as being concerned about others by telling you that he is the kind of person who is concerned about others or by telling you about his work in a mental institution and an orphanage that reveals such concern.

What kinds of self-presentation are likely to be effective in increasing one's interpersonal attractiveness? The ingratiator should obviously try to convey that he possesses positive characteristics, and try to avoid sending out cues that he possesses traits that are negative or undesirable. In deciding what kind of a self-presentation to employ, he can use two sources of information. First, he can pay attention to the target person's idiosyncratic preferences. He might present himself in different ways as a function of his perceptions of the target person's likes and dislikes. This technique was apparently practiced by Lord Chesterfield, who commented that "With the men I was a Proteus, and assumed every shape to please them all: among the gay, I was the gayest; among the grave, the gravest …"(1901, p. 139). Of course, in order to practice this technique successfully, an individual must be able to intuit the target person's preferences. A second possibility is to present oneself as possessing those virtues that are generally admired in our culture, such as being friendly to others or being concerned with their welfare. The obverse of this strategy is that the individual should try to avoid conveying impressions that are viewed negatively in this culture. In the American culture, for example, a person probably reduces his attractiveness to others when he conveys an impression of boastfulness and conceit, of rudeness and lack of consideration, of spitefulness and malice, or of deceit.

THE TROUBLE WITH SELF-PRESENTATIONAL CLAIMS When we present ourselves in a certain way, there are a number of attributions of causality that the target person may make about our behavior. For example, suppose you tell an acquaintance all about your successes on a Saturday night date. First, he may conclude that you are exaggerating or fabricating your experiences in order to impress him. This attribution will probably lead him to decrease, rather than increase, his opinion of you. Second, he may believe that you really did have success with the girl, but feel that the reason you told him was to impress him. Although he may increase his opinion of you because of your great amorous qualities, his conclusion that you were trying to impress him will probably decrease his estimation of you. The net effect of this attribution, then, is not likely to be much of a change in interpersonal attraction. Third, he may believe your self-presentation, and it may not occur to him that you are attempting to make yourself more attractive to him. If he admires the traits that you present yourself as possessing, this conclusion on his part will probably be quite effective in eliciting interpersonal attraction. Thus, the ingratiator's goal is a complex one. He must demonstrate to the target person that he possesses attributes that are positive and desirable. But he must avoid creating the impression that he is trying to impress the target person with these attributes, or worst of all, that his claims are exaggerated or unfounded.

As we have already emphasized, one thing that is likely to alert the target person to the possibility of manipulative intentions is the salience of the benefit desired to the ingratiator. When it is clear to the target person that the ingratiator has something to gain by impressing him, the ingratiator must eschew the more obvious self-presentation tactics. In such situations, we suspect, the more positively the ingratiator tries to portray himself, the more suspicious the target person is likely to be.

These factors create a dilemma for the ingratiator who possesses positive attributes and wants the target person to know about them. Mentioning such traits is likely to signify manipulative intentions to the target person, especially if the ingratiator is dependent upon him. But by not mentioning such traits, the ingratiator deprives the target person of information that would probably make him more attractive to the target person. For example, suppose that you have received outstanding grades at a good college, were elected president of your class, and have received a prestigious fellowship for graduate study. Suppose you have just met a young lady and wish to impress her with your positive [22] qualities. If you tell her all of these things, she is likely to conclude that you are trying to impress her, and she may therefore decide that you are insecure and somewhat pathetic. But if you don't mention your credentials, she may conclude that you are a high school dropout or run-of-the-mill, at best. The ingratiator would probably do well to structure the conversation so that the target person asks him about his accomplishments. It is relatively common for individuals to ask one another where they are going to school, what kinds of activities they are engaged in, and so on. If the ingratiator mentions these things in response to a direct question, the target person is unlikely to think that he is bragging.

In general, it is probably a good idea for the ingratiator to look for indirect ways of communicating his positive attributes to the target person, rather than mentioning them directly. He may try to have them conveyed by a third party. Or he may try to arrange settings so as to demonstrate his positive attributes by his performance. Rather than telling the target person that he is a good cook, an ingratiator can invite the target person to a gourmet dinner. It is much more effective to convince others by our behavior that we are thoughtful and considerate than by telling them that we possess these traits.

And, of course, there are other indirect ways of communicating positive attributes that do not require bragging on our part. An individual can communicate positive attributes by his nonverbal cues, his manner of dress, his choice of friends and residence, and so on. For example, an individual can convey that he is self-confident by the way he walks, speaks, and carries himself. He can convey that he is popular by always being surrounded by friends. And he can convey that he has good taste by decorating his apartment with distinguished prints.

THE FRUITS OF MODESTY—ARE THEY EXAGGERATED? The previous discussion has considered some of the ways that an individual might make himself more attractive by engaging in positive or enhancing self-representation. The obverse of self-aggrandizement is, of course, self-deprecation or humility, which under some circumstances, may also have value as an ingratiation strategy. Modesty, humility, and the acknowledgement of one's dependence may derive their effectiveness as ingratiation tactics from their contribution to an implicit other-enhancement. By emphasizing his weaknesses rather than his strengths, a person implies the superiority of the target person and reduces the likelihood of being considered a competitive threat by him.

Of course, a person who is modest or self-deprecating runs a certain risk. Suppose you are talking to a friend about intelligence, and you modestly point out that you don't think you have a very high IQ. He may admire your modesty. But if he also admires high intelligence, his opinion of you is likely to be reduced to the extent that he believes your self-deprecating statement. This reasoning suggests that modesty is most likely to be an ingratiation strategy if a person's strengths and virtues are considerable and already a matter of public knowledge. It also suggests that if one's virtues are not a matter of public record, he should try to exhibit modesty on unimportant attributes rather than important ones. For example, a career girl may tell another that she has no talent at all for sewing. By adopting this strategy, an individual can gain credit for being modest without losing credit for possessing important negative attributes.

Another condition under which it is probably a good idea for an individual to be modest or self-deprecating is when he anticipates criticism from another. As Carnegie has suggested: "Say about yourself all the derogatory things you know the other person intends to say, and say them before he has a chance to say them—and you take the wind out of his sails. The chances are a hundred to one that he will then take a generous, forgiving attitude (toward you) and minimize your mistakes" (1940 p. 130).

Since self-enhancement and self-deprecation are clearly contradictory presentational tactics, it is important to establish the conditions under which one is more effective than the other. We have suggested that if one adopts a self-enhancing strategy, he should avoid the appearance of being boastful, since boastfulness and conceit are generally not admired in our culture. He should try to structure his self-presentation in such a way that the target person does not conclude that he is trying to be impressive. We have speculated that modesty may be a good idea if the target person would be threatened by a positive self-presentation. We have also suggested that modesty is a good strategy when a person's assets are known and, when a person's assets are not known, can be employed effectively if he displays modesty on dimensions that are trivial or unimportant. Finally, we have conjectured that modesty or self-deprecation is likely to be an effective strategy if the target person is about to criticize the ingratiator anyway. Hopefully, future research will add more substance to these speculations.

Before concluding our discussion of self-enhancement and self-deprecation, we would like to mention a study by Jones and Gordon (1972). This study dealt with a related topic: How do individuals react to an ingratiator when he reveals something positive or negative about his past? Jones and Gordon conjectured [23] that an individual's reaction may depend on whether the disclosure occurs early or late in the relationship. They reasoned that if a person has something good about himself to disclose, he may seem immodest if he discloses it early in the relationship. In the case of bad fortune, it was more difficult for Jones and Gordon to make a prediction. If someone waits a long time before disclosing something bad about himself, it may seem as though he is ashamed of this fact and hoped to conceal it. On the other hand, if a person discloses something bad about himself at the beginning of a relationship, it may seem as though he is making a plea for sympathy, and people may react negatively for this reason.

In an experiment designed to explore these possibilities, Jones and Gordon manipulated three variables: whether the stimulus person's fortune was good or bad, whether or not he was responsible for this fortune, and whether he disclosed this fact early or late in the interview. Subjects were told that they would be listening to an interview between a student and his advisor recorded earlier in the year. The experimenter played one of eight preselected tapes for the subject. On each of the tapes it was explained that the student has lost a semester during his junior year at prep school, resulting in his transfer to the local high school. In the early information conditions, the reason for this change was given early in the interview. The stimulus person gave some bland information about his background and then stated, "I think the people listening should know that ...." In the bad fortune–responsible version, the student revealed that he was expelled from prep school for cheating. The bad fortune–not responsible condition revealed that he left school because of the litigation involved in his parents' divorce. In the good fortune–responsible condition, he revealed that he had spent a semester in Europe on an American Field Service Scholarship. In the good fortune–not responsible condition, he mentioned that he had spent a semester in Europe with funds inherited from his uncle.

In the late information conditions, the stimulus person did not mention why he had left school at the beginning of the interview. At the end of the interview, the interviewer asked him specifically why he had transferred. At this point, he explained why he had transferred in exactly the same manner used for the four early information conditions.

The major dependent variable of the study was the subject's attraction to the stimulus person. The results revealed that when the stimulus person had something good to reveal, he was liked better when he delayed in revealing his fortune than when he mentioned it early in the interview. When bad fortune was involved, however, it made a difference whether the target person was responsible for his unfortunate outcome. If the target person was responsible for his bad fortune, as in the case of cheating, he was liked better if he revealed the information early. If he was not responsible, as in the case of a parental divorce, it was better to reveal the information late in the interaction. Perhaps when a person discloses a handicapping experience early in a relationship, others feel he is trying to elicit sympathy.

It may seem surprising that the timing of the disclosure has so much impact on interpersonal attraction that a cheater who quickly admits his fault is liked as well as a fellowship winner who discloses his good fortune early and liked better than the early-disclosing inheritor or son of divorced parents. It should be understood, of course, that timing of disclosure is closely related conceptually to variations in the reluctance to disclose. In Jones and Gordon's experiment, subjects in the early information condition revealed the information of their own free will; subjects in the late information condition did so in response to a probing question from the experimenter. We have already mentioned that it may be better to let others ask us about our virtues than to mention them spontaneously. Jones and Gordon's results presumably reflect this variation in perceived reluctance, though technically reluctance was confounded with time variations per se.

THE SIMILARITY TACTIC   Of course, a target person's reaction to the ingratiator is likely to be affected by factors other than how self-enhancing or modest the ingratiator is. One factor that seems to be an important determinant of interpersonal attraction is the personal similarity of the ingratiator to the target person. We have already discussed the fact that individuals seem to like individuals who agree with them. There is also a substantial body of literature (see, e.g., Byrne, Griffit, & Stefaniak, 1967; Secord & Backman, 1964) that supports the assertion that people like others whose personalities are similar to their own.

If this is the case, then the ingratiator should be able to make himself more attractive by presenting himself as being personally similar to the target person. Of course, there are probably exceptions to this rule, and unfortunately, they have not been clearly spelled out by previous research. There is evidence that, for some personality traits, we like others whose personalities are complementary to our own. For example, it has been shown that dominant individuals prefer submissive rather than dominant ones, and vice versa (cf. Winch, 1958). And no research has been conducted to determine whether we like those who possess similar personality traits if the traits are negative.

THE SAME-BOAT PHENOMENON   Another potentially [24] effective strategy may be to emphasize a shared orientation to a past or present situation. War veterans may increase mutual attractiveness when they discover that they both fought at Anzio or Guadalcanal. The cementing realization that you and another attended the same Ivy League college might have the same kind of attraction-enhancing effect. We have all doubtless experienced many occasions when the discovery of a common situational bond made us feel more comfortable with and more attracted toward another.

It may be especially true that we like people in the same boat when the same boat is not a very pleasant place to be. Latané, Eckman, and Joy (1966) showed that subjects who experienced electric shock together tended to like each other better than comparable subjects in a no-shock condition. However, this finding was only of marginal significance except in the case of firstborn children. In line with much previous research (Schachter 1959) showing that firstborns are more affiliative when anxious than lateborns are, it is not surprising that firstborns are more attracted to others when affiliation is possible.

The weakness of these results is nevertheless surprising in view of the common folklore that deep and lasting attractions develop toward those who share foxholes, prison cells, and other stressful situations together. Clearly the same-boat phenomenon is a worthy target for additional research.

The Ingratiator's Dilemma Again

Now that we have discussed other-enhancement, opinion conformity, rendering favors, and self-presentation in some detail, are there any general statements we can make about these strategies? One generalization is that, if it is clear to the target person that the ingratiator has something to gain by impressing him, then all of these ingratiation tactics are less likely to be effective. We have already referred to this as the "ingratiator's dilemma," but perhaps we are now in a better position to formalize the underlying notion that the extremity or obviousness of ingratiation overtures interacts with the degree of apparent social dependence to determine whether or not attraction will be gained. This complex statement may be clarified with reference to the model depicted in Figure 15.2. In this model, the target person's (A's) judgment of the ingratiator (B) is expressed as a joint function of the degree to which the subject is dependent on the target person and the extremity or obviousness of his

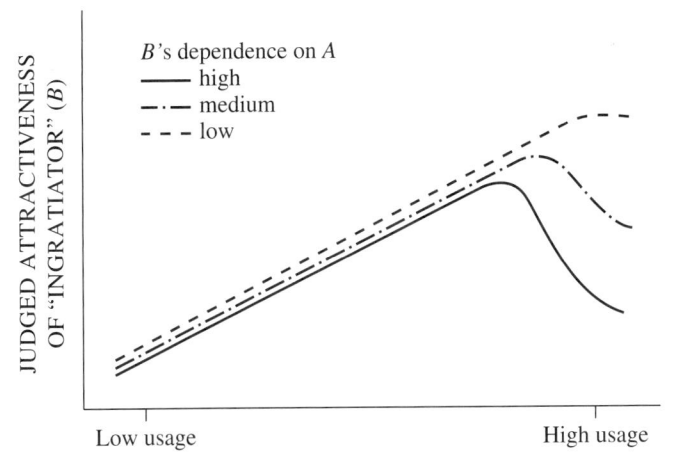

Figure 15.2 Theoretical Relationship between Use of Ingratiation Tactics and Judged Attractiveness of the Ingratiator

ingratiation overtures. As Figure 15.2 shows, *A*'s attraction for *B* increases throughout most of the range of using such tactics as compliments and conformity for gaining favor. But *A*'s attraction will diminish under circumstances of extreme tactical use, and this will be especially true when the ingratiator is obviously dependent on the target person.

The assumptions underlying this predicted family of curves are fairly simple. We have noted at several points in previous discussions that the ingratiator faces a problem of attribution management. He must agree, compliment, or serve without raising the specter of ulterior motivation. In other words, he must maintain his credibility as a communicator. Credibility is primarily determined by the sheer amount, intensity, and consistency of ingratiating overtures, though clearly it is also affected by situational factors. The model shows how the most relevant set of situational factors—the degree of the ingratiator's dependence—combines with behavioral extremity to control attraction received.

In the section on other-enhancement, we presented the results of a study by Dickoff (1961) along with a figure reflecting results that are very compatible with this model. To assess the generality of the model, we [25] can look also at studies of reactions to conformity. There is evidence from experiments by Jones, Jones, & Gergen (1963) and Jones, Stires, Shaver, & Harris (1968) that individuals get credit if they avoid slavish conformity when dependence is very high. Jones, Jones, & Gergen asked subjects to listen to a tape-recorded interchange between two other students. One of these students always expressed his opinions second. Depending on the treatment condition, the second speaker either agreed continually with the first ("same" condition) or expressed opinions that were a mixture of agreement and disagreement with the first subject ("variable" condition). Crosscutting this manipulation was a variable designed to manipulate the extent to which the second student on the taped interchange was dependent on the first. In some cases, the students on the tape were told that it was to their advantage to be compatible. It was explained that compatible pairs would have a chance to earn extra money in future sessions, and that compatibility would be determined by each peer's rating of the other (high-dependence condition). In other cases, the students on the taped interchange were told that they were in a first-impression situation and the emphasis was on forming an accurate impression of one another (low-dependence condition).

After listening to the opinion exchanges, the subjects were asked to predict how the first speaker would rate the second on a series of questionnaires. They were also asked to give their own rating of the second speaker. Regardless of rating set, the second speaker was rated as self-promotive and lacking in candor in the "same" high-dependence condition. The results also indicated that when dependence was high, subjects liked the "same" evaluator significantly less than the "variable" speaker. Interestingly, however, subjects thought that the first speaker would be more taken in by the agreeing tactics of the second speaker than they themselves were.

The second speaker was also rewarded with increased attraction for resisting the urge to use tactical conformity. The "variable" speaker was liked better in the high-dependence than in the low-dependence condition. The results are described by Figure 15.3, which agrees generally with the model otherwise. It would appear that there is an "extra credit" effect when a potential ingratiator clearly resists the temptation to conform plausibly and instead maintains his credibility.

Would these results replicate in a "live" setting where subjects are confronted with slavish or variable agreement? This question was explored in two experiments by Jones,

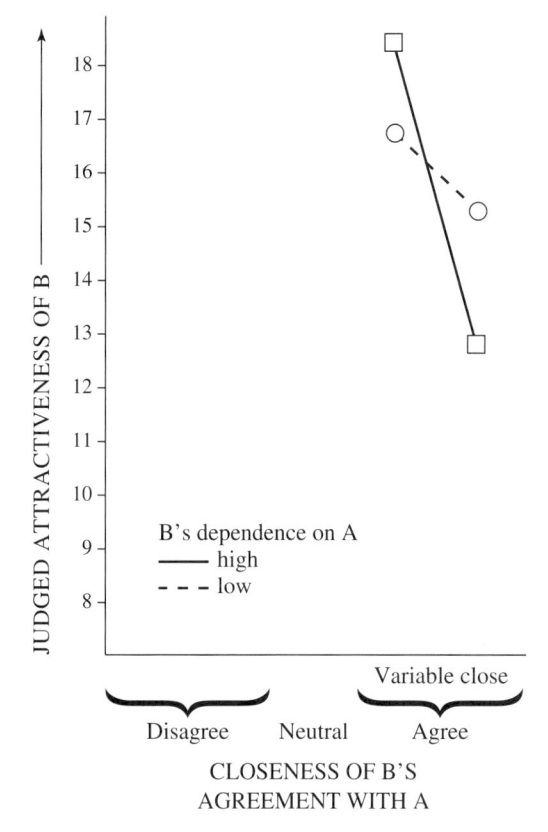

Chapter 15 Ingratiation: An Attributional Approach **315**

Figure 15.3 Personal Attractiveness Ratings as a Function of Experimental Conditions

Stires, Shaver, & Harris (1968). In the first experiment, female subjects were asked to discuss an opinion issue with another subject, who was actually a confederate of the experimenter. The confederate either came to agree with the subject or remained autonomous (but in no way disagreeably contrary) in her views. After the exchange of opinions, half of the subjects learned that the confederate had been urged to use various attraction-seeking maneuvers in her interaction with the subjects. The remaining subjects learned that the confederate had been instructed to be spontaneous. Subjects were asked to rate how much they liked the confederate.

In a second experiment, subjects were exposed to tape recordings representative of the sessions run in the first experiment. The subjects were asked to indicate how they thought the involved subjects would react to the confederate and how they themselves would rate her. In both experiments, the agreeing confederate was liked better when she had nothing to gain from the subject's approval than in the high-dependence condition. The autonomous confederate, on the other hand, again created an especially favorable [26] impression by retaining her own views in the face of incentives to be agreeable. Thus, the "extra credit effect" for not taking the conformity bait when dependence is high does replicate in a "live" setting.

If these findings are generally valid, what should the ingratiator do when the target person controls resources for the ingratiator and knows it? The results of the experiments by Dickoff (1961), Jones, Jones, & Gergen (1963), and Jones, Stires, Shave, & Harris (1968) do not suggest that the ingratiator should shun all ingratiation overtures when his dependence on the target person is obvious. In Dickoff's experiment, individuals who were extremely flattering when they had something to gain were still liked more than those who were neutral toward the subject under the circumstance. And in the Jones, Stires, Shaver, & Harris experiment, subjects liked the agreeable person just as well as the autonomous one when dependence was high. Only in the experiment by Jones, Jones, & Gergen did subjects actually react negatively to someone agreeing for tactical reasons. However, these subjects were mere bystanders to the interaction. Further, the agreement manifested by the subjects was quite extreme in nature: Taken as a whole, these experiments suggest that the individual should try to be a little less extreme and more subtle in his approach if his dependence on the target person is obvious. In fact, with a pinch of disagreement here and a dash of criticism there, the ingratiator may win favor precisely in those conditions where dependence is most obvious and extreme. This, again, is the "extra credit" principle.

It is clear, in conclusion, that the situation changes for an ingratiator when it is quite clear to both him and the target person that he has a lot to gain by making a good impression.

Status Differences and Their Implications

How does the problem of successful ingratiation for a low-status person compare with the same problem for a high-status individual? From our immediately prior reasoning we may extract the general hypothesis that low-status persons, vis-à-vis those higher in status, should confine their ingratiating maneuvers to more oblique and subtle tactics. If we consider the tactics presented earlier—other enhancement, conformity, favor-doing, and self-presentation—there are reasons why conformity might be a good choice for the typical subordinate. Conformity to the opinions of a superior stands a good chance of being effective because it is difficult to discriminate between conformity and genuine attitude similarity. Opinion agreement can bolster the validity of the superior's views without raising obvious questions about devious intentions. Moreover, the low-status person should avoid the appearance that he is changing, without resistance or intervening thought, from initial disagreement to agreement with the high-status superior. Other-enhancement and rendering favors are probably less likely to be effective because they are such obvious tactics for attempting to curry favor. Nor are tactics involving self-presentation likely to be helpful for the low-status person. If he presents himself favorably, the high-status person may conclude that he is trying to curry favor; furthermore, by engaging in a positive self-presentation, he may appear to the target person as though he were trying to usurp the latter's power. And a modest self-presentation is also unlikely to do him much good. Blau (1960, p. 550) has pointed out that if a person is not impressive to begin with, self-deprecation will probably tend to make him seem even less attractive.

The psychological position of a high-status person is quite different. When he makes an ingratiating overture, he doesn't have to worry too much about the low-status person suspecting his motives. However, he faces another problem in trying to enlist the liking and spontaneous loyalty of his subordinates. He must win the subordinate's support, which involves elements of affectional attraction, without undermining his own respectability and power. In surveying the tactics of ingratiation discussed previously, the tactic of conformity seems the least likely to succeed. In his interactions with his subordinates, the high-status leader must demonstrate his capacity to form independent judgments in areas where his experience and his role render him likely to be more competent than the subordinates. While the leader may seek out opinion issues on which he can safely agree with his subordinates, he has much to lose if his conformity is indiscriminate. Also, the leader who adopts the tactic of conformity will soon find that he cannot agree with all of his subordinates, unless they agree among themselves.

Concerning self-presentation, there are again problems that the high-status person must watch out for. As Blau (1960) has pointed out, the high-status person faces the problem of impressing others without causing them to lose their affection for him. The more impressive a person becomes, the more unapproachable he becomes, and the more difficult it is to initiate social interchanges with him. The high-status person must therefore find ways to demonstrate his approachability without, at the same time, destroying his impressiveness, or his follower's respect for him. As Blau implies, he can do this by presenting himself in a modest or self-deprecating [28] manner, but the self-deprecation cannot be indiscriminate. The high-status person must not deprecate himself on those characteristics central to his status. This would only undermine the subordinate's respect for him. He must demonstrate his approachability by acknowledging actual or alleged defects on nonsalient, unimportant attributes.

Whereas the dangers of conformity and self-presentation are obvious for high-status ingratiators, compliments and favors are likely to be effective tactics. After all, it is quite reasonable for the high-status person to assume the role of evaluator and to pass out compliments in the spirit of judicious judgment. Rendering favors is also compatible with the traditions of *noblesse oblige.*

Although there is no research evidence that bears directly on the problem of how people react to tactical overtures as a function of the ingratiator's status, a series of studies provides some support for our argument that a high-status person will be found more attractive if he makes himself more approachable. A study by Aronson, Willerman, and Floyd (1966) demonstrates that a high-status person will be found more attractive if he commits an embarrassing blunder or pratfall. These investigators were led to their study by attempting to understand why President Kennedy's popularity showed a sharp increase immediately after the Bay of Pigs fiasco, which was certainly one of history's great avoidable disasters. Why should people increase their liking for a president after he commits such a blunder? Aronson, Willerman, and Floyd reasoned that people may have regarded Kennedy as too perfect. He was a young and handsome president who was exceedingly wealthy, had a "perfect" wife and two adorable children, and came from a famous and close-knit family. They reasoned that some evidence of fallibility could have served to make him appear more human and, therefore, more likable.

In order to provide a test for their reasoning, Aronson, Willerman, and Floyd conducted an experiment in which they varied whether a stimulus person was high-status or low-status and whether he committed a blunder or not. Subjects were asked to listen to a tape recording containing an interview with a candidate for the College Quiz Bowl.

For half of the students, the interviewer was portrayed in such a manner that he seemed to be nearly perfect. He answered a series of difficult test questions with little trouble, and he revealed in response to personal questions that he had had a very distinguished career in high school. The remaining students listened to a different tape in which the stimulus person was portrayed as quite ordinary and average. He answered only a minority of the test questions correctly and revealed that his years in high school had been quite undistinguished. Near the end of the interview, half of the students in each condition heard the stimulus person commit an embarrassing blunder. Specifically, he clumsily spilled a cup of coffee all over himself. For the remaining subjects, the interview simply ended, and no blunder was committed.

The main dependent measure was how much the subject liked the stimulus person. The results revealed that subjects found the stimulus person most attractive when he was portrayed as a superior person who committed a blunder. The least attractive person was the one of average ability who committed a blunder.

A blunder may have served to make the superior person seem more approachable to the subject and may have increased his attractiveness for this reason. This suggests committing an embarrassing blunder might be a good ingratiation strategy if one is sure that others view him as superior. However, later studies (see, e.g., Helmreich, Aronson, & Lefan, 1970; Mettee & Wilkins, 1972) have suggested that this effect holds only when the target person (i.e., the subject perceiving the pratfall) is of average self-esteem, and other investigators have not been able to replicate the finding that a blunder makes a high-status individual more attractive. Therefore, it would be premature to recommend blundering as a tactic of high-status ingratiation, but the notion of approachability seems a very plausible one and deserves considerably more research.

We have suggested that the particular tactics that are likely to work best will probably be affected by the status of the ingratiator and the target person. Another factor that probably should govern the use of the ingratiation tactics is the sex of the parties involved. We will not present a detailed discussion of this topic, since it should be obvious that a tactic may convey one thing when directed toward a man and something altogether different when used on a woman. For example, continued eye contact or touching may increase attractiveness of one woman for another. A man who received these tactics from another man may regard him with some alarm, however.

THE NAIVE PSYCHOLOGY OF INGRATIATION—OR WHAT PEOPLE THINK WILL MAKE THEM MORE ATTRACTIVE TO OTHERS

In the previous sections, we described several tactics that might be successfully employed by the ingratiator. In discussing the probable success of these tactics, we cited experiments in which subjects were exposed to people employing them and were asked to indicate how much they liked these people. In this chapter, we will focus on a complementary question. When an individual is motivated to gain another's approval, what does he actually do? Does he flatter the other, agree with him, do favors for him? Does he become self-enhancing or self-deprecating? Does he ask the other for advice or reveal intimate secrets to him? Specifically, what kinds of tactics does he adopt in order to make himself more attractive? And, a more complicated question, how does the choice of tactics vary with the context of the social interaction?

Fortunately, several experiments that shed light on these questions have been conducted. Some of these studies have approached the problem by using role-playing instructions. Half of the subjects are told to try and make a good impression, and the remainder are told to present themselves accurately. This may be considered a rather direct "make the horse drink" approach, but there is no guarantee that it captures the essence of ingratiation, with all its subtleties, in the natural environment. Another problem is that the accuracy instructions do not necessarily create a control condition, since ruthless honesty may be exceptional in normal social intercourse.

Other experiments have, instead, maneuvered the horse in the general vicinity of water by varying the subject's dependence on the target person. Rather than simply instructing the subject to be attractive, this second procedure explores the antecedents of attraction-seeking behavior. The outcome of the more indirect (and more theoretically interesting) approach can then be compared with the behavior observed in the role-playing experiments.

Making the Horse Drink: Effects of Instructions to Ingratiate

The first experiment of the role-playing variety was conducted by Jones, Gergen, & Davis (1962). In their study, female subjects were told that they would be interviewed by graduate students in the practicum course for clinical psychology trainees. The subjects were then given instructions designed to provide a particular context, or set, for the interview. Half of the subjects were given instructions designed to create an accuracy set: "… Just be yourself. Present yourself to the interviewer as you actually see yourself and try not to overemphasize your good points or to play up your failings" (Jones, Gergen, & Davis 1962, p. 5). The remaining subjects were given instructions designed to create an ingratiation set: "Let us suppose that some foundation put up a large sum of money to finance traveling fellowships for a representative group of American college students. Students who qualify for the fellowships will be sent abroad for the summer.… Let's suppose further that the interviewers … will have a large say in whether or not you are considered qualified for one of the fellowships. In such a situation, it would naturally be to your advantage to say the kinds of things calculated to make the interviewer think highly of you. This is what I'd like you to do in the coming interview. Try to figure out what kind of a person the interviewer probably likes and then try to act like such a person … even though it does not accurately reflect the picture you have of yourself" (pp. 5–6).

During the interview that followed, the interviewer asked a series of preliminary questions and then proceeded to administer orally a triads test. Every subject was handed a stack of cards, each of which contained three self-descriptive phrases. One phrase was a very positive, self-accepting statement; one was slightly self-accepting or belittling; the final phrase was definitely self-derogating. The subject was to examine the phrases on each card and to indicate the one she considered most characteristic and least characteristic of herself. From the responses to the test, it was possible to obtain an estimate of the subject's tendency to present herself favorably or unfavorably. The results revealed that subjects in the ingratiation set were far more positive in their self-presentation than subjects in the accuracy set.

Similar results were obtained in an experiment by Gergen (1965). In his study, half of the subjects were instructed to present themselves accurately to an interviewer. The remaining subjects were told to try to make a favorable impression. The results closely parallel those obtained by Jones, Gergen, & Davis (1962). When told to make a favorable impression on the interviewer, the subjects responded to this task by exaggerating their strengths and minimizing their weaknesses.

These experiments suggest that when individuals are trying to impress another, they adopt a positive or self-enhancing self-presentation. Experiments by Gergen & Wishnov (1965) and Schneider & Eustis (1972) suggest that the degree of self-enhancement will depend on information they have about the target person's own self-presentational style. They propose that individuals will adopt a self-presentation similar to that of the target person when they are trying to create a good impression. Although Gergen & Wishnov did not vary whether subjects were motivated to be ingratiating, they exposed some subjects to a target person who was very positive about himself, some to [29] a target person who was slightly positive, and some to a target person who was quite negative in describing himself. Their results revealed that subjects tended to match the self-presentation of the target person to whom they were exposed. Subjects interacting with an egotistical other described themselves more positively, while subjects who were exposed to a self-deprecating partner described themselves more negatively.

Schneider & Eustis (1972) replicated and extended this experiment. In addition to target positiveness, these investigators manipulated how revealing a person the target person was. They also manipulated ingratiation motivation. Half of the subjects were instructed to "try to make as good an impression as you can upon your partner"; the remaining subjects were given no instructions about how to present themselves. Subjects were more positive to a positive partner than to a neutral one, and more self-revealing to a high-revealing partner than to a low-revealing one. These effects were statistically significant for subjects in the ingratiation condition, but were not significant for subjects in the control condition.

The experiments by Gergen & Wishnov and Schneider & Eustis suggest that when an individual is motivated to make a good impression on another, he will present himself similarly to the way that the target person presents himself. Schneider & Eustis suggest that the self-presentation of the target person provides useful information for the ingratiator about what is appropriate and permissible behavior in the situation. Of course, another possibility is that subjects "match" a person's behavior when they are trying to impress him, in order to demonstrate their similarity to him. Gergen & Wishnov have suggested a third possibility: that subjects become positive about themselves in the face of a positive other in order to maintain a position of power relative to the other. Perhaps future experiments can determine precisely what subjects hope to gain by engaging in this matching strategy.

These studies provide some insight into the effects on self-presentations of variations in the target person's self-descriptions. Experiment by Lefebvre (unpublished) and Rosenfeld (1966) have also varied the "instructional set" given to the subject and have investigated the subject's use of a variety of ingratiation tactics. In addition to self-presentation, Lefebvre examined the tendency of subjects to engage in other-enhancement, conformity, and smiling behavior. Rosenfeld examined the subjects' tendency to engage in a wide range of verbal and nonverbal behaviors when instructed to be ingratiating. Furthermore, both of these experiments varied the sex of the subjects to explore the possibility of systematic sex differences.

In the experiment by Lefebvre, each subject was told that he would be interviewed by a fellow student. In reality, the "fellow student" was an accomplice of the experimenter. The subject was informed that the interview would proceed according to a standardized sequence. This sequence was designed to provide opportunities for ingratiation via self-presentation, opinion conformity, other-enhancement, and the nonverbal behavior of smiling.

Lefebvre manipulated whether subjects operated under an "ingratiation" or "spontaneous" set. Subjects in the ingratiation condition were told to present themselves as attractively as possible, and to attempt to win over the other. Subjects in the spontaneous condition were told to act spontaneous and to present themselves as honestly, sincerely, and objectively as they possibly could. Lefebvre also manipulated the sex of the subject and the sex of the target person or accomplice.

To summarize the very complex results as briefly as possible, Lefebvre found that when subjects are instructed to be ingratiating, they present themselves more favorably, conform more, engage in other enhancement to a greater extent, and smile more than they do when they are trying to be natural or spontaneous. There is a hint from Lefebvre's results that women adopt modesty rather than self-enhancement when trying to impress other women. In general, ingratiation overtures seem to be more frequent in heterogeneous (male–female) than in homogeneous dyads.

In Rosenfeld's experiment (1966), subjects were scheduled in same-sex pairs, half of which were female and half of which were male. The member who arrived first (designated the "naive" member) was taken into an experimental room and told to wait for the other subject, who would be arriving shortly. When the second member (designated the "instructed" member) arrived, he or she was taken into a separate room and told that the study concerned behavior in social situations. The subject was further told that another subject was waiting in the next room and that he would be interacting with this subject in a few moments.

At this point, subjects were given instructions concerning their interaction with the other. Half of the instructed subjects (approval-seeking condition) were told to imagine that the other was a person to whom they were immediately attracted and that they wanted very much for this person to like them. They were told to act as they normally would if they wanted to gain the other's approval. The remaining subjects (approval-avoiding condition) were told to imagine that the other was a person whom they found personally [30] undesirable and unattractive. "Although you don't want to come right out and hurt his feelings, ... you want him to get the idea that you are not interested in becoming his friend." Subjects in both conditions were told that everything would be explained to the other subject at the end of the experiment.

After receiving these instructions from the experimenter, the "instructed" subject was taken into the room with the "naive" subject. Their conversation was recorded by trained observers who noted the frequency of smiles, positive and negative head nods, gesticulations, and such verbal behaviors as length of utterances, questions, etc. After five minutes, the experimenter entered and gave questionnaires to both subjects containing additional dependent measures.

The results (See Table 15.6) revealed that approval-seeking (AS) subjects emitted a significantly higher percentage of smiles and a significantly lower percentage of negative head nods than did approval-avoiding (AA) subjects. AS subjects were also found to gesticulate significantly more than AA subjects, but this difference was primarily attributable to female subjects; male AS subjects did not gesticulate more than male AA subjects. On the other hand, men tend to emit more head nods when they are seeking approval than when they are avoiding it, and yet there is little difference between conditions in the head nods emitted by women.

Analysis of the subjects' verbal behaviors revealed that AS subjects emitted significantly lengthier speeches and utterances than did AA subjects. The AS subjects also emitted significantly more recognitions (brief utterances that indicate attentiveness to the preceding statement, e.g., "really," "um-humm"). The author suggests that AA subjects generally tried to avoid approval by talking only in response to questions from their naive peers and keeping their answers short.

The author examined correlations between these verbal and nonverbal responses of the instructed subjects and the attraction ratings of the naive peer, who was asked to form an impression of the "instructed" subject immediately after their conversation. Interestingly, none of these correlations reached significance in the AS condition. In the AA condition, the number of recognitions was significantly related to attraction received from naive peers. Also, positive head nods were positively related to attraction

Table 15.6 Response of Instructed Subjects as a Function of Instructions and Sex[a]

	M				F score		
	AS		AA				
Response category	Male (N = 13)	Female (N = 13)	Male (N = 11)	Female (N = 9)	Instructions (I)	Sex (S)	I × S
Gestures (frequency)	42.9	54.9	27.0	17.7	7.4***	<1	1.2
% Smiles	28.8	28.6	17.7	24.9	5.0**	<1	2.0
% Positive head nods	28.9	20.5	15.6	24.0	1.5	<1	3.5*
% Negative head nods	6.3	7.0	18.6	11.9	8.0***	<1	<1
% Gesticulations	9.2	22.4	7.5	2.1	12.0***	<1	9.0***
% Self-manipulations	23.5	20.9	32.3	33.2	2.8	<1	<1
Speeches (frequency)	33.4	37.2	20.3	15.4	29.2***	<1	1.77
Mean length (utterances)	1.7	1.5	1.5	1.2	7.2**	5.4**	<1
Utterances (frequency)	53.9	57.4	30.4	19.7	37.6***	<1	1.6
Mean length (words)	6.5	6.5	5.9	4.7	8.5***	2.6	3.0*
% Questions	19.8	18.1	20.9	17.2	<1	<1	<1
% Answers	10.2	11.2	19.7	33.8	15.7***	3.3*	2.4
% Recognitions	13.5	17.0	9.4	9.8	6.0**	<1	<1
% Initiations	49.4	48.5	44.8	32.2	3.7*	<1	<1
Words (frequency)	349.5	379.9	188.4	107.7	25.6***	<1	1.6
% Self	6.9	8.1	8.8	9.5	3.5*	1.1	<1
% Other	3.4	3.5	3.8	2.1	<1	1.4	1.6
% 3rd person	3.8	4.4	2.7	2.9	2.0	<1	<1
% Speech disturbances	8.3	6.5	6.0	2.9	7.7***	5.5**	<1

[a] From Rosenfeld (1966).
*$p < 0.10$.
**$p < 0.05$.
***$p < 0.01$.

received, while self-manipulations (e.g., scratching) were negatively related to attraction. The author, surprised by the fact that these correlations were significant only in the AA conditions, suggests that "positive" social responses are likely to induce approving reactions from others either when performed unintentionally or when performed in a context of relative deprivation of positive responses. [31]

Rosenfeld obtained some interesting information concerning the "naive psychology" of the subjects by asking the "instructed" subjects to indicate what they had done to try to make a good impression or a poor impression on the other, and by asking the "naive" subjects what they liked and disliked about the instructed subjects. The categories of behavior that instructed AS subjects reported most often used to make a good impression were "act friendly," "ask questions," "converse freely," and "smile." The first two categories were about equally common for men and women, but the last two were listed almost entirely by women. The categories cited most often by AA subjects as used to avoid approval were "avoid or minimize participation in conversation," "criticize," "avoid visual contact," and "act conceited." Except for criticism, these categories were listed about twice as often by women as by men. Naive subjects reported that they most liked the other when he was friendly, interested, interesting, nice looking, intelligent, and had things in common with them. Friendliness and appearance were listed approximately twice as often by women as by men. Naive subjects reported that they most disliked the other's "unwillingness to carry on a conversation," "nervousness," and "presumptuousness."

STATUS DIFFERENCES IN TACTICAL USE Jones, Gergen, & Jones (1963) also conducted an experiment that varied the instructions given to the subjects. This study has a number of methodological weaknesses, most notably that the ingratiation condition was run one year and the accuracy condition was run the following year, and thus subjects were not assigned randomly to the two conditions. However, it will be discussed here since it is one of the few studies to focus on the different ways that high- and low-status persons respond to pressures to be ingratiating. We speculated earlier that low-status individuals have to worry more about suspicions of ulterior motivation from their target person and, therefore, may be better off using opinion conformity rather than other-enhancement, rendering favors, or self-presentation. We also mentioned the problem faced by high-status individuals of maintaining respect from their subordinates without becoming "unapproachable" and therefore unattractive.

In order to shed light on this problem, Jones, Gergen, & Jones varied both status and instructional set in their experiment. The subjects were freshmen and upperclassmen in a naval ROTC program. They were run in pairs comprising one freshman (low-status individual) and one upperclassman (high-status individual). During the experiment they were instructed to communicate by exchanging information about themselves. This exchange of information made it possible for the experimenters to determine the tendency of both high- and low-status individuals to engage in opinion conformity, self-presentation, and other-enhancement.

During the first year of the experiment, subjects were instructed that it was very important for them to be compatible and were asked to make a special effort to get the other to like them. During the second year, subjects were told that it was very important that they be accurate in exchanging information about themselves. One side of the exchange was actually controlled by the experimenter since subjects received standardized communications.

The results revealed that on the opinion measure both high- and low-status subjects conformed more in the ingratiation condition than in the control. High-status subjects conformed more on miscellaneous items than on items relevant to the status differential, apparently trying to show their approachability while maintaining their power position. Low-status subjects conformed more on the items relevant to the status differential than on miscellaneous items, apparently because they were concerned with deferring to the power differential while maintaining credibility. These results are portrayed in Figure 15.4. **[32]**

On a self-presentation segment of the "exchange," high-status subjects became more modest when under pressure to make themselves more attractive. Surprisingly, low-status subjects showed the same tendency on items rated as "important," but became more self-enhancing on the unimportant items (see Figure 15.5) The authors suggest that the low-status person may avoid describing himself favorably on important attributes so that he will not be viewed as a presumptive upstart, and he will not appear to be claiming leadership qualities in a way that would thereby threaten the leader's authority.

On a final segment permitting a measure of other enhancement, there was a tendency for low-status subjects to be more flattering in their appraisals of high-status subjects than the high-status subjects were or their low-status partners. Appraisals by both high- and low-status individuals were more favorable under ingratiation than under control conditions.

Finally, all subjects were told that their partner found them quite attractive, and subjects were then asked to indicate whether they thought their partner had manipulative intentions. Interestingly, high-status subjects in the ingratiation condition were distinctly more suspicious of the motives of their low-status partners than vice versa.

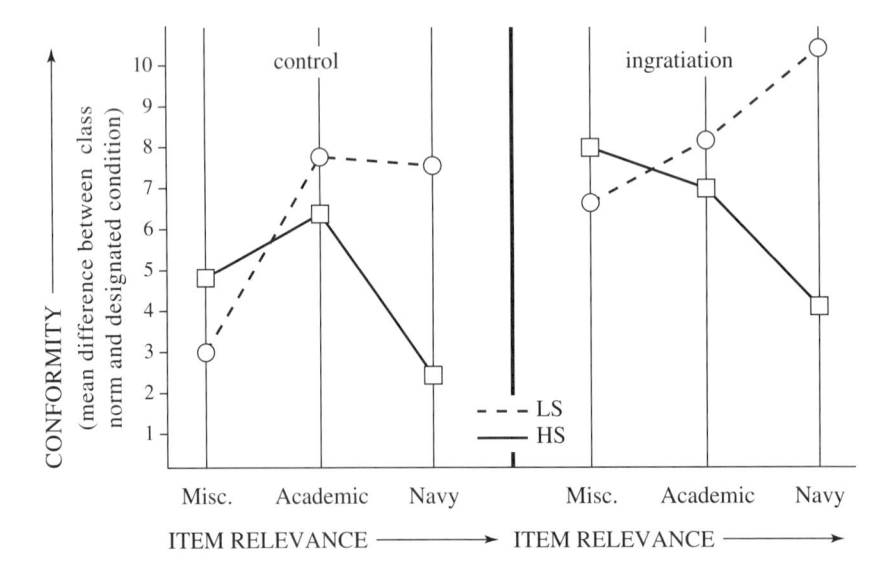

Figure 15.4 Conformity as a Function of Issue Relevance

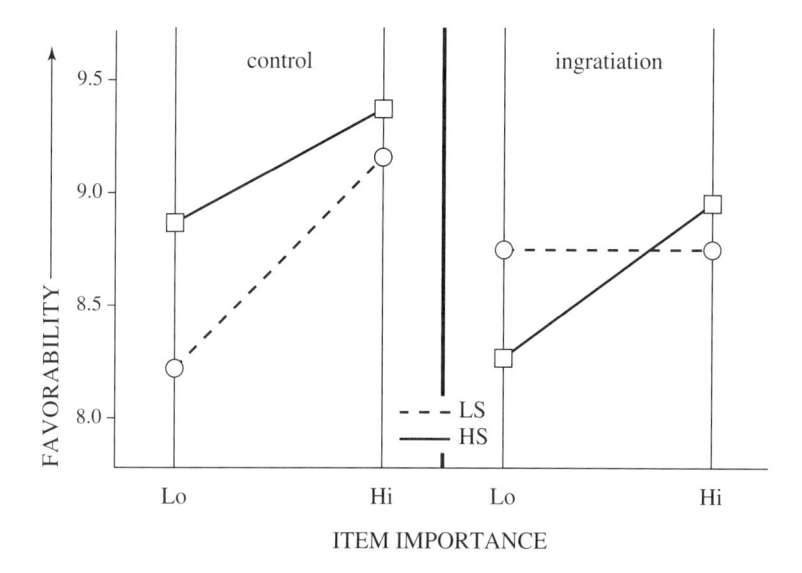

Figure 15.5 Favorability of Self-Presentation on Items Varying in Importance

Taken together, these results imply that low-status individuals cannot resist flattering their superiors, even though this is not an effective ingratiation tactic.

Leading the Horse Near Water: Variations in Dependence

The experiments that we have discussed so far in this chapter attempted to study ingratiation by instructing some subjects to be ingratiating and comparing their behavior with subjects instructed to be accurate. R. G. Jones & E. E. Jones (1964), Jones, Gergen, Gumpert, & Thibaut (1965), and Stires & Jones (1969) used a different approach in investigating this topic. Instead of telling some subjects to be compatible or to make themselves attractive, these studies manipulated whether the subjects had anything to gain by being ingratiating. Half of the subjects were placed in a dependent situation where it was clearly to their advantage to make themselves attractive to a target person. Their behavior was compared to that of subjects whose outcomes were not controlled by the target person and who therefore had little ulterior reason to impress him. Furthermore, these studies contained conditions in which the subject was led to believe that the target person was aware of his power over them. Such awareness on the part of the target person presumably makes the ingratiator's task more difficult, invoking the "ingratiator's dilemma." This is in marked contrast to the situation facing subjects in the studies described earlier. Subjects in these studies had to decide how to cope with the task of creating a positive impression. However, except in the Jones, Gergen, & Jones ROTC study (1963), they were led to believe that the target person was unaware that they had received instructions to manage an impression.

In the experiment by Jones and Jones (1964), male subjects were instructed to exchange opinion ballots with a target person. Each opinion statement was printed twice with a 12-point scale, ranging from agreement to disagreement under each printing. The situation was set up so that the target person always expressed his opinion on the first scale. For each item, the subject was asked to express his opinion on the second scale. He was also asked to indicate his confidence that his opinion was correct, with the understanding that both his opinion and confidence rating would then be returned to the target person.

In reality, the opinions of the target person were programmed by the experimenter to create the various experimental conditions. The subjects had previously recorded their opinions in a "neutral" classroom setting, so it was possible to arrange the incoming opinion [33] ratings to coincide with the subject's prior ratings on every item (same treatment) or to be systematically different from them (discrepant treatment). If the subject were to hold to his originally stated opinions, then he would present himself as behaviorally conforming in the same condition and as distinctly independent in the discrepant condition.

Jones and Jones reasoned that the subject in the same condition would find himself in a dilemma if his dependence on the target person were obvious—that is, if it were important to win the target person's approval, and the latter were clearly aware of his power in this respect. Under the circumstances, the same subject could not remain true to his opinions without appearing to conform for ulterior purposes. Since this would spoil his chances of creating a positive impression, or at least put his chances in jeopardy, the dependent-same subject, by modifying his initial opinions, should attempt to avoid the appearance of overconformity.

Subjects in the discrepant treatment should be in an entirely different psychological position, and variation in the subject's dependence on the target person should have quite the opposite effect from that expected in the same treatment. Jones and Jones reasoned that the more important it was to create a positive impression, the more the discrepant subject would attempt to reduce the discrepancy between his opinions and the target person's by conforming to the target person's views to some degree.

Jones and Jones manipulated dependence by setting the stage for half of the subjects in such a way that it was to their best interest to create a positive impression, while instructing the remaining subjects to strive for accuracy in expressing their opinions. Subjects arrived at the lab in groups of five and were informed that the purpose of the experiment was to study productivity in groups. Students in the high-dependence condition were told that one of them would be randomly selected to be the supervisor on an anticipated task and that the supervisor would assign the remaining subjects to a number of jobs. The anticipated task was to involve the preparation of advertising copy. It was explained that prior to this task, the supervisor would exchange opinions with the other workers, and would be asked to form an impression of them on the basis of their opinions. Subjects were told that the person judged to be most attractive by the supervisor would be assigned the job of production manager and the one judged least attractive would be the worker; the other two would be copywriters. Subjects were led to expect that following these assignments, all of them would work on the advertising copy task for 30 minutes. There were, therefore, two good reasons for each subject to secure the supervisor's approval—he would receive a more interesting job, and everyone would know that the supervisor had rated him highly. Subjects in the low-dependence treatment were told that one of them would be randomly selected to make some evaluations of the rest of them and that these evaluations would be based on opinion exchanges. The importance of providing accurate opinions to the person making the evaluations was stressed.

In summary, Jones and Jones put subjects in a situation in which they had to indicate their opinion after seeing the opinion of the target person. For half of the subjects, the target person expressed the same opinion that they had expressed earlier in the semester. For the remaining subjects, the target person expressed opinions that were very different from their own. Half of the subjects were led to believe that it would be in their best interest to impress the target person; the remaining subjects were instructed to be very accurate in conveying their opinions to the target person. In addition to these experimental groups, some control groups were run to determine whether the subjects' opinions were stable over time. If the majority of subjects had changed their opinions from those they endorsed at the group session preceding the experiment, then those in the same condition would not feel that their private opinions had been preempted by the target person.

Unfortunately, the data from the control groups did suggest that subjects' opinions were relatively unstable over time. The results showed that the dependence variation produced quite different results in the same versus the discrepant condition. In the discrepant condition, subjects in the high-dependence cell conformed to the target person's views significantly more than subjects in the low-dependence cell. However, contrary to the hypothesis that some subjects would move away from their prior position (and thus away from conformity), subjects in the same condition stuck fairly close to their prior opinions. Although there was significantly more conformity in the high-dependence discrepant condition than in the comparable same condition, this probably reflects largely the fact that the former subjects had more room for the movement in the target person's direction.

The Jones and Jones study was primarily concerned with the potential dilemma facing subjects in the high-dependence same condition. As originally planned, the dilemma was to emerge out of competing pressures to be true to one's own opinions while avoiding the appearance of slavish conformity. Because of the instability of the subjects' opinion ratings, and the resulting [34] fact that their opinion during the experimental session was not really preempted by repeating their previously recorded ratings, there is serious question that such a dilemma was, in fact, created. However, there is some indication that subjects in the high-dependence same condition faced a more benign dilemma: how to gain the target person's attraction by conforming without appearing to conform for manipulative purposes. Interestingly, subjects in the high-dependence same condition expressed more confidence in their opinions than did subjects in all other treatments combined. Furthermore, as Table 15.7 shows, only in the high-dependence

Table 15.7 Relations between Opinion Conformity and Confidence[a]

	High dependence	Low dependence
Same	.671	−.213
Discrepant	.076	−.149

[a]From Jones and Jones (1964).

same condition was there a high correlation between conformity and the amount of confidence expressed. A plausible interpretation of this correlation is that subjects who think they may have agreed too much can attempt through high confidence rating to convince the target person of their autonomy in the agreement process. Those who are concerned that they may have disagreed too much can soften the impact of this disagreement by their lack of expressed self-confidence.

THE ROLE OF OPENNESS TO INFLUENCE The degree of conformity shown by a dependent subject may also depend on his estimate of the subjective probability of successful ingratiation. This, in turn, will depend on the personality of the target person, and the value he places on congeniality and agreement. This hypothesis was investigated by Jones, Gergen, Gumpert, & Thibaut (1965). The experiment was an attempt to show that ingratiation will occur in a work setting when (a) the worker feels that it will be difficult to gain high outcomes through effortful performance, (b) the supervisor has some freedom to develop and modify his standards of performance evaluation, and (c) the supervisor places a value on group solidarity and "getting along" well with others. The design was a 2 × 2 factorial in which both the target person's openness to influence and his personal values were varied.

The experimental procedures involved rather elaborate stage setting, and each subject was exposed to a complicated sequence of events. Fifty male volunteers appeared for the experiment in pairs and were introduced to an experimental accomplice identified as a graduate student in the School of Business Administration. The subjects were informed that they were to be players in a game designed to simulate the features of a real business concern. The graduate student was to serve as the supervisor in the game. He was to evaluate the performance of the two subjects and to give or take away points accordingly.

The experimenter then explained that the period would be divided into three parts. First there was to be a practice session in which the subjects would learn how the game was played. Then there was to be a "get-acquainted" session in which the subjects and the supervisor would get to know each other a little better as persons. Finally, a game consisting of several business problems was to be played for points. Although the final game was continually referred to as the climax of the experiment, the task toward which everything else was to lead, it was not actually played.

First, the supervisor's openness to influence was manipulated. Half of the workers (open condition) were told that the supervisor would be free to decide, after each problem, whether a solution was correct. The remaining workers (closed condition) were led to believe that the supervisor was committed to a series of problem solutions that he had worked out in advance. After the open or closed variation had been included, the supervisor was taken to an adjoining room to finish looking over his materials.

The subjects were then taken to individual booths and exposed, in turn, to a practice game, information about the supervisor's values, and the get-acquainted session. By prearranged performance feedback on the practice game, each subject was led to expect that he would do poorly in the actual game and that the other subject would do well. Subjects were expected to conclude from the practice game that it would be difficult for them to gain good outcomes through effortful task participation alone.

Next, each subject listened over earphones to an (actually tape-recorded) interview of the supervisor by the experimenter. The purpose of exposing subjects to this interview was to manipulate their impression of the supervisor's values with respect to leadership in business and industry. Half of the subjects heard the supervisor emphasize the "human side" of business: the importance of morale, getting along with others, cooperation, and mutual supportiveness. In view of the emphasis [35] on solidarity, the supervisor in this condition is hereafter referred to as Sol. The remaining subjects were exposed to interview responses in which the supervisor stressed the quality and quantity of job performance above all else. In view of his emphasis on productivity, the supervisor in this condition is hereafter referred to as Prod.

Each subject then engaged in a "get-acquainted session," actually a pseudo-interaction with the supervisor designed to provide opportunities for ingratiation. The subject completed a self-rating questionnaire to be transmitted to the supervisor, a shortened version of an opinion questionnaire he had completed earlier in the semester, and finally, he rated the supervisor on the same questionnaire form used for the self-ratings. As he confronted the task of recording his opinions, each subject was exposed to ratings on the same opinions allegedly made by the supervisor. These incoming opinion messages had been predoctored by the experimenter so that the ratings agreed with the subject's preexperimental opinions on some items, but disagreed rather markedly on others. (The pattern of agreement and disagreement was constant from subject to subject.)

The major hypothesis of the business game study concerned the interactive impact of both independent variables on the degree to which subjects would conform to the supervisor's opinions. Specifically, it was predicted that subjects in the open judgment conditions would conform more to Sol and less to Prod than would subjects in the closed conditions. As detailed above, conditions for estimating the degree of conformity were established by having the supervisor appear to transmit his own ratings, some of which were systematically discrepant from the earlier expressed opinions of the subject. The subject was instructed to respond to each of the supervisor's opinions with his own.

One way of measuring the degree of conformity was to sum the ultimate discrepancies between the supervisor's and the subject's opinion ratings. Disregarding the magnitude of this change on any given item, a score of one was assigned for each rating falling between the prerating and two points beyond the supervisor's rating; all other items were simply assigned a zero. The decision to include movement slightly beyond the supervisor's rating seemed psychologically reasonable and was an a priori decision. The choice of two points beyond, rather than one or three, was arbitrary. The means of this "movement index" are presented in Table 15.8.

It is clear that the major prediction was nicely confirmed. Looking first at the closed condition, it is apparent that Prod stimulates greater agreement than Sol when there is no reason for the subject to be ingratiating. This may be attributable to any of a variety of factors (including chance, since the

Table 15.8 Opinion Conformity: Measure of Movement toward Supervisor[a]

	Judgment context[b]	
	Open	Closed
Solidarity	8.9	6.9
Productivity	6.7	7.6

[a]Adapted from Jones, Gergen, Gumpert, & Thibaut (1965).

[b]The higher the score, the greater the incidence of movement toward the supervisor. For each subject, each of the 20 discrepant items was assigned a score of +1 for movement toward the supervisor and a zero otherwise.

difference is not statistically significant). A plausible explanation is that Prod exerts more informational influence, more expertise and therefore the subjects show greater agreement with his stands. Under the open-to-influence condition, however, the pattern shifts dramatically. If anything, subjects confronting Prod conform *less* when they are motivated to increase their attractiveness, whereas subjects confronting Sol show substantially greater conformity.

Measures of self-presentation and other-enhancement were also obtained, but the results on these measures were not so clear-cut. In describing themselves on traits reflecting either personal competence or affability and approachability, subjects did emphasize the competence traits in the open-to-influence conditions (relative to the affability traits). No differences at all emerged on the other-enhancement ratings, and it is likely that the complex experimental inductions had lost their potency by the time these ratings took place.

The main importance of the study is the evidence it provides that subjects are very sensitive to contextual factors in expressing their opinions to a target person. Only under conditions where the target person is potentially open to influence, and only when he appears susceptible because of his value orientation does ingratiating conformity occur.

THE ROLE OF AWARENESS OF DEPENDENCE The experiments by Jones & Jones (1964) and by Jones, Gergen, Gumpert, & Thibaut (1965) made it clear to subjects in the high-dependence condition that the target person was aware of his power over them. In both studies subjects engaged in a variety of subtle strategies in order to avoid the appearance of slavish conformity. An experiment by Stires & Jones (1969) actually manipulated whether the target person was aware that the subject had something to gain by winning his approval. Using self-presentation as the main dependent variable, these investigators predicted that a [36] would-be ingratiator, when interacting with a target person who is unaware of his power over desired resources, will adopt a strategy of self-enhancement. An ingratiator who knows that his target is aware of his dependence, on the other hand, will adopt a more complicated strategy and will tend to be self-enhancing in some and modest in other aspects of his self-presentation.

Male subjects arrived at the laboratory in groups of four and were introduced to a male experimenter and a confederate who again posed as a graduate student in business administration. The experimenter explained that the study dealt with the performance of work groups. He told them that the experiment would require an additional session and that they would participate in a work group in that session. Subjects were led to believe that each group would consist of two workers and a supervisor, the confederate being assigned the latter role. They were told that one of the workers would be performing a very attractive job, while the other would perform a dull and monotonous job. The experimenter explained how the assignment to these jobs would be made, and his explanation varied according to the experimental condition. There were three experimental treatments. In the dependence–supervisor-aware condition, subjects were led to believe that the supervisor would assign the workers to the two jobs on the basis of their self-presentation. It was emphasized that the supervisor was aware that his decision would determine job assignment. In the dependence–supervisor-unaware condition, subjects were told that the supervisor would make the assignments, but that he would not be aware that his opinions actually determined job assignment. He was to think that these assignments were determined by the flip of a coin, "in order to avoid potential embarrassment." In the no-dependence (control) condition, subjects were told that job assignments would be made by flipping a coin.

At this point, the experimenter administered a self-presentation form to the subjects and told them that this form would be given to the supervisor. This form consisted of 25 antonym pairs. About half concerned task competence and half described socially relevant personal qualities. Crosscutting this division was a further distinction between items that are reputational, or best gauged by the consensus of others (e.g., "popular"), and those which could be indicative of an intention on the part of the subject (e.g., "friendly"). Subjects were also asked to rate themselves on the trait "modest–arrogant." After rating themselves on these items, they were asked to indicate their degree of confidence in their ratings. Changes in self-presentation were determined by comparing each subject's response on this self-presentation form to one he had filled out at a prior group testing session.

The results: Dependent subjects with an unaware supervisor were found to be significantly more self-enhancing than nondependent (control) subjects. Subjects in the dependence–supervisor-aware condition tended to be less self-enhancing than those in the unaware condition and more self-enhancing than those in the control condition, but these comparisons did not reach significance.

A more refined analysis in terms of type of scale item showed that it made a difference whether the subjects were rating themselves on items describing task competence or socially relevant personal qualities (see Table 15.9). Subjects in both of the dependence conditions were more self-enhancing than control subjects on the competence items. There was no comparable difference on the personal items. However, dependent subjects with an unaware supervisor were found to be significantly more self-enhancing on reputational–personal [37] items than either of the other two groups. Subjects in

Table 15.9 Change in Self-Presentation as a Function of Dependence and Awareness of It[a]

	Item type[b]			
	Competence		Personal qualities	
	Reputational	Intentional	Reputational	Intentional
Dependent, supervisor aware	0.87	0.98	0.34	0.59
Dependent, supervisor unaware	0.77	0.91	0.93	0.68
Control (not dependent)	0.35	0.31	0.39	0.60

[a]Adapted from Jones, Gergen, Gumpert, & Thibaut (1965).
[b]The higher the score, the greater the incidence of movement toward the supervisor. For each subject, each of the 20 discrepant items was assigned a score of +1 for movement toward the supervisor and a zero otherwise.

the dependence–aware condition were about as modest as control subjects on these items. These results suggest that when subjects confront a target person who is aware of his power over them, they are reluctant to claim positive attributes like "popular," "interesting," and "well-informed"—traits that are usually subject to verification by peer judgment.

There is some evidence that subjects with an aware supervisor used rather subtle strategies to enhance the credibility of their ratings. Subjects in this condition who described themselves most favorably did not also claim undue modesty. In addition, subjects who described themselves favorably expressed relatively high confidence in their ratings. Within the high-dependence–aware condition, the negative correlation between modesty and self-enhancement and the positive correlation between confidence and self-enhancement are in marked contrast to those obtained in the high-dependence–unaware and the control conditions.

A SUMMARY OVERVIEW   What have we learned from the preceding experiments about the kinds of tactics individuals employ when they are trying to make themselves more attractive? Either in response to leading instructions or rigged dependence conditions, subjects will resort to self-enhancing ratings, opinion conformity, other-enhancement, smiling behavior, and doubtless many other strategies that are designed to elicit approval. We seem to be on the right track in identifying these forms of strategic behavior, but we are far from understanding the precise conditions under which certain tactics are favored over others. There is some evidence that the target person's awareness of his potential power affects the patterning of ingratiation attempts. When the target person is in a position to be aware of his power, the ingratiator tends to be more cautious and subtle in his self-presentational claims. We suspect, from our understanding of the ingratiator's dilemma, that such subtlety would also show up in opinion conformity and public appraisals of the other's characteristics.

We have also presented preliminary evidence concerning the roles of social status, sex, and the personal values of the target person in making and shaping ingratiation. Low-status subjects have a credibility problem and tend to handle the ingratiator's dilemma by asserting their independence on trivial or irrelevant opinions while conforming on important issues. High-status subjects show the opposite pattern in their attempt to maintain their status while advertising their approachability. The sex variable has been examined in connection with nonverbal behavior and the results are inconclusive at best. Lefebvre reports that smiling is not used by males when they are trying to gain the approval of other males, but no such sex differences are suggested by Rosenfeld's results. Clearly more systematic study of sex differences in tactical preference is called for.

As for the target person's revealed values, we have reported several studies that emphasize the importance of this variable. Subjects conform more to a target person who obviously appreciates congeniality and social support. Subjects also attempt to utilize information about the target person's self-presentation to bring their own presentations into line. We would expect that there are many other ways to bring about variations in tactical behavior by varying information about the target person.

In order to determine which of these many sources of variation are worth pursuing, we need to develop a clearer picture of the dynamics of ingratiation—its cognitive and motivational basis. Thus far, we have a taxonomy without a theory. We now turn to examine, at the more general level of concepts, the theoretical determinants of ingratiation.

COGNITIVE AND MOTIVATIONAL DETERMINANTS OF INGRATIATION

To the extent that ingratiation may be distinguished from other forms of socially responsive behavior, it becomes pertinent to attempt a systematic analysis of the circumstances giving rise to this attraction-oriented cluster of responses. When does a person make a special effort to be agreeable, complimentary, or personally appealing in an effort to gain attraction? In this section, we will describe three sets of factors that are likely to affect the use of ingratiating strategies: incentive-based determinants, the ingratiator's subjective probability of success, and the perceived legitimacy of engaging in tactics to curry favor.

Incentive-Based Determinants

Ingratiation is motivated behavior directed toward the goal of eliciting increased attraction from a particular person. There are several reasons why an individual may seek attraction. First, attraction implies something about his worth as a person. If others like him, for whatever reason, there must be something there to like. Second, by making himself attractive, an individual may increase his chances of obtaining a specific goal, such as a raise, a promotion, or an invitation [38] to club membership. Or he may reduce his chances of receiving a negative outcome, such as a cut in pay or a demotion. In any case, the incentive value of ingratiation should be a function of the following variables: (a) the importance or value of the goal to the ingratiator and (b) the perceived uniqueness of the target person as a source of the benefit desired.

INCENTIVE MAGNITUDE Turning first to the importance of the benefit to the ingratiator, we can specify a number of conditions that enhance the value of attraction or approval. Some of the conditions are undoubtedly dispositional; because of his personal motivational structure or self-concept, each person brings into his social situations a need to be loved, approved, or admired. One can imagine some of the individual differences that might correlate with such a disposition: stability of self-esteem, need for affiliation, fear of rejection or failure.

In addition to dispositional factors, there are obviously situational conditions that increase or decrease the importance of social approval. Some of these are simply the transient or momentary replicas of the dispositional variables discussed above. For example, an individual who has just been criticized or belittled in a convincing way may have his need for positive feedback aroused because of his momentary lowered self-esteem. One can imagine the value of approval fluctuating, then, as a function of success and failure experiences in the immediate past.

Some support for this expectation comes from experiments by Walster (1965), Jacobs, Berscheid, & Walster (1971), and Schneider (1969). Schneider's experiment is especially relevant to our current concerns. Its purpose was to determine whether varying subjects' feelings of competence affected their tactical self-presentation.

Schneider argued that a person who has just failed on an important task, and therefore has a temporarily lowered estimate of his abilities, will want to obtain approval from others in order to reestablish a more positive self-evaluation. He suggests that for this reason, failure leads individuals to be self-enhancing to others who are in a position to provide feedback. In contrast to subjects who have recently failed, subjects who have recently succeeded will be primarily motivated to avoid disapproval. They will therefore adopt rather conservative tactics of self-presentation because, by presenting a moderate self, they will give an evaluator little reason to act negatively. In this way, successful subjects can hope to protect their recently gained positive self-evaluation.

Male subjects entered the laboratory individually and were given one form of a self-presentation test. They were then told that the experiment concerned social sensitivity, and a social sensitivity test was administered to them. Depending on the experimental condition, subjects were told that they had succeeded on this test, that they had failed, or they were not told how well they did. Then subjects were interviewed by a "trained' interviewer who was to assess their social sensitivity from a different perspective. The interviewer administered a questionnaire that was another form of the self-presentation test the subjects had taken at the beginning of the session. Subjects in the feedback condition were told that the interviewer would discuss his evaluation of their social sensitivity with them. Subjects in the no-feedback condition were told that it would not be possible for the interviewer to discuss his evaluation with them.

As expected, subjects who had failed were more positive about themselves under the feedback condition than under no feedback, and the successful subjects were marginally more modest under the feedback than under no feedback. In further support of his reasoning, Schneider found that the subjects who had failed tended to emphasize positive points about themselves, while the control and successful subjects de-emphasized negative points.

UNIQUENESS OF THE TARGET PERSON In addition to the importance of the goal desired, the uniqueness of the target person as a source of this goal is likely to be an important factor governing the incentive to be ingratiating. A person may have powerful needs for approval, but a certain target person may be only one of many individuals who can satisfy this need. It may be stated as a testable proposition that the strength of the motive to be ingratiating to a particular person varies inversely with the number and saliency of other persons who can also produce the benefit the ingratiator desires.

Uniqueness is likely to be of special importance in cases where the ingratiator's goal is to evoke signs of worthiness. In this case, such factors as the target person's role, his level of information about the ingratiator, and the nature of their relationship may be critical. A person may not place much value on approval from just anybody, but may be especially interested in signs of approval from his son, his analyst, or his employer. In general, we would expect individuals to be more impressed by approval from those who have more information about them, since such approval would seem to imply more about a person's basic worth.

In line with this reasoning, we would expect approval from an individual who is a casual acquaintance to have less significance than the approval of a close friend. However, Aronson (1969) has considered the matter from another perspective and makes just **[39]** the opposite prediction. Aronson argues that once we have become certain of the good will of a person such as a spouse or a good friend, that person may become less potent as a source of reward than a stranger. He maintains that since we have grown accustomed to positive feedback from such people, their behavior does not provide any gain in interpersonal attraction. Pointing to the results of the previously discussed study by Aronson & Linder (1965), he maintains that a gain in esteem is likely to have a greater influence on an individual than continual positive evaluation. He uses the following example to clarify his point "... After ten years of marriage, a doting husband and his wife are leaving their house for a cocktail party. He compliments her on her appearance—'Gee, honey, you look great.' Her response might well be a yawn. She already knows that her husband thinks she's attractive.... Mr. and Mrs. Doting arrive at the cocktail party, and a total stranger engages Mrs. Doting in conversation. After a while he says, with great sincerity, that he finds her very attractive. My guess is that she would not find this boring. It represents a distinct gain, makes her feel good, and increases the attractiveness of the stranger" (Aronson, 1969, p. 168).

This principle is generally referred to as Aronson's Law of Marital Infidelity and raises some interesting speculations for future research. It is certainly possible that the relationship between acquaintance duration and the impact of approval is a very complex one. It may, for example, be curvilinear. Some knowledge about the person being evaluated seems essential for the evaluation to be taken seriously by the target person. At more advanced levels of acquaintanceship, however, complimentary remarks from a moderately knowledgeable acquaintance may mean more than remarks from a highly knowledgeable one.

Another consideration related to the uniqueness of the source of the benefit desired is the possibility that the ingratiator may produce this benefit himself. Can the ingratiator accomplish his goal through his own direct efforts? If so, what cost is likely to be incurred by the target person in producing the desired outcome? If a person's goal is approval to gain certification of his worth, it is clear that he is in a poor position to provide these goals for himself. But he can obtain many other kinds of benefits on his own effort and initiate. For example, a student may strive mightily to excel through endless hours of effort and application, or he may scan his assignments and try to ingratiate himself with the graduate student grader. The study by Kipnis & Vanderveer (1971) discussed earlier compared a supervisor's response to a superior performer with his response to an average performer who made an ingratiating comment. The supervisor tended to give both workers higher performance evaluations than a third worker who was average in output but did not attempt to ingratiate himself. The study provides an instance, then, of the potential trade-off of task performance and ingratiation. Under some conditions, at least, the successful ingratiator need not work quite as hard for the same performance evaluation as the worker who eschews attraction-seeking strategies.

Subjective Probability of Success

The incentive value of the ingratiator's goal and the uniqueness of the target person as a source of this goal are necessary but not sufficient determinants of ingratiation. Unless other conditions are favorable, even the most extreme dependence on approval responses from others will not initiate attraction-seeking tactics. One important class of conditions is the set of variables associated with the ingratiator's subjective probability that the tactic he employs will succeed in eliciting attraction from the target person. What factors are likely to affect his assessment of his chances for successful ingratiation?

One thing that an ingratiator will probably keep in mind in estimating his chances for success is how much the target person will like or value the ingratiation tactic. He may ask himself whether the strategies available to him are ones that the target person would appreciate. In the Jones, Gergen, Gumpert, & Thibaut experiment (1965) discussed in the preceding section, the results indicated quite clearly that conformity only occurred when the target person was presented as someone likely to appreciate it. Aside from variations in the target person's values, the target person's momentary need for what the ingratiator has to offer must be considered. If the target person is essentially satiated with approval, if he has such strongly supported beliefs that agreement by one more person is incidental, or if he has such vast resources that gifts would be superfluous, it is unlikely that the range of tactics available to most of us would be very effective.

A related consideration is whether the conditions are such that the target person is apt to be especially appreciative of, or vulnerable to, the tactics that the ingratiator may employ. For example, in the case where the tactic being considered is other-enhancement, the vanity or conceit of the target person may be important. Perceived conceit or vanity in the target person should raise the ingratiator's subjective probability that ingratiation will succeed. Of course, it may well be that a vain person is not any more receptive to flattery than a modest one, or one who is uncertain [40] of his positive attributes. But as long as the ingratiator thinks that the target person will be more susceptible, he will be more likely to engage in flattery.

Another factor that is relevant to calculations of success probability is the salience of the benefit desired in the target person's response hierarchy. There are cases where a person is favorably disposed toward another but remains unaware of the benefit that the other really desires. The wife who abundantly demonstrates her love for her husband, but never mentions her respect for his professional skill, may be a case in point. Another example might be the son who wants more time with his father, but instead succeeds by his suppliant overtures only in securing increases in his allowance. If a person knows that the benefit he desires is not likely to be present in the target person's response hierarchy, then he should be less likely to engage in ingratiating overtures. Of course, he may be able to exert some influence on the salience of the target person's responses by evoking relevant imagery, or in other ways subtly arranging the proper situational props. For example, the son cited above may develop skills and interests similar to his father's so that spending time with him becomes a naturally salient alternative to his father. Of course, increasing the salience of the benefit one desires must be done with finesse and subtlety. We would be very surprised to overhear such a statement as, "I have been agreeing with your comments lately because I would like you to ask me to go sailing with you on your new yawl," except, of course, in jest.

A second set of factors that may affect the ingratiator's subjective estimate of success is his assessment of the target person's personality. There is some evidence from the research literature that ingratiation attempts are more likely to be made to some personality types than to others. Kaufman & Steiner (1968) found that individuals engaged in tactical conformity less if they had information that the target person was high-authoritarian than if he was portrayed as a low-authoritarian. The authors suggest that subjects may have felt the high-authoritarians were too rigid or moralistic to be easy targets for ingratiation, but it may simply be that the particular sample of subjects was less receptive to authoritarian ideology and unwilling to move in that direction. Schneider & Eustis (1972) found that individuals were more self-enhancing when interacting with a high-revealing target person than when interacting with a target person who did not have a tendency to reveal personal information about himself. They suggest that high-revealing targets may be perceived as more gullible, receptive, or in need of friendship than low-revealing targets, and that subjects may feel that they can get away with saying positive things about themselves to such a target.

The ingratiator's subjective probability of success is also likely to be affected by his control over situational resources that are relevant to his interaction with the target person. If the ingratiator can manipulate the time, place, and social context of his interaction with the target person, his chances for successful ingratiation are likely to be improved. For one thing, the more the situation allows for communicative subtlety on his part, the better his chances should be for winning the target person's approval. If the situation governing their interaction confines communication to one or two channels, successful ingratiation is likely to be more difficult. For example, if the only time that a new executive sees his supervisor is in a board meeting, it may be hard for him to engineer ingratiating overtures. Many types of comments and responses are inappropriate in such a setting. But if the rising executive can arrange a more informal meeting (say, over coffee or lunch), his chances may improve. In this type of situation, he can explore mutual interests and common experiences and express his opinions in a highly differentiated, and therefore credible, way.

There is another reason why it helps if the ingratiator has control over the situational resources. If he then has a chance to maneuver the target person into settings where the salience of the benefit he desires is low, his chances of successful ingratiation are likely to improve. The prevalent belief that customers, buyers, or prospects can be more successfully influenced over cocktails, or in noncommercial social gatherings, seems to bear testimony to this argument.

Furthermore, if the ingratiator has control over situational resources, he can try to arrange his overtures so that they occur in pleasant surroundings. A recent experiment by Griffit & Veitch (1971) examined the effects of temperature and population density on interpersonal attraction, and found that individuals were less attracted to a stranger when they were exposed to him under crowded than under low-density conditions. Subjects also tended to respond with less attraction for the stranger if the experiment was conducted in a warm room (93.5 degrees Fahrenheit) as opposed to a comfortable room. It is not clear from this study *why* individuals respond less positively to others under uncomfortable conditions. Perhaps these conditions put them in a bad mood, and then they mistakenly attribute their negative feelings to the person with whom they are interacting.

One final factor that is likely to affect the ingratiator's subjective probability of success has already been mentioned several times: whether it is clear to the target [41] person that the ingratiator has something to gain by impressing him. The probability of success may seem low if the ingratiator thinks the target person will be suspicious of his overtures. And, in fact, the target person will probably react negatively if he thinks the ingratiator is trying to curry favor. The transparent flatterer does not end up where he started when his blandishments fail; he loses ground and suffers from the attempt.

As noted earlier, this creates a dilemma for the potential ingratiator. The situation in which he has the most to gain by successful ingratiation is also the one in which he has the most to lose, should the attempt backfire. What can we predict, then, about the occurrence of ingratiation when the target person is aware of his power over the ingratiator? Kaufman & Steiner (1968) focused on this problem and argued that the probability of payoff will seem low to the ingratiator, in two very different kinds of situations when the ingratiator perceives the target person as unwilling or unable to provide the desired reward to those who elicit his attraction (low salience of ingratiation), or when the ingratiator perceives the situation to be one in which opportunity and incentive to employ ingratiation techniques are so obvious to the target person that he will recognize any attempts that occur, and react negatively (high salience of ingratiation). They predicted, and found, that the occurrence of ingratiation is highest when the salience of ingratiation is moderate.

They manipulated three variables that they expected to influence the salience of ingratiation as a technique of obtaining valued payoffs: the Machiavellianism of the ingratiator (his dispositional tendency to endorse Machiavellian sentiments), the perceived power of the target person to control the ingratiator's resources, and the discrepancy between the attitudes of the ingratiator and the target person. The results were generally as predicted. Subjects engaged in ingratiating conformity least when all three variables were set at high levels. Conformity was low also when all three variables were at low levels. As anticipated, greater conformity occurred when one or two of the variables were set at high levels. Subjects in the very high salience group actually conformed less than did a group of control subjects who were asked their opinions after seeing those of the target person, but who did not expect the target person to see their opinions. This suggests that subjects under very high salience conditions may be reluctant to reveal even genuine agreements that a target person may construe as evidence of ingratiation.

Perceived Legitimacy

We have defined ingratiation as an illicit attempt to win favor and, more loosely, as an illegitimate member of the social exchange family. The decision to indulge in strategic other-enhancement, conformity, or artful self-presentation is, then, a decision hedged by ethical constraints. To the extent that the individual can convince himself that tactical maneuvering is morally justifiable and ethically legitimate, we should expect him to indulge more readily in effect-oriented maneuvers. For this reason, perceived legitimacy is put forth as a third major determinant of ingratiation.

Many generations of scholars and commentators have grappled with the ethics of hypocrisy, dissimulation, and flattery. A brief survey of references to flattery in such compendia as Stevenson's *Home Book of Quotations* and Bartlett's *Familiar Quotations* will reveal many comments that vehemently excoriate the flatterer. But most of the quotations mix righteous indictment of the flatterer with liberal criticism of those who succumb to the compliments of others:

> He that rewards flattery begs it. Thomas Fuller, *Gnomologa*. No. 2269.

> He that loves to be flattered is worthy o' the flatterer.
> Shakespeare, *Timon of Athens,* Act. I, Sc. 1, 1.232.

Every flatterer lives at the expense of the person who listens to him.
La Fontaine, *Fables,* i, 2.

Especially in Lord Chesterfield's "Letters," one finds flattery justified by the vanity, and therefore the gullibility, of the target person. Chesterfield walks a delicate tightrope in advising his son:

> Do not mistake me, and think that I mean to recommend to you abject and criminal flatteries: no; flatter nobody's vices or crimes; on the contrary, abhor and discourage them. But ... if a man has a mind to be thought wiser, and a woman handsomer than they really are, their error is a comfortable one to themselves, and an innocent one with regard to other people; and I would rather make them my friends, by indulging them than my enemies, by endeavoring ... to undeceive them (1901, I. p. 25).

In contemporary American society, the ethics of ingratiation are no less complicated and ambiguous. While it would be difficult to find a clear endorsement of insincere and manipulative social behavior in statements of the moral arbiters of our times, there is a vast gray area of moral ambiguity within which Dale Carnegie and others like him have been able to operate. The great success of *How to Win Friends and Influence People* (Carnegie, 1940) may itself say something about the American penchant for treating personality as a marketable commodity. In any event, the essence of Carnegie's confrontation of the ethics of deliberate impression management is that the right hand does not quite know what the left hand is doing. In a chapter entitled "How to Make People Like You Instantly," Carnegie expresses fury at the implication [42] that he would compliment someone because he was trying to get something out of him: "Great God Almighty!!!" If we are so contemptibly selfish that we can't radiate a little happiness and pass on a bit of honest appreciation without trying to screw something out of the other person in return—if our souls are no bigger than sour crab apples, we shall meet with the failure we so richly deserve" (p. 99). And yet the remainder of the chapter consists of a sequence of anecdotes in which the complimenter clearly gains material or social advantage from the target person, and this is the obvious message of the stories. Along these same lines, an interesting and delightfully circular maxim appears in an earlier book by Webb and Morgan (1930) entitled *Strategy in Handling People:* "Personal charm arises chiefly from a feeling of deep and sincere interest in other people and a genuine liking for them. By acquiring the habit of success in dealing with people, you strengthen your interest in them and with it your power to charm them" (p. 158).

In general, what are some of the ways that individuals handle the ethical dilemma of employing ingratiation tactics for their own personal gain? One way of solving this problem is for the ingratiator to convince himself that the statements he is making are true. If he has engaged in other-enhancement, he can try to convince himself that the person really deserves the compliments he has given. If he has engaged in a flattering self-presentation, he can come to view his statements as accurate reflections on his characteristics and traits. Studies by Jones, Gergen, & Davis (1962), Upshaw & Yates (1968), and Schneider (unpublished) suggest that subjects do adopt this strategy, at least when the ingratiation attempt is crowned with success. In the study by Jones,

Gergen, & Davis, for example, half of the subjects were instructed to distort their self-presentation in order to gain the approval of the target person. The remaining subjects were instructed to present themselves accurately. Crosscutting this variable, half of the subjects later found that they had made an unfavorable, half a favorable impression. Subjects who received a positive evaluation from the target person indicated that their self-presentation had been more accurate than subjects who received a negative evaluation, even when they obviously had distorted their self-picture in order to win this approval.

A second way of dealing with the ethical dilemma posed by ingratiation is for a person to admit that his statement or behavior does not reflect his true feelings, but to attribute this to benign, rather than manipulative or self-seeking, motives. Especially when he engages in other-enhancement, he may convince himself that he was "only trying to be nice," or that he "didn't want to hurt the person's feelings." It is even possible to stretch this rationalization to cover a kind of self–fulfilling prophecy: "If I tell this person that he is really good, this will bolster his self-confidence and he will actually become good." Contemporary social psychology is quite receptive to the idea that people will perform better and therefore be happier when their self-esteem has been bolstered by others. This is, in part, the message of Rosenthal's & Jacobson's *Pygmalion in the Classroom* (1968), the report of a study in which children, who were (randomly) identified to their teachers as superior, actually ended up with better test scores. The notion of compliments resulting in good behavior is implied also by Aronson & Mettee's study (1968). They gave arbitrary feedback to subjects concerning their personalities and found that those who received negative evaluations were more inclined to cheat in a subsequent card game. The implied strategy is even recommended by *The Sensuous Woman,* who suggests: "Praise his sexual prowess. Even great lovers need to have their talents reaffirmed, and your man is not immune to being told how terrific he is. Your admiration will probably spur him on to even greater sexual heights, and there's nothing wrong with that!" Garrity, 1969, p. 150).

While it is very reassuring to believe that being nice to people actually increases their effectiveness and their pleasure, one needs to give serious consideration to whether it is always nice to compliment someone when the compliment is actually undeserved. In many performance evaluation situations, an undeserved compliment may leave the performer with a temporary warm glow of success, but it also may mislead him in the long run about the reach of his abilities and coax him into performance settings where he is bound to fail. The recipient of undeserved compliments about intellectual power may, to take one example, apply for a college or graduate program where he would be clearly overmatched. This is obviously an area in which more research is needed because important practical consequences are involved.

A third way of handling the ethical dilemma is for a person to admit that he has engaged in ingratiation, but that under the circumstances, his behavior was morally justifiable. There are a number of ways that he may look at the situation in order to make such behavior seem less "immoral." One possible way of justifying his behavior is to compare it with the behavior of others. If an individual can convince himself that others in his reference group are also engaging in ingratiation strategies, then his own behavior is unlikely to seem unethical to him. For example, a college man may feel a slight twinge of guilt because he flattered a young lady in order to increase his chances

[43] of "making out" with her. But if he notices that all of his male friends also engage in these tactics, his moral misgivings may be conveniently muted.

An individual can also view ingratiation as legitimate if he comes to perceive the target person as a natural enemy who does not deserve equitable treatment. This may occur especially in those social settings where the ingratiator feels that the target person has unfairly obtained a position of power relative to his own position. A decade or so ago, prior to effective civil rights litigation and the use of black power, it is fair to say that relationships between southern whites and blacks were suffused with ingratiation. Uncle Tomism may not have been the heroic ideal, but it was widely tolerated by southern blacks as a way of getting along.

Another factor that may affect perceived legitimacy is whether an individual's interaction with, and relationship to, the target person is a voluntary one. If a young man is drafted into the army and finds himself confronted with a nasty drill sergeant, he may view any means of "survival" as legitimate. Furthermore, the individual in this situation who succeeds in improving his power position, by whatever nefarious strategies, is often applauded and admired by his peers. Sergeant Bilko was primarily a figure of triumphant dazzling manipulative skill. The script rarely took him to task for the immorality of his ingrating exploits with officers as target persons.

An additional factor that may affect perceived legitimacy may develop out of an understanding of the plight of extreme dependence. While ingratiation directed toward improving one's position is generally frowned upon in our culture, we may at least be prone to tolerate tactical overtures when the ingratiator has been dealt a severe blow by fate. From the ingratiator's point of view, the fact that he finds himself in desperate need of resources, through no fault of his own, may promote the convenient rationalization that ingratiating maneuvers are justified. In this case, the ingratiator may perceive that ingratiation may be indulged in without implications for the self-image.

Before we terminate our discussion of perceived legitimacy, we should at least mention an additional factor that may be important: individual differences in personality. It is quite conceivable that some individuals may adopt a cynical view of human nature, allowing them to operate within a wider area of legitimacy than those with a less misanthropic view. Over a period of several years, Christie has been concerned with the measurement of individual differences in cynicism or misanthropy. Although his work with the Mach Scale (a measure based on the endorsement of Machiavellian sentiments and described more fully in Christie & Geis [1970]), confirms that this personality distinction is a meaningful one, there is as yet no clear evidence that it is related to frequency or duration of ingratiation overtures. Jones, Gergen, & Davis (1962), for example, found no clear evidence that high scorers on the Mach Scale were more inclined than low scorers to adapt their self-presentations for the purpose of gaining approval.

In summary, then, we have suggested that a person's decision to engage in ingratiation will depend on three factors: the incentive value of the benefit desired, the person's subjective estimate of his chances for success, and the perceived legitimacy of the behavior. How these three factors combine is, unfortunately, far from clear. It might be argued that the combination is multiplicative since, if any factor is zero, ingratiation will presumably not occur. Intuitively, it may turn out that perceived legitimacy is more a dichotomous variable than either incentive value or subjective probability. Moral decisions tend to have an either–or quality about them. This would suggest that incentive value and subjective probability combine multiplicatively to produce a strong or weak tendency to ingratiate. Legitimacy then plays its role as a threshold factor, providing a go or stop signal for the behavior once the tendency to ingratiate reaches a certain strength. Thus, a person may flatter or ingratiate even though he knows this behavior is illegitimate, once the importance and the likelihood of obtaining a benefit reach a certain combined value.

EFFECTS OF INGRATIATION OVERTURES

Now that we have described the tactics of ingratiation and enumerated some of the factors governing their use, it is time to consider some of the effects that ingratiating statements are likely to have. We will first consider their probable effect on the target person. We will then speculate on some of the ways that these tactics affect the ingratiator himself. Finally, we will conclude with a brief discussion of how ingratiation overtures affect the nature of the interaction between the ingratiator and the target person and the quality of interpersonal relationships, in general.

Effects on the Target Person

The target person is bound to be affected, to some extent, by the praise, agreement, or favors that he receives from the ingratiator. It should go without saying that how these statements affect the target person will depend on his attributions of motivation. We have already enumerated the factors that are likely to affect these attributions, and there is no need to repeat them [44] here. If the target person takes the ingratiator's comments at face value, these comments may have a profound effect on his view of reality. Comments from others may strongly influence our views on such issues as politics, religion, and morals. And, of course, comments from others are likely to be especially important in determining how we view ourselves. In order for us to make the wisest decisions about our future, we must have an accurate estimation of our abilities and traits. But since it is difficult for the average person to tell how handsome, how creative, or how popular he is, he is likely to be strongly influenced by others' estimation of him.

If the statements made by the ingratiator have some basis in fact, they are likely to be quite helpful to the target person in formulating ideas about reality. But if the ingratiator has designed his statements primarily to further his own image, and thereby makes statements to the target person that depart from his private beliefs, the target person's attempts at valid appraisals of reality will certainly be threatened. The ingratiator's compliments may lead the target person to draw inaccurate inferences about himself, and the ingratiator's agreement on opinion issues may lead him to draw ill-founded conclusions about the world.

If the target person is in a position of power, there are additional reasons why the feedback he receives from the social environment may be ambiguous. Thibaut and Riecken (1955) have pointed to an affliction of tyrannical governments that takes the form of mistrusting the citizens' motives for compliance. Since the reasons for loyalty are ambiguous when a person has the power to enforce obedience, he has poor devices for detecting the spontaneous quality of compliance. This leads to a vicious circle in which mistrust of the genuineness of loyalty leads to increased surveillance, which leads to increased ambiguity of feedback and further mistrust. Strickland (1955) has shown the validity of this reasoning in a simple supervisory setting in which initial performance monitoring leads to continued monitoring because of the absence of developed trust.

We have referred several times to the awareness variable and emphasized the contribution of awareness of the dependence relationship to the ingratiator's dilemma. We now recognize the other side of this dilemma—the fact that the more powerful target person cannot easily assess the reliability of the information he receives from others. He does not know whether dependent others *really* admire him and share his beliefs. Is the agreeable feedback he is apt to receive, in other words, directed to his position or his person? In some settings, the target person's informational dilemma can be partly solved by the use of trusted listeners, informants, and suggestion boxes. In the more ubiquitous informal settings of social influence, however, the target person is at the mercy of his readings of those subtle cues suggesting the credibility of the potential ingratiator.

Effect of Ingratiating Overtures on the Ingratiator

How will the ingratiator himself ultimately be affected by his attempts to curry favor? There are a number of possibilities. Saying positive things about himself might lead him to change his self-view. Saying positive things about others, and doing favors for them, might lead him to view them more positively. And expressing conforming opinions may have some influence on his private opinions and beliefs.

We will first consider some of the ways that engaging in ingratiation strategies may affect a person's self-view. First, a person may say positive things about himself in order to impress others, and then come to believe these self-enhancing statements he has made. Of course, it is important to understand what leads an individual's behavior to be assimilated to his self-concept. One important set of conditions is suggested by Festinger's theory (1957) of cognitive dissonance. This theory suggests that the more compelling the justification for ingratiating behavior, the less this behavior will affect subsequent attitudes toward the self. Factors that may affect the justification have been mentioned in the preceding section—the value of the benefit desired, the likelihood of successful ingratiation, and the perceived legitimacy of trying to curry favor. Thus, if an individual has a number of good reasons for making self-enhancing statements, he will attribute his behavior to these reasons. For example, suppose an individual says positive things about himself to his boss. He may clearly realize that he said these things in order to get the boss to like him because this particular boss only promotes his friends. But if he makes these self-enhancing statements when there is little possibility for pay-off or success, or when he feels there are ethical problems in doing so, he is likely to change his private attitudes and come to believe the positive things be said about himself.

An individual's self-enhancing statements may also affect his self-view if others respond favorably to his self-enhancing claims. They may either respond positively, indicating how much they like him or how impressed they are with his virtues, or they may respond by agreeing with him. It seems reasonable that if others respond favorably to our self-enhancing [45] claims, we should come to view ourselves more positively.

VARIATIONS IN THE SIGNIFYING VALUE OF ATTRACTION   However, there is a certain dilemma facing the individual who extols his virtues in order to receive praise. We have said that a person may attempt to create a positive impression so that the signs of approval may be taken as evidence of his worth as a person. The paradox is that the greater the ingratiator's efforts to elicit attraction, the less the signifying value of the attraction response. Attraction should be relevant to our basic worth only when we have not unduly distorted our characteristics in the attraction-winning attempt.

This reasoning suggests that the more an individual has tried to impress the target person, the less impact the target person's approval should have on the ingratiator's self-concept. Some interesting evidence bearing on this proposition comes from the experiments by Jones, Gergen, & Davis (1962) and Gergen (1965) cited earlier.

In the study by Jones, Gergen, & Davis, it will be recalled, female subjects described themselves under ingratiation or accuracy instructions, and learned that they had created a positive or a negative impression. Subjects who were seeking approval described themselves much more favorably on the triads test than subjects instructed to present themselves accurately. Furthermore, the subjects rated the approving source much more highly than the disapproving source. Of more interest to the present discussion, however, is the finding that subjects who received positive feedback reported their self-presentation to be more accurate than those who received negative feedback. This was even true when the subjects had distorted their characteristics in order to get the feedback. In fact, subjects in the accuracy–disapproval condition reported slightly lower accuracy of self-presentation than the subjects in the ingratiation–approval condition. When individuals receive approval from another, they seem to forget the fact that they have dissimulated in order to get it, and come to believe that their self-enhancing statements were accurate.

In Gergen's experiment (1965), female subjects were also instructed either to present themselves accurately, or to make a positive impression on the interviewer. Half were told that the interviewer had been instructed to be as natural and spontaneous as possible (personal condition); the remaining subjects were told that the interviewer would merely be practicing interview techniques, and that she would not even be able to see the subject during the interview (impersonal condition). The subjects were given a series of triads during the interview, and were asked to distribute ten points among the three statements in each triad, according to how characteristic each phrase was of them. Throughout her self-presentation on the triads tests, the interviewer reinforced the subject (saying "Yes,' or "Very good," or "I agree") for saying positive things about herself. For comparison, a group of control subjects were interviewed under neutral or nonreinforcing conditions, the interviewer remaining impassive throughout.

After the interview was completed and the interviewer left, the experimenter administered another group of triads. Their purpose was to examine effects of generalization— to determine whether subjects would continue to be positive about themselves with the reinforcement stopped. Following this, subjects were asked to fill out a standard test of self-esteem. It was expected to provide a more remote test of generalization than the triads. Both of these measures provided an opportunity to examine temporary changes in the self-concept that might occur as a result of the self-presentation and the feedback.

As would be expected, and as noted in a previous section, subjects who were reinforced by the interviewer became more favorable in their self-presentation during their interview. Figure 15.6 presents the average difference by experimental conditions between each subject's level of evaluation in a "neutral" classroom situation and his level of evaluation on the same items during the experiment. The vertical axis therefore represents the degree to which the subjects assigned more points to the positive statements of

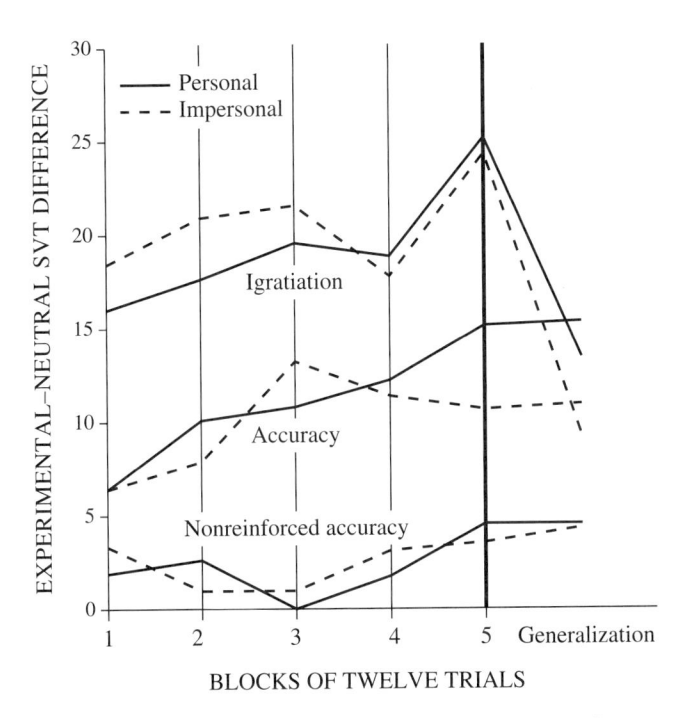

[Figure 15.6: Mean SVT Experimental–Neutral Difference Scores across Blocks of Trials for All Conditions. Y-axis: EXPERIMENTAL–NEUTRAL SVT DIFFERENCE (0 to 30). X-axis: BLOCKS OF TWELVE TRIALS (1–5, Generalization). Lines labeled Personal (solid) and Impersonal (dashed) for conditions: Igratiation, Accuracy, Nonreinforced accuracy.]

Figure 15.6 Mean SVT Experimental–Neutral Difference Scores across Blocks of Trials for All Conditions

each triad in the experimental than in the classroom situation. As can be seen, subjects in the ingratiation condition started out assigning more positive points to themselves, and continued to do so throughout the interview. This finding serves to replicate the finding of Jones, Gergen, & Davis (1962) that individuals respond to instructions to create a positive impression by exaggerating their strengths and minimizing their weaknesses.

However, even subjects in the accuracy-reinforced condition were more positive about themselves in the experimental than in the classroom situation. Subjects in the reinforced accuracy conditions were significantly more self-enhancing than control subjects who were not reinforced. As Figure 15.6 shows, all of the nonreinforced subjects were operating under accuracy instructions. There was no comparable control for subjects in the ingratiation condition.

Is there any evidence that the public self-enhancement produced by the reinforcing interviewer has an impact on the average subject's private self-assessment? [46] Figure 15.6 shows that there were striking differences in the generalization value of reinforcement as a function of prior instructional set. Subjects in the ingratiation conditions showed a sharp decline in the favorability of self-description when asked to respond to a final block of triads after the interviewer had left. Subjects in the accuracy conditions, on the other hand, maintained the positive level of self-appraisal that their responses had reached by the end of the interview. The loss in favorability of self-evaluation from the fifth learning block to the generalization block was, as predicted, significantly greater in the ingratiation conditions than in the control conditions.

However, there is another way of viewing Figure 15.6 and considering the effects of generalization. This is to ignore the actual amount of decrease from the end of the interview and to concentrate instead on the "generalization gain" as measured against the baseline of the response to these items in the prior classroom setting. Here it emerges that subjects in the ingratiation conditions ended up with roughly the same enhanced view of themselves as did those in the accuracy conditions. And the results of the self-esteem scale revealed that subjects in the ingratiation conditions, like those in the accuracy-reinforced conditions, ended up viewing themselves more positively after the reinforcing interview. The results suggest, then, that the ultimate result of being reinforced for saying positive things about oneself was roughly the same in both accuracy and ingratiation conditions. This implies that an individual will enhance his self-esteem upon receiving positive feedback from others, even if he has distorted his self-picture in order to get this positive feedback.

THE (MUTED) ROLE OF PERSONALISM So far we have not said anything about the personalism variable included in this study, but an examination of Figure 15.6 reveals that its effect was less than overwhelming. Gergen (1965) predicted that reinforcement from the personal interviewer would be more effective in influencing the subject's self-image than reinforcement from the impersonal interviewer, and that this would be revealed by self-presentational changes during the interview and greater subsequent generalization effects. However, analysis of the data revealed no clearly significant difference as a function of the personalism variable. What could be responsible for this negative result?

In the personal condition, every effort was made to emphasize the spontaneity of the interview, and to make the subject feel that the interviewer was responding to her as an individual. In contrast, subjects in the impersonal condition were told that the interviewer would merely be practicing interviewing techniques when she responded to the subject. Subjects in the personal condition were introduced to the interviewer, and the interviewer remained in the room while the experimenter asked several questions about their background, and instructed them to recount an incident that made them feel proud or embarrassed. In contrast, subjects in the impersonal condition never met the interviewer or revealed any personal information to her. Furthermore, the interview was conducted with the subject and the interviewer separated by a one-way mirror. It was carefully explained to the subject that, whereas she could see the interviewer, the interviewer was not able to see her.

Given the confines of a laboratory situation, it is hard to imagine a more extreme variation in the interpersonal context in which reinforcement is delivered. In the impersonal condition, obvious pains were taken to deprive the reinforcement of its signification value and make it difficult for the subject to conclude that she, personally, was found attractive by the interviewer. On the postexperimental questionnaire, subjects were asked to indicate to what extent the interviewer was acting naturally and spontaneously, and to what extent she seemed bound to a set of rules governing her behavior during the interview. Subjects' answers to these questions revealed that the two interviewer roles were perceived as intended. And yet, a striking thing [47] about the self-presentation results summarized in Figure 15.6 is the similarity of the findings in the comparable personal and impersonal conditions.

Subjects were also asked to predict the interviewer's true feeling about them on a number of traits. The mean score in the ingratiation impersonal condition is significantly lower than the ingratiation personal condition and almost significantly lower than the accuracy impersonal mean. Apparently, the combination of instructions to ingratiate, and the emphasis on impersonality of approving feedback, does inhibit the tendency to assume that the approving remarks reflect a genuinely positive appraisal. Signs of approval are apparently accepted at face value when these particular conditions do not exist in combination. The person who is trying to get approval considers the approval genuine if it is delivered in a personal context, and the person who is trying to be accurate with others considers the approval genuine regardless of strong evidence that it may be perfunctory and based on specified role requirements.

REINFORCING SELF-ENHANCEMENT Both the experiments by Jones, Gergen, & Davis (1962) and Gergen (1965) suggest, then, that individuals take positive feedback from others quite seriously, and do not correct sufficiently for their strategies for obtaining it. At this point, it might be a good idea to consider the nature of the feedback that a person is likely to receive after making self-enhancing statements to another. There would seem to be two reasons why the feedback a person gets after self-enhancement may be inaccurate. First of all, well-established norms of politeness or face-work (Goffman, 1955) govern the way we respond to people when they extol their virtues to us. If an individual tells us how superior he is on a variety of dimensions, we may not express vigorous assent, but at the very least, we will refrain from anything approaching a challenge. Most likely, we will unthinkingly nod our agreement, and this type of "reinforcing" response is likely to occur even if our true reaction to the ingratiator is quite negative.

In addition to norms of politeness, there is another reason why we might respond positively even though we are not really impressed—we may be trying to ingratiate the ingratiator! We may agree publicly with people's self-enhancing statements in order to win their affection or approval, even though we don't really believe these statements. These two factors may lead the self-enhancing ingratiator to develop a false picture of himself, since he seems to interpret such "reinforcement" as genuine, and modify his self-concept alter receiving it.

We have suggested that ingratiation attempts may alter a person's self-concept because he will tend to believe at least some of the positive things he has said about himself, especially when his remarks are reinforced by the target person. Another condition under which ingratiation may affect the self-concept has been suggested by Upshaw and Yates (1968). These authors point out that, in general, an individual's self-esteem will increase if he is successful at a task that he has undertaken. They suggest, therefore, that if a person makes an effort to receive a positive impression from another and then finds out that he has been successful, his self-esteem should increase. They argue that feelings of task success may explain the results of Jones, Gergen, & Davis (1962) and Gergen (1965). In order to test their reasoning, they conducted the following experiment. Subjects entered the lab in groups. The experimenter described a new and unusually reliable and valid personality test to the subjects. He told them the purpose of the experiment was to see whether this test was sensitive to deliberate misrepresentation by a person trying to create a false impression.

The test used in this study was the Edwards Social Desirability Scale. Half of the subjects were instructed to fill out this test so as to create the best possible impression. The remaining subjects were told to fill it out so as to create the worst possible impression. Subjects' responses were then presumably sent to a computer, which analyzed the subjects' personality and printed out a diagnosis. Half of the subjects received a personal evaluation that was favorable; the remaining subjects an unfavorable evaluation. After reading the computer's statements about them, subjects were asked to evaluate the extent to which the test had succeeded in detecting their true personalities despite their attempts at impression management. Subjects were also asked to complete a second form of the personality test, this time responding as accurately as possible. This form was used to detect effects of impression management and feedback on self-esteem.

Consistent with the results obtained by Jones, Gergen, & Davis (1962), subjects rated the favorable feedback as more accurate than the unfavorable feedback. However, the groups receiving positive feedback were not significantly more positive about themselves, on the final personality test than subjects receiving negative feedback. As Upshaw and Yates expected, subjects were more positive in their self-ratings when they tried to be positive and received positive feedback, and when they tried to be negative and received negative feedback.

Since subjects did not increase their self-evaluation [48] after receiving positive feedback, these results are inconsistent with those obtained by Gergen (1965). What factors may account for this discrepancy? Some suggestions have been made in a recent paper by Schneider (unpublished). As noted previously, Lipshaw & Yates used the Edwards Social Desirability Scale to measure subjects' self-presentations. As Schneider points out, subjects trying to create a favorable impression marked an average of 18 out of 19 possible socially desirable items, while those in the unfavorable impression condition marked only 3 in the socially desirable direction. Schneider concluded that subjects in the Upshaw & Yates experiment seem to have presented themselves more extremely than subjects in other ingratiation experiments. He suggests that this factor may account for the difference between the results obtained by Upshaw & Yates and those of Gergen. The self-ratings may have been more extreme in the Upshaw & Yates study because there was no real social risk involved in dealing with a computer rather than a flesh-and-blood target person.

According to Schneider, a person may accept reinforcement as genuine only when his self-presentation remains relatively credible. As his self-presentation becomes more extreme, it may be more difficult for an individual to believe that the reinforcement he has received reflects his positive characteristics. In order to test this reasoning, Schneider conducted an experiment in which positivity of self-evaluation, extremity of self-presentation, and positivity of feedback received were varied. Female subjects were told that they would be interviewed. Half of the subjects were told to try to obtain a positive self-presentation from the interviewer; the remaining subjects were instructed to get a negative evaluation. Crosscutting this variable was a manipulation of extremity of self-presentation. Subjects in the moderate condition were told to merely exaggerate a little bit and were told that they either could give themselves the benefit of the doubt (positive condition), or that they should be a little bit more self-critical than normal (negative condition). Girls in the extreme conditions were told to lie about themselves all they wanted. They were specifically told to be quite extreme in their presentations.

During the interview, the interviewer read a series of self-presentation items to the subject, and she indicated the extent to which each one applied to her. Following the interview, the interviewer evaluated each subject. Half were led to believe that they had made a good impression on the interviewer. The remaining subjects were told that the interviewer had a negative impression of them. After reading this evaluation, the subject was met by the experimenter, who administered a number of questionnaires; these included some self-evaluation scales and a questionnaire designed to tap their feelings about the interviewer.

The results generally supported Schneider's reasoning. He predicted that the moderate and extreme self-presentation subjects would react differently to the feedback, and this appears to be the case. Subjects in the moderate conditions were more positive about themselves after approval than disapproval. Thus, their responses were quite similar to those made by subjects in Gergen's experiment (1965). For subjects who had presented themselves in an extreme fashion, the only significant effect was an interaction between positivity of the presentation and evaluation. The results in this condition were similar to those obtained by Upshaw & Yates (1968). Subjects' self-evaluations were most positive when the feedback they received was consistent with the evaluation they were trying to get. When asked to indicate how accurate they had been in portraying themselves, subjects who were asked to be positive reported that they were more accurate than subjects asked to be negative. Not surprisingly, subjects giving a moderate self-presentation indicated that they were more accurate in describing themselves than subjects asked to give an extreme presentation. And in support of the findings by Jones, Gergen, & Davis (1962), subjects reported that they had been more accurate when they received a positive evaluation than when they received a negative one.

These studies suggest that there are two reasons why an individual may come to view himself more positively after receiving positive feedback. First, he generally accepts this feedback as genuine and his self-presentation as accurate even when he has distorted his self-view in order to get it. Second, if he has been making a conscious effort to gain approval, he views positive feedback as evidence that he was successful. Such evidence may lead him to view himself more positively. He presumably sees himself as competent in social skills, and this may generalize to other esteem-related characteristics. We have already mentioned that self-aggrandizing statements will probably elicit positive feedback from others, even though the others may not really be taken in by the self-enhancing claims. As a consequence of making self-enhancing claims, then, an individual is likely to develop an overly positive picture of himself.

In addition to altering his self-view, one's ingratiation overtures may affect his view of the target person, and his attitudes about various opinion issues. There [49] are a number of factors that may lead an individual to become more favorable toward the target person. First, he may come to believe the positive things he has said about the target person. As we have noted previously, dissonance theory (cf. Festinger, 1957) suggests that the more compelling the circumstances that justify saying positive things about another, the less we will come to believe these statements. If we are positive toward another when there is no good reason for it—when there is little to be gained from complimenting the other, when subjective probability of success is low, or when there are ethical problems involved—then we should come to view the other as more attractive. Suppose, for example, that an individual has just told a plain young thing that she is a raving beauty, in order to pave the way for sexual favors. The cognition, that he had lied to the girl for his own gain, may be disturbing to him. Therefore, he may attempt to convince himself that he believed what he said and in this ,way avoid the self-attribution that he is manipulative and self-seeking.

An individual may also come to view a target person more favorably if he has expressed agreement with the target person and there are few justifications for such agreement. This phenomenon seems to occur in the experiment by R. G. Jones & E. E. Jones (1964) cited earlier. Half of the subjects in this study were told that it would be to their advantage to make themselves attractive to another. The remaining subjects were told to be as accurate as possible in their interchanges with the other. Subjects were told that they would receive a series of cards from the other, each containing the other's opinion on a certain issue. On the bottom of each card, they were supposed to indicate their own opinion and their degree of confidence in it. They were then supposed to return the card to the other. In this manner, all subjects were given an opportunity to engage in opinion conformity. When they began the interchange, half of the subjects found out that the other's opinions were quite similar to theirs (same condition); the remaining subjects discovered that the other's opinions were very different from theirs (discrepant conditions).

As we mentioned earlier, in a more detailed analysis of the results, subjects in the high-dependence–same condition seemed to be involved in convincing themselves that their agreement with the target person was not contrived for ulterior purposes. Only in this condition was there a highly significant correlation between conformity and expressed liking for the target person. This can best be explained as an attempt on the part of the subject to justify to himself the validity of his expressed opinions. Since the measure of liking was derived from the postexperimental questionnaire, the favorable ratings could not have been part of any strategy to impress the target person. Instead, the correlation between conformity and liking seems a product of the subject's wish to emphasize to himself that agreement was coincidental. By liking the target person, the conformist in this condition may justify his conformity on grounds other than manipulative intent.

This reasoning suggests, then, that attraction may develop as a way of dealing with conflict of dissonance when conformity has occurred. This interpretation is quite similar to one proposed by Gerard (1961) to account for his results. The novel thing about Gerard's experiment is that the subject was led to believe he had a strong tendency to conform to group judgments or deviate from them. Much as in the present case, subjects who found themselves conforming to the group also became more attracted to it.

Just as our attitudes toward the target person may become more positive, it is conceivable that our opinions and values might change as a result of engaging in ingratiating behaviors. This is probably most likely to occur when we have conformed with someone and have little justification for doing so. Then we may change our attitudes so that they are in line with the conforming statements we have made. However, as the Jones & Jones experiment (1964) suggests, we may also change our attitudes toward the target person in order to justify our conformity to ourselves. More research is needed to determine the conditions under which each of these types of attitude change is likely to occur.

Effect of Ingratiating Overtures on the Quality of Interpersonal Relationships

It has been implied by the preceding discussions that ingratiation pervades social life. Especially when there is differential power—where resources are unevenly distributed—

we would expect a tendency toward strategic behavior as a response to social dependence. Overt ingratiation may be inhibited by legitimacy considerations, or eschewed because of the strategic risks involved. But the tendency toward (temptation toward?) strategic behavior is nevertheless there.

We now suggest—as we have implied throughout—that ingratiating overtures are rarely the result of conscious or deliberate tactical planning. True, some of us some of the time are aware of an explicit conflict between expressing our private beliefs and agreeing with different beliefs held by those with high status or power over us. By and large, however, the kinds **[50]** of strategic overtures with which we have been mainly concerned in this book are overlearned responses to the condition of dependence. Through a long and complex socialization process, the average person develops deeply embedded reaction tendencies that are triggered by settings of differential resources or power. Most of the time, we believe, the attraction-seeking response is relatively automatic or unthinking. Alternatives of utter openness and candor are not even considered as the dependent person nods, smiles, agrees, or compliments. For the dependent person, such congenial behavior may seem completely natural under the circumstances.

The socialization process is, obviously, not monolithic in a complex culture such as ours. For some people the ingrained tendency to be ingratiating may be strong; for others it may be very weak. There are undoubtedly individual differences in threshold, or the degree of dependence required to trigger off ingratiation, and in personal preferences for particular forms of tactical behavior. Some of us are conformers, others favor flattery, and still others proceed with a charming humility. Different subcultures will be discernibly different in these same respects: Northerners vs. Southerners, blacks vs. whites, males vs. females. But we would argue that, regardless of differences in cultural and behavioral topography, tendencies toward ingratiation pervade any social system in which people are dependent on each other for unevenly distributed resources. We are suggesting, then, that ingratiation becomes a factor to the extent that all social transactions cannot be handled through equitable social exchange.

But what are the sociocultural implications of this pervasive phenomenon? In approaching an answer to this question, it might be of some value to imagine a society in which ruthless candor was pandemic. And as long as we are imagining, let us further provide that each individual must carry a little signal light that flickers whenever he misrepresents his private views, or behaves inconsistently from one social context to the next. Such a signal would fortify the candor norm, permitting sanctions to be applied in response to a telltale flicker. We might speculate that in such a society, people would become avoidant and isolated one from another. As compared with our own society, other people would be more valuable from an informational point of view, but also more threatening from the point of view of emotional support and reinforcement. It is plausible to expect the development of a series of rigid hierarchies based on observable talents, physical beauty, or universally acknowledged charm. The ugly and the untalented would constantly be reminded of their shortcomings, whereas the strong would receive entrenching feedback. Courtships would have to weather more storms of candor than is presently the case. Families would become "encounter groups" at the dinner table, with members expressing either powerful positive or negative things about each other over the meat and potatoes. Groups would move slowly toward consensus, if at all, and leaders would often have to function without the security-giving benefits of social support. And so on.

The imagery conjured up by this stark fantasy is that of an abrasive, unforgiving, hierarchical culture. It would be a culture of revealed differences and one in which animosities as well as attractions would be clearly "worn on the sleeve." There is no reason why such a culture could not survive, especially if people established new adaptation levels and learned to tolerate disagreement, expressed disfavor, and intense affection. And there would, of course, be the benefits that would come with candor and credibility. We would know where we stood, our channels of social information would be clear and informative, and our resources for reality testing would certainly be greater than they are in our present culture. But the benefits of information clarity would be purchased at a cost that might be intolerably high from the point of view of maintaining the social system.

Returning to our present culture in which, as we have argued, ingratiation pervades social interaction, we now are in a better position to see precisely what functions ingratiation serves for society. We have already noted that the ingratiator muddies the informational waters. He puts noise into social feedback and makes it difficult for individuals to gain an accurate reading of their standing and impression. This dilemma is highlighted in Buber's remarks:

> … Imagine two men, whose life is dominated by appearances, sitting and talking together. Call them Peter and Paul. Let us list the different configurations which are involved. First, there is Peter as he wishes to appear to Paul, and Paul as he wishes to appear to Peter. Then there is Peter as he really appears to Paul, that is Paul's image of Peter, which in general does not in the least coincide with what Peter wishes Paul to see; and similarly there is the reverse situation. Further, there is Peter as he appears to himself, and Paul as he appears to himself. Lastly, there are bodily Peter and the bodily Paul, two living beings and six ghostly appearances, which mingle in many ways in the conversations between the two. Where is there room for any genuine interhuman life? (1957)

But ingratiation is also a social lubricant that facilitates interaction and helps to neutralize status differences. When a successful ingratiation attempt [51] occurs, the target person should feel more personally secure, while at the same time the ingratiator has augmented his own power by increasing his attractiveness. It might even be added that the pervasiveness of ingratiation helps to prevent people from taking social feedback too seriously, and this is facilitative because we can work with others compatibly without being drawn too deeply into relations of intense affect.

We are essentially proposing that effective group functioning requires a delicate balance between valid social information and constructive social support. A group that leans too far in the direction of emphasizing ruthless candor is likely to require various reparative processes to smooth over the frictions of disagreement and hostility. But a group so wrapped up in social support activities that little valid information gets through has obvious problems of another sort. Such a group misses out on the kind of triangulation process that is so valuable for reality testing. Somehow, then, the society, the subculture, or the group finds its own way to construct this balance in order to survive as a social system and maintain effective interaction with the environment. Perhaps adaptive social life requires a little blarney now and then to mute the impact of disagreement, antagonism, and even love.

Perhaps, in other words, social life requires some degree of unreliability in statements of personal evaluation so that the delicate balance can survive.

A FEW FINAL WORDS

We have presented an account of the social psychology of ingratiation or attraction seeking—its forms, its determinants, and its consequences. It should be perfectly apparent to the reader who has persevered this far that the topic of ingratiation represents a confluence, an intersection point, for a variety of different concerns. An attempt to understand ingratiation involves the study of conformity, source credibility, social exchange processes, self-presentation, causal attribution, power relations, and many other theoretical and investigative traditions.

In the present paper, we have chosen an attributional emphasis because it is so appropriate for illuminating the unique properties of an ingratiation episode. The effectiveness of attraction-seeking overtures depends on the ingratiator's success in manipulating the causal attributions for his behavior. If his behavior is seen as shaped primarily by strategic considerations, the ingratiation attempt will founder. We have noted other problems associated with attributing behavior to the person ("That's the way he is") and to the situation ("Anybody would have done it"). The successful ingratiator must manipulate the target person's attributions so that he is seen as credible, sincere, and yet as treating the target person as an individual rather than a position. He must go beyond the norm to change power relationships rather than merely complying so as to confirm them.

There is no simple way to summarize the attributional approach in a few sentences. Indeed, this entire essay may be seen as an attempt to explore in some detail the strategies most likely to be effective in managing the subtle attributional problems involved in ingratiation. Along the way, we did present two heuristic models that supplement the attributional approach. The first was a model relating the extremity or obviousness of strategic behavior to the degree of elicited attraction. Up to a point, the more effusive the compliments, the stronger the self-presentational claims, the greater the degree of agreement, the greater will be the attraction elicited. Beyond a certain level of extremity, however, the degree of dependence on the target person plays an increasingly important role. The greater the dependence, the more likely that extreme strategic behavior will elicit less rather than more attraction. There is empirical evidence consistent with this model, though an interesting modification may be necessary: Under high-dependence conditions, the would-be ingratiator appears to receive extra attraction credits for moderate disagreement or autonomy.

A second model involved an attempt to specify three antecedent variables determining the occurrence of ingratiation. The incentive value of the resources uniquely controlled by the target person is the first of these variables. The second is the subjective probability of success. The potential ingratiator will hesitate if his dependence is terribly obvious, or if the target person seems, for whatever reason, unsusceptible to the available tactics of conformity, self-enhancement, other-enhancement, or favor giving. Finally, the perceived legitimacy of ingratiation in the specific context is a third important variable. Thus, a normative or moral consideration is added to the conventional probability times incentive function that is used in many theoretical statements about human motivation. The three-component model is crude, but it has been remarkably useful in stimulating research and providing a conceptual home for the results.

Thus, certain theoretical considerations have emerged from the many studies dealing with attraction and strategic behavior. Much of the work that remains to be done involves refining the theoretical statements we now have so that not only the occurrence, but the form of ingratiation may be better predicted. Challenging [52] exploration of empirical generality also remains. We need to know more about the vicissitudes of ingratiation in various everyday settings, across cultural boundaries, and over different personalities. We hope that the present essay will help to stimulate such further explorations and to convince the reader of the importance of theoretical clarification.

BIBLIOGRAPHY

Aronson, E. (1969). Some antecedents of interpersonal attraction. In W. J. Arnold and D. Levine, (Eds.), *Nebraska Symposium on Motivation* (pp.143–173). Lincoln, NE: University of Nebraska Press.

Aronson, E., & Linder, D. (1965). Gain and loss of esteem as determinants of interpersonal attractiveness. *Journal of Experimental Social Psychology,* 1, 156–171.

Aronson, E., & Mettee, D.R. (1968). Dishonest behavior as a function of differential levels of induced self-esteem. *Journal of Personality and Social Psychology,* 9, 121–127.

Aronson, E., Willerman, B., &. Floyd, J. (1966). The effect of a pratfall on increasing interpersonal attractiveness. *Psychonomic Science,* 4, 227–228.

Backman, C.W., & Secord, P.F. (1959). The effect of perceived liking on interpersonal attraction. *Human Relations,* 12, 379–384.

Bartlett, J. (1955). *Familiar Quotations.* New York: Little Brown.

Blau, P.M. (1960). A theory of social integration. *American Journal of Sociology,* 65, 545–556.

Brehm, J.W., & Cole, A.H. (1966). Effect of a favor which reduces freedom. *Journal of Personality and Social Psychology,* 3, 420–426.

Buber, M. (1957). Elements of the interhuman. *Psychiatric,* 20, 105–113.

Byrne, D. (1961). Interpersonal attraction and attitude similarity. *Journal of Abnormal and Social Psychology,* 62, 713–715.

Byrne, D. (1969). Attitudes and attraction. In L. Berkowitz.(Ed.), *Advances in Experimental Social Psychology* (Vol 4., pp.35–89). New York: Academic Press.

Byrne, D., & Griffit, W. (1966). A developmental investigation of the law of attraction. *Journal of Personality and Social Psychology,* 4, 699–702.

Byrne, D., Griffit, W., & Stefanak, D. (1967). Attraction and similarity of personality characteristics. *Journal of Personality and Social Psychology,* 5, 82–90.

Byrne, D., Nelson, D., & Reeves, K. (1966). Effects of consensual validation and invalidation on attraction as a function of verifiability. *Journal of Experimental Social Psychology,* 2, 98–107.

Byrne, D., & Rhamey, R. (1965). Magnitude of positive and negative reinforcements as a determinant of attraction. *Journal of Personality and Social Psychology,* 2, 884–889.

Carnegie, D. (1940). *How to Win Friends and Influence People.* New York: Simon & Schuster, Pocket Book edition (Original published 1936).

Earl of Chesterfield (Philip Darmer Stanhope), (1901). *Letters to His Son* (Walter M. Dunne, Ed.). New York: Wiley. (Original published 1774).

Christie, R., &. Geis, F.L. (1970). *Studies in Machiavellianism.* New York: Academic Press.

Clore, G.L., & Baldridge, B. (1970). The behavior of item weights in attitude-attraction research. *Journal of Experimental Social Psychology,* 6, 177–186.

Cozby, P.C. (1972). Self-disclosure, reciprocity, and liking. *Sociometry,* 35, 151–160.

Deutsch, M., & Solomon, L. (1959). Reactions to evaluations by others as influenced by self-evaluations. *Sociometry,* 22, 93–112.

Dickoff, H. (1961) *Reactions to evaluations by another person as a function of self-evaluations and the interaction context.* Unpublished doctoral dissertation, Duke University.

Dittes, J. E. (1959). Attractiveness of group as function of self-esteem and acceptance by group. *Journal of Abnormal and Social Psychology,* 59, 77–82.
Ehrlich, H. J., & Graeven, D. B. (1971). Reciprocal self-disclosure in a dyad. *Journal of Experimental Social Psychology,* 7, 389–400.
Farson, R. E. (1963). Praise reappraised. *Harvard Business Review,* 41, 61–66.
Festinger, L. (1957). *A theory of cognitive dissonance.* New York: Row, Peterson.
Garrity, J. (1969). *The sensuous woman.* New York: L. Stuart.
Gerard, H.B . (1961). Some determinants of self-evaluation. *Journal of Abnormal and Social Psychology,* 62, 288–293.
Gerard, H. B., & Greenbaum, C.W. (1962). Attitudes toward an agent of uncertainty reduction. *Journal of Personality,* 30, 485–495.
Gergen, K. J. (1965). The effects of interaction goals and personalistic feedback on the presentation of self. *Journal of Personality and Social Psychology,* 1, 413–424.
Gergen, K. J., & Wishnov, B. (1965). Others' self-evaluation and interaction anticipation as determinants of self-presentation. *Journal of Personality and Social Psychology,* 2, 348–358.
Goffman, E. (1955). On face-work. *Psychiatry,* 18, 213–231.
Greenberg, M. S., & Frisch, D. M. (1972). Effect of intentionality on willingness to reciprocate a favor. *Journal of Experimental Social Psychology,* 8, 99–111.
Griffit, W., & Veitch, R. (1971). Hot and crowded: Influences of population density and temperature on interpersonal affective behavior. *Journal of Personality and Social Psychology,* 17, 92–98.
Harvey, O. J., & Clapp, W. F. (1965). Hope, expectancy, and reactions to the unexpected. *Journal of Personality and Social Psychology,* 2, 45–52.
Heider, F. (1958). *The psychology of interpersonal relations.* New York: Wiley.
Helmreich, R., Aronson, E., & Lefan, J. (1970). To err is humanizing—sometimes: Effects of self-esteem, competence, and a pratfall on interpersonal attraction. *Journal of Personality and Social Psychology,* 16, 259–264. **[53]**
Hewitt, J. (1972). Liking and the proportion of favorable evaluations. *Journal of Personality and Social Psychology,* 22, 231–235.
Jacobs, L., Berscheid, E., &. Walster, E. (1971). Self-esteem and attraction. *Journal of Personality and Social Psychology,* 17, 84–91.
Jellison, J.M., &. Zeisset, P.T. (1969). Attraction as a function of the commonality and desirability of a trait shared with another. *Journal of Personality and Social Psychology,* 11, 115–120.
Johnson, S., & Johnson, D.W. (1972). The effects of other's actions, attitude similarity, and race on attraction toward the other. *Human Relations,* 25, 121–130.
Jones, E. E. (1964). *Ingratiation.* New York: Appleton-Century.
Jones, E. E. (1965). Conformity as a tactic of ingratiation. *Science,* 149, 144–150.
Jones, E. E., Bell, L., & Aronson, E. (1972). The reciprocation of attraction from similar and dissimilar others: A study in person perception and evaluation. In C. C. McClintock, (Ed.), *Experimental Social Psychology.* (pp. 142–179). New York: Holt, Rinehart and Winston.
Jones, E. E., Gergen, K. J., & Davis, K. E. (1962). Some determinants of reactions to being approved or disapproved as a person. *Psychological Monographs,* 76 (Whole No. 521).
Jones, E. E., Gergen, K. J., Gumpert, P., & Thibaut, J. W. (1965). Some conditions affecting the use of ingratiation to influence performance evaluation. *Journal of Personality and Social Psychology,* 1, 613–625.
Jones, E. E., Gergen, K. J., & Jones, R. G. (1963). Tactics of ingratiation among leaders and subordinates in a status hierarchy. *Psychological Monographs,* 77 (Whole No. 566).
Jones, E. E., & Gordon, E. M. (1972). Timing of self-disclosure and its effects on personal attraction. *Journal of Personality and Social Psychology,* 24, 358–365.
Jones, E. E., Hester, S. L., Farina, A., & Davis, K. E. (1959). Reactions to unfavorable personal evaluations as a function of the evaluator's perceived adjustment. *Journal of Abnormal and Social Psychology,* 59, 363–370.
Jones, E. E., Jones, R. G.,& Gergen, K. J. (1963). Some conditions affecting the evaluation of a conformist. *Journal of Personality,* 31, 270–288.
Jones, E. E., Stires, L. K., Shaver, K. C., & Harris, V. A. (1968). Evaluation of an ingratiator by target persons and bystanders. *Journal of Personality,* 36, 385.
Jones, E. E., & Wein, G. (1972). Attitude similarity, expectancy violation, and attraction. *Journal of Experimental Social Psychology,* 8, 222–235.

Jones, R. G., & Jones, E. E. (1964). Optimum conformity as an ingratiation tactic. *Journal of Personality, 32*, 436–158.

Jones, S. C. (1973). Self and interpersonal evaluations: Esteem theories versus consistency theories. *Psychological Bulletin, 79*, 185–199.

Jones, S. C., & Ratner, C. (1967). Commitment to self-appraisal and interpersonal evaluations. *Journal of Personality and Social Psychology, 6*, 442–447.

Jones, S. C., & Schneider, D. J. (1968). Certainty of self-appraisal and reactions to evaluations from others. *Sociometry, 31*, 395–403.

Kaufman, D. R., & Steiner, I. D. (1968). Some variables affecting the use of conformity as an ingratiation technique. *Journal of Experimental Social Psychology, 4*, 400–414.

Kiesler, S. B. (1966). The effect of perceived role requirements on reactions to favor doing. *Journal of Experimental Social Psychology, 2*, 198–210.

Kipnis, D., & Vanderveer, R. (1974). Ingratiation and the use of power. *Journal of Personality and Social Psychology, 17*, 280–286.

Kleinke, C. L., Staneski, R. A., & Weaver, P. (1972). Evaluation of a person who uses another's name in ingratiating and noningratiating situations. *Journal of Experimental Social Psychology, 8*, 457–466.

Landy, D., & Aronson, E. (1968). Liking for an evaluator as a function of his discernment. *Journal of Personality and Social Psychology, 9*, 133–141.

Latané, B., Eckman, J., & Joy, V. (1966). Shared stress and interpersonal attraction. *Journal of Experimental Social Psychology, Supplement, 1*, 80–94.

Lefebvre, L.M. *An experimental approach on the use of ingratiation under homogeneous and heterogeneous dyads.* Unpublished manuscript, University of Louvain, Belgium. (Editor's note: This paper was subsequently published as Lefebvre, L. M. (1973). An experimental approach to the use of ingratiation tactics under homogeneous and heterogeneous dyads. *European Journal of Social Psychology, 3*, 427–445).

Lowe, C.A., & Goldstein, J.W. (1970). Reciprocal liking and attributions of ability; Mediating effects of perceived intent and personal involvement. *Journal of Personality and Social Psychology, 16*, 291–298.

Mettee, D. R. (1971a). The true discerner as a potent source of positive affect. *Journal of Experimental Social Psychology, 7*, 292–303.

Mettee, D. R. (1971b). Changes in liking as a function of the magnitude and affect of sequential evaluations. *Journal of Experimental Social Psychology, 7*, 157–172.

Mettee, D. R., & Wilkins, P. L. (1972). When similarity hurts: Effects of perceived ability and a humorous blunder on interpersonal attraction. *Journal of Personality and Social Psychology, 22*, 246–258.

Nemeth, C. (1970). Effects of free versus constrained behavior on attraction between people. *Journal of Personality and Social Psychology, 15*, 302–311.

Rosenbaum, M. E., & deCharms, R. (1960). Direct and vicarious reduction of hostility. *Journal of Abnormal and Social Psychology, 60*, 105–112.

Rosenfeld, H. M. (1966). Approval-seeking and approval-inducing functions of verbal and nonverbal responses in the dyad. *Journal of Personality and Social Psychology, 4*, 597–605.

Rosenthal, R., & Jacobson, L. (1968). *Pygmalion in the classroom: Teacher expectation and pupils' intellectual development.* New York: Holt, Rinehart and Winston.

Schachter, S. (1959). *The Psychology of Affiliation.* Palo Alto, CA: Stanford University Press.

Schneider, D. J. (1969). Tactical self-presentation after success and failure. *Journal of Personality and Social Psychology, 13*, 262–268.

Schneider, D. J. *The effects of extremity and positivity of self-presentation and other evaluation on self-evaluation.* Unpublished manuscript, Brandeis University.

Schneider, D. J., & Eustis, A. C. (1972). Effects of ingratiation motivation, target positiveness, and revealingness on [54] sell-presentation. *Journal of Personality and Social Psychology, 22*, 149–155.

Schopler, J., & Thompson, V. D. (1968). Role of attribution processes in mediating amount of reciprocity for a favor. *Journal of Personality and Social Psychology, 10*, 243–250.

Secord, P. F., & Backman, C. W. (1964). Interpersonal congruency: Perceived similarity, and friendship. *Sociometry, 27*, 115–127.

Sigall, H. (1970). Effects of competence and consensual validation on a communicator's liking for the audience. *Journal of Personality and Social Psychology, 16*, 251–258.

Skolnick, P. (1971). Reactions to personal evaluations: A failure to replicate. *Journal of Personality and Social Psychology,* 18, 62–67.

Stapert, J. O., & Clore, G. L. (1969). Attraction and disagreement produced arousal. *Journal of Personality and Social Psychology,* 13, 64–69.

Stevenson, E. E. (1934). *The home book of quotations.* New York: Dodd, Mead.

Stires, L. K., & Jones, E. E. (1969). Modesty versus self-enhancement as alternative forms of ingratiation. *Journal of Experimental Social Psychology,* 5, 172–188.

Strickland, L. H. (1958). Surveillance and trust. *Journal of Personality,* 26, 200–215.

Taylor, D. A., Altman, I., & Sorrentino, R. (1969). Interpersonal exchange as a function of rewards and costs and situational factors: Expectancy confirmation–disconfirmation. *Journal of Experimental Social Psychology,* 5, 324–339.

Thibaut, J. W., & Riecken, H. W. (1955). Some determinants and consequences of the perception of social causality. *Journal of Personality,* 24, 113–133.

Tognoli, J., & Keisner, R. (1972). Gain and loss of esteem as determinants of interpersonal attraction: A replication and extension. *Journal of Personality and Social Psychology,* 23, 201–204.

Upshaw, H. S., & Yates, L. A. (1965). Self-persuasion: Social approval, and task success as determinants of self-esteem following impression management. *Journal of Experimental Social Psychology,* 4, 143–152.

Walster, E. (1965). The effect of self-esteem on romantic liking. *Journal of Experimental Social Psychology,* 1, 184–197.

Webb, E. T., & Morgan, J. B. (1930). *Strategy in handling people.* Garden City, NJ: Garden City Publishers.

White, R. W. (1959). Motivation reconsidered: The concept of competence. *Psychological Review,* 66, 297–333.

Winch, R. F. (1958). *Mate-selection: A study of complementary needs.* New York: Harper and Row.

Worthy, M., Gary, A. L., & Kahn, C. M. (1969). Self-disclosure as an exchange process. *Journal of Personality and Social Psychology,* 13, 59–63. **[55]**

Author's Note: This paper incorporates some of the material presented earlier in *Ingratiation,* a volume now out of print. Our intent has been to review the recent relevant literature and to achieve an updated statement of the earlier volume. The authors thank David J. Schneider for his helpful comments on the manuscript.

Chapter 16

Toward a General Theory of Strategic Self-Presentation

Edward E. Jones
Princeton University
Thane S. Pittman
Gettysburg College

We hope that the initial word of our title diminishes its pretentiousness. The present chapter is offered as a preliminary formulation that will obviously be modified to accommodate new data. Nevertheless, we believe that the self-presentation area has been slow to develop in social psychology because of the lack of comprehensive theorizing (as well as the difficulty of doing theory-based experimental research). Self-presentational phenomena are ubiquitous in social life, and yet we have no conceptual framework to relate and understand these phenomena. The present chapter attempts to outline such a framework to facilitate the organization—and indeed the identification—of self-presentation research.

A DEFINITION AND SOME EXCLUSIONS

One problem in coming to terms with self-presentation is its very omnipresence. No one would seriously challenge the general idea that observers infer dispositions from an actor's behavior, or that actors have a stake in controlling the inferences drawn about

---

Reprinted with permission from J. Suls (Ed.), *Psychological Perspectives on the Self.* (Vol. 1, pp. 231–260). Hillsdale, NJ: Erlbaum, ©1982, Lawrence Erlbaum Associates.

them from their actions. Goffman crystallized one viewpoint on impression management with his classic dramaturgical account in 1959, one that essentially gave us the label of *self-presentation,* and provided enough descriptive variety and richness to convince us that here was an important area for social psychological analysis. Goffman's emphasis, however, was on the subtle ways in which actors project or convey a definition of the interaction situation as they see it. Attempts on the part of the actor to shape others' impressions of his personality received only secondary emphasis. Jones (1964), and Jones & [231]* Wortman (1973) focused on our interest in getting others to like us, and developed a theoretical framework that combined motivational, cognitive, and evaluative features.

A number of experiments have since addressed the determinants and social consequences of "self-disclosure" (Cozby, 1973; Jourard, 1964; and others). Solid conclusions in this area have proved hard to come by. All the while, we have been occasionally edified, sometimes amused, and often appalled by a popular literature dealing with power, manipulation, and self-salesmanship (Carnegie, 1936; Korda, 1975; Ringer, 1973; Webb & Morgan, 1930).

Impression management concerns have found their way into many areas of social psychology. Tedeschi, Schlenker, and their associates (1971) have argued that such concerns can explain most of the phenomena that others have attributed to cognitive dissonance reduction. Orne (1962), Rosenthal (1966), Rosenberg (1965), and others have written at length about the concerns of experimental subjects with how they will be evaluated by an experimenter.

And yet, in spite of the volume of seemingly relevant literature and research, the topic of self-presentation suffers from an amorphous identity with insecure underpinnings in motivational and cognitive theory. Our intent is to provide such underpinnings and demarcate the area of concern more clearly than previous treatments.

To these ends, we start with definitions first of the phenomenal self, and then of what we mean by strategic self-presentation. The *phenomenal self* was defined by Jones & Gerard (1967) as: "a person's awareness, arising out of interactions with his environment, of his own beliefs, values, attitudes, the links between them, and their implications for his behavior [page 716]." We accept this view that each of us has a potentially available overarching cognition of his or her interrelated dispositions. The notion of a phenomenal self implies that memories of past actions and outcomes are available in integrated form to clarify current action possibilities. The evolution of this overarching phenomenal self is greatly facilitated by the fact that other people, in their attempt to render *their* social environment more predictable, endow us with stable attributes and respond to us as enduring structures. It is not surprising that we learn to take ourselves as definable social objects and become concerned with the consistency of our actions over time.

But the words "potentially available" are important in approaching the phenomenal self. The phenomenal self is not always salient; we are not always self-focused or preoccupied with self-consistency. A consequence of being socialized in a particular culture is that sequences of action become automatic, triggered off by contextual cues in line with past reinforcements. We are often, in effect, "mindless" (Langer & Newman, 1979). In many of

---

*Bracketed bold numbers refer to original page numbers. Page numbers indicate where the original page ended.

the routine social interchanges of everyday life, therefore, the phenomenal self is not aroused, does not become salient. Conflict and novelty do, however, give rise to mindfulness and self-salience. When we do not have preprogrammed response sequences, the phenomenal self becomes a reference point for decision-making, as we review the [232] implications of our beliefs and values for action. Pressures toward self-consistency (and long-range adaptation) may then compete with pressures toward shorter-range social gains in creating the conflicts and dilemmas of social life. These dilemmas are often cast in moral terms as the individual assesses the relative virtues of integrity, consistency, and authenticity on the one hand, as against the virtues of adaptive effectiveness and personal security gained through power augmentation on the other. Jones & Wortman (1973) have argued, however, that this conflict is often avoided as adaptive social responding becomes automatic in the face of well-established recurrent cues. Thus, the contextual cue that defines our momentary social position as "dependent" may trigger off ingratiating actions or other attempts at impression management without necessarily evoking the phenomenal self.

A vital point to stress is that, in spite of certain pressures toward self-stability and consistency over time, the phenomenal self: (1) shifts from moment to moment as a function of motivational state and situational cues, and (2) is constantly evolving and changing in ways that incorporate, or come to terms with, one's actions or one's outcomes. The impact of self-presentation on the self-concept receives our recurrent attention throughout this chapter.

But, now, what exactly do we mean by strategic self-presentation? Most would agree that self-presentation involves an actor's shaping of his or her responses to create, in specific others, an impression that is, for one reason or another, desired by the actor. Most, if not all, of these reasons can be subsumed under an interest in augmenting or maintaining one's *power* in a relationship. The actor uses his behavior to convey something about him or herself, regardless of what other meaning or significance the behavior may have.[1] Formally, we define strategic self-presentation as *those features of behavior affected by power augmentation motives designed to elicit or shape others' attributions of the actor's dispositions.* "Features," of course, include the most subtle aspects of style and nonverbal expressions, as well as the contents of overt verbal communications. The definition also makes clear that we are unlikely to find a given response, or set of responses, that are intrinsically or universally self-presentational. Rather, self-presentation is likely to be intimately intertwined in social responses that have other significances as well. It is also by no means implied that strategic self-presentation features are necessarily false, distorted, or seriously discrepant from the phenomenal self. As we subsequently argue in more detail, such features typically involve selective disclosures and omissions, matters of emphasis and toning, rather than of deceit and simulation.

In view of the difficulties created by the intertwining of self-presentational and other features of behavior, about the only way to identify the presence of strategic self-presentation is to arouse particular impression-management motives experimentally, and to observe the features that distinguish ensuing responses from behavior without such implanted motivation. This is easier said than done, [233] but at least it provides a starting point for ostensive definition and is more or less the prescription followed in the ingratiation area (Jones, 1964; Jones & Wortman, 1973).

---

[1] The pronouns *he, his,* and *him* are used throughout this chapter to refer to both sexes.

It may be helpful to continue this definitional discussion by paying some attention to those conditions likely to inhibit self-presentational concerns. In other words, let us list some examples of settings in which strategic self-presentation behaviors are absent or minimal:

1. Behavior under conditions of high task involvement. This essentially refers to those settings that arouse "subjective self-awareness" in Duval & Wicklund's (1972) terms. The individual is absorbed by physical or intellectual challenge that, to use a Freudian image, totally captures the libidinal cathexis. The demands of the task (whether it involves hem stitching, observing, reading, or involvement in an athletic contest) preclude self-consciousness. Even lecturers and actors, though addressing an audience, may be so engrossed in their material as to elude momentary concern with its response.

2. Purely expressive behavior—anger, mirth, joy—may escape self-presentational shaping at or near the moment of provocation. Some emotions apparently overwhelm the concerns of impression management, if only for a brief moment before we start to worry whether our reactions are "appropriate" to the occasion.

3. We would also set aside as *not* self-presentational a large class of over-learned, ritualized social interchanges. Actors are often apt to forego the self-presentational possibilities of divergent ways of conducting routine commercial transactions, driving through traffic, or checking out library books—though the opportunities for impression management are very much available in these instances for the person who is constantly obsessed with his public image.

4. Finally, for psychological completeness, we might include those occasions when persons are, above all, concerned with the integrity or authenticity of their actions. They want their actions to be self-fulfilling and self-disclosing. They reach inward for available traces of beliefs, values, and feelings, which they try to capture in self-revealing comments or nonverbal expressions. Therapy sessions, encounter groups, and intimate relationships often motivate us to portray the phenomenal self with maximum fidelity, concealing and distorting as little as possible. This is not, however, to suggest that such contexts normally preclude a concern with managing the attributions of others. What we sincerely believe is "authentic" may vary with our audience and our purpose.

We would emphasize that self-presentation is an important subcategory of social behavior, but, nevertheless, it is a *sub*category. To summarize, our actions in the presence of others are relatively unaffected by our concern with their impressions of us to the extent that the behavior in question is task centered, spontaneously expressive, normatively ritualized, or deliberately self-matching. On the other hand, self-presentational features will be intertwined with behavior whenever **[234]** the actor cares, for whatever reasons, about the impression others have of him. We now move on to show what some of the reasons are, and how some of them are linked to recognizably different self-presentational strategies.

A TAXONOMY OF ATTRIBUTIONS SHAPED BY SELF-PRESENTATIONAL STRATEGIES

We believe strongly that a theory of strategic self-presentation must be anchored in identifiable social motives. Self-presentation involves the actor's linkage of particular motives to his or her strategic resources. In short:

1. A wants to make secure, or to augment, his power to derive favorable outcomes from B.
2. The desired growth or consolidation of power may or may not be directed toward these outcomes in the immediate future. A may invest his strategic outcomes in a "power bank," whose resources may be tapped in unspecified future encounters with B.
3. A's getting the kind of power he wants will be facilitated if B has a certain impression of A.
4. Creating that impression will be easy or difficult depending on A's resources, which, in turn, are defined by A's cognitive and behavioral capacities within the settings available for interaction with B.
5. The linkage of a particular power motive with the self-presentational features of social behavior is mediated by cognitive processes in the self-presenting actor. The behavior is further shaped by evaluative or moral constraints. The complex interaction of motive, cognition, and morality determines the choice of self-presentational strategies.

Hoping that the reader keeps these assumptions in mind, we offer a taxonomy of five classes of self-presentational strategies. The defining feature of each class is the particular attribution sought by the actor. The taxonomy consists of ingratiation, intimidation, self-promotion, exemplification, and supplication. In our view, these rubrics, although not entirely exhaustive, encompass most instances of strategic self-presentation.

Ingratiation

Ingratiation is undoubtedly the most ubiquitous of all self-presentational phenomena. Much of our social behavior is shaped by a concern that others like us and attribute to us such characteristics as warmth, humor, reliability, charm, and physical attractiveness. The ingratiator's goals may shift back and forth among these specific attributional foci, but by definition the ingratiator seeks to achieve the *attribution of likability*. Consistent with this orientation, ingratiation has been formally defined by Jones & Wortman (1973) as "a class of strategic behaviors illicitly designed to influence a particular other person concerning the attractiveness of one's personal qualities" [p. 21]. Ingratiating actions are illicit because **[235]** they are directed toward an objective that is typically not contained in the implicit contract underlying social interaction. In fact, the very success of ingratiation usually depends on the actor's concealment of ulterior motivation or of the importance of his stake in being judged attractive. The illicit nature of ingratiation may also lead ingratiators to deceive themselves concerning either the importance of being judged attractive, or the relationship between this desired goal and the strategic features invading their action decisions. A tantalizing conspiracy of cognitive avoidance is common to the actor and his target. The actor does not wish to see himself as ingratiating; the target wants also to believe that the ingratiator is sincere in following the implicit social contract.

A considerable volume of research has been conducted in the ingratiation area, much of it summarized by Jones & Wortman (1973). Such prominent subclasses as conformity, other enhancement, doing favors, and various forms of direct and indirect self-description have been dealt with extensively. The general finding is that placing an actor in a position of dependence vis-à-vis a more powerful target person, in comparison to control conditions in which actor and target person have equal power, gives rise to greater conformity (Jones, 1965), self-enhancement (Jones, Gergen, & Davis, 1962), and other enhancement (Jones, Gergen, & Jones, 1963). Typically, however, the dependent actor's behavior is complicated to increase credibility (Jones, 1965). Bystanding observers react negatively to conformity and other ingratiating overtures, when such overtures are obvious or excessive, and the power discrepancy between the actor and the target is great (Jones, Jones, & Gergen, 1963). It is also true, however, that target persons respond more positively to a highly agreeable actor dependent on them than do bystanders watching the interchange on film (Jones, Stires, Shaver, & Harris, 1968). A number of more subtle considerations qualify these findings, but the broad outlines of ingratiation research basically show that people are responsive to ingratiation "incentives"; they tend to avoid the more blatant forms of ingratiating behavior; and, if an actor's overtures are blatant, he is readily identified by outside observers as responding to ulterior motives—and less readily charged with ulterior motivation by the high-power target person himself.

The theoretical treatment of ingratiation has been more fully developed than the theoretical bases of other self-presentational strategies. The particular form that ingratiation will take (conformity versus favors versus other-enhancement versus self-enhancement) is, no doubt, determined in complex ways by the ingratiator's resources and the nature of the setting. It is easier for the applicant to be self-enhancing than conforming in an employment interview situation. It is easier to be flattering after observing a performance, or meeting an offspring of the target, than in an informal discussion of world affairs. High-status persons with a low-status target are more likely to use flattery to gain attraction than conformity or agreement. Thus, the time, the place, and the nature of the relationship promote the likelihood of particular attraction-seeking strategies. Individual difference factors undoubtedly also play a role both in the generation of ingratiating behavior and in bystander evaluations of ingratiation (Jones & **[236]** Baumeister, 1976). Nevertheless, a general theoretical account of the ingratiation process is plausible and consistent with known data. Such an account stresses three underlying determinants of attraction-seeking overtures:

1. Incentive value—the importance of being liked by a particular target. This varies directly with the dependence of the actor on the target, and inversely with the degree of his power over the target. In most nonritualized, nontransient relationships, the incentive value is greater than zero, because the actor is unlikely to be indifferent toward others' evaluations of his attractiveness as a person.

2. Subjective probability—the choice of a particular ingratiation strategy is also determined by the subjective probability of its success, and the inverse probability that a boomerang effect (decreased attraction) will occur. Thus, the motivational determinant, incentive value, is qualified or constrained by the cognitive determinant, subjective probability, in its effects on behavior. The *ingratiator's dilemma* is created by the fact that as the actor's dependence on the target goes up, his motivation to ingratiate goes up, whereas the subjective probability of its success goes down. This occurs because dependence makes salient to the target, as well as any bystanding observers, the possibility of ulterior purposes in actions that are commonly seen as eliciting attraction. The dilemma for the ingratiator is that the more important it is for him to gain a high-power target's attraction, the less likely it is that he will be successful. Attempts to avoid or minimize the effects of this dilemma can lead to the complication of strategic overtures noted previously. The actor must go out of his way to establish his credibility, especially in those settings where extreme dependence might make his credibility suspect. Matters of timing are also important. We have already noted that individuals may invest the profits from strategic overtures in a power bank for use on future occasions. The far-sighted ingratiator may thus avoid the greater risks of failure attendant upon maneuvers specifically linked to those times when his dependence is most apparent and his need for approval the most imperative.

3. Perceived legitimacy—in addition to the contribution of motivational and cognitive factors, ingratiation is further shaped and constrained by moral or evaluative factors. We have already noted that the forms of ingratiating behavior vary with opportunity and resources, including appropriateness within a setting. Perceived legitimacy adds another dimension of appropriateness: the extent to which one's presentations of self are consistent with the phenomenal self and with the norms governing acceptable departures (for reasons of kindness or courtesy) from candor. Each of us internalizes a set of moral standards defining the reprehensibility of dissimulation and deceit in human relations. The moral situation is complicated, however, by the inculcation of other values favoring the promotion of self-interest and the legitimacy of self-salesmanship. Thus, out of a complex mixture of moral forces pushing here for "authenticity" and there for "impression management," the individual must decide on the best strategic combination in his dealings with others.

Because of various ambiguities connected with the "business ethic," many [237] would-be ingratiators can find considerable freedom of movement in their strategic choices. The press to perceive ingratiation as legitimate undoubtedly increases with other features defining the relationship: ingratiation is likely to be perceived as legitimate in settings where self-salesmanship is sanctioned by the individualistic norms of the business world, where the target is not respected by the actor, in the absence of bystanders, and where the actor feels that his dependence is unfair or inequitable. Other possibilities are discussed by Jones (1964; Jones & Wortman, 1973). Many of these reflect the importance of consensus or perceived consensus. What "everybody does" is all right for one to do. Other factors stress the readiness of actors (1) to deny that their behavior was insincere, and (2) to insist that their intentions were benign and socially supportive.

The theory of ingratiation does not specify clearly how these three major determinants interact. Perhaps they combine multiplicatively because, if any factor is zero, ingratiation will presumably not occur. Though normative factors undoubtedly shape the form as well as the occurrence of ingratiation, it may turn out that perceived legitimacy is more a dichotomous variable than either incentive value or subjective probability. Moral decisions tend to have an either–or quality about them. This would suggest that incentive value and subjective probability multiply to produce a strong or weak tendency to ingratiate. Legitimacy then plays its role as a threshold factor, providing a go or stop signal depending on the strength of incentive value and subjective probability. Thus, a person may flatter or ingratiate even though he knows this behavior is not entirely legitimate once the importance and the likelihood of obtaining a benefit reach a certain combined value.

Intimidation

Whereas the ingratiator attempts to convince a target person that he is likable, the intimidator tries to convince a target person that he is *dangerous*. Whereas successful ingratiation reduces or blunts the target person's power by causing him to avoid doing anything that would hurt or cost the actor, the intimidator advertises his available power to create pain, discomfort, or all kinds of psychic costs. The actor seeks to receive the attribution that he has the resources to inflict pain and stress *and* the inclination to do so if he does not get his way. Quite unlike the ingratiator, the intimidator typically disdains any real interest in being liked; he wants to be feared, to be believed.

The intimidation prototype is the sidewalk robber who extracts money from a pedestrian by brandishing a gun or a knife. The robber is successful when the pedestrian believes the threat: if I do not give him my money, he will kill or maim me. A more benign, and more psychologically interesting prototype is an older person in some position of authority within an organization. He is gruff, austere, impatient with shoddy performance. He does not suffer fools gladly. Underlings do his bidding because they fear the consequences of his response to failure or inadequate performance. In some cases, he may not even make his expectations or [238] desires clear, thus leaving his dependent subordinates in an uncomfortable position of edgy anxiety. In any event, it is clear in these cases that the intimidator has managed to project and elicit an attribution from others that supports his continuing social control.

Though it is perhaps more common for intimidation to flow from high-power to low-power persons than vice versa, relationships without some element of counterpower are almost inconceivable in contemporary society. And where there are elements of counterpower, there is the opportunity for intimidation. It is by no means farfetched to speak of the power of children to intimidate adults. In fact, we suggest that the occurrence of filial intimidation is indeed common. Children learn in infancy the rewards of tears and tantrums. Especially as they progress into adolescence, our offspring can blunt the exercise of parental power by having previously established that they are quite capable of making a "scene." The anticipated likelihood of such scenes can deter the most conscientious mother from asking her son to clean his room or to do the company dishes. Parents will sometimes go to great lengths to avoid the disharmony that follows in the wake of demands on their children for services that are reasonable and equitable.

The counterpower resource of making a scene is also available to otherwise impotent employees, students, servants, or prisoners. There are, of course, a number of self-abnegating variants such as hunger strikes and passive resistance. Of special importance in the attributional context is the threat, usually created quite unwittingly, of emotional breakup or collapse. An otherwise impotent person can gather considerable power by acquiring the reputation of one who cannot stand stress or disappointment without responding with hysterical weeping, coronary distress, or suicidal depression. The costs of acquiring such a reputation may be too great for most of us, but there are milder variations on this theme of manipulation that have considerable controlling power in many organizational contexts. The employer who fails to criticize the inept performance of an emotionally unstable employee, in the interests of avoiding a breakdown on his part, may end up unable to fire him because the employer has never given him fair warning. Similarly, it is natural for one spouse to avoid actions and conversational topics that upset the other. It is just as natural for a spouse to signal through incipient distress those mannerisms or topics that he or she wishes to eliminate from the repertory of the other spouse.

When the potential intimidator has enough power to be a credible aggressive threat, incipient anger is a very common controlling device in his relations with others. A man with a short fuse can often dominate a relationship or a group, especially if his ultimately provoked overt anger is likely to be explosive or consequential. President Eisenhower had a very mobile face, whose expressions ranged from the famous grin to a dark and forbidding glower. The latter often appeared when a particular line of questioning began in a press conference, and we are tempted to speculate concerning the controlling potential of such "incipient rage," especially in view of our knowledge of his blood pressure problem. [239]

The concept of threat is obviously central to a discussion of intimidation, but we would stress the implicit nature of most interpersonal threats and note that their effectiveness depends on the manipulation of attributions to the actor by those he desires to control. We may summarize this descriptive account of intimidation variants by suggesting some of the more common alternative attributional goals:

Attribution 1. I cannot tolerate much stress, and if I am placed under stress, I will develop symptoms or engage in behaviors that will cost or embarrass you.

Attribution 2. I am willing to cause myself pain or embarrassment in order to get my way with others.

Attribution 3. I have a low threshold for anger, and when angered, I behave unpredictably and irrationally.

Attribution 4. I have a low threshold for anger, and when angered, I have the resources to be effectively vindictive.

Attribution 5. I am not likely to be deterred in my actions by sentiment, compassion, or the wish to be liked by others.

In theoretical terms, intimidation is, in many respects, the obverse of ingratiation. Intimidating gestures are likely to make the intimidator less, rather than more, attractive. As such, intimidation drives people apart and creates pressures toward withdrawal and avoidance by the target person. This is why we have stressed that intimidation most commonly occurs in relationships that have nonvoluntary status: families, marriages, student–teacher relationships, employers and employees, and military service. It is important that the intimidator have a clear conception of the strength of nonvoluntary bonds. Because intimidation generates avoidance pressures, miscalculations can result in divorces, delinquency, disinheritance, job switching, and various forms of sabotage and insurgency.

A glance at the preceding list of alternative attributions also suggests that intimidation is limited in other respects. The high-power intimidator must often forego affection and a number of attributions that are highly prized in our society. The low-power intimidator must often undergo humiliation or pain in order to carry out such threats as "making a scene," getting drunk, or becoming ill, to say nothing of carrying out such ultimate threats as suicide.

But we must also remember that much of the intimidation range is rather benign and involves transitory sequences in relationships that are otherwise stable and even, on balance, affectionate. Rather than destroy a relationship, patterns of intimidation may redefine it so that certain kinds of interaction are avoided. Thus, marital adjustments may involve a considerable amount of mutual intimidation within a framework of affection and love.

To summarize this introductory view of intimidation, interpersonal power may be exerted by credible threats that create fears of negative consequences for a target person. As a class of self-presentational strategies, intimidation involves the manipulation of attributions that support the credibility of such threats of negative consequences. The threats may be exceedingly vague or implicit. The intimidator [240] may or may not be aware of the strategic goals of his self-presentations. His actions may, as in the case of the ingratiator, represent an overlearned response to a particular pattern of social conditions, rather than a self-conscious strategy of manipulation. There are almost no empirical data concerning the conditions favoring intimidation as currently defined. From the preceding discussion, however, we may extract the following suggestions about the antecedent conditions under which intimidation is most likely to occur:

1. When relationships are nonvoluntary, involve commitments difficult to abrogate, or when alternative relationships are unavailable to the target person.
2. When the potential intimidator has readily available resources with which to inflict negative consequences (weapons, wage control, sexual availability).
3. When the potential target person has weak retaliatory capacities (inhibitions regarding direct aggression toward the young or less fortunate, small stature, lack of confidence in capacity to make verbal rejoinders).
4. When the potential intimidator is willing to forego affection and the attributions of compassion, generosity, and humility—either because he has "given up" on such attributions or can obtain them in alternative relationships.

Self-Promotion

Although using self-descriptions to enhance one's attractiveness was originally presented (Jones, 1964) as one form of ingratiation, we would like to separate out an important class of self-descriptive communications that seek the attribution of competence rather than likability. For such communications, we reserve the name self-promotion. Within the overall self-presentation taxonomy, then, we speak of an actor as "self-characterizing" when he describes himself with the ulterior goal of increasing his personal attractiveness. We speak of the actor as "self-promoting" when he seeks the attribution of competence, whether with reference to general ability level (intelligence, athletic ability) or to a specific skill (typing excellence, flute-playing ability).

At the outset, it should be noted that self-promotion partakes of certain features of both ingratiation and intimidation. In fact, the fusion or combination of attributional goals is common in all forms of self-presentation. We may wish to be both liked for our attractive personal qualities and respected for our talents and capacities. Or we may wish to appear competent so that we gain the social privilege of being intimidating: so that, for example, we can "get away with" depriving others for inferior performance. There is a sense in which competence itself is intimidating. We defer in awe to Einsteins, Horowitzes, and Borgs. The projection of a competent image is often an important part of the intimidator's baggage. But self-promotion is not equivalent to intimidation. We can convince others of our competence without threatening them or striking fear in their hearts.

A brief digression may delineate the difference. In 1973, R. Ringer wrote a best seller called *Winning Through Intimidation*. By the current taxonomy, this book actually said very little about intimidation and a great deal about self-promotion. **[241]** Ringer describes again and again various ploys and mannerisms for convincing others that you are worthy of their time, their attention, their business. In describing his own success as a real-estate broker, he notes the importance of flying to the potential client's city in a private Lear jet and sweeping into the office with expensive portable dictating equipment and a personal secretary. But these "trappings of power" seem less designed to threaten the client than to reassure him that the broker knows what he is doing. If he were an incompetent broker, after all, he could hardly afford a Lear jet or a traveling secretary.

There are obviously many contexts in which we are eager to impress others with our competence. Some of the more obvious ones are students confronting teachers, applicants being interviewed for professional schools or jobs, actors trying out for a play, and athletes trying to make a team. But for many of us, self-promotion is almost a full-time job. The phenomenal self is typically organized in such a way that some talents, some areas of competence, are clearly more important than others. We laugh at our own ineptitude at music, bridge, or ping-pong, but we are deadly serious about our ability to diagnose an ailment, or to design a house, or to raise a family. Many self-promoters parade their ineptitude in minor areas to establish the credibility of their claims of competence in crucial areas (Jones, Gergen, & Jones, 1963).

The ingratiation strategist must cope with the problems of establishing sincerity and authenticity. The intimidator must cope with the costs and potential dangers of his threatening behavior. The self-promoter must cope with the apparent ease with which many areas of competence may be objectively diagnosed. One might wonder if a person can get away with claims of competence for very long before being observed in some form of diagnostic performance. Within long-range relationships among spouses, academic colleagues, or business associates, competence claims can ordinarily be tested against the data of performance.

Chapter 16   Toward a General Theory of Strategic Self-Presentation   **369**

An experiment by Baumeister & Jones (1978) demonstrates how people cope with diagnostic information about them to which others have access. Subjects took a personality test, the (bogus) results of which were shown to them, and (so they believed) to a fellow subject with whom they were later to interact. When subjects were then given the opportunity to communicate further information about themselves to the other subject in the form of self-ratings, these ratings depended crucially on the particular personality profiles allegedly in the other subjects' hands. If the profile was generally negative, subjects rated themselves negatively on traits disparaged by the profile, but strongly compensated by positive self-descriptions on dimensions not specifically mentioned. If the profile was positive, on the other hand, subjects were typically modest on all their communicated self-ratings. The relevance of these data for the current discussion of self-promotion lies in the fact that these same self-description tendencies were absent when only the subjects themselves (and not the "other subject") saw their personality profile. The compensation effect noted in the negative profile case (positive self-descriptions on traits unrelated to the profile) was not present when only the subject was the recipient, and the notable modesty in the positive profile **[242]** case also disappeared when the subject thought he was describing himself to someone who knew nothing as yet about him. It is apparent, then, that people develop fairly standard ways of coming to terms with self-referent information that is publicly known. They manage their self-presentations so as not to contradict directly any known information that is negative in implications. When the information others have is generally positive, however, people apparently strive for the extra social rewards that accompany modesty, without the risk of appearing incompetent.

It is relatively easy to think of instances where the data of performance or other diagnostic information are not readily available to contradict self-promoting claims. One example is the claim of an older man that he was a star athlete, or an older woman that she was a polished dancer. There are certain crucial decisions of selection, or admission, that are often based largely on claims alone, though some information about previous performance is typically available as well. Nevertheless, the admissions committee or the selection officer is usually aware of the fact that prior performance in one setting may be a poor predictor of good performance in the setting to which they control access. Finally, some people may claim important attributes like a high IQ without fearing that their IQ will ever by publicly assessed. Thus, there are occasions when all we can go by in judging another's competence are his claims, and many more occasions when the claims can be only indirectly tested and never totally refuted if false.

This leaves most of us with considerable freedom to maneuver, but if there is "an ingratiator's dilemma" (see earlier), there is also a "self-promoter's paradox." Most of us learn that many people exaggerate their abilities, and therefore their competence claims can often be, at least partly, discounted. In fact, the paradox arises because it is often the case that competence claims are *more* likely when competence is shaky than when it is high and securely so (as evident in Baumeister & Jones's modesty findings). Even if direct competence claims are credible, the attribution of competence may be achieved along with less favoring attributions of arrogance, insecurity, or at least dreariness.

However, the gifted self-promoter will not be totally inhibited by this paradox. He will seek indirect ways to enable the target person to reach the conclusion that he is competent in the desired respects. The adroit social climber is not likely to claim membership in the upper class to establish his aristocratic origins. He will do so by subtle patterns of consumption (clothing, house, cars, furniture) that convince others he is not just a pretentious or gauche nouveau arrivé. Similarly, college, job, and professional school applicants can establish the *likelihood* that they will succeed, if accepted, by noting factors that would normally be expected to facilitate success: middle-class family background, educated parents, previous entry to a prestigious school, diverse summer employment experiences, elections to leadership positions, etc.—and noting them in the most matter-of-fact way.

Quattrone & Jones (1978) investigated self-presentational priorities in a role-playing **[243]** experiment in which subjects either did or did not have the opportunity for a diagnostic performance. In one vignette, for example, subjects were to imagine themselves trying out for a coveted dramatic role and were told to be motivated to convince the director that they were versatile actors, suitable for roles in future plays as well. Some subjects were to assume that they impressed the director with a highly relevant performance audition. Others were to assume that no such audition took place. In the latter case, as predicted, subjects chose to disclose to the director those designated facts about themselves that were evaluatively positive and would normally facilitate the likelihood of doing well in the part (e.g., they chose to disclose readily that they had acted the same part previously). When an audition occurred and the subject's performance was applauded by the director, however, subjects chose to assign disclosure priority to facts that would normally make it *less* likely that they could perform the particular role (e.g., they had received good notices in a play where their role was the opposite kind of person from that in the role to be currently filled). Thus, when correspondent, diagnostic behavior is possible and successful, the individual will present *inhibitory* background factors to augment the significance of his general ability or his perseverance or his innate courage. When there is not an opportunity for correspondent performance, on the other hand, the individual will disclose features that normally are seen to *facilitate* the likelihood that subsequent performance will be successful.

This study has several strategic implications and especially suggests that we often do not merely wish to establish that we are competent at X, Y, or Z. Beyond this, whenever possible, we want to convince the target person that our talents stem from causal conditions that enhance our attractiveness or respect worthiness. We may wish our competence as a musician to be attributed to great natural ability rather than hard work and, thus, fail to disclose the long practice hours in our past. We may for similar reasons conceal that we have taken lessons in golf. On the other hand, if we are a member of a seminar in which the appraisal of our performance is very much a matter of the instructor's subjective judgment, we may go out of our way to impress him that we have worked harder than other seminar members in preparing papers for the course. Though he may influence the instructor to give him a higher grade in this particular course, however, the seminar member who follows this strategy also runs the risk of being evaluated as a little too limited and overconscientious for consideration as a top candidate for subsequent academic positions. Following the line of reasoning developed by Quattrone & Jones, the appropriate graduate student strategy might be to marshal all the relevant facilitatory factors for presentation to the department before admission, and to emphasize the inhibitory factors once having been admitted. The applicant might, for example, stress his Yale education prior to admission but talk much more about growing up in Appalachia once in graduate school.

To summarize the subclass of self-presentation strategies that we have labeled here as self-promotion: Individuals commonly have a stake in convincing particular [244] target persons that they are competent in one or more areas where there are no readily available, highly criterial competence tests. Their success may be an important factor in gaining access to such important goals as prestigious school admission and responsible jobs. There are strategic problems associated with straightforward competence claims, however, in that the most persistent claimants are often the most insecure about the talents being claimed. For this reason, it is a superior strategy for the self-promoter to arrange for others to make claims in his behalf, but even these can range in impact because the outside claimant may be far from an objective judge. Professors often have a stake in the success of their students and are unlikely to be ruthlessly candid in their letters of reference for a mediocre protégé. On the whole, there is no substitute for diagnostic performance itself—especially if this can be managed under conditions that implicate desirable causal origins for the demonstrated competence. The individual who wants her professional success to be attributed to her natural brilliance will obviously behave in a different way than one who wants others to attribute her success to hard work and self-denial. Self-promotion thus has a property of being multitiered, with attributions underlying attributions. It is desirable to be seen as competent, but it is even more desirable to be seen as competent for the most admired causal reasons—whatever they may be in a particular culture or situational context.

Exemplification

The ingratiator wants to be liked and the intimidator wants to be feared. The self-promoter and the exemplifier both want to be respected, to be admired, but there are subtle and important differences in the attributions they seek. Whereas the self-promoter wants to be seen as competent, masterful, olympian, the exemplifier seeks to project *integrity and moral worthiness*. Once again, we emphasize that there is nothing mutually exclusive about these goals. Many of us would love to be seen as simultaneously competent, likable, and morally worthy. Nevertheless, we single out exemplification because of its distinct strategic qualities and its special relationship to the behavior of emulation and the internal conditions of guilt and shame.

The exemplifier (in Western society at least) typically presents himself as honest, disciplined, charitable, and self-negating. He is the saint who walks among us, the martyr who sacrifices for the cause. But to be successful he must not cross over the line into self-righteousness. For appropriate social effect he must exemplify morality and not merely claim it. But what *is* the appropriate social effect? Exemplary actions may be sincere and self-consistent: The actor may have so strongly internalized the ideal values of a society that his consistently virtuous behavior is unaffected by the response of others to its expression. Insofar as this is true, we are not dealing with strategic self-presentation as we have defined it earlier. There may be such people. We suspect that totally autonomous, self-consistent, and self-expressive exemplifiers—true "exemplars"—are rare. [245] In keeping with our interests in strategic behavior, we turn to the more common everyday self-presenter who wants others to perceive, validate, and be influenced by his selfless integrity, even though he might vigorously deny such motivation and, indeed, be unaware of it.

The prototype for the exemplifier is, of course, the religious leader who lives a life of apparent Christian (Buddhist, Moslem, etc.) virtue in return for persuasive power. In celebrated and unusual cases, the exemplifier seeks martyrdom or, at least, passively accepts incarceration, torture, institutionalized deprivation. Examples such as Gandhi, Martin Luther King, the Ayatollah Khomeini come to mind. The power that may accrue from such dramatic exemplifiers may be used for a variety of specific objectives: recruiting a following, raising funds, changing a law, fomenting a revolution.

A variant of exemplification is ideological militancy, though the relationship of militancy to self-presentation is undoubtedly complex because militancy is typically more a collective than an individual phenomenon. Nevertheless, individuals may, in the service of an ideological belief, exploit self-deprivation to influence such institutionalized power sources as employers, legislators, judges, and government executives. This self-deprivation may often be coupled with violent confrontation. This is obvious in the case of "pro-life" advocates who vandalize abortion clinics, or student militants who take over administration buildings. Anti-nuclear and pro-environmental forces seem to have similar potential. In all such cases, the exemplifier attempts to trade on the worthiness of his cause and not solely on the physical power of his coalition with like-minded colleagues. We would label him an exemplifier, because he attempts to arouse guilt in those who otherwise have the power to control the possibilities of physical confrontation. He presents himself as taking an exclusively worthy stand for which he is willing to undergo abstinence, arrest, expulsion, and so on. The target persons to whom he presents this selfless image can reduce their resulting guilt by, if not undergoing the same deprivations, at least supporting the same cause and implicitly recognizing the worthiness of the militant advocate.

Such confrontations have a less dramatic counterpart in many instances of social influence and self-presentation. Parental socialization of children relies heavily on exemplification. Most parents attempt to put their best foot forward in front of their children. They attempt to exemplify the values of the culture in the hopes that their children will model these values and feel guilty when falling short of parental standards. We refer here not so much to the kinds of response modeling discussed by Bandura (1971) and other social-learning theorists, but rather to the sequence of self-presentation, eliciting an attribution of moral worth, providing the conditions for potential guilt in a target person, who, in turn, is motivated to emulate or model the exemplifier. Even in the context of socialization, the sequence implies that the child has clearly acquired a sufficient "feel" for idealized cultural values, so that he can recognize and appreciate the exemplary status of his parents.

Exemplification as a self-presentational strategy is probably as ubiquitous as [246] the other strategies we have discussed (and is often fused with them). The fellow alumnus who calls for a contribution to the college class fund is exemplifying because *he* is making the kind of sacrifice he wants, and expects, you to make. The neighbor who bicycles to the train station arouses our guilt as we climb into our commodious gas guzzler. The housewife who eats peanut butter sandwiches for lunch and wears clothes from the 60's can have a decisive moral edge over her self-indulgent husband with his three-martini lunch. Employers and supervisors who arrive early and leave late may exert exemplifying pressure on their subordinates, even though they may take long lunches, play midday tennis, or seclude themselves for an afternoon nap. In general, to practice what you preach is to give the preaching that much more force, but exemplification may also be effective when the preaching is not explicit.

In summary, aside from wanting others to think of us as competent and likable, we usually want them to think of us as morally worthy: honest, generous, self-sacrificing. Furthermore, attributed worthiness may provide considerable strategic leverage when asking others for support or self-sacrifice. Most would agree that President Carter was more prone to use exemplification as an influence strategy than were Presidents Johnson or Nixon. It is difficult to assess the extent to which this helped to alert the nation to the virtues of physical exercise or the need for self-sacrifices in the energy sector. The present discussion merely scratches the surface of a complex subject, but we believe that the attribution of worthiness is often sought for strategic purposes, and that "worthy" persons often find it difficult to avoid exploiting the power inherent in their own apparent virtue.

Supplication

A final self-presentational strategy may be available to those who lack the resources implied by the preceding strategies: a person may exploit his own weakness and dependence. When the wolf feels overwhelmed by superior fighting power, it displays its vulnerable throat. This appears to evoke some form of instinctive inhibition in the attacker so that the supplicant wolf is spared. We venture to suggest an analogy in interpersonal relations. By stressing his inability to fend for himself and emphasizing his dependence on others, the human supplicant makes salient a norm of obligation or social responsibility (Berkowitz & Daniels, 1963) that is more or less binding on target persons with greater resources. Supplication—the strategy of advertising one's dependence to solicit help—works best when there appears to be an arbitrary or accidental component in the power differential (Schopler & Matthews, 1965). If through an accident of birth one enjoys such resources as physical strength, intelligence, natural beauty, or money, and another is born handicapped in some physical or mental way, social responsibility norms impose an obligation on the former to care for the latter. Matters may be somewhat different when the "self-made" man confronts the "indolent" welfare applicant, but even here there are general, if less imperative, norms that those who need have some claim over those who have more than they [247] need. The prototype of the self-presenting supplicant is the sexist female paired with the sexist male. The classic female supplicant (against ERA to the core) is nearly helpless in coping with the physical world. She cannot change a tire, understand algebra, read a legal document, carry a suitcase, or order wine. Her classic male counterpart, of course, rushes in to fill the breach. His vanity is touched by the indispensability of his contributions to her survival in the world. Regardless of the ultimate psychological or social consequences of this symbiosis, the supplicant female influences the male to expend energy on her behalf; to do things for her that she would like to have done. She accomplishes this at the small cost of being considered totally incompetent by her vain and dedicated husband or suitor.

We hasten to reaffirm that not all females are supplicants; nor, we now add, are all supplicants females. One suspects that many children exaggerate their ineptitude at common household chores in order to influence their parents to complete the chores themselves. Similarly, husbands often avoid learning to sew, iron, or change diapers, in order to ensure that their wives will continue to perform these functions for them, or instead of them. In a typical job setting, A may entreat B for substantial help on a project for which A gets the credit. A may then pay with an expression of gratitude, but the more important hidden payment may be A's implicit acknowledgment of B's superiority. Such exchanges of help for competence validation are undoubtedly common in group life, whether they involve students, siblings, or job colleagues. Even more common, however, are relationships sustained by mutual dependence in which A is better than B in some areas, and B is better than A in others. Complementary aid, in such cases, can result in a stable and satisfactory division of labor, expertise, or advice.

The exploitation of one's dependence is a risky strategy and presumably one that is normally of last resort. There may be heavy costs to one's self-esteem in acknowledging, or even advertising, one's helplessness and incompetence. And there is always the good possibility that the resource-laden target person is insensitive to the social responsibility norm. Even if he responds initially with a helpful or noble gesture, he may arrange to avoid getting entrapped by the supplicant in the future by breaking off the relationship ("tell him I'm not in"). It is not too difficult for an impoverished graduate student to wrangle a free lunch from his professor at a campus restaurant; it is substantially more difficult to bring about such an event a second time. The professor may start bringing sandwiches to work or eat at odd hours to avoid further exploitation by the student—who may feel that the economic deprivation that goes with student status entitles him to trade on noblesse oblige from the more affluent professor.

Summary

We have introduced taxonomy of self-presentational strategies classified in terms of the kinds of attributions sought by the presenter. In all cases, we conceive of the underlying goal as the augmentation or protection of the strategist's [248] power to influence and control his social environment. The ingratiator augments his power by reducing the likelihood that the target person will deliver negative outcomes, and increasing the prospects for positive ones. The intimidator more directly enhances his power by increasing the likelihood that he will use the negative part of the range of outcomes that he can deliver to the target person. The self-promoter enhances his putative instrumental value as a problem solver for the target person. Because he obviously has something to offer, he may extract money or other outcomes in exchange. The exemplifier trades on the power of recognized social norms undergirded by the judged consensus about proper values and aspirations. He influences by successfully reflecting these norms. The supplicant also gains the power provided by the sheltering norm of social responsibility. By relinquishing his claims to more immediate personal power, he places himself at the mercy of more powerful others who are, he hopes, sensitive to the dictates of noblesse oblige.

We have, in passing, noted that these five strategies need not be mutually exclusive, though some combinations may be more plausible and therefore more likely than others. There is a certain incompatibility between ingratiation and intimidation, though self-promotion may fit nicely with either. The exemplifier may be intimidating if he can arouse guilt and fear simultaneously. Supplication is the obverse of self-promotion, though the supplicant can obviously be ingratiating and even, in a certain sense, intimidating. And so on. It is also undoubtedly the case that the same act can serve different functions for different audiences. The militant picketer may intimidate management, while being an exemplifier to passersby. We separate the strategies in our taxonomy not to segregate personal types or behavior episodes, but rather to distinguish the particular attributional goal, the "self" presented in the strategic act. Figure 16.1 presents a summary of the taxonomy in terms of the attribution sought, negative attributions risked, the emotion aroused, and prototypical actions.

THE IMPLICATIONS OF THE PHENOMENAL SELF FOR STRATEGIC SELF-PRESENTATION—AND VICE VERSA

We now consider the relations between self-presentation and the phenomenal self. We ultimately want to know both how strategic self-presentations are influenced by the immediately salient features of the phenomenal self, and how the phenomenal self is altered or shaped by particular self-presentational strategies. It is perhaps self-evident that socially oriented actions should, in some way, reflect the phenomenal self, though there is surprisingly little evidence on this point. We here deal with the issue very briefly.

The Phenomenal Self as a Determinant of Strategy Choice

We have already commented on the existence of various social norms that support [250] and give social value to personal consistency. The concept of "integrity" is tied in with

	Attributions sought	Negative attributions risked	Emotion to be aroused	Prototypical actions
1. Ingratiation	Likable	Sycophant, conformist, obsequious	Affection	Self-characterization, opinion conformity, other-enhancement, favors
2. Intimidation	Dangerous (ruthless, volatile)	Blusterer, wishy-washy, ineffectual	Fear	Threats, anger (incipient), breakdown (incipient)
3. Self-promotion	Competent (effective, "a winner")	Fraudulent, conceited, defensive	Respect (awe, deference)	Performance claims, performance accounts, performances
4. Exemplification	Worthy (suffers, dedicated)	Hypocrite, sanctimonious, exploitative	Guilt (shame, emulation)	Self-denial, helping, militancy for a cause
5. Supplication	Helpless (handicapped, unfortunate)	Stigmatized, lazy, demanding	Nurturance (obligation)	Self-deprecation, entreaties for help

Figure 16.1 A Taxonomy of Self-Presentational Strategies Classified Primarily by Attribution Sought

an individual's capacity to avoid being different things to different people—in effect, to avoid being overly influenced by strategic concerns. These norms coalesce in the concept of perceived legitimacy, which constrains the circumstances under which strategic self-presentations take place. We have not discussed the role of perceived legitimacy in determining the most acceptable *form* of strategic behavior once it takes place, but such considerations obviously relate to the current concern with how the phenomenal self influences the presented self. It seems likely, for example, that a person who (momentarily or characteristically) sees himself as tough and competitive is more likely to be intimidating or self-promotive than supplicating or ingratiating. Someone who has just given to charity or helped a friend move, and whose worthiness is therefore phenomenally salient, is more likely than others to adopt the strategies of exemplification. Clearly, there is a wide-open field of study involved in charting the role that individual differences play in preferences for particular forms of strategic behavior. Immediate prior experiences may also affect strategic choice, however, and this avenue of experimentation should not be ignored.

Self-Enhancement, Approval, and Self-Esteem

We ultimately want to know both how strategic self-presentations are influenced by the immediately salient features of the phenomenal self, and how the phenomenal self is temporarily affected by a particular choice of self-presentational strategy. Turning to effects of self-presentation on the phenomenal self, research on this question has been largely restricted to the consequences of ingratiation for the actor's self-esteem. We review this research briefly and then speculate concerning the consequences for the phenomenal self of self-presentations involving the remaining strategies.

Let us begin by picturing an actor who is asked to characterize himself in a setting where he has a stake in gaining attraction from a target person. Typically, ingratiation research shows an actor in such a setting will be more self-enhancing than one in more neutral settings where attraction is less of an issue (Gergen, 1965; Jones, Gergen, & Davis, 1962; Jones, Gergen, & Jones, 1963). Self-enhancement will be reduced and self-characterization will be more modest to the extent that the actor's dependence on the target person is salient (Stires & Jones, 1969). If we could subsequently gain access to the undistorted phenomenal self, would it reflect, in any way, the preceding self-characterization? What circumstances might augment, and what might lessen, the impact of such self-characterization on the phenomenal self?

First of all, it is abundantly clear that if an actor is positively reinforced for characterizing himself in a very enhanced way, his phenomenal self will subsequently shift in the direction of the characterized self. Indirect evidence on this point is presented by Jones, Gergen, & Davis (1962). Subjects instructed to play the role of fellowship applicants with an interviewer were considerably [251] more self-enhancing than control subjects instructed to present themselves accurately to a counselor trying to help them. Half the subjects in each condition then learned that they had impressed the interviewer favorably; the other half learned that the interviewer was unfavorably impressed. Regardless of whether subjects were in the ingratiation or control (accuracy) conditions, those with positive feedback rated their behavior in the interview as "more representative" of their true selves than those with negative feedback.

More direct evidence along the same lines comes from Gergen's (1965) experiment, in which subjects in an ingratiation condition were instructed to make a positive impression on an interviewer, and those in an accuracy condition were instructed to help the interviewer get to know them. All subjects in the ingratiation condition and half the accuracy condition subjects were then reinforced by the interviewer's head nods and expressions of agreement each time they characterized themselves in a positive way on a special triads test. The remaining accuracy subjects were not reinforced at all. Finally, all subjects filled out a self-esteem scale for the experimenter to gauge the extent to which the reinforcement generalized. The results showed a considerable elevation of self-esteem scores in the reinforcement conditions. Although ingratiation subjects were significantly more self-enhancing in the interview than accuracy subjects, both groups ultimately showed approximately the same degree of self-esteem elevation. This seems to indicate that even though subjects in the ingratiation condition realized that their self-characterizations were somewhat unrealistic, as measured by the decline in self-evaluation from the interview situation to the final self-ratings in a more neutral setting, they nevertheless did not lower their self-esteem back to its original level. In both Gergen's experiment and the earlier one of Jones, Gergen, and Davis, positive feedback was an important factor in determining resultant self-esteem levels.

Recent studies by Jones, Rhodewalt, Berglas, & Skelton (1981) took a different approach to the question of the impact of self-presentation on the phenomenal self. If subjects can be induced to characterize themselves positively without explicit instructions to fabricate or distort their characteristics, this may be sufficient to elevate subsequent self-esteem, even in the absence of positive feedback. Why might this be so? Two possibilities suggest themselves: dissonance reduction and biased scanning. If we were to assume that actors have stable phenomenal selves and that ingratiation incentives induced them to describe their characteristics in ways that differ from this stable self-picture, dissonance would be aroused. If the dissonance could not be reduced by attributing responsibility for the discrepancy to experimental instructions, it could most conveniently be reduced by a change in the phenomenal self in the direction of the ingratiating self-characterization. This would be yet another instance of attitudes reflecting behavior in a situation where the actor has some choice and responsibility for his actions (Wicklund & Brehm, 1976).

The biased-scanning approach (Janis & Gilmore, 1965) assumes that the selves phenomenally available to the same person over time are highly variable **[252]** in many respects, including favorability; that is, situational cues and immediate push experiences elevate the salience of certain self-features more than others. It follows that inducing a subject to describe himself in a highly favorable way is not necessarily dissonant with some of the phenomenally available selves and will not motivate the subject to *change* his stable self-concept in the direction of a new phenomenal self. Instead, the biased-scanning hypothesis assumes selective attention to those aspects of the phenomenal self that are most consistent with the actor's strategic goals. A subject induced to characterize himself very favorably, for example, will typically do this without clear dissimulation or misrepresentation. He will put his best foot forward, but it is nevertheless his foot. Subsequently, because of the recent biased scanning of favorable instances and self-appraisals, the actor will show the kind of elevated self-esteem observed in Gergen's study.

Jones & Berglas (Experiment I in Jones et al., 1981) set out to explore some of the conditions under which self-presentation produces a shift in subsequent self-esteem. They invited prospective college student subjects to participate for money as members of small teams that would be observing high school student encounter groups. (This activity was selected as a highly desirable one for most undergraduates.) Subjects were informed, however, that selection as an observer team member was contingent on (1) doing well on a social sensitivity test and (2) impressing the team leader with their attractive qualities during an interview. The social sensitivity test involved looking at videotaped excerpts of three previous interviewees responding, allegedly, to the same ingratiation-promoting instructions. The subject was asked to indicate which of the three received the highest attraction ratings by the interviewer. This observation and rating task provided a means of varying the perceived legitimacy of highly favorable versus rather modest self-characterizations. Half the subjects saw tapes of highly self-enhancing behavior in all three interviewees. For the remainder, the interviewees were uniformly modest and self-deprecating. Crosscutting this variation in the direction of the consensus about how to be ingratiating, the order of events was varied. Some subjects were exposed to the taped interview segments before their own interview; others saw the tapes after the interview. The interview itself included a series of items from which a self-enhancement score could be derived.

After the two procedures, whatever their order, all subjects were asked as an incidental afterthought to fill out some questionnaires for a colleague of the experimenter at another university. Their responses would be anonymous and would be mailed directly to him. This afterthought questionnaire provided a measure of self-esteem in a totally different format than that used for the behavioral measure in the interview, and the setting was itself neutral, nonstrategic, and anonymous. Results showed a striking carryover from self-presentation to subsequent self-esteem. Subjects who saw the consensus tapes prior to their interviews were much affected by them; those exposed to the self-enhancing consensus were themselves much more self-enhancing than those exposed to the self-deprecating consensus. These differences continued to be [253] reflected in highly significant differences on the supposedly unrelated self-esteem task. Subjects exposed to the tapes *after* their interview were unaffected by the apparent consensus. Thus, the self-esteem carryover is more than a simple effect of what is perceived to be legitimate or normative in a situation. It depends crucially on whether the actor has been induced to modify his behavior.

Although powerful carryover effects were obtained in this study, their bearing on the dissonance biased-scanning controversy is not clear. The results are very compatible with the biased-scanning hypothesis, because subjects presented a selective pattern of strengths or weaknesses that could easily have made salient either an optimistic or pessimistic view of the self. Dissonance theory would have more trouble handling the results, because it is not clear why dissonance should have been aroused by the procedures—at least by those in the self-enhancing conditions. Why should there be dissonance when a subject describes himself positively in the same setting in which he has seen others describing themselves positively as well? Presumably, self-enhancement should have high perceived legitimacy in such a setting. Dissonance arousal would be prevented by the presence of a consensus justifying any exaggerations or distortions in characterizing the self.

In a follow-up study (Experiment III in Jones et al., 1981) subjects were instructed to present themselves either in a self-enhancing or a self-deprecating way in a contrived interview situation. The interviewer supposedly did not know the situation was contrived. Half the subjects were explicitly told that they could withdraw from the experiment at this point. The remaining subjects were given no such option. This intended manipulation of cognitive dissonance produced variations in self-esteem carryover, but only in the self-deprecating conditions. Thus, those who, in effect, chose to participate in an interview under self-deprecation instructions later rated their self-esteem lower than those who deprecated themselves without being told they had the option to withdraw.

Although the choice manipulation had no effect on self-esteem carryover in the self-enhancing interviews, a biased-scanning manipulation did. Half the subjects generated their own responses to the interview instructions; the remaining subjects were yoked to these so that their responses in the interview were specified to them. This variation in the degree of self-reference had no effect on self-esteem carryover in the self-deprecation conditions, but clearly affected carryover after the self-enhancing interviews. Those who had generated their own self-enhancing interview responses later showed higher self-esteem than yoked subjects constrained to make exactly the same responses.

These results are complex but comprehensible. Jones et al. (1981) suggest that the self-concept is not inflexibly structured. Like other attitudes, it has a latitude of acceptable attributes—things that the individual is willing to believe about himself—and a latitude of rejection. Subjects in the self-enhancing condition are basically operating within the latitude of acceptable attributes. Therefore, following the proposal of Fazio, Zanna, & Cooper (1977), self-concept changes should be explainable in terms of self-perception theory (Bem, 1972). **[254]** According to this theory, subjects' self-concepts should be heavily influenced by their recent behavior, as long as that behavior is seen as self-relevant. Presumably, subjects in the yoked conditions do not see their behavior as self-relevant since the specific content is specified by someone else. Self-deprecating subjects, on the other hand, are acknowledging self-attributes that fall in the latitude of rejection. Thus, again according to Fazio, Zanna, & Cooper (1977), dissonance is created to the extent that there is perceived choice to describe oneself in a self-deprecating way.

The results of this final experiment in the series reported by Jones et al. (1981) suggest that self-presentation can influence the phenomenal self both through biased-scanning and dissonance-reduction processes, depending importantly on the conditions and the content of the self-presentation episode.

Performance Authenticity, Self-Handicapping, and Social Feedback

The effects of other presentational tactics on the phenomenal self are contingent both on the social feedback they elicit and the "authenticity" of the presented self. The ingratiator wants to be liked, but it is especially rewarding if he is viewed as attractive, having not misrepresented himself. Jones (1964) refers to this as the "signifying" value of feedback, noting each actor's interest in verifying or validating his self-concept by reading the social responses of others, and also noting that the signification value of approval is less meaningful to the extent that the actor has gone out of his way to achieve it. As Lord Chesterfield (1774) proposed, furthermore, approval is especially valued if we are uncertain about whether we deserve it. We believe that very similar points could be made with regard to self-promotion and the desire for respect. It is nice if someone believes we are competent, it is better if the same person confirms our own beliefs in our competence, and it is even better if someone convinces us we are competent in an area where we were previously uncertain.

The fact that approval is especially valuable following an authentic or representative performance, puts pressures on the actor that have consequences for the phenomenal self. On the one hand, perceived legitimacy considerations constrain his self-presentations so that they are at least loosely tethered to the phenomenal self. On the other hand, given the fact that some self-presentations occur in settings that tempt the actor to make questionable claims, we can imagine pressures on the individual to bring his phenomenal self in line with these claims. Only in this way can he maximize the signification value of any approval received.

The desire for self-validating approval may become especially strong when events conspire to threaten cherished features of the phenomenal self. Thus, the rejected suitor may try especially hard to be charming and likable around his female friends; the solid citizen arrested for speeding might decide to increase his community service work. In such cases, threats to the phenomenal self lead to self-presentations designed to secure restorative feedback. To the extent that the threatened actor sustains his counteractive [255] behavior, or to the extent that the counteractive behavior involves effortful and costly commitments, social confirmation will have the restorative power sought.

Such validation-oriented self-presentations involve a kind of "positioning" to optimize the value of self-presentational success. An observer's respect for a self-promoting actor is more valuable when it confirms the actor's own image of self-competence. And the actor's subjective competence image may itself evolve from, or be protected by, self-handicapping strategies. Jones & Berglas (1978) used this term to denote a widespread tendency to avoid unequivocal information about one's own abilities when that information might suggest incompetence. To this end, people may arrange performance circumstances that create impediments in the path of optimal performance (thus, the word *handicapping*). In this way, responsibility for success may be triumphantly internalized and for failure, discounted. Berglas & Jones (1978) present the data from two experiments to show subjects will protect ill-gotten performance gains (in their experiments, a "success" derived from luck or chance) by choosing a performance-inhibiting, rather than a performance-facilitating, drug prior to retest. The notion of self-handicapping fits into a more general framework of "egotism" in self-attribution (Snyder, Stephan, & Rosenfield, 1978). From the present point of view, self-handicapping and other egotistic maneuvers may be seen as one way to position one's self so that signs of respect from others for one's competence will not be dismissed as ill-gotten or undeserved gain. At the same time, such maneuvers reduce the impact of failure or disparaging criticism.

Other Carryover Effects

INTIMIDATION   To what extent must the intimidator come to terms with his potential to hurt others and his willingness to exploit that potential? We have noted that intimidation requires a relationship that is, to some extent, nonvoluntary. This fact has the important consequence that the intimidator may seldom receive the attributional feedback that his actions deserve. Instead of learning that he is ruthless or dangerous or violence prone, he may receive signals of admiration and fealty. Thus, intimidation can elicit ingratiation or supplication often enough for the intimidator to be quite misled concerning the attributions he has actually elicited in those who do his bidding. This is reminiscent of the tyrant's dilemma noted by Thibaut & Riecken (1955): A tyrant may exert successful control over his subjects, but the more he applies his power, the less information he receives concerning their spontaneous goodwill and affection. Thus, the intimidator may bask in the unwarranted inference that people are doing things for him because they like him or respect him, rather than because they are afraid not to.

On the other hand, there may be circumstances that shatter such illusions and leave the intimidator with the realization that his power is truly based on his willingness to apply negative sanctions. Here, perhaps, the intimidator can and does protect his phenomenal self from the negative implications of his behavior by one **[256]** of a number of justifications: The world is a jungle, it's for your own good, it's my neck if we fail, war is hell.

EXEMPLIFICATION It is an intriguing fact that exemplifiers often present themselves as mediators or spokesmen for external agencies. Thibaut (1964) has written of the paradoxical mixture of activism and fatalism in the lives of great exemplars: "In many cases, there appears to be a strong dependence on a powerful external agency of control, which may sometimes be a form of deity, an ineluctable historical force, an institution (the army), etc. It is as though the man belonged to a coalition that gave him greater strength to strive or to resist than could be commanded by any single individual" [p. 87]. Thibaut suggests a number of reasons why such an imagined coalition with a powerful agency might lead to a high level of striving and influence and accomplishment. In the present context, however, we are more interested in some of the paradoxical consequences for the phenomenal self of acting on behalf of an all-powerful force. One's immediate associations might suggest that servile "humility" would be the self-image most compatible with exemplification. But there are many conflicting data that involve instances of arrogance and exploitation, even if we avoid the totally fraudulent cult leaders and evangelists who deliberately dissimulate for power or cash. There are enough cases in which initially humble, selfless exemplifiers were transformed into arrogant exploiters to pose a challenge for social psychological analysis. Perhaps because of the coalition with an omnipotent agency mentioned previously, the exemplifier may come to believe in his own moral invulnerability and lose contact with normally effective social and legal sanctions. The case of Jim Jones and his voracious sexual exploitations seems pertinent here, along with the ultimate homicidal behavior of Charles Hedrick, the founder of Synanon. There are doubtless other cases in which the exemplifier gets carried away with his own moral authority. Such transformations seem to be extreme instances of the impact of a self-presentational strategy on the phenomenal self.

Turning to the more casual everyday exemplifier, we suspect that there is considerable strain inherent in maintaining an impeccable moral posture. The exemplifier may find himself on a perpetual treadmill, for behavioral departures from worthiness claims can elicit ridicule and contempt. Here, perhaps, it might seem important to distinguish between the implicit exemplifier and the more explicit claimant to worthiness.

To the extent, however, that the actor attempts to trade on his worthiness in the market of social influence, he becomes a claimant whether or not this is made explicit. Implicit or explicit worthiness claims place a greater burden on the exemplifier than competence claims do on the self-promoter. To overestimate one's competence may be seen as part of the game of life; to parade one's worthiness is at the very least to heighten one's vulnerability to charges of hypocrisy, self-righteousness, or fraudulent piety. There is something paradoxical about expressing pride in one's humility, or exerting influence through self-denial. In addition, whereas one can be competent at x but not at y or z, worthiness is a more either/or quality, a more indivisible whole.

A consequence of the constant pressure on the exemplifier may be the use of [257] "time-outs" or the segregation of on-stage from back-stage performances (Goffman, 1959). Thus, the exemplifier may be able to maintain a consistent moral posture in front of one audience, whereas behaving differently in private or with other audiences. The priest may be a secret heavy drinker or visit brothels in a neighboring city. The father may be profligate and self-indulgent at a convention, although emphasizing the virtues of self-denial to his children.

SUPPLICATION   The phenomenal self of the supplicant is by definition incomplete. The supplicant's self-esteem must be threatened by his cultivation of dependence and ineptitude. We speculate that this might be countered by a form of "identification with the aggressor" that may provide psychological sustenance. To take pleasure in the outcomes and achievements of those who control your fate may be an important form of vicarious gratification that gives closure to the self-concept. An emphasis of the team, the organization, the family, the ethnic group may perhaps be a saving feature of the supplicant's phenomenal self. If one is dependent on others, it may be comforting to think in terms of larger symbiotic units when reflecting on one's identity.

An alternative possibility is that the supplicant can view himself as deserving the largesse of others more fortunate than he. This may coincide with a broader ideological conviction that those who have gained more should be expected to give more. Equity, not equality, is the watchword. Or the dependent supplicant may feel that the system let him down; therefore, the conviction that the system "owes him" is woven into an ideology of embittered and peevish passivity.

SUMMARY AND CONCLUSIONS

The strategic self-presentation rubric encompasses much, though by no means all, of interpersonal behavior. The present essay has drawn attention to five distinct strategies designed to manipulate a target person's attributions to an actor. The attributions sought are in the ultimate interest of power maintenance or augmentation. It should be emphasized that, most of the time, these strategies are not self-consciously pursued. We assume that because power-reducing actions are maladaptive for the person, he learns—indeed overlearns—those ways of behaving that have power-augmenting implications for the self. By and large, these ways of behaving become semiautomatic reactions triggered by interpersonal threats and opportunities.

The strategy of *ingratiation* is undoubtedly the most ubiquitous, as well as the most highly researched. It is hard to imagine a person who is totally indifferent to the affective reactions he induces in others; we all would rather be liked than ignored or disliked. And efforts to be liked are presumably boosted when we find ourselves in a dependent or low-power position. Research has highlighted the dilemma facing the would-be ingratiator; the greater or more obvious the dependence, the greater the target person's defensive sensitivity to ingratiating overtures. Nevertheless, target persons are often trapped by their own vanity. **[258]** Just as the ingratiator wants to believe in his own sincerity, the target person wants to believe in the sincerity of the compliments or agreements he receives. This clearly mutes the ingratiator's dilemma. Nevertheless, establishing credibility is a major task for the ingratiatory—precisely in those settings where he most wants to be liked.

Intimidation is a second strategy, and one quite distinct from ingratiation in emphasizing threat and the manipulation of fear rather than the more positive emotions associated with affection. Intimidation also requires credibility for its effectiveness, but even credible intimidation may be a self-defeating strategy in relationships that may be easily abrogated or avoided. However, the more subtle forms of intimidation are often woven through relationships that are basically founded on affection, respect, and other positive emotions. Subtle intimidation pressures may shape the flow of behavior and lead to consistent conversational omissions or diversions. Intimidators are generally (though not necessarily) in positions of high power relative to their targets. To the extent that this is true, the intimidator is not likely to learn that the target's compliances are based on fear. In such settings of clear differential power, intimidation often breeds ingratiation and thus provides the intimidator with misleading feedback concerning the attributions actually suggested by his actions.

Self-promotion, the third strategy discussed, is a close cousin to ingratiation with the emphasis on competence and respect rather than personal attractiveness and affection. A distinctive feature is the potential availability of independent evidence concerning ability. This raises the danger of false claims with which the self-promoted may be discredited. But the lines of inference from performance to attributed ability are usually tenuous enough to permit considerable strategic maneuvering. Self-handicapping strategies are not only useful for deceiving oneself; they can be very important in arranging one's self-presentations before influential audiences. The self-handicapper can always make sure that his performances are given under less than optimal circumstances, thus guaranteeing that poor performance will be attributionally ambiguous, and that good performance will yield high competence attributions. In addition, research has shown that people are well aware of the relative attractiveness of certain causal factors underlying competence, and we assume that they will arrange their self-presentations to suggest the existence of these attractive causal factors. Most of us would rather be considered as relaxed but brilliant, for example, than as plodding overachievers. There are occasions, however, when the latter attribution might be acceptable or even preferred.

Exemplification, the fourth strategy, runs the gamut from the explicit manipulations of muckrakers and religious leaders to the subtleties of serving as a modest moral model in the parent or teacher role. Attempting to exemplify virtue or culture-defined worthiness has different implications for the actor than attempting to promote one's competence image. Worthiness is a more seamless whole attribute than competence. A man who has been a model of virtue all his life, but who one day is caught with his hand in the till, is suddenly but a parody **[259]** of virtue, a fraudulent hypocrite. A performer who occasionally fails to live up to expectations is easily excused as having a bad day.

The final strategy, *supplication,* may be considered a strategy of last resort, but it may nevertheless be a highly effective way of avoiding the negative reaches of others' power when one's own power resources are limited. By throwing himself at the mercy of the high-power target person, the supplicant counts on social responsibility norms to reduce the risk of being even further exploited because he has advertised his dependence. His reading of the target person's susceptibility to such normative pressure is obviously very important.

We propose that these five strategies are interwoven in much of social behavior, though the behavior almost always serves other purposes as well as power augmentation. We do not propose that this is somehow a typology of persons, even if for expositional purposes, we have written about intimidators, exemplifiers, and supplicants. Though we do not think much would be gained by a psychometric individual-difference approach to self-presentational strategies, it would not be altogether surprising to find that certain experiences and certain personal resources would make one strategy much more prominent than others in a particular actor's repertory. It is clear also that the strategies are often linked or fused so that one precedes or gives way to another. This is particularly true of the trio, ingratiation, self-promotion, and exemplification. On the other hand, ingratiation and intimidation seem to be rather incompatible strategies, as are self-promotion and supplication. Finally, one actor's strategy may trigger counterstrategies in the target person. We have noted that intimidation can lead to ingratiation, but the opposite may also be true if target persons rise to take advantage of those who appear to like them. Self-promotion might, in some cases, give rise to competing self-promotion in the target; or in other circumstances, it could evoke supplication or ingratiation. All of which makes it extremely difficult to think of promising research strategies for pinning down determinants and conditions. We hope and suspect, however, that the provision of the present taxonomy will not only stimulate such research, but provide a framework for a fair amount of existing research that was produced under different labels for different theoretical purposes. We ourselves intend to pursue these possibilities in our future work. **[260]**

REFERENCES

Bandura, A. (1971). *Psychological modeling: Conflicting theories.* Chicago: Aldine-Atherton.

Baumeister, R. F., & Jones, E. E. (1978). When self-presentation is constrained by the target's knowledge: Consistency and compensation. *Journal of Personality and Social Psychology,* 36, 604–618.

Bem, D. (1972). Self-perception theory. In L. Berkowitz (Ed.), *Advances in experimental social psychology* (Vol. 6). New York: Academic Press.

Berglas, S., & Jones, E. E. (1978). Drug choice as a self-handicapping strategy in response to noncontingent success. *Journal of Personality and Social Psychology,* 36, 405–417.

Berkowitz, L., &. Daniels, L. R. (1963). Responsibility and dependency. *Journal of Abnormal and Social Psychology,* 66, 664–669.

Carnegie, D. (1936). *How to win friends and influence people.* New York: Simon & Schuster.

Chesterfield, Earl of (Philip Darmer Stanhope). (1901). *Letters to his son* (Walter M. Dunne, Ed.). New York: Wiley. (Original published 1774).

Cozby, P. C. (1973). Self-disclosure: A literature review. *Psychological Bulletin,* 79, 73–91.

Duval, S., & Wicklund, R.A. (1972). *A theory of objective self awareness.* New York: Academic Press.

Fazio, R. H., Zanna, M. P., & Cooper. J. (1977). Dissonance and self perception: An integrative view of each theory's proper domain of application. *Journal of Experimental Social Psychology,* 13, 464–479.

Gergen, K. J. (1965). The effects of interaction goals and personalistic feedback on the presentation of self. *Journal of Personality and Social Psychology,* 1, 413–424.

Goffman, E. (1959). *The presentation of self in everyday life.* Garden City, N.Y.: Doubleday.

Janis, I. L., & Gilmore, J. B. (1965). The influence of incentive conditions on the success of role playing in modifying attitudes. *Journal of Personality and Social Psychology,* 1, 17–27.

Jones, E. E. (1975). *Ingratiation: A social-psychological analysis.* New York: Appleton-Century-Crofts, Irvington.

Jones, E. E. (1965). Conformity as a tactic of ingratiation. *Science,* 149, 144–150.

Jones, E. E., & Baumeister, R. (1976). The self-monitor looks at the ingratiator. *Journal of Personality,* 44, 654–674.

Jones, E. E., & Berglas, S. (1978). Control of attributions about the self through self-handicapping strategies: The appeal of alcohol and the role of underachievement. *Personality and Social Psychology Bulletin,* 4, 200–206.

Jones, E. E., & Gerard, H. B. (1967). *Foundations of social psychology.* New York: Wiley.

Jones, E.E., Gergen, K.J., & Davis, K.E. (1962). Some determinants of reactions to being approved or disapproved as a person. *Psychological Monographs,* 76 (2, Whole No. 521).

Jones, E.E., Gergen. K.J., & Jones, R.G. (1963). Tactics of ingratiation, among leaders and subordinates in a status hierarchy. *Psychological Monographs,* 77 (3, Whole No. 566).

Jones, E.E., Jones, R.G., & Gergen, K.J. (1963). Some conditions affecting the evaluation of a conformist. *Journal of Personality,* 31, 270–288.

Jones. E.E., Rhodewalt, F., Berglas, S., & Skelton, J. A. (1981). Effects of strategic self-presentation on subsequent self-esteem. *Journal of Personality and Social Psychology,* 41, 407–421.

Jones, E.E., Stires, L.K., Shaver, K.G., & Hams, V.A. (1968). Evaluation of an ingratiator by target persons and bystanders. *Journal of Personality,* 36, 349–385.

Jones, E.E., & Wortman, C. (1973). *Ingratiation: An attributional approach.* Morristown, N.J.: General Learning Press.

Jourard, S. M. (1964). *The transparent self.* Princeton, N.J.: Van Nostrand.

Korda, M. (1975). *Power: How to get it, how to use it.* New York: Random House. **[261]**

Langer, E., & Newman, H.M. (1979). The role of mindlessness in a typical social psychology experiment. *Personality and Social Psychology Bulletin,* 5, 295–298.

Orne, M.T. (1962). On the social psychology of the psychology experiment. *American Psychologist,* 77, 776–783.

Quattrone, G. A., & Jones, E. E. (1978). Selective self-disclosure with and without correspondent performance. *Journal of Experimental Social Psychology,* 14, 511–526.

Ringer, R.J. (1973). *Winning through intimidation.* Los Angeles: Los Angeles Book Publishers Company.

Rosenberg, M.J. (1965). When dissonance fails: On eliminating evaluation apprehension from attitude measurement. *Journal of Personality and Social Psychology,* 1, 28–42.

Rosenthal, R. (1966). *Experimenter effects in behavioral research.* New York: Appleton-Century-Crofts.

Schopler, J., & Matthews, M. W. (1965). The influence of the perceived causal locus of partner's dependence on the use of interpersonal power. *Journal of Personality and Social Psychology,* 1965, 2, 609–612.

Snyder, M.L., Stephan, W.G., & Rosenfield, D. (1978). Attributional egotism. In J.H. Harvey, W. J. Ickes, & R. F. Kidd (Eds.), *New directions in attribution research* (Vol. 2). Hillsdale, N.J.: Lawrence Erlbaum Associate.

Stires, L.K., & Jones, E.E. (1969). Modesty vs. self-enhancement as alternative forms of ingratiation. *Journal of Experimental Social Psychology,* 5, 172–188.

Tedeschi, J.T., Schlenker, B.R., & Bonoma, T.V. (1971). Cognitive dissonance: Private ratiocination or public spectacle? *American Psychologist,* 26, 685–695.

Thibaut, J.W. (1964). The motivational effects of social dependence on a powerful agency of control: In W.W. Cooper, H. J. Leavill, & M.W. Shelley II (Eds.), *New perspectives in organization research.* New York: Wiley.

Thibaut, J.W., & Riecken, H.W. (1955). Some determinants and consequences of the perception of social causality. *Journal of Personality,* 24, 113–133.

Webb, E. T., & Morgan, J. J. B. (1930). *Strategy in handling people.* Garden City, N.J.: Garden City Publishers.

Wicklund, R. A., & Brehm, J.W. (1976). *Perspectives on cognitive dissonance.* Hillsdale, N.J.: Erlbaum. **[262]**

SELF-HANDICAPPING

Chapter 17

Drug Choice as a Self-Handicapping Strategy in Response to Noncontingent Success

Steven Berglas
Harvard Medical School
Edward E. Jones
Princeton University

ABSTRACT: In two closely related experiments, college student subjects were instructed to choose between a drug that allegedly interfered with performance and a drug that allegedly enhanced performance. This choice was the main dependent measure. The drug choice intervened between work on insoluble problems and a promised retest on similar problems. In Experiment 1, the subjects received success feedback after their initial problem solving attempts, thus creating one condition in which the success appeared to be accidental (noncontingent on performance), and one in which the success appeared to be contingent on appropriate knowledge. Males in the noncontingent success condition were alone in preferring the

---

Reprinted with permission from *Journal of Personality and Social Psychology,* 36, 405–417 (1978). Copyright © 1978 by the American Psychological Association.

performance-inhibiting drug, presumably because they wished to externalize probable failure on the retest. The predicted effect, however, did not hold for female subjects. Experiment 2 replicated the unique preference shown by males after noncontingent success and showed the critical importance of success feedback.

The present research is concerned with one kind of attempt to control the esteem implications of performance feedback by the choice of netting in which performance occurs. Specifically, we present two experiments designed to show an important set of conditions under which people will choose to take a drug *because* it is authoritatively alleged to interfere with performance. We cautiously suggest that such conditions commonly exist in socialization, and may serve as an important precursor of the appeal of alcohol and other substances with performance-inhibiting reputations.

A ubiquitous assumption in psychology is that persons are generally eager to receive accurate information about the nature of their environment and reliable diagnostic feedback about their capacities to act on that environment. Such an assumption is the starting point for Festinger's (1954) theory of social comparison processes. It is also a widely accepted premise of attribution theory (Heider, 1958) that people are typically motivated to penetrate accurately the causal structure of the social world and to gain control through adequate understanding (cf. Kelley, 1971).

A separate tradition, anchored in the theory of achievement motivation, emphasizes individual differences in the tendency to seek unequivocal information regarding one's own competence. Atkinson (1957) proposed that individuals high in achievement motivation prefer tasks of moderate difficulty. Weiner et al. (1972) have argued that this tendency stems from the interest among high-need achievers in obtaining accurate feedback concerning their abilities. Trope (1975; Trope & Brickman, 1975) showed that it is indeed the diagnostic informational value of a task that makes it appealing to those high in achievement motivation. But it is also true that subjects high in fear of failure show a tendency [**405**]* to prefer either very simple or very difficult tasks, tasks typically low in diagnosticity. As early as 1961, McClelland noted that not everyone wants to have "concrete knowledge of results of their choices of actions" (p. 231).

The present experiments attempt to capitalize on this insight and to point to one set of antecedent conditions that promote the desire to avoid diagnostic information. The search for such conditions begins with the hunch that diagnostic information will be avoided when the chances are good that such information will indicate inferior competence. Ideally, performers should seek out those settings in which only success can be internally attributed—linked to the self-esteem of the performer. *Self-handicapping* strategies serve this goal. We define such strategies as any action or choice of performance setting that enhances the opportunity to externalize (or excuse) failure and to internalize (reasonably accept credit for) success. Self-handicapping exploits the performer's understanding of Kelley's (1971) augmentation principle.

This principle may be seen with the example of alcohol use. Alcohol may be viewed as an inhibitory cause of successful performance, whereas ability is a facilitative cause. The inference that ability is the most likely potential cause of a successful

---

*Bracketed bold numbers refer to original page numbers. Page numbers indicate where the original page ended.

performance is augmented by the presence of alcohol. Regardless of what the performance outcome is, then, the self-handicapper cannot lose. Some other examples of self-handicapping are getting too little sleep or underpreparing before an examination, exaggerating the effects of illness or injury, or, in general, embracing impediments and plausible performance handicaps. (The concept of self-handicapping and its determinants is more fully discussed in Jones & Berglas, 1978.)

Any use of self-handicapping that involves more than cognitive distortion presumably decreases the chances of success. Mettee (1971) has explored some of the conditions under which people deliberately choose failure over success, tying this choice primarily to the desire to avoid raising unfulfillable expectations for future performance. Marecek and Mettee (1972) have shown that those who are low in self-esteem and certain of it, are especially prone to avoid success when it is most likely to be attributed to their ability. Our present reasoning is that self-handicapping strategists do not primarily set out to ensure failure; they are willing to accept (probable) failure if it can be explained away *and* if (possible) success will have augmented value for self–esteem.

No doubt some persons are more prone to adopt self-handicapping strategies than are others. We propose that there is probably a modest correlation between such strategic preferences and the appeal of performance-affecting substances like drugs and alcohol. Our present interest, however, is in isolating in the laboratory at least one set of conditions that should promote self-handicapping; in this case, the choice of performance-inhibiting drugs. The hope is that this will provide an analogue to comparable conditions in the prior socialization environment of the alcohol- or drug-prone adult.

We speculate that self-handicapping tendencies reflect a basic uncertainty concerning how competent one is. People who know they have the talent and resources to master life's challenges are not likely to hide behind the attributional shield of self-handicapping. Such persons have, presumably, learned the close relationship between their goal-directed actions and the desirable effects these actions are designed to bring about. They have also presumably learned that the better their information is about the tasks at hand, the better their control can be over effective performance.

At the other extreme are individuals who rarely enjoy success at anything and who have been forced to scale down their expectations about the effects of their actions. They are "klutzes," and they know it. They have learned to avoid chronic failure by tackling only the most attainable objectives and, perhaps, by aligning themselves with others more capable of control and mastery over the environment. But they do not succumb to the ready self-delusion implicit in self-handicapping because they are also dependent on an accurate reading of "task difficulty." They need to know, on a given occasion, whether there is any point in trying, and to find out they must monitor environmental demands and challenges with a certain detached realism. **[406]**

We now propose that self-handicappers fall between these two extremes and that their strategic orientation stems from a capricious, chaotic reinforcement history. It is not that their histories are pocked with repeated failure; they have been amply rewarded, but in ways and on occasions that leave them deeply uncertain about what the reward was for. These individuals may feel, for example, that they have been rewarded for extraneous realms such as beauty, some unrelated past success or the ascribed status of simply being a family member. This description is reminiscent of Seligman's (1975) theory of helplessness and depression as conditions growing out of noncontingent reward histories. Of particular present relevance is the "success depression" (pp. 95–99), in which rewards have been ample but uninformative regarding one's competence image.

To the extent that individuals have passed through a history of noncontingent reward, they may have a strong sense of being impostors or pretenders. They do not deserve their rewards because they did not really do anything to earn them. They were just lucky, they happened to be in the right place at the right time, the evaluation standards were lax—any of these subjective hypotheses are consistent with the underlying fear that (a) successful performance cannot be repeated or sustained and (b) impostors must eventually pay for their inequitable current receipts.

We suggest that the victims of noncontingent success are never clearly reconciled to the fact that their success is something arbitrarily bequeathed to them and out of their control. There is almost always sufficient ambiguity to feed the processes of self-deception and wishful thinking about competence. It is true that the anticipation of accurate future performance evaluation inhibits the more obvious kinds of autistic thinking. People are willing to settle for modest appraisals of their own competence in the face of upcoming further assessments (Eagly & Acksen, 1971; S. C. Jones, 1973; Wortman, Costanzo, & Witt, 1973). But strategies of self-handicapping can preserve the ambiguity of such further assessments. As long as people can avoid clearly diagnostic feedback settings, they may maintain the precarious illusion of control. They may, paradoxically, deliberately run the risk of being out of control—through drug abuse, or inadequate preparation, or not trying—to protect their belief in ultimately being capable of control when it is really necessary, when the chips are down. Among other things, this strategy fits in with the mañana fantasies so commonly observed in budding alcoholics and in the early stages of drug addiction. These fantasies involve thoughts about how successful they will be *when* they break the drinking habit or could be *if* they did.

One question remains before we turn to a description of experimental procedures. The notion of a strategy may suggest that self-handicapping is directed only to a public effect, that we are talking essentially about the self-presentational control of *others'* attributions concerning our basic, underlying competence. Although the possible effects on an audience, including an experimenter or test administrator, may augment the tendency to choose performance settings that obscure the drawing of correspondent inferences about competence (cf. Jones & Davis, 1965), we propose that the basic purpose behind such strategic choices is the control of the actor's *self*-attributions of competence and control. The choice of self-handicapping settings should occur, therefore, even if the susceptible person were being tested under conditions of total privacy.

Experiment 1 was designed to test the proposition linking self-handicapping strategies—in this case, the choice of a performance-inhibiting drug—to a recent history of noncontingent success. Noncontingent success refers specifically to an operation where success feedback follows a performer's attempt to offer solutions to insoluble problems. More conceptually, the performers do not see that the outcome is appropriate to their performance. They feel that they lack the knowledge or control that success feedback implies. This lack generates the anxious uncertainty that an effective performance cannot be repeated at will because the degree of control may have been misjudged or incorrectly indexed in the first place—that luck or measurement error may have been involved. **[407]**

In addition, the experiment provided for an evaluation of whether such self-handicapping is exclusively a maneuver designed to influence the attributions of an audience or serves purely self-protective functions as well. To this end, subjects were recruited for an experiment allegedly designed to measure the effects of drugs on intellectual performance. Some subjects were exposed to insoluble problems and others to readily soluble problems before being given enthusiastic success feedback. Subjects were then allowed to choose between performance-facilitating and performance-inhibiting drugs whose effect would be active during a retest on comparable problems. In half of the cases, the experimenter administering the drugs was clearly unaware of the subject's prior intellectual performance; in the remaining cases, he was obviously aware. The main prediction was that noncontingent-success subjects, in both the private and public knowledge conditions, would choose the performance-inhibiting drug more than contingent-success subjects.

EXPERIMENT 1

Method

SUBJECTS Introductory psychology students (68 males and 43 females) volunteered for an experiment entitled "Drugs and Intellectual Performance" as part of a research participation requirement. Thus, there was initial selection of subjects willing to take drugs as part of a psychology experiment. After 15 subjects were excluded because of heavy drug usage, procedural errors, or suspicion, the finally analyzed sample consisted of 60 males and 36 females.

PROCEDURE Each subject was greeted at the lab by a male experimenter. After preliminary probing of drug-usage history and establishing that subjects were of majority age, the experimenter explained that the present experiment had been designed to determine if either of two (actually bogus) drugs used to treat metabolic disorders had an effect on intellectual performance. To make this determination, the subject was to take two parallel forms of a difficult intellectual performance test, separated by the ingestion of one of the two drugs. The purpose of this procedure was to compare the subject's initial test score, achieved while free from the influence of a drug, with the test score achieved while under its influence.

The subject was told that one of the two drugs being tested, Actavil, was expected to facilitate intellectual performance, whereas the other drug, Pandocrin, was expected to inhibit or disrupt intellectual performance. The experimenter added that the predicted performance effects were not certain to occur, and thus the present experiment was needed in order to gather more reliable data.

The experimenter then described the nature of the intellectual performance test. Subjects were told that they would be taking two 20-question tests, each of which contained a randomly selected group of analogies and progressions borrowed from two nationally used aptitude tests. It was further explained that the tests were "designed to discriminate the uppermost levels of intellectual potential." Subjects were told to expect scores no higher than "between the 60th and 70th percentiles," and then shown two relatively easy examples of the questions that would follow. After each subject solved the sample questions, the experimenter called his testing assistant (a female) to the room. After introductions, the experimenter left the room.

CONTINGENCY MANIPULATION The testing assistant administered a 20-question test of analogies and progressions, and their difficulty level, plus the subsequently announced success, defined the contingency manipulation. In the noncontingent conditions, the problems were largely insoluble; in the contingent conditions, they were largely soluble. All subjects then received success feedback.

In administering the test, the testing assistant handed the subjects individual multiple-choice questions printed on index cards. Subjects were told to respond orally to each item within 15 seconds. Furthermore, their answer on each trial was to be accompanied by a subjective probability estimate of its accuracy, expressed in terms of a percentage between 0 and 100.

The testing assistant randomly assigned subjects to either contingent- or noncontingent-success conditions. Subjects in the noncontingent conditions were given 16 insoluble questions and 4 questions that were easily solved. In spite of this, noncontingent-success subjects were given feedback to the effect that they had successfully solved 16 out of 20 problems. The contingent-success outcome was achieved by tailoring the problems given to subjects in such a way as to tax them, but nevertheless insure that they would perform quite well. This was accomplished by having the assistant shift through a variety of (presealed) question difficulty levels so that if a subject began to solve too many problems, the assistant moved to a more difficult level, and if the subject began to have difficulty with the questions, an easier question was selected for the following trial. The actual number of problems solved in the contingent-success condition ranged from 9 to 16, but the vast majority of the scores were between 12 and 14 correct. Subjects in the contingent success conditions were always provided with their actual scores following the test. Regardless of what condition subjects were in, upon completion of the test, they were congratulated by the testing assistant and told that they had done exceptionally well: "Yours was one of the best scores seen to date!"

It may be noted that the subjective probability estimates were included to strengthen the manipulation **[408]** of feedback contingency. During the pretesting, it became apparent that it was quite difficult to establish a noncontingent-success condition. Subjects proved to be very facile in explaining to themselves and to the testing assistant how they managed to get a correct answer on an insoluble problem. Thus, the confidence ratings were introduced to anchor the noncontingent-success subject's realization that he did not have good control over the test. It was predicted that the subjective probability ratings would be quite low in the noncontingent conditions, making it difficult for those subjects to conclude later that they really understood the contingency between their responses and the success feedback.

PUBLICITY MANIPULATION When the testing session was completed, the experimenter was signaled to return and either was or was not told about the subject's performance. In the public feedback condition, the experimenter asked how the subject had done, and when he was told by the assistant that the subject attained one of the highest scores recorded, he expressed his congratulations. In the private feedback conditions, the experimenter specifically admonished subjects not to say anything about their performance so that he could remain blind in order to maintain experimental control. Subjects in this condition were given a "subject record sheet" with a subject number to protect their anonymity and told that their data would be turned in to a secretary who would code their responses for computer analysis. Following this manipulation, the testing assistant left the room.

At this point, both independent treatments had been established. It is important to note that the experimenter was kept blind as to which contingency condition the subject was in. Furthermore, the testing assistant was kept blind as to the publicity treatment until the end of the testing session.

The experimenter then prepared the subject for the drug ingestion part of the experiment. However, prior to this procedure, the experimenter informed the subject of a modification in scoring the post-drug-ingestion intellectual performance test. After providing an appropriate rationale for the change in procedures on the post-test, the experimenter informed subjects that an incorrect response to a question would be penalized, that is, subtracted from the total score, whereas simply choosing to "pass" on an item would produce neither a credit nor a debit. This penalty for guessing, which increased the likelihood of a lower score on the post-test, should have exacerbated the concern of subjects in the noncontingent condition with "being discovered."

Following a brief "medical" examination consisting of a pulse count, blood pressure measurement, and pupillary dilation check—intended to entrench more firmly the cover story—the experimenter provided subjects with "all necessary and pertinent" information about the two drugs. This information was intended to make salient the probable consequences for future performance of taking each drug. Subjects were first presented with a pair of line graphs depicting some pilot data collected on the effects of Actavil and Pandocrin. The graphs clearly illustrated that, for the most part, subjects who had taken Actavil showed improvement in their intellectual performance between the first and second tests, whereas those subjects who had taken Pandocrin tended to have poorer performances on their postdrug test. However, subjects were cautioned that these pilot data were not conclusive, since an insufficient number of cases were considered and because there were several reversals in the two trends.

Subjects were next given a "preliminary" PDR (Physicians' Desk Reference) report for both Pandocrin and Actavil. These (actually bogus) reports provided information about the chemistry and benign side effects of each drug and the critical information about each drug's influence on intellectual performance. One report noted that Actavil should facilitate intellectual performance through "stimulation of associative processes and a general heightening of cognitive acuity." The report for Pandocrin indicated that this drug should disrupt intellectual performance as a result of decrements in "cognitive association, ... attention, and powers of concentration," as well as "information retrieval processes." Following the presentation of the two PDR reports, the experimenter repeated his assurances that no previous subject had experienced any unpleasant side effects from either drug and that, although there would probably be performance effects, they would most probably occur without the subject's awareness. Furthermore, subjects were assured that if the drugs did in fact affect their performance, this effect would be transitory.

DEPENDENT MEASURES The major dependent measure in this study was the drug and dosage level selected by the subject. Following the presentation of the PDR reports, subjects were shown a Lucite tray on which drugs and dosages were arrayed as if in a scale, from the maximum 10-mg dosage of Actavil on the left to the maximum 10-mg dosage of Pandocrin on the right. Intermediate dosages of 2.5, 5, and 7.5 mg of each drug were clearly marked along the tray, as well as a blank space in the center of the tray labeled "Control."

Subjects were instructed to choose which drug and which dosage level they wished to take. Though they had the option of taking neither drug ("since control subjects were needed"), some pressure was exerted to take one of the larger dosages of either Actavil or Pandocrin. However, the experimenter clearly stated, "I don't want you to take either drug at any particular dosage level to please me ... Select either drug or no drug at all according to your own personal preference, according to what you will find most interesting."

After indicating which drug and dosage level they would be taking, subjects were asked to complete a series of manipulation checks disguised as a "Midpoint Questionnaire." In addition to standard questions probing for suspicion or an awareness of the hypothesis being tested, subjects were asked to indicate how they felt the chosen drug would affect both the average individual's and their own intellectual performance. In addition, subjects were asked **[409]** to indicate how difficult they felt the intellectual performance test was, and to indicate the extent to which luck versus ability accounted for their test scores. The experiment was then terminated, and the subject was completely debriefed.

Results

VALIDATION OF MANIPULATIONS Because of the differences in problem solubility that constituted the contingency manipulation, subjects in the noncontingent-success condition should have registered lower confidence scores after each problem solution than contingent-success subjects. Each subject's confidence scores were totaled. The contingent-success subjects ($M = 64.40$) indeed expressed greater confidence in the accuracy of each problem solution than the noncontingent-success subjects ($M = 45.32$); $F(1, 88) = 102.72, p < .001$. As Table 17.1 shows, both males and females also saw the test version used in the noncontingent condition as greater in difficulty, $F(1, 88) = 12.89, p < .001$. This is especially true in the private condition, as reflected in a significant Contingency X Publicity interaction, $F(1, 88) = 6.31, p < .01$.

Of somewhat greater theoretical interest, subjects in the contingent-success condition attributed their intellectual performance more to ability (versus luck) than noncontingent-success subjects, $F(1, 88) = 34.43, p < .001$. It seems abundantly clear that the contingency manipulation was successful in the expected direction and that subjects who were "successful" on problems that actually had no correct solution acknowledged a certain amount of luck, their overall mean being slightly on the "luck-only" side of the midpoint.

The *public–private variable* entered into two significant effects for the male subjects. When rating the difficulty level of the test, male subjects in the public conditions did not distinguish between the soluble and insoluble items. Those in the private condition, however, distinguished sharply between them, a difference between differences that is reflected in the highly significant interaction effect, $F(1, 56) = 15.83, p < .001$, involving contingency and publicity (see Table 17.1). Subjects in the public condition may have let their ratings be slightly affected by self-presentational concerns. Since the experimenter collecting

Table 17.1 Mean Difficulty Estimates, Ability Attributions, and Drug Choice

| | Difficulty[a] ||| Ability[b] ||| Drug choice[c] ||||||
| | Male (n = 60) | Female (n = 36) | Total (n = 96) | Male (n = 60) | Female (n = 36) | Total (n = 96) | Male (n = 60) || Female (n = 36) || Total (n = 96) ||
Condition							Scale value	% Pandocrin	Scale value	% Pandocrin	Scale value	% Pandocrin
Contingent success												
Private	9.13	9.60	9.32	10.87	9.80	10.44	2.2	13	5.0	40	3.5	24
Public	10.87	9.44	10.33	11.27	10.33	10.92	2.3	13	2.8	11	2.5	13
Noncontingent success												
Private	12.73	12.00	12.50	7.20	6.29	6.91	6.1	73	4.4	29[d]	5.5	59[d]
Public	10.67	10.70	10.68	9.53	7.80	8.84	6.3	67	5.4	50	5.9	60

[a]Question 5: How difficult did you feel the intellectual performance test was? (1 = extremely easy; 15 = extremely difficult)
[b]Question 6: To what factors do you attribute your intellectual performance score? (1 = luck only; 8 = ability and luck; 15 = ability only)
[c]Scale values run from 1, the highest dosage of Actavil, to 9, the highest dosage of Pandocrin. % Pandocrin indicates the percentage of subjects choosing Pandocrin in that condition.
[d]One subject in this condition chose "no drug."

the questionnaires knew they had done well, it was important for subjects not to claim that the problems were very easy (which puts down the other subjects who did not do as well, and which may seem to contradict the congratulating experimenter) or very difficult (which suggests boastfulness).

In addition, public subjects attributed their successful performance to ability more than private subjects did, $F(1, 88) = 5.97$, $p < .05$. Although this effect is small compared to the contingency effect, we may speculate that public subjects hesitated to claim too much luck in front of an experimenter who knew that they did very well, since this would tend to impugn the reliability of the test.

These speculations are only that, however, and though we can point to significant statistical effects to support the claim that the public–private manipulation had an impact, it is difficult to articulate the precise nature of that impact. All we should argue, perhaps, is that the link of knowledge between the two experimenters was less salient in the private than in the public conditions, and this differential saliency had a detectable effect on subjects' experiential reports.

As for our success in conveying potential drug effects, the information was clearly accepted. Subjects responded that most people do better after Actavil and worse after Pandocrin, $t(93) = 30.96$, $p < .001$, and their expectancies concerning their own intellectual performance were also significantly affected by the anticipated drug choice, $t(93) = 13.54$, $p < .001$. Since subjects were told that the pretest data were not firm or highly reliable (thus the present study) and that a few previous subjects had done better under Pandocrin and worse under Actavil, it is quite appropriate that their own expectations were less affected by the choice of drug than their general expectations about "most people."

DRUG CHOICE The last three columns of Table 17.1, indicate the effects of the crosscutting conditions (and sex of subject) on drug choice. The overall effect of performance contingency on drug choice using the scale value measure is highly significant, $F(1, 88) = 18.28$, $p < .001$, but it is clear from the [411] Contingency × Sex interaction, $F(1, 88) = 6.51$, $p < .05$, and the separate analyses for male and female, that the effect is attributable largely to the male subjects, $F(1, 56) = 33.93$, $p < .001$. Overall, 70% of the males following a noncontingent-success experience chose Pandocrin; only 13% of those males whose success was contingent on performance chose Pandocrin. For females, the percentages were, respectively, 40% and 26%.

In line with prediction, the publicity of the subject's success was not a significant factor in this drug choice. With the more robust male sample, the public and private conditions produced almost identical drug-choice distributions. With the female sample, there is the hint of an interaction between contingency and publicity, $F(1, 32) = 2.66$, the females tending to follow the drug-choice predictions only in the public conditions.

As for the possible bases of this sex difference, there is some evidence that the entire experimental situation had less impact on the females than on the males. As Table 17.1 shows, females were less inclined than males to attribute their performance to ability, $F(1, 88) = 5.67$, $p < .05$. Since their attributions to luck were thus more generous, the need for strategic handicapping through Pandocrin choice may have been reduced.

In the confidence data, there was a significant interaction between contingency and sex, $F(1, 88) = 5.05$, $p < .05$. The males were more confident than the females in the contingent conditions and less confident than the females in the noncontingent condition. In this respect, then, the contingency manipulation had more impact on the males' crucial subjective feelings of control than on the females' feelings. Also, in the private conditions, male subjects thought the contingent problems were easier and the noncontingent problems harder than the female subjects did. This feeling contributes to the highly significant interaction between contingency and publicity for males on ratings of task difficulty; this interaction does not approach significance for females.

Discussion

The male data are clearly consistent with the underlying assumption of attributional control as well as the more particular derivation concerning drug choice. However the data by no means compel agreement concerning the processes involved. There are two sources of evidence regarding such processes: (a) the subjects' own verbalized accounts of the reasons behind their choice and (b) evidence inherent in the comparisons provided by the research design itself.

Turning first to the self-report data collected just prior to debriefing, only 2 out of 30 noncontingent-success Pandocrin takers explained their choice in defensive terms. The remaining Pandocrin choosers either claimed that the choice was completely arbitrary or that they were helping to make the experiment "work" because, having scored 16 out of 20 on the first test, they had more room for downward than upward movement. Thus the effects of the drug could be easier to see with Pandocrin than with Actavil. The self-report data, then, are of little help in confirming the theoretical reasoning about self-handicapping.

The design of the present experiment was limited to the crucial contingency variable and an attempt to manipulate whether the knowledge about performance was shared by the two experimenters. For males, at least, the public–private variation had no effect on drug choice, though it did have effects on attributions to ability and problem difficulty. This result is intriguing because it suggests that under the proper circumstances, people will choose to avoid diagnostic information about themselves that cannot be discounted, even when only they will know the significance of the information. To stretch rather widely for an analogy in the natural environment, the concept of self-handicapping helps to explain the solitary as well as the social drinker.

While the design yields information concerning the self-knowledge implications of self-handicapping, it is not sufficiently complex or differentiated to rule out some of the available alternatives. Several alternative explanations question the importance of success on the first test items. Is it the fact that subjects succeeded on the insoluble items that is important or just that they knew the items were, and would be, very difficult? [412]

It is possible that emotional factors took precedence over the attributional implications of success and failure in the choice of Pandocrin. Perhaps subjects became so frustrated with trying to solve the insoluble problems that they wanted to take the Pandocrin in order to "drop out" of the situation psychologically. The only evidence we have that frustration reduction was not the key factor in taking Pandocrin comes from noncontingent-success pretest subjects prior to the institution of the confidence ratings and restructured scoring of the second task. These subjects took Actavil almost without exception, and yet they had been exposed to the same insoluble problems. Also, one might imagine that the success feedback would go a long way toward removing the emotional residue of struggling with insoluble problems. Nevertheless, the frustration-reduction hypothesis remains a possibility that cannot entirely be dismissed.

Especially if we take seriously the Pandocrin subjects' own comments, another possibility looms as an alternative explanation of the findings. A few Pandocrin choosers in the noncontingent conditions clearly stated that they took Pandocrin to help the experimenter. Since they scored so high that there was not much room to improve with Actavil, the best way to test for drug effectiveness (and therefore make it a useful experiment) was to take Pandocrin. It will be recalled that, on the average, contingent-success subjects did not score as high as the alleged score of 16 out of 20 in the noncontingent-success conditions. Their average score was 12.5. There are two bits of evidence arguing against this plausible alternative. First, contingent-success Pandocrin takers were as likely as noncontingent-success Pandocrin takers to mention helping the experimenter. Second, within the combined contingent-success conditions, the correlation between actual test score and drug preference score was $-.381$ ($n = 50, p < .01$). In other words, within the limited range of actual scores, the better the contingent success subject did, the *less* likely he or she was to choose Pandocrin. This is precisely the opposite from what would be predicted if the "help-the-experimenter" alternative were of importance in the present results.

Nevertheless, because of these interpretive loose ends, a second experiment was planned with three purposes in mind. First, and most important, the role of problem solubility was examined by varying whether success feedback was provided. Second, when feedback was given, both contingent- and noncontingent-success subjects received the identical feedback count—16 out of 20 correct. This means that feedback in the contingent-success condition was only approximately accurate. Finally, we wished to see if the sex differences observed in Experiment 1 would be replicated. Thus, the design of Experiment 2 varied sex of subject, whether the problems were soluble, and whether subjects received feedback (which was always "success").

EXPERIMENT 2

Method

A total of 87 subjects were assigned to the eight-condition design. Assignment was random except that approximately twice as many subjects were assigned to each of the two critical conditions: male, insoluble problems, success feedback and male, insoluble problems, no feedback. An additional 9 volunteers were dismissed prior to drug choice. Five subjects were dismissed at the outset of the experiment for medical reasons or strong suspicion. The remaining 4 subjects were dismissed when it was clear that they did not accept the experimenter's final drug-choice spiel.

The procedural details were precisely the same in Experiment 2 as in the public conditions of Experiment 1 except that (a) conditions were added so that exposure to either soluble or insoluble problems was not followed by feedback of any kind, (b) subjects in the success feedback conditions were told that they had solved 16 out of 20 problems and that this was exceptionally good, and (c) the experimenter neither asked about the subjects' performance nor stressed the importance of his not knowing about it.

The same two experimenters played the same two roles, and the subjects were recruited from a comparable subject pool approximately 1 year after those participating in Experiment 1. Again, the testing assistant was blind until the last moment to the feedback condition, and the drug administrator was blind to problem solubility.

Results

VALIDATION OF MANIPULATIONS Again, subjects in the soluble-problems conditions were on the average more confident in their solutions [413] ($M = 65.52$) than subjects exposed to insoluble problems ($M = 57.08$); $F(1, 79) = 46.20, p < .001$. No other effects approached significance on this measure.

Also, as expected, the insoluble problems were seen as more difficult than the soluble ones, $F(1, 79) = 26.60, p < .001$. There were, however, main effects of sex and feedback on this measure. Males rated the task as more difficult than females, $F(1, 79) = 5.23, p < .05$, and success-feedback subjects rated the task as less difficult than subjects receiving no feedback, $F(1, 79) = 4.34, p < .05$. The condition means for this measure are provided in Table 17.2. Not surprisingly, it is especially clear that task difficulty is rated highest when the subject is exposed to insoluble problems without subsequent feedback.

Subjects who worked on the soluble problems were more likely than those who worked with insoluble problems to attribute their performance to ability, $F(1, 79) = 10.03, p < .01$. In Experiment 1, males were significantly more likely than females to attribute their performance to ability. The same tendency held in Experiment 2, though the difference was not quite significant, $F(1, 79) = 3.85 \ p < .10$. In any event, the results on the confidence, difficulty, and ability indices all strongly validate the manipulation of problem solubility or difficulty, and the major results to follow also make clear that subjects were very cognizant of the feedback in assessing their performance.

As in Experiment 1, subjects clearly comprehended that most people do better after Actavil and most people do worse after Pandocrin, $t(85) = 25.91, p < .001$. Also, once again subjects thought their own performance would be somewhat less affected by the drug taken, but it still would be clearly affected, $t(85) = 14.20, p < .001$.

DRUG CHOICE Experiment 2 was designed to answer three basic questions: (a) Do the sex differences replicate? (b) Is success feedback important? And (c) could the results of Experiment 1 have been affected by differential information concerning the number of problems solved? The prediction was that subjects would prefer the performance-inhibiting drug only in the condition in which the problems were insoluble and they had received success feedback. The last three columns of Table 17.2 show that this prediction was clearly confirmed, and again this result was true for males only. An unweighted-means analysis of variance produces a significant triple-order interaction, $F(1, 79) = 6.80, p < .05$, indicating that solubility, feedback, and sex all play roles as determinants of drug choice. Examination of the means makes clear that this interaction reflects the uniqueness of the male noncontingent-success condition. Though the mean scale score of the female insoluble-problem no-feedback condition appears close to the mean of this crucial cell, 3 out of 8 subjects in this condition chose not to take either drug. Thus, the percentages choosing Pandocrin in two conditions are substantially different.

Table 17.2 Mean Difficulty Estimates, Ability Attributions, and Drug Choice

	Difficulty[a]			Ability[b]			Drug choice[c]						
							Male (n = 53)		Female (n = 34)		Total (n = 87)		
Condition	Male (n = 53)	Female (n = 34)	Total (n = 87)	Male (n = 53)	Female (n = 34)	Total (n = 87)	Scale value	% Pandocrin	Scale value	% Pandocrin	Scale value	% Pandocrin
Soluble problem												
Success	10.10	8.78	9.44	10.67	10.44	10.56	2.11	11	3.56	22	2.84	17
No feedback	10.13	9.22	9.68	9.75	9.00	9.38	3.13	25	2.78	11[d]	2.96	18
Insoluble problem												
Success	11.67	10.25	10.96	9.56	8.00	8.78	5.72	61	3.38	25	4.55	50
No feedback	12.56	12.38	12.47	8.78	7.75	8.27	2.50	11	4.75	25[e]	3.63	15

[a]Question 5: How difficult did you feel the intellectual performance test was? (1 = extremely easy; 15 = extremely difficult)
[b]Question 6: To what factors do you attribute your intellectual performance score? (1 = luck only; 8 = ability and luck; 15 = ability only)
[c]Scale values run from 1, the highest dosage of Actavil, to 9, the highest dosage of Pandocrin. % Pandocrin indicates the percentage of subjects choosing Pandocrin in that condition.
[d]One subject in this condition chose "no drug."
[e]Three subjects in this condition chose "no drug."

Since the design was intended to emphasize the comparison of the success versus no-feedback, insoluble-problems conditions for males, and twice the number of subjects were assigned to these conditions, the unweighted-means analysis is highly conservative in this case. A direct comparison between the two crucial conditions shows a much higher level of Pandocrin choice when male subjects have received success feedback after working on insoluble problems than after no feedback, $t(51) = 4.63$, $p < .001$. There is no hint of this difference among female subjects.

BASIS OF SEX DIFFERENCES In the report of Experiment 1, we cited evidence that the experimental situation had less impact on the female than on the male subjects. In both experiments, females were less inclined than males to attribute their performance to ability, though the tendency only approached significance ($p < .10$) in the present case. We earlier noted that greater attribution to luck in the crucial noncontingent-success cell may have reduced the need for self-handicapping through Pandocrin choice.

Differences on the confidence ratings did not replicate. In Experiment 1, males were significantly more confident than females in the contingent-success condition and less confident than females in noncontingent-success condition. There was a nonsignificant trend for males in Experiment 2 to be more confident in both success feedback conditions. **[415]**

GENERAL DISCUSSION

The basic assumption underlying the present experiments is that people arrange their environments to influence the dispositions that can be attributed to them—by themselves as well as by others. In particular case of the present experiments, people are shown to select the available environment best designed to protect their image of self-competence in the event of poor performance. Male subjects choose a performance-inhibiting drug in a condition in which they have just experienced a success apparently based substantially on luck. In this way, their claim on this success cannot be rudely challenged by a subsequent failure. At least their choice has provided them with a ready external attribution for any downward change in performance.

The results of Experiment 1 permitted a plausible alternative explanation: It could have been the insolubility of the problems rather than the noncontingency of the success that prompted the choice of a performance-inhibiting drug. The results of Experiment 2, however, clearly rule out this alternative. When an insoluble-problems–no-feedback condition is compared to an insoluble-problems condition with success feedback, there is no tendency for subjects in the former condition to prefer the performance-inhibiting drug. The contribution of success feedback, so important for the theoretical argument, is emphasized by this final set of results.

SEX DIFFERENCES Quite surprisingly, in view of the reliability of these results among male subjects, the female subjects do not show the predicted response to noncontingent success in either experiment. Even the directional trend in Experiment 1, under public feedback conditions, did not replicate in Experiment 2 where the experimenter did not mention the importance of his not knowing the test results. It is conceivable that the experimenter's public congratulations stimulated self-handicapping among the female subjects in Experiment 1.

There is some evidence in both experiments that the female subjects attributed their performance to luck more than the male subjects did. This tendency has been noted in numerous other studies comparing the attributions of male and female subjects after success feedback (e.g., Deaux & Farris, 1977; cf. Frieze, Fisher, Hanusa, McHugh, & Valles, 1978). It might be that females chose this attributional option (luck) to blunt the impact of experimental conditions. Females may have seen less reason to protect a success readily acknowledged to be based on luck. One might wonder whether those females who did attribute their success to ability tended to choose Pandocrin in the noncontingent-success or insoluble-problem condition. There is strong support for the relation between ability attribution and Pandocrin choice in only one condition: the female public condition of Experiment 1. Here the correlation ($r = .76$, $n = 10$) shows that those females who attributed to ability also tended to choose Pandocrin. However, females in the private condition of Experiment 1 and in Experiment 2, which was essentially public, showed no such relationship. It is difficult to know what conclusion to draw about the females, given the discrepancy between experiments and the public–private conditions of Experiment 1. Our general caution concerning the meaning of the female results is further increased by the realization that the results might have been different with a female experimenter.

Although any conclusions must be restricted to male subjects at this point, the present results make more tenable the proposition that alcohol and certain forms of drug usage may be facilitated by prior experiences of success, unaccompanied by subjective feelings of mastery and control. Such experiences promote strategies designed to protect ill-gotten performance gains and a fragile but positive competence image.

REFERENCES

Atkinson, J. W. (1957). Motivational determinants of risk-taking behavior. *Psychological Review*, 64, 359–372.

Deaux, K., & Farris, E. (1977). Attributing causes of one's own performance: The effects of sex, norms, and outcomes. *Journal of Research in Personality*, 11, 59–72.

Eagly, A. H., & Acksen, B. A. (1971). The effect of expectancy to be evaluated on change toward favorable and unfavorable information about oneself. *Sociometry*, 34, 411–422. **[416]**

Festinger, L. (1954). A theory of social comparison processes. *Human Relations*, 7, 117–140.

Frieze, I. H., Fisher, J., Hanusa, B., McHugh, M. C., & Valle, V. A. (1978). Attributions of the causes of success and failure as internal and external barriers to achievement in women. In J. Sherman & F. Denmark (Eds.), *Psychology of women: Future dimensions of research*. N.Y., New York: Psychological Dimensions, Inc.

Heider, F. (1958). *The psychology of interpersonal relations*. New York: Wiley.

Jones, E. E., & Berglas, S. (1978). Control of attributions about the self through self-handicapping strategies: The appeal of alcohol and the role of underachievement. *Personality and Social Psychology Bulletin*, 4, 200–206.

Jones, E. E., & Davis, K. E. (1965). From acts to dispositions: The attribution process in person perception. In L. Berkowitz (Ed.), *Advances in experimental social psychology* (Vol. 2). New York: Academic Press.

Jones, S. C. (1973). Self and interpersonal evaluations: Esteem theory versus consistency theories. *Psychological Bulletin*, 79, 185–199.

Kelley, H. H. (1971). *Attribution in social interaction*. Morristown, N.J.: General Learning Press.

Marecek. J., & Mettee, D.R. (1972). Avoidance of continued success as a function of self-esteem, level of esteem certainty, and responsibility for success. *Journal of Personality and Social Psychology*, 22, 98–107.

McClelland, D.C. (1961). *The achieving society.* Princeton, N.J.: Van Nostrand.

Mettee, D.R. (1971). Rejection of unexpected success as a function of the negative consequences of accepting success. *Journal of Personality and Social Psychology,* 17, 332–341.

Seligman, M. P. (1975). *Helplessness.* San Francisco: Freeman.

Trope, Y. (1975). Seeking information about one's own ability as a determinant of choice among tasks. *Journal of Personality and Social Psychology,* 32, 1004–1013.

Trope. Y., & Brickman, P. (1975). Difficulty and diagnosticity as determinants of choice among tasks. *Journal of Personality and Social Psychology,* 31, 918–925.

Weiner, B., I. Frieze, Kukla, A., Reed, L., Rest, S., & Rosenbaum, R. M. (1972). Perceiving the causes of success and failure. In E. E. Jones, D. E. Kanouse, H. H. Kelley, R. E. Nisbett, S. Valins, & B. Weiner (Ed.), *Attribution: Perceiving the causes of behavior* (pp. 95–120). Morristown, NJ: General Learning Press.

Wortman, C.B., Costanzo, P.R., & Witt, T.R. (1973). Effect of anticipated performance on the attributions of causality to self and others. *Journal of Personality and Social Psychology,* 27, 372–381. **[417]**

SELF-HANDICAPPING

Chapter 18

Control of Attributions about the Self through Self-Handicapping Strategies: The Appeal of Alcohol and the Role of Underachievement

Edward E. Jones
Princeton University
Steven Berglas
Harvard Medical School

> ABSTRACT: Explores the hypothesis that alcohol use and underachievement may serve as strategies to externalize the causation of poor performance and to internalize the causation of good performance. Such a strategy may be prominently used, especially by those who have a precarious, but not entirely negative, sense of self-competence. The etiology of this strategic preference may follow either of two scenarios. The child may attach desperate importance to this competence image because competence is the

---

Reprinted with permission from *Personality and Social Psychology Bulletin,* 4, 200–206. Copyright ©1978 Sage Publications, Inc.

condition for deserving parental love. Or the child may have been rewarded for accidental attributes or performances that do not predict future success, thus leaving him in a position of one who has reached a status he fears he cannot maintain through his own control. The linkage of alcohol appeal to underachievement strategies is stressed; both are seen as expressions of the same overconcern with competence.

Let us proceed from the premise that people use attributional principles in the service of self-image protection. We believe that people actively try to arrange the circumstances of their behavior so as to protect their conceptions of themselves as competent, intelligent persons. This is part of a general pattern of self-presentation that goes beyond the verbal claims and disclosures that are usually considered under that heading. We shall explore the hypothesis that the appeal of alcohol can be understood with reference to its strategic role in obscuring the meaning of performance feedback. We shall try to relate this discussion of strategic alcohol use to the similarly obscurant possibilities of underachievement and overachievement, here seen as strategies for controlling self-attributions by withdrawing or augmenting one's effort.

If there is any novelty in our premise, perhaps it lies in the suggestion that we sometimes do things to *avoid* diagnostic information about our own characteristics and capacities. Social comparison theory (Festinger, 1954) posits a fundamental motive to gain an accurate view of reality and a discriminating appraisal of our abilities to cope with it. Indeed, attribution theory itself is typically couched in terms of stabilizing the distal features of the environment and accurately penetrating the causal structure of the social world. Harold Kelley (1972) makes this very explicit in his emphasis on the relationship between accurate or stable attributions and control through understanding. But do people always want to know precisely who they are and exactly what they are capable of accomplishing at their best? We doubt it, and we suggest that social psychologists have overlooked each person's need for certain kinds of ambiguity to allow room for self-sustaining and self-embellishing fantasies.

To illustrate the dangers of too much self-knowledge, we offer this brief excerpt from the musings of Denison Andrews (1975) upon learning from his old grade school principal that his measured IQ is only 125: **[200]***

> Keep cool. Control wobbly knees. 125. Not brilliant. Not undiscovered genius. Ordinary bright. Everyday bright like everyone else … No brighter than my stockbroker. No brighter than insurance agent. Did they laugh when I applied to medical school? … IQ has no meaning. Totally discredited. No one takes it seriously … Who was Otis anyway? I test badly. IQ doesn't measure creativity. Winston Churchill. Maybe I was depressed. Maybe I had an earache. A bad night's sleep. Maybe I lost time daydreaming. Creatively …

Here we see the tortured efforts of posterior defensive attribution, but our present argument is that people actively select those settings for action that render performance feedback ambiguous, thus anticipating the kinds of excuses Andrews is forced lamely to offer.

---

*Bracketed bold numbers refer to original page numbers. Page numbers indicate where the original page ended.

Chapter 18   Control of Attributions through Self-Handicapping Strategies   **405**

The hypothesis, specifically, is that an important reason why some people turn to alcohol is to avoid the implications of negative feedback for failure and to enhance the impact of positive feedback for success. This is part of the more general notion that people drink to escape from responsibility for their actions, but it is more specific than that notion, and it trades on the public assumption that alcohol generally interferes with or disrupts performance. This assumption paves the way for what we shall call self-handicapping strategies. By finding or creating impediments that make good performance less likely, the strategist nicely protects his sense of self-competence. If the person does poorly, the source of the failure is externalized in the impediment, perhaps in the glass or the bottle. In the terms of Jones and Davis (1965), it is difficult for the strategist and for others to make a "correspondent inference" about competence. If the person does well, then he or she has done well in spite of less than optimum conditions. According to Kelley's (1972) augmentation principle, then, the person's competence should receive a boost. Alcohol is what Kelley refers to as an inhibitory cause of a successful performance effect, whereas ability is a facilitative cause. The presence of ability as an inferred potential cause of a given performance level is augmented by the presence of alcohol. Regardless of what the outcome is, the self-handicapping strategist cannot lose, at least in those settings where the attributional implications of performance are more important that the success of the performance itself.

Before going any further, it might be helpful to run through some other examples of self-handicapping to show that alcohol appeal is only one subset of a variety of strategic instances. The high school senior who gets but two hours of sleep before taking his SAT exams may be a self-handicapper. The ingratiator who avoids disclosing his true preferences or opinions protects himself from the ultimate implications of rejection as a person. Even if he gets rejected, this isn't so bad if he was "just trying to be nice," if he held his true self in reserve. Similarly, the professional actor may build a career around the externalization aspect of self-handicapping by constantly retreating to roles so that failure is never attached to the real self. We have all seen the occasional talk show guest who, actor or comedian by profession, is petrified by the assigned "role" of being himself. Self-handicappers are legion in the sports world, from the tennis player who externalizes a bad shot by adjusting his racket strings, to the avid golfer who systematically avoids taking lessons or even practicing on the driving range.

Therapists have long been aware of the appeal of the "sick" role to those who wish temporarily to drop out of life's competition. This is a form of self-handicapping where the body is seen as outside the system of personal responsibility. Many clinicians have noted that even the roles of "neurotic" or "mental" [201] patients may be partly strategic in nature. Carson (1969), for example, points out that "acquisition of the label 'mentally ill' is not invariably treated as a major disaster by the person so labeled ... it is an excellent 'cover story' for various types of rulebreaking ('it's not me who is doing this—it's my illness')" (p. 228).

The self-handicapper, we are suggesting, reaches out for impediments, exaggerates handicaps, embraces any factor reducing personal responsibility for mediocrity and enhancing personal responsibility for success. One does this to shape the implications of performance feedback both in one's own eyes and in the eyes of others. Handicapping is a self-defending maneuver whose significance is probably augmented by the presence of an audience, but we emphasize that the public value of the strategy is not its original impetus. This lies in the exaggerated importance of one's own private conception of self-competence and the need to protect that conception from unequivocal negative feedback, even in the absence of others.

UNDERACHIEVEMENT AS A STRATEGY TO PROTECT SELF-ESTEEM

The same defensive dynamic may underly the strategy of underachievement, a strategy that involves the subtraction of facultative effort rather than the imposition of inhibitory performance barriers. The underachiever, like the impediment-seeking externalizer, wishes to avoid the most drastic implications of possible failure. If one is excessively worried about his basic competence and simply cannot face the prospect of being judged incompetent, it is better to exert less than total effort, thus inviting probable (but not inevitable) failure, than to try and risk a possible failure that would implicate the self more irrevocably. In the unlikely event of successful achievement, the performer who has only casually or half-heartedly involved himself gains the added esteem award of ability-relevant positive feedback.

At this point, there are two broad questions that must be confronted. The first is whence derives this intense concern with the maintenance of a competence image? The second is what determines the choice of alcohol or underachievement over other strategic alternatives within the self-handicapping family?

THE CHOICE OF THE ALCOHOL STRATEGY

Considering the latter question first, it must be clearly understood that the appeal of alcohol is a function of many things beside the personality of the drinker or the stresses inherent in his life. Jessor and his colleagues (1973), for example, have noted that drug abuse and problem drinking may be (1) a learned way of coping with personal frustrations and anticipated failure, (2) an expression of opposition to or rejection of conventional society—including the very norms that define the behavior as a problem, (3) a negotiation or claim on status transformation or developmental transition, or (4) a manifestation of solidarity with the peer subculture. So we are interested at best in one set of factors that predispose individuals to alcohol use, though it may well be the set that is most likely to lead to serious problem drinking.

The path from use to abuse to addiction involves many complexities that take us beyond our present concern. What interests us, at this point, are the factors that predispose a person toward alcohol use and which enhance the reinforcement value of such an agent. Our basic proposition rests on the fact that alcohol has the reputation of reducing one's responsibility for good performance. But it has other properties that undoubtedly enhance its attractiveness to the self-handicapper Here, the relationship between alcohol appeal and underachievement must be specifically stressed. Beckett (1974) notes that alcohol and drug addicts are almost always distinct underachievers. Jessor and his colleagues (1973) also stress the negative relationship between achievement value and the appeal of drugs and alcohol. While the conventional interpretation would emphasize the direct effects of problem drinking on performance capability, our present view suggests that both [202] alcohol appeal and underachievement may be symptoms of the same self-protective strategy. For reasons that we shall explore below, the problem drinker and the underachiever are fearful of receiving the unequivocal message that they are unworthy and incompetent. They perhaps suspect this might be true and are very afraid of being "discovered." So much follows directly from the original hypothesis of self-handicapping: such a person would be motivated to get equivocal or biased information from the environment about self-worth.

Another aspect of the appeal of alcohol is that it lends itself to a subjectively temporary strategic commitment. The drinker does not set out to achieve addiction. He believes that he can control the agent that temporarily lowers his performance capacity. This belief fits nicely into *mañana* fantasies that are so common in alcohol use. These fantasies involve thoughts about how successful one will be *when* he breaks the drinking habit or could be *if* he did. The problem drinker tells himself that he will report for meaningful social measurement when he's good and ready, but typically he never is. The suspected truth is too horrible to risk, and in the meantime, he may prosper in fantasies of glorified competence.

There is no question that alcohol has direct physiological effects on nervous system functioning. The appeal of alcohol has been commonly attributed to its euphoric and anxiety-reducing effects (Cappell & Herman, 1972: Kingham, 1958). Our present line of argument adds a psychological dimension to the anxiety-reduction phenomenon. It suggests that anxiety is typically centered around one's competence or respectworthiness, and that it is reduced when the alcohol provides an excuse for marginal performance. This oversimplifies the complex interactive effects of alcohol and mood, since there are legendary as well as vividly real examples of drink-induced morosity (e.g., the "crying jag"). But the euphoric effects of alcohol are certainly more commonly observed and therefore built into the expectations of the drinker himself. Self-handicapping agents like alcohol may in fact enhance performance for those with an inordinate fear of the competence implications of failure. Weiner and Sierad (1975), in a fascinating study, examined the digit symbol performance of subjects high in need for achievement and those low in need for achievement (but high in fear of failure). Half of these subjects ingested a placebo under the impression that it would interfere with visuo-motor performance. All subjects were given periodic failure feedback and their performance was measured. The high fear of failure subjects actually performed better after taking the performance-inhibiting placebo than those in the control condition. The subjects high in need for achievement performed better in the control condition in line with their normal tendency to attribute failure to low effort and to try harder. When the pill obscured this attributional line, they did not perform as well. Although this is not Weiner and Sierad's exact interpretation, we would suggest that the high fear-of-failure subjects do better in the pill condition because the placebo removes the competence implications of failure, and this reduction in anxiety actually releases energy for attention, motivation, and therefore improved performance.

THE COMPETENCE IMAGE

But now let us return to the question of etiology and consider the special reasons why strategies to protect one's competence image are necessary. Why is it so important for the potential alcoholic to avoid information implying that he is unworthy and incompetent?

Imagine the following developmental scenario: The potential problem drinker, like the rest of us, early realizes that reward follows good behavior. However, social rewards have either or both of two meanings. The first of these is the *exchange* implication, reward rendered for costs incurred. The child who receives thanks for wiping the dishes may accept this [203] merely as a quid pro quo, rather than drawing any deep inferences about his or her basic worthiness. On the other hand, there may be something about the "thanks" that does carry a self-esteem increment. The reward may have *signifying* implication as well as an exchange value (cf. Jones, 1964).

The potentially dual meaning of reward introduces a complexity which the developing child may find difficult to penetrate. A part of this complexity is the difficulty of establishing whether the love of significant others is unconditional. The child may reflect on whether the parental rewards received are solely contingent on performance (exchange) or whether they are signals of parental love and esteem (signification). We can imagine the child attempting to separate these implications, these parental messages, by experimental tests to find out whether there is love in the absence of performance. One source of the "competence complex" that we theoretically attribute to the potential problem drinker may be the tentative discovery that he or she is not unconditionally loved. The very unpleasantness of this experimental outcome may support the disinclination to conduct similar unconfounded experiments in the future.

REACTIONS TO CONDITIONAL LOVE SUSPICIONS

Here there is a crucial choice point. The child can confound subsequent experimental tests of parental love by oversufficient effort and application. Such a child is driven to zeal by an overdetermined fear of failure; for failure may invite further evidence that love is conditional on performance. The vicious circularity of this strategic course is apparent in the attributional implications of overachievement. The more one tries, the more essential it is that one avoid failure, for failure under conditions of high effort carries unequivocal implications about ability. In this way, perhaps, trying can lead only to more trying. The overachievement strategy is a precarious one, but with sufficient talent, appropriate choice of performance setting, and luck, it may effectively propel the person into relative emotional security. Even the overachiever, though, may be periodically attracted to alcohol and to nonperformance settings in which he may escape the burdens of being tested while competence is fully engaged.

The other path is more self-destructive and involved. The feedback from the child's conditional love experiment goes beyond the simple exchange implication to carry a more complicated message. The child reads the message as saying "You can do it if you try, and that's why we love you." And if the child does occasionally succeed, the only reward is a "We knew it all along," which vindicates the parents more than it reinforces the child. These messages create the bind of the underachiever. He who tries and fails loses everything. He who fails without trying maintains a precarious hold on the illusion of love and admiration. The resulting strategy of lowered motivation may be buttressed by a culturally derived competence elitism. We live in a world in which people are (sometimes secretly) admired for their talents and intelligence regardless of the quality of actual performances. This may be a residual of the many myths stressing the inevitable genetic superiority of the aristocracy and the nobly born (going back at least to Oedipus).

It may also be a not unreasonable interpretation of Calvinist predestination doctrines. The vital importance of underlying competence may be stressed by the parents who are motivated to see their children as the carriers of their own superior genetic potential.

This line of argument seems to fly in the face of the results of Weiner and his colleagues (1972) who have shown that the low-ability person who tries hard is rewarded more than the able slacker by subjects playing a teacher role. In such a teacher–student context, the exchange model may emphasize the importance of [204] doing one's best. However, it is another matter when we ask whether the average person would rather be a highly motivated dummy or a highly competent low achiever. Theoretically, the competent person has more potential control over performance outcomes than the incompetent person. Motivation can be turned on at some later time; competence is more irrevocably fixed. Some results by Nicholls (1975) support this notion that performance linked to ability is more gratifying than performance linked to effort.

Thus the self-handicapper, whether seeking to impose external performance impediments or to withdraw effort, may in many ways be similar to the overachiever. Each is fearful that failure will implicate competence. Each has an abnormal investment in the question of self-worth. One succeeds in avoiding failure through persistent effort, the other embraces failure as an alternative to self-implicating feedback. We have suggested that each strategy originates in a conditional love experiment in which the child draws different conclusions from the evidence that the signs of love are actually potentially absent after failure.

THE ROLE OF REINFORCEMENT CONTINGENCY

An alternative scenario points to the contingency of rewards and performance as more crucial than the signification value of parental messages. Perhaps the self-handicapping path is followed by those whose reinforcement history has been capricious or chaotic. It is not that they have been unrewarded; it is that they have not been able to determine consistently what the reward was for, or they suspect that they have been rewarded for extraneous reasons such as beauty or the ascribed status of simply being a family member. We are reminded here of Seligman's (1975) theory of depression as a condition growing out of noncontingent reward histories. Of particular interest is the "success depression" where rewards have been ample, but uninformative regarding one's competence image.

The notion of self-protecting strategies implies, after all, that the strategist has something to protect. There has to have been some experience of success, something in the person's history that has created a fragile and ambiguous, but not a wholly negative, self-concept. The perpetual loser may not be the prime candidate for alcohol abuse. He may be more likely to handle his problems by drastically lowering his aspirations to fit realistically his meager talents.

No doubt success-avoidance has other motivational origins as well. For one thing, success often incurs a future obligation to perform at a high level (cf. Jones 1973). A performance Peter Principle often operates such that success propels a person into new and more demanding challenges where the risk of failure increases. This would seem to amplify further the appeal of self-handicapping strategies for both the failure-avoider and the success depressive.

These alternative etiologies describe different reinforcement histories. In the first version, the potential problem drinker responds to what he fears might happen if he were to commit himself to maximal effort or establish ideal conditions for a performance. In the second version, the emphasis is more on the protection of ill-gotten gains. Both etiological versions, however, emphasize the potential addict's vital concern with the signifying implications of performance for his self-image of competence. Both assume that this image has become a deep and overriding consideration. Both further assume that the individual is willing to settle for confounded performance feedback rather than taking the chance on repeated tests of the conditional love hypothesis under maximally informative conditions. The problem drinker and the underachiever are willing to forego success to protect the illusion that they have the competence to be consistently successful. [205]

From the viewpoint of advice to parents, however, the implications of the two scenarios appear antithetical. On the one hand, we imply that parents should avoid tying rewards exclusively to performance. On the other hand, we inveigh against noncontingent reinforcement schedules. What is the poor parent to do in the ostensible no-win situation? Somehow, the parent must segregate his or her signifying response from those which provide informative feedback about performance. Interest and affection should not be withdrawn in the absence of achievement but contingent tutelage is essential to give the child a sense of adaptive control or effectance. Often, we suspect, the parents divide their roles so that the cross-sex parent emphasizes noncontingent, signifying love, whereas the same-sex parent emphasizes feedback contingent on performance (in part, through serving as a performance model). The two roles combine in the ideal case to provide emotional security and a sense of mastery of the environment. To the extent that signification and exchange feedback are inextricably tangled in the family setting, there is potential for the kind of competence concern that leads to disturbances in achievement strivings and/or the subsequent appeal of such performance inhibitors as alcohol.

REFERENCES

Andrews, D. (1975). Stupid. *Harvard Magazine,* 78, 6–8.

Beckett, H. D. (1974). Hypotheses concerning the etiology or heroin addiction. In P. G Bourne (Ed.). *Addiction.* New York: Academic Press.

Cappell, H., & Herman, C. P. (1972). Alcohol and tension reduction: A review. *Quarterly Journal of Studies on Alcohol,* 33, 33–64.

Carson, R.C. (1969). *Interaction concepts of personality.* Chicago: Aldine.

Festinger, L. (1954). A theory of social comparison processes. *Human Relations,* 7, 117–140.

Jessor, R., Jessor, L. S., & Finney, J. (1973). A social psychology of marijuana use: Longitudinal studies of high school and college youth. *Journal of Personality and Social Psychology,* 26, 1–15.

Jones, E. E. (1964). *Ingratiation.* New York: Appleton-Century-Crofts.

Jones, E. E., & Davis. K. E. (1965). From acts to disposition: The attribution process in person perception. In L. Berkowitz (Ed.), *Advances in experimental social psychology,* Vol. 2. New York: Academic Press.

Jones, S. C. (1973). Self- and interpersonal evaluations: Esteem theories versus consistency theories. *Psychological Bulletin,* 79, 185–199.

Kelley, H. H. (1972). Attribution in social interaction. In E. E. Jones, D. E. Kanouse, H. H. Kelley, R. E. Nisbett, S. Valins, & B. Weiner (Ed.), *Attribution: Perceiving the causes of behavior* (pp. 1–26). Morristown, NJ: General Leaning Press.

Kingham, R. J. (1958). Alcoholism and the reinforcement theory of learning. *Quarterly Journal of Studies on Alcohol,* 19, 320–330.

Nicholls, J. G. (1975). Causal attributions and other achievement-related cognitions: Effects of task outcome, attainment value, and sex. *Journal of Personality and Social Psychology,* 31, 379–389.

Seligman, M. E. P. (1975). *Helplessness.* San Francisco: W. H. Freeman.

Weiner, B., I. Frieze, Kukla, A., Reed, L., Rest, S., & Rosenbaum, R. M. (1972). Perceiving the causes of success and failure. In E. E. Jones, D. E. Kanouse, H. H. Kelley, R. E. Nisbett, S. Valins, & B. Weiner (Ed.), *Attribution: Perceiving the causes of behavior* (pp. 95–120). Morristown, NJ: General Learning Press.

Weiner, B., & Sierad, J. (1975). Misattribution for failure and enhancement of achievement strivings. *Journal of Personality and Social Psychology,* 31, 415–421. **[206]**

SELF-HANDICAPPING

Chapter 19

The Framing of Competence

Edward E. Jones
Princeton University

> ABSTRACT: The challenge of how to appear competent (to oneself and others) is closely tied to the attributional relationship between ability (can) and effort (try). Data are presented to support the layperson's understanding of the discounting principle that describes this relationship: Holding performance constant, the lower the apparent effort and the more difficult the task, the greater the attributed ability. It is proposed that people in our culture attach great value to the appearance of basic, or "natural," ability. Depending on available opportunities, people will withdraw effort, emphasize task difficulty, and even handicap themselves to protect their competence image. Experimental results also make clear that self-promoters must avoid claims that are refutable, excessive, or seen as out of context.

What is competence? Thirty years have passed since R. W. White (1959) stimulated considerable discussion of the concept of competence, defining it in the broad terms of effective interaction with the environment, and linking it to what he called "effectance motivation." Psychologists share a long and illustrious history of more specific attempts to define and measure the skills and aptitudes that are the most relevant for adaptive performances in our society. This history will not be part of my focus here, although I share with it the premise that one's competence is an extremely valuable attribute, an attribute closely linked to self-esteem, to social status, and to feelings of

---

Reprinted with permission from *Personality and Social Psychology Bulletin,* 15, 477–492. Copyright © 1989 Sage Publications, Inc.

control, personal security, and mental health. My topic instead is the *appearance* of competence, a concern justified by the extreme value we attach to it. How do people communicate competence? How is a political candidate, or a job applicant, or a suitor, going to convince us that he or she has it? How, in terms reminiscent of Erving Goffman (1974), do we go about framing our actual competences so that they can be displayed in a salient and credible form?

Attempts to answer this question involve research on the management of impressions through self-presentation, but I am concerned with self-presentations that are directed both to an audience and to the self. I shall make little or no attempt to distinguish between strategies to convince others and strategies to convince ourselves. Just as we frame our competence for the consumption of others who are important to us, so we frame our competences as part of our self-definition or identity. [477]* The processes are often similar, if not the same, and both trade heavily on one's understanding of attributional relationships and assumptions.

Indeed, my primary starting point for this inquiry is Fritz Heider's (1958) famous account of the naive psychology of action. A central feature of this account is the trade-off between ability (can) and effort (try); the same performance may be a reflection of high effort compensating for low ability or of high ability requiring minimal effort. Unless a performance is outstanding—that is, either very good or very poor—there is inherent attributional ambiguity in the evidence that I or someone else has turned in a certain level of performance. Of course, we may have other evidence, such as the manner or style of the performance, but the point I wish to emphasize is that achievements are typically not direct indexes of competence. And it is this indirect relationship between performances and underlying competence that provides the elbow room for framing processes. Within this elbow room, the strategies of self-promotion are often directed toward the casting of good performances as a reflection of stable abilities, and the casting of poor performances as the consequence of inhibiting external factors, or of the temporary withdrawal of effort. Thus, a study of the framing of competence lands us in such interesting domains as excuse making, more subtle efforts at self-handicapping, and the kinds of persistent withdrawal of effort that we designate as academic underachievement.

Heider suggested that a certain primitive algebra connected the various possible determinants of performance. In particular, ability and motivation are multiplicatively related in that performance would be zero in the absence of either. Situational factors and personal factors are related in an additive way, implying that one could substitute for the absence of the other—a wind can remove the leaves from the lawn just as surely as a man with a rake.

John Darley and George Goethal (1980) have tried to capture Heider's reasoning in the formula presented in Figure 19.1. This formula expresses Heider's algebra, capturing the multiplicative relation of ability and motivation as well as the additive relation between both of these internal factors and the external factors of task difficulty and luck. Darley and Goethals have added something else, however, noting that some ability factors and some motivational factors are more stable than others. Certain things

---

*Bracketed bold numbers refer to original page numbers. Page numbers indicate where the original page ended.

$P = [(A - A') \times (M \pm M')] + (D \pm D') + L$

P = performance
A = stable ability factors
A' = temporary ability constraints
M = stable motivational factors
M' = temporary motivational factors
D = usual difficulty level
D' = temporary factors affecting difficulty
L = luck

Source: After Darley & Goethals, 1980.

Figure 19.1 Attributes Underlying Variations in (and Explanations of) Performance

can happen to affect our ability temporarily, such as a bad head cold or a hangover. These are the kinds of conditions Darley and Goethals want to identify as A'. Similarly, M' may refer to the general tendency to persist, to delay gratification or to possess a high level of achievement motivation, whereas M' refers to the more transient conditions of momentary concentration and exertion.

I would now like to argue that, in large segments of our society, individuals are hard at work manipulating the perceived causes of a performance so as to emphasize the importance of the more stable forms of competence, represented by the boxed stable ability factor. This is far from a self-evident proposition—indeed, it seems to be in the face of our desire to emphasize those good things over which we have personal responsibility—but I believe that there is ample anecdotal and experimental evidence to back it up. Those of us in academic life are particularly aware of the enormous importance assigned to intelligence—whether we call it IQ, or *g*, or **[478]** "smarts." In evaluating potential graduate students, how completely we ignore letters of recommendation that emphasize hard work and a pleasing personality! But the importance of intelligence may extend far beyond the realm of academe. Even a cursory monitoring of children's conversations will reveal the repeated use of *stupid* and *dummy* as epithets. The same cannot be said for the use of *lazy* or *loafer*. Edgerton (1967), in his fascinating study of retarded citizens trying to live in the community, emphasizes over and over again their preference for any explanation of their performances or current position other than inadequate intelligence. These retarded citizens **[479]** would much rather attribute their difficulties to emotional problems or family interference than to their assigned fate of limited intellectual competence.

In the sports world, there is, of course, a shift in emphasis from intelligence to speed, strength, and coordination, but once again priority is typically assigned to uncontrollable native ability factors while motivation and learned skills take a back seat. On the sports pages of the *New York Times* (July 19, 1988), for example, we read that Danta Whitaker was drafted by the New York Giants even though "during his senior year at Mississippi Valley State College, the tight end caught just one pass [and] his team won only 1 of 11 games." A scout for the Giants ignored this kind of performance evidence because Whitaker can run 40 yards in 4.6 sec and was outstanding on weightlifting tests.

It is not entirely clear why *native* ability factors, as indicated in Figure 19.1, are treasured—and therefore framed—more than acquired or learned talents. A logical reason is the very real fact that our genes can define our ultimate capacity to perform, and such ultimate capacities are terribly important to our fantasies about future achievement, to our "possible selves." Moreover, the innate capacity to learn and master new skills (if there is such an innate capacity) may be realistically valued by others—it is obviously of great potential value to any employer or other beneficiary of our ultimate capacities to perform. There are probably some less logical reasons for the emphasis on native talents, including the emulation of aristocracy and noble birth. There may even be some residue of Calvinistic fatalism in our reading of the "gift" of intelligence as a sign of being among the elect. In certain upper-class strata of our society, the importance of native endowments is protected by the avoidance of any competition that would belie or jeopardize their apparent existence. Although times may have changed, it was not so long ago that members of Harvard College's "final clubs" deliberately avoided any participation in demanding athletic competition and gave credence through their academic indifference to the appealing notion of the "gentleman's C."

Richard Huber (1971) convincingly documents a change in American culture from an emphasis on hard work and strength of character to what he refers to as the "personality ethic." As a reaction to the economic depression of the 1930s, the idea of success through striving and self-discipline gave way to success through the wonders of impression management. I would go beyond Huber's argument to suggest that the personality ethic has substituted competence for diligence as a major component of the desired self-image. In addition, the personality ethic is often infused with patrician symbols that mute the signs of crass ambition, play down the themes of "humble origin," and substitute the consumption patterns, tastes, and apparent values of the aristocracy. These values include a special emphasis on "style" and "charisma," both of which must be seen as "natural" to be effective, and both of which imply a certain kind of competence that cannot be contrived.

I will readily concede that there still are contexts in which we may wish to frame our strenuous effort or persistence or, more generally, our strength of character. It is also undoubtedly true that as we get along in life, our performances themselves become more closely linked to our identities—more and more we become what we **[480]** have accomplished rather than what we might be capable of accomplishing. When a person achieves a certain status or level of accomplishment, no one (including the person involved) cares that much anymore about the particular attributional ingredients that made his or her success possible. In fact, in most cases with mature adults, we are dealing with complex fusions of character, native ability, and acquired skills that defy the easy partitioning implied by attribution theory. Dweck and Leggett (1988) present some evidence suggesting that people who are "mastery-oriented" and who seek challenges for their instructive value also view ability as malleable and as fused with, rather than inversely related to, effort.

Nevertheless, in the American psyche there is something special about the appeal of natural talent, whether it is in the genius of an Einstein or Mozart, or in the athletic talents of a Jackie Joyner-Kersee. Most of us would rather be a little gifted than a lot dogged, unless we can also convince ourselves that being dogged is part of a strong character, which is, in turn, a highly stable—maybe even naturally endowed—attribute.

If we accept the premise that we generally would like to "frame" the *A* factors, how do we use our understanding of these various causal formulas derived from Heider and from Darley and Goethals to accomplish this task? A number of strategies are implicit in the Darley and Goethals formula. Generally, if we hold performance constant, then anything that reduces motivations should increase the attribution of ability. Similarly, anything that either increases the difficulty level or reduces ability has the same effect of signaling impressive and stable ability factors.

Another way to think of these trade-offs is in terms of what Harold Kelley (1972) has called the "discounting" and "augmentation" effects. These effects are an essential consequence of attributional arithmetic. Assume a performance as an effect of certain causes: assume further that some causal attributes are normally seen to facilitate that effect and others are assumed to inhibit it. If there are many facilitating causes, the contributions of any single cause can be proportionately discounted. If both facilitating and inhibiting causes are present, then the stronger or the more numerous the inhibiting attributes, the stronger the facilitating causes must be to achieve the same level of performance. A self-presentational logic follows from this: If I want to emphasize my ability, I can do whatever it takes to make salient all those attributes that can inhibit its expression. Recalling the Darley–Goethals formula, this would include calling my attention to temporary handicaps (emphasizing D'), or making it clear that I am not putting forth maximum effort (emphasizing M').

An experiment by George Quattrone and myself (Quattrone & Jones, 1978) showed that people are capable of exploiting their understanding of the augmentation effect in determining the best strategy for framing their competence. Subjects in one experimental scenario were asked to imagine that they were trying out for the role of Scrooge in a Broadway production of *A Christmas Carol,* and were given an opportunity to convey selected information about themselves to the play's director. Half the subjects were to imagine that they had been through an audition for the part followed by enthusiastic applause from an audience that included the director, whereas no audition was mentioned in the hypothetical scenario given to the remaining subjects. [481] When subjects were confident of meeting the specific self-presentational objective of winning the Scrooge role—in other words, when they were led to believe that the audition had been a successful one—they went out of their way to emphasize inhibitory factors that made their performance difficult or unlikely, and therefore all the more diagnostic of a more general (or "natural"?) underlying competence. Specifically, the successful audition subjects were eager to disclose that they had previously received excellent notices for their performance in another play in the role of a generous, lovable sucker—just the opposite of the Scrooge role. Subjects without the opportunity of a Scrooge audition indicated that they would avoid the disclosure of this information, presumably because it would have been damaging to their effort to convince the director that they could be a plausible Scrooge. Results for an entirely different scenario with the same conceptual features were almost identical.

Thus the successful audition subjects seem to be saying, "My ability to play the Scrooge role is part of a broader and more basic versatility." The moral of the story in a related domain might be: When a senior from Penn or Yale or Cornell is applying for graduate school, it is surely a good idea for her to convey her Ivy League credentials. Once she is admitted, however, she may frame her native competence by letting everyone know that she grew up in a small mining town in the hills of West Virginia.

Although our experiment was a role-playing study, and as such it is but a plausibility confirmation, there are obvious examples of how the augmentation principle is often used on the political scene. In the 1988 presidential campaign, the Democrats' keynote speaker at the nominating convention attempted to question Bush's competence and to emphasize the absence of testing adversity in his background by noting that he was born with "a silver foot in his mouth." The original movie $M*A*S*H$ and many episodes of the ensuing television series can also be seen as celebrating the competence of the heroes through augmentation. Sodden with martinis made from medical alcohol, exhausted from sleepless nights devoted to practical jokes on Major Burns and Hot Lips Houlihan, Hawkeye and his buddies perform amazing feats of delicate emergency surgery on shipments of wounded GIs. Imagine what they could do under less trying or inhibiting circumstances

THE APPEAL OF ATTRIBUTIONAL AMBIGUITY

Self-Handicapping

In circumstances where individuals are uncertain about the level of performance that they can expect from themselves, especially when they have an inordinate investment in their competence image and must still face the possibility of failure, there may be good reasons for avoiding diagnostic information about such a stable attribute as one's IQ. Consider the fate of poor Denison Andrews (1975), a freelance writer who describes his reaction when he makes the mistake of finding out his IQ from the principal of his old grade school. The principal breaks the rules, retrieves Andrews's school folder, and tells him he scored 125 on a fifth-grade Otis Beta test. **[482]**

> Bombshell! Not genius! Not even brilliant! Unbelievable! Thank Principal and leave. Keep cool. Control wobbly knees. 125. Not brilliant. Not undiscovered genius.... How can I tell my wife? ... Did they laugh when I applied to medical school?
>
> ... I.Q. has no meaning. Totally discredited. No one takes it seriously.... All it measures is ability to take I.Q. tests. Who was Otis anyway? ... I.Q. doesn't measure creativity. Winston Churchill ... Maybe I had an earache. A bad night's sleep. Maybe I lost time daydreaming. Creatively ... cultural bias. But ... cultural bias all in my favor!
>
> Wife: National Merit Scholar, skipped two grades. Photos as child show strange bulging forehead. Genius for sure. We lie awake in bed, not touching.... Is she talking more slowly than usual, rephrasing things to make sure I understand? "What's it like not to be brilliant?" she wants to know. "What kinds of thoughts don't you get? What do you do in the long wait between ideas?" (Andrews, 1975, pp. 6–8)

Obviously the author of this confessional piece would have been better off had he left room for more attributional ambiguity. Steven Berglas and I (Jones & Berglas, 1978) introduced the concept of "self-handicapping" to designate a cluster of strategies designed either to augment or to protect the kinds of stable competence we have designated as *A*. Such strategies typically make use of various kinds of attributional ambiguity (Snyder & Wicklund, 1981). The basic message with regard to self-handicapping is that people routinely use attributional principles in the service of protecting their competence image. We know that people are good at making excuses, but self-handicapping strategies go beyond retrospective self-serving accounts in that they are designed to put a person into a position that makes excuses unnecessary. To an important extent, an actor can arrange the settings he enters into so that his actions will be attributed to himself when they are praiseworthy and attributed to the environment or to some transient, easily correctable personal characteristic when they are not.

In our initial study of self-handicapping, Berglas and I (1978) were able to show that subjects in an intelligence test–retest situation will try to protect a precarious sense of intellectual competence by choosing a drug alleged to be performance-inhibiting, rather than performance-facilitating, in an interval between taking two parallel forms of an intelligence test. This precarious competence was induced by telling some subjects they had performed exceedingly well on an important "high-level intelligence test," most of whose items were in fact unsolvable. Subjects in this "noncontingent success" condition had ample reason to doubt that their "success" could be reproduced.

The basic finding that subjects will choose settings known to inhibit success when they have been initially successful but do not know why has since been replicated by several other investigators with such diverse self-handicapping agents as choosing to ingest alcohol, enduring the pain of ice water while solving problems, and listening to distracting music (see Arkin & Baumgardner, 1985). Hence, I am confident that a precarious competence image does lead to self-handicapping tendencies. In the terms **[483]** laid out by Darley and Goethals (see Figure 19.1), this series of experiments shows that people who are insecure about their talent (but have some evidence that they might indeed be talented) will self-select temporary handicaps (A') in order to protect this fragile competence image. In other words, their belief in their intellectual potential or their native ability becomes more important than successful performance itself.

Underachievement

Another common means of protecting a vital but fragile competence image by creating attributional ambiguity involves the withdrawal of effort. In attributional terms, this involves a subtraction of a performance-facilitating cause, thereby strengthening attributions for success to the remaining causes—especially to competence. Failure, of course, can be attributed to a correctable absence of effort, which, in this case, plays the role equivalent to an inhibitory cause. The crucial implication is that if and when an underachiever *does* try, she will succeed, or at least do noticeably better than she is doing now.

We are aware of examples of illusory effort withdrawal in the interest of the framing of augmented competence. Indeed, Stephen Potter long ago named this the Harvard–Edinburgh Gambit under the more general heading of Universitymanship. He tells us about famed Harvard man J. Fitzjames, who

> disappeared suddenly from college midway through January reading period, just about the time his friends began studying in earnest. Then, on the day of his first exam, he would return, strolling into the examination room five minutes late, dressed in a light Palm Beach suit and heavily tanned. Sitting down next to a friend he would inspect his papers casually, and begin to write slowly. Later it became known that Fitzjames received an A in the course. What was the explanation? Fitzjames has been holing himself up in a miserable rented room in Boston surrounded by the total reading assignment including the optional books, and has been working

like a dog for three weeks, stripped to the waist between two sunlamps.
(Potter, 1962, p. 287)

But more often than we would like to see, the withdrawal of effort is real; academic performance suffers, and we have problem cases of underachievement on our hands. Two related Princeton dissertations, by Janet Riggs (1982) and Beth Preston (1983), involve attempts to study the dynamics of underachievement in an experimental analogue. Both Riggs and Preston wanted to show that academic underachievers were indeed more concerned with framing and protecting their competence image than overachievers were. The analogue they chose involved a controlled presentation of digit-symbol problems on a computer terminal. Subjects were led to believe that by squeezing a hand dynamometer attached to the computer, they could, on the average, control the length of time the problem would be displayed and therefore increase the chances of successful performance. Although the dynamometer actually had no effect on the length of the presentation, accurate measures of the actual effort could be, and were, obtained. These were calculated for each subject, partialing out physical strength in order to obtain a pure measure of effort when actually attempting to solve the experimental problems. **[484]**

Both studies used high school students as subjects, some of whom were previously defined as overachievers and some as underachievers on the basis of whether their grades were over or under the regression line predicting grade point average from a standard aptitude score. In other words, overachievers got better grades from the aptitude scores predicted, and underachievers got worse scores. All subjects were told that the test they would be taking was a highly reliable indicator of an important aspect of intelligence.

Two intriguing findings are relevant here, findings that held across both of these similar studies. First of all, underachievers tended to underestimate the amount of effort they expended, and this was in spite of the fact that they actually expended more effort than overachievers. One interpretation of this tendency to underestimate effort is the likelihood that the underachievers have been told so many times by parents and teachers that they are not trying hard enough in school that this has become a protective form of self-labeling. Underachievers may have become confused about how much effort they are, in fact, putting out, and have merely learned to accept the fact that it is not enough.

In both studies, also, underachievers and overachievers behaved quite differently as a function of their understanding of the relative importance of effort and ability in solving the intelligence test problems. As Figure 19.2 shows, if an overachiever believed that effort was important for performance, he or she tended to exert more effort. What could be more reasonable! But it is reasonable only if we assume that doing well is more important than certain other things—for example, protecting one's competence image. When we look at the underachievers in both studies, if they think the task is very sensitive to the amount of effort expended, *they withdraw effort.* This makes sense only if we assume that, for them, performance is important only to the extent that it is diagnostic of their ability or their competence. If effort is more relevant to success on the task, and effort is withdrawn, a poor performance can only reflect insufficient effort. If ability is more clearly linked to performance, however, the application of effort naturally follows, in order to ensure a maximum level of performance. Obviously, this implies a certain amount of self-deception. The underachievers appear to be playing attributional games to protect their sense of self-competence. Overachievers seem to care less about

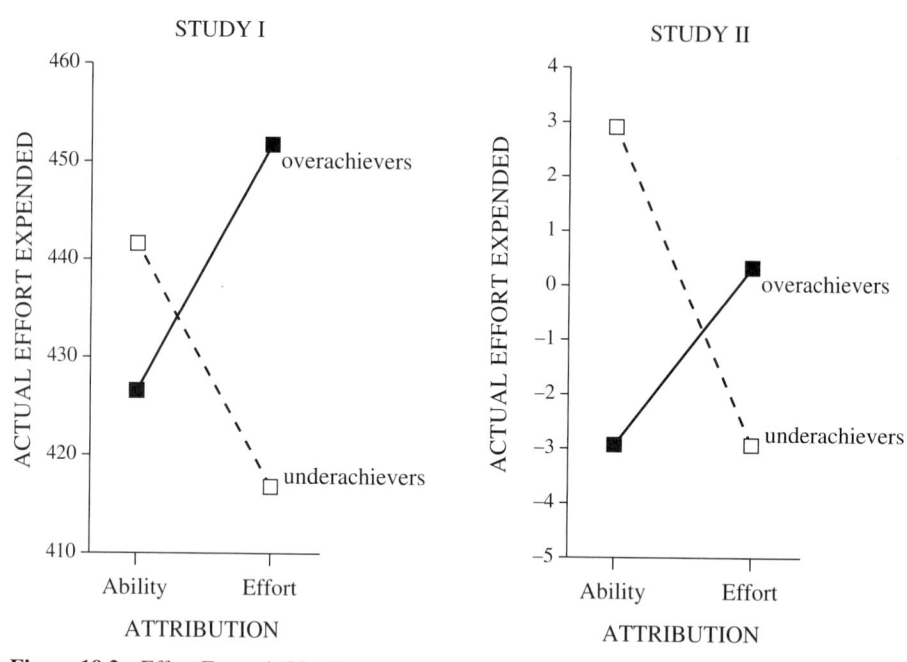

Figure 19.2 Effort Expended by Over- and Underachievers Who Believe that Successful Task Performance Is Largely a Function Either of Ability or of Effort

underlying attributions and merely want to do whatever it takes to perform well on the assigned task.

These studies merely scratch the surface of what we need to know to understand the dynamics of underachievement. The results are consistent, however, with the hypothesis that underachievers are unduly obsessed with their competence image and that this takes precedence, under some circumstances at least, over performing well. Berglas and I once proposed (Jones & Berglas, 1978) that underachievers come out of families whose parents constantly reiterate to them, "Johnny, if you only tried harder and took your studies more seriously, you would do much better." Johnny is not so sure, but he may suspect that if he does ostentatiously apply himself and he still ends up with mediocre grades, he will shatter his parents' expectations and perhaps lose their love. Thus the underachiever's preoccupation with competence is but a reflection of a parental obsession. The parents have made it clear to their [485] underachieving offspring that his or her possession of the natural gift of intellectual competence is terribly important to them. The parents are much more comfortable believing that Johnny is lazy than that he is simply stupid.

Self-Promotion

In an essay on self-presentation, Thane Pittman and I (Jones & Pittman, 1982) included self-promotion as one of five major self-presentation strategies. We tried to distinguish a concern with promoting one's competence from the more ubiquitous objectives of ingratiation—one's interest in being liked and in being seen as warm, charming, and personally attractive. A crucial feature of the framing of competence through self-promotion is, of course, the relationship between one's performances and one's direct or indirect competence claims. The Quattrone and Jones (1978) study tells part of the story by showing that performances can be framed in such a way as to point to underlying attributes of versatility and natural talent—and that subjects are quite capable of seizing such a framing opportunity.

We are taught to deprecate those who are truly arrogant or conceited, who take their talents so seriously in their public self-depictions that they quickly become targets of ridicule. As Pittman and I argue, there is even a "self-promoter's paradox" suggesting that those who are truly secure in their talents are, if anything, *less* likely to refer to them than those who have self-doubts. This may be the case in part because if we are truly secure about our own competence, there is no need to seek confirmation from the accolades of others. But it is also usually the case that truly competent people can let their performances speak for them without any self-presentational embellishment.

It certainly seems to be true that we admire modesty in those whose talents are well established because we have observed their impressive performances, but there remain a number of complexities here that need to be identified. Some of these emerged in a study that Roy Baumeister and I (Baumeister & Jones, 1978) did several years ago. The study basically concerned how people cope with diagnostic information about themselves to which others have access. Subjects took a personality test, the (bogus) results of which were shown to them and (so they believed) to a fellow subject with whom they were later to interact. The results were in the form of a paragraph mostly emphasizing a particular set of strengths or a more negative paragraph describing the subject as selfish, shallow, and emotionally immature. When subjects were then given the opportunity to communicate further information about themselves to the other subject in the form of self-ratings, these ratings depended crucially on the particular personality profiles allegedly in the other subject's hands. If the profiles were generally negative, subjects rated themselves negatively on traits disparaged by the profile itself, but they then proceeded to compensate for this negative self-presentation by describing themselves positively on dimensions that were not specifically mentioned. If the bogus personality profile was positive, however, subjects were typically modest on all their communicated self-ratings. We can tell that these differences were a function of self-presentational strategies because the same self-description tendencies were absent when only the subjects themselves [487] saw their personality profiles. It is apparent, then, that people develop fairly standard ways of coming to terms with information referring to themselves that is publicly known. They manage their self-presentation so as not to contradict directly any known information, even when it is negative in implications. When the information others have is generally positive, however, people apparently strive for the extra social rewards that accompany modesty, without the risk of appearing incompetent. These results are summarized in Figure 19.3.

In the everyday environment, those interested can not only choose how to appear and what to say, they can also choose the settings and the occasions for enacting their appropriate strategic behavior. There remain, however, many occasions when the potential self-promoter cannot choose his or her own arena to display the correlates of competence. A classic example is the job interview were the interviewee must be impressive in a highly constraining situation—where it is patently obvious that everyone would go

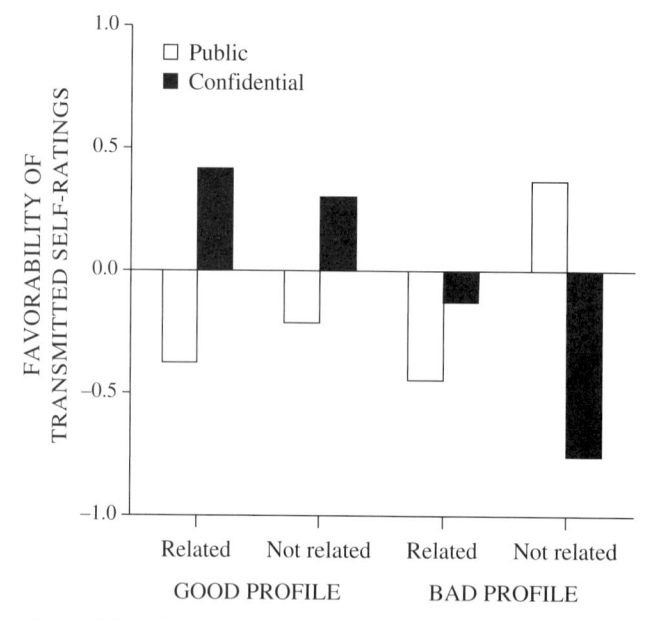

Figure 19.3 Presenting Favorable or Unfavorable Information about Oneself as a Function of What Is Already Known

out of his or her way to try to be impressive. Deborah Godfrey, Charles Lord, and I (Godfrey, Jones, & Lord, 1986) attempted a straightforward study of self-promotion and ingratiation in a similar kind of constraining interview situation. Our specific interest was in showing that ingratiation and self-promotion are separate and distinctive strategies. Thus it should follow that subjects instructed to pursue one, but not the other, of these two strategies will behave very differently. The experimental procedure was simple and straightforward. Pairs of naive subjects were brought together for a get-acquainted interview. They talked for 20 minutes and then rated each other on a variety of characteristics, including competence and likability. They returned a week later for a second 20-minute discussion. In the meantime, a randomly chosen member of each pair had been taken aside and instructed to focus in the second interview on convincing the naive partner that he or she was a highly competent person, *or* the subject was instructed to do everything possible to get the partner to like him or her more than the partner had after the first interview session. These strategic self-presenters were not told how they had initially been rated, but the self-promotion subjects were led to believe that there was room for improvement in their competence ratings, and those in the ingratiation were led to believe that they could improve on their likability ratings.

The actual changes in ratings showed that ingratiators did indeed become more likable in response to the instructions in their condition. However, not only did self-promoters fail to convince their partners that they were more competent than the partner originally assumed, but their efforts to do so also caused their partners to rate them as less likable the second time around.

A major prediction of the study was that ingratiators would talk less during the second discussion than they had in the first. Our reasoning was that the best way to be liked is to be responsive to the other person, to draw him or her out, and to be sympathetic and agreeing. Self-promoters, in contrast, must use the discussion time to convey information about themselves. They therefore should attempt to take charge of the conversation and to talk more during the second session. This prediction turned out to be confirmed. A content analysis of the two discussions also showed that ingratiators accelerated their rate of agreement with their partners during the second [488] discussion, whereas self-promoters reduced their tendency to confirm their partners' opinions. (This, of course, may explain why they were less liked.)

A more intensive analysis focusing on the first 5 minutes of the second session also showed that ingratiators nodded and smiled more, showed an abrupt decline in the use of first-person pronouns, and in various other ways performed those standard verbal and nonverbal behaviors that we associate with trying to be liked. This was especially true, incidentally, of those who were successful in improving their likability. Not surprisingly, furthermore, ingratiators increased their tendency to flatter and to give compliments, while self-promoters showed a decrease in these tendencies.

For our present purposes, the most intriguing feature of the results was that those who attempted to be self-promoting were generally unsuccessful in framing their competence. In fact, as it turns out, those in the self-promotion condition who were [489] successful tended to behave as the ingratiators did, and the ingratiators were generally at least as successful as the self-promoters in securing elevated ratings of competence. If this is the case with an unsuspecting discussion partner, one can well imagine that blatant attempts at self-promotion would be even less fruitful in a highly constrained job interview setting.

Although we can only speculate about the effects of job interview constraints on the effectiveness of ingratiation attempts, one conclusion that might be drawn from the present results is that the discussion context is a more favorable milieu for ingratiation than it is for self-promotion. It did seem that subjects were generally at a loss to implement the strategic goals of self-promotion, unless they were clever enough to do so indirectly by the kinds of ingratiation tactics that were more available in the discussion context.

CONCLUDING REMARKS

The Godfrey, Jones, and Lord study reminds us of some of the obvious hazards involved in verbal self-promotion attempts. But I hope I have conveyed in the remainder of this article a sense of competence framing that goes well beyond what a person says about himself or herself in an interview. I have emphasized the relationship between one's performances and the settings in which one chooses to perform; I have stressed the strategic casting of performances so as to highlight such appropriate underlying attributions as native intelligence, or acting versatility, or being a natural athlete. Direct claims of competence, unrelated to, or in the absence of, supporting performance, appear to be a rather drastic and dangerous last resort. The credentials displayed must be related to the competence image one desires to display, but they must not be so directly related that one's claims denote only the importance of conveying a desired impression or the arrogance of the insecure.

Although I have focused thus far on how we manage to convince *others* of our competence, it is important to realize that the competence framing may have important consequences for coping and achievement. Our "self-efficacy," in Bandura's (1982) term, is not given. It is to an important extent a self-constructed label, one that is subject to our own attributional manipulations, manipulations that involve not only strictly cognitive processes but also the judicious uses of social comparison and feedback from constructive choices of tasks in those performance settings most suitable for the framing of competence.

In a recent article, Taylor and Brown (1988) have presented impressive evidence concerning the role of illusions about one's positive attributes in contributing to mental health. Among other consequences of overly positive self-evaluations are increased motivation, task persistence, and generally effective performance. Such consequences presumably can reflect an illusory sense of mastery or control. The framing of competence can undoubtedly contribute to this illusory sense—and, on occasion, to a self-fulfilling prophecy of competence confirmation. Insofar as we are successful in convincing ourselves that we have certain kinds of talents, a range of potential activities may beckon and challenge us. We may quickly learn, of course, that we cannot follow through on the competences we have framed, but we also may [490] succeed in a bootstrapping self-validation of the framed ability. After all, our framed competence beliefs may lead us to fail, but without them we would not even attempt to succeed.

And yet, our results suggest a dark underside to the rosy glow of positive illusions about one's competence. There is a realistic chance that even the most cleverly framed competence claims can be irrefutably disconfirmed. Awareness of this discontinuation potential can push us in directions that can actually sabotage performance and undermine the authenticity of any competence claim. Thus, alcohol abuse and underachievement may reflect strategies designed to protect one's competence image while generating data that ultimately discredit one's pretensions to competence.

In the final analysis, then, the framing of competence may have many consequences, some of which are salutary, and some of which are eventually self-destructive. We live in an era where one's unframed competence is often overshadowed by another's more meager talents that are more adroitly framed. We may take a moral stance of disdain when encountering such triumphs of pretension, but the topic of competence framing should not be shunned simply because it portrays a seamy side of human nature. The fact remains that our self-defined or socially confirmed competence is a central ingredient of our identity and our social value. Different cultures will obviously attach different weights to the underlying attributes that contribute to adaptive performances. I have argued that the more stable attributes that define our given, or natural, abilities are particularly valued in many areas of our own society. And I have also argued that it is these underlying attributes, rather than the performances themselves, that can become the goals we seek to reach through our interactive behavior. In any event, since one's underlying competence is only indirectly reflected in performance, it remains important to understand how the truly valued attributes of competence can be separated from counterfeit claims and strategic displays—and to try to determine whether and when the authenticity of such claims actually makes much of a difference.

REFERENCES

Andrews, D. (1975). Stupid. *Harvard Magazine,* 78, 6–8.
Arkin, R. M., & Baumgardner, A. H. (1985). Self-handicapping. In J. H. Harvey & G. Weary (Eds.), *Attribution: Basic issues and applications.* Orlando, FL: Academic Press.
Bandura, A. (1982). Self-efficacy mechanism in human agency. *American Psychologist,* 37, 122–147.
Baumeister, R. F., & Jones, E. E. (1978). When self-presentation is constrained by the target's knowledge: Consistency and compensation. *Journal of Personality and Social Psychology,* 36, 606–618.
Berglas. S., & Jones, E. E. (1978). Drug choice as a self-handicapping strategy in response to non-contingent success. *Journal of Personality and Social Psychology,* 36, 405–417.
Darley, J. M., & Goethals. J. R. (1980). People's analyses of the causes of ability-linked performances. In L. Berkowitz (Ed.), *Advances in experimental social psychology* (Vol. 13, pp. 2–37). Orlando, FL: Academic Press.
Dweck, C. S., & Leggett, E. L. (1988). A social-cognitive approach to motivation and personality. *Psychological Review,* 95, 256–273. **[491]**
Edgerton, R. B. (1967). *The cloak of competence: Stigma in the lives of the mentally retarded.* Berkley: University of California Press.
Godfrey, D., Jones, E. E., & Lord, C. G. (1986). Self-promotion is not ingratiating. *Journal of Personality and Social Psychology,* 50, 106–115.
Goffman, E. (1974). *Frame analysis.* New York: Harper & Row.
Heider, F. (1958). *The psychology of interpersonal relations.* New York: Wiley.
Huber, R. M. (1971). *The American idea of success.* New York: McGraw-Hill.
Jones, E. E., & Berglas, S. (1978). Control of attributions about the self through self-handicapping strategies: The appeal of alcohol and the role of underachievement. *Personality and Social Psychology Bulletin,* 4, 200–206.
Jones, E. E., & Pittman, T. (1982). Toward a general theory of strategic self-presentation. In J. Suls (Ed.). *Psychological perspectives on the self* (Vol.1). Hillsdale, NJ: Erlbaum.
Kelley, H. H. (1972). Attribution and social interaction. In E. E. Jones, D. E. Kanouse, H. H. Kelley, R. E. Nesbitt, S. Valins, & B. Weiner (Eds.), *Attribution: Perceiving the cause of behavior* (pp. 1–26). Morristown, NJ: General Learning Press.
Potter, S. (1962). *Threeupmanship.* New York: Holt, Rinehart and Winston.
Preston, E. A. (1983). *The role of effort expenditure in academic achievement.* Unpublished doctoral dissertation, Princeton University.
Quattrone, G. & Jones, E. E. (1978). Selective self-disclosure with and without correspondent performance. *Journal of Experimental Social Psychology,* 14, 511–526.
Riggs, J. M. (1982). *The effect of performance attributions on choice of achievement strategy.* Unpublished doctoral dissertation, Princeton University.
Snyder, M., Wicklund, R. A. (1981). Attribute ambiguity. In J. H. Harvey, W. Ickes, & J. F. Kidd (Eds.), *New directions in attribution research* (Vol. 3). Hillsdale: Erlbaum.
Taylor, S. E., Brown, J. D. (1988). Illusion and well-being: A social psychological perspective on mental health. *Psychological Bulletin,* 103, 193–210.
White, R. W. (1959). Motivation reconsidered: The concept of competence. *Psychological Review,* 66, 279–333. **[492]**

Bibliography of E.E. Jones

1954

Jones, E. E. (1954). Authoritarianism as a determinant of first-impression formation. *Journal of Personality,* 23, 107–127.

Jones, E. E., & Bruner, J. S. (1954). Expectancy in apparent visual movement. *British Journal of Psychology,* 45, 157–165.

1956

Jones, E. E., & Aneshansel, J. (1956). The learning and utilization of contravaluant material. *Journal of Abnormal and Social Psychology,* 53, 27–33.

1957

Jones, E. E., & deCharms, R. (1957). Changes in social perception as a function of the personal relevance of behavior. *Sociometry,* 20, 75–85.

1958

Jones, E. E., & deCharms, R. (1958). The organizing function of interaction roles in person perception. *Journal of Abnormal and Social Psychology,* 57, 155–164.

Jones, E. E., & Kohler, R. (1958). The effects of plausibility on the learning of controversial statements. *Journal of Abnormal and Social Psychology,* 57, 315–320.

Jones, E. E., & Thibaut, J. W. (1958). Interaction goals as bases of inference in interpersonal perception. In R. Tagiuri & L. Petrullo (Eds.), *Person perception and interpersonal behavior* (pp. 151–178). Stanford, CA: Stanford University Press.

Jones, E. E., Wells, H. H., & Torrey, R. (1958). Some effects of feedback from the experimenter on conformity behavior. *Journal of Abnormal and Social Psychology,* 57, 207–213.

1959

Jones, E. E., & Daugherty, B. N. (1959). Political orientation and the perceptual effects of an anticipated interaction. *Journal of Abnormal and Social Psychology,* 59, 340–349.

Jones, E. E., Hester, S. L., Farina, A., & Davis, K. E. (1959). Reactions to unfavorable personal evaluations as a function of the evaluator's perceived adjustment. *Journal of Abnormal and Social Psychology,* 59, 363–370.

1960

Davis, K. E., & Jones, E. E. (1960). Changes in interpersonal perception as a means of reducing cognitive dissonance. *Journal of Abnormal and Social Psychology,* 61, 402–410.

Strickland, L. H., Jones, E. E., & Smith, W. P. (1960). Effect of group support on the evaluation of an antagonist. *Journal of Abnormal and Social Psychology,* 61, 73–81.

1961

Jones, E. E., Davis, K. E., & Gergen, K. J. (1961). Role playing variations and their informational value for person perception. *Journal of Abnormal and Social Psychology,* 63, 302–310.

1962
Jones, E. E., Gergen, K. J., & Davis, K. E. (1962). Some determinants of reactions to being approved or disapproved as a person. *Psychological Monographs, 76* (Whole No. 521).

1963
Gergen, K. J., & Jones, E. E. (1963). Mental illness, predictability and affective consequences as stimulus factors in person perception. *Journal of Abnormal and Social Psychology, 67*, 95–104.

Jones, E. E., Jones, R. G., & Gergen, K. J. (1963). Some conditions affecting the evaluation of a conformist. *Journal of Personality, 31*, 270–288.

Jones, E. E., Jones, R. G., & Gergen, K. J. (1963). Tactics of ingratiation among leaders and subordinates in a status hierarchy. *Psychological Monographs* (Whole No. 566).

1964
Jones, E. E. (1964). *Ingratiation*. New York: Appleton-Century-Crofts.

Jones, J. G., & Jones, E. E. (1964). Optimum conformity as an ingratiation tactic. *Journal of Personality, 32*, 436–458.

1965
Jones, E. E. (1965). Conformity as a tactic of ingratiation. *Science, 149*, 144–150.

Jones, E. E., & Davis, K. E. (1965). From acts to dispositions: The attribution process in person perception. In L. Berkowitz (Ed.), *Advances in Experimental Social Psychology* (Vol. 2, pp. 219–266). New York: Academic Press.

Jones, E. E., Gergen, K. J., Gumpert, P., & Thibaut, J. W. (1965). Some conditions affecting the use of ingratiation to influence performance evaluation. *Journal of Personality and Social Psychology, 1*, 613-625.

1967
Jones, E. E., & Gerard, H. B. (1967). *Foundations of social psychology*. New York: Wiley.

Jones, E. E., & Harris, V. A. (1967). The attribution of attitudes. *Journal of Experimental Social Psychology, 3*, 1–24.

Linder, D.E., Cooper, J., & Jones, E. E. (1967). Decision freedom as a determinant of the role of incentive magnitude in attitude change. *Journal of Personality and Social Psychology, 6*, 245–254.

1968
Jones, E. E., Rock, L., Shaver, K. G., Goethals, G. E., & Ward, L. M. (1968). Pattern of performance and ability attribution: An unexpected primacy effect. *Journal of Personality and Social Psychology, 10*, 317–340.

1969
Cooper, J., & Jones, E. E. (1969). Opinion divergence as a strategy to avoid being miscast. *Journal of Personality and Social Psychology, 13*, 23–30.

Stires, L. K., & Jones, E. E. (1969). Modesty versus self-enhancement as alternative forms of ingratiation. *Journal of Experimental Social Psychology, 5*, 172–188.

1971
Jones, E. E., & Goethals, G. R. (1971). Order effects in impression formation: Attribution context and the nature of the entity. In E. E. Jones, D. E. Kanouse, H. H. Kelley, R. E. Nisbett, S. Balins, & B. Weiner (Eds.) Attribution: Perceiving the causes of behavior (pp. 27–46). Morristown, NJ: General Learning Press.

Jones, E. E., Kanouse, D. E., Kelley, H. H., Nisbett, R. E., Valins, S., & Weiner, B. (1971). Attribution: Perceiving the causes of behavior. Morristown, NJ: General Learning Press.

Jones, E. E., & Nisbett, R. E. (1971). The actor and the observer: Divergent perceptions of the causes of behavior. In E. E. Jones, D. E. Kanouse, H. H. Kelley, R. E. Nisbett, S. Valins, & B. Weiner (Eds.), *Attribution: Perceiving the causes of behavior* (pp. 79–94). Morristown, NJ: General Learning Press.

Jones, E. E., & Sigall, H. (1971). The bogus pipeline: A new paradigm for measuring affect and attitude. *Psychological Bulletin*, 76, 349–364.

Jones, E. E., Worchel, S., Goethals, G. R., & Grumet, J. F. (1971). Prior expectancy and behavioral extremity as determinants of attitude attribution. *Journal of Experimental Social Psychology*, 7, 59–80.

1972

Cooper, J., Jones, E. E., & Tuller, S. M. (1972). Attribution, dissonance and the illusion of uniqueness. *Journal of Experimental Social Psychology*, 8, 45–57.

Jones, E. E., Bell, L., & Aronson, E. (1972). The reciprocation of attraction from similar and dissimilar others: A study in person perception and evaluation. In C. C. McClintock (Ed.), *Experimental Social Psychology* (pp. 142–179). New York: Holdt.

Jones, E. E., Goethals, G. R., Kennington, G. E., & Severance, L. (1972). Primacy and assimilation in the attribution process: The stable entity proposition. *Journal of Personality*, 40, 250–274.

Jones, E. E., & Gordon, E. H. (1972). The timing of self-disclosure and its effects on personal attraction. *Journal of Personality and Social Psychology*, 24, 358–365.

Jones, E. E., & Wein, G. A. (1972). Attitude similarity, expectancy violation, and attraction. *Journal of Experimental Social Psychology*, 8, 222–235.

1973

Jones, E. E., & Johnson, C. A. (1973). Delay of consequences and the riskiness of decisions. *Journal of Personality*, 41, 613–637.

Jones, E. E., & Sigall, H. (1973). Where there is ignis, there may be fire. *Psychological Bulletin*, 79, 260–262.

Jones, E. E., & Wortman, C. (1973). *Ingratiation: An attributional approach*. Morristown, NJ: General Learning Press. [54 pages]

1974

Snyder, M., & Jones, E. E. (1974). Attitude attribution when behavior is constrained. *Journal of Experimental Social Psychology*, 10, 585–600.

Snyder, M., Schulz, R., & Jones, E. E. (1974). Expectancy and apparent duration as determinants of fatigue. *Journal of Personality and Social Psychology*, 29, 426–434.

1976

Jones, E. E. (1976). How do people perceive the causes of behavior? *American Scientist*, 64, 300–305.

Jones, E. E., & Archer, R. (1976). Are there special effects of personalistic self-disclosure? *Journal of Experimental Social Psychology*, 12, 180–193.

Jones, E. E., & Baumeister, R. F. (1976). The self-monitor looks at the ingratiator. *Journal of Personality*, 44, 654–674.

Jones, E. E., & Berglas, S. (1976). A recency effect in attitude attribution. *Journal of Personality*, 44, 433–448.

Jones, E. E., & McGillis, D. (1976). Correspondent inferences and the attribution cube: A comparative reappraisal. In J. H. Harvey, W. J. Ickes, and R. F. Kidd (Eds.), *New directions in attribution research* (Vol. 1, pp. 389–420). Hillsdale, NJ: Erlbaum.

Stevens, L., & Jones, E. E. (1976). Defensive attribution and the Kelley Cube. *Journal of Personality and Social Psychology*, 34, 809–820.

1978

Baumeister, R. F., & Jones, E. E. (1978). When self-presentation is constrained by the target's knowledge: Consistency and compensation. *Journal of Personality and Social Psychology*, 36, 608–618.

Berglas, S., & Jones, E. E. (1978). Drug choice as a self-handicapping strategy in response to noncontingent success. *Journal of Personality and Social Psychology,* 36, 405–417.

Jones, E. E., (1978). Update of "From acts to dispositions": The attribution process in person perception. In L. Berkowitz (Ed.), *Advances in experimental social psychology* (Vol. 2, pp. 219–266). New York: Academic Press.

Jones, E. E., & Berglas, S. (1978). Control of attributions about the self through self-handicapping strategies: The appeal of alcohol and the role of underachievement. *Personality and Social Psychology Bulletin*, 4, 200–206.

Quattrone, G.A., & Jones, E. E. (1978). Selective self-disclosure with and without correspondent performance. *Journal of Experimental Social Psychology*, 14, 511–526.

1979

Jones, E. E. (1979). The rocky road from acts to dispositions. *American Psychologist*, 34, 107–117.

Jones, E. E., Riggs, J. M., & Quattrone, G. A. (1979). Observer bias in the attitude attribution paradigm: Effect of time and information order. *Journal of Personality and Social Psychology,* 37, 1230–1238.

1980

Jones, E. E. (1980). Social psychology. In G. A. Kimble, N. Garmezy, & E. Zigler (Eds.), *General psychology* (pp. 307–329). New York: Wiley.

Jones, E. E., Wood, G. C., & Quattrone, G. A. (1980). Perceived variability of personal characteristics in in-groups and out-groups: The role of knowledge and evaluation. *Personality and Social Psychology Bulletin*, 7, 523–528.

Linville, P. W., & Jones, E. E. (1980). Polarized appraisals of out-group members. *Journal of Personality and Social Psychology,* 38, 689–703.

Quattrone, G. A., & Jones, E. E. (1980). The perception of variability within in-groups and outgroups: Implications for the law of small numbers. *Journal of Personality and Social Psychology,* 38, 141–152.

1981

Jones, E. E., Rhodewalt, F., Berglas, S., & Skelton, J. A. (1981). Effects of strategic self-presentation on subsequent self-esteem. *Journal of Personality and Social Psychology*, 41, 407–421.

Miller, A. G., Jones, E. E., & Hinkle, S. (1981). A robust attribution error in the personality domain. *Journal of Experimental Social Psychology,* 17, 587–600.

1982

Cantor, N., Pittman, T. S., & Jones, E. E. (1982). Choice and atttitude attribution: The influence of constraint information on attributions across levels of generality. *Social Cognition,* 1, 1–20.

Jones, E. E., & Pittman, T. S. (1982). Toward a general theory of strategic self-presentation. In J. Suls (Ed.), *Psychological perspectives on the self* (Vol. 1, pp. 231–262). Hillsdale, NJ: Erlbaum.

1983

Jones, E. E., Schwartz, J. & Gilbert, D. T. (1983/1984). The perception of moral expectancy violation: The role of expectancy source. *Social Cognition,* 2, 273–293.

1984
Jones, E. E., Farina, A., Hastorf, A. H., Markus, H., Miller, D. T., & Scott, R. A. (1984). *Social stigma: The psychology of marked relationships.* New York: Freeman.

Jones, E. E., & Lord, G. C. (1984). Social cognition and social behavior. In G. A. Kimble, N. Garmezy, & E. Zigler (Eds.). *Principles of psychology,* (pp. 586–609). New York: Wiley.

Jones, E. E., & Lord, G. C. (1984). Social influence and group processes. In G.A. Kimble, N. Garmezy, & E. Zigler (Eds.). *Principles of psychology.* (pp. 610–636). New York: Wiley.

1985
Jones, E. E. (1985). History of social psychology. In G. A. Kimble, & K. Schlesinger (Eds.), *Topics in the history of psychology.* (Vol. 2, pp. 371–402). Hillsdale, NJ: Erlbaum.

Jones, E. E. (1985) Major developments in social psychology during the past five decades. In G. Lindzey and E. Aronson (Eds.), *The handbook of social psychology* (Vol. 1, pp. 47–107). New York: Random House.

Jones, E. E. (1985). Social psychology. In A. Kuper & J. Kuper (Eds.), *The social science encyclopedia* (pp. 780-783). London: Routledge & Kegan Paul.

Jones, E. E. (1985). Stereotypes. In A. Kuper & J. Kuper (Eds.), *The social science encyclopedia* (pp. 827–828). London: Routledge & Kegan Paul.

Jones, E. E. (1985). Stigma. In A. Kuper & J. Kuper (Eds.), *The social science encyclopedia.* (pp. 829–830). London: Routledge & Kegan Paul.

1986
Galanis, C. M. B., & Jones, E. E. (1986). When stigma confronts stigma: Some conditions enhancing a victim's tolerance of other victims. *Personality and Social Psychology Bulletin*, 12, 169–177.

Gilbert, D. T., & Jones, E. E. (1986). Exemplification: The self-presentation of moral character. *Journal of Personality*, 54, 101–123.

Gilbert, D. T., & Jones, E. E. (1986). Perceiver-induced constraint: Interpretations of self-generated reality. *Journal of Personality and Social Psychology,* 50, 269–280.

Godfrey, D., Jones, E. E., & Lord, C. (1986). Self-promotion is not ingratiating. *Journal of Personality and Social Psychology,* 50, 106–115.

Jones, E. E. (1986). Interpreting interpersonal behavior: The effects of expectancies. *Science*, 234, 41–46.

1987
Gilbert, D. T., Jones, E. E., & Pelham, B. W. (1987). Influence and inference: What the active perceiver overlooks. *Journal of Personality and Social Psychology,* 52, 861–870.

Ginzel, L. E., Jones, E. E., & Swann, W. B. (1987). How naive is the naive attributor? Discounting and augmentation in attitude attribution. *Social Cognition,* 5, 108–130.

Jones, E. E. (1987). Retrospective review: The seer who found attributional wisdom in naivety. *Contemporary Psychology*, 32, 213–216.

1988
Jones, E. E. (1988). Impression formation: What do people think about? In T.K. Srull & R.W. Wyer (Eds.), *Advances in social psychology* (Vol. 1, pp. 83–90). Hillsdale, NJ: Erlbaum.

1989
Jones, E. E. (1989). The framing of competence. *Personality and Social Psychology Bulletin,* 15, 477–492.

Jones, E. E. (1989). Expectancies, actions, and attributions in the interaction sequence. In J. P. Forgas & J. M. Innes (Eds.), *Recent advances in social psychology: An international perspective* (pp. 63–80). Amsterdam: Elsevier, North Holland.

1990

Jones, E. E. (1990). Constrained behavior and self-concept change. In J. Olson & M. Zanna (Eds.), *Self-inference processes: The Ontario symposium* (Vol. 6, pp. 69–86). Hillsdale, NJ: Erlbaum.

Jones, E. E. (1990). *Interpersonal perception*. New York: Freeman.

Jones, E. E., Brenner, K. J., & Knight, J. G. (1990). When failure elevates self-esteem. *Personality and Social Psychology Bulletin*, 16, 200–209.

1992

Aronson, J. M., & Jones, E. E. (1992). Inferring abilities after influencing performance. *Journal of Experimental Social Psychology*, 28, 277–299.

1993

Jones, E. E. (1993). Afterword: An avuncular view. *Personality and Social Psychology Bulletin*, 19, 657–661.

Jones, E. E. (1993). The social in cognition. In G. Harman (Ed.), *Conceptions of the human mind: Essays in honor of George A. Miller* (pp. 85–98). Hillsdale, NJ: Erlbaum.

Weisz, C., & Jones, E. E. (1993). Expectancy disconfirmation and dispositional inference: Latent strength of target-based and category-based expectancies. *Personality and Social Psychology Bulletin*, 19, 563–574.

In press

Jones, E. E. (In press). Major developments in five decades of social psychology In D. T. Gilbert, S. T. Fiske, & G. Lindzey (Eds.), *The handbook of social psychology*. New York: McGraw Hill.